Inside Social Life

Readings in Sociological Psychology and Microsociology

Fifth Edition

Spencer E. Cahill
University of South Florida

Roxbury Publishing Company
Los Angeles, California

Library of Congress Cataloging-in-Publication Data

Inside social life: readings in sociological psychology and microsociology / [compiled by] Spencer E. Cahill. — 5th ed.
    p. cm.
Includes bibliographical references.
ISBN 978-1-933220-23-9 (alk. paper)
1. Social psychology. 2. Microsociology. I. Cahill, Spencer.
HM1033.I57 2007
 302–dc21   2006037150

Publisher: Claude Teweles
Managing Editor: Dawn VanDercreek
Production Editor: Carla Plucknett
Copy Editor: Cheryl Adam
Proofreaders: Renee Ergazos and Christy Graunke
Typography: Jerry Lenihan
Cover Design: Chris Carrier

Printed on acid-free paper in the United States of America. This paper meets the standards for recycling of the Environmental Protection Agency.

ISBN - 978-1-933220-23-9

Instructor's Manual/Testing Program Available

ROXBURY PUBLISHING COMPANY
P.O. Box 491044
Los Angeles, California 90049-9044
Voice: (310) 473-3312 • Fax: (310) 473-4490
Email: roxbury@roxbury.net
Website: www.roxbury.net

Contents

Part I: Human Being and Social Reality

Peter Berger and Thomas Luckmann

Berger and Luckmann's classic statement about how humans socially construct and maintain reality and how it shapes individuals' experiences of
the world and themselves.

Gerald Handel, Spencer Cahill, and Frederick Elkin

A brief summary of recent research on the centrality of neurological flexibility or plasticity to human development.

Eviatar Zerubavel

An examination of how individuals socially divide reality into discrete categories of experience, or islands of meaning.

Part II: The Social Construction of Self

Charles Horton Cooley

This is the classic statement of Cooley's theory of the "looking-glass self."

George Herbert Mead

Mead's analysis of the social origins and character of the self inspired the
development of a distinctively sociological psychology.

---

* Denotes chapters new to the Fifth Edition.

Part III: The Social Construction of Subjective Experience

Part IV: The Self and Social Interaction

---

* Denotes chapters new to the Fifth Edition.

Part V: The Organization of Social Interaction

Part VI: Social Interaction and Relationships

* Denotes chapters new to the Fifth Edition.

Part VII: Structures of Social Life

---

* Denotes chapters new to the Fifth Edition.

Part VIII: The Construction of Social Structures

Part IX: The Politics of Social Reality

---

* Denotes chapters new to the Fifth Edition.

Part X: Postmodern Social Reality

* Denotes chapters new to the Fifth Edition.

Introduction

Sociology is a topically vast area of study. It is popularly associated with large-scale surveys of such topics as Americans' shrinking social networks and with reanalysis of governmental statistics to examine topics like residential segregation between whites and blacks. However, sociologists study everything from the operation of the global social system to the turn-by-turn organization of conversation. Given this topical range, many distinguish between macrosociology, or the study of broad patterns of social life, and mircrosociology.

Macrosociological studies provide a kind of aerial view of social life. They enable identification of the distinguishing features of the social landscape. However, in order to understand the actual social processes responsible for such broad patterns of social life, it is necessary to get closer to the ground—to the actual places where everyday social life is lived.

That is the purview of microsociology. Microsociology concerns the daily details of how actual people create and sustain the social worlds that they inhabit. They include the social worlds of preschools, playgrounds, basketball courts, public bathrooms, sororities, and street corners. Microsociologists go to such places to observe and sometimes participate in the activities that occur there so as to identify the patterns of interaction that characterize such social settings. They interview participants in depth to learn about the meanings that guide their conduct. Some even examine conversations in detail to investigate how particular social situations are talked into being. The goal is to understand the social processes that serve to produce and reproduce the social relationships, organizations, and systems that macrosociology studies in the abstract.

Many sociologists do not stop there but also look inside the hearts and minds of individuals who inhabit different social worlds. They examine relationships between people's social and subjective experience—their thoughts, feelings, and private views of themselves. Sociologists share this field of study with psychologists, and it is commonly referred to as *social psychology*. However, sociologists and psychologists generally approach the study of interrelations between social life and individuals' inner lives from different directions. Psychologists tend to look for the operation of universal principles of human psychology in social life, while sociologists consider the social variability of subjective experience to be more significant and informative. This has led to the cumbersome expressions *sociological social psychology* and *psychological social psychology*. But there is a more economical way of drawing this distinction. Psychologists can retain the title of *social psychology* if sociologists claim the title of *sociological psychology* as their own. This latter expression clearly refers to a psychology based on a distinctively sociological understanding of the human condition in all its varied forms.

The concerns of microsociology and sociological psychology are not unrelated to those of macrosociology. Both types of study are essential for a comprehensive understanding of human social life. Although individuals daily produce and reproduce the social worlds that they inhabit, they do not do so under circumstances of their own choosing. Recurring patterns of interaction result in relatively stable features or structures of social life. For example, people routinely place one another into different gender, ethnic, and other categories, treating one another differently based on such identifications. Organized patterns of social life result in unequal distributions of resources and power among people. They influence where people live and with whom they are likely to interact. Such social divisions and hierarchies or social structures influence interaction in ways that tend to lead to their perpetuation. As previously suggested, microsociology examines how individuals interactionally produce and reproduce the social divisions, organizations, institutions, and systems that macrosociology studies in the abstract. Microsociology and sociological psychology also address how social structures influence different individuals' social lives and subjective experiences. They thereby complement macrosociology and bring alive the study of human social life.

The readings collected in this volume provide an introduction to sociological psychology and microsociology. College students are often introduced to these fields of study in courses with titles like Social Psychology or The Individual and Society. This volume is intended for them and for other readers who are interested in the inner workings of social life and how each of us influences and is influenced by it. The volume includes both statements of theoretical positions and empirical studies that draw and elaborate upon those positions.

Some of the selections included herein are considered classics of sociological psychology and microsociology. Others are more recent and have yet to weather the test of time. This combination of classic and more current readings is intended to give readers a sense of the intellectual roots of sociological psychology and microsociology, as well as their continuing vitality. The selections can be read in any order, although I have tried to arrange them so that they build on the ideas

and empirical findings that have preceded each. In whatever order the articles may be read, my hope is that they convey an appreciation of the intricate artfulness of daily social action and the fascinating variety of human social experience.

Microsociologists have long maintained that language is central to the social shaping of human experience, so I would like to add a note about some of the language in this anthology. Because many of the selections were originally published some years ago, a few use the masculine generic and contain other references to gender that may seem insensitive to the contemporary reader. Rather than change that language, I have left most of it intact, in part because there is a microsociological lesson in our reactions to such gender usage. It indicates just how much our thinking about gender has socially changed since those selections were written. Other language in this volume may offend ethnic and racial sensibilities. This language is found in empirical studies that report, as accurately as possible, what was actually observed, including the language that was actually used. If we are to understand human social life, it is essential that we confront such everyday language, however uncomfortable it may make us.

This Fifth Edition of *Inside Social Life* is much changed from the Fourth Edition. I have included ten new selections. These new chapters address such topics as the following:

- The social construction of human experience
- The neurological plasticity of the developing human brain
- Young children's ethnic and racial definitions of self
- The historical transformation of grief in America
- The experience of taking psychiatric drugs
- The presentation of "cyberselves" on the Internet

- The conversational delivery of bad diagnostic news
- Young adult children's negotiations with parents over cars
- The challenges of living in impoverished, inner-city neighborhoods
- The processes that resulted in the design and establishment of the Vietnam Veterans Memorial

Introductions to each section *and* chapter identify and explain central issues, key concepts, and relationships among topics.

This volume is not a product of my efforts alone. I was greatly aided in this revision by the comments and evaluations that instructors forwarded to the publisher. I am most grateful to Emma G. Bailey (University of Western New Mexico), Angela Garcia (University of Cincinnati), Matthew Green (University of Arizona), Sara Horsfall (Texas Wesleyan University), Ann Marie Kinnell (University of Southern Mississippi), Jean Lynch (Miami University), James P. Marshall (University of Northern Colorado), Erica Owens (Marquette University), and David Rohall (Western Illinois University) for their thoughtful and constructive comments on the Fourth Edition. I also thank Sclafani Louis-Jeune for her clerical assistance and technical wizardry. As I did in the introduction to the First Edition, I thank Gerald Handel for first suggesting, fifteen years ago, that I undertake this project. I am deeply grateful to Claude Teweles for his continuing encouragement and support and to Donileen Loseke for everything. Finally, I thank my former students and colleagues at Skidmore College and my current students and colleagues at the University of South Florida for their stimulation, inspiration, guidance, and support. ✦

Uses of the Selections

I *nside Social Life* can be used effectively as a single assigned text. However, for instructors who wish to use this anthology to supplement another text, the following chart may be helpful. It groups the chapters in this volume by topics conventionally used to organize courses in social psychology and microsociology. Primary and secondary emphases are listed separately. (Parentheses indicate an alternative primary use for a chapter.) ✦

Topic	Primary Emphasis	Secondary Emphasis
Cognition and Perception	1, 2, 3, 8	5, 11
Emotions	10, 18, (9), (31)	4, 11, 22
Self and Identity	4, 5, 7, 13, 14, 15, 24, 37	11, 12, 32, 33, (6), (36)
Socialization	6, (10)	4, 5, 8, 20, 24, 29, (2), (20)
Social Interaction	12, 16, 17, 19	28, (13), (30)
Social Relationships	20, 21, 22, (15), (23), (24)	18, 25, (9)
Culture	35	9, 25, (1)
Social Organizations and Institutions	26, 28, 31, (21), (25)	35, (27)
Gender	29	25, (26)
Class and Ethnicity	25, 26, 27, 30, (6), (7)	20
Deviance and Social Control	32, 33	11, 22, 23, 30, (27), (37)
Social Problems	23, 34	27, 30, 35
Social Change	9, 36	34, 35, 37

About the Contributors

Patricia Adler is Professor of sociology at the University of Colorado. She is the author of *Wheeling and Dealing* (1985) and coauthor (with Peter Adler) of *Paradise Laborers* (2004).

Peter Adler is Professor of sociology at the University of Denver. He is the coauthor (with Patricia Adler) of *Backboards and Blackboards* (1991) and *Peer Power* (1997).

Elijah Anderson is the Charles and William L. Day Professor of Social Sciences at the University of Pennsylvania. He is the author of *A Place on the Corner* (1976), *Streetwise* (1990), and *The Code of the Street* (1999).

Arnold Arluke is Professor of sociology at Northeastern University. He is a coauthor of the award-winning *Regarding Animals* (1996) and author of *Just a Dog* (2006), among other books.

Peter Berger is Professor of sociology and theology at Boston University. His many authored and coauthored books include *An Invitation to Sociology* (1963), *The Sacred Canopy* (1963), and *Modernity, Pluralism, and the Crises of Meaning* (1995).

Alexandra Berkowitz recently received her Ph.D. in sociology from Indiana University and is currently a researcher at the Centers for Disease Control and Prevention.

Amy Best is Professor of sociology at George Mason University and author of *Prom Night* (2000) and *Fast Cars, Cool Rides* (2005).

Joel Best is Professor of sociology at the University of Delaware. His many books include *Threatened Children* (1990), *Damn Lies and Statistics* (2001), and *Why Serious People Fall for Fads* (2006).

Herbert Blumer (1900–1987) was a prominent advocate for the sociological perspective of symbolic interactionism and Professor of sociology at the University of California, Berkeley, before his death. Among his many articles and books, the most widely read is *Symbolic Interactionism: Perspective and Method* (1969).

Spencer E. Cahill is Professor of sociology at the University of South Florida and the editor of this volume.

Charles Horton Cooley (1864–1929), an economist turned sociologist, had a long teaching career at the University of Michigan. His major works are *Human Nature and Social Order* (1902), *Social Organization* (1909), and *Social Process* (1919).

Robin Eggleston is a practicing social worker in upstate New York.

Frederick Elkin is Professor Emeritus of sociology at York University, Toronto. He was the original author of *Child and Society* (1960).

Joe R. Feagin is the Ella C. McFadden Professor of Liberal Arts at Texas A&M University. He is the author and coauthor of many books, including *White Racism* (1995), *Double Burden* (1998), and *Black and Blue* (2004).

Kathryn J. Fox is Professor of sociology at the University of Vermont and a coauthor of *Ethnography Unbound* (1991).

Arthur W. Frank is Professor of sociology at the University of Calgary and the author of *At the Will of the Body* (1991), *The Wounded Storyteller* (1995), and *The Renewal of Generosity* (2005).

Frank Furedi is Professor of sociology at the University of Kent. His books include *Culture of Fear* (1997), *The Silent War* (1998), and *Paranoid Parenting* (2001).

Kenneth J. Gergen is Professor of psychology at Swarthmore College. He is the author of several books, including *The Saturated Self*

(1991) and *An Invitation to Social Construction* (1999).

Erving Goffman (1922–1982) was the Benjamin Franklin Professor of Anthropology and Sociology at the University of Pennsylvania and president of the American Sociological Association at the time of his death. His many highly influential books include *The Presentation of Self in Everyday Life* (1959), *Asylums* (1961), *Relations in Public* (1971), and *Frame Analysis* (1974).

Jaber F. Gubrium is Professor and Chair of sociology at the University of Missouri. His many books include *Oldtimers and Alzheimers* (1986), *Out of Control* (1992), and *The Self We Live By* (2000).

Gerald Handel is Professor Emeritus of sociology at The City College of New York. His many edited, authored, and coauthored books include *Making a Life in Yorkville* (2000).

James A. Holstein is Professor and Chair of sociology at Marquette University. Among other books, he is the author of *Court-Ordered Insanity* (1993) and coauthor of *The Self We Live By* (2000).

Leslie Irvine is Professor of sociology at The University of Colorado and the author of *Codependents Forevermore* (1999) and *If You Tame Me* (2004).

David A. Karp is Professor of sociology at Boston College. He is the author of the award-winning *Speaking of Sadness* (1966) and of *The Burden of Sympathy* (2001), among other books.

Sherryl Kleinman is Professor of sociology at the University of North Carolina. She is the author of *Equals Before God* (1984) and *Opposing Ambitions* (1996).

Thomas Luckmann was Professor of sociology at the University of Konstanz in Germany. Since 1994 he is professor emeritus and he lectures internationally. He is a coauthor of *The Social Construction of Reality* (1966) and *The Structures of the Life-World* (1974).

Douglas Maynard is Professor of sociology at the University of Wisconsin–Madison.

He is the author of *Inside Plea Bargaining* (1984) and *Bad News, Good News* (2003).

George Herbert Mead (1863–1931) profoundly influenced early generations of American sociologists while he was Professor of Philosophy at the University of Chicago. His published lectures and other work provided the basis for a distinctively sociological psychology and include *Mind, Self, and Society* (1934) and *The Philosophy of the Act* (1938).

Melissa Milkie is Professor of sociology at the University of Maryland and coauthor of the forthcoming *Changing Rhythms of American Family Life*.

Nancy Naples is Professor of sociology and women's studies at the University of Connecticut. Her books include *Grassroots Warriors* (1998) and *Feminism and Method* (2003).

Irene Padavic is Professor of sociology at Florida State University and coauthor of *Women and Men at Work*, now in its second edition (2002).

Greta Foff Paules is a cultural anthropologist and the author of *Dishing It Out* (1991).

Barry Schwartz is Professor Emeritus of sociology at the University of Georgia. His books include *Vertical Classification* (1981) and *Abraham Lincoln and the Forge of National Memory* (2000).

Allen C. Smith III has long been involved in medical education and is the former Dean of Student and Academic Affairs at the Northeastern Ohio Universities College of Medicine.

Peter N. Stearns is Provost and Professor of history at George Mason University. His many books include *American Cool* (1994), *The Battleground of Desire* (1999), and *Anxious Parents* (2003).

Barrie Thorne is Professor of sociology and women's studies at the University of California, Berkeley. She is a coauthor of *She Said/He Said* (1976) and the author of *Gender Play* (1993).

Debra Van Ausdale is Professor of sociology at Syracuse University and coauthor of *The First R* (2000).

Lev Vygotsky (1896–1934) was an influential Russian psychologist who died of tuberculosis only ten years after beginning his study of psychology. Among his extensive writing during that decade, *Language and Thought* (1934) is the most widely read today.

Robin Wagner-Pacifici is Professor of sociology at Swarthmore College. She is the author of *Discourse and Destruction* (1994) and *Theorizing the Standoff* (2000).

Dennis D. Waskul is Professor of sociology at Minnesota State University, Mankato. He is the author of *Self-Games and Body Play* (2003) and editor of *net.seXXX: Readings on Sex, Pornography and the Internet* (2004).

Eviatar Zerubavel is Professor of sociology at Rutgers University. He is the author of several books, including *Hidden Rhythms* (1981), *Social Mindscapes* (1997), and *Time Maps* (2003). ✦

Part I

Human Being and Social Reality

The study and understanding of any subject must start with something—with some general ideas about that subject. The subject of sociological psychology and microsociology is human experience both shared and private. Thus, sociological psychology and microsociology must start with some general ideas about human nature, human experience, and social existence. The three selections in this section advance some ideas about these fundamental questions. They provide conceptual foundations on which a study and understanding of human social life and experience can be built. All three provide conceptual pillars that securely support sociological psychology and microsociology. They also remind us that more popular ways of thinking about human beings and social life may not do justice to their fascinating complexity. ✦

1

The Social Foundations of Human Experience

Peter Berger and Thomas Luckmann

Most people today are at least vaguely aware of the wide variety of human cultures or ways of life that populate the globe. Although they may consider their own way of life superior to that of others, they recognize that other people hold radically different beliefs and observe wildly different customs than they do. It is as if such people inhabit different worlds than they do, and, in an important sense, they do. Humans at all times and in all places do not experience the same reality. Rather, they experience a socially constructed reality that their predecessors have bequeathed to them and that they routinely reproduce. In this selection, sociologists Peter Berger and Thomas Luckmann briefly explain why humans must construct their own reality, how that reality is transmitted from one generation to the next and routinely confirmed, and some implications for understanding the relation of the individual to society.

As Berger and Luckmann argue, humans' biological constitution does not adequately order their relationship to their environment. Instead, they must interpret, define, and endow their environment with meanings so as to respond to it effectively. Human meanings provide the regulation and order to human conduct that human

biology does not. However, individual humans do not construct these meanings alone but collectively. They endow their environment with shared meanings that promote the coordination of action. Moreover, because those meanings are shared or intersubjective, they assume an objective status, as existing apart from any particular individual's experience.

The seeming objectivity of socially constructed realities is further enhanced by the fact that human infants are born into a world already interpreted and organized by others. The significant others who care for the infant transmit the prevailing definitions and interpretations of reality in their society to him or her. To the naïve child, this construction of reality is simply given and inevitable. In addition, the significant others who care for infants and children also transmit messages to them concerning their own socially defined identities. They might tell a child that she is and treat her as a girl, an African American, pretty, a tomboy, and the like. Eventually, the child comes to define herself similarly and acquires a self, a process that will be discussed in far more detail later in this volume.

As Berger and Luckmann note, the term *socialization* is commonly used to refer to this process whereby children are inducted into a society and its shared or objective reality. One goal of socialization is to establish a correspondence between that shared or objective reality and the individual's own subjective experience. This is initially accomplished during primary or childhood socialization by the seeming inevitability of the significant others' definitions of reality. These definitions provide the child with their most basic *nomic structure*, or ways of meaningfully ordering their experience. Subsequent or secondary socialization into particular roles builds on this primary reality.

Yet, correspondence between socially shared or objective reality and subjective experience is never established once and for all. It must be constantly confirmed and maintained. According to Berger and Luckmann, the most important means of reality maintenance is conversation. Conversation with others continually reaffirms social definitions of reality, not so much by what is said but by what is taken for granted and unde-serving of comment. Conversation also maintains the shared reality through the language in which it is conducted. Language classifies, typifies, and defines experience. Because it is shared, it gives the reality it constructs the accent of objectivity.

Yet, the organization of individuals' experience does change. Sometimes they undergo radical transformations of subjective experience or alternations, involving a kind of resocialization. More commonly, individuals' subjective experience and selves are gradually transformed through secondary socialization and gradual changes in social experience. In societies in which such change is common, socially standard explanations are available that minimize inconsistency between the individual's past and present, helping to maintain a correspondence between the socially objective reality and individual experience.

Social definitions of reality also include definitions of the types of people who populate society and of how they think, feel, and act. Berger and Luckmann refer to these as *theories of identity*, but they might better be called *psychologies*. These "psychologies" are always embedded in more comprehensive definitions of reality and cannot be fully understood apart from those broader constructions of reality. This implies that assessments of psychological functioning are always relative to particular definitions of reality. What may seem quite insane in one society may be quite normal in another. Hence, in an important sense, there is no such thing as human psychology, except in the vaguest sense. There are only human psychologies, psychologies as numerous as the human societies, cultures, and realities that populate and have populated the earth.

. . . [H]umans'] relationship to [their] environment is characterized by world-openness. Not only [have humans] succeeded in establishing [themselves] over the greater part of the earth's surface, [their] relationship to the surrounding environment is everywhere very imperfectly structured by [their] own bi-

ological constitution. The latter, to be sure, permits [humans] to engage in different activities. But the fact that [they] continued to live a nomadic existence in one place and turned to agriculture in another cannot be explained in terms of biological processes. This does not mean, of course, that there are no biologically determined limitations to [humans'] relations with [their] environment; [their] species-specific sensory and motor equipment poses obvious limitations on [their] range of possibilities. The peculiarity of [humans'] biological constitution lies rather in its instinctual component.

[Humans'] instinctual organization may be described as underdeveloped, compared with that of the other higher mammals. [Humans do] have drives, of course. But these drives are highly unspecialized and undirected. This means that the human organism is capable of applying its constitutionally given equipment in a very wide and, in addition, constantly variable and varying range of activities. This peculiarity of the human organism is grounded in its [individual] development . . . [T]he developing human being not only interrelates with a particular natural environment, but with a specific cultural and social order, which is mediated to him [or her] by the significant others who have charge of him [or her]. Not only is the survival of the human infant dependent upon certain social arrangements, the direction of his [or her] organismic development, and indeed a large part of his [or her] biological being as such, are subjected to continuing socially determined interference.

Despite the obvious physiological limits to the range of possible and different ways of becoming [human] in this double environmental interrelationship the human organism manifests an immense plasticity in its response to the environmental forces at work on it. This is particularly clear when one observes the flexibility of [humans'] biological constitution as it is subjected to a variety of socio-cultural determinations. It is an ethnological commonplace that the ways of becoming and being human are as numerous as [humans'] cultures. Humanness is socioculturally variable. In other words, there is no human nature in the sense of a biologically fixed substratum. There is only human nature in the sense of anthropological constants (for example, world-openness and plasticity of instinctual structure) that delimit and permit [humans'] socio-cultural formations. But the specific shape into which this humanness is molded is determined by those socio-cultural formations and is relative to their numerous variations. While it is possible to say that [humans have] a nature, it is more significant to say that [humans construct] their own nature, or more simply, that [humans produce themselves]. . . .

The period during which the human organism develops towards its completion in interrelationship with its environment is also the period during which the human self is formed. The formation of the self, then, must also be understood in relation to both the ongoing organismic development and the social process in which the natural and the human environment are mediated through the significant others. The genetic presuppositions for the self are, of course, given at birth. But the self, as it is experienced later as a subjectively and objectively recognizable identity, is not. The same social processes that determine the completion of the organism produce the self in its particular, culturally relative form. The character of the self as a social product is not limited to the particular configuration the individual identifies as himself [or herself] (for instance, as a "man," in the particular way in which that identity is defined and formed in the culture in question), but to the comprehensive psychological equipment that serves as an appendage to the particular configuration (for instance, "manly" emotions, attitudes, and even somatic reactions). It goes without saying, then, that the organism and, even more, the self cannot be adequately understood apart from the particular social context in which they were shaped. . . .

It should be clear from the forgoing that the statement that [humans produce themselves] in no way implies some sort of Promethean vision of the solitary individual. [Humans'] self-production is always, and of necessity, a social enterprise. [Humans] *together* produce a human environment, with the totality of its socio-cultural and psychological formations. None of these formations may be understood as products of [humans'] biological constitution, which, as indicated, provides only the outer limits for human productive activity. Just as it is impossible for [a human] to develop as [human] in isolation, so it is impossible for [a human] in isolation to produce a human environment. Solitary human being is being on the animal level (which, of course, [humans] share with other animals). As soon as one observes phenomena that are specifically human, one enters the realm of the social. [Humans'] specific humanity and [their] sociality are inextricably intertwined. . . .

The human organism lacks the necessary biological means to provide stability for human conduct. Human existence, if it were thrown back on its organismic resources by themselves would be existence in some sort of chaos. . . . The question then arises: From what does the . . . existing stability of human order derive? An answer may be given on two levels. One may first point to the obvious fact that a given social order precedes any individual organismic development. That is, world-openness, while intrinsic to [humans'] biological make-up, is always pre-empted by social order. One may say that the biologically intrinsic world-openness of human existence is always, and indeed must be, transformed by social order into a relative world-closedness. While this reclosure can never approximate the closedness of animal existence, if only because of its human produced and thus "artificial" character, it is nevertheless capable, most of the time, of providing direction and stability for the greater part of human conduct. The question may then be pushed to another level. One may ask in what manner social order itself arises.

The most general answer to this question is that social order is a human product, or more precisely an ongoing human production. . . . Social order is not biologically given or derived from any biological *data* in its empirical manifestations. Social order, needless to add, is also not given in [humans'] natural environment, though particular features of this may be factors in determining certain features of social order (for example, its economic or technological arrangements). Social order is not part of the "nature of things," and it cannot be derived from the "laws of nature." Social order exists *only* as a product of human activity. No other ontological status may be ascribed to it without hopelessly obfuscating its empirical manifestations. Both in its genesis (social order is the result of past human activity) and its existence in any instant of time (social order exists only and insofar as human activity continues to produce it) it is a human product.

* * *

The individual . . . is not born a member of society. He [or she] is born with a predisposition toward sociality, and he [or she] becomes a member of society. In the life of every individual, therefore, there *is* a temporal sequence, in the course of which he [or she] is inducted into participation [in society]. . . . The ontogenetic process by which this is brought about is socialization, which may be . . . defined as the comprehensive and consistent induction of an individual into the objective world of a society or sector of it. Primary socialization is the first socialization an individual undergoes in childhood, through which he [or she] becomes a member of society. Secondary socialization is any subsequent process that inducts an already socialized individual into new sectors of the objective world of his [or her] society. . . .

It is at once evident that primary socialization is usually the most important for an individual, and that the basic structure of all secondary socialization has to resemble that of primary socialization. Every individual is born into an objective social structure within which he [or she] encounters the significant others who are in charge of his [or her] socialization. These significant others are imposed upon him [or her]. Their definitions of his [or her] situation are posited for him [or her] as objective reality. He [or she] is thus born into not only an objective social structure but also an objective social world. The significant others who mediate this world to him [or her] modify it in the course of mediating it. They select aspects of it in accordance with their own location in the social structure, and also by virtue of their individual, biographically rooted idiosyncrasies. The social world is "filtered" to the individual through this double selectivity. Thus, the lower-class child not only absorbs a lower-class perspective on the social world, he absorbs it in the idiosyncratic coloration given it by his parents (or whatever other individuals are in charge of his [or her] primary socialization). The same lower-class perspective may induce a mood of contentment, resignation, bitter resentment, or seething rebelliousness. Consequently, the lower-class child will not only come to inhabit a world greatly different from that of an upper-class child, but may do so in a manner quite different from the lower-class boy next door. . . .

In primary socialization, then, the individual's first world is constructed. Its peculiar quality of firmness is to be accounted for, at least in part, by the inevitability of the individual's relationship to his [or her] first significant others. The world of childhood, in its luminous reality, is thus conducive to confidence not only in the persons of the significant others but in their definitions of the situation. The world of childhood is massively and indubitably real. Probably this could not be otherwise at this stage of the development of consciousness. Only later can the individual afford the luxury of at least a modicum of doubt. . . . [T]he world of childhood is so constituted as to instill in the individual a nomic structure in which he may have confidence that "everything is all right"—to repeat what is possibly the most frequent sentence mothers say to their crying offspring. The later discovery that some things are far from "all right" may be more or less shocking, depending on biographical circumstances, but in either case the world of childhood is likely to retain its peculiar reality in retrospection. It remains the "home world," however far one may travel from it in later life into regions where one does not feel at home at all. . . .

Secondary socialization is the [induction into] institutional or institution-based "subworlds." . . . Forgetting for a moment its other dimensions, we may say that secondary socialization is the acquisition of role-specific knowledge, the roles being directly or indirectly rooted in the division of labor. There is some justification for such a narrow definition, but this is by no means the whole story. Secondary socialization requires the acquisition of role-specific vocabularies, which means, for one thing [systems of meaning] structuring routine interpretations and conduct within the institutional area. At the same time "tacit understandings," evaluations and affective colorations of these [systems of meaning] are also acquired. The "subworlds" internalized in secondary socialization are generally partial realities in contrast to the "base-world" of primary socialization. Yet they too are more or less cohesive realities. . . .

The formal processes of secondary socialization are determined by its fundamental problem: it always presupposes a preceding process of primary socialization; that is, that it must deal with an already formed self and an already internalized world. It cannot construct subjective reality [out of nothing]. This presents a problem because the already internalized reality has a tendency to persist. Whatever new contents are now to be internalized must somehow be superimposed upon this already present reality. There is, therefore, a problem of consistency between the original and the new internalizations. The problem may be more or less difficult of solution in different cases. Having learned that cleanliness is a virtue in one's own person it is not difficult to transfer the same virtue to one's horse. But having learned that certain obscenities are reprehensible as a pedestrian child, it may need some explanation that they are now [required] as a member of the cavalry. To establish and maintain consistency secondary socialization presupposes conceptual procedures to integrate different bodies of knowledge. . . .

Since socialization is never complete and the contents it internalizes face continuing threats to their subjective reality, every viable society must develop procedures of reality maintenance to safeguard a measure of symmetry between objective [shared] and subjective [individual] reality. . . . [T]he reality of everyday life [generally] maintains itself by being embodied in routines. . . . Beyond this, however, the reality of everyday life is ongoingly reaffirmed in the individual's interaction with others. Just as reality is originally internalized by a social process, so it is maintained in consciousness by social processes. . . .

The most important vehicle of reality-maintenance is conversation. One may view the individual's everyday life in terms of the working away of conversational apparatus that ongoingly maintains, modifies and reconstructs his [or her] subjective reality. Conversation means mainly, of course, that people speak with one another. This does not deny the rich aura of non-verbal communication that surrounds speech. Nevertheless speech retains a privileged position in the total conversational apparatus. It is important to stress, however, that the greater part of reality-maintenance in conversation is implicit, not explicit. Most conversation does not in so many words define the nature of the world. Rather, it takes place against the background of a world that is silently taken for granted. Thus an exchange such as, "Well, it's time for me to get to the station," and "Fine, darling, have a good day at the office" implies an entire world *within which* these apparently simple propositions make sense. By virtue of this implication the exchange confirms the subjective reality of this world.

If this is understood, one will readily see that the great part, if not all, of everyday conversation maintains subjective reality. Indeed, its massivity is achieved by the accumulation and consistency of casual conversation—conversation that can *afford to be casual* precisely because it refers to the routines of a taken-for-granted world. The loss of casualness signals a break in the routines and, at least potentially, a threat to the taken-for-granted reality. Thus one may imagine the effect on casualness of an exchange like this: "Well, it's time for me to get the station," "Fine, darling, don't forget to take along your gun."

At the same time that the conversational apparatus ongoingly maintains reality, it ongoingly modifies it. Items are dropped and added, weakening some sectors of what is still being taken for granted and reinforcing others. Thus the subjective reality of something that is never talked about comes to be shaky. It is one thing to engage in an embarrassing sexual act. It is quite another to talk about it beforehand or afterwards. Conversely, conversation gives firm contours to items previously apprehended in a fleeting and unclear manner. One may have doubts about one's religion; these doubts become real in a quite different way as one discusses them. One then "talks oneself into" these doubts; they are objectified as reality within one's consciousness. Generally speaking, the conversational apparatus maintains reality by "talking through" various elements of experience and allocating them a definite place in the real world.

This reality-generating potency of conversation is already given in the fact of linguistic objectification. . . . Language objectifies the

world, transforming the [ragged cloth] of experience into a cohesive order. In the establishment of this order language *realizes* a world, in the double sense of apprehending and producing it. Conversation is the actualization of this realizing efficacy of language in the face-to-face situations of individual existence. In conversation the objectifications of language become objects of individual consciousness. Thus the fundamental reality-maintaining fact is the continuing use of the same language to objectify unfolding biographical experience. In a sense, all who employ this same language are reality-maintaining others. The significance of this can be further differentiated in terms of what is meant by a "common language"—from the group—idiosyncratic language of the primary groups to regional or class dialects to the national community that defines itself in terms of language. There are corresponding "returns to reality" for the individual who goes back to the few individuals who understand his in-group allusions, to the section to which his accent belongs, or to the larger collectivity that has identified itself with a particular linguistic tradition—in reverse order, say, a return to the United States, to Brooklyn, and to the people who went to the same public school.

In order to maintain subjective reality effectively, the conversational apparatus must be continual and consistent. Disruptions of continuity and consistency [necessarily] posit a threat to the subjective reality in question. . . . Subjective reality is thus always dependent upon specific plausibility structures, that is, the specific social base and social processes required for its maintenance. One can maintain one's self-identification as a man of importance only in a milieu that confirms that identity; one can maintain one's Catholic faith only if one retains one's significant relationship with the Catholic community; and so forth. Disruption of significant conversation with the mediators of the respective plausibility structures threatens the subjective realities in question. . . . The individual may resort to various techniques of reality-maintenance even in the absence of actual conversation, but the reality-generating potency of these techniques is greatly inferior to the face-to-face conversations they are designed to replicate. The longer these techniques are isolated from face-to-face confirmation, the less likely they will be to retain the accent of reality. The individual living for many years among people of a different faith and cut off from the community of those sharing his [or her] own may continue to identify himself [or herself] as say, a Catholic. Through prayer, religious exercises, and similar techniques his old Catholic reality may continue to be subjectively relevant to him [or her]. At the very least the techniques may sustain his [or her] continued self-identification as a Catholic. They will, however, become subjectively empty of "living" reality unless they are "revitalized" by social contact with other Catholics. To be sure, an individual usually remembers the realities of his past. But the way to "refresh" those memories is to converse with those who share their relevance. . . .

Everything that has been said so far on socialization implies the possibility that subjective reality can be transformed. To be in society already entails an ongoing process of modification of subjective reality. To talk about transformation, then involves a discussion of different degrees of modification. [The extreme case is that of] near-total transformation; that is, in which the individual "switches worlds." . . . Such transformations we . . . call alternations.

Alternation requires processes of re-socialization. These processes resemble primary socialization, because they have to radically reassign reality accents and, consequently, must replicate to a considerable degree the strongly affective identification with the socializing personnel that was characteristic of childhood. They are different from primary socialization because they do not start [from nothing], and as a result must cope with [the]

problems of dismantling, disintegrating the preceding nomic structure of subjective reality. . . . The historical prototype of alternation is religious conversion [but other] examples are in the areas of political indoctrination and psychotherapy. . . .

There are in practice . . . many intermediate types between resocialization . . . and secondary socialization that continues to build on the primary internalizations. In these there are partial transformations of subjective reality or designated sectors of it. Such partial transformations are common in contemporary society in connection with the individual's social mobility and occupational training. Here the transformation of subjective reality can be considerable, as the individual is made into an acceptable upper-middle-class type or an acceptable physician, and as he internalizes the appropriate reality-appendages. But these transformations typically fall short of re-socialization. They build on the basis of primary internalizations and generally avoid abrupt discontinuities within the subjective biography of the individual. As a result, they face the problem of maintaining consistency between the earlier and later elements of subjective reality. This problem, not present in th[e] form of resocialization, which ruptures the subjective biography and reinterprets the past rather than correlating the present with it, becomes more acute the closer secondary socialization gets to resocialization without actually becoming it. . . .

The procedures for maintaining consistency also involve a tinkering with the past, but in a less radical manner—an approach dictated by the fact that in such cases there is usually association with persons and groups who were significant before. They continue to be around, are likely to protest too fanciful reinterpretations, and must themselves be convinced that such transformations as have taken place are plausible. For example, in the case of transformations occurring in conjunction with social mobility, there are ready-made interpretive schemes that explain what has happened to all concerned *without* positing a total metamorphosis of the individual concerned. Thus the parents of such an upwardly mobile individual will accept certain changes in the latter's demeanor and attitudes as necessary, possibly even desirable, accompaniment[s] of this new station in life. "Of course," they will agree, Irving has had to de-emphasize his Jewishness now that he has become a successful doctor in suburbia; "of course" he dresses and speaks differently; "of course" he now votes Republican; "of course" he married a Vassar girl—and perhaps it will also become a matter of course that he only rarely comes to visit his parents. Such interpretative schemes, which are ready-made in a society with high . . . mobility and already internalized by the individual before he himself is actually mobile, guarantee biographical continuity and smooth inconsistencies as they arise. . . .

* * *

Identity is, of course, a key element of subjective reality . . . and is formed by social processes. Once crystallized, it is maintained, modified, or even reshaped by social relations. The social processes involved in both the formation and the maintenance of identity are determined by the social structure. Conversely, the identities produced by the interplay of organism, individual consciousness, and social structure react upon the given social structure, maintaining it, modifying it, or even reshaping it. Societies have histories in the course of which specific identities emerge; these histories are, however, made by [humans] with specific identities. . . .

Identity is a phenomenon that emerges from the [interrelationship] between the individual and society. Identity *types*, on the other hand, are social products [through and through], relatively stable elements of objective social reality (the degree of stability being, of course, socially determined in its turn). As such, they are the topic of some form of theorizing in any society, even if they are sta-

ble and the formation of individual identities is relatively unproblematic. Theories about identity are always embedded in a more general interpretation of reality. . . . Identity remains unintelligible unless it is located in a world. Any theorizing about identity—about specific identity types—must therefore occur within the framework of the theoretical interpretation within which it and they are located. . . .

If theories about identity are always embedded in the more comprehensive theories about reality, this must be understood in terms of the logic underlying the latter. [It should be stressed . . . that we are here referring to theories of identity as a social phenomenon, that is, without prejudice as to their acceptability to modern science.] For example, a psychology interpreting certain empirical phenomena as a possession by demoniacal beings has as its matrix a mythological theory of the cosmos, and it is inappropriate to interpret it in a non-mythological framework. Similarly, a psychology interpreting the same phenomena in terms of electrical disturbances of the brain has as its background an overall scientific theory of reality, both human and non-human, and derives its consistency from the logic underlying this theory. Put simply, psychology always presupposes cosmology.

This point can be well illustrated by reference to the much used psychiatric term "reality-oriented." A psychiatrist trying to diagnose an individual whose psychological status is in question asks him [or her] questions to determine the degree of his [or her] "reality-orientedness." This is quite logical; from a psychiatric viewpoint there is obviously something problematic about an individual who does not know what day of the week it is or who readily admits he [or she] has talked with departed spirits. Indeed, the term "reality-oriented" itself can be useful in such a context. The sociologist, however, has to ask the additional question, "*Which*" reality? Incidentally, this addition is not irrelevant psychiatrically. The psychiatrist will certainly take it into account, when an individual does not know the day of the week, if he [or she] has just arrived on a jet plane from another continent. He [or she] may not know the day of the week simply because he [or she] is still "on another time"—Calcutta time, say, instead of Eastern Standard Time. If the psychiatrist has any sensitivity to the socio-cultural context of psychological conditions he will also arrive at different diagnoses of the individual who converses with the dead, depending on whether such an individual comes from, say, New York City or from rural Haiti. The individual could be "on another reality" in the same socially objective sense that the previous one was "on another time." In other words, questions of psychological status cannot be decided without recognizing the reality-definitions that are taken for granted in the social situation of the individual. To put it more sharply, psychological status is relative to the social definitions of reality in general and is itself socially defined. . . .

Reprinted from: Peter Berger and Thomas Luckmann, *The Social Construction of Reality*. Copyright © 1966 by Peter L. Berger and Thomas Luckmann. Used by permission of Doubleday, a division of Random House, Inc. ✦

2

Human Neural Plasticity and Socialization

Gerald Handel,
Spencer Cahill, and
Frederick Elkin

There is a long-standing debate regarding whether biological factors or experience are largely responsible for the course of human development and individuals' consequent abilities and characteristics. Some argue that almost all human characteristics are products of genetic inheritance. Others argue that humans are almost totally products of their experience. This debate is often called the "nature versus nurture" controversy, as if human biology and experience were easily separable. Although there are those who still promote biological determinism and wholly environmental positions, there is a growing recognition among both biological and social scientists that most human characteristics result from complex interactions between biological processes and experience. Probably the most telling research in this regard is that on human neural plasticity or the responsiveness and adaptability of the human brain to experience.

This selection summarizes some of the research findings regarding human neural plasticity and the interplay between neurology and socialization in human development. Consistent with the earlier selection by Berger and Luckmann, it cites research evidence that human infants have a "predisposition toward sociality." The authors of this selection observe that this innate responsiveness to other humans initiates a complex interplay between biological processes and social experience that is the essence of human socialization and development.

A particularly important consequence of this complex interplay is the shaping of the functional circuitry of the brain, patterns of brain activity involved in the acquisition and retention of different skills and abilities, in the triggering of emotional reactions, the processing of sensory input, and the regulation of bodily movement. This circuitry forms through the development of synapses, or connections between nerve cells or neurons, and patterns of synaptic activity. As this selection notes, most synaptic connections in humans develop after birth and are subject to experiential influences. Millions of new synapses form in the brain of a human infant every day. Those that are stimulated by environmental inputs are strengthened, while those that are not are gradually weakened and eventually "pruned" or eliminated. Experience thereby shapes the functioning circuitry of the human brain and the skills and abilities the individual acquires, his or her emotional reactions, perceptions, and physical capabilities.

Language learning provides one important example. As this selection notes, human children seem "primed" to learn and understand spoken language, and do so quite rapidly when exposed to a language. However, the realization of that remarkable capacity depends on exposure to a language or languages, to experience. Moreover, the mastering of a particular language seems to interfere with the later learning of a second language. As this selection notes, there is even evidence that quite early in life children lose their ability to recognize different phonemes or vocal sounds that their native or original language does not distinguish. Children can learn to speak a second or even third language proficiently and virtually accent free, but that capacity declines with age, apparently because the neural circuitry of the brain becomes less flexible as it is continually reactivated by repeated experience.

11

Although human neural plasticity declines with age and the corresponding accumulation of experience, it never disappears. This selection is limited to the importance of neural plasticity during primary or childhood socialization. However, according to one of the leading experts on human neural plasticity, research indicates "that there is considerable residual malleability of the brain" among adults (Huttenlocher 2002, 188). And, it is because of such human neural plasticity that humans require nurture or social experience to complete their nature. In an important sense, as Berger and Luckmann noted in an earlier selection, humans construct their own nature.

Until recently, social scientists could only point to the wide variability among human societies as evidence of the biological plasticity of the human organism. However, recent discoveries of neurological research provide more direct evidence of humans' remarkable degree of *neural plasticity* (Huttenlocher 2002). These research findings suggest that the biological development, structure, and functioning of the human brain is "largely environmentally regulated" (Huttenlocher 2002, 189).

The development of the brain does occur within what many neurologists call "a particular genetic envelope" (Johnson 1997, 182). For example, all of the neurons or nerve cells that will make up the human brain have been produced and most moved or migrated into what will be their permanent location in the brain halfway through gestation or fetal development. However, "the real business of brain development is in synapse formation" or *synaptogenesis* (Elliot 1999, 26). A synapse is a junction that links one neuron to another. Once neurons are in their permanent location they sprout branches called *dendrites* and a kind of trunk called an *axon*. Everyplace where a dendrite comes close to an axon there is a potential for synapse formation. If stimulated, the axon releases a "chemical messenger" or neurotransmitter that may

then "bind" to a receptor chemical of a nearby dendrite of another neuron, forming a synapse (Elliot 1999, 23). This is the means through which neurons "communicate" or transfer information, leading to the coordinated functioning of systems of neurons (Barnet and Barnet 1998, 17). The development of such functioning neural systems apparently underlies the acquisition and retention of varied skills and abilities. In humans some synapses are formed before birth, but over eighty percent of the growth of dendrites and consequent formation of synapses occurs after birth when neurons are subject to the influence of sensory stimulation or experience (Elliot 1999, 27). Genes may lay the foundation for the functioning human brain, but experience largely determines what is built upon that foundation.

Most of the regulation of human intellect, emotions, as well as sensory and motor processes in humans takes place in the cerebral cortex or outer layer of the brain. Yet, at birth, there are few synaptic connections in that "rumpled gray mantle that covers the brain" (Barnet and Barnet 1998, 17). Most synaptic connections there form during the first year of life when the size of the brain rapidly expands to near-adult size (Huttenlocher 2002, 41), and an estimated 1.8 million new synapses form each second (Elliot 1999, 27). However, these synapses are not "hard-wired." Those that are routinely stimulated and activated are stabilized or strengthened while less active ones are weakened (Elliot 1999, 30). Hence, the initial burst of synaptic formation over the first one or two years of life is followed by "a much longer period of elimination or pruning of . . . synaptic connections."

It is generally believed that this early "overproduction" and subsequent pruning of synaptic connections accounts for humans' remarkable neural plasticity and capacity to learn. For example, the brains of human infants and young children have a remarkable capacity for functional self-repair. In an infant or young child with localized brain damage from stroke or injury, the undamaged parts of the cerebral cortex commonly "take over" functions normally carried out by the damaged region (Huttenlocher 2002, 2). For example, language processing is normally localized in certain regions of the left side or hemisphere of the brain. However, language processing is often taken over by the right hemisphere if those regions of the left hemisphere are damaged or removed for medical reasons at a young age (Huttenlocher 2002, 136). Hence, individuals with such early brain damage can become as proficient in language use as those whose brains are fully intact, although there are limits to such neural plasticity. Extensive brain injury or damage can result in the crowding of neurological functions into smaller than normal areas of the brain resulting in impairment of those functions and the associated abilities. Yet, the human brain has a remarkable capacity to "rewire" itself, especially early in life, and commonly does so in response to environmental inputs, especially those from the social environment.

Varied research suggests that human infants seem biologically "primed" to attend to other people. For example, research shows that within two to four months of birth infants tend to look significantly more at a schematic drawing of a human face than at either an empty circle or a circle containing scrambled facial features (Johnson 1997, 99–117). Two month old infants also "show signs of becoming attuned to the eyes as a privileged communicative feature" (Rochart 2001, 138), and by six months of age they smile significantly more at an adult who looks directly at them compared to one who slightly averts her or his gaze (Hains and Muir 1996). Similarly, infants seem inherently responsive to human facial expressions of emotions. For example, in one study, newborns were observed while facing an experimenter who displayed, in succession, exaggerated expressions of happiness, sadness, and surprise. The newborns tended to widen

their lips in response to the display of happiness, to protrude their lower lips during the expression of sadness, and to increase the opening of their eyes and mouth when the experimenter looked surprised (Feld et al. 1982). Such seemingly innate responsiveness to human stimulation arguably invites human interaction and thereby helps initiate the complex interplay of biological processes and social experience involved in human socialization.

Unfortunately, not all human newborns seem biologically primed to encourage social interaction and, thereby, their own socialization. For example, research suggests that some newborns who are later diagnosed with infantile autism tend to find novel forms of stimulation, including human stimulation, aversive that other newborns find pleasurable. That may be why autistic children tend to withdraw into so-called stereotypic forms of self-stimulation such as repeatedly rocking back and forth, flipping a light switch, or persistently rubbing a piece of carpet. However, the developmental psychologist Stanley Greenspan (1997, 159) and his colleagues have dramatically illustrated that autistic children's apparent aversion to human stimulation need not be an insurmountable barrier to adequate socialization. In their therapy with autistic children, Greenspan and his colleagues treat these children's stereotypic behavior not merely as symptoms but as opening wedges for human connection and, later, socialization. For example, they instructed the mother of a two-year-old girl who repeatedly rubbed a favorite piece of carpet to lie down on the floor and place her hand next to her daughter's. The girl pushed her mother's hand away, but each time she did so, her mother gently returned it. After three days, the girl began to smile at her mother when pushing her hand away and, from that small beginning, their play and interactions became progressively richer until, before long, the girl began to speak to her mother. At age seven, the girl had "a range of age-appropriate emotions, warm friendships and . . . score[d] in the low superior IQ range" (Greenspan 1997, 17). According to Greenspan (1997, 159), the crux to adequate socialization in such cases is finding the "environmental keys" that will unlock biological doors.

There are undoubtedly biological conditions that make socialization virtually impossible, but, because of human neural plasticity, they may be far fewer than previously thought. For example, a condition like congenital deafness could prove a major barrier to socialization if we relied on verbal sounds and language to communicate with deaf children. Yet, nonverbal languages such as American Sign Language can easily overcome such a biological barrier to human interaction, communication, and, thereby, socialization. Such languages are environmental keys that unlock biological doors to adequate socialization. They can unlock those doors because of the remarkable neural plasticity of the human brain. For example, among humans who are born deaf, the processing of visual information "appears to expand into" regions of the brain usually used for "auditory functions" (Huttenlocher 2002, 101).

Like hearing children, children who are born or "congenitally" deaf seem biologically "primed" to acquire language. The most compelling evidence for humans' biological propensity for language is that children learn whatever language to which they are exposed, spoken or signed, without specific instruction, and in a remarkably regular way.

> A baby goes from speaking no words at birth, to 50 to 100 words and two-word phrases at eighteen months or thereabouts, to nearly 600 words by age two and a half, to intricate and wordy constructions by three or four. A first-grader can understand 13,000 words and expertly deploys tenses, embedded clauses, compounds, and combinations using rules only a grammarian could explicate. (Barnet and Barnet 1998, 36)

Yet, the door to this remarkable human potential for language acquisition does not open automatically. It requires the environmental key of exposure to human language, and that exposure is always to a particular language or, in some cases, languages.

Although human infants apparently have the capacity to learn any human language, they end up proficiently speaking and understanding only the language or languages to which they are exposed relatively early in life. Research suggests that newborns can recognize differences between all the possible phonemes or distinctive vocal units of speech of all human languages. Yet, by the time they are around a year old, they have lost that ability and recognize only those sound combinations and contrasts that occur in the language to which they have been exposed or what is commonly called their "native language." For example, research indicates that Japanese babies can distinguish between the sounds "ra" and "la," but, a year later, they have lost this ability, apparently because these sounds are equivalent in Japanese (Barnet and Barnet 1998, 47).

Research findings such as these suggest that there may well be a critical or "sensitive" period for language learning. . . . That is, humans' capacity to acquire a language and speak it proficiently may decline with age. Grammatical aspects of language and proficient pronunciation may be most "sensitive" to the timing of language acquisition. For example, ninety percent of deaf children in the United States are born to hearing parents and differ greatly in the age at which they are first exposed to American Sign Language. As such, they provide important insights into the possible effects of learning a first language at varying ages (National Research Council and Institute of Medicine 2000, 134). Much of the research on language acquisition in deaf children has focused on their use of grammar because it seems especially sensitive to early experience. Among fluent users of American Sign Language, "subtle differences in hand-shape, as well as the spatial location and movement of individual signs," denote similar logical relations as word endings and order, articles, prepositions, and pronouns in spoken languages (Elliot 1999, 361). However, research indicates that only "native signers" or children who are exposed to sign language within the first two or three years of life make full use of these grammatical capabilities of American Sign Language. Those who learn American Sign Language when they are between four and six perform well but not as fluently as "native" signers, and those who do not learn American Sign Language until after they are twelve consistently sign in ungrammatical ways even after using it for thirty years or more (Elliot 1999, 362).

Studies of second language learning reveal similar patterns. The earlier in life individuals acquire a second language the more likely they are to speak it proficiently and accent free. For example, one study asked Chinese and Korean immigrants to the United States to listen to a few hundred English sentences, about half of which were ungrammatical, and indicate whether the sentences sounded "correct." "Only those who had immigrated by the age of seven performed as well as native English speakers, which is to say almost flawlessly." Among the rest, performance steadily declined in relation to the age at which they had immigrated and learned English (Elliot 1999, 362–363; National Research Council and Institute of Medicine 2000, 134–135). Other research indicates that the ability to speak a second language accent free is also related to the age at which that second language is acquired. For similar languages, like English and German, this window of opportunity for accent free speech may extend into early adolescence but for dissimilar languages, like English and Korean, it may close much earlier (Huttenlocher 2002, 149).

Research on the timing of language acquisition and subsequent fluency in its use suggests a more general lesson about the interplay of nature and nurture in human socialization: There may be temporal or chronological constraints on the experientially shaped "circuitry" of the human brain. The countless synaptic connections and potential connections in young children's brains enable the formation of varied neural circuits and, hence, the learning of varied skills and information. Yet, the formation of neural circuits in response to environmental stimulation tends to localize different neural functions into specific areas of the brain, and the associated loss or pruning of synaptic connections that are not stimulated limits the subsequent plasticity of the brain. As the brain's neural circuitry becomes more organized and specialized, it becomes more inflexible. Consequently, skills and abilities that might be easily acquired at an earlier age may be quite difficult or even impossible to acquire at a later age.

However, if there are critical or "sensitive" periods for acquiring different skills and capabilities, it would be misleading to consider them solely a matter of biological maturation. Whatever children experience, synaptic connections are being activated, strengthened and stabilized while others are being weakened. The consequent neural circuitry of their brains are organized and specialized to process the kind of environmental stimulation to which they have been exposed. That circuitry may be ill-suited to process other kinds of environmental stimulation and interfere with the acquisition of new and different skills and abilities. For example, areas of the brain that normally process language may become devoted to other neural functions in children who are not exposed to human language earlier in their lives. If so, then their ability to process and proficiently use human language has not so much been lost as replaced by some other, experientially regulated neurological capability. Even the limits of our neural plasticity and capacity to learn are arguably products of the continual interplay of nature and nurture in our lives.

Moreover, the retention of acquired skills and capabilities also depends on this intricate dance between biology and experience in human life. Synaptic transmissions are facilitated by frequent activation, resulting in increased speed and accuracy in the performance of associated skills and abilities, while lack of activation can lead to the loss of neural pathways and the associated skills and abilities. For example, young children who learn to use a second language proficiently will rapidly lose that ability if they are not continually exposed to and use it. Experience not only shapes the neural circuitry of the human brain, it also sustains it. The biology of the brain organizes our experience, but experience just as profoundly organizes the biology—the functioning neurological circuitry—of our brains.

This complex interplay of nature and nurture is likely implicated in humans' acquisition of not only socially shared characteristics, such as a particular language, but personal ones as well. For example, research indicates that infants tend to react with more or less inhibition when encountering novel situations such as a strange human or a mechanical toy that moves toward them (see Kagan 1994). These early differences in "temperament" are apparently inborn and may well be genetically determined. They also tend to be long-lasting. Relatively fearful infants tend to become timid children and shy adults, and relatively fearless infants tend to become bold children and outgoing adults. Yet, it is doubtful that the persistence of such traits is simply a matter of genetic inheritance.

. . . [S]ocialization is an interactive process of mutual influence. Infants' behaviors influence how parents and other caregivers respond to them, and those responses, in turn, influence infants. For example, parents are likely to expose babies to novel stimulation who seem to delight in it and to avoid irritating babies who find such stimulation upsetting. They consequently and quite inadvertently may perpetuate and even deepen infants' inherent boldness or timidity. On the other hand, research conducted by the child psychologist Jerome Kagan (1994) indicates that about a third of inhibited babies outgrow their timidity by kindergarten. He speculates that they do so because their parents made a conscious effort to "engineer emboldening experiences" by expressing interest in unfamiliar objects and new experiences and encouraging their child to do the same. Genes undoubtedly influence what human infants are and what they may become, but what humans most fundamentally are is biologically plastic or flexible.

Human biology, especially the neural plasticity of the human brain, provides the necessary foundation for human socialization. In turn, socialization shapes the very biological functioning of the human organism. In that sense, humans have not a single but a dual nature. We are born with a biological nature that enables and even requires the acquisition of a second nature through nurture. . . . As the anthropologist Clifford Geertz (1973, 45) observes, humans "all begin with the natural equipment to live a thousand kinds of life but end in the end having lived only one." Socialization largely determines the kind of life out of those thousand possibilities that we end up living.

References

Barnet, Ann, and Richard Barnet. 1998. *The Youngest Minds*. New York: Simon & Schuster.

Elliot, Lise. 1999. *What's Going On in There: How the Brain and Mind Develop in the First Five Years of Life*. New York: Bantam Books.

Feld, T. M., R. Woodson, R. Greenberg, and D. Cohen. 1982. "Discrimination and Imitation of Facial Expression by Neonates." *Science* 218: 149–181.

Geertz, Clifford. 1973. *The Interpretation of Cultures*. New York: Basic Books.

Greenspan, Stanley. 1997. *The Growth of the Mind*. Reading, MA: Addison-Wesley.

Hains, S. M. and D. W. Muir. 1996. "Infant Sensitivity to Adult Eye Direction." *Child Development* 67: 1940–1951.

Huttenlocher, Peter. 2002. *Neural Plasticity: The Effects of Environment on the Development of the Cerebral Cortex.* Cambridge, MA: Harvard University Press.

Johnson, Mark. 1997. *Developmental Cognitive Neuroscience.* Cambridge, MA: Blackwell.

Kagan, Jerome. 1994. *Galen's Prophecy: Temperament in Human Nature.* New York: Basic Books.

National Research Council and Institute of Medicine. 2000. *From Neurons to Neighborhoods: The Science of Early Childhood Development,* edited by Jack Shonkoff and Deborah Phillips. Washington, DC: National Academy Press.

Rochart, Philippe. 2001. *The Infant's World.* Cambridge, MA: Harvard University Press.

3

Islands of Meaning

Eviatar Zerubavel

The previous selection implied that human infants are born with a predisposition to distinguish human faces, and probably voices, from other sensory stimuli. However, apart from that, initially human perception is probably a kaleidoscope of smells, sounds, sights, and tactile sensations. We are confronted with a dizzying array of unique objects and events. If we are to order our relations with our environment, we must organize our perceptual experience. Regulating our responses to the environment requires that we regularize our experience. We must treat certain groups of objects and events as similar to one another and other groups of objects and events as distinctly different. Hence, classification and typification are basic building blocks for ordering humans' relation to their environments. They are the most fundamental means through which humans define, interpret, and endow their world with meaning—through which they construct their own realities. And, as Berger and Luckmann suggest in the first selection, humans do not do so alone but in concert with one another. The systems they use to classify and typify their experience are shared or intersubjective and, consequently, are experienced as objective. Moreover, as previously noted, humans are born into a world already interpreted and organized by others. They learn socially prevailing systems of classification and typification in the course of their socialization and thereby come to experience the organized worlds that other members of their society do.

In this selection, Eviatar Zerubavel examines how humans sort their experiences into distinct categories or what he describes as "islands of meaning." We lump together things we consider similar, ignoring their differences, and separate them from other things, ignoring similarities and exaggerating differences. The world we experience does not come prepackaged in such categories. We pack it into them, and, as Zerubavel observes, our packaging of experience into discrete categories of meaning is an "inevitably arbitrary act." There are an indefinite variety of ways to break up reality into such discrete islands of meaning, as the cultural and historical variety of human classification systems attests.

Zerubavel notes that language largely guides our classification of our experience. We learn a logic of classification when we learn a language and other symbol systems. In this way society teaches us how to perceive our world, shape it into discrete islands of meaning, and construct reality. This is one of the ways in which socialization completes our unfinished human nature. It provides social lenses through which we can see meaningful shapes in our largely shapeless experience. And individuals who acquire the social lenses of different societies see, and therefore live, in different realities. We must understand what others are seeing in order to understand how they think, feel, and act, and that requires inspection of the social lenses—the systems of classification and typification—through which they are looking.

Although classification and typification are necessary if humans are to relate to their environment effectively, they also have their dark side. For example, every human society classifies and typifies its own members, at least in regard to sex category—male or female—and to age or general stage of life. Some societies, like our own, also classify their members into races on the basis of visible physical characteristics and typifies one or another race as superior to others. Of course, these and other systems of classification and typification are subject to dispute and historical change. Indeed, they are often sources of protracted human conflict. What is at stake in such conflicts is the very construction of social reality. Classification and typification are, then, very serious business.

We transform the natural world into a social one by carving out of it mental chunks we then treat as if they were discrete, totally detached from their surroundings. The way we mark off islands of property is but one example of the general process by which we create meaningful social entities.

In order to endow the things we perceive with meaning, we normally ignore their uniqueness and regard them as typical members of a particular class of objects (a relative, a present), acts (an apology, a crime), or events (a game, a conference). After all, "If each of the many things in the world were taken as distinct, unique, a thing in itself unrelated to any other thing, perception of the world would disintegrate into complete meaninglessness."[1] Indeed, things become meaningful only when placed in some category. A clinical symptom, for instance, is quite meaningless until we find some diagnostic niche (a cold, an allergic reaction) within which to situate and thus make sense of it. Our need to arrange the world around us in categories is so great that, even when we encounter mental odds and ends that do not seem to belong in any conventional category, we nonetheless "bend" them so as to fit them into one anyway, as we usually do with the sexually ambiguous or the truly novel work of art. When such adjustment does not suffice, we even create special categories (avant-garde, others, miscellaneous) for these mental pariahs. . . .

Creating islands of meaning entails two rather different mental processes—lumping and splitting. On the one hand, it involves grouping "similar" items together in a single mental cluster—sculptors and filmmakers ("artists"), murder and arson ("felonies"), foxes and camels ("animals"). At the same time, it also involves separating in our mind "different" mental clusters from one another—artists from scientists, felonies from misdemeanors, animals from humans. In order to carve out of the flux surrounding us meaningful entities with distinctive identities, we must experience them as separate from one another.

Separating one island of meaning from another entails the introduction of some mental void between them. As we carve discrete mental chunks out of continuous streams of experience, we normally visualize substantial gaps separating them from one another. Such mental versions of the great divides that split continuous stretches of land following geological upheavals underlie our basic experience of mental entities as situated amid blank stretches of emptiness. It is our perception of the void among these islands of meaning that makes them separate in our mind, and its magnitude reflects the degree of separateness we perceive among them.

Gaps are critical to our ability to experience insular entities. The experiential separateness of the self, for example, is clearly enhanced by the actual gap of "personal space" that normally envelops it. By literally insulating the self from contact with others, such a gap certainly promotes its experience as an insular entity. A similar experience of an island situated in a vacuum often leads us to confine our horizons to, and never venture beyond, our neighborhood, hometown, or country. The great divides we visualize between women and men, children and adults, and blacks and whites likewise promote our perception of such entities as discrete. . . .

I have thus far drawn a deliberately one-sided picture of reality as an array of insular entities neatly separated from one another by great divides. Such discontinuity, however, is not as inevitable as we normally take it to be. It is a pronouncedly mental scalpel that helps us carve discrete mental slices out of reality. . . . The scalpel, of course, is a *social* scalpel. It is society that underlies the way we generate meaningful mental entities.

Reality is not made up of insular chunks unambiguously separated from one another by sharp divides, but rather, of vague, blurred-edge essences that often "spill over" into one another. It normally presents itself not in black and white, but, rather, in subtle shades of gray, with mental twilight zones as well as intermediate essences connecting entities. Segmenting it into discrete islands of meaning usually rests on some social convention, and most boundaries are, therefore, mere social artifacts. As such, they often vary from one society to another as well as across historical periods within each society. Moreover, the precise location—not to mention the very existence—of such mental partitions is often disputed even within any given society. . . .

Breaking up reality into discrete islands of meaning is, thus, an inevitably arbitrary act. The very existence of dividing lines (not to mention their location) is a matter of convention. It is by pure convention, for example, that we regard Danish and Norwegian as two separate languages yet Galician as a mere dialect of Portuguese. It is likewise by sheer convention that we draw a line between heroin and other lethal substances such as alcohol and tobacco (not to mention its own chemical cousins, which we use as pain-killers or as controlled substitutes for heroin itself). It is mere convention that similarly leads us to regard cooking or laundering as "service" occupations and fishermen or raftsmen as less skilled than assembly-line workers or parking-lot attendants. Just as arbitrary is the way in which we carve supposedly discrete species out of the continuum of living forms, separate the masculine from the feminine, cut up continuous stretches of land into separate continents (Europe and Asia, North and Central America), or divide the world into time zones. Nor are there any natural divides separating childhood from adulthood, winter from spring, or one day from the next (both my children, indeed, used to refer to the morning before their last afternoon nap as "yesterday"), and if we attribute distinctive qualities to decades ("the Roaring Twenties") or centuries ("nineteenth-century architecture"), it is only because we happen

to count by tens. Had we used nine, instead, as the basis of our counting system, we would have undoubtedly discovered the historical significance of 9-, 81-, and 729-year cycles and generated fin-de-siècle and millenary frenzy around the years 1944 and 2187. We probably would also have experienced our midlife crisis at the age of thirty-six!

It is we ourselves who create categories and force reality into supposedly insular compartments. Mental divides as well as the "things" they delineate are pure artifacts that have no basis whatsoever in reality. A category, after all, is "a group of things [yet] things do not present themselves . . . grouped in such a way . . . [Nor is their resemblance] enough to explain how we are led to group . . . them together in a sort of ideal sphere, enclosed by definite limits."[2] Classification is an artificial process of concept formation rather than of discovering clusters that already exist. Entities such as "vitamins," "politicians," "art," and "crime" certainly do not exist "out there." The way we construct them resembles the way painters and photographers create pictures by mentally isolating supposedly discrete slices of reality from their immediate surroundings. In the real world, there are no divides separating one insular "thing" from another. . . .

And yet, while boundaries and mental fields may not exist "out there," neither are they generated solely by our own mind. The discontinuities we experience are neither natural nor universal, yet they are not entirely personal either. We may not all classify reality in a precisely identical manner, yet we certainly do cut it up into rather similar mental chunks with pretty similar outlines. It is indeed a mind that organizes reality in accordance with a specific logic, yet it is usually a group mind using an unmistakably social logic (and therefore also producing an unmistakably social order). When we cut up the world, we usually do it not as humans or as individuals but rather as members of societies.

The logic of classification is something we must learn. Socialization involves learning not only society's norms but also its distinctive classificatory schemes. Being socialized or acculturated entails knowing not only how to behave, but also how to perceive reality in a socially appropriate way. An anthropologist who studies another culture, for example, must learn "to see the world as it is constituted for the people themselves, to assimilate their distinctive categories.... [H]e may have to abandon the distinction between the natural and the supernatural, relocate the line between life and death, accept a common nature in mankind and animals."[3] Along similar lines, by the time she is three, a child has already internalized the conventional outlines of the category "birthday present" enough to know that, if someone suggests that she bring lima beans as a present, he must be kidding.

Whenever we classify things, we always attend some of their distinctive features in order to note similarities and contrasts among them while ignoring all the rest as irrelevant. The length of a film, for example, or whether it is in color or black and white is quite irrelevant to the way it is rated, whereas the color of a dress is totally irrelevant to where it is displayed in a department store. What to stress among what is typically a "plethora of viable alternatives" is largely a social decision,[4] and being socialized entails knowing which features are salient for differentiating items from one another and which ones ought to be ignored as irrelevant. It involves learning, for example, that, whereas adding cheese makes a hamburger a "cheeseburger," adding lettuce does not make it a "lettuceburger," and that it is the kind of meat and not the condiment that goes with it that gives a sandwich it distinctive identity. It likewise involves learning that the sex of the person for whom they are designed is probably the most distinctive feature of clothes (in department stores men's shirts are more likely to be displayed alongside men's paja-

mas than alongside women's blouses), and that the way it is spelled may help us locate an eggplant in a dictionary but not in a supermarket. Similarly, we learn that in order to find a book in a bookstore we must attend its substantive focus and the first letters of its author's last name (and ignore, for example, the color of its cover), yet that in order to find it in a book exhibit we must first know who published it. (We also learn that bookstores regard readers' ages as a critical feature of books, thus displaying children's books on dogs alongside children's books on boats rather than alongside general books on dogs). We likewise learn that, in supermarkets, low-sodium soup is located near the low-sugar pineapple slices ("diet food"), marzipan near the anchovy paste ("gourmet food"), and canned corn near the canned pears (rather than by the fresh or frozen corn). And so we learn that, for the purpose of applying the incest taboo, brotherhood "counts" as a measure of proximity to oneself, whereas having the same blood type is irrelevant.

Separating the relevant (figure) from the irrelevant (ground) is not a spontaneous act. Classifying is a normative process, and it is society that leads us to perceive things as similar to or different from one another through unmistakably social "*rules* of irrelevance"[5] that specify which differences are salient for differentiating entities from one another and which ones are only negligible differences among variants of a single entity. Ignoring differences which "make no difference" involves some social pressure to disregard them. Though we often notice them, we learn to ignore them as irrelevant, just as we inhibit our perception of its ground in order to perceive the figure. Along the same lines, ignoring the stutter or deformity of another is not a spontaneous act but rather a social display of tact. It is rules of irrelevance that likewise lead judges, professors, and doctors to display "affective neutrality"[6] and acquit innocent defendants, reward good students, and do their best to save patients' lives even when they personally despise them. They also lead bureaucrats who screen applications to exclude applicants' sex or race from their official considerations even if they are personally attentive to it.

The social construction of discontinuity is accomplished largely through language:

> We dissect nature along lines laid down by our native languages. The categories . . . we isolate from the world of phenomena we do not find there because they stare every observer in the face. . . . [T]he world is presented in a kaleidoscopic flux of impressions which has to be organized by our minds. We cut nature up . . . as we do, largely because we are parties to an agreement to organize it in this way—an agreement that . . . is codified in the patterns of our language. . . . [W]e cannot talk at all except by subscribing to the organization and classification of data which the agreement decrees.[7]

Not only does language allow us to detach mental entities from their surroundings and assign them fixed, decontextualized meanings, it also enables us to transform experiential continuums into discontinuous categories ("long" and "short," "hot" and "cold"). As we assign them separate labels, we come to perceive mental essences such as "professionals," "criminals," or "the poor" as if they were indeed discrete. It is language that allows us to carve out of a continuous voice range the discrete categories "alto" and "soprano," distinguish "herbs" (basil, dill) from leaves we would never allow on our table, define vague discomfort in seemingly sharp categories such as "headache" or "nausea," and perceive aftershave lotion as actually different from eau de toilette or cologne. At the same time, it is our ability to assign them a common label that also allows us to lump things together in our mind. Only the concept "classical," for example, makes Ravel's music similar to Vivaldi's, and only the concept "alcoholic" makes wine seem "closer" to vodka than to grape juice.

Since it is the very basis of social reality, we often forget that language rests on mere convention and regard such mental entities, which are our own creation, as if they were real. . . .

By the same token, as we divide a single continuous process into several conceptual parts ("cause" and "effect," "life" and "death") we often commit the fallacy of misplaced concreteness and regard such purely mental constructs as if they were actually separate. We likewise reify the mental divide separating "white-collar" from "manual" labor as well as the purely mental outlines of such entities as races, classes, families, and nations. Like the dwellers of Plato's proverbial cave, we are prisoners of our own minds, mistaking mere social conceptions for actual experiential perceptions.

It is society that helps us carve discrete islands of meaning out of our experience. Only English speakers, for example, can "hear" the gaps between the separate words in "perhapstheyshouldhavetrieditearlier," which everyone else hears as a single chain of sound. Along similar lines, while people who hear jazz for the first time can never understand why a seemingly continuous stretch of music is occasionally interrupted by bursts of applause, jazz connoisseurs can actually "hear" the purely mental divides separating piano, bass, or drum "solos" from mere "accompaniment." Being a member of society entails "seeing" the world through special mental lenses. It is these lenses, which we acquire only through socialization, that allow us to "perceive things." The proverbial Martian cannot see the mental partitions separating Catholics from Protestants, classical from popular music, or the funny from the crude. Like the contours of constellations, we "see" such fine lines only when we learn that we should expect them there. As real as they may feel to us, boundaries are mere figments of our minds. Only the socialized can "see" them. To all cultural outsiders they are totally invisible.

Only through such "glasses" can entities be "seen." As soon as we remove them, boundaries practically disappear and the "things" they delineate fade away. What we then experience is as continuous as is Europe or the Middle East when seen from space or in ancient maps, or our own neighborhood when fog or heavy snow covers curbs and property lines, practically transforming familiar milieu into a visually undifferentiated flux. This is the way reality must appear to the unsocialized—a boundless, unbroken world with no lines. That is the world we would have inhabited were it not for society.

Notes

1. George G. Simpson, *Principles of Animal Taxonomy* (New York: Columbia University Press, 1961), p. 2.

2. Emile Durkheim and Marcel Mauss, *Primitive Classification* (Chicago: University of Chicago Press, 1973), pp. 7–8.

3. Rodney Needham, "Introduction" to Durkheim and Mauss, *Primitive Classification*, p. viii.

4. Steven J. Gould, "Taxonomy as Politics: The Harm of False Classification," *Dissent*, Winter 1990, p. 73.

5. Erving Goffman, *Encounters* (Indianapolis: Bobbs-Merrill, 1961), pp. 19–26.

6. Talcott Parsons, *The Social System* (New York: Free Press, 1964), pp. 60, 435, 458–62.

7. Benjamin Whorf, "Science and Linguistics," in *Language, Thought, and Reality* (Cambridge: MIT Press, 1956), pp. 213–214.

Part II

The Social Construction of Self

The experience of self is central to being human. Humans could not experience a meaningful reality unless they could symbolically convey meanings to themselves as well as to others. In order to do so, they must think of and act toward themselves as if they were someone else. We get angry at, talk to, encourage, and congratulate ourselves much as we do one another. From the perspective of sociological psychology, this is the essence of the human self: to be both the subject and object of one's own thoughts and actions. And the self that is the object of our thoughts and actions is as much socially constructed as any other object of our experience. Our self becomes real to us as we act toward ourselves as others do. We interpret and define our thoughts, feelings, and actions in terms of shared symbols. The selections in this section examine the social character of the self, the process of its acquisition, and the social influences that continually shape it. ✦

4

The Self as Sentiment and Reflection

Charles Horton Cooley

Charles Horton Cooley was an economist by training who made important contributions to the development of sociological psychology. The influence of Adam Smith's theory of human sentiments is obvious in this selection, which was written around the turn of the twentieth century. In *Theory of Moral Sentiments* (1759), Smith maintains that individuals' sympathetic identification with one another's situation provides the moral foundation of human social life. For Cooley, the human self also rests on individuals' emotional responsiveness to one another. He argues that sentiment is the core of the human self and is central to its development. Accordingly, a sense of appropriation is the source of this self-feeling. The individual not only appropriates people and material objects by claiming them as "mine," but he or she also appropriates images of himself or herself reflected in others' treatment of him or her.

This is what is commonly known as Cooley's theory of "the looking-glass self." Cooley suggests that the individual can only reflect upon and form images of himself or herself through the imaginary adoption of someone else's perspective. The individual imagines how he or she must appear to someone, imagines how that person must be judging his or her appearance and behavior, and consequently feels either pride or shame. Such socially reflected images inform the individual of who and what she or he is, and the consequent feelings of pride and shame provide the grounds for her or his sense of self-worth or esteem.

Cooley's young daughter M. was an important source of inspiration for his theory of the looking-glass self. He closely observed and took meticulous notes on her behavior. Cooley was particularly taken by her use of first-person pronouns like "mine" and "my." As Cooley notes, unlike most other expressions, these pronouns mean something or someone quite different, depending on who is speaking. M. could only have learned to use pronouns correctly by reflecting how others used them—by the imaginary adoption of other people's perspectives. Cooley was also amazed at how early in life M. was aware of her influence over others. She recognized the reflections of her own actions in how others responded to her. For us, as for M., others' responses are the looking glass in which we see reflected images of ourselves. It is from these socially reflected images that we construct a self and our feelings about it.

It is well to say at the outset that by the word "self" in this discussion is meant simply that which is designated in common speech by the pronouns of the first person singular, "I," "me," "my," "mine," and "myself." "Self" and "ego" are used by metaphysicians and moralists in many other senses, more or less remote from the "I" of daily speech and thought, and with these I wish to have as little to do as possible. What is here discussed is what psychologists call the empirical self, the self that can be apprehended or verified by ordinary observation. I qualify it by the word social not as implying the existence of a self that is not social—for I think that the "I" of common language always has more or less distinct reference to other people as well as the speaker—but because I wish to emphasize and dwell upon the social aspect of it.

The distinctive thing in the idea, for which the pronouns of the first person are names, is apparently a characteristic kind of feeling which may be called the my-feeling or sense of appropriation. Almost any sort of ideas may be associated with this feeling, and that alone, it would seem, is the determining factor in the matter. As Professor James says in his admirable discussion of the self, the words "me" and "self" designate "all the things which have the power to produce in a stream of consciousness excitement of a certain peculiar sort. . . ." The social self is simply any idea, or system of ideas, drawn from the communicative life, that the mind cherishes as its own. Self-feeling has its chief scope within the general life, not outside of it. . . .

That the "I" of common speech has a meaning which includes some sort of reference to other persons is involved in the very fact that the word and the ideas it stands for are phenomena of language and the communicative life. It is doubtful whether it is possible to use language at all without thinking more or less distinctly of someone else, and certainly the things to which we give names, and which have a large place in reflective thought, are almost always those which are impressed upon us by our contact with other people. Where there is no communication there can be no nomenclature and no developed thought. What we call "me," "mine," or "myself" is, thcn, not something separate from the general life, but the most interesting part of it, a part whose interest arises from the very fact that it is both general and individual. That is, we care for it just because it is that phase of the mind that is living and striving in the common life, trying to impress itself upon the minds of others. "I" is a militant social tendency, working to hold and enlarge its place in the general current of tendencies. So far as it can, it waxes, as all life does. To think of it as apart from society is a palpable absurdity of which no one could be guilty who really *saw* it as a fact of life. . . .

If a thing has no relation to others of which one is conscious, he is unlikely to think of it at all, and if he does think of it, he cannot, it seems to me, regard it as emphatically *his*. The appropriative sense is always the shadow, as it were, of the common life, and

when we have it, we have a sense of the latter in connection with it. Thus, if we think of a secluded part of the woods as "ours," it is because we think, also, that others do not go there. . . .

The reference to other persons involved in the sense of self may be distinct and particular, as when a boy is ashamed to have his mother catch him at something she has forbidden; or it may be vague and general, as when one is ashamed to do something which only his conscience, expressing his sense of social responsibility, detects and disapproves; but it is always there. There is no sense of "I," as in pride or shame, without its correlative sense of you, or he, or they. Even the miser gloating over his hidden gold can feel the "mine" only as he is aware of the world of men over whom he has secret power; and the case is very similar with all kinds of hidden treasure. Many painters, sculptors, and writers have loved to withhold their work from the world, fondling it in seclusion until they were quite done with it; but the delight in this, as in all secrets, depends upon a sense of the value of what is concealed.

In a very large and interesting class of cases, the social reference takes the form of a somewhat definite imagination of how one's self—that is, any idea he appropriates—appears in a particular mind; and the kind of self-feeling one has is determined by the attitude toward this attributed to that other mind. A social self of this sort might be called the reflected or looking-glass self:

> "Each to each a looking-glass
> Reflects the other that doth pass."

As we see our face, figure, and dress in the glass, and are interested in them because they are ours, and pleased or otherwise with them according as they do or do not answer to what we should like them to be; so in imagination we perceive in another's mind some thought of our appearance, manners, aims, deeds, character, friends, and so on, and are variously affected by it.

A self-idea of this sort seems to have three principal elements: the imagination of our appearance to the other person; the imagination of his judgment of that appearance; and some sort of self-feeling, such as pride or mortification. The comparison with a looking glass hardly suggests the second element, the imagined judgment, which is quite essential. The thing that moves us to pride or shame is not the mere mechanical reflection of ourselves, but an imputed sentiment, the imagined effect of this reflection upon another's mind. This is evident from the fact that the character and weight of that other, in whose mind we see ourselves, makes all the difference with our feeling. We are ashamed to seem evasive in the presence of a straightforward man, cowardly in the presence of a brave one, gross in the eyes of a refined one, and so on. We always imagine, and in imagining share, the judgments of the other mind. A man will boast to one person of an action—say some sharp transaction in trade—which he would be ashamed to own to another. . . .

[This] view [of] "self" and the pronouns of the first person . . . was impressed on me by observing my child M. at the time when she was learning to use these pronouns. When she was two years and two weeks old, I was surprised to discover that she had a clear notion of the first and second persons when used possessively. When asked, "Where is your nose?" she would put her hand upon it and say "my." She also understood that when someone else said "my" and touched an object, it meant something opposite to what was meant when she touched the same object and used the same word. Now, anyone who will exercise his imagination upon the question of how this matter must appear to a mind having no means of knowing anything about "I" and "my," except what it learns by hearing them used, will see that it should be very puzzling. Unlike other words, the personal pronouns have apparently no uniform meaning, but convey different and even opposite ideas when employed by different persons. It seems remarkable that children should master the problem before they arrive at the considerable power of abstract reasoning. How should a little girl of two, not particularly reflective, have discovered that "my" was not the sign of a definite object like other words, but meant something different with each person who used it? And, still more surprising, how should she have achieved the correct use of it with reference to herself which, it would seem, *could not be copied from anyone else*, simply because no one else used it to describe what belonged to her? The meaning of words is learned by associating them with other phenomena. But how is it possible to learn the meaning of one which, as used by others, is never associated with the same phenomenon as when properly used by one's self? Watching her use of the first person, I was at once struck with the fact that she employed it almost wholly in a possessive sense, and that, too, when in an aggressive, self-assertive mood. It was extremely common to see R. tugging at one end of a plaything and M. at the other, screaming, "My, my." "Me" was sometimes nearly equivalent to "my" and was also employed to call attention to herself when she wanted something done for her. Another common use of "my" was to demand something she did not have at all. Thus, if R. had something the like of which she wanted, say a cart, she would exclaim, "Where's *my* cart?"

It seemed to me that she might have learned the use of these pronouns as follows. The self-feeling had always been there. From the first week she had wanted things and cried and fought for them. She had also become familiar by observation and opposition with similar appropriative activities on the part of R. Thus, she not only had the feeling herself, but by associating it with its visible expression had probably defined it, sympathized with it, resented it, in others. Grasping, tugging, and screaming would be associated with the feeling in her own case and would recall the feeling when observed in others.

They would constitute a language, precedent to the use of first-person pronouns, to express the self-idea. All was ready, then, for the word to name this experience. She now observed that R., when contentiously appropriating something, frequently exclaimed, "my," "mine," "give it to *me*," "I want it," and the like. Nothing more natural, then, than that she should adopt these words as names for a frequent and vivid experience with which she was already familiar in her own case and had learned to attribute to others. Accordingly, it appeared to me, as I recorded in my notes at the time, that " 'my' and 'mine' are simply names for concrete images of appropriativeness," embracing both the appropriative feeling and its manifestation. If this is true, the child does not at first work out the I-and-you idea in an abstract form. The first-person pronoun is a sign of a concrete thing, after all, but that thing is not primarily the child's body, or his muscular sensations as such, but the phenomenon of aggressive appropriation, practiced by himself, witnessed in others, and incited and interpreted by a hereditary instinct. This seems to get over the difficulty mentioned above, namely, the seeming lack of a common content between the meaning of "my" when used by another and when used by one's self. This common content is found in the appropriative feeling and the visible and audible signs of that feeling. An element of difference and strife comes in, of course, in the opposite actions or purposes which the "my" of another and one's own "my" are likely to stand for. When another person says "mine" regarding something which I claim, I sympathize with him enough to understand what he means, but it is a hostile sympathy, overpowered by another and more vivid "mine" connected with the idea of drawing the object my way.

In other words, the meaning of "I" and "mine" is learned in the same way that the meanings of hope, regret, chagrin, disgust, and thousands of other words of emotion and sentiment are learned: that is, by having

the feeling, imputing it to others in connection with some kind of expression, and hearing the word along with it. As to its communication and growth, the self-idea is in no way peculiar that I see, but essentially like other ideas. In its more complex forms, such as are expressed by "I" in conversation and literature, it is a social sentiment, or type of sentiments, defined and developed by intercourse. . . .

I imagine, then, that as a rule the child associates "I" and "me" at first only with those ideas regarding which his appropriative feeling is aroused and defined by opposition. He appropriates his nose, eye, or foot in very much the same way as a plaything—by antithesis to other noses, eyes, and feet, which he cannot control. It is not uncommon to tease little children by proposing to take away one of these organs, and they behave precisely as if the "mine" threatened were a separable object—which it might be for all they know. And, as I have suggested, even in adult life, "I," "me," and "mine" are applied with a strong sense of their meaning only to things distinguished as peculiar to us by some sort of opposition or contrast. They always imply social life and relation to other persons. That which is most distinctively mine is very private, it is true, but it is that part of the private which I am cherishing in antithesis to the rest of the world, not the separate but the special. The aggressive self is essentially a militant phase of the mind, having for its apparent function the energizing of peculiar activities, and, although the militancy may not go on in an obvious, external manner, it always exists as a mental attitude. . . .

The process by which self-feeling of the looking-glass sort develops in children may be followed without much difficulty. Studying the movements of others as closely as they do, they soon see a connection between their own acts and changes in those movements; that is, they perceive their own influence or power over persons. The child appropriates the visible actions of his parent or nurse, over which he finds he has some control, in quite the same way as he appropriates one of his own members or a plaything; and he will try to do things with this new possession, just as he will with his hand or his rattle. A girl six months old will attempt in the most evident and deliberate manner to attract attention to herself, to set going by her actions some of those movements of other persons that she has appropriated. She has tasted the joy of being a cause, of exerting social power, and wishes more of it. She will tug at her mother's skirts, wriggle, gurgle, stretch out her arms, etc., all the time watching for the hoped-for effect. . . .

The young performer soon learns to be different things to different people, showing that he begins to apprehend personality and to foresee its operation. If the mother or nurse is more tender than just, she will almost certainly be "worked" by systematic weeping. It is a matter of common observation that children often behave worse with their mother than with other and less sympathetic people. Of the new persons that a child sees, it is evident that some make a strong impression and awaken a desire to interest and please them, while others are indifferent or repugnant. Sometimes the reason can be perceived or guessed, sometimes not; but the fact of selective interest, admiration, and prestige is obvious before the end of the second year. By that time a child already cares much for the reflection of himself upon one personality and little for that upon another. Moreover, he soon claims intimate and tractable persons as *mine*, classes them among his other possessions, and maintains his ownership against all comers. M., at three years of age, vigorously resented R.'s claim upon their mother. The latter was "*my* mamma," whenever the point was raised.

Strong joy and grief depend upon the treatment this rudimentary social self receives. . . . At about fifteen months old [M.] had become "a perfect little actress," seeming to live largely in imaginations of her effect upon other people. She constantly and obvi-

ously laid traps for attention, and looked abashed or wept at any signs of disapproval or indifference. At times it would seem as if she could not get over these repulses, but would cry long in a grieved way, refusing to be comforted. If she hit upon any little trick that made people laugh, she would be sure to repeat it, laughing loudly and affectedly in imitation. She had quite a repertory of these small performances, which she would display to a sympathetic audience, or even try upon strangers. I have seen her at sixteen months, when R. refused to give her the scissors, sit down and make-believe cry, putting up her underlip and sniffling, meanwhile looking up now and then to see what effect she was producing. . . .

Progress from this point is chiefly in the way of a greater definiteness, fullness, and inwardness in the imagination of the other's state of mind. A little child thinks of and tries to elicit certain visible or audible phenomena, and does not go beyond them; but what a grown-up person desires to produce in others is an internal, invisible condition which his own richer experience enables him to imagine, and of which expression is only the sign. Even adults, however, make no separation between what other people think and the visible expression of that thought. They imagine the whole thing at once, and their idea differs from that of a child chiefly in the comparative richness and complexity of the elements that accompany and interpret the visible or audible sign. There is also a progress from the naive to the subtle in socially self-assertive action. A child obviously and simply, at first, does things for effect. Later there is an endeavor to suppress the appearance of doing so; affection, indifference, contempt, etc., are simulated to hide the real wish to affect the self-image. . . .

Reprinted from: Charles Horton Cooley, "The Self as Sentiment and Reflection" in *Human Nature and the Social Order*, pp. 168–170, 179–184, 189–194, 196–199. Copyright © 1983 by Transaction Publishers. Reprinted by permission. ✦

5

The Self as Social Structure

George Herbert Mead

George Herbert Mead is probably the most important figure in the development of sociological psychology. His characterizations of the self and its development are central to distinctively sociological understandings of the human condition. This selection is taken from *Mind, Self, and Society*, which is Mead's best-known work, even though he did not actually write it. It was reconstructed from the class notes of students who took a course of that same title from Mead at the University of Chicago in the 1920s. Mead makes a number of important points about the human self in this selection: the self is separate from the body; it arises in social experience; but it is more than a mere product of socially reflected self-images.

According to Mead, language is crucial to the development of the self. When we speak, we hear ourselves and respond to what we are saying in similar ways, as do those whom we are addressing. In speaking, we are both the subject and an object of our own action. Moreover, because what we say means more or less the same to us as to those being addressed, we can assume their role and anticipate their likely reaction to what we are saying. Mead observes that, once children start to acquire language, they literally begin to take on the roles of others in play. They play at being a mother, father, or superhero. In so doing, the child addresses himself or herself in the role of those whom Mead calls significant others and responds accordingly. At this stage, the child develops separate selves that answer to each role

he or she plays. That is why, Mead argues, a multiple personality is, in a certain sense, normal. It is when the child starts playing games that he or she begins to tie these multiple selves together into a unified whole.

Games involve the rule-governed coordination of a variety of distinct roles. In order to successfully play a game, the child must simultaneously assume the roles of all the other players. For example, in Mead's favorite example of baseball, a first baseman cannot successfully complete a double play unless she or he takes the role and anticipates the reactions of both the shortstop and the second baseman to a ground ball hit in their direction. By simultaneously assuming such interrelated roles, the individual adopts the perspective of an organized community or generalized other toward himself or herself. Such a generalized perspective provides the individual with a unified view of self. As Mead notes, this implies that the structure of the self will reflect the structure of the various groups of which the individual is a member.

However, in Mead's view, the self consists of more than the "me" that is the object of others' actions. The self is both subject and object. The subject or "I" responds to the object or "me," sometimes questioning and challenging it. The self is not a thing but a process—a continuous interchange between subject and object, "I" and "me."

Mead provides a profoundly social, although not socially deterministic, view of the self. The self is profoundly social not only in the sense that it arises in social experience, but also in the sense that it is a social process—a continuous inner conversation between an "I" and a "me." Social experience may make that conversation possible, but it does not determine what will emerge from it. It can be as lively, creative, and unpredictable as the most entertaining conversation among individuals.

The self has the characteristic that it is an object to itself, and that characteristic distinguishes it from other objects and from the body. It is perfectly true that the eye can see the foot, but it does not see the body as a whole. We cannot see our backs; we can feel certain portions of them, if we are agile, but we cannot get an experience of our whole body. There are, of course, experiences which are somewhat vague and difficult of location, but the bodily experiences are for us organized about a self. The foot and hand belong to the self. We can see our feet, especially if we look at them from the wrong end of an opera glass, as strange things which we have difficulty in recognizing as our own. The parts of the body are quite distinguishable from the self. We can lose parts of the body without any serious invasion of the self. The mere ability to experience different parts of the body is not different from the experience of a table. The table presents a different feel from what the hand does when one hand feels another, but it is an experience of something with which we come definitely into contact. The body does not experience itself as a whole, in the sense in which the self in some way enters into the experience of the self.

It is the characteristic of the self as an object to itself that I want to bring out. This characteristic is represented in the word "self," which is a reflexive, and indicates that which can be both subject and object. This type of object is essentially different from other objects. . . .

The self, as that which can be an object to itself, is essentially a social structure, and it arises in social experience. . . . The individual experiences himself as such, not directly, but only indirectly, from the particular standpoint of other individual members of the same social group, or from the generalized standpoint of the social group as a whole to which he belongs. For he enters his own experience as a self or individual, not directly or immediately, not by becoming a subject to himself, but only insofar as he first becomes an object to himself, just as other individuals are objects to him or in his experience; and he becomes an object to himself only by taking the attitudes of other individuals toward himself within a social environment or context of experience and behavior in which both he and they are involved.

After a self has arisen, it in a certain sense provides for itself its social experiences, and so we can conceive of an absolutely solitary self. But it is impossible to conceive of a self arising outside of social experience. When it has arisen, we can think of a person in solitary confinement for the rest of his life, but who still has himself as a companion, and is able to think and to converse with himself as he had communicated with others. . . . We are continually following up our own address to other persons by an understanding of what we are saying, and using that understanding in the direction of our continued speech. We are finding out what we are going to say, what we are going to do, by trolling the process itself. In the conversation of gestures, what we say calls out a certain response in another and that in turn changes our own action, so that we shift from what we started to do because of the reply the other makes. The conversation of gestures is the beginning of communication. The individual comes to carry on a conversation of gestures with himself. He says something, and that calls out a certain reply in himself which makes him change what he was going to say. One starts to say something, we will presume an unpleasant something, but when he starts to say it, he realizes it is cruel. The effect on himself of what he is saying checks him; there is here a conversation of gestures between the individual and himself. We mean by significant speech that the action is one that affects the individual himself, and that the effect upon the individual himself is part of the intelligent carrying out of the conversation with others. Now we, so to speak, amputate that social phase and dispense with it for the time being, so that one is talking to one's self as one would talk to another person. . . .

We have discussed the social foundations of the self. . . . We may now explicitly raise the question as to the nature of the "I" which is aware of the social "me." . . . The "I" reacts to the self which arises through taking the attitudes of others. Through taking those attitudes, we have introduced the "me" and we react to it as an "I."

The "I" is the response of the individual to the attitude of the community as this appears in his own experience. His response to that organized attitude in turn changes it. . . . [T]his is a change which is not present in his own experience until after it takes place. The "I" appears in our experience in memory. It is only after we have acted that we know what we have done; it is only after we have spoken that we know what we have said. The adjustment to that organized world which is present in our own nature is one that represents the "me" and is constantly there. But if the response to it is a response which is of the nature of the conversation of gestures, if it creates a situation which is in some sense novel, if one puts up his side of the case, asserts himself over against others and insists that they take a different attitude toward himself, then there is something important occurring that is not previously present in experience. . . . Such a novel reply to the social situation . . . constitutes the "I" as over against the "me."

The problem now presents itself as to how, in detail, a self arises. We have to note something of the background of its genesis. . . . We have seen . . . that there are certain gestures that affect the organism as they affect other organisms and may, therefore, arouse in the organism responses of the same character as aroused in the other. Here, then, we have a situation in which the individual may at least arouse responses in himself and reply to these responses, the condition being that the social stimuli have an effect on the individual which is like that which they have on the other. That, for example, is what is implied in language; otherwise, language as significant symbol would disappear, since the individual would not get

the meaning of that which he says. . . . It is out of that sort of language that the mind of Helen Keller was built up. As she has recognized, it was not until she could get into communication with other persons through symbols which could arouse in herself the responses they arouse in other people that she could get what we term a mental content, or a self.

Another set of background factors in the genesis of the self is represented in the activities of play and the game.

We find [among] children . . . invisible, imaginary companions. . . . [Children] organize in this way the responses which they call out in other persons and call out also in themselves. Of course, this playing with an imaginary companion is only a peculiarly interesting phase of ordinary play. Play in this sense, especially the stage which precedes the organized games, is a play at something. A child plays at being a mother, at being a teacher, at being a policeman; that is, he is taking different roles, as we say. We have something that suggests this in what we call the play of animals: a cat will play with her kittens, and dogs play with each other. Two dogs playing with each other will attack and defend, in a process which if carried through would amount to an actual fight. There is a combination of responses which checks the depth of the bite. But we do not have in such a situation the dogs taking a definite role in the sense that a child deliberately takes the role of another. This tendency on the part of the children is what we are working with in the kindergarten where the roles which the children assume are made the basis for training. When a child does assume a role he has in himself the stimuli which call out that particular response or group of responses. He may, of course, run away when he is chased, as the dog does, or he may turn around and strike back just as the dog does in his play. But that is not the same as playing at something. Children get together to "play Indian." This means that the child has a certain set of stimuli which call out in itself the responses that they would call out in others, and which answer to an Indian. In the play period the child utilizes his own responses to these stimuli which he makes use of in building a self. The response which he has a tendency to make to these stimuli organizes them. He plays that he is, for instance, offering himself something, and he buys it; he gives a letter to himself and takes it away; he addresses himself as a parent, as a teacher; he arrests himself as a policeman. He has a set of stimuli which call out in himself the sort of responses they call out in others. He takes this group of responses and organizes them into a certain whole. Such is the simplest form of being another to one's self. It involves a temporal situation. The child says something in one character and responds in another character, and then his responding in another character is a stimulus to himself in the first character, and so the conversation goes on. A certain organized structure arises in him and in his other which replies to it, and these carry on the conversation of gestures between themselves.

If we contrast play with the situation in an organized game, we note the essential difference that the child who plays in a game must be ready to take the attitude of everyone else involved in that game, and that these different roles must have a definite relationship to each other. Taking a very simple game such as hide-and-seek, everyone, with the exception of the one who is hiding, is a person who is hunting. A child does not require more than the person who is hunted and the one who is hunting. If a child is playing in the first sense he just goes on playing, but there is no basic organization gained. In that early stage he passes from one role to another just as a whim takes him. But in a game where a number of individuals are involved, then the child taking one role must be ready to take the role of everyone else. If he gets in a "ball nine," he must have the responses of each position involved in his own position. He must know what everyone else is going to do in order to carry out his own play. He has to

take all of these roles. They do not all have to be present in consciousness at the same time, but at some moments he has to have three or four individuals present in his own attitude, such as the one who is going to throw the ball, the one who is going to catch it, and so on. These responses must be, in some degree, present in his own make-up. In the game, then, there is a set of responses of such others so organized that the attitude of one calls out the appropriate attitudes of the other.

This organization is put in the form of the rules of the game. Children take a great interest in rules. They make rules on the spot in order to help themselves out of difficulties. Part of the enjoyment of the game is to get these rules. Now, the rules are the set of responses which a particular attitude calls out. You can demand a certain response in others if you take a certain attitude. These responses are all in yourself as well. There you get an organized set of such responses as that to which I have referred, which is something more elaborate than the roles found in play. Here there is just a set of responses that follow on each other indefinitely. At such a stage we speak of a child as not yet having a fully developed self. The child responds in a fairly intelligent fashion to the immediate stimuli that come to him, but they are not organized. He does not organize his life as we would like to have him do, namely, as a whole. There is just a set of responses of the type of play. The child reacts to a certain stimulus, and the reaction is in himself that is called out in others, but he is not a whole self. In his game he has to have an organization of these roles; otherwise, he cannot play the game. The game represents the passage in the life of the child from taking the role of others in play to the organized part that is essential to self-consciousness in the full sense of the term.

The fundamental difference between the game and play is that in the [former] the child must have the attitude of all the others involved in that game. The attitudes of the other players which the participant assumes organize into a sort of unit, and it is that organization which controls the response of the individual. The illustration used was of a person playing baseball. Each one of his own acts is determined by his assumption of the action of the others who are playing the game. What he does is controlled by his being everyone else on that team, at least insofar as those attitudes affect his own particular response. We get then an "other" which is an organization of the attitudes of those involved in the same process.

A multiple personality is in a certain sense normal. . . . There is usually an organization of the whole self with reference to the community to which we belong, and the situation in which we find ourselves. What the society is, whether we are living with people of the present, people of our own imaginations, people of the past, varies, of course, with different individuals. Normally, within the sort of community as a whole to which we belong, there is a unified self, but that may be broken up. To a person who is somewhat unstable and in whom there is a line of cleavage, certain activities become impossible, and that set of activities may separate and evolve into another self. Two separate "me's" and "I's," two different selves result, and that is the condition under which there is a tendency to break up the personality. There is an account of a professor of education who disappeared, was lost to the community, and later turned up in a logging camp in the West. He freed himself of his occupation and turned to the woods where he felt, if you like, more at home. The pathological side of it was the forgetting, the leaving out of the rest of the self. This result involved getting rid of certain bodily memories which would identify the individual to himself. We often recognize the lines of cleavage that run through us. We would be glad to forget certain things, get rid of things the self is bound up with in past experiences. What we have here is a situa-

tion in which there can be different selves, and it is dependent upon the set of social reactions that is involved as to which self we are going to be.

The unity and structure of the complete self reflects the unity and structure of the social process as a whole; and each of the elementary selves of which it is composed reflects the unity and structure of one of the various aspects of that process in which the individual is implicated. In other words, the various elementary selves which constitute, or are organized into, a complete self are the various aspects of the structure of that complete self answering to the various aspects of the structure of the social process as a whole; the structure of the complete self is thus a reflection of the complete social process. The organization and unification of a social group is identical with the organization and unification of any one of the selves arising within the social process in which that group is engaged, or which it is carrying on.

The organized community or social group which gives to the individual his unity of self may be called "the generalized other." The attitude of the generalized other is the attitude of the whole community.

I have emphasized what I have called the structures upon which the self is constructed, the framework of the self, as it were. . . . We cannot be ourselves unless we are also members in whom there is a community of attitudes which control the attitudes of all. We cannot have rights unless we have common attitudes. That which we have acquired as self-conscious persons makes us such members of society and gives us selves. Selves can exist only in definite relationships to other selves. No hard-and-fast line can be drawn between our own selves and the selves of others, because our own selves exist and enter as such into our experience only insofar as the selves of others exist and enter as such into our experience also. The individual possesses a self only in relation to the selves of the other members of his social group; and the structure of his self expresses or reflects the general behavior pattern of this social group to which he belongs; just as does the structure of the self of every other individual belonging to this social group.

Reprinted from: George Herbert Mead, "The Self as Social Structure" in Charles Morris (ed.), *Mind, Self, and Society*, pp. 136–137, 138, 140–141, 142–143, 144–145, 149–154, 163–164, 173–174, 196. Copyright © 1962 by The University of Chicago Press. Reprinted by permission. ✦

6

Young Children's Racial and Ethnic Definitions of Self

*Debra Van Ausdale and
Joe R. Feagin*

Both Cooley and Mead propose that the individual acquires a self by taking the attitude of others toward him- or herself. What they imply, but do not explicitly address, is that the attitude of others toward the individual, the way they respond to her or him, is guided by social meanings. We define one another in terms of shared systems of social classification and typification. We attribute different identities and different characteristics to one another based on those classifications, and respond to one another accordingly. As individuals come to respond to themselves as others do, they define themselves similarly and assume the identities and characteristics others attribute to them. For example, within moments after birth, most newborns are identified as either female or male, and from that moment forward are responded to as either a girl or a boy. As children come to understand gender classification, they also start to understand the gender-related meanings of names others call them and ways others treat them. Responding to themselves as others do, they adopt the gender identity others attribute to them as their own and take on the characteristics others attributed to them based on that identification. Gender identity thereby becomes an important dimension of the self. By the age of five, if not earlier, most children emphatically identify themselves as either a girl or a boy and insist on dressing, playing with toys, and generally acting in ways that confirm that identity.

Similarly, in a racially and ethnically diverse and conscious society like our own, racial and ethnic identity often is an important dimension of the self. This selection examines young children's use of racial identities in a preschool that promotes racial and ethnic diversity and tolerance. Although many developmental theories argue that very young children cannot understand racial and ethnic distinctions, this study demonstrates otherwise. It illustrates how children use skin color, family background, national origin, and other racial and ethnic "markers" to define themselves and others. More tellingly, it suggests that preschool-age children adopt the racial and ethnic identities others attribute to them as their own.

Although most children eventually do adopt the racial and ethnic identities others attribute to them, they do not passively acquire racial and ethnic identities but actively explore racial and ethnic classification in their interactions with others. Their racial and ethnic classifications often do not correspond to those of adults, but they clearly recognize that such classifications are of some importance. Others', including their peers', responses to their racial and ethnic identifications deepen their understanding of and sharpen their skill in applying the socially prevailing system of racial and ethnic identification. Unfortunately, as this study illustrates, young children consequently learn that different racial and ethnic identities are not equally valued. On the other hand, children's creative uses of racial and ethnic identities reveal just how arbitrary racial and ethnic identification is. The grounds on which they racially and ethnically identify themselves and others are questionable only if the grounds on which adults do so remain unquestioned. Yet, however arbitrary, racial and ethnic identification is an important dimension of self in our own and many other societies. We find ourselves on what might be called, borrowing the language of Zerubavel's earlier selection, racial and ethnic islands of meaning separated by a wide gulf from those on other islands. This separation is not natural but a product of how others have responded to us.

In this [selection] we examine when, where, and how children make use of racial and ethnic understandings and distinctions to define themselves and others in their everyday lives. . . . Our [empirical information] come[s] from extensive observations of fifty-eight preschool age children over nearly a year in a large preschool in an urban setting. The children involved in this study ranged in age from barely three to more than six years of age. . . . The preschool had several racially and ethnically diverse classrooms and employed a popular antibias curriculum. The school's official data on children in the classroom we observed was as follows: white (twenty-four); Asian (nineteen); Black (four); biracial (for example, Black and white, three); Middle Eastern (three); Latino (two); and other (three). . . .

Debra Van Ausdale, who did the classroom observations, made a conscious effort to play down or eliminate the researcher/adult role and to remain nonauthoritarian and supportive in her interactions with the children. While some of the children were initially puzzled by her behavior, they soon accepted that an adult could actually not be in charge of anything or anyone . . . Debi was able to operate as a nonsanctioning playmate-adult. Debi's activities in the day care center evolved to become a combination of teacher's helper, children's playmate, and official lap for children who needed comforting. Debi was soon accepted by the children as a nonthreatening, uninteresting component of the preschool world. . . .

The obvious, physically grounded racial and ethnic markers of skin color, facial features, and hair color and texture were widely used within the children's interactions with each other. A variety of other, more subtle symbols also came into play. . . . Children as young as three invented complex combinations of racial meaning, for themselves and for others, and incorporated social relationships and physical characteristics to produce explanations for how their world was racially constructed and maintained. . . .

[For example, in one] episode in the classroom, skin color . . . takes center stage. It is just after nap, and Mark, a white teacher's aide, is sitting with Lu (3, Chinese), Susan (4, Chinese), Corinne (4, African/white), and Mike (4, Black). The children are listening to a story read by another teacher. The purpose of stories after naptime is to delay the children from racing to the snack tables before their hands are washed. They are required to sit and listen until they are released, and this release is accomplished by allowing only a few children at a time to leave the room. This prevents them from lining up and destroying each other while they wait. A favorite device for delay is to play the "color of the day" game, where children must remain seated unless they are wearing a particular color of clothing. Jeanne, the teacher, finishes her reading and announces, "If you have something brown on, you can get up and wash you[r] hands for snack."

The children look around and seem to collectively decide that this invitation includes brown skin, hair, and eyes. Mike jumps up, yelling "I have brown skin on!" and rushes to the sink to be the first in line for food. Upon seeing this, Corinne also smiles widely, yells, "Me too!" and dashes away. Mark, regarding Lu with a smile, leans over and tells her, "You have brown skin too." Lu retorts, "I do NOT!" She appears to be very indignant. "I have white skin." Lu looks to Susan to support her. Susan verifies this, telling Mark, "Lu's skin is white, Mark, not brown." Mark seems surprised, then says, "My skin is brown from the sun." Susan nods, remarking, "Lu, you have brown eyes." Lu looks her over and smiles saying, "So do you!" Susan peers deeply into Mark's face, asking him, "Do I have brown eyes?" Mark gazes back, pretending to think deeply. "Why yes, you do have brown eyes!" he finally declares. "So we can both go get snack," Susan declares. All three of them rise and go to the next room.

The desirability of whiteness, of white identity and esteem, is . . . evident in [this] exchange . . . Lu . . . insists that she . . . is white, not brown, despite the fact that she would probably not be construed by others as white since her skin has an olive tone. She angrily denies having brown skin and draws another child in to support her evaluation. . . . One significant aspect of Lu's denial is her anger at being assumed to have darker skin. She is annoyed that Mark would make such an error and appeals to another child to verify her skin color for him. Her indignation at his mistake is a clear indicator of the importance she is already attaching to her physical appearance and, more importantly, to valuing the category of whiteness. She seems to want to deny that she could possibly be dark or close to the category of Blackness.

Here we see an Asian child trying to find her place in a white-dominated society that implicitly and explicitly accents a racist continuum running from positive whiteness to undesirable Blackness. [C]hildren's actions and understandings in their interactive settings reveal aspects of the larger society and its deep-lying historical roots. As they have entered and increased in number in the United States, each new group of color has usually been placed, principally by the dominant white group, somewhere on a white-to-Black status continuum, the common gauge of social acceptability. . . . This long standing continuum accents physical characteristics and color coding in which European-like features and cultural norms tend to be highly privileged. Not surprisingly, all children in this society learn at an early age that, generally speaking, whiteness is privileged and darkness is not—and thus their choices in this regard are usually not surprising. In particular, Asian and Latino American children, like their parents, may often find themselves

placed by whites on the continuum without their active involvement, and thus they may struggle for a better placement, and definition, of themselves on that white-originated continuum. . . .

* * *

Adult definitions and reconstructions of children's activities have a strong influence on . . . children's lived realities. . . . In [the following] episode, . . . we see . . . that the presence of adults radically changes the nature of interaction between children. . . . [C]hildren realize that adults disapprove of some of their activity. Their awareness of adults' opinions prompts them to avoid confrontations or arguments with grown people, choosing instead to merely acquiesce to adult demands.

Debi is sitting with . . . three children on the steps to the deck, playing Simon Says. Brittany (4, white) is Simon. While Debi stays in the background, Rita (3, white/Latina) and Joseph (3, Black) discuss what racial group they belong to. Keep in mind that this conversation is unprompted by adult influence and that the only adult on the scene so far is Debi, who is being thoroughly ignored. Joseph informs Rita, "I'm Black, and you're white." "No," she retorts angrily, "I'm not white, I'm mixed." The two debate back and forth for a few moments, their voices getting louder and angrier. Joseph maintains his definition of Rita, and she as vigorously denies it, reiterating and reinforcing her own conception. Debi listens and watches quietly, ready to intercede if the children get too upset. However, the noise attracts the attention of a teacher who enters the scene from inside the building and approaches as Rita shouts, "I'm mixed, you stupid!" into Joseph's face. He merely rolls his eyes at her, making her even angrier.

Patricia, an African American teacher, enters this scene from inside the classroom . . . [and joins] the children on the playground. She listens to Rita's last declaration, quickly evaluates the situation, and intervenes. "You're not mixed, Rita, you're Spanish. What race am I?" Patricia is making an attempt to change the subject between the two, in hopes of calming the argument. Rita looks up at Patricia and reluctantly replies, "Mixed." "Mixed!?" Patricia responds, laughing. "Mixed with what?" Rita ponders for a moment, looking uncomfortable. "Blue," she says finally. Patricia is wearing an entirely blue outfit today. "Oh," Patricia says, "I'm Black too, like Joseph; I'm not mixed. What an interesting conversation you guys are having." Patricia smiles ineffectively at the children, which prompts them to begin squirming and looking for a way out. Rita says nothing in response, and Joseph has remained silent throughout Patricia's exchange with Rita. The child leading Simon Says (Brittany) finally tells the kids to go to the playground, and Rita and Joseph run off in different directions. Patricia smiles at Debi, shaking her head, but offers no comments. . . .

Here, the teacher seems to allow no mixed category for a child's identity and self-conception. This is suggestive of a common adult tendency to limit children's understandings of the nuances of racial meaning. In Rita's case, her use of the term "mixed" probably referred to her knowledge of her parents' origins. Her mother and father were from different countries in Latin America. While she appeared white to outside observers, with pale skin and curly dark hair, her assessment of herself was that she was mixed. Joseph's insistence that she was white finally provoked her into an angry retort, complete with name-calling. Rita's racial-ethnic group status is very important to her. She reacts to the teacher's inquiry by becoming relatively uncommunicative. Clearly not wishing to engage in the argument with a teacher, Rita and Joseph abandon their interaction and address the more urgent need of responding to an adult. The lesson is not lost on them, however, given their behavior. It is better, in their world, to submit to the adults' definitions of racial matters than to attempt to enter an argument. Young children quickly learn that

debates with adults are typically unproductive.

The Children's Views

Both teachers and children regularly seized upon the connections between skin color and other markers of differences between people, although for different reasons. The celebration of ethnic and racially oriented holidays precipitated considerable interaction among the children, and at times this interest incorporated skin color and its salience to ethnic identity. Children were keenly interested in any information about unfamiliar customs and holidays. Non-Jewish children, regardless of race, delighted in activities oriented around Hanukkah, such as the making of challah and storytime books about the Festival of Lights. White children displayed intense interest in explanations of Kwanzaa, asking questions and listening quietly as teachers read books about this holiday. The history of Kwanzaa's origins was covered in the curriculum and was made a point of discussion by the teachers. That different holidays were connected to different racial and ethnic groups was not missed by the children. In the case of Kwanzaa, teachers explicitly connected the holiday to African Americans, as is appropriate. The children, however, refined and extended this meaning on their own. In this next situation, one child uses skin color as a determinant of what kind of ethnic activity another child can do.

Aaron (4, white) taunts Amy (4, Black/white). She is alone, playing quietly near the gazebo. He approaches her and sticks his tongue out, informing her, "You can't celebrate Kwanzaa, you're not Black." Amy retorts, "Oh yes I am. You don't know. You're stupid." "I am not," he replies, sniffing at her and adding, "and you're not Black." "I am too Black!" Amy responds hotly. "My Dad is Black and so is his parents, my granddad and grandma." "Stupid!" he shouts at her. "You're stupid!" she yells right back. "You don't know nothing about me." She rises and faces Aaron with an angry glare on her face. Aaron responds in kind, and they glare at each other until he finally backs down and leaves. Amy resumes her play.

It is immediately apparent that Aaron defined Amy's qualifications to participate in Kwanzaa celebrations according to her skin color. He has named and imposed his comprehension of what Black identity is and how it is to be measured and noted. Amy's skin was pale, and she had curly, dark blond hair. According to Aaron's interpretation, Kwanzaa was for "Black" people as he mentally defined them, and thus Amy was not to be included. She was, to all outward appearances, white. Amy, however, relied on her family history and her knowledge of black and white ancestry and its meaning to define her capacity to be included in Kwanzaa. Each child was basing their interpretation of Amy's status on different criteria, each using a different model of explanation. For the white child, another's skin hue was decisive. For the Black child, skin color was but one gauge. Far more important were her ancestry and knowledge of her family. Her skin color was not a key factor for her. . . .

In yet another situation, skin color provides the opportunity for extensive comparison with the colors of other objects and the color of people. In this scene, Taleshia [3, Black] makes use of color to categorize other things and other people in order to draw a contrast with herself. Her understanding of self, as an abstraction, is evident in this exchange.

Debi sits on the rug, cross-legged, with Taleshia leaning up against her. This is a common position for Debi, and children at times will vie for the use of her as a cushion. They are waiting for a teacher-led activity to begin. Taleshia snuggles up and says, "Your T-shirt is black." Debi agrees and adds, "I really like black. It's a pretty color." Taleshia nods, announcing, "Your hair is black." Again Debi

agrees. The child continues, "And so is Mike's hair and Steven's hair and Mitchell's hair and Elizabeth's hair." She has named all the Asian and African American children currently in the room. Debi nods, "Black hair is prettier than T-shirts." Taleshia laughs, touches Debi's arm and remarks, smiling, "I'm Black too." Debi says, "Yes, and so is Mike." Taleshia nods again and says, "And Joseph." She holds her hand up, turns it from side to side. "See?" she asks. "I'm *Black!*" She shouts the last word, delighted; holds up her hands; and sings loudly, "I'm Black, Black, Black." By now she is in Debi's lap. She holds her arm up against Debi's legs. "I'm *real* black," she notes, eyeing the contrast between the two skin tones. "And I'm *real white*," Debi replies, imitating her emphasis. Again Taleshia laughs and sings, "I'm Black, Black, Black!" The two remain in contact, with Taleshia singing and Debi serving as her perch, until the teacher-led activity begins.

The contrast between Debi's pale skin and Taleshia's dark skin is striking. The conversation she started was a device employed to engage Debi, first in a maneuver to gain possession of Debi's lap. Then Taleshia moved her comparisons from clothing to hair color to skin color. She made a game of it, moving with ease from one object to another, all the while proclaiming her awareness and delight in her own color. She also managed to get exclusive control over an adult's attention, quite an achievement for a preschool child. . . .

More mental pictures are created in the next account, with color and skin again incorporating nonhuman objects. There are several rabbits in residence at this school. The two males are gray and white and black and white, and the solitary female is solid white. True to their nature, the rabbits have indulged in procreation, and the result was six bunnies: two solid black in color, three white, and one black and white spotted. Corinne (4, African/white) and Sarah (4, white) are playing with the bunnies, which are temporarily contained in a galvanized bucket while a teacher cleans out their cage. The bunnies are about a week old and are an object of great interest for the children. The two girls count the tiny rabbits and discuss their colors. Corinne announces, "The black ones are girls, and the white ones are boys." Sarah gazes into the bucket, then looks skeptical and asks, "How do you know?" Corinne instructs, "My mommy is Georgine and she is Black and she is a girl, so the black ones are girls. My daddy is David and he is white and he is a boy, so the white ones are boys." Sarah giggles. She picks up the lone black and white spotted bunny and asks Corinne, "Well, what's this one, then?" Corinne gets a huge smile on her face and yells, "That's *me!*" at the top of her lungs. Both girls dissolve into silliness, abandon the bunnies, and run off.

The dual nature of Corinne's origins is very important to her, and she makes great efforts to explain and clarify this to anyone needing educating, whether child or adult. Like all people, she experiments with what she knows to sharpen, deepen, and crystallize her understandings. She makes use of a variety of objects and situations to point out her skin color and its origin. Color matching seems to be one way of drawing out and explaining the relationship of skin color to self. For Corinne, the meaning of skin color and identity is complicated, and she does not try to simplify her explanation. She incorporates gender as well as color and family history to construct an explanation of each to another child. She is exploring the many meanings of racial group, gender, relationships, and color and experimenting with different definitions for each. Clearly, she is developing a strong sense of her multiracial identity and a positive sense of her self, in spite of the constant questioning she must endure from adults . . . about these matters. Faced with the negative imagery that is generally imposed on Black children and biracial children like herself, Corinne presses forward with a very positive interpretation and delineation of her biracial identity.

Drawing on her awareness of her own racial group and her relationship to her parents, she supplies some of those meanings to her friend, extending her awareness of her family's characteristics and her biracial identity to another child. That she is incorrect in her system for assessing the bunnies' gender is inconsequential to the importance of her own self-definition. Her analogies make some experimental sense, to her and another child, affording each with an enhanced idea of the meaning of color differences.

In a separate episode, another child makes use of the center's animals to examine this relationship between color, gender, and self, again expanding and refining the base of personal knowledge. One day, a pregnant cat took up residence near the playground. For weeks, the mother cat evaded capture and cared for her babies, but eventually the animal control staff was successful in capturing her. Her kittens had become habituated to people, and the center's director decided that they would be placed in adoptive homes. Debi volunteered to take the kittens to her veterinarian and have them checked. On her return from this trip, the following exchange with a child took place.

Debi enters the classroom with the carrier full of kittens, and meets Mike (5, Black), who runs up and asks, "Whatcha got?" Debi responds, "These are the kittens that were under the deck." "Oh, I want one!" he replies loudly, snatching at the carrier. "They already have homes, honey," Debi tells him. He ignores her, stating, "I'll have that black one, because I'm Black and me and my mommy are Black." Told again that the kittens already have homes, he says, "Oh. You want to play a game?" He immediately loses interest in the kittens when Debi tells him she must wait for the parents to pick up their new pets and that she cannot play right now. Similar to the way in which Corinne explained her parentage, Mike determines that since one kitten is black it qualifies as a pet for him and his family. In this case, color matching takes on still another meaning. . . .

Racial markers and skin color are also used to point out differences between people. Once again, for Black children and for the children who are of mixed racial-ethnic heritages or from other countries these variables are compelling. One teacher, Jeanne, is reading a storybook to the kids. Afterward, the children respond eagerly to Jeanne's question, drawn from the story, "How are we the same and different at the same time?" The children mention hair, age, and skin color. No prompting or suggestions are needed to get them going. Taleshia sits next to Debi, with her hand on Debi's leg. She studies the contrast once again, then turns and says to Debi, "We're different colors." She continues to study the skin tones, turning her arm over and back several times. Other children make observations about height, hair, and other physical characteristics. Corinne offers, "My mommy and I have the same skin, but my daddy doesn't. But we're one family." For children in families where difference is a part of daily life the nature of racial group, skin color, and other differences may assume particular importance. The more differences are noticed, in any context, the more they become part of dialogue and behavior among the children.

On one occasion talk about racial group and color involved a group of four children. The dialogue begins with a discussion of clothing colors, which moves into a comparison of clothing, hair, and skin colors. Debi is pushing Taleshia (3, Black), Christine (3, Asian), and Amber (3, Asian) on the tire swing. Brittany (4, white) comes over and informs Debi, "You have on white shoes and black socks and then black shorts." "Sure do," Debi replies; "and you have on white socks and blue shorts and a blue shirt." This technique of simply repeating what the children told her has proven to be very effective in carrying on child-centered conversations. Brittany grins, looking down and regarding

her clothing with some amusement. The similarity between her clothing and Debi's is apparent. Also apparent is Brittany's ultimate design: she seeks a spot on the tire swing. Taleshia then informs Debi that Debi has black hair. Debi replies, "Yes, but really I have black and white hair. See?" Debi bends toward the children and gestures to the gray streaks in her dark hair. Taleshia looks closely and then nods her head. Debi continues to push the swing, while the three girls chat.

"You," Taleshia says emphatically to Debi, "are white." "Yes," Debi agrees and continues, "and you are Black," once again imitating a child's remarks. Taleshia grins delightedly. "She's white too," Taleshia continues, pointing at Peggy, who has now joined the group. "Yes, she is white too," Debi agrees. Taleshia regards Elizabeth (3.5, Chinese) for a moment and then announces, "She's not white." "She's not white," Taleshia repeats. Debi agrees with the child's assessment and responds, "No, she's not white, she's Chinese." Debi extends Taleshia's remark to include nationality. "She's from China," Taleshia states, verifying Debi's remark and providing evidence that she realizes the connection between "Chinese" and China. "Yes, she is," Debi agrees, while Elizabeth laughs, apparently delighted that another person is bringing her into the conversation. "She's from China too," says Taleshia, pointing at Amber. "Yes, she is from China too," Debi tells her. "She's got black hair like you do," Taleshia continues. "She sure does," Debi notes. "So does Elizabeth. Very pretty black hair," Debi adds, making Elizabeth smile. Taleshia throws her head back and laughs. "Everybody's got black hair," she says. "No," Debi disagrees, "not everybody. Who doesn't have black hair?" Debi asks her. "Robin," she replies. Taleshia thinks for a moment and adds, "Sarah." "Anybody else?" Debi asks. "Peggy!" Taleshia shouts. "Sure enough," Debi says, "but what color is it?" "Brown," Taleshia again shouts, delighted that she is getting the right answers to this game. "Right again. Is that the same as

Robin's?" "No!" she shouts again. "What color is Robin's hair?" Debi asks. "Yellow."

Suddenly tired of the talk, Taleshia leans back and begins to sing, "Nanny, nanny, boo, boo, you can't get me!" to Sarah, who is passing by. "I want off now," she demands, and Debi lifts her down from the swing, replacing her with Peggy. Taleshia and Sarah enter a game of chase. Elizabeth and Amber begin to chant, "Ahhhh," starting low and rising up until it ends in screeching laughter as the tire swing moves from low to high.

The details of this scene are complex. Here the children are discussing and playing with various color and cultural issues, sometimes individually, sometimes all at once. They are quite excited by the game. A discussion of clothing quickly dissolved into an activity featuring categorization of different persons into racial and ethnic groups. The children begin their talk with a simple comparison of clothing, but the game soon evolves into a complex dialogue adding racial group, skin color, and national origins. Debi's responses to the children were primarily imitations of those addressed to her. Taleshia demonstrated a sophisticated ability to categorize the other children, recognizing that Elizabeth and Amber are not white. Yet she did not dichotomize color, reducing it to a matter of either black or white. Instead, color, racial group, and nationality are combined. Taleshia extended her evaluation of the Asian girls' color to incorporate their national origin and racial group, noting that while they were not Black, they also certainly were not white. It became necessary to use yet another category: Chinese. This category was not a new one for the children. Taleshia knew immediately that being Chinese meant a person was from China. The complicated nature of difference is not lost on this child, who strives to keep a complex matter intact.

A word here on Debi's involvement in the conversation: All the while she was engaged with the children, it was on her mind that she not lead them to conclusions. When she offered a name for the "not white" category, she was drawing on her knowledge, shared by the children, that Chinese was a category of people. The ideas of nationality and ethnicity were well known to these children. They had been exposed to many different racial, ethnic, and national labels, through their experiences with each other and through structured lessons delivered by the teaching staff. Food, language, dress, and other markers had been widely shared. That Taleshia eagerly concurred with Debi indicates that this view was not novel. Much of what Debi did in this interaction was in imitation of the children, a practice that the children themselves engage in often. . . .

In the next scene the differences between the children become an occasion for mass comparisons. We are at the tire swing again, and Debi is pushing three children, Dao (4, Asian), Rita (3, white/Latina), and Trevor (3, white), and listening to their conversations. Joseph (3, Black) joins them. Rita remarks to Debi, "You know what? I like his hair." She points to Joseph's head. His hair is done in five or six rows of plaits that run from front to back and are gathered in a knot in the back. "It's curly," Rita continues, reaching out and patting Joseph on the head. Joseph smiles at Rita as she touches his head. He says nothing. "I like his hair too," Debi tells Rita. Trevor says to Rita, "That's because he's Black." Rita agrees, adding, "Yeah, and my hair is curly too. And it's getting long and pretty. But I'm not Black, I'm Spanish." Trevor says, "My hair is straight. Debi's hair is straight too, and really, really, really, long. Right?" He looks at Debi for confirmation. "Yup," Debi agrees with him, "my hair is straight and long and dark brown with lots of gray streaks." Trevor adds, "Because you're old." Debi nods. "Old as the hills, right Dao?" Debi addresses another child. Dao nods and says, in a low voice, "My hair is straight and short and dark." This remark is unusual for Dao, who is usually very quiet, rarely saying anything. During this exchange Joseph says nothing, although he has pointed out to Debi in the past that he is Black. . . .

In this case, [the] children feel obliged to point out differences in coloring and hair type and are intrigued by these distinctions. Perhaps they suspect that other children would not notice or comment on differences unless attention is directed toward them. The exchange demonstrates the everyday nature of racial and ethnic comparisons within the center. At least eleven children were involved in the previous two dialogues, a figure that represents a substantial percentage of the center's classroom population. The children sought out differences and remarked on them in detail and at length, often with some sophistication. They are dealing with racial and ethnic identities, as well as racial-ethnic histories and cultural matters. They incorporated into their interactions many aspects of ethnicity and racial group that are not generally believed to be part of preschool children's repertoires of abilities. The extent of this sharing allows them to ask questions, support each other's conclusions, and contribute to the direction of discussion, skills developed to a significant degree outside the teacher-dominated spheres of center life. They are in charge here, acting on their thoughts and considerations. These scenes illustrate how peer relations become a critical aspect in learning about the meaning of racial and ethnic differences. No teacher initiated these conversations. Only one adult was involved and that involvement was limited. The topic of discussion was both salient and spontaneous for the children.

The children here were wrestling with complicated and socially important ideas. These markers of racial and ethnic origin informed them about each other. They named, indicated, and discussed several aspects of racial group and ethnicity. These were frank and curious discussions of social markers useful in understanding the nature of the larger world and relationships within both

that world and the more constrained and circumscribed world of the preschool.

Sharing Ideas About Racial Group and Ethnicity

Since the center housed a racially and ethnically diverse population, there was plenty of opportunity for discussion about children's backgrounds. For individual children, skin color was not the only element in the creation of self-identity and self-concept. Nationality and ethnicity also occupied the center of recurring interactions in the classroom and on the playground. Sometimes this discussion arose from an activity or from an adult question to a child. On more than one occasion, however, the children themselves initiated dialogue with each other about their nationality or ethnic background.

In one situation, Kumar (6, Asian), who is visiting the classroom; Corinne (4, African/white); and Susan (4, Chinese) are discussing their origins. Susan says to Kumar, "You're not American. Where are you from?" Kumar replies, "Yes, I am American, I was born here." Susan shakes her head, "You don't look American." Kumar just looks at her, apparently waiting for further remarks, with some irritation on his face. Susan then informs him, "I'm from China. That makes me Chinese." Corinne adds, "Yes, see, she is from Chinese." "No, silly, not Chinese," says Susan, "China. China is the country. Chinese are the people." Corinne volunteers, "I'm from Africa." Susan nods, "Yes, you are from Africa, and now you are here." Corinne nods and smiles. Kumar says, "My brother is from Africa, and my mother and father are from Asia." "How can your brother be from Africa and your mother and father from Asia?" questions Susan. "That's silly. You can't be from different places." "Yes you can!" retorts Kumar. "I am from here and my brother is from Africa and my mommy and daddy are from Asia. We move around a lot," he offers in explanation. "So what *are* you?" Susan asks Kumar. "A person," he replies. He then leaves the group and goes to get a drink from the water fountain.

Kumar offered a detailed and precise explanation of his family's multiple ethnic origins. Not only was he able to describe the complexity of his family, but he offered a reasonable explanation for it. Though originally from Asia, his family had at one time lived in Africa, where a brother was born. He had been born in the United States. Susan questions him in detail, demanding explanations for what appear to her to be contradictions. Kumar was able to provide her with a detailed and accurate accounting of his family's complex national origins. Susan also observes that dark-skinned Kumar doesn't look like an American, a remark that causes him to fluff up in anger. We see that the discussion of nationality and ethnicity among children can arouse strong emotions. Kumar's response indicates that he is aware of what he looks like and that being born in the United States makes him an American. Yet Susan's categorization of what is an "American" does not seem to include dark-skinned, black-haired youngsters. She doesn't explicitly state what "American" looks like, but it is fairly clear that she is confounding a certain light-skinned appearance with American. Clearly, Kumar is uncomfortable with the entire dialogue. His final evaluation of himself is that he is a person, a status with little emotional baggage, but one with great dignity.

This example illustrates key aspects of our arguments about how children use and process ideas, understandings, and language about ethnic, racial, and nationality distinctions. A child has picked up an embedded feature of the surrounding white-dominated society and is experimenting with it in her everyday interactions. One issue here is the general understanding of what an "American" is. In most media reports, in the minds of most white Americans, and in the minds of many other people in the United States and around the globe, "American" is synonymous with native-born white American. . . . In the case above, even a four-year-old Asian child sees another child, whose parents have lived in Africa and southern Asia, as not looking "American." At the same time, she is clearly experimenting with the ideas and is willing to discuss the matter fully.

Experimentation with racial and ethnic concepts was part of most of the children's activities at the center. For the American-born children, trying out new concepts was enhanced by the ready availability of children from other countries. The diversity provided these children with opportunities to juxtapose their developing sense of self with their recognition of others as different, contrasting a sense of self-identity with their growing awareness of others. Racial and ethnic markers became useful tools for the task. The children from other lands often found that their origins became a source of conversation and interaction with others. Their racial, ethnic, and nationality backgrounds afforded them opportunities to engage in personal interaction, thereby gaining attention and increasing their knowledge of how these concepts functioned in social life.

The children of foreign-born parents afforded us with opportunities to watch deep explorations of racial and ethnic meanings and understandings. For example, Corinne, the four-year-old child of a white American parent and a Black African parent, incorporated several social variables in her young life. She was a rich source of information about racial-ethnic understandings among young children. Her biracial, dual-continent origins were questioned on numerous occasions, yet this girl successfully negotiated her biracial identity: not merely Black but also white, not only American but also distinctively African. Her multiple identities confused many adults and other children, yet she easily accounted for and understood her identities and was able to explain them and their meanings to others. She had created an extraordinarily strong sense of her self, one that she defended and explained with great dexterity.

One day, close to parent pickup time, Corinne, Mike (4, Black), and Debi are sitting at a picnic table. The two children are coloring, ignoring Debi and the other children around them. Corinne's father, David, arrives to pick her up, and when she spots him she leaps up and runs to him. They walk back to the table together, holding hands, and sit down again with Mike and Debi. David greets Debi, remarking that he would like to wait and meet his wife here.

"Who's that?" Mike demands, looking at Corinne's father. "That's my daddy," she replies, beaming at her father. Mike regards the man unsmilingly, then sniffs and shakes his head vigorously. "Uh, uh," he declares, indicating his disbelief. Corinne stares at Mike for a moment, then says, "Yes he is!" David looks on in amusement, a smile on his face. "How come he ain't Black?" Mike asks Corinne. "Because he's not," she retorts, glaring at Mike and grabbing her father's hand. "Uh, uh, you can't have a white dad. Black kids have Black dads," Mike states, smiling. "Yes I can. I do. We're from Africa." Corinne's tone has now taken on a quieter quality, but she still frowns at Mike. "Uh, uh," Mike insists, "nope." David sits smiling gently, as though he cannot quite believe what is going on in front of him.

"Stop it!" Corinne is now yelling at Mike, which prompts David to intercede. "Corinne's mommy is Black," he explains to Mike, retaining his smile. Mike does not respond to him, instead staring at the man as though he does not exist. Corinne sticks her tongue out at Mike, who ignores her and continues to stare at David. "When Black people and white people fall in love and get married they have beautiful brown babies," David continues, hugging Corinne and smiling at Mike, who does not reply. At this point, Mike's mother also arrives to pick him up from school, distracting him and ending the episode.

Mike adamantly refused to acknowledge that Corinne's father was white, despite the facts that a white man was sitting right in front of him and that Corinne declared this man to be her father. Mike justified his disbelief by referring to a rule he had garnered from his own experience: Black children could not have white parents. Mike's denial of Corinne's origins, and by implication her multiracial identity, was met with opposition from her and an explanation from her father, but he persisted. As far as he was concerned, Corinne was a Black child, and Corinne's skin color and facial features confirmed his evaluation. Hence she could not have a white parent, since in his experience Black children invariably had Black parents. The contradiction of Corinne's parentage was too much for him to bear.

Mike was not the only person who challenged Corinne's explanation of her origins. Adults, too, questioned whether or not Corinne really knew who, and what, she was. One day, during a sharing circle, Corinne was invited to describe her family and her home. She eagerly launched into a description of her home in Africa, elaborating the story with a tale about riding elephants in the backyard. As Corinne spoke, Debi overheard Cindy and Lynne, two center employees, remarking on her story. "Isn't that cute!" Cindy said, "That little girl thinks she's from Africa." Lynne smiled and said, "Oh, she probably heard her parents say that she was African American and is just confused." Corinne continued with her story, blissfully unaware of the disbelief evident on the adults' faces. . . .

Neither children nor adults had difficulty accepting that several of the children were born in Europe or Asia. Yet, whenever Corinne offered to a newcomer her story that she was from Africa, there was disbelief, especially on the part of adults. The task of explaining her origins became a recurring chore for Corinne. She was forced to continually defend herself, especially to adults, the authority figures in her life. They provided her with the most difficulties. Eventually, she acquiesced and no longer attempted to talk to adults about her origins or correct their mistaken beliefs. One day, when once again instructed by a well-meaning adult that she was African American, Corinne merely rolled her eyes and replied, "Whatever." She had learned a valuable lesson: Adults often do not believe what small children tell them, even if it is true. . . .

The belief held by most white adults that young children have little awareness of their racial-ethnic characteristics and identities acts to exacerbate a child's task of explaining herself to others. Teacher-led activities often did not lend themselves to encouraging children to explain and describe their own racial-ethnic understandings. These teacher-children activities were almost always designed around teacher questions and children's answers to those predetermined questions. This assertion is not an effort to blame teachers, or to suggest that they are somehow scheming to ignore or denigrate youngsters. This is merely the virtually universal nature of the schoolroom. Teachers ask questions; children answer. The nature of the teacher-child interaction in most cases of racial-ethnic sharing did not permit the children to engage in elaborate dialogue or provide detailed stories as they did in interaction with other children or with Debi. The children were usually limited to simple yes/no answers or an occasional explanation of an unusual custom or word. The following episode is illustrative of the pattern present when adults were in charge of self-description.

On a few occasions, especially when a new semester started or new children entered the facility, teachers led activities designed to introduce children to each other. These sharing circles were occasions for reporting all aspects of oneself, including racial group and ethnicity. Shortly after the center reopened from a holiday break, Dean, a teacher from another classroom, arranged to present new students from his room to our

classroom. He begins the activity by announcing his name and that he is from the United States. The children then take turns sharing where they are from. "I'm from China," says Susan, predictably. "I'm from Korea," an Asian boy responds. "Where are you from?" Dean asks a boy, whose name tag reads "Emile." Before the child can reply, another teacher in the circle responds, "France." However, Emile vigorously shakes his head no on hearing this and points to the ground. "Are you from here, Emile?" Dean asks. Emile nods and continues to point at the ground, a smile on his face. "Are your parents from France?" Dean continues, smiling at the child. "I don't know," Emile shrugs. Dean turns his attention to the next child in the circle. "I'm from Sweden," a tall blond girl contributes. Most of the children seem to know where they or their parents are from but offer no detail. However, Kumar breaks from this pattern and tells a long, involved story about how he is from the United States, his brother is from Africa, and his parents are from Asia. "My dad is there now," he adds. "Where is your mom?" another boy asks. "She's here," replies Kumar.

Dean interrupts him, moving on to Corinne. She heaves a deep sigh and reports, "I'm from Africa." She waits, looking around her. "Really?" Dean replies, "Are you African American?" The look on Corinne's face is simply priceless. In a display of comical exaggeration, she rolls her eyes, shrugs her shoulders, and flops her hands into her lap in helpless resignation. "Nope, just plain old, stupid African," she sighs, obviously wishing this activity was over. Dean obliges her and moves on without remark. Given the question-and-answer format of these activities, the children learn that adults are not really interested in in-depth discussions with children, or in the racial-ethnic worlds in which they live and interact every day. . . .

Conclusion

In this chapter we showed how white children and children of color use the racial-ethnic concepts widely found in the surrounding societal environment to interact and build and define the meaning of their own selves and the selves of others. We saw how they interact with each other and with adults—fine-grained data that are only available from extensive observations. . . . The episodes we observed in children's lives demonstrate how children obtain and organize ethnic and racial information from others and then use this information to construct their social lives. Racial and ethnic attitudes, group preferences, and self-identity are all parts of the same process: building a racial-ethnic reality.

In our study we see that the children are learning from cumulative experiences with racism, color coding, and racial-ethnic identities. Negative and positive experiences accumulate over time and in elaborate interaction, eventually, with a wide variety of different others. This makes such experiences longitudinal and significant as social phenomena. How children come to know themselves in racial-ethnic terms arises in part from their grounding in a racist society and in part from their own daily interaction with other children and with adults. Despite the fact that they might not be aware of the workings of the world in a refined, adult way, they have substantial abilities to employ self, color, and racial concepts by the time they are three. In general, the children we observed were able to use color coding consistently and in detailed comparisons, whether the color was of skin, clothing, hair, eyes, or inanimate objects. They routinely created complex explanations for themselves and each other based on skin color and offered descriptions and verification of physical characteristics in a variety of ways. Some, particularly children of color and those whose parents included someone from another country, were able to construct and maintain very complicated self-identities that incorporated aspects of racial group and ethnicity.

7

Media Images' Influence on Adolescent Girls' Self-Concepts

Melissa Milkie

Mead argues that the individual acquires a complete self by taking the attitude of the "generalized other" or whole community toward her- or himself but does not explain how the individual learns of that generalized attitude toward her or him. A strong case can be made that, in contemporary societies, the mass media are important sources of information about the generalized other. As this selection illustrates, the process through which the mass media influence individuals' self-concepts—their definitions and assessments of who and what they are—is a complex one. It suggests that media images exert their influence in two ways, through social comparisons and reflected appraisals. Social comparisons occur when an individual defines and evaluates herself or himself in relation to a reference group of similar people who share with her or him such current or desired social identities as ethnicity or future occupation. Individuals also define and evaluate themselves on the basis of what they feel others think of them, in terms of reflected appraisals. These are two aspects of what Cooley called "the looking glass self," of the reflected self-images we use to define ourselves. As this study demonstrates,

those reflected images are increasingly found on television screens and in the pages of popular magazines.

This study examines the influence of beauty images in girls' magazines and other mass media on adolescent girls' self-concepts. Melissa Milkie, the author of the study, surveyed and interviewed a variety of high school girls about their uses and opinions of popular girls' magazines. Most of the girls reported reading and discussing those magazines, although white girls did so more often than African-American girls, and most criticized as unrealistic and unattainable the beauty images found in their advertisements and fashion pages. Yet, despite those criticisms, white girls still tended to judge themselves in terms of those images, although the African-American girls did not. Milkie explains this racial difference in terms of social comparisons and reflected appraisals. White girls considered the magazines for "girls like them" and compared themselves to the ideal beauty images in them despite their criticisms of those images. African-American girls, in contrast, did not consider that such magazines were for or about girls like them and so did not negatively compare themselves to the beauty ideals the magazines conveyed. Moreover, the white girls believed that "other girls" and "boys" evaluated their appearance in relation to the beauty images portrayed in those magazines and other media. In contrast, the African-American girls believed that other African-American girls and many boys found a much wider range of appearances attractive. In other words, while the beauty images of popular media influenced reflected appraisals of the white girls, the African-American girls discounted the influence of those images on those whose appraisals they took seriously.

This study demonstrates that while the mass media can affect our self-concepts, their effects are neither assured nor direct. Like the African-American girls in this study, some may simply conclude that the images the media convey are irrelevant to them. On the other hand, like the white girls, some may be critical of those images, yet believe others use them to judge others. In such cases, we imagine that others are judging us in relation to those images and so compare ourselves to them. When those images are idealized and unrealistic, these social comparisons and reflected appraisals can have a devastating effect on self-esteem. Although indirect, the beauty images in popular girls' magazines and other media apparently had such an effect on the self-esteem of the white girls in this study. At least they considered themselves less attractive and had lower self-esteem than the African-American girls who did not negatively compare themselves to those images or believe that those whose opinions they valued did so.

This study also illustrates that what Mead called the complete self is never completed, but is continually subject to social influence and revision. The girls in this study were continually comparing themselves to others, evaluating themselves in terms of reflected self-appraisals, and revising their self-concepts accordingly. The African-American girls' more positive self-concepts do not indicate that they were immune to social influence, but that they took the attitude of a different generalized other than the white girls. While the white girls took the attitude of the generalized other expressed through the popular media toward themselves, the African-American girls evaluated themselves in comparison to other African-American girls and women and in terms of the assumed appraisals of the African-American community. Like the rest of us, neither group escaped the relentless influence of one or another generalized other on their self-concepts.

Questions of whether and how media influence self-concept—both self-identities and self-evaluations—as well as their impact on beliefs, values and behaviors underlies much media research. . . . In this study I . . . [analyze] the extent to which people's power to make critical assessments of [media] content (for example, believing that stereotyped portrayals of one's group are unrealistic or unimportant) may prevent that content from negatively affecting the self. I take the case of feminine beauty images in media, and assess the relative power of critical interpretations in countering harmful effects on the self-concept, specifically on self-esteem. To clarify how media can affect people indirectly, I draw on basic principles in social psychology which point to the key role of *others* in self processes, and discuss these in terms of some unique properties of mass media. . . .

How Media Affect the Self: Incorporating Social Psychological Principles

A unique quality of media is their public pervasiveness and people's knowledge that the images or ideas they see are also seen by many others—often millions of others. In addition, individuals believe that *others are more strongly affected* by media portrayals than they themselves are (Davison 1983; Perloff 1993). This belief reflects either a misperception of how others view or are influenced by media or, as Davison (1983) points out, perhaps an underestimation of the media influence on the self. Evidence for this belief—known as the "third-person effect"—includes studies showing that people believe that other people's children are affected by commercials more strongly than their own, and that others in their communities are affected by political campaigns more strongly than they are (see Davison 1983; Perloff 1993).

How does a belief that media images are powerful for others matter for individuals? The third-person effect suggests that effects of media in which the content *directly* influences the self, attitudes, or behavior may not be the only important kind of influence. A complex, indirect effect may also occur as people account for the effects of the pervasive imagery in media on others in their social networks, *and are themselves influenced by perceptions of the way others see the media-distorted world*. Much of what we know and understand about others outside our community—who they are, what they value, indeed, what is happening in the broader society—is filtered through the distorted lens of the media; and for some, this information may even come to represent the society (Altheide and Snow 1988). Indeed, media may have become a significant part of the generalized other—that is, the "society" we know—whose views we take into account in understanding and evaluating our self. Because media effects may involve how we believe *others* see such images, self processes involving significant others—specifically social comparisons and reflected appraisals—must be considered.

Social comparisons affect how we learn about and see ourselves in relation to individuals, groups, or social categories. Are we the same or different? Better or worse? Social comparison theories suggest that we tend to compare ourselves with similar others, though we have selectivity in making such comparisons, that is, relative freedom to select the referents by whom we evaluate ourselves (Rosenberg 1986; Singer 1981). Theoretically, given freedom of comparison, people could use selectivity to escape media images that they dislike or to which they compare negatively—by ignoring or discounting them and by not using such images as a basis for social comparison. Yet because of the pervasiveness of media, and the way in which people believe that media affect others, it may be difficult to avoid some social comparisons with media images and felt evaluations (reflected appraisals) based on the media-depicted world. Media images may alter ideas of what is normative or ideal or of what one thinks *others* believe is normative or ideal, while offering an additional pervasive standard of comparison that goes beyond local cultures. If people believe that others use such images to evaluate them, they cannot simply shift away from this constraining comparative referent.

Reflected appraisals, or how people believe that others view them, can further explain the indirect impact of media. . . . At least two areas of research on reflected appraisals are important for understanding media im-

pact. First, research shows that people cannot easily distinguish how a particular significant other views them. Instead, reflected appraisals appear to be a proxy for the generalized other—the attitudes of an entire group (Felson 1989). Given the place of media in representing society's (generalized others') norms and ideals, it is crucial to consider how media relate to the self via reflected appraisals.

Second, it is essential to consider the relevance and importance of reflected appraisals. Rosenberg (1986) cautions researchers to examine the conditions under which reflected appraisals in fact will affect the self. Ultimately those reflected appraisals must be important to the individual in order to exert influence. For example, Rosenberg argues that a racist society does not simply cause a negative impact on black children's self-esteem because black children are not necessarily aware of others' (whites') views, may not agree with them, may not find them relevant to the self, or may not care about the opinions of those others. Similarly, people might be affected (indirectly) by media images only when they believe that those important to them are so affected. The theoretical and empirical research on social comparisons and reflected appraisals is important in considering how media criticism could be deflated. Even if someone believes that her group is portrayed unrealistically and does not like the portrayal, she may not know or believe that others *share* her criticisms. In other words, individuals see themselves through the eyes of others who they assume have been affected significantly by mass media imagery. It is clear that people ignore, dislike, and belittle media portrayals, and may not wish to make a social comparison that is negative for the self. Yet the extent to which such critical assessment of media is effective, or can negate effects, may depend on the extent to which individuals know that significant others have assessed the symbols critically in the same way. . . . Alternatively, peers may be a means of validating critical assessment if the peer network also is critical of such portrayals *and* if the individual knows the views of that group accurately. In such a case, an individual can act on criticisms, or they can be meaningful in protecting her self-evaluations, because she knows that the network or group devalues those images as well.

Analytic Strategy and Research Questions

. . . I examine the case of pervasive beauty ideals disseminated through mass media, which many suggest are harmful to young women. These images, particularly in regard to body shape, are extremely unlike "real" American women. The gap between the image and the reality has grown in recent years, as the media images have become slimmer and Americans have grown heavier (Wiseman et al. 1992). The in-depth interviews focus on a tangible, explicit embodiment of idealized femininity—girls' magazines—which saturate their target audience (Evans 1990). The images presented therein are also pervasive in other media such as movies and television. I address these broad research questions: How do girls interpret the female image in media, how do they critique it, and how do they perceive its influence? How do girls view peers' interpretations of these images? How important are critical views of the imagery in protecting girls' self-esteem?

Data and Method

The data come from in-depth interviews with a subsample of 60 girls who were part of a larger survey. . . . I obtained permission from the principals of two high schools to conduct the study, and from grade 9 and grade 10 teachers to gain access to their classrooms. To examine how media interpretations might vary by ethnicity and locale, I chose an ethnically diverse urban high school and an all-white rural high school in the mid-

west. This choice of schools allowed comparisons of whites' interpretations of popular national media images across localities, and permitted a comparison of ethnic groups in a single locale . . .

Of the 60 girls interviewed, 49 were white and 11 were minorities (10 African-American and one Asian-American). About two-thirds were interviewed individually, and the remainder in groups of two (and, in one case, three) friends. The interviews took place in a private room during the subject's study hall or lunch period, or during a class period in which a teacher had approved her absence . . .

Results

Ethnic status sharply differentiated whether girls identified with the images, supposedly intended for and about all adolescent girls. This status created an important filter for social comparisons and reflected appraisal processes, and thus influenced the effectiveness of critical interpretations for shielding harm to self-concept. First I discuss how the magazines and the images they contain were a part of white girls' culture at both the rural and the urban school, but how black girls generally rejected the images as part of their reference group even though they occasionally read popular girls' magazines. Both white and black girls interpreted the images as largely unrealistic; many wanted more normal or more "real" girls in the images.

Next I show that theoretical work on social comparisons and reflected appraisals helps to explain how critical interpretations of media do not necessarily preclude effects of media. Social comparisons with the images were distinguished strongly by ethnicity, with variations in the desire to emulate the images. Even though the white girls compared themselves negatively with the images and felt poorly about themselves in relation to the ideal, they felt it difficult to opt out of such a comparison. The utility of the criticisms relates to reflected appraisals, demonstrating the limitations of "resistance" when media images are presumed to affect significant or generalized others.

Reference Groups, Media Interpretation, and Criticism of Images

Explicit in cultural products labeled *Seventeen* or *Teen* is the notion that such products provide images and information relevant to particular groups of people. . . . In interviews, the white girls clearly indicated that they regarded the images as directed toward *adolescent girls*. Much of the content directly advises or discusses issues pertaining to females, and the girls' responses indicated their understanding that femininity was central in these cultural products.

Girls' magazines, like other media, were part of the white girls' peer culture in both schools. They helped these girls to assess how well they fit into, or were similar to, their reference group. . . . The magazines gave advice on, and were perceived to help with, girls' concerns about "fitting in" and being accepted by others. In the interviews, for example, many girls stated that any hypothetical girl who does *not* read girls' magazines does not care about others' opinions or is very independent. This comment implies that the information contained in these media pertains to conforming to the "norm" of adolescent femininity.

The respondents considered reading the magazines an enjoyable leisure activity: 95 percent of the white girls surveyed read them occasionally or more often; more than half read them "always." Magazine reading as a part of peer culture, and the relative amount of interaction centered around the cultural products themselves, differed somewhat in the two locales. At the rural school, where girls made slightly higher use of the imagery and evaluated it more positively, cliques regularly discussed content during school hours and after school over the telephone. They

read the magazines in the lunchroom, the hallways, and the school library, and even during class. Subscribers often shared their magazines with friends, reading them either together or to each other, and passing on copies to those who did not subscribe. Indeed, for rural white girls, a great deal of peer interaction surrounded these magazines. This is not surprising because in rural areas, media may be an important means of understanding the larger world and the variety of people in it, with which the rural dwellers have much less contact.

Urban white girls also said they discussed the magazines or particular items in the magazines with friends, but they reported this experience less often. Perhaps because more varied activities are available to the urban girls, magazine reading is less salient. Yet in a quantitative analysis examining how often white girls read the magazines alone or with friends, I found no differences between schools. Indeed, more white girls at the urban school than at the rural school subscribed to at least one girls' magazine (64 percent versus 50 percent).

Black respondents less often read mainstream girls' magazines, both individually and as a collective activity: 86 percent of the black girls surveyed read them at least occasionally, but only 11 percent always read them. Even though, in recent years, black models have appeared regularly in the four magazines with the greatest circulation, the magazines are perceived as largely for white girls. Most of the black girls read *Ebony* or *Essence*, aimed at black adults and black women respectively, magazines about music directed toward black youth, and hairstyle publications. Thus, in contrast to white girls, these respondents largely regard mainstream girls' magazines as something they do not want to or should not orient themselves toward because they view the magazines as for and about white girls. They define the images as irrelevant to their reference group for this social aspect of the self. . . . Tanya, in responding to how people would understand "girls" if they had only girls' magazines to look at, said:

> I think this is mainly toward . . . white females . . . you really wouldn't see too many black people in here—so if this is all you saw, you'd be kinda scared when you saw one like me or something. (May 9, 1994; urban black girl)

Minority girls were quite critical about the realism of the images. Part of this critique was that normative adolescent femininity was portrayed as white femininity. Although ethnicity differentiated the respondents' use of these mainstream magazines, both African-American and white girls seemed to hold common perceptions about the unreality of the images.

When asked to describe the magazines to a girl who had never seen them, most of the respondents interpreted them as conveying very traditional aspects of femininity, such as appearance and romance. They mentioned fashion, makeup, styles—all related to appearance—and relationships with males. . . . Barb's explanation is similar to how most girls described the magazines:

> They're about how girls can do their hair, what's in fashion. They give advice on boys; sometimes they give you advice on your body and stuff like that—how to get in shape. They've got how to do your makeup right, hair—I think I already said that—what's the right jewelry. They talk a lot about stars and stuff like that, they also talk a lot about boys. (May 9, 1994; urban Asian girl)

Secondarily, the respondents reported that the magazines were about girls' "problems." This view is closely related to the above observation. The information presented about appearance and relationships with boys was interpreted by the girls as advice about problems of traditional femininity which they were experiencing or which were common to adolescent females. A minority of the girls described the magazines more

broadly as about "teenagers' lives" or "everything." Only two of 60 respondents described the magazines in what might be considered feminist terms, as about girls' "being independent," although these two girls also discussed appearance as an important component of the magazines.

The great majority of the respondents, even those who seldom read the magazines, liked them as a whole or liked certain parts. The girls stated that they read them because they were interesting, entertaining, and informative. An important feature of the girls' enjoyment and interest was learning about themselves and assessing their lives and their problems in relation to their peers. Linda, a grade 9 student, explained this:

> The girls will write in, and you kind of realize they have the same problems as you do . . . you know they [other girls] kinda make you feel like you're not the only one. (May 19, 1994; urban white girl)

Researchers have suggested that one reason why people are critical of media is that the media distort reality and reflect groups in distorted ways. Most of the respondents were critical in that they said media images of girls were not realistic at all, and they made negative comments about the lack of "normal" girls. In general, the respondents indicated that the feminine images in the magazines presented an unrealistic appearance, both in the styles of clothing and in the perfection of their faces, hair, and bodies in comparison with the largely imperfect local girls. A few respondents said that the girls in the magazines were somewhat realistic; sometimes, they referred to the pages that focused on "real" girls' problems or compared the images with the most popular or most beautiful girls in the school. The black girls were quite critical of the magazine models' physical appearance in general and tended to be critical about the lack of ethnic diversity or representation.

In discussing how the models looked, the respondents were likely to comment that they were *too* perfect, especially in body shape, weight, hair, facial features, and complexion. Sandra, a grade 10 student, discussed the message sent by the magazines:

> They mainly focus on models . . . they make them look perfect, which nobody is. Makes everyone's expectations really high of their self, and they don't need it. I don't think they show the true girl. You know, nobody is perfect, and they all have their mistakes, and some of these people look like they never make a mistake. (April 21, 1994; rural white girl)

In fact, many viewed the images not merely as unrealistic, but as artificial. A girl who had recently lost a good deal of weight remarked that some models shown in the magazines have altered their "true" selves:

> I think some of them might be fake. Like get contacts to change their eye color, cake on their makeup, starve themselves. Like they're really not that skinny, but they just starve themselves. (May 25, 1994; urban white girl)

Generally, the respondents disliked the fact that these pervasive media images deviated so much from reality. They remarked, as noted above by Sandra, that the media created an uneasy gap between image and reality. Barb, while looking at the title of a girls' magazine article in front of her, observed that even the so-called "problem" bodies shown in the magazines are perfect:

> Oh, if I read that "Four Weeks to a Better Body," I'd probably . . . these magazines are trying to tell you "Do this and do that." Sometimes they have . . . swimsuits and stuff, and what you can do if you have a problem body. If you got a big butt, big chest . . . what to do. And these girls that they are showing don't have that problem. I mean you can tell they don't, and that makes me mad. . . . They say if you got a stick figure, wear a one-piece and . . . colorful and I'm looking at the girl and she doesn't have a stick figure. If you

got big hips, if you got a big stomach—she doesn't have it—you can never understand that. (May 9, 1994; urban Asian girl)

In response to open-ended questions about whether they would change anything about the magazines, particularly anything that was emphasized too much or was not included, more than one-third of the respondents specified that the magazines should change the feminine image to be more realistic or "normal." Amy believes that "normal" people are missing from the images:

> One thing I guess would be just more normal people . . . not like the models, but just average. Other people that haven't really had modeling experience. (May 25, 1994; urban white girl)

Similarly, Suzanne suggests that magazine editors should be more realistic:

> Probably tell them to be more realistic about the situations, and who they have in their magazines . . . people that are everyday teenagers, not just celebrities and people like that. (May 20, 1994; urban white girl)

The majority of the girls indicated that the unrealistic images were a problem for themselves, and/or for some, most, or all girls. Leslie, who had discussed her "underweight" friends' concern about eating anything fatty, said:

> If all you ever see is all these people with the perfect teeth, the perfect complexion, with a skinny body, then they may not think that they're perfect and then they start to worry about being skinny and getting braces, wearing lots of makeup to cover up their face. (May 25, 1994; urban white girl)

Similarly, Brittany discussed what she would tell the editors of girls' magazines:

> To quit stressin' so much that you need to be so skinny for bathing suits and stuff 'cause it just makes teenagers feel bad

about themselves. (May 2, 1994; rural white girl)

In sum, most of the respondents regarded media images of females, particularly those which are common in ads or fashion pages, as unrealistic. Many disliked the images for this reason, considered them harmful to themselves or to others and advocated that media producers should alter their products to include more "real," ordinary, or "normal" girls.

Media and Social Comparison Processes

Social comparison theories argue that we compare ourselves with similar and nearby others, and that social structural factors influence which referents will be chosen. Although researchers generally suggest that we are motivated and free to make comparisons that are favorable to us (Rosenberg 1986; Singer 1981) there are limits; comparisons that disfavor us may be unavoidable if we cannot leave a group. . . . This point may help to explain how cultural images of one's reference group, although rarely considered in social comparison research, may constitute an inescapable "group" that can have negative consequences as it is incorporated into local culture. Insofar as one views media "others" as attractive and identifies with them as they are brought into one's peer group, they may become comparative referents, although such comparison to images is likely to have negative consequences for the self. In this section, I discuss how the mainstream female image, although most respondents view it as unrealistic and criticize it, becomes an oppressive negative referent for whites who cannot escape it easily, but not for blacks, who feel distant from it.

Both the white and the African-American respondents, but especially the white girls, liked the magazines, even though they criticized the lack of realism of the girls pictured therein. The white respondents used the images and ideas in the magazines to assess themselves. They said frequently that they "felt better" or more normal when reading about the problems and experiences of other girls their age. This feeling came from the numerous articles and advice columns that dealt with problems of relationships with boyfriends and family members, peer group pressures, and health, beauty, and fashion issues. The respondents particularly liked to assess themselves in relation to their reference group by taking quizzes that evaluated them on topics such as relationships (e.g., "How Good a Friend Are You?"). These quizzes provide scores that categorize the reader as a certain type of person and explain how she tends to act in situations in comparison with others. Jackie explains why she reads the magazines:

> I guess I like to see what . . . the clothes, like what people are wearing. And like questions-answers, like what people are . . . curious about, and see if I'm the same, I guess. (May 23, 1994; urban white girl)

The respondents often told how they learned about themselves through other girls' problems or experiences discussed in the magazines, and thus about how they compared with their peers on adolescent issues that were often troubling developmental concerns, such as sexuality. Many girls appreciated the magazines for helping with their problems. Yet just as the white girls sought to learn about and evaluate themselves in reference to their "media peers'" emotions, problems, behavior, and experiences, they did so with their media peers' physical appearance, though with less enthusiasm. The ordinary girls featured in the text and the atypical professional models featured in the accompanying pictures are very different types of media peers; perhaps this coexistence of "real" girls with problems (in the text) and "ideal" girls (pictured) makes the comparison to beauty images even more likely and leads to negative self-evaluations. Because of their perception that these images, however distorted, constituted others' views of adolescent femininity, the white respondents could not easily opt out of a social comparison and self-evaluation in which they were sure to fall short. . . .

Social comparison theories assume some degree of freedom in choosing comparison referents; such choices are presumed to be partly governed by motivations for self-enhancement (Singer 1981; Rosenberg 1986). Yet the girls who saw the images as unrealistic and disliked this nonrealism, and for whom comparisons would not invite self-enhancement, nonetheless made comparisons. The great majority of white girls wanted to look like the ideal girls featured in the magazines, connecting such imagery to rewards such as male attention, and inevitably compared themselves with the "perfect" girl. Beth indicated why "everybody" wants to be like this:

> They're so beautiful and everything and they have these really great bodies and they have the perfect hair, the perfect boyfriend, the perfect life, and they're rich and everything. (April 25, 1994; rural white girl)

Similarly, Amber explained how she believed the magazines influence girls:

> I think they, just girls in general, kind of want to be like the girls in there. Like the models. I think they want to be like those models . . . [because] they think if they're like that they're gonna get lots of guys and stuff. (April 28, 1994; rural white girl)

Although the vast majority of white girls appeared to use the information and images as a reference group with which they identified and whose physical appearance they emulated, four respondents stated that they did not want to change themselves to be like anybody else. For example, Beth, who commented about what "everybody wants," said:

> Well, everybody wants to be a model but . . . I just like myself as myself. I wouldn't

really . . . change anything about myself. (April 25, 1994; rural white girl)

The minority respondents, in sharp contrast, did not emulate these images nor compare themselves as negatively with the models. Even though most of the black girls occasionally read the mainstream publications, they considered the images less relevant, belonging to "white girls' " culture and not part of a reference group toward which they oriented themselves. Strikingly, 10 of the 11 minority girls (nine black and one Asian-American) said unequivocally that they did not want to be like these girls; one mixed-race respondent (African-American and white) said that she "sometimes" did. The black girls indicated that they did not relate to the images and did not wish to emulate the rigid white beauty ideal. Tamika described why she generally did not read mainstream girls' magazines:

> Well, I don't see a lot of black girls. . . . I don't see a lot of us . . . maybe if they had more, maybe I could relate to that. I don't know. 'Cause obviously we can't wear the same makeup or get our hair the same way . . . things like that. So maybe if they had more. (May 11, 1994; urban black girl)

In sum, for the great majority of white girls in both locales, national media images and information about the reference group served as an additional social comparison introduced into the local context. The white girls evaluated their own behavior, problems, emotions, and importantly, physical appearance in comparison with these media others. Even though they knew that the images were unrealistic, the white girls saw themselves as part of the reference group being portrayed, and compared their "problems" with adolescent females' problems. They reported that they often (reluctantly) made social comparisons with the perfect physical appearance of media images because they knew that these images were what "everybody" wants. The minority respondents and a very few of the white respondents did not emulate these feminine images in media, did not bring them meaningfully into peer groups, and seemingly did not make social comparisons unfavorable to themselves. . . .

Although the white girls liked the magazines a good deal and enjoyed finding out that they were "normal" on the basis of other girls' behaviors and problems, many said that they personally or that "girls" in general felt abnormal and inferior in relation to the idealized feminine image. A key influence of the magazines, then, is that the great majority of white respondents said they wanted to look like the girls pictured therein, *even though most saw the images as unrealistic and unattainable.* These girls necessarily experienced relative deprivation because they could not attain the valued image promoted by the pervasive display of this unique part of the reference group. Although they generally understood that the images were unrealistic, the girls perceived that other girls in the school, and especially males, valued such an appearance. Thus it was difficult for critical appraisal of media images to become meaningful in local interaction, a phenomenon that I discuss below.

A rural white respondent, Patty, demonstrated the complexity of being aware of nonrealism and critical of images, while simultaneously striving to achieve such an appearance. She indicated that the magazines influence girls "quite a bit," and explained that they did so by making girls, including herself, feel as if they wanted and *needed* to look like the media portrayals:

> [Girls are influenced by magazines] . . . by havin' to look that way. I mean by their body and stuff 'cause they're all really tall and skinny so everybody tries to be all really tall and skinny. . . . I think most girls don't realize that they're bigger boned than [that] . . . I'm [from a] very big-boned family . . . most girls just don't realize that there's *no way* in the world they could

look like that. (April 22, 1994; rural white girl; respondent's emphasis)

Patty underestimated the degree of critical assessment by girls: most respondents *did* realize that they could not attain the look. Similarly, Alana, a tall, slim 15-year-old who had been recruited by a modeling agency, said that she and others felt as if they should measure up:

> The thing with being skinny—you think sometimes "Maybe I should be skinny too." But then you sit back and you're thinking "Oh my God . . . what am I thinking—thinking that I'm going to be perfect like one of them." But there's a lot of girls, like I said, that get into that—they try to be all of that. (May 12, 1994; urban white girl)

The white respondents made negative social comparisons even while they recognized the media distortion. They indicated that the comparisons were difficult to opt out of and made them or "girls" feel worse about themselves because the girls inevitably looked worse than the glamorized exceptional females in the media. In . . . data from the larger group of girls surveyed ($N = 210$) the white girls felt significantly worse about themselves compared with the images . . . than the minority girls. . . .

The black girls' criticisms of media imagery, in contrast to the white girls', may be effective in reducing the impact of media in this case, because the black subculture as a whole is more critical of mainstream beauty ideals. The black girls in this study, although as concerned about appearance as the white respondents, perceived themselves as better-looking and were more satisfied with their appearance than were the white girls, and their self-esteem was higher. Though the black girls objectively are farther from the mainstream ideals of beauty in skin color, hair style, and weight . . . they compared themselves more favorably with mainstream media images than did the white girls. Evidence from interviews also indicates that black girls perceived the white ideal as narrow or as less applicable to them. Eliza discussed how minority girls may strive less often to be like the images of girls shown in these magazines:

> This is kind of a stereotype, but more of my white friends than my black friends are into [trying to be like feminine images in magazines]. I mean a lot of them are going on a diet or "I want that body so bad"—I don't know how anybody can be like that. (May 27, 1994; urban black girl)

Lakoff and Scherr (1984) suggest that ethnic minority women, although evaluated by whites as inferior in relation to a model of white beauty which is impossible for them to achieve, currently may consider a *wider* range of looks as beautiful or normal within their subculture. They cite black women's magazines: Although these publications advertise hair straighteners (for a more mainstream model of beauty), they also show a wide variety of African facial features when demonstrating hair styles, as well as a range of body types, with information about how to "get bigger" as well as smaller (Lakoff and Scherr 1984). Indeed, *Essence,* a magazine targeted to African-American women, received a media award for its more realistic portrayal of females, including its depiction of a wider variety of body shapes (Chambers 1995). . . .

Although the black girls surveyed as part of the larger study . . . felt that they were significantly better looking than white girls and were more satisfied with their looks overall . . . the interviews indicated a good deal of concern and dissatisfaction about hair, which the girls felt must be altered from its natural state for a more "beautiful" look. Indeed, hair straighteners are advertised in the very publications directed to black women which have been praised for their wide variety of body shapes and facial features.

As the above analysis shows, the effects of media imagery are complex. Social psycho-

logical work on reference groups and social comparison processes can help to elucidate how the consequences of pervasive media images vary for girls of different ethnicities. Social comparison research suggests that we compare ourselves with similar others, and although media images generally have not been examined as part of reference groups, it is likely that people shown in the media may serve this function for self assessment (Snow 1983).

The data reported here show that a peer group depicted through media can be an important social comparison group, even though it creates negative consequences for self-evaluation. In addition, the freedom to *select* this comparison referent may be limited. The relative freedom of choosing similar others to compare oneself to for self-enhancement purposes, as suggested in research on social comparison (see Singer 1981), is shown to be very restricted in this case. Rather, the public pervasiveness and the esteemed, glamorized position of these "perfect" female peers apparently restrict white girls' ability to ignore or downplay this comparison despite its negative consequences. Indeed, because the images are presented in a variety of media formats such as television, magazines, film, and the Internet, the impact of the images may be much more powerful. . . .

It was striking that the urban white girls' interpretations of the images and their beliefs about the place of those images in others' eyes were more similar to the rural white girls' interpretations and beliefs than to those of their black urban classmates. The black girls in this integrated school did not report that the mainstream model of female beauty was relevant to them, and thus did not generally compare themselves unfavorably with these media peers. As Rosenberg (1986) points out in his study of black and white children's self-esteem—blacks generally made comparisons within their own group, not with whites, on aspects of self-evaluation such as physical appearance. Similarly, the black girls studied here reported that the media figures with whom they identified were black performers, not white or "whitened" models; the performers had a wide range of appearances, and the girls did not appear to compare themselves negatively with these women.

In sum, although many white girls understood that the images were unrealistic, and although they disliked the anxiety-producing gap between their own physical appearance and a media-generated ideal, they still desired such an appearance, attempted to attain it, and felt bad when they did not measure up to the media image of femininity. Some of this lack of efficacy in the white girls' critical interpretations, due to continued negative social comparisons, may be explained by reflected appraisal processes.

Reflected Appraisals: How Media Images Can Affect the Self Indirectly

Research suggests that reflected appraisals may be a proxy for the perceived attitudes of a generalized other rather than for perceived views of particular others (Felson 1989). This finding helps to explain how media images may affect us indirectly insofar as they are an important part of the generalized other; indeed, as I explain in this section, media images may represent society's views. In addition, research on reflected appraisals points to the relevance and importance of these perceived attitudes toward us, and our agreement with these attitudes as mediators of reflected appraisals' impact on the self (Rosenberg 1986). This phenomenon explains the variability in the power of critical interpretations of media. For whites, beliefs about how important others—white peers—consider these images may thwart their own power to meaningfully express criticism. For blacks, this "white" generalized other is less relevant, and the evaluations of those who find the image desirable are less important; thus critical interpretations of these media images are more effective.

In interviews, the respondents distinguished between the importance of appearance to them and to others (they almost always considered appearance more important to others), and discussed how different groups of others might use and interpret media images. Close girlfriends usually were not regarded as holding the respondents to idealized media standards, but "other" girls—those in the school or beyond—often were viewed in this light. The white girls did not believe that criticisms of images were widely shared; the black girls, however, indicated that their close friends were equally critical. Mary, an African-American respondent interviewed with a close friend, said:

> It seems like sometimes we're the only two people in this entire school that don't want to hear this stuff . . . Everybody else might, I'm not sure, but everybody else might be enjoying it, and we're the only [girls] being different and we don't want to hear it. . . . I know my friends, I know they're probably not any of them . . . worried about this stuff . . . in these magazines, like that magazine [refers to magazine in front of her] said "How to Kiss Better." My friends are worried about stuff like how to take care of yourself and learn how to be independent. They're worried about real things that are going to help you. Like who's going to hire you just cause you can kiss good? (May 27, 1994; urban black girl)

Note Mary's distinction between her friends and "other" girls. . . .

In addition to "other girls," the white girls believed overwhelmingly that males are influenced by the unrealistic images and are uncritical of those images. The great majority of white girls perceived that males *evaluated them on the basis of females' unrealistic appearance in media imagery.* Some girls indicated that boys explicitly discuss media models such as Cindy Crawford, and/or insult girls who deviate from the unrealistic standards represented by such models. Although boys rarely are exposed to these images through girls' magazines, the same models and images appear in magazines and other media formats directed to males and to general audiences. Most respondents perceived that males wanted this appearance in girls, even if they had not heard males talk about it. Alison described how boys may use these images:

> Guys mostly look at . . . the ones that are like supermodels, an' then they look at you, an' balance the scales, (and) kinda look more towards the model [laughs]. (April 5, 1994; rural white girl)

Lenore and Andrea commented:

Lenore: I think it kind of influences guys 'cause I think the guys a lot just [go for] looks and I think that makes them look more . . . for looks cause they see them.

Andrea: They see them and they try to compare all of us to them . . . I just get that perception. (May 13, 1994; urban white girls)

The idea that males want females to be physically attractive complements abundant research on adolescent relations. . . . In this study, however, the respondents indicated that rather than local standards, they may be evaluated by the standards of the media, a public, glamorized, and unrealistic portion of the social group with which they compare unfavorably. Because the ideal—a rare extreme in women's body shape . . . and socially constructed "perfection" of physical features—is commonly displayed, and acknowledged, it may seem that *others* whose views are important to the girls perceive the image as attainable and normative (Snow 1983).

Body image is a particularly important aspect of the effect of media culture on white girls' local culture. The girls reported that they often talked about looks and that they had friends who asked frequently if their appearance was acceptable and often commented on their weight. . . . Several respondents made connections between the media and the girls' warped views of themselves, particularly in regard to body size. For exam-

ple, often before they were questioned directly about body weight, shape, or perceptions among their peers, a significant number of girls stated that friends or girls they knew often talked about being overweight. The respondents indicated, however, that those who said these things were not actually overweight.

Tanya, an African-American girl who was rare in having close interracial friendships, observed how her white friends were affected by the unrealistic media images. She pointed to reflected appraisals in citing their unhappiness with their appearance:

> I think that's why some girls . . . think they're too fat and try to lose weight. They look at her [points to a girl in the magazine] and they think they should look like that because they heard a guy say that she's pretty or whatever. So they feel that they should look like her and they try to go on a diet and all that stuff. So I think some people just don't know what they [others] are saying, and people hear them, and so they automatically assume they should do this and do that for other people . . . I hear a lot of girls that are . . . smaller than I am talking about "I'm so fat." I say "if you're fat, then I'm obese." . . . [They say] "I'm on a diet, I can't eat." [I say] "Did you eat breakfast?" [They say] "no." [I say] "if I eat lunch, are you going to eat something?" [They say] "I can't, I'm on a diet." And I say "You're already skinny! How much do you want to weigh? 100 pounds?" (May 9, 1994; urban black girl)

Even when respondents were aware of peers' misperceptions of weight and did not have this misperception themselves, the media's distorted images shift the local standards for what is normative. Tanya's comment to her friends, "If you're fat, then I'm obese," indicates how the media affect local cultures, including those in which girls are aware and critical of unrealism in cultural products.

Thus, because media images were a part of the white girls' peer culture, and because these girls perceived that significant others—other girls and especially boys in their local networks—evaluated them on the basis of media ideals that were nearly unattainable, they were influenced regardless of how strongly they criticized the imagery. Especially important were body shape "norms" in the media, which tended to warp average-weight and thin girls' perceptions of their weight and attractiveness, or at least made them over-concerned about weight at objectively normal, healthy, weights. Even girls who articulated the distorted nature of peers' views of attractiveness seemed to feel compelled to abide by the shifted "norm" of body shape.

The wider range of physical appearances and body shapes that the black girls seemed to accept as good-looking in themselves and others was related to a more inclusive beauty ideal promoted in the "black" media. In addition, the black girls were more tentative about suggesting that males evaluated them on the basis of mainstream (white) media images. Most girls indicated that some males might do so but that others would not. This belief that males (often specified as black) rejected the "whitened" image was important in reducing black girls' negative self-evaluations especially related to body size. Several minority girls said they believed at least some black males desire women who are not extremely thin. Nadia discussed the "normal" appearance preferred by black females and males:

> They're [black females] not trying to have little bodies. They want to be thick. They don't want to be fat, they just want to be thick . . . a nice size behind, nice big bra . . . they want to be a nice normal size. They don't want to be skinny . . . 'cause black men don't like skinny people that much. Some of 'em do, but they'd rather have a thick person. . . . We don't think skinny is pretty. (May 23, 1994; urban black girl)

Thus, the black girls interpreted the media differently than the white girls. In particular, most perceived that the images were intended for other, white girls. They appeared to be affected less negatively by a narrow media image of female beauty. The black girls defined themselves outside the dominant culture and cultural imagery; therefore they seemed to be able to reject the images *as a group.* Reflected appraisals allow criticisms of nonrealism to be practically effective: Because the black girls believe that African-American males also reject the narrow, "white" feminine ideal prominent in the media and define a wider range of black feminine appearances as beautiful or "normal," they can express and act on such criticisms of mainstream beauty ideals within their subculture. The white girls' (segregated) social networks constrained the avenues for meaningfully expressing criticism of media imagery; those of the black girls facilitated media criticism.

In sum, reflected appraisal processes are important in considering how media can affect the self indirectly, even when such images are disliked or criticized. The media are presumed to affect others; for the white girls, as noted above, an important part of the interpretations is that others use the images and find them important and attainable, even when they themselves do not. Reflected appraisal processes indicate the importance of beliefs about how others view us; thus the usefulness of a critical interpretation is thwarted by imagining that others use the extremely unusual image of women that pervades the media. The black girls however, do not view the mainstream images as part of the reference group. In addition, they believe that those important to them, generally within their ethnic group, are critical of the images as well. Thus, they are protected to some degree from negative comparisons. The opinions of the mainstream white "others," who are presumed to find the image desirable and realistic, are generally not deemed important for African-American girls' view of self (see Rosenberg 1986).

Conclusion

. . . This research . . . shows the utility of examining how even critically interpreted media content may negatively affect individuals' self-concept, attitudes, or behavior through "mediated" social comparisons and reflected appraisals. Virtually all of the white respondents said that they wanted to achieve an appearance like that featured in the media, even though most regarded the images as unrealistic and many wished to see more "real" girls in the media. The influence of the media on white girls appears to lie mainly in publicly presenting, directly and repeatedly, a unique part of the reference group which is glamorized. This media subgroup is oppressive in that it shifts the self-evaluations of the population of real white girls downward. They perceive, through the "media-filled" eyes of others who matter—white peers—that their own appearance is judged negatively. . . .

The black girls generally criticized the artificiality of females' appearance and the lack of diversity in these media; however they were more immune to unfavorable social comparisons than were the white respondents. This immunity relates to the black girls' belief that girlfriends and at least some black males are also critical of these media images and appreciate a wider array of "normal" or attractive appearances.

This research attests to the importance of studying media influence as it actually operates in the empirical world. . . . It makes clear that the images are not simply accepted or interpreted individually. Rather, the media are understood in everyday experience to be part of the collectivity of individuals' social worlds, in and beyond their local context. . . . [T]his . . . work suggests that social comparisons and reflected appraisals . . . may be more complex today, when much information about others and their views comes from media; and when one "knows" the media images which others see and which supposedly influence them.

References

Altheide, David L., and Robert P. Snow. 1988. "Toward a Theory of Mediation." Pp. 194–223 in *Communication Yearbook,* edited by James A. Anderson. Newbury Park, CA: Sage.

Chambers, Veronica. 1995. "The Essence of Essence." *New York Times Magazine,* June 16, p. 24.

Davison, W. Phillips. 1983. "The Third Person Effect in Communication." *Public Opinion Quarterly* 47: 1–15.

Evans, Ellis D. 1990. "Adolescent Females' Utilization and Perception of Contemporary Teen Magazines." Presented at the biennial meetings of the Society for Research on Adolescence, Atlanta.

Felson, Richard B. 1989. "Parents and the Reflected Appraisal Process: A Longitudinal Analysis." *Journal of Personality and Social Psychology* 56: 965–971.

Lakoff, Robin Tolmach, and Raquel L. Scherr. 1984. *Face Value: The Politics of Beauty.* Boston: Routledge.

Perloff, Richard M. 1993. "Third Person Effect Research 1983–1992: A Review and Synthesis." *International Journal of Public Opinion* 5: 167–184.

Rosenberg, Morris. 1986. *Conceiving the Self.* Melbourne, FL: Krieger.

Singer, Eleanor. 1981. "Reference Groups and Social Evaluations." Pp. 66–93 in *Social Psychology: Sociological Perspectives,* edited by M. Rosenberg and R. H. Turner. New York: Basic Books.

Snow, Robert P. 1983. *Creating Media Culture.* Beverly Hills: Sage.

Wiseman, Claire V., James J. Gray, James E. Mosimann, and Anthony H. Ahrens. 1992. "Cultural Expectations of Thinness in Women: An Update." *International Journal of Eating Disorders* 11: 85–89.

Part III

The Social Construction of Subjective Experience

In the earlier selection, "The Self as Social Structure," Mead observes that once the self has arisen, individuals have themselves as companions. They are able to think and converse with themselves as they have communicated with others. They are able to define and interpret their own experience through inner conversations. Yet, individuals can do so only because they have communicated with others. The language, symbols, and understandings that individuals draw upon in conversing with themselves are not of their own invention. They are used by and learned from others with whom the individual has communicated. Thus, the individual's inner reality is as much socially constructed as the outer reality that she or he shares with others.

The selections in this section address the social construction of subjective experience. They examine the social shaping of individuals' thoughts, emotions, and perceptions. Each illustrates that sociological study and understanding, rather than being skin deep, reach deep inside individuals' minds and hearts. They can do so because the social life among individuals gets under their skin, creating social lives within each person. ✦

8

The Development of Language and Thought

Lev Vygotsky

Lev Vygotsky was a research fellow at the Moscow Institute of Psychology from 1924 up until his untimely death in 1934 at 38 years of age. Although a prolific writer during that decade, few outside the former Soviet Union knew of Vygotsky's writing until the early 1960s, when his book *Thought and Language* was first published in English. This selection is from a later edition of that volume and demonstrates what many Western readers now know: Vygotsky, like Mead and Cooley, provided a basis for the development of a distinctively sociological psychology.

Throughout his writing, Vygotsky stressed the social origins of human thought. He proposed that the initial direction of human psychological development runs from the "interpsychological" to the "intrapsychological," or from the social to the individual. This proposal directly challenged what was then, and still remains, the prevailing view of psychological development as a gradual accommodation of subjective desires and thoughts to social existence and objective reasoning. The cognitive developmental theory of Jean Piaget, a popular example of this general view, was the principal target of Vygotsky's criticism in this selection.

As Vygotsky notes, Piaget's general view of human psychological development was not unique but rather was borrowed from psychoanalysis. Like Freud, Piaget assumed that the individual is born with unrealistic desires and thoughts. According to Freud, the individual is initially governed by the pleasure principle, but the gratification of his or her innate desires is frustrated by the necessity of adapting to the environment in order to survive. The ego develops out of this clash between the pleasure and reality principles, resulting in the repression of the individual's unrealistic desires and thoughts within the unconscious realm of the id. The individual then confronts the additional demands of the social environment, giving rise to a superego or social conscience.

Piaget's proposed stages of cognitive development mirrored Freud's sequence of psychosexual development. According to Piaget, the individual's thought is initially idiosyncratic and fantastic or "autistic." It then becomes egocentric, as the individual attempts to change the environment to her or his needs and desires. This self-centeredness gradually disappears, as the individual interacts with others and learns that there are other perspectives besides his or her own. His or her thought gradually becomes socialized, directed, and objective rather than subjective. The intrapsychological is gradually replaced by the interpsychological.

Piaget based this proposed sequence of cognitive development on his observation of children's play. He observed that preschool-age children talk to themselves or engage in what he termed egocentric speech far more than school-age children who engage in more socialized speech.

Vygotsky was unconvinced by this evidence. He proposed an alternative explanation of young children's so-called egocentric speech, based on the results of his own experiments. Those experiments indicated that children's egocentric speech increases when they confront a problem. Vygotsky therefore concluded that this egocentric speech is not self-centered, but self-directing. Children are apparently attempting to talk themselves through the problem, much as others have verbally directed them through problems in the past. Egocentric speech is not, then, a preliminary to socialized or communicative speech, but rather its product. According to Vygotsky, it is a transitional stage in the development from communicative to inner speech. Inner speech or thought is merely egocentric speech that has become silent. The development of human speech and thought moves from the intersubjective to the subjective, rather than the reverse, as Piaget and Freud would have it. As Vygotsky suggested, thought—even autistic thought—is impossible without a language and symbols with which to think. And language and symbols are acquired through communication with others. That is the source of even our most private, idiosyncratic, and fantastic thoughts.

Psychology owes a great deal to Jean Piaget. It is not an exaggeration to say that he revolutionized the study of the child's speech and thought. He developed the clinical method for exploring children's ideas that has since been widely used. He was the first to investigate the child's perception and logic systematically; moreover, he brought to his subject a fresh approach of unusual amplitude and boldness.

Piaget, however, did not escape the duality characteristic of [modern] psychology. He tried to hide behind the wall of facts, but facts "betrayed" him, for they led to problems. Problems gave birth to theories, in spite of Piaget's determination to avoid them by closely following the experimental facts and disregarding, for the time being, that the very choice of experiments is determined by hypotheses. But facts are always examined in the light of some theory and, therefore, cannot be disentangled from philosophy.

According to Piaget, the bond uniting all the specific characteristics of the child's logic is the egocentrism of occupying an intermediate position, genetically, structurally, and functionally, between autistic and directed thought.

The idea of the polarity of directed and undirected . . . thought is borrowed from psychoanalysis. . . . We find the same idea in Freud, who claims that the pleasure principle precedes the reality principle. . . . Piaget says:

Directed thought is conscious, i.e., it pursues an aim which is present to the mind of the thinker; it is intelligent, which means that it is adapted to reality and tries to influence it; it admits of being true or false (empirically or logically true), and it can be communicated by language. Autistic thought is subconscious, which means that the aims it pursues and the problems it tries to solve are not present in consciousness; it is not adapted to reality, but creates for itself a dream world of imagination; it tends not to establish truths, but to satisfy desires, and it remains strictly individual and incommunicable as such by means of language. On the contrary, it works chiefly by images, and in order to express itself, has recourse to indirect methods, evoking by means of symbols and myths the feeling by which it is led. (Piaget 1959:43)

Directed thought is social. As it develops, it is increasingly influenced by the laws of experience and of logic proper. Autistic thought, on the contrary, is individualistic and obeys a set of special laws of its own:

Now between autism and intelligence there are many degrees, varying with their capacity for being communicated. These intermediate varieties must, therefore, be subject to a special logic, intermediate too between the logic of autism and that of intelligence. The chief of those intermediate forms, i.e., the type of thought, which like that exhibited by our children seeks to adapt itself to reality but does not communicate itself as such, we propose to call *egocentric* thought. (Piaget 1959:45)

While its main function is still the satisfaction of personal needs, it already includes some mental adaptation, some of the reality orientation typical of the thought of adults. The egocentric thought of the child "stands midway between autism in the strict sense of the word and socialized thought" (Piaget 1969:208). This is Piaget's basic hypothesis.

Piaget emphasizes that egocentric speech does not provide communication. . . . [It] is, therefore, useless. It plays no essential role in child behavior. It is speech for the child's sake, which is incomprehensible for others and which is closer to a verbal dream than to a conscious activity.

But if such speech plays no positive role in child behavior, if it is a mere accompaniment, it is but a symptom of weakness and immaturity in the child's thinking, a symptom that must disappear in the course of child development. Useless and unconnected with the structure of activity, this accompaniment should become weaker and weaker until it completely disappears from the routine of the child's speech.

Data collected by Piaget seemingly supports this point of view. The coefficient of egocentric speech decreases with age and reaches zero at the age of seven or eight—which means that egocentric speech is not typical for school children. Piaget, however, assumes that the loss of egocentric speech does not preclude children from remaining cognitively egocentric. Egocentric thought simply changes the form of its manifestation, appearing now in abstract reasoning and in the new symptoms that have no semblance to egocentric talk. In conformity with his idea of the uselessness of egocentric speech, Piaget claims that this speech "folds" and dies out at the threshold of school age.

We in our turn conducted our own experiments aimed at understanding the function and fate of egocentric speech. The data obtained led us to a new comprehension of this phenomenon that differs greatly from that of Piaget. Our investigation suggests that egocentric speech does play a specific role in the child's activity.

In order to determine what causes egocentric talk, what circumstances provoke it, we organized the children's activities in much the same way Piaget did, but we added a series of frustrations and difficulties. For instance, when a child was getting ready to draw, he would suddenly find that there was no paper, or no pencil of the color he needed. In other words, by obstructing his free activity, we made him face problems.

We found that in these difficult situations the coefficient of egocentric speech almost doubled, in comparison with Piaget's normal figure for the same age and also in comparison with our figure for children not facing these problems. The child would try to grasp and to remedy the situation in talking to himself: "Where's the pencil? I need a blue pencil. Never mind, I'll draw with the red one and wet it with water; it will become dark and look like blue."

In the same activities without impediments, our coefficient of egocentric talk was even slightly lower than Piaget's. It is legitimate to assume, then, that a disruption in the smooth flow of activity is an important stimulus for egocentric speech. This discovery fits in with two premises to which Piaget himself refers several times in his book. One of them is the so-called law of awareness, which was formulated by Claparede and which states that an impediment or disturbance in an automatic activity makes the author aware of this activity. The other premise is that speech is an expression of that process of becoming aware.

Indeed, the above-mentioned phenomena were observed in our experiments: egocentric speech appeared when a child tried to comprehend the situation, to find a solution, or to plan a nascent activity. The older children behaved differently: they scrutinized the problem, thought (which was indicated by long pauses), and then found a solution. When asked what he was thinking about, such a child answered more in a line with the "thinking aloud" of a preschooler. We thus assumed that the same mental operations that the preschooler carries out through voiced egocentric speech are already relegated to soundless inner speech in school children.

Our findings indicate that egocentric speech does not long remain a mere accompaniment to the child's activity. Besides being a means of expression and of release of tension, it soon becomes an instrument of thought in the proper sense—in seeking and planning the solution of a problem. An accident that occurred during one of our experiments provides a good illustration of one way in which egocentric speech may alter the course of an activity: a child of five and a half was drawing a streetcar when the point of his pencil broke. He tried, nevertheless, to finish the circle of [the] wheel, pressing down on the pencil very hard, but nothing showed on the paper except a deep colorless line. The child muttered to himself, "It's broken," put aside the pencil, took watercolors instead, and began drawing a *broken* streetcar after an accident, continuing to talk to himself from time to time about the change in his picture. The child's accidentally provoked egocentric utterance so manifestly affected his activity that it is impossible to mistake it for a mere by-product, an accompaniment not interfering with the melody. Our experiments showed highly complex changes in the interrelation of activity and egocentric talk. We observed how egocentric speech at first marked the end result or a turning point in an activity, then was gradually shifted toward the middle and finally to the beginning of the activity, taking on a directing, planning function and raising the child's acts to the level of purposeful behavior. What happens here is similar to the well-known developmental sequence in the naming of drawings. A small child draws first, then decides what it is that he has drawn; at a slightly older age, he names his drawing when it is half-done; and finally, he decides beforehand what he will draw.

The revised conception of the function of egocentric speech must also influence our conception of its later fate and must be brought to bear on the issue of its disappearance at school age. Experiments can yield indirect evidence but no conclusive answer about the causes of this disappearance.

There is, of course, nothing to this effect in Piaget, who believes that egocentric speech simply dies off. The development of inner speech in the child receives little specific elucidation in his studies. But since inner speech and voiced egocentric speech fulfill the same function, the implication would be that if, as Piaget maintains, egocentric speech precedes socialized speech, then inner speech also must precede socialized speech—an assumption untenable from the genetic point of view.

However, Piaget's theoretical position apart, his own findings and some of our data suggest that egocentric speech is actually an intermediate stage leading to inner speech. Of course, this is only a hypothesis, but, taking into account the present state of our knowledge about the child's speech, it is the most plausible one. If we compare the amount of what might be called egocentric speech in children and adults, we would have to admit that the "egocentric" speech of adults is much richer. From the point of view of functional psychology, all silent thinking is nothing but "egocentric" speech. John B. Watson would have said that such speech serves individual rather than social adaptation. The first feature uniting the inner speech of adults with the egocentric speech of children is its function as speech-for-oneself. If one turns to Watson's experiment and asks a subject to solve some problem thinking aloud, one would find that such thinking aloud of an adult has a striking similarity to the egocentric speech of children. Second, these two forms also have the same structural characteristics: out of context they would be incomprehensible to others because they omit to mention what is obvious to the speaker. These similarities lead us to assume that when egocentric speech disappears, it does not simply atrophy but "goes underground," i.e., turns into inner speech.

Our observation that at the age when this change is taking place children facing difficult situations resort now to egocentric speech, now to silent reflection, indicates that the two can be functionally equivalent. It is our hypothesis that the processes of inner speech develop and become stabilized approximately at the beginning of school age and that this causes the quick drop in the egocentric speech observed at this stage.

The above-mentioned experiments and considerations hardly support Piaget's hypothesis concerning the egocentrism of six-year-olds. At least the phenomenon of egocentric speech, viewed from our perspective, fails to confirm his assumptions.

The cognitive function of egocentric speech, which is most probably connected with the development of inner speech, by no means is a reflection of the child's egocentric thinking, but rather shows that under certain circumstances egocentric speech is becoming an agent of realistic thinking. Piaget assumed that if 40–47 percent of the speech of a child of six and a half is egocentric, then his thinking must be egocentric within the same range. Our investigation showed, however, that there can be no connection between egocentric talk and egocentric thinking whatsoever—which means that the major implication drawn from Piaget's data might be wrong.

We thus have an experimental fact that has nothing to do with the correctness or falsity of our own hypothesis concerning the fate of egocentric speech. This is the factual evidence that the child's egocentric speech does not reflect egocentric thinking, but rather carries out an opposite function, that of realistic thinking.

Limited in scope as our findings are, we believe that they help one to see in a new and broader perspective the general direction of the development of speech and thought. In Piaget's view, the two functions follow a common path, from autistic to socialized speech, from subjective fantasy to the logic of relations. In the course of this change, the influence of adults is deformed by the psychic processes of the child, but it wins out in the end. The development of thought is, to Piaget, a story of the gradual socialization of deeply intimate, personal, autistic mental states. Even social speech is represented as following, not preceding, egocentric speech.

The hypothesis we propose reverses this course. Let us look at the direction of thought development during one short interval, from the appearance of egocentric speech to its disappearance, in the framework of language development as a whole.

We consider that the total development runs as follows: the primary function of speech, in both children and adults, is communication, social contact. The earliest speech of the child is, therefore, essentially social. At first it is global and multifunctional; later, its functions become differentiated. At a certain age the social speech of the child is quite sharply divided into egocentric speech and communicative speech. (We prefer to use the term *communicative* for the form of speech that Piaget calls *socialized*, as though it had been something else before becoming social. From our point of view, the two forms, communicative and egocentric, are both social, though their functions differ.) Egocentric speech emerges when the child transfers social, collaborative forms of behavior to the sphere of inner-personal psychic functions. The child's tendency to transfer to his inner processes the behavior patterns that formerly were social is well known to Piaget. He describes in another context how arguments between children give rise to the beginnings of logical reflection. Something similar happens, we believe, when the child starts conversing with himself as he has been doing with others. When circumstances force him to stop and think, he is likely to think aloud. Egocentric speech, splintered off from general social speech, in time leads to inner speech, which serves both autistic and logical thinking.

Egocentric speech as a separate linguistic form is the highly important genetic link in the transition from vocal to inner speech, an intermediate stage between the differentiation of the functions of vocal speech and the final transformation of one part of vocal speech into inner speech. It is this transitional role of egocentric speech that lends it such great theoretical interest. The whole conception of speech development differs profoundly in accordance with the interpretation given to the role of egocentric speech. Thus, our schema of development—first social, then egocentric, then inner speech—contrasts . . . with Piaget's . . . sequence—from non-verbal autistic thought through egocentric thought and speech to socialized speech and logical thinking.

The . . . most serious conclusion that can be drawn from our critical analysis concerns the alleged opposition of two forms of thinking: autistic and realistic. This opposition served as a basis for Piaget's theory, as well as for the psychoanalytical approach to child development. We think that it is incorrect to oppose the principle of satisfaction of needs to the principle of adaptation to reality. The very concept of need, if taken from the perspective of development, necessarily contains the notion of satisfaction of need through a certain adjustment to reality.

Need and adaptation must be considered in their unity. What we have in well-developed autistic thinking, i.e., an attempt to attain an imaginary satisfaction of desires that failed to be satisfied in real life, is a product of a long development. Autistic thinking, therefore, is a late product of the development of realistic, conceptual thinking. Piaget, however, chose to borrow from Freud the idea that the pleasure principle precedes the reality principle.

We see how different is the picture of the development of the child's speech and thought, depending on what is considered to be a starting point of such development. In our conception, the true direction of the development of thinking is not from the individual to the social, but from the social to the individual.

References

Piaget, Jean. 1959. *The Language and Thought of the Child.* London: Routledge and Kegan Paul.

———. 1969. *Judgement and Reasoning in the Child.* London: Routledge and Kegan Paul.

9

The Historical Transformation of American Grief

Peter N. Stearns

Social experience not only provides us the language with which we think. It also profoundly shapes how we feel. Different human societies have different emotional cultures or beliefs, rules, and practices regarding emotional expression and feelings. Through socialization, children learn and adopt those beliefs, rules, and practices as their own. Those beliefs, rules, and practices consequently come to shape not only our emotional expression but also what we actually feel under different circumstances. Whatever the biological or natural bases of human emotions, we acquire a second emotional nature through social experience. Feelings that seem "only natural" to us in response to particular circumstances may seem quite unnatural and bizarre to members of other societies.

Some of the most telling evidence of the social relativity of human emotions comes from historical studies of changes in emotional culture. This selection, written by the social historian Peter Stearns, is excerpted from a larger study of the historical transformation of the intense emotional culture of nineteenth-century, middle-class Americans into the emotional "cooler" or subdued culture of their twentieth-century counterparts. It illustrates that broader historical transformation with the example of grief. Stearns uses the expression *emotionology* throughout this selection as a synonym for emotional culture. He adopts this term because it is more easily changed into an adjective, emotionological, than is the expression emotional culture.

As Stearns documents, our nineteenth-century Victorian ancestors considered intense and enduring grief a natural response to the loss of loved ones. It encouraged such deeply felt and lingering grief in both adults and children. Over time, however, deep and lingering grief fell out of favor among middle-class Americans. It and the Victorian mourning practices that supposedly encouraged intense grief were condemned as morbid and superstitious.

This change in prevailing standards regarding grief was, in part, a response to declining mortality rates in America, especially among the young. Death had become a less common presence in everyday life than in the past and increasingly occurred after a long life. However, it also reflected a more general trend away from emotional intensity toward a "cooler" emotional style. Although grief was still recognized as a natural reaction to the loss of a loved one, purveyors of new emotional standards argued that it should be of relatively short duration so that the bereaved could "get on with their lives." They considered those who did not get over their grief in a reasonable amount of time candidates for professional therapy. They condemned mourning practices that they believed encouraged or intensified grief, and advised parents to shield children from death as much as possible. And, over time, many middle-class Americans came to consider intense grief embarrassing in both themselves and others.

Of course, historical change is never complete or permanent. As Stearns notes, there was increasing criticism of the modern approach to death, dying, and mourning during and after the 1960s. For example, support groups for the bereaved proliferated and the hospice movement attempted to reintegrate death more fully into family life. However, these criticisms and movements have arguably had a negligible effect on prevailing cultural standards regarding grief. Normal grief is still considered a temporary state from which the bereaved should quickly recover. Most of us still find intense public displays of grief discomforting. The intense and enduring grief that seemed only natural to our Victorian ancestors strikes us as quite abnormal. On the other hand, our Victorian ancestors would probably consider our calmer and relatively short-lived grief unloving and callous. This contrast illustrates that what we feel and how we feel is largely a matter of social definition, interpretation, and meaning. Even our most private feelings are in large part products of our social experience.

[This selection analyzes, using the example of grief,] a major change in American middle-class emotional culture, a change that took place between approximately the end of World War I and mid-century. In the last half of the nineteenth century, a complex emotional culture flourished among the Victorian middle-class, exerting a powerful influence on the entire range of social relationships. This influence extended into the twentieth century, but by the 1920s Victorian standards were being irrevocably transformed, preparing the way for a cooler approach to emotional expression. . . .

Emotional culture is an important topic. . . . It affects the way people describe their own emotional experience. Interesting in its own right as part of cultural identity, emotionological change also affects social interactions and elements of emotional life itself. . . . Emotional culture forms the basis for constructing reactions to one's own emotions, and in some respects the emotions themselves. . . .

This study focuses primarily on the middle-class of business people and professional families. . . . Emotional culture forms an aspect of middle-class standards that had [widespread influence], both in its nineteenth-century version and, more extensively though more subtly, in its twentieth-century formulation. . . . The middle-class did not entirely triumph, however. Therefore, the distinction between my primary emphasis—the middle-class—and American society seen as a complex combination of classes, ethnic groups, and subcultures must be constantly recalled. . . .

Source materials for this [study] cluster primarily, though not exclusively, in what is generally known as prescriptive literature. Victorian popularizers, and their readers, felt a need for guidance in various aspects of emotional socialization, and the popularity of the numerous manuals directed at parents and youth has been well documented. . . . For the Victorian period [these] manuals . . . form a vital starting point. Most of them addressed various kinds of emotional standards. Popular short stories . . . etiquette books, and hortative stories for older children and youth add to the prescriptive mix. Many of these genres continued in the transition decades of the twentieth century . . . Marital advice manuals and popular magazines for men as well as for women increased in volume and utility, while childrearing advice in various forms remained central. . . . The cumulation of this various material, combined with many other studies that provide additional evidence on key points—such as recent interview and questionnaire data and private letters from the Victorian period—yields a fairly full picture of emotional culture and its audience.

* * *

Victorian Grief

Victorian engagement with emotional intensity showed clearly in the embrace of grief. Grief was, in the first place, a vital component in the cultural arsenal. It was frequently discussed, a staple not only of story but also of song. Grief was heartrending. . . . The depth of grief followed directly, in fact, from the emphasis on great love, for Victorian convention held that even the temporary absence of a loved one was a real sorrow. As Nathaniel Hawthorne put it in a letter to Sarah Peabody in 1840: "Where thou are not, there it is a sort of death." Death itself, correspondingly, would move one to the core. Despite its pain, the essence of grief was a vital part of Victorian emotional life. Children were prepared for it by frequent references, while adults developed various conventions to permit its open expression. In its intensity and its link to love, grief indeed could have a bittersweet quality: immensely sad, but almost a welcome part of a full emotional experience. It would express and enrich the very love Victorian culture sought. As a Protestant minister put it in a family advice manual of 1882: "It may truly be said that no home ever reaches it highest blessedness and sweetness of love and its richest fullness of joy till sorrow enters its life in some way."[1]

Efforts to present grief and death to children in a benign though sorrowful context continued through the later nineteenth century. In *McGuffy's Fourth Eclectic Reader* (1866), sixteen of twenty nine "poetical lessons" dealt with death, including one entitled "What is Death?"

> *Child. Mother, how still the baby lies.*
>
> *I cannot hear his breath;*
>
> *I cannot see his laughing eyes;*
>
> *They tell me this is death.*
>
> *They say that he again will rise,*
>
> *More beautiful than now;*
>
> *That God will bless him in the skies;*
>
> *O mother, tell me how.*

In this case, the mother responds with the image of a butterfly emerging from a lifeless chrysalis. In other poems, again in school readers, the dominant theme was reunion of loved ones after death in heaven.

> *Oh. we pray to meet our darling*
>
> *For a long, long sweet embrace.*
>
> *Where the little feet are waiting—*
>
> *And we meet her face to face.*

Tragic death scenes remained commonplace in stories for children, as they were asked to live through the sorrows of illness and passing while being assured that an outpouring of emotion was valid and ultimately healthy: "Elsie's grief was deep and lasting. She sorrowed as she might have done for the loss of a very dear brother, . . . a half remorseful feeling which reason could not control or entirely relieve; and it was long ere she was quite her own bright, gladsome sunny self again." Louisa May Alcott wrote of a sister's "bitter cry of an unsubmissive sorrow," of "sacred moments, when heart talked to heart in the silence of the night, turning affliction to a blessing, which chastened grief and strengthened love."[2] Mother's assurances, repeated references to protecting angels, and the increasing theme of familial reunion in heaven all linked the power of grief to hope and love; but the power was not evaded. Stories of death were now disengaged from fear and from moral admonitions about life's transiency to become part of the characteristic Victorian emotional style, in which intense emotions served as a desirable part of life and, ultimately, an enhancement of human ties. The starkness of death disappeared under sentimental overlays in these portrayals, but the inescapability, even the benefit, of a period of deep grief was generally confirmed. . . .

Rituals after death . . . clearly changed in the nineteenth century to accommodate heightened emotion. Victorian funeral procedures, unlike those before or since, were intended both to remove the fear of death and to allow open expression of grief through ritual. Increasing use of cosmetics on corpses, and ultimately the rise of professional undertakers and embalmers who took over the handling of death from bereaved families, expressed mainly the desire to allay fear and to direct emotions away from decaying flesh to the bittersweet grief at a loved one's loss. The practice of wearing mourning clothing spread. Funerals became more elaborate, cemeteries and tombstones more ornate and evocative. Scholars have legitimately argued over whether the paraphernalia of middle-class Victorian funerals expressed simply growing wealth and status rivalry, or real grief, and the sensible conclusion has been that both were involved. Families really need rituals that would allow them to show their grief. . . .

[T]he Victorians who expressed themselves in letters, diaries, and often in ritual commonly expected, articulated, and felt the sharpness that grief was supposed to generate. The intensity resulted above all from the attachments of love, but it was heightened by emotionological approval of grief itself, such that its presence was expected, its absence a potential occasion for guilt. Grief applied most poignantly to death but also to departures and other separations. Nellie Wetherbee recorded in her diary as she left her family to head west, "I only cried as the steamer sailed away—bitter, bitter tears." The death of children produced almost overwhelming emotion, as an 1897 diary reported: "Jacob is dead. Tears blind my eyes as I write . . . now he is at rest, my little darling Jacob. Hope to meet you in heaven. God help me to bear my sorrow." Here, clearly, not only the pain of grief but also the conscious handling of grief with references to reunion and divine support reflect the currency of the larger Victorian culture. Men as well as women expressed their sorrow. A Civil War soldier leaves his family in 1863, crying for days before the final departure, then musing in his diary both on his great love and on the "cruelty" of the separation. A minister, coincidentally in the same year, asks Jesus to "support me under this crushing blow"—his brother's death. Another man, recording in 1845 the death of a brother-in-law, ended his entry: "Oh! What sorrow burst in upon us at the melancholy news of his death. . . . All is sorrow and weeping." Even nostalgic recollection brought grief, as when Sarah Huntington recalled a loss of two years earlier: "Reading these letters revived all the exclu-

siveness and intenseness of my love for him I once called husband."[3]

Some facets of grief varied, to be sure. Different personalities responded differently to death. Death could still call up diary entries dwelling on the transience of life and the uncertainties of God's judgment. Some diaries report that intense grief followed death for a month or so, then tapered off; others record a fresh renewal of grief well over a year after a death or separation. In the main, however, the obligation to record grief and the felt intensity of grief as a direct reaction to love rather than to fears of death reflected real-life experiences of the culture's emotional standards. Deep loss, hopes for reunion in the afterlife, bittersweet recollections of the ongoing love—all were commonplace in the private reportage. . . .

Grief was . . . accepted. Its functions of building supporting relationships to cushion loss seem normally to have worked. Many adults drew close on the death of a child as they accepted each other's grief and the terms in which it could be consoled. Grieving diarists commented on the "sympathy of friends" and importance of shared ritual. Etiquette books emphasized appropriate rituals for expressing grief and channeling reactions to it, but they too acknowledged the validity of the emotion and the need of supportive friends and relatives to respond to it. Writers on manners deplored any disruptive potential in conversation, to be sure. A few, in this vein, urged that signs of mourning be ignored in dealings with mere acquaintances. This advice, particularly common in the first half of the century, recognized emotional intensity—"any allusion to the subject of his grief [is] very painful to him"—but recommended an aloof reaction. More common was the recommendation that good manners obliged people of good breeding to call on a bereaved family and then take the cue from the family's own tone. If the family was attempting to put up a brave front, one should keep the conversation distracting; but "if they speak of their misfortune," one should "join them" by speaking well of the dead and showing active, saddened sympathy. Almost all manners authors felt compelled to address grief as a significant part of public interactions.

Of course, as in previous centuries, grief might go on too long in certain individual cases and require assistance from doctor or minister. But emphasis was placed on the enhancement to spiritual love that might be derived from emotional sharing, not on the degree of excess. It is possible indeed that Victorian culture encouraged acknowledgement of grief over an unusually long span, as in the case of the father who noted long after the death of a child, "There are some wounds which are never healed—which break out afresh and trouble the afflicted heart . . . I find but abatement of that yearning and longing for his dear face."

References to grief in letters and diaries are notable for their open expressions of the intensity of grief, but they are equally as notable for their uniform assumption of emotional harmony as families and friends grouped to help each other articulate and cope with grief. Mourners frequently recorded the importance of family and community support. A father, grieving for a dead son, recalled the "substantial and visible tokens of sympathy from our numerous friends and neighbors." Along with religion, this support made grief endurable. "The sympathy of friends is valuable but vain is all that man can do if the love of God be wanting. . . . We feel confident that it is well with our dear boy and that our loss is his gain."[4]

* * *

Twentieth-Century Grief

The transformation of twentieth-century grief has yet to be explicitly studied. Commentary on twentieth-century reactions to death from historians like Philippe Aries and psychologists like Elisabeth Kübler-Ross indicates an increasing distaste for death; a desire to isolate it in alienating hospital environments; and (though more rapidly in Europe than the United States) an increasing preference for cremation as a replacement for traditional memorials and rituals. Lack of adequate outlets for mourning resulting from the decline of formal periods and markings of grief has also been noted. But the actual historical process by which a rich Victorian grief culture yielded to the colder reactions of the twentieth century has not been examined.[5]

[G]rief did not exactly become a negative emotion, [but] the experience of grief was regarded as unpleasant, lacking the saving graces that Victorian culture had provided for it. Even more important, its potentially consuming qualities inevitably drew growing disapproval. Precisely the feature of grief that had seemed most suitable to nineteenth-century observers—its capacity to take a person out of normal reality in reaction to loss—now became menacing. Thus . . . grief . . . began to encounter a combination of concern and neglect that marked a pronounced shift from nineteenth-century standards.

The initial reconsideration of the Victorian valuation of grief began in the 1890s, mainly through the medium of opinion articles in middle-class magazines. Although preliminary to a full emotionological change, this reconsideration entered into the process of reshaping basic standards as magazines like *Outlook*, the *North American Review*, and others offered an array of articles on death and its emotional overtones from the 1890s through World War I.

Two factors, at least, accounted for the early start on a revisionist approach. First, death rates began to drop rapidly in the United States from the 1880s to the 1920s, particularly among children.[6] It was almost inevitable that such a dramatic development would have cultural repercussions. Second, and perhaps even more important to the editorials about death, discussions of Victorian ideas about mortality followed from the "warfare between science and theology" generated by the debates over evolution.[7] Death proved to be one of the areas where enlightened modern opinion found it easy to attack old religious beliefs, Victorian among others, and while this focus was not directly emotional, it had emotional implications that were gradually taken up. . . .

One subtle source of attack on Victorian grief really involved an . . . extension of Victorianism itself: If death involved quick union with God and only brief separation from loved ones on earth, why bother to grieve at all, and why dread death? "Why should it not be to all of us the Great Adventure? Why should we not look forward to it with anticipation, not with apprehension?" In this upbeat Christian rendering, joy, not grief, should predominate, and the bittersweet ambivalence of Victorian culture was muscled aside in favor of assertions of perpetual happiness. In 1907 Jane Belfield wrote on death for *Lippincott's Magazine*, stressing the folly of great pain. After all, not only death but also reunion with family is certain, so death need not involve intense feelings at all but rather "emotions and aspirations hushed." Another tack, slightly different from Christian optimism, increasingly emphasized the debilities of old age, such that death could and should be calmly greeted if, as was increasingly the case, it had the courtesy to wait until people had passed through normal adulthood. *Outlook* also took up this theme, stressing death as a pleasant release from decrepitude: "The stains of travel were gone, the signs of age had vanished; once more young, but with a wisdom beyond youth, she started with buoyant step and with a rising hope in her heart; for through the soft mist beautiful forms seemed to be moving, and faint and far she heard voices that seemed to come out of her childhood, fresh with the freshness of the morning, and her spirit grew faint for joy at the sound of them." Clearly, in this picture,

neither fear for one's own death nor grief at the passing of an older relative made much sense.[8] . . .

Other commentary on emotions associated with death flowed from a series of articles on foreign death practices, which could be used to highlight American gains in objectivity. Another popular theme involved critiques of expensive funeral practices and the increase of professional morticians. A *North American Review* article of 1907 distinguished between appropriate recognition of the gravity of death and the exploitative ceremonies that played on grief. "Nobody goes to see a man born, but the entire community turns out to see him buried." Funerals had become perverse. "We could never understand why old women should, as they unquestionably do, love to attend funerals, or how anybody could be induced, except as a matter of duty, to make a business or profession of the handling of corpses." The only undertaker worth his salt was the progressive practitioner interested in helping a family save money and curtail needless agonizing, though the author granted that traditional grief should not be assailed too frontally. A *Harper's Weekly* piece echoed these sentiments, with emphasis on minimization and low cost: a cheap funeral should be entirely adequate "to satisfy anyone except those who want really unnecessary display." *The Survey*, for its part, condemned grasping undertakers. "Nothing less than ghoulish are some of the stories of the pressure put upon grief-distracted people to honor their dead at excessive expense." Emphasis, of course, rested on economic good sense, but a corollary implication was that sensible people would not let themselves be so overcome by emotion as to fall prey to the greedy.[9]

Finally, a trickle of articles played up a somewhat different theme of modern life, noting the rise of death-defying behavior in auto racing and flying. Thrill seeking here transcended caution, and death receded to the background. And just as the new moderns defied the fear of death, so should those confronted with the sudden death of an acquaintance handle the situation coolly. "The best psychology of life is equally the best psychology of death: be glad to live and gladly die." Even religious authors had to agree that nineteenth-century death attitudes had been rather "vulgar and morbid," resulting in funeral practices that were often "in bad taste"; they also castigated the "old idea" of grief as heartbreak.[10]

While death itself received more explicit attention than emotional reactions to it, up-to-date authors did comment on grief as well. As the *Independent* noted in 1908, "Probably nothing is sadder in life than the thought of all the hours that are spent in grieving over what is past and irretrievable." Time wasted was only part of the problem; loss of control was the other: "It is only man [of all the species] that allows his sorrow so to overcome him that he spends hours calling up the pictures of past happiness which cannot be brought back." People know this, but their grief overwhelms their reason, with the result that they nurse sorrow rather than looking for happy distraction. Here was a direct attack on Victorian emotionology: grief has no function, its effort to maintain contact with the departed being foolish at best, unhealthy at worst. Modern "psycho-therapeutics" must be invoked to help people escape conventional grief, and medical attention was necessary to combat any physical causes of "melancholic feelings." A bit of grief might be tolerable, but weeks of tears suggested "something morbid, either mental or physical." Women of course were the worst offenders: "When a woman cannot rouse herself . . . from her grief there is need of the care of the physician." The *Independent* editorial acknowledged that grief used to seem consoling, when a young spouse, for example, mourned the death of a partner, but went on to say that a great deal of unscientific nonsense used to be written about pining away from grief when often the cause was "the

transmission of the bacillus tuberculosis." "This may seem a very crude and heartless way to look at such a subject, but it is eminently practical and above all has the merit of being satisfactorily therapeutic. Nothing is more calculated to arouse people from the poignancy of their grief than the realization of a necessity to care for their health." Thus, although grief might always be with us to a degree, Victorian wallowing had become ridiculous. Modern medicine suggested that mental and physical healing often make grief entirely unnecessary. Even religion might be legitimately used, if all else fails, to pull people out of their misery. Whatever the remedy, grief "in excess" must be attacked. As the editorial concluded, in an orgy of scientism, grief is a "contradiction in the universe, an attempt on the part of a drop in the sea to prevent the tidal progress of the ocean of life of which it is so small a part, yet every atom of which is meant to serve a wise purpose in all its events."[11]

The new view of death and grief was both confirmed and enhanced by recommended reactions to the massive slaughter of World War I. This event, which might have prompted a return to older notions of the comfort and bonding qualities of grief (and doubtless it did, in individual cases), in fact served in most public commentary as yet another sign of grief's misplaced, even offensive qualities. The dominant theme emphasized the need to put grief aside—as a British article put it, "to efface as far as possible the signs of woe" . . . [T]his approach . . . downplay[ed] grief in the interests of carrying on, even providing cheerful encouragement. The idea of death as routine and unemotional gained ground in this approach: "we are beginning to hold [death] in contempt." *Current Opinion* summed up the dominant thought in an essay on "the abolition of death," specifically noting the new revulsion in both England and America against Victorian habits, including elaborate, mournful funerals. The *Literary Digest* built on this theme in 1917: "Death is so familiar a companion in war-time that a revision of our modes of dealing with its immediate presence is pertinent to the relief of human anguish." The old Christian bugaboo, fear of death, must be put aside, as even Christian outlets admitted. Funerals should be joyful so that they do not distract from the ongoing purposes of life. People who still wanted "an old-fashioned chamber of horrors show"—the tearful funeral—must be brought into line. Referring to some neighbors who were resistant to the new approach to grief, the *Literary Digest* article explained, "Some of them protested at first . . . but before it was over they all took off their hats . . . and let civilization have the right of way." Another journal wanted to use the war to effect permanent improvement in the area of emotion, "evolving greater wisdom and good sense in our mourning usages." Grief should, in this revealing argument, become embarrassing: "To strive to be as natural as possible at such a time is surely the healthy attitude." Self-control, not excessive sorrow, should predominate, and formal mourning practices, which merely encourage grief, must yield accordingly. "Let us have more sweetness—and light—in our commemorating of our dear ones." As another author put it, "When you squeeze the pusillanimous eloquence and sentimentality out of the most elegant funeral discourse, I doubt if what remains is a [fitting] tribute to the essential qualities of a brave man's character."[12] . . .

[After a] brief postwar flurry, the long debate over how to end Victorian approaches to grief and death came to a close. Middle-class magazines turned to other topics as the issue of death and its emotional environment faded from view. Transitional themes like the attack on death as painful largely shut down. Beleaguered defenses of Victorianism also ceased in the mainstream magazines. Even the interest in criticizing gouging funeral directors seemed to disappear. Yet the attack on Victorian concepts of grief had three ongoing results that incorporated the

new hostility to the emotion more fully in middle-class emotionology. First, while discussions of death and grief became far less common, the occasional comment reminded the middle-class audience of the accepted emotional rules; second, the agreement reached about seeking to reduce grief translated into dominant therapeutic emphases; and third, advice to parents sought to develop appropriate socialization strategies to remove intense grief from childhood.

The first result was the growing silence itself. Into the later 1950s discussions of death and emotional reactions to it seemed out of bounds, either not worth pen and ink or too risky to evoke. After this period, by the 1960s, observers of American (and European) death culture . . . began to talk of death as a modern taboo.[13] They exaggerated slightly, as we will see, but the contrast between the 1890s–World War I decades, when active discussion was almost an essayist's staple, and the subsequent cessation of comment was genuinely striking. Either editors assumed that their audience had come to terms with appropriate attitudes or judged that elaborately evoking the topic was risky precisely because the new, upbeat standards were too shakily established to warrant exposure.

Whatever the reasons for it, grief now generated widespread avoidance. . . .

Whether this relative silence reflected a desire to make death taboo, however, is debatable. It may instead have followed from a sense among the popularizing pundits that the relevant issues were closed, that by now everyone knew the new rules. The largest number of articles during the late 1920s and the 1930s—and they too were infrequent—suggested an assurance that modern Americans were rapidly moving toward appropriate enlightenment about death and grief. Beatrice Blankenship, writing of many family deaths, noted how rarely death intruded on the routines of modern life. She criticized ritual remnants such as irrational fear of death or disturbing funerals. Death, even a child's death, while it might elicit some grief, should be treated rationally and calmly, even as modern people were losing the false certainty of an afterlife. More bombastically, Mabel Ulrich wrote in 1931 of the decline of religious beliefs and their replacement by scientific curiosity and self-control. Only a few backsliders remained: "Is it too far-fetched a hope that to these when they have forsaken their wavering misty image of heaven there may come a consciousness . . . of the amazing relevance of life?" "Modern knowledge . . . offers to the intelligent person today a conception of living which is a positive answer to old death fears." The *American Mercury* proudly boasted that in contrast to emotion-sodden Europe, "America Conquers Death." "Death, which dominates Europeans' thought, has been put in its proper place on this side of the water." This article praises modern Americans for triumphing over their cultural past, when death once hovered much closer to home. In 1940 *Scholastic* acknowledged real grief but urged the possibility of allowing life to go on equably even after a death in the immediate family. Distorting grief, the author argued, usually resulted from some "unpleasant and mystifying experience" in connection with death during one's childhood—another indication that appropriately low levels of grief . . . depended on up-to-date child training[14] . . .

The second result of the reconsideration of Victorian grief involved the dominant therapeutic approach. By the 1920s, partly as a result of Freudian influence but partly, as we can now appreciate, because of shifts in more general middle-class prescriptions, most therapists dealing with grief moved toward what has been called a "modernist" approach. Freud had valued grief as a means of freeing individuals from ties with the deceased, but he had made it clear that detachment was the ultimate goal and had warned against the stunting that could result if grief were not transcended fairly quickly. Later modernists downplayed grief even further, viewing it as a

form of separation anxiety, an inappropriate or dysfunctional attempt to restore proximity. In most instances, of course, grief played itself out as mourners gradually abandoned hope that the lost person would return; but from the therapeutic perspective there was constant danger that a more durable imbalance might form. The therapeutic goal, whether outside help was needed or not, was severance of bonds with the deceased or departed. Therapy or counseling should work toward this process of withdrawal, and those who retained grief symptoms must be regarded as maladjusted. By the 1970s even counseling with older widows encouraged the development of new identities and interests and promoted the cessation of grief and its ties to the past.[15] "Grief work" meant work against grief and an implicit attack on Victorian savoring of this emotional state. Appropriate terms were developed for excessive grief—two from the 1960s were "mummification" and "despair." "Chronic grief syndrome" applied to a situation of clinging dependency, most common among women, when a parent or spouse died. The idea that grief followed from love was also attacked; psychologists argued that in cases of spouse death, grief developed particularly strongly when a love-hate tension had existed, grief then picking up on a sense of guilt for the hate rather than a nostalgia for the love. Mental health meant breaking bonds and avoiding dependency. Grief, contradicting both goals, became a target for attack[16] . . .

The third area in which the new antigrief regime manifested itself from the 1920s onward lay in a more familiar realm—advice to parents on how to socialize children. Here, the general aversion to Victorian grief was compounded by two factors: the rapid decline in child mortality, which made it progressively easier to dissociate childhood from traditional concern with death; and the rising anxiety about children's fears. From D. H. Thorn in the mid-1920s onward, discussions of children's fears frequently embraced the subject of death as popularizers tried to help parents deal with irrational worries about such fanciful prospects as being buried alive. The same new breed of experts warned against the common assumption that children developed attention to death only after their initial years, and they also cautioned that conventional Victorian euphemisms, such as the equation between death and sleep, actually might increase childish fear. As Sidonie Gruenberg noted, " 'They go to sleep' is one example of a convenient but dangerous evasion which could make a child approach bedtime with alarm."[17] This new approach to death in the childrearing advice was facilitated by the removal of death from the family context, not only because of rapidly dropping child mortality rates but also because of removal of sick adults to hospitals, grandparents to separate residences, and the dead themselves to funeral homes. Further, the decline in adult mourning that followed from the attack on Victorian ceremony also made it easier to separate children from active comment on death, as did the distancing of cemeteries.

In the new context children's fears of death provoked complex reactions among the popularizers. On the one hand, general instructions about fear urged frankness, talking things out. On the other hand, adults themselves were being urged to keep death at an emotional distance, which made it difficult to follow the general line where this particular fear was concerned. A clearer conclusion was that traditional Victorian approaches would not work. Children should not be widely exposed to death ceremonies, and they should not be filled with stories of angels and heavenly reunions. *Parents' Magazine* cautioned against "conjuring up a heaven of angels and harp playing," for "inevitably the small girl or boy will discover that mother and father are not certain about the after life. Such a discovery augments the fear of death." One handbook urged parents to emphasize death's humorous side, while carefully avoid-

ing ridicule—a clear effort to desensitize. Other authors suggested carefully evasive phrasing so that the child would receive no images that he could easily apply to himself. Referring to a grandparent's death as "all through" might thus be a good idea. "Fear of death arises when the child imagines not mother or grandmother, or the bird, but himself being covered up with dirt. That much the child can imagine; that much is within the child's observable experience. But if the child gets the idea that a dead person is 'all through,' the identification of himself with the dead person or animal is more difficult."[18] . . .

Experts urged parents to tell children that most death resulted from old age. "If such an explanation is grossly inappropriate," added Alan Fromme, "reference may be made to a most unusual illness which none of us is likely to get." This approach dearly enabled avoidance. To be sure, when the subject of death could not be avoided and grief did emerge, advice givers urged parents to reassure their children—though this theme received greatest emphasis before 1920. "To childish grief we should give the same loving sympathy that we should give to real grief in any other phase of life. It is a mistake to repress tears or sobs which arise from such a cause; it is far better to let the child 'cry it out' unless the current of his thoughts can be turned in another direction." But parents should avoid showing emotion on their own. One of the reasons for abandoning mourning and its colors was to help children ignore death to the greatest extent possible. When information had to be conveyed, "let us give the facts to the child with as little emotion as possible." For older children, factual, scientific information would help separate death from powerful emotion—here was a child-socialization variant of the medical modernization approach in adult contexts. Parents were advised to tell children about other cultures' ideas about death, and to talk to them about medical data when their understanding permitted, but to keep the whole subject dispassionate. Some authorities also urged not only dry facts but maximum avoidance. Fromme, for example, advising that children be kept away from funerals, wanted to prevent any glimpse of intense adult mourning. Death itself should be acknowledged quickly, lest children suspect dark secrets, but ceremonies as well as emotions might best be removed.[19] . . .

As we have seen, adult grief issues were increasingly minimized, shrouded in silence, or at most addressed through therapeutic approaches directed toward recovery from the emotion as if from a disease. The approach recommended for children—keeping them away from death—rounded out a consistent picture. After several decades of diverse kinds of attacks on Victorian grief assumptions, middle-class culture resolutely worked around grief. The emotion became unpleasant, potentially overwhelming, lacking in any positive function. . . .

* * *

Application of the anti-intensity theme to grief . . . produced ambiguous results. Many people continued to grieve as they had in the nineteenth century, mourning the deaths of children or young adults with great sorrow. Here, the biggest change may have been not culture but demographic reality, as child death rates declined greatly and thus greatly reduced the occasions for grief manifestations. At the same time, awareness of new grief rules spread, making some people comfortable with relatively little show of outward sorrow and causing others who were genuinely grief-stricken to question or criticize their own reactions. Therapists reported problems with patients who adamantly insisted that there must be something wrong with them because their grief "cures" did not occur as rapidly as the general culture urged or simply because they occurred in less recognizable phases. "I feel like I am just at a standstill in my life, really, just kind of stopped there," said one patient actively fighting her

deep grief. The need for therapy itself, though not unprecedented, was a sign of growing discomfort with spontaneous emotional reactions to sorrow. Many marriages now split apart during grief over the death of a child, and this newly common family disruption reflected not only hostility to the grief of others but also confusion over one's own reactions; shared grief, that staple of Victorian culture, became harder to achieve.[20] . . .

[Grief was a victim] of the growing intolerance for emotional intensity on the part of others. . . . [E]tiquette manuals, picking up on the new aversion to intense grief, argued in terms of the emotion's unpleasantness for other people, "who might find it difficult to function well in the constant company of an outwardly mourning person." Stories also dealt with the problems of peer reactions—"her friends were again feeling a little critical of her, saying to one another that it would be a pity if poor Marian should allow grief to make her 'queer.' " From the 1920s onward formal mourning declined. Special clothes were abandoned except for funerals themselves, and increasingly even for funerals. Markings on homes progressively disappeared. Employers became increasingly reluctant to allow time off for mourning apart from a funeral day or half-day. And, always granting variety in personal reactions, many Americans became impatient with the need to listen to the grief of others, particularly after an initial this-should-do-it exchange. The removal of death to hospitals, where few people were allowed to participate in the receipt of the final news, was not directly caused by the new aversion to handling grief, but it certainly furthered the process. Avoidance of grief situations seemed to make the new emotionology work well.[21]

But grief itself did not decline as rapidly as did public tolerance for it. Stories might note the decline of conventional mourning and of sacred symbols of the departed, but their recommendations for alternatives remained rather vague: "Slowly, slowly we come out of all this. Slowly we learn that the one way to keep our own forever with us, is to lift into the aura of his spiritual permanence." By the 1950s certain categories of grief-stricken Americans, such as people who lost a child or spouse at an untimely age, began to form voluntary groups of kindred souls, providing emotional support for each other on the basis of their shared experience and their common realization of the lack of extensive sympathy from the wider society. Support groups like Theos and the Compassionate Friends spread to most American cities.[22] This new bond elevated strangers to a position of emotional importance simply on the basis of the unavailability of sympathetic others, including, often, friends. The bond might fill the void, but it also testified to the growing distaste for other people's intensities even at times of crisis. The pressure to maintain control of oneself and the convenient belief in the immaturity of others' outbursts supported a major change in emotional interactions in many middle-class families and acquaintance groups. . . .

Beginning in the 1960s, concerns about the limitations of "modern" grief standards began to circulate, spearheaded by gurus like Elisabeth Kübler-Ross. As death and dying courses proliferated for a time on college campuses, it became fashionable to assert that contemporary Americans had lost the ability to die well or to mourn well. Much of the criticism was directed at doctors and hospitals wedded to a death-fighting stance, but grief came in for comment as well. According to some experts, contemporary society, having removed death from home and family and become focused on the shallow joys of work and material acquisition, had shunted grief, not only damaging the process of dying but also leading to severe psychological stress among those left behind, perhaps even causing unnecessary depression and even suicide. New movements like the creation of hospices attempted to reintegrate the family with death, allowing more "natural" grief in the process. Therapists began to rethink their

penchant for damping down grief, wondering if the emotion should not be encouraged instead. There was no full revolution in standards, and indeed a steady increase in the use of cremation in the United States reflected a continued wish to handle death in an emotionally unobtrusive fashion. But there is no question, either, that grief had been turned into a problem case . . . and was being rethought in some quarters.

Notes

1. Nathaniel Hawthorne to Sarah Peabody, 15 March 1840, *Hawthorne Collection,* Harvard University; Lystra, *Searching the Heart* 50; Reverend J. R. Miller, *Homemaking* (Philadelphia, 1882), 299.

2. *McGuffey's Fourth Eclectic Reader* (1866); Richard Evans, "The Golden Stein," *Analytical Fourth Reader,* 1888; Martha Finley, *Elsie's Girlhood* (New York, 1872), 156; Louisa May Alcott, *Little Women* (New York, 1868), 472, 488.

3. Paul C. Rosenblatt, *Bitter, Bitter Tears: Nineteenth-Century Diarists and Twentieth Century Grief Theories* (Minneapolis, Minn., 1983), 21, 38, 93 and passim; *Diary of Nellie Wetherbee,* unpublished manuscript, Bancroft Library, University of California, Berkeley, 1860.

4. *The Art of Pleasing*; or, *The American Lady and Gentleman's Book of Etiquette* (Cincinnati, Ohio, 1855); Robert V. Wells, "Taming the 'King of Terrors' "; *The Handbook of the Man of Fashion* (Philadelphia, 1847), 85; Cecil B. Hartley, *The Gentleman's Book of Etiquette and Manual of Politeness* (Boston, 1873), 80; Paul C. Rosenblatt, *Bitter, Bitter Tears.*

5. Phillipe Aries, *The Hour of Our Death* (New York, 1981); Ralph Houlbrooke, ed., *Death, Ritual, and Bereavement* (London, 1989); Elisabeth Kübler Ross, ed., *Death: The Final Stage of Growth* (New York, 1975); Ivan Illich, *Medical Nemesis* (London, 1976).

6. Peter Uhlenberg, "Death in the Family," in N. Ray Hiner and Joseph M. Hawes, eds., *Growing Up in America: Children in Historical Perspective* (Urbana, Ill., 1985), 243–246.

7. Andrew White, *The Warfare of Science with Theology* (New York, 1894).

8. Rev. W. R. Inge, "The Vesper Hour," *Chautauqua* 62 (April 1911): 260; "The Great Adventure," *Outlook* 103 (22 March 1913): 605; Jane Belfield, "The Passing: An Emotional Monotone," *Lippincott's Magazine* 80 (September 1907): 374; "At the End of the Journey," *Outlook* 70 (25 January 1902): 216.

9. Richard Fisguill, "Death and La Mort," *North American Review* 199 (January 1914): 95–107; "The German Idea of Death," *Living Age* 286 (August 1915): 523–29; "Editor's Diary," *North American Review* 186 (October 1907): 307–308; Arthur Reeves, "The High Cost of Dying," *Harper's Weekly* 52 (January 1913): 15; Graham Taylor, "Pioneer Inquiries into Burial Lots," *Survey* 28 (September 1911): 815–24.

10. "The Psychology of Sudden Death," *Literary Digest* 47 (December 1912): 1120; "Grieving," *Independent* 64 (1908): 476–477.

11. "Grieving," 476–77.

12. "The New Mien of Grief," *Literary Digest* 52 (February 1916): 202. See also "The Presence of Death," *The New Republic* 11 (May 1917): 45–47; "Poor Death," *Living Age* 290 (September 1918): 360; "The Abolition of Death," *Current Opinion* 62 (April 1917): 270–271; "The Unseemliness of Funerals," *Literary Digest* 54 (April 1917): 1170; "And the Mourners Go About the Streets," *Unpartizan Review* 12 (July 1919): 176; Corra Harris, "Politics and Prayers in the Valley," *Independent* 71 (1916): 195.

13. Geoffrey Gorer, *Grief and Mourning in Contemporary Britain* (New York, 1965).

14. M. Beatrice Blankenship, "Death Is a Stranger," *Atlantic Monthly* 154 (December 1934): 649–57; Mabel S. Ulrich, "What of Death in 1931," *Scribner's Magazine* 89 (June 1931): 559–60; Milton Weldman, "America Conquers Death," *American Mercury* 10 (February 1927): 216–17; "Problems of Living," *Scholastic* 36 (April 1940): 31.

15. Margaret Stroebe et al., "Broken Hearts in Broken Bonds," *American Psychologist* 47 (1992): 1205–12; I am grateful to Baruch Fischoff for this reference. H. Lopata, "On Widowhood: Grief Work and Identity Reconstruction," *Journal of Geriatric Psychiatry* 8 (1975): 41–58.

16. Stroebe, *Broken Hearts;* James R. Averill and E. P. Nunley, "Grief as an Emotion and a Disease; A Social Constructionist Perspective," *Journal of Social Issues* 44 (1988): 79–95; J. Bowlby, *Attachment and Loss*, 3 vols. (Harmondsworth, England, 1971–1980).

17. D. A. Thom, *Child Management* (Washington, D.C., 1925), 14; Daniel Anthony Fiore, "Grandma's Through": Children and the Death Experience from the Eighteenth Century to the Present, unpublished honors paper, Pittsburgh, 1992; Peter Stearns and Timothy Haggerty, "The Role of Fear: Transitions in American Emotional Standards for Children, 1850–1950," *American Historical Review*, (Feb. 1991); S. M. Gruenberg, ed., *The Encyclopedia of Child Care and Guidance* (New York, 1954), 170.

18. Ruth Sapin, "Helping Children to Overcome Fear," *Parents' Magazine* 8 (August 1933): 16; see also Donald A. Laird and Eleanor C. Laird, *The Strategy of Handling Children* (New York, 1949), 77; C. W. Hunicutt, *Answering Children's Questions* (New York, 1949), 22; Harold H. Anderson, *Children in the Family* (New York, 1941), 104–5.

19. Allan Fromme, *The Parents Handbook* (New York, 1956), 66; Mrs. Theodore [Alice] McLellan Birney, *Childhood* (New York, 1905), 28, 239; Dorry Metcalf, *Bringing Up Children* (New York, 1947), 62–63.

20. Paul Rosenblatt, *Bitter, Bitter Tears: Nineteenth-Century Diarists and Twentieth-Century Grief Theories* (Minneapolis, 1983); Margaret Stroebe, Mary Gergen, Kenneth Gergen, and Wolfgang Stroebe, "Broken Hearts and Broken Bonds," *American Psychiatry* 54 (1991); Charles W. Brice, "Paradoxes of Maternal Mourning," *Psychiatry* 54 (1991); E. Lindermann, "The Symptomology and Management of Acute Grief," *American Journal of Psychiatry* 101 (1944): 141–48.

21. Amy Vanderbilt, *New Complete Book of Etiquette* (New York, 1954), 127; Anne Shannon Moore, "Golden Sorrow," *Good Housekeeping* 80 (April 1925): 176; Phillipe Aries, *The Hour of Our Death* (New York, 1981); Elisabeth Kübler-Ross, ed., *Death: The Final Stage of Growth (New York 1975).*

22. Moore, "Golden Sorrow," 181; Brice, "Maternal Mourning." On therapists' debates over the appropriate approach to grief, see Stroebe, Gergen, Gergen, and Stroebe, "Broken Hearts."

10

Managing Emotions in Medical School

Allen C. Smith III and
Sherryl Kleinman

For many years, students of social life ignored emotions. That changed in the late 1970s when a number of sociologists began to study and write about the social shaping and consequences of human emotions. Among them, Arlie Russell Hochschild proposed that human emotions are shaped by learned but implicit "feeling rules." According to her, individuals manage not only their outward expression of emotions but also their very feelings in order to conform to such rules. They not only express but also attempt to feel what they think they should be feeling. Further, Hochschild suggested that feeling rules vary not just historically and cross-culturally but also within societies. For example, she illustrated that feeling rules vary among occupations within our own society.

If that is the case, then occupational training necessarily involves some emotional socialization. Initiates into an occupation need to learn new feeling rules and develop new emotion management skills. Such emotional socialization may be most apparent in professional schools. As Zerubavel noted in an earlier selection, professionals such as judges, professors, and doctors are expected to put personal feelings aside and display "affective neutrality" in their work. That expectation may be most difficult for doctors who must touch and treat the human body in ways that would evoke repulsion or arousal in most of us.

This selection examines the emotional socialization of medical students. As Smith and Kleinman document, medical students' education includes subtle instruction in the feeling rules of their chosen occupation and practice in emotion management. Students learn, if they do not already know, that doctors do not let their emotions interfere with their work. Yet, the students' contact and treatment of the human body during their training often provokes professionally inappropriate and uncomfortable emotions. Although these feelings are seldom explicitly discussed, medical school encourages students to adopt emotion management strategies through which emotions are shaped to conform to professional feeling rules. Over time, most students come not only to display affective neutrality toward the human body, but also to feel affectively neutral about it. However, as Smith and Kleinman note, that too can cause problems if they carry this affective neutrality into their personal lives.

This example provides a particularly clear picture of how emotions are socially shaped. For the most part, we learn feeling rules and how to manage emotions gradually over many years. It is only when we must suddenly conform to new feeling rules, as medical students must, that our management of emotions becomes self-conscious and obvious to us. Yet, medical students' management of emotions merely helps us see what we are all doing less self-consciously most of the time—managing emotions.

All professionals develop a perspective different from, and sometimes at odds with, that of the public. "Professionals" are supposed to know more than their clients and to have personable, but not personal, relationships with them. Social distance between professional and client is expected. Except for scattered social movements within the professions in the late 1960s and 1970s . . . professionals expect to have an "affective neutrality" (Parsons 1951) or a "detached concern" for clients (Lief and Fox 1963). Because we associate authority in this society with an unemotional persona, affective neutrality reinforces professionals' power and keeps clients from challenging them. One element of professional socialization, then, is the development of appropriately controlled affect.

Medicine is the archetypal profession, and norms guiding the physician's feelings are strong. Physicians ideally are encouraged to feel moderate sympathy toward patients, but excessive concern and all feelings based on the patient's or the physician's individuality are proscribed. Presumably, caring too much for the patient can interfere with delivering good service. Other feelings such as disgust or sexual attraction, considered natural in the personal sphere, violate fundamental medical ideals. Doctors are supposed to treat all patients alike (that is, well) regardless of personal attributes, and without emotions that might disrupt the clinical process or the doctor-patient relationship. . . . [D]etachment presumably helps doctors to deal with death and dying, with the pressure of making mistakes, and with the uncertainty of medical knowledge.

In this paper we examine another provocative issue—the physical intimacy inherent in medicine—and ask how medical students manage their inappropriate feelings as they make contact with the human body with all of their senses. We look closely at the situations that make them most uncomfortable: disassembling the dead human body (i.e., autopsy and dissection) and making "intimate" contact with living bodies (i.e., pelvic, rectal, and breast examinations). From the beginning of medical training, well before students take on clinical responsibility, dealing with the human body poses a problem for them. Clothed in multiple meanings and connected to important rituals and norms, the body demands a culturally defined respect and provokes deep feelings. Even a seemingly routine physical calls for a physical intimacy that would evoke strong feelings in a personal context, feelings which are unacceptable in medicine.

The ideology of affective neutrality is strong in medicine; yet no courses in the medical curriculum deal directly with emotion management, specifically learning to change or eliminate inappropriate feelings (Hochschild 1983). Rather, two years of participant observation in a medical school revealed that discussion of the students' feelings is taboo; their development toward emotional neutrality remains part of the hidden curriculum. Under great pressure to prove themselves worthy of entering the profession, students are afraid to admit that they have uncomfortable feelings about patients or procedures, and hide those feelings behind a "cloak of competence" (Haas and Shaffir 1977). Beneath their surface presentations, how do students deal with the "unprofessional" feelings they bring over from the personal realm? Because faculty members do not address the problem, students are left with an individualistic outlook: they expect to get control of themselves through sheer will-power.

Despite the silence surrounding this topic, the faculty, the curriculum, and the organization of medical school do provide students with resources for dealing with their problem. The culture of medicine that informs teaching and provides the feeling rules also offers unspoken supports for dealing with unwanted emotions. Students draw on aspects of their experience in medical school to manage their emotions. . . . In this case study of the professionalization of emotions, we examine how students learn to handle unsettling reactions to patients and procedures in a context in which faculty members expect students to socialize themselves.

Methods and Setting

We studied students as they encountered the human body in clinical situations during the first three years of their training at a major medical school in the southeast. The first author conducted participant observation for two and one-half years. . . . Over the same period we conducted open-ended, in-depth interviews with 16 first-year, 13 second-year, and 15 third-year students, and with 18 others, including residents, attending physicians, nurses, spouses, and a counselor in the student health service. . . .

The school is a well-established university-based program with a traditional four-year curriculum. . . . Students have direct contact with the human body in a variety of situations. They begin dissection in gross anatomy on the third day of the first year. For 70 hours they progressively disassemble a preserved human body (cadaver), removing, examining, and discarding tissue while searching for specific "structures." Beginning in the first year, students spend 20 hours practicing a limited set of physical examination skills on each other. Although they do not examine the breasts, genitals, or rectum in these sessions, the practice still becomes uncomfortable at certain points, such as listening to the heart and examining the abdomen.

In the second year, students also practice examination skills for about 10 hours with patients in the hospital. Again, the breasts, genitals, and rectum are excluded unless a specific instructor requires them for his or her group of students. In a special session in the second year, students learn to conduct the gynecological examination. . . . Each student practices the basic examination once. Another special session, the autopsy, also is required in the second year. The autopsy is more upsetting to students than dissection, largely because the body is freshly dead and is accompanied by personal information in the patient's medical record. As one student put it, the body is "much closer to life than the smoked herring (cadaver) in gross anatomy."

In the third-year clerkships, the students conduct physical examinations and assist with a wide variety of tests and procedures. Depending on the relationships they establish with residents and faculty, clerks are in-cluded in much of the clinical service offered in the hospital. . . .

The Student's Problem

As they encounter the human body, students experience a variety of uncomfortable feelings including embarrassment, disgust, and arousal. Medical school, however, offers a barrier against these feelings by providing the anesthetic effect of long hours and academic pressure.

> You know the story. On call every third night, and stay in the hospital late most other evenings. I don't know how you're supposed to think when you're that tired, but you do, plod through the day insensitive to everything. (Third-year male)

Well before entering medical school, students learn that their training will involve constant pressure and continuing fatigue. Popular stories prepare them for social isolation, the impossibility of learning everything, long hours, test anxiety, and the fact that medical school will permeate their lives. These difficulties and the sacrifices that they entail legitimate the special status of the profession the students are entering. They also blunt the students' emotional responses.

Yet uncomfortable feelings break through. Throughout the program, students face provocative situations—some predictable, others surprising. They find parts of their training, particularly dissection and the autopsy, bizarre or immoral when seen from the perspective they had "for 25 years" before entering medical school.

> Doing the pelvis, we cut it across the waist. . . . Big saws! The mad scientist! People wouldn't believe what we did in there. The cracking sound! That day was more than anxiety. We were really violating that person. . . . Drawn and quartered. (First-year male)

> I did my autopsy 10 days ago. That shook me off my feet. Nothing could have pre-

pared me for it. The person was my age. . . . She just looked (pause) asleep. Not like the cadaver. Fluid, blood, smell. It smelled like a butcher shop. And they handled it like a butcher shop. The technicians. Slice, move, pull, cut . . . all the organs inside, pulled out in 10 minutes. I know it's absurd, but what if she's not really dead? She doesn't look like it. (Second-year female)

The "mad scientist" and the "butcher" violate the students' images of medicine. Even in more routine kinds of contact, the students sometimes feel that they are ignoring the sanctity of the body and breaking social taboos.

Much of the students' discomfort is based on the fact that the bodies they have contact with are or were *people*. Suddenly students feel uncertain about the relationship of the person to the body, a relationship they had previously taken for granted.

It felt tough when we had to turn the whole body over from time to time (during dissection). It felt like real people. (First-year female)

OK. Maybe he was a father, but the father part is gone. This is just the body. That sounds religious. Maybe it is. How else can I think about it? (First-year male)

When the person is somehow reconnected to the body, such as when data about the living patient who died are brought into the autopsy room, students feel less confident and more uneasy.

Students find contact with the sexual body particularly stressful. In the anatomy lab, in practice sessions with other students, and in examining patients, students find it difficult to feel neutral as contact approaches the sexual parts of the body.

When you listen to the heart you have to work around the breast, and move it to listen to one spot. I tried to do it with minimum contact, without staring at her tit . . . breast. . . . The different words

(pause) shows I was feeling both things at once. (Second-year male)

Though they are rarely aroused, students worry that they will be. They feel guilty, knowing that sexuality is proscribed in medicine, and they feel embarrassed. Most contact involves some feelings, but contact with the sexual body presents a bigger problem.

On occasion students feel unsure about differences between the personal and the professional perspectives. Recalling the first day of "surface anatomy," when they are expected to remove their shirts in order to examine each other's backs before beginning dissection of the back, students remember an unspoken tension. The lab manual suggests that women wear bathing suit tops, but few students read it in advance. Some of the few women who comply wear bras.

I remember surface anatomy. That first day when they asked us to take our shirts off, including the girls. That was real uncomfortable. You know (pause) seeing some of the girls in bras. Some of them were wearing swimsuit tops. But (pause) and drawing on their chests. So I got a guy for a partner. (First-year male)

What's the difference between a bra and a bathing suit top? Don't know. But there is one! (First-year female)

When students are standing in the anatomy lab beside the cadavers, the difference between a bra and a bathing suit is surprisingly hard to describe. The differences are clear from a personal perspective, but in the technical objectivity of the laboratory, the details and meanings of the personal perspective seem elusive and irrational.

Students also feel disgust. They see feces, smell vomit, touch wounds, and hear bone saws, encountering many repulsive details with all of their senses.

One patient was really gross! He had something that kept him standing, and coughing all the time. Coughing phlegm, and that really bothers me. Gross! Just something I don't like. Some smelled real bad. I didn't want to examine their axillae. Stinking armpits! It was just not something I wanted to do. (Second-year female)

When the ugliness is tied to living patients, the aesthetic problem is especially difficult. On opening the bowels of the cadaver, for example, students permit themselves some silent expressions of discomfort, but even a wince is unacceptable with repugnant living patients.

To make matters worse, students learn early on that they are not supposed to talk about their feelings with faculty members or other students. Feelings remain private. The silence encourages students to think about their problem as an individual matter, extraneous to the "real work" of medical school. They speak of "screwing up your courage," "getting control of yourself," "being tough enough," and "putting feelings aside." They worry that the faculty would consider them incompetent and unprofessional if they admitted their problem.

> I would be embarrassed to talk about it. You're supposed to be professional here. Like there's an unwritten rule about how to talk. (First-year female)

> It wouldn't be a problem if I weren't in medicine. But doctors just aren't supposed to feel that way. (Interviewer) How do you know? (Student) I don't know how, just sense it. It's macho, the control thing. Like, "Med student, get a grip on yourself." It's just part of medicine. It's a norm, expected. (First-year male)

The "unwritten rule" is relaxed enough sometimes to permit discussion, but the privacy that surrounds these rare occasions suggests the degree to which the taboo exists. At times, students signal their uncomfortable feelings—rolling their eyes, turning away, and sweating—but such confirmation is limited. Exemplifying pluralistic ignorance, each student

feels unrealistically inadequate in comparison with peers (yet another uncomfortable feeling). Believing that other students are handling the problem better than they are, each student manages his or her feelings privately, only vaguely aware that all students face the same problem.

The silence continues in the curriculum; discomfort with medical intimacy is not mentioned officially. The issue is broached once or twice in class with comments such as "You can expect to be aroused sometimes, examining an attractive woman." Yet there is no discussion, and such rare exceptions occur only according to individual faculty members' initiative. . . .

Emotion Management Strategies

How do students manage their uncomfortable and "inappropriate" feelings? The deafening silence surrounding the issue keeps them from defining the problem as shared, or from working out common solutions. They cannot develop strategies collectively, but their solutions are not individual. Rather, students use the same basic emotion management strategies because social norms, faculty models, curricular priorities, and official and unofficial expectations provide them with uniform guidelines and resources for managing their feelings.

Transforming the Contact

Students feel uncomfortable because they are making physical contact with people in ways they would usually define as appropriate only in a personal context, or as inappropriate only in a personal context, or as inappropriate in any context. Their most common solution to this problem is cognitive. Mentally they transform the body and their contact with it into something entirely different from the contacts they have in their personal lives. Students transform the person into a set of esoteric body parts and change their intimate contact with the body into a mechanical or analytic problem.

> I just told myself, "OK, doc, you're here to find out what's wrong, and that includes the axillae (armpits)." And I detach a little, reduce the person for a moment. . . . Focus real hard on the detail at hand, the fact, or the procedure or question. Like with the cadaver. Focus on a vessel. Isolate down to whatever you're doing. (Second-year female)

> Well, with the pelvic training (pause) I concentrated on the procedure, the sequence, and the motions. . . . With the 22-year-old, I concentrated on the order, sequence (pause), and on the details to check. (Second-year male)

Feeling guilty about "mangling" a cadaver, one student begins to ask difficult questions about nerves in the neck. Feeling "uneasy" about a pelvic exam, another student concentrates on the Bartholin gland, which is hidden under more disturbing flesh. Distinct from the body as a whole, these anatomical and procedural details become personally insignificant but academically important. Students learn to recognize them, even if they do not always understand how the specifics will be important in medicine. In the process, the body loses its provocative, personal significance.

Students also transform the moment of contact into a complex intellectual puzzle, the kind of challenge they faced successfully during previous years of schooling. They interpret details according to logical patterns and algorithms, and find answers as they master the rules.

> It helped to know that we were there for a training experience. My anxiety became the anxiety of learning enough. We saw a movie on traumas, like gunshots, burns, explosions. If I had just come off the street, I would have felt sick. But I focused on learning. Occupying my mind with learning and science. (Second-year male)

> The patient is really like a math word problem. You break it down into little pieces and put them together. The facts you get from a history and physical, from the labs and chart. They fit together, once you begin to see how to do it. . . . It's an intellectual challenge. (Third-year female)

Defining contact as a part of scientific medicine makes the students feel safe. They are familiar with and confident about science, they feel supported by its cultural and curricular legitimacy, and they enjoy rewards for demonstrating their scientific know-how. In effect, science itself is an emotion management strategy. By competing for years for the highest grades, these students have learned to separate their feelings from the substance of their classes and to concentrate on the impersonal facts of the subject matter. In medical school they use these "educational skills" not only for academic success but also for emotion management.

The curriculum supports the students' efforts to focus on subpersonal facts and details. In 20 courses over the first two years, texts and teachers disassemble the body into systems and subsystems. Students are presented with an impossibly large number of anatomical and pathophysiological details which define the body as a collection of innumerable smaller objects in a complex system. Furthermore, faculty members reward students for recognizing and reciting the relevant facts and details and for reporting them in a succinct and unemotional fashion. Intellectualization is not merely acceptable; it is celebrated as evidence of superior performance in modern medicine. The curriculum equips the students with the substantive basis for their intellectual transformations of the body, and rewards them for using it.

The scientific, clinical language that the students learn also supports intellectualization. It is complex, esoteric, and devoid of personal meanings. "Palpating the abdomen" is less personal than "feeling the belly."

When we were dissecting the pelvis, the wrong words kept coming to mind, and it was uncomfortable. I tried to be sure to use the right words, penis and testicles (pause) not cock and balls. Even just thinking. Would have been embarrassing to make that mistake that day. School language, it made it into a science project. (First-year female)

Further, the structure of the language, as in the standard format for the presentation of a case, helps the students to think and speak impersonally. Second-year students learn that there is a routine, acceptable way to summarize a patient: chief complaint, history of present illness, past medical history, family history, social history, review of systems, physical findings, list of problems, medical plan. In many situations they must reduce the sequence to a two- or three-minute summary. Faculty members praise the students for their ability to present the details quickly. Medical language labels and conveys clinical information, and it leads the students away from their emotions.

Transformation sometimes involves changing the body into a nonhuman object. Students think of the body as a machine or as an animal specimen, and recall earlier, comfortable experiences in working on that kind of object. The body is no longer provocative because it is no longer a body.

After we had the skin off (the cadaver), it was pretty much like a cat or something. It wasn't pleasant, but it wasn't human either. (First-year female)

(The pelvic exam) is pretty much like checking a broken toaster. It isn't a problem. I'm good at that kind of thing. (Second-year male)

You can't tell what's wrong without looking under the hood. It's different when I'm talking with a patient. But when I'm examining them it's like an automobile engine....There's a bad connotation with that, but it's literally what I mean. (Third-year male)

Working on a cat, a toaster, or an engine, the student effaces the person and proceeds "as if" contact were something entirely different (Hochschild 1983). The secularized body is sometimes disturbing to students ("It's just like any meat"). At other times it is reassuringly neutral; contact becomes truly impersonal.

The curriculum supports these dehumanizing transformations by eliminating the person in most of the students' contact with the body. Contact is usually indirect, based on photographs, X-rays (and several newer technologies), clinical records, diagrams, and written words. Students would have to make an effort to reconnect these images to the people they remotely represent. It is harder to disregard the person in direct contact, but such contact constitutes a very small part of the students' school time in the first three years. In addition, a large part of the students' direct contact occurs with a cadaver in the anatomy lab. Contact with living persons represents less than three percent of their school time over the first three years. Students must take the final step in transforming the body into a specific nonhuman thing, but the curriculum provides the first step by separating the body from the person.

Accentuating the Positive

As we hinted in the previous section, transforming body contact into an analytic event does not merely rid students of their uncomfortable feelings, producing neutrality. It often gives them opportunities to have good feelings about what they are doing. Their comfortable feelings include the excitement of practicing "real medicine," the satisfaction of learning, and the pride of living up to medical ideals. Students identify much of their contact with the body as "real medicine," asserting that such contact separates medicine from other professions. As contact begins in dissection and continues through the third-year clinical clerkships, students feel excited about their progress.

I can't remember what it was like before coming. It's enveloping. When I wake up I start thinking about being in med school. It's like a honeymoon, knowing I'll be a MD some day. It's just a real good feeling. I don't know how long it will last. And the work is demanding, almost all my time. But it is real, and it does make gross (lab) easier. Lab makes it real, even if it is gross. (First-year male)

This (dissection) is the part that is really medical school. Not like any other school. It feels like an initiation rite, something like when I joined a fraternity. We were really going to work on people. (First-year male)

After years of anticipation, they are actually entering the profession; occasions of body contact mark their arrival and their progress. The students also feel a sense of privilege and power.

This is another part that is unique to med school. The professor told us we are the only ones who can do this legally. It is special (pause) and uneasy. (First-year female)

I remember my second patient. An older guy. . . . There I was, a second-year student who didn't know much of anything, and I could have done anything I wanted. He would have done whatever I told him. (Second-year male)

Eventually students see contact as their responsibility and their right, and forget the sense of privilege they felt at the beginning. Still, some excitement returns as they take on clinical responsibility in the third year. All of these feelings can displace the discomfort which also attends most contact.

Contact also provides a compelling basis for several kinds of learning, all of which the students value. They sense that they learn something important in contact, something richer than the "dry facts" of textbooks and lectures. Physicians, they believe, rely on touch, not on text.

I guess I learned the intuitive part in the practice sessions (on physical examination skills). After all that training in science, this was different . . . Like feeling someone's side. Feeling (pause) it begins to mean something. . . . All the courses don't mean anything 'til I have them in my fingertips, my ears. (First-year male)

The bimanual (in the pelvic exam) was different. Like I knew that I was supposed to feel (with my hands), but I didn't feel anything. Like when you palpate the spleen. Most people never feel it. So this is just another of those. I had read the book on the exam, and it seemed like an ancient rite. It felt good to have a sense of it after that evening. . . . (Second-year male)

Students also develop clinical intuition and a fascination for the body and the "personality" of its parts. They find the learning that occurs with contact gratifying, sometimes satisfying a long-standing curiosity, and frequently symbolizing the power of medicine.

Similarly, students can intensify the good feelings that come with practicing medical ideals. By attending to those ideals, students can feel a pride which overrides any spontaneous discomfort.

If it's something uneasy, like moving her (breast) to listen to her heart, I also know that I'm doing the right thing. It's both, and it feels good to know I'm doing it right. (Second-year male)

The personal stuff just doesn't apply to the real exam of a patient. This is a completely different relationship than any other in my life. It's my job. It would be inappropriate if I didn't examine them, touch them. It's expected. (Second-year female)

In proceeding with contact despite their discomfort, the students are "doing it right," and that feels good. Some feel pleased about passing important landmarks in their training. Some feel proud of "practicing good medicine." Pride and self-respect diminish awkwardness and embarrassment.

There are two ways in which students accentuate their pride and excitement. First, they can "go with" the good feelings that arise spontaneously. Second, they can create good feelings when they do not arise naturally. By transforming an uncomfortable contact into an analytic event, students can produce the feelings of excitement and satisfaction that they have learned to associate with problem solving. Transformation and accentuating the positive are mutually reinforcing strategies.

Using the Patient

Students sometimes take patients' feelings into account as a means of managing their own discomfort. They do this in two different ways: empathizing with the patient and blaming the patient. When they are uncomfortable, students can control their feelings by shifting their awareness away from their own feelings and to the patient's. Empathizing with the patient, they distract themselves from their own feelings. At the same time, they can feel good about "putting the patient first."

> Sure, my feelings matter. But theirs do too, even more. I'm here for them, and it's only right to give theirs priority. It feels good to listen to them, to try to understand (pause) to care. And I don't feel so weird. (Second-year male)

Empathy, then, can be an effective emotion management strategy as well as an appropriate professional quality.

Students sometimes use the patient as an external locus for their own uncomfortable feelings. They make the patient responsible for their feelings, blaming the patient or simply projecting their own feelings onto the patient. A student can manage feelings of sexual awkwardness, for example, by defining the patient as inappropriately sexual.

> I know he is embarrassed. I would be. (Interviewer) Are you embarrassed too?

(Student) Yeah. Maybe part of it's mine. No just his. Embarrassed isn't quite the right word. Uneasy. But he might be embarrassed too! (Second-year female)

> My very first patient was a young girl, 14 years old. I had been told she was a pediatrics patient, but I sure didn't expect a 14-year-old (pause) and well-developed. I think she was promiscuous. I forgot to do the heart at first. Went all the way to the end and then said, "I'll have to listen to your heart." It was extremely uncomfortable. (Third-year male)

Labeling the patient as "promiscuous," the student can forgive himself his awkwardness and perhaps replace it with feelings of superiority or anger. Patients can be difficult in many ways. . . . Yet in order to manage their own feelings, students sometimes manufacture or exaggerate negative conclusions about the patient or project their own feelings onto the patient, where they are less threatening.

Laughing About It

Students can find or create humor in the situations that provoke their discomfort. Humor is an acceptable way for people to acknowledge a problem and to relieve tension without having to confess weaknesses. In this case, joking also lets other students know that they are not alone with the problem.

> When the others are talking it's usually about unusual stuff, like jokes about huge breasts. . . . Talking in small groups would help. The sexual aspect is there. Are they normal or abnormal? What's going on? (Second-year male)

> The way we talk. Before we wouldn't talk about the penis or vagina. Now we do casually, with folks in medicine. And we say more about what's happening with us sexually. Lots of comments about ejaculation, orgasms, getting it back in less than 20 minutes, that kind of thing. Some of it is serious learning conversation. Sometimes it's just joking banter. (Second-year female)

By redefining the situation as at least partially humorous, students reassure themselves that they can handle the challenge. They believe that the problem can't be so serious if there is a funny side to it. Joking also allows them to relax a little and to set ideals aside for a time.

Where do students learn to joke in this way? The faculty, including the residents (who are the real teachers on the clinical teams), participate freely, teaching the students that humor is an acceptable way to talk about uncomfortable encounters in medicine.

> We get all our grandmotherly types around the first day of (gross anatomy) lab, in case some of (the students) wimp out. Wonder why it's such a problem. (Faculty member)

> If I had to examine her I'd toss my cookies. I mean she is enormous. That's it! Put it in the chart! Breasts too large for examination! (Resident) (The team had just commented on a variety of disturbing behaviors that they observed with the patient.)

None of these comments is particularly funny out of context and without the gestures and tone of voice that faculty members use to embellish their words. Yet the humor is evident in person. . . . Eager to please the faculty and to manage their emotions, students quickly adopt the faculty's humor. Joking about patients and procedures means sharing something special with the faculty, becoming a colleague. The idea implicit in the humor, that feelings are real despite the rule against discussing them, is combined with an important sense of "we-ness" that the students value.

Unlike the students' other strategies, joking occurs primarily when they are alone with other medical professionals. Jokes are acceptable in the hallways, over coffee, or in physicians' workrooms, but usually are unacceptable when outsiders might overhear. Joking is backstage behavior. Early in their training, students sometimes make jokes in public, perhaps to strengthen their identity as "medical student," but most humor is in-house, reserved for those who share the problem and have a sense of humor about it.

Avoiding the Contact

Students sometimes avoid the kinds of contact that give rise to unwanted emotions. They control the visual field during contact, and eliminate or abbreviate particular kinds of contact.

> We did make sure that it was covered. The parts we weren't working on. The head, the genitals. All of it really. It is important to keep them wrapped and moist, so they wouldn't get moldy. That made sense. But when the cloth slipped, someone made sure to cover it back up, even if just a little (pubic) hair showed. (First-year female)

Keeping personal body parts covered in the lab and in examinations prevents mold, maintains a sterile field, and protects the patient's modesty. Covers also eliminate disturbing sites and protect students from their feelings. Such nonprofessional purposes are sometimes most important. Some students, for example, examine the breasts by reaching under the patient's gown, bypassing the visual examination emphasized in training.

Students also avoid contact by abbreviating or eliminating certain parts of the physical examination, moving or looking away, or being absent. Absence is usually not an option, but many students use the less obvious variations.

> I had most trouble with the genitalia. . . . Quite an ordeal. Taking the skin off. The girls did the actual dissection. I went into the corner and read. Turned my back. Didn't want to be involved. (First-year male)

> At the genitals, I was embarrassed. I had never touched a guy's genitals before. Even though this was medical, it was a pretty quick exam. I mimicked the preceptor, but I didn't really have any knowl-

edge of it. It was not comfortable. (Second-year female)

The students explain their limited and "deferred" examinations by claiming inexperience or appealing to the patient's needs: "Four or five others will be doing it. Why should I make the patient uncomfortable?" Some students admit they use these arguments to avoid or postpone disturbing contact.

Conveniently, the faculty do not supervise students' contact with patients in the second and third years. When the faculty members are present they do the work themselves, leaving the students to observe. This lack of supervision gives students the freedom to learn without the pressure of criticism. It also gives them opportunities to avoid the kinds of contact that make them uncomfortable.

Also, faculty members protect students from contact with the parts of the body that make them most uneasy. There is no pressure to continue with "surface anatomy," where students examine each other in the region of the body to be dissected. In fact, students stop after the first three or four sessions; some students do not participate at all. There are limits on the range of physical examination skills that the students practice with each other and in the gynecological training session: the student does not examine the breasts and does not conduct the rectal component of the examination in this session. There is a policy excluding the genitals and the rectum in practice sessions with patients in the second year. The faculty rarely challenge students who "defer" the breast, rectal, and genital examinations in the clerkships, and they abbreviate such contact in their own work.

Mostly, (the residents) don't do the breasts, pelvic, or rectal. We had a woman with a vaginal discharge (noted in the chart), but I didn't do a pelvic on the workup. Almost never. Sometimes a quick external check. That is the extent of

their concern. For most docs and residents those are outside their area of expertise. If they think an exam should be done, they call in a consult, like GYN. . . .

On medicine, the rectal is often important. I did a couple. Hopefully, the resident or attending did it. We thought we should do screening on the breasts, but I only did one or two. (Third-year male).

If you skip the genitals or rectal, and you note "exam deferred" in the chart, there's no problem. Sometimes they tell you to go ahead and do it, but there's no problem. So long as they don't think you just forgot. Just say "pelvic deferred." (Third-year female)

Silent acceptance of the boundary around the sexual parts of the body suggests that the faculty *do* regard and treat the sexual body as "different," despite the official line (neutrality) that conceals the difference. As neutrality fails and feelings arise, the faculty give the students, and themselves, permission to reduce or eliminate the kinds of contact they find most upsetting.

Taking Medicine Home

In their studies, students gradually come to see the human body as an interesting object, separate from the person. This new, intellectualized body is stripped of the meanings the students knew before coming to medical school. The impersonal body is relatively neutral and easy to contact clinically, but students have a vague and unsettling sense of loss.

The heart. I know it's just a blood pump. Mostly muscle. Valves. But it's something more, too. Interesting to touch it, see it. But it felt funny. Like (pause) I went up in my head when we lifted out his heart. Funny feeling (pause) partly physical. Won't be any place to go when we open his head. (First-year female)

I had to confront the fact that we are just flesh, made of flesh, like the animals we eat. It took a week to work it out, partly. (Second-year male)

According to the official perspective of the school, the body is "just" a complex object. The heart may be an awesome, marvelous pump, but something which has been valuable is lost during professionalization. Mysterious and romantic meanings are publicly discarded, and students are not sure what their world will be like without them. They try to shift culturally sacred meanings from the body to the abstract person, and their efforts do diminish the uncomfortable feelings that spill over into medicine from their personal lives. Yet the new perspective is sometimes awkward at school, and it creates other issues for students as medical neutrality spills over into their personal lives.

For some students, medical training creates a problem as new meanings for the body and for body contact go home with them at night. The clinical perspective enters into moments of contact with spouses and friends, an arena where personal meanings are important.

I have learned enough to find gross problems. And they taught us that breast cancer is one of the biggest threats to a woman's health. OK. So I can offer my expertise. But I found myself examining her, right in the middle of making love. Not cool! (Second year male)

I'm learning, but it's still a little uncomfortable. I'm sure glad I could talk about it with my wife. It felt like something about my masculinity. In GYN you don't think so much in sexual terms. Not with that big piece of metal (the speculum) in her. But there's no metal at home, and I still don't feel the same about it. They say you get over this pretty quick. I wonder how. What will it be like later? (Third-year male)

Particularly in the sexual domain, the progressive neutralization of the body threatens personal meanings that the students have long attached to physical intimacy. Without alternative meanings that could promise a comparable sense of attachment and gratification, some students fear that the special power of intimacy may be lost as they neutralize the body for medicine. Acknowledging the threatening quality of intimacy in personal life, some students are also concerned that they may bring their emotion management strategies home and use them in unhealthy ways to minimize personal pains.

For other students, neutralizing the body at school helps them to achieve greater intimacy at home. If intimacy has been over romanticized in their personal relationships, for example, it can become less awesome and more manageable as they redefine it for medicine.

Well, it's been fun, trying things on him. I'd practice things like the ear exam, or (pause) we didn't do the (male) genitals at school. I tried it at home. He was real good about it, and I think I learned something. I was glad to have a chance before trying it on a real patient. And we talked afterward, more than we usually do. (Second-year female)

I had fallen way behind in touching (in my personal life). It had gotten so touching wasn't an option for me. But I'm catching up. It's an option. It's allowed. Almost like I'm practicing on my patients. . . . I don't know if that makes sense. Like I have been blocking on touching every time. But with patients I get beyond the blocks, and I can sense a little of what it's like. Look! I'm out here beyond the blocks, and it's OK! Then I can try it a little more in my personal life. (Third-year female)

As some special meanings are stripped away, these students can proceed more comfortably with personal intimacy. Their training demystifies physical intimacy, making it easier to discuss it with personal partners. In some cases they find it easier to initiate contact. Whether the effect is comfortable or threatening, the fact that students bring home their professional perspective on the body indicates the strength of the training process, particularly as it affects the personal body. Maintaining a personal perspective at home becomes yet another challenge that many students face.

Conclusion

Medical students sometimes feel attracted to or disgusted by the human body. They want to do something about these feelings, but they find that the topic is taboo. Even among themselves, students generally refrain from talking about their problem. Yet despite the silence, the culture and organization of medical school provide students with supports and guidelines for managing their emotions. Affective socialization proceeds with no deliberate control, but with profound effect. . . .

Analytic transformation is the students' primary [emotion management] strategy, and it does tend to produce affective neutrality. As we stated, however, the medical culture provides other strategies that involve strong feelings instead of the neutrality of medical ideals. The particular feelings allowed by faculty members and by the culture fit with the basis of all occupations that have achieved the honorific title of "profession": acquiring hierarchical distance from clients (if not always emotional indifference). Much of the humor that students learn puts down patients who are aesthetically, psychologically, or socially undesirable. . . . Blaming patients and avoiding uncomfortable contact lend power to the physician's role. Even the effort to accentuate the comfortable feelings which come with learning contributes to the distance. In concentrating on the medical problem, students distance themselves from their patients. . . . All of these strategies maintain the kind of professional distance that characterizes modern medical culture, a dis-

tance which provides for comfortable objectivity as well as scientific medical care.

One of the students' strategies, however, operates differently. Empathizing with patients diminishes the students' discomfort and directs attention to the patient's feelings and circumstances. Students are taught that excessive concern for patients can cloud their clinical judgment, but moderate concern allows them to manage their own feelings *and* to pay close attention to the patient. . . .

We suspect that the patterns we found in medical education occur as well in other professional schools and situations. Most health professionals face similar challenges and maintain a similar silence about them (Pope, Keith-Spiegel, and Tabachnik 1986). Comparably provocative challenges exist elsewhere, requiring potentially similar strategies of change and control. . . .

Our study suggests that the emotional socialization of professional training will influence the character of performance in the workplace and will have consequences for life outside the workplace. Medical students accept that they must change their perspective on the body in order to practice medicine, but they worry about the consequences. Often using the word "desensitization," they are concerned that medical training will dull their emotional responses too generally.

> Those feelings just get in the way. They don't fit, and I'm going to learn to get rid of them. Don't know how yet, and some of the possibilities are scary. What's left when you succeed? But what choice is there? (Second-year female)

> It's kind of dehumanizing. We just block off the feelings, and I don't know what happens to them. This is pretty important to me. I'm working to keep a sense of myself through all this. (Third-year male)

Quietly, because their concern is private and therefore uncertain, students ask questions we might all ask. Will we lose our sensitivity to those we serve? To others in our lives? To ourselves? Will we even know it is happening?

References

Haas, J. and W. Shaffir. 1977. "The Professionalization of Medical Students: Developing Competence and a Cloak of Competence." *Symbolic Interaction* 1: 71–88.

Hochschild, A. 1983. *The Managed Heart*. Berkeley: University of California Press.

Lief, H. and R. Fox. 1963. "Training for Detached Concern in Medical Students." Pp. 12–35 in *The Psychological Basis of Medical Practice*, edited by H. Lief. New York: Harper and Row.

Parsons, T. 1951. *The Social System*. New York: Free Press.

Pope, K., P. Keith-Spiegel, and B. Tabachnik. 1986. "Sexual Attraction to Clients: The Human Therapist and the (Sometimes) Inhuman Training System." *American Psychologist* 42(2): 147–158.

11

Mental Illness, Psychiatric Drugs, and the Elusive Self

David A. Karp

Many of us occasionally have thoughts and feelings that we believe people like us should not have, which is to say, socially inappropriate thoughts and feelings. Most, although not all, of us find such thoughts and feelings distressing. In our contemporary society, such socially inappropriate thoughts and feelings are considered potential symptoms of mental illness. Hence, when such distressing thoughts and feelings are recurrent, many seek the help of professional psychiatrists. Today, that help usually comes in the form of psychiatric medications. The prevailing psychiatric, and popular, view of mental illness is that it results from chemical imbalances in the brain that can be corrected, or at least masked, with an appropriate drug or combination of drugs. Yet, the prevailing psychiatric view neglects the fact that drugs affect not just brain chemistry but also the individual's entire sense of being.

Over the years, social scientists have documented that drug-induced experiences are not a direct product of a drug's physiological effects but of how the individual defines and interprets those effects. For example, a drug-induced hallucination might be interpreted as a sign of mental breakdown or of divine revelation, or simply as an exotically pleasurable experience. How individuals interpret a drug's effects largely depends upon the interpretations to which they have been socially exposed. Members of different societies often react to the same drug quite differently, and members of recreational drug-using subcultures often interpret a drug's effects quite differently from those who first experiment with the drug.

Psychiatric drugs pose a particularly perplexing interpretive puzzle. The individual who begins taking psychiatric medication implicitly admits that she or he has a mental illness. That, in turn, implies that she or he is not in complete control of her or his own thoughts and feelings. Hence, the individual must now question whether her or his thoughts and feelings are their own or are products of her or his diseased brain chemistry. Psychiatric medications complicate this interpretive challenge. Is what I am now experiencing because of my illness, the drug, or what I really think and feel? Many who take psychiatric medications continually struggle with this interpretive puzzle even when the drugs relieve their distressing "symptoms."

This selection poignantly documents psychiatric patients' struggle to make sense of their experience. Its author, David Karp, has suffered from depression most of his adult life and has taken psychiatric medications for years. Those experiences led him to investigate the experience of depression, of caring for the mentally ill (see Chapter 22), and of taking psychiatric medications. In each case, he has relied on the testimony of those who actually live those experiences.

Here his focus is on psychiatric patients' attempts to determine who and what they really are. He documents patients' reluctance to take psychiatric drugs and accept the identity of being mentally ill as well as how that identity complicates their sense of self. He shows how patients struggle with the question of whether their thoughts and feelings are their own or "just the meds." Some resolve that struggle by simply accepting that the medications enable them to be their normal or "true" selves. Others worry that the medications have robbed them of something valuable, including who they really are. These latter patients often experiment with their prescribed regimen of medications in an attempt to minimize their use of such drugs. They continue to puzzle over whether their thoughts and feelings are "their own," symptoms of their disease, or "just the meds."

There is a larger lesson to learn from these psychiatric patients' experiences. Our experience of internal bodily states is not a direct product of physiologically based perceptions. As with our perceptions of the external environment, we define, interpret, and endow perceptions of internal states with meaning. We cannot make anything we want out of either the external environment or our internal states, but they can be interpreted and defined in an indefinite variety of ways. Social experience is the source of those possible interpretations and definitions. It shapes drug-induced and sexual experiences, experiences of illness and pain, and various other internal states. It shapes our subjective experience as much as it shapes our experience of the external environment.

Here I give fifty people with a diagnosed mental illness a platform for describing their experiences with psychiatric drugs. Emotionally ill people and their families rarely get to speak their minds . . . about their illness. Rather, most of our information on these matters comes from professional experts. . . . [This selection], in contrast, will be organized around [some] central, repeating, and common dimensions of psychotropic drug use that become discernible only when one listens to a variety of personal narratives focused explicitly on that subject. . . .

I talked with people who were being treated with medications for either depression or manic depression. Initially, I recruited several of my interviewees through my membership in an organization called MDDA—The Manic-Depressive and Depressive Association. I have attended MDDA's weekly "sharing and caring" support groups with some regularity for about fifteen years. The stories I hear in this forum astonish me by their poign-

ancy, courage, and drama. Almost invariably, the accounts turn to the efficacy and meaning of medications. Although most people acknowledge that the drugs prevent their worst "episodes," they also express distress about the ways the medications affect their bodies and minds.

* * *

[T]he people I interviewed for this book . . . were . . . clearly changed by the drugs they were taking. Almost to a person they felt that medication made them different. . . . [S]uch transformations almost always provoke puzzling questions about identity and authenticity. Whatever their life circumstances, every human being wonders, at some point, "Who am I really? Is there an essential self that distinguishes me from others? How does my sense of self change over time?" . . .

Psychiatric drugs add another layer to the search for self because they influence our feelings and moods. They alter our consciousness, and in doing so, they potentially refashion who we believe ourselves to be. To the degree that we associate ourselves with our feelings—we are, in large measure, what we feel—it should come as no surprise that drug-induced changes in feelings can arouse substantial reflection about selves gained and lost.

Drugs, like all objects, assume meanings that are socially imposed, vary across groups and cultures, and change over time. And yet contemporary medicine, based on rational, scientific principles, largely restricts its purview to the biological effects of medications on body cells. It fails to consider the ways psychotropic drugs affect the identities of those who use them. To varying degrees, taking antidepressants required all the people I interviewed to think about three issues: (1) whether they were ready to cross what they viewed as a significant identity boundary; (2) what it means to feel like oneself; and (3) whether one's "true" self is revealed or obscured by the pills one takes. . . .

Crossing Identity Boundaries

Among the people I interviewed were several who sought drug treatment from the onset of their illness, who welcomed the relief that they thought psychiatric drugs would provide, or who were so desperate that they would do anything to escape the pain of depression. We might well expect that as drug companies market their products more widely, more people will actively seek them out. To be sure, the explosive growth of psychotropic drug use suggests that an increasing number of Americans see pills as an appropriate response to a wide array of human problems. At the same time, most of the people in my sample were resistant to medication, at least initially. Over and again, they expressed a deep reluctance to take medication despite the urging of friends, family, and physicians. To take a pill was to cross an important identity line. . . .

Here is how a teacher described his fears about taking the first pill:

I remember when I was about to take my first pill. I . . . was determined I was going to take it that hour or that evening. [I was a] little bit bathed in self-pity, almost. Poor Frank, you're losing part of yourself. Part of yourself is being taken away from you because you have to take this medicine. Isn't this too bad that you have whatever you have because it means you have to take this pill and you're losing part of yourself. . . . It was the fact of being altered. Now I'm no longer going to be who I was. Because these chemicals do something and so [there is] this notion of integrity of a human being, of how everything interacts. . . . When you take these pills [you] somehow alter the structure inside you, which is not a simple structure. And [it's a structure] which we don't know [much about] . . . I was losing part of myself.

Most of my interviewees who initially resisted taking medication were afraid of being labeled mentally ill. The following . . . express[es] this common theme:

Part of me still didn't want to accept or had a hard time accepting that I was . . . I had a mental illness. That I was depressed enough . . . clinically that someone was wanting to have me try certain medications to alleviate the illness, you know—the mental illness, not the physical illness. . . . It's very confusing. I think the whole experience . . . you sort of keep questioning yourself why are you doing this. (female homemaker, aged 28)

Many expressed the feeling that a diagnosis of mental illness and the suggestion that they take medications made them feel "defective":

I had been diagnosed when I was twelve with bipolar. I had been hospitalized twice. I had a suicide attempt at twelve. And so it was already known. It was already labeled there's something just wrong with her. There's just something wrong with her . . . and it just spilled into everything. It was in the context especially within my family, but I think it spilled . . . into relationships and because there really was something fundamentally wrong with me. I wasn't fixable. I wasn't changeable. You talk about an identity, but it's just an identity of yuckiness. (female sociology student, aged 20)

The symbolic importance of doctor-prescribed pill-taking as a kind of identity point of no return is powerfully illustrated by Sarah's case . . . Sarah's persistent insomnia had caused her, in her own words, to abuse over-the-counter remedies for many years. However, she had steadfastly refused to visit a psychiatrist or to take prescribed medications. Then, after her mother's death, she had found a large stockpile of Xanax, a powerful antianxiety drug, among her mother's belongings. She had begun using the pills liberally, until eventually she became dependent on them. Even with this long history of drug use, however, she resisted the idea of taking pills prescribed by a doctor:

> I did go to the doctor when I was in my early thirties. And I said, "You know, I can't sleep. I get very anxious . . ." He said, "I am giving you a prescription for Valium." I didn't want to take it . . . To me it would be like labeling me that I needed a prescription for Valium . . . [But] the over-the-counter thing was something I [could do]. You know, if I were just messing around with over-the-counter stuff [I was okay]. . . . I always entertained the thought that by doing the over-the-counter thing I could stop whenever I wanted to.

At first Sarah's thinking seems paradoxical. She freely consumes large volumes of pills found on pharmacy shelves and then becomes hooked on a drug prescribed for someone else. At the same time, she refuses to accept her doctor's recommendation that she take a minor tranquilizer. Perhaps, though, her behavior makes more sense when viewed in the context of a general cultural ambivalence about whether we should each be in control of our emotions. As long as Sarah resists the patient role by treating herself, she maintains at least the illusion of personal control over her feelings and, thus, responsibility for them.

The society in which we live offers contradictory messages about personal responsibility. On the one hand, the biomedical model of mental illness as a product of broken brains is welcome because it relieves people of responsibility for their circumstances. On the other hand, relieving people of responsibility for how they feel can result in a sense of powerlessness. One man I interviewed captured the paradox:

> You talk about personal identity. The good news is that it's biogenic [and] therefore it's not my fault. The bad news is it's biogenic because I'm just a passenger on life's way, and I have no idea of who's driving me where and to what destination.

Despite the popularity of biological explanations for mental illness, as a society we expect people to manage their emotions, and we have very little tolerance for those who cannot. . . . With remarkable regularity the people I interviewed expressed uneasiness about controlling their feelings with a pill. The notion that one ought to "tough it out" without medication is evident in th[is] remark:

> I didn't want to rely on something to make me feel better. I'm supposed to do it by myself because I'm a human being. Everyone else can do it by themselves, so why can't I? (female sociology student, aged 20)

As th[is] account show[s], people's self-esteem and sense of integrity are deeply connected to their ability to control their personal problems. The people I spoke with had difficulty accepting fully the idea that emotional illnesses are no different from physiological problems such as heart disease or diabetes. It may be comforting to hear that antidepressant medications correct chemical imbalances in the brain just as insulin controls diabetes. But most of those I interviewed assigned different meanings to mental and physical conditions. When asked directly, they affirmed that psychiatric drugs are far more likely than other medications to make them feel bad about themselves:

> It's a different species of being. It is the magical thinking that I will be this . . . that whatever is causing these instabilities and these tremendous mood swings will eventually be set on the right course. I won't have to think about taking medications that serve as a constant reminder that I have this psychiatric illness . . . which is stigmatizing. (male media consultant, aged 52)

My conversations also revealed that resistance to psychiatric medications is tied up in complex ways with people's feelings about altering their minds and brains. Although many classes of medication affect brain chemistry, there is something especially frightening about using drugs that "mess around with my brain." . . .

> The fact that I was going to take something that would affect my mind . . . was very scary to me. I mean, talk about your feeling of losing control. They are powerful drugs, and it was frightening to me that I was going to go in and mess around with my mind. It was very scary . . . That's my life up there. So it was scary to me. (female technical writer, aged 50)

To be sure, antidepressants do alter brain chemistry and thereby affect feelings, perceptions, thoughts, and moods. Virtually everyone in my sample continued to question how psychotropic medications affect who they are at their core. But the eradication of painful symptoms can also call forth questions about what constitutes one's self.

Feeling Like Oneself

. . . [S]everal people I interviewed reported that medication miraculously restored them to "normalcy." The interviews contain comments like these: "He gave me amitriptyline, which is . . . supposed to take two weeks to six weeks to work. It took two weeks [and] I felt like a brand-new person." "And sure enough within four or five weeks I started . . . even before that, maybe a week or two, I started feeling well." "When you find one that works, for the period of time when it's working, it's worth its weight in gold and platinum." As the last comment suggests, medication miracles are too often shortlived, although many individuals did experience significant long-term relief from their symptoms. People struggled to explain some of the subtle ways in which the medications dulled feelings they greatly valued. Often the descriptions they offered were simultaneously distressing and uplifting. A doctor spoke of "finding my eyes again" (that is, having courage to tell people what he really feels) while losing the capacity to feel appropriate sadness:

> I've lost tears. I heard something on the radio and it clearly reminded me of my mother, some early stuff that she would sing to me from the song "Lightly Like a Rose." . . . I was at [the] cemetery taking a walk. It was a beautiful morning. The lilacs were out. The lilies of the valley that my mother loved were out. Everything was really nice, and on the radio was . . . a jazz piano player, sweetly playing "Lightly Like a Rose," [and it] immediately caught me. And I listened to it. I wanted to cry. I just couldn't do it. It was clear that the trough had been cut off. And I knew, and I knew that it was the Prozac. . . . And I said, "Fuck you, Prozac, I want to cry for my mom." (male physician, aged 54)

Thus far, the people we have heard in this section have been commenting on the relatively subtle ways medications have changed their feelings. Sometimes the connections between drug use and emotional changes are unclear. In other cases, however, alterations in moods, feelings, and emotions are sufficiently intense after taking a medication that there is no mistaking cause. The drug then has two opposing effects: desirable feelings are either gained or lost. Drug success stories center on the eradication of unwanted feelings and the availability of feelings that make life more manageable:

> I've had one fabulous reaction. I took Celexa and I was happy and I was laughing. And it wasn't like sarcastic, you know—I'm very sarcastic and I enjoy sarcasm and dry humor and I'll laugh at that. But it was like laughing and I walked down the street, and if I see someone whistling or hear someone whistling . . . to me someone whistling is symbolic of this happiness that I want to achieve. And I can remember what it's like. People don't whistle if they're depressed. You know, nobody depressed is walking around the street whistling. You don't whistle unless

you are like psyched and you are loving life. . . . And when I was on Celexa, it was just . . . my sister described it as just this person who she always knew I was but was just underneath everything. And she just felt so happy that I was able to come out, and I just felt like this freedom. . . . And my depression is always just weighing me down and [now] . . . it was a freedom and a lightness. And I could go to the gym because I was light enough. It was . . . there was nothing weighing me down. [long pause] Sometimes I feel like that, you know, without being on Celexa or without being on medication, but it's very fleeting. And I'd like to think that I am the person who I was on Celexa. (female psychology student, aged 20)

Psychiatric drugs typically have more mixed results, however. They are clearly a powerful tool for relieving extreme depression or mania, but the relief is too often partial and inconsistent. Frequently, it also comes at a heavy price. Many people told me they felt robbed of feelings that were central to their view of themselves. Even when the medications "worked" they repeatedly complained that they had lost important parts of themselves:

I think there is a definitely serious identity question. I don't feel like the same person on drugs. I feel as though maybe I'm a better person, but it's not who I am. . . . I mean, maybe you might get to see the bad side [without medications], but that's still part of who I am, you know, the bad side. It's an identity issue to me, I think. (male education student, aged 20)

I'm a complicated person and it's a difficult life and I make mistakes. But I'm there and then I take the pills, and my therapist told me that the pills would make me more like me. . . . I go back to her and I say, "It's not happening." You know, the pills take me away from me, they do something else. The lithium sort of organizes me, the Wellbutrin lifts me up, the Benadryl puts me down. But it's not me. (female office worker, aged 60)

In *Prozac Diary* Lauren Slater [1998] observes that though a great deal has been written about what happens to people when they become sick, very little has been said about the equally powerful consequences of becoming well. Like the inmates portrayed in the movie *The Shawshank Redemption* who cannot deal with freedom after decades of institutionalization, some of my interviewees found it difficult to contemplate—and sometimes live—a life free of depression or mania. They missed their illness because it is who they fundamentally define themselves to be. While the vast majority of those who suffer from affective disorders choose pills over pain, the choice is not as easy as one might imagine:

I always had these very deep feelings, and I used to write poetry to express how I felt. On medication, I'm not so hot to do that. And so I think it does take a piece away from me, a more poetic and maybe creative part of me. And that's another one of those trade-offs. . . . I notice when I'm off the Celexa . . . I just sometimes feel things so acutely. . . . I think I was born this way. I have a very strong empathetic streak. I don't always like those feelings because they're uncomfortable. . . . I guess it's all about tolerating feelings. Can I tolerate the feelings that feel bad to me in order to experience . . . who I am? These drugs are wonderful and can really help a person, but . . . there is a compromise there. (female technical writer, aged 50)

People suffering from depression may also have difficulty understanding whether their troubles arise from their illness or from some independent, core self. Those with a long history of psychiatric drug use face an additional challenge—to distinguish the pill from the person. That is, after years of drug-taking, most of those I interviewed longed to know who they would be in the absence of the drugs. Even those who felt well, even cured, on their medications often fiddled with dosage levels and considered stopping their medication altogether. For many, the urge to know one's own true self prompted ongoing experimentation with medications.

Searching for a True Self

Because psychiatric medications are designed to change moods, feelings, and behaviors, people taking them for prolonged periods of time often begin to wonder: *Is this me or is it the drug?* No one can know for sure.

> I appreciate what medication has done for me, and I recognize that medications like Zoloft, with all its issues, and Wellbutrin, the miracle drug, have improved my life a thousand times over—I don't know where I'd be without them. . . . Would I be a completely different person? And will I ever know that? And can I ever say, "This is who I am" as long as I'm on these? That's my issue with drugs. (female drama student, aged 19)

It is not possible . . . to live two lives to determine the true impact of a single factor (medication vs. no medication, or even illness vs. no illness) on one's self. There are always intervening circumstances for instance, changing careers, love relationships, or exercise regimens—that may have as much to do with our moods and outlooks as medication does. For the people in my study, this unclear distinction between cause and effect resulted in a great deal of confusion:

> And one of the mysteries about it for me is [that] it's hard to know . . . the cause [of my recent pessimism]. Is it the condition itself? Is it the medication? I've been trying cognitive therapy, but it's hard to know how to deal with it when you don't have the facts and you don't know where the problem lies. (male professor, aged 59)

People ask themselves, "If I experience X, is it because of the illness, the medication, or is it 'just me'?" Such confusion not only under-

cuts the ability to manage one's own illness, as expressed above, but also raises questions about personal identity. The inability to trace with any certainty the causal relationships between one's life experiences, one's illness, and one's drug regimen renders obscure the nature of the authentic self that most of us believe we possess:

> Lots of times I haven't had any sense of what's normal for me. Because it's up or down, up or down, and many times in my life I'll say, "What's the real me? What am I really without the illness?" (female counselor, aged 59)

There is a subtle but profound sense of loss associated with such uncertainty. The longing to know the "real me" is often so powerful that it leads many people to experiment with their medication, sometimes without the knowledge of their doctors—from trying new drugs or new combinations of drugs to lowering doses or stopping medication altogether—in the hopes of determining who they really are. In a few cases, experimenting with medication did help people clear up some of the confusion created by their illness. For instance, one man, who had been having serious marital trouble during a deep depression, thought his illness might have been causing his relationship problems until he removed the depression as a variable:

> It's [trying Prozac] made me realize that . . . my marriage isn't in bad shape because I'm depressed. [It's] in bad shape because we've got shit. . . . The evidence is clear that [after] Prozac . . . my wife and I are [not] . . . being goo-goo, gaa-gaa, and fighting less. (male physician, aged 54)

Going on medication gave this man an opportunity to test a hypothesis about the source of his marital discord. Once he saw that Prozac improved his depression but not his marriage, he had to revise the explanation for his domestic unhappiness.

Many of the people I interviewed experimented by manipulating their dosages of antidepressants. In explaining their motivation for doing so, they spoke of wanting to "go it alone," of experimenting to see if they could handle their problems "on their own." Several described ongoing struggles to reduce the amount of medication they were taking, frequently expressing their ultimate desire to become medication-free. As one male education student, aged twenty, put it: "I mean, I'm kind of working the path to not taking it [Zoloft]. I mean, I'm taking less dosages . . . I'd like to think, eventually, a year or two maybe, I'll be off the drug completely."

For many, dosage levels were a meaningful indicator of the severity of their illness or, conversely, the degree of their normalcy. Echoing the observations of several respondents, one man explained, "The goal [is] to keep the dosages as low as possible . . . [because] it would be nice to just be a normal person and not have to think about the medications and so forth." This man and many others equated less medication with greater authenticity, as if the lower the dosage the more clearly they could claim their feelings, thoughts, and actions as their own rather than as effects of the drugs. As one woman put it, "I wondered if I could sleep without this stuff—and I did it! . . . I was two pills away from being me." Such sentiments imply a shared belief in the existence of a real self that medications obscure, making a drug-free life the desirable if elusive goal for many.

The way individuals interpret the relationship between medications and authenticity affects their attitude toward drug treatments. If, for instance, someone views her ill self as "the real me," it is not surprising that she would view medication as an undesirable detour from her "true" path, however much it may make her feel better. One woman described her drug treatment as "a deal with the devil" that she one day hoped to be free of:

My goal is to not be on medication. I don't want to be on meds. I know how helpful they are, and I know that they help me and can improve my life . . . I think of the manic-depressive people—the famous ones . . . whose talent comes from the fact that they have learned how to harness that disability, and I want to be able to do the same . . . I don't want to ignore it or make it go away, because it's there. Even when I'm on medication, it's still there, it's just being dealt with because of the pill. I'd much rather learn to deal with it . . . because it's a part of me. Depression is a huge part of my life . . . [It taught me] to be able to read myself really well in order to function. So now . . . I can read a situation really well, and it's one of those things I pride myself on. . . . And I don't want to lose that skill. . . . It's something that developed because of my depression . . . I want to explore it for a while . . . I've decided that I really want to make theater something big in my life. If I can turn depression into something I can use on stage or as a director that would be a skill. (female drama student, aged 19)

Like several other interviewees, this woman understood her depression not only as an undeniable part of who she was, but also as a teacher, offering valuable skills (and, in her case, even a career) that carried more meaning than the improved moods achieved by medication.

Others interpreted the relationship between medication and authenticity differently. Several respondents expressed the belief that their medications did not mask but rather enabled their true selves, as conveyed by the remarks of a thirty-year-old man who said, after several years of taking Zoloft, "It's incredible to discover who I really am." For this man and others, psychotropic drugs were the means to recovering a lost self, thus making the thought of returning to a life before medication unappealing:

I think it was a huge turning point when I wanted to *make* things better for myself and I wanted to become authentic in the most true sense that I could become authentic. Instead of thinking I was becoming inauthentic by taking medication, I realized that I was totally inauthentic when I wasn't taking medication because I was doing things that made me somebody that I didn't want to be. So it was this sort of paradox in terms of realizing that the medication stood for something positive instead of negative. It took me a while to get there and it wasn't easy, but I got there. (female sociology student, aged 20)

Some individuals may be reluctant to tinker with their drug regimens because they don't want to mess with what works. Several people shared the view expressed by one man who said that "whether it's the real me or not, this is the me that I like." In other words, they so value the ability to function at a high level that they are willing to live with the suspicion that the drugs might somehow distance them from their authentic selves. . . .

In this chapter we have heard different accounts of the ways psychotropic drugs affect users' senses of themselves. In some cases medication allowed people to realize their authentic selves or to function at a higher level. In this sense their narratives are success stories, even miracles. In other cases, by contrast, people described psychiatric drugs as masking or even devastating their authentic selves. As a result they were typically resistant to or ambivalent about medication.

Although it is impossible to sort out the precise connections among genuine selves, theories of self, and unique life experiences, my interviewees searched within themselves to reclaim or restore lost feelings caused by illness or by medications. Despite different attitudes and life experiences, they shared the common goal of realizing a valued, authentic identity.

Reference

Slater, Lauren. 1998. *Prozac Diary*. New York: Random House.

Part IV

The Self and Social Interaction

The self not only arises in social experience, as discussed in Part II, but is also sustained and changed through social interaction. The individual continually interacts with others. Each of those interactions provides the individual with reflected images of himself or herself. The way that others respond to the individual conveys their attitude toward him or her; and, as Cooley and Mead explained, the individual takes each attitude in kind. The self-images reflected in others' responses to the individual sometimes confirm, occasionally undermine, and gradually alter the individual's view of himself or herself.

However, the individual is not a passive participant in these interactions with others. Social interaction is a process of mutual influence. The individual influences as much how others view and respond to her or him as they influence the individual. Through influence over others, the individual can shape the very self-images that others reflect back. Moreover, the individual converses with herself or himself, whether interacting with others or alone.

The individual can inwardly challenge and counter the self-images that external life reflects, at least for a while. One's inner conversations may temporarily drown out others' external voices, especially if they are not in unison. If they are, however, the individual will have difficulty preventing those voices from echoing throughout these inward conversations. ✦

12

The Presentation of Self

Erving Goffman

The name Erving Goffman is virtually synonymous with microsociology. Throughout his life, Goffman argued that social interaction should be studied as a topic in its own right. He maintains that social interaction has its own logic and structure, regardless of the participants' personality characteristics or the social organizational and institutional context in which it occurs. That position is the basis for Goffman's very novel and influential analysis of the self. He was not interested in the individual's subjective self or inner conversations but rather in the social definition and construction of the public self during social interaction.

Goffman's approach to this topic is commonly described as dramaturgical. That is, Goffman views the self, social interaction, and life as dramatic or theatrical productions. Individuals are social actors who play different parts in the varied scenes of social life. Every time individuals interact with one another, they enact a self, influencing others' definition of them and of the situation. They usually arrive at a working consensus concerning the definition of each other's self and of the situation that consequently guides their interaction. Although social actors' performances are sometimes clumsy and unconvincing, they generally cooperate to save each other's individual shows and their collective show as a whole.

Goffman's dramaturgical analysis is more than a creative use of metaphor. We humans cannot peer into one another's hearts and minds, nor can we ever know another's "real" or "true" self.

Our knowledge of each other is limited to what we can observe. Our definition of one another's self is necessarily based on appearance, conduct, and the settings in which we interact. In turn, we present a self to one another through how we look and act, and where we go. Regardless of whether these self-presentations are intentional or unintentional, honest or dishonest, they are nonetheless performances. The self is not a material thing that the individual carries around and can show others. It must be dramatically realized on each and every occasion of social interaction.

Goffman wrote this selection in the 1950s and a few of his illustrative examples trade upon prevailing stereotypes of women at that time. Although contemporary readers may find those dated examples to be sexist, they do not detract from Goffman's insight into the drama of everyday social life.

When an individual enters the presence of others, they commonly seek to acquire information about him or to bring into play information about him already possessed. They will be interested in his general socioeconomic status, his conception of self, his attitude toward them, his competence, his trustworthiness, etc. Although some of this information seems to be sought almost as an end in itself, there are usually quite practical reasons for acquiring it. Information about the individual helps to define the situation, enabling others to know in advance what he will expect of them and what they may expect of him. Informed in these ways, the others will know how best to act in order to call forth a desired response from him.

For those present, many sources of information become accessible and many carriers (or "sign-vehicles") become available for conveying this information. If unacquainted with the individual, observers can glean clues from his conduct and appearance which allow them to apply their previous experience with individuals roughly similar to the one before them or, more important, to apply untested stereotypes to him. They can also assume from past experience that only individuals of a particular kind are likely to be found in a given social setting. They can rely on what the individual says about himself or on documentary evidence he provides as to who and what he is. If they know, or know of, the individual by virtue of experience prior to the interaction, they can rely on assumptions as to the persistence and generality of psychological traits as a means of predicting his present and future behavior.

However, during the period in which the individual is in the immediate presence of the others, few events may occur which directly provide the others with the conclusive information they will need, if they are to direct wisely their own activity. Many crucial facts lie beyond the time and place of interaction or lie concealed within it. For example, the "true" or "real" attitudes, beliefs, and emotions of the individual can be ascertained only indirectly, through his avowals or through what appears to be involuntary expressive behavior. Similarly, if the individual offers the others a product or service, they will often find that during the interaction there will be no time and place immediately available for eating the pudding that the proof can be found in. They will be forced to accept some events as conventional or natural signs of something not directly available to the senses. In Ichheiser's terms,[1]

> the individual will have to act so that he intentionally or unintentionally expresses himself, and the others will in turn have to be *impressed* in some way by him.

Taking communication in both its narrow and broad sense, one finds that when the individual is in the immediate presence of others, his activity will have a promissory character. The others are likely to find that they must accept the individual on faith, offering him a just return, while he is present before

them, in exchange for something whose true value will not be established until after he has left their presence. (Of course, the others also live by inference in their dealings with the physical world, but it is only in the world of social interaction that the objects about which they make inferences will purposely facilitate and hinder this inferential process.) The security that they justifiably feel in making inferences about the individual will vary, of course, depending on such factors as the amount of information they already possess about him; but no amount of such past evidence can entirely obviate the necessity of acting on the basis of inferences.

Let us now turn from the others to the point of view of the individual who presents himself before them. He may wish them to think highly of him, or to think that he thinks highly of them, or to perceive how in fact he feels toward them, or to obtain no clear-cut impression; he may wish to ensure sufficient harmony, so that the interaction can be sustained, or to defraud, get rid of, confuse, mislead, antagonize, or insult them. Regardless of the particular objective which the individual has in mind and of his motive for having this objective, it will be in his interests to control the conduct of the others, especially their responsive treatment of him. This control is achieved largely by influencing the definition of the situation which the others come to formulate, and he can influence this definition by expressing himself in such a way as to give them the kind of impression that will lead them to act voluntarily in accordance with his own plan. Thus, when an individual appears in the presence of others, there will usually be some reason for him to mobilize his activity, so that it will convey an impression to others, which it is in his interests to convey. Since a girl's dormitory mates will glean evidence of her popularity from the calls she receives on the phone, we can suspect that some girls will arrange for calls to be made, and Willard Waller's finding can be anticipated:

It has been reported by many observers that a girl who is called to the telephone in the dormitories will often allow herself to be called several times, in order to give all the other girls ample opportunity to hear her paged.[2]

I have said that when an individual appears before others, his actions will influence the definition of the situation which they come to have. Sometimes the individual will act in a thoroughly calculating manner, expressing himself in a given way solely in order to give the kind of impression to others that is likely to evoke from them a specific response he is concerned to obtain. Sometimes the individual will be calculating in his activity but be relatively unaware that this is the case. Sometimes he will intentionally and consciously express himself in a particular way, but chiefly because the tradition of his group or social status require this kind of expression and not because of any particular response (other than vague acceptance or approval) that is likely to be evoked from those impressed by the expression. Sometimes the traditions of an individual's role will lead him to give a well-designed impression of a particular kind, and yet he may be neither consciously nor unconsciously disposed to create such an impression. The others, in their turn, may be suitably impressed by the individual's efforts to convey something, or may misunderstand the situation and come to conclusions that are warranted neither by the individual's intent nor by the facts. In any case, in so far as the others act *as if* the individual had conveyed a particular impression, we may take a functional or pragmatic view and say that the individual has "effectively" projected a given definition of the situation and "effectively" fostered the understanding that a given state of affairs obtains.

There is one aspect of the others' response that bears special comment here. Knowing that the individual is likely to present himself in a light that is favorable to him, the others may divide what they witness into two parts: a part that is relatively easy for the individual to manipulate at will, being chiefly his verbal assertions, and a part in regard to which he seems to have little concern or control, being chiefly derived from the expressions he gives off. The others may then use what are considered to be the ungovernable aspects of his expressive behavior as a check upon the validity of what is conveyed by the governable aspects. In this a fundamental asymmetry is demonstrated in the communication process, the individual presumably being aware of only one stream of his communication, the witnesses of this stream and of one other. For example, in Shetland Isle one crofter's wife, in serving native dishes to a visitor from the mainland of Britain, would listen with a polite smile to his polite claims of liking what he was eating; at the same time, she would take note of the rapidity with which the visitor lifted his fork or spoon to his mouth, the eagerness with which he passed food into his mouth, and the gusto expressed in chewing the food, using these signs as a check on the stated feelings of the eater. The same woman, in order to discover what one acquaintance (A) "actually" thought of another acquaintance (B), would wait until B was in the presence of A but engaged in conversation with still another person (C). She would then covertly examine the facial expressions of A as he regarded B in conversation with C. Not being in conversation with B, and not being directly observed by him, A would sometimes relax usual constraints and tactful deceptions, and freely express what he was "actually" feeling about B. This Shetlander, in short, would observe the unobserved observer.

Now given the fact that others are likely to check up on the more controllable aspects of behavior by means of the less controllable, one can expect that sometimes the individual will try to exploit this very possibility, guiding the impression he makes through behavior felt to be reliably informing. For example, in gaining admission to a tight social circle, the participant observer may not only wear an accepting look while listening to an informant, but may also be careful to wear the same look when observing the informant talking to others; observers of the observer will then not as easily discover where he actually stands. A specific illustration may be cited from Shetland Isle. When a neighbor dropped in to have a cup of tea, he would ordinarily wear at least a hint of an expectant warm smile as he passed through the door into the cottage. Since lack of physical obstructions outside the cottage and lack of light within it usually made it possible to observe the visitor unobserved as he approached the house, islanders sometimes took pleasure in watching the visitor drop whatever expression he was manifesting and replace it with a sociable one just before reaching the door. However, some visitors, in appreciating that this examination was occurring, would blindly adopt a social face a long distance from the house, thus ensuring the projection of a constant image.

This kind of control upon the part of the individual reinstates the symmetry of the communication process, and sets the stage for a kind of information game—a potentially infinite cycle of concealment, discovery, false revelation, and rediscovery. It should be added that since the others are likely to be relatively unsuspicious of the presumably unguided aspect of the individual's conduct, he can gain much by controlling it. The others, of course, may sense that the individual is manipulating the presumably spontaneous aspects of his behavior, and seek in this very act of manipulation some shading of conduct that the individual has not managed to control. This again provides a check upon the individual's behavior, this time his presumably uncalculated behavior, thus re-establishing the asymmetry of the communication process. Here, I would like only to add the suggestion that the arts of piercing an individual's effort at calculated unintentionality seem better developed than our capacity to manipulate our own behavior; so that, regardless of how many steps have occurred in the information game, the witness is likely to have the advantage over the actor, and the initial asymmetry of the communication process is likely to be retained.

When we allow that the individual projects a definition of the situation when he appears before others, we must also see that the others, however passive their role may seem to be, will themselves effectively project a definition of the situation by virtue of their response to the individual and by virtue of any lines of action they initiate to him. Ordinarily, the definitions of the situation projected by the several different participants are sufficiently attuned to one another so that open contradiction will not occur. I do not mean that there will be the kind of consensus that arises when each individual present candidly expresses what he really feels and honestly agrees with the expressed feelings of the others present. This kind of harmony is an optimistic ideal and in any case not necessary for the smooth working of society. Rather, each participant is expected to suppress his immediate heartfelt feelings, conveying a view of the situation which he feels the others will be able to find at least temporarily acceptable. The maintenance of this surface of agreement, this veneer of consensus, is facilitated by each participant concealing his own wants behind statements which assert values to which everyone present feels obliged to give lip service. Further, there is usually a kind of division of definitional labor. Each participant is allowed to establish the tentative official ruling regarding matters which are vital to him but not immediately important to others, e.g., the rationalizations and justifications by which he accounts for his past activity. In exchange for this courtesy, he remains silent or non-committal on matters important to others but not immediately important to him. We have then a kind of interactional *modus vivendi*.

Together, the participants contribute to a single over-all definition of the situation, which involves not so much a real agreement as to what exists, but rather a real agreement as to whose claims concerning what issues will be temporarily honored. Real agreement will also exist concerning the desirability of avoiding an open conflict of definitions of the situation. I will refer to this level of agreement as a "working consensus." It is to be understood that the working consensus established in one interaction setting will be quite different in content from the working consensus established in a different type of setting. Thus, between two friends at lunch, a reciprocal show of affection, respect, and concern for the other is maintained. In service occupations, on the other hand, the specialist often maintains an image of disinterested involvement in the problem of the client; while the client responds with a show of respect for the competence and integrity of the specialist. Regardless of such differences in content, however, the general form of these working arrangements is the same.

In noting the tendency for a participant to accept the definitional claims made by the others present, we can appreciate the crucial importance of the information that the individual *initially* possesses or acquires concerning his fellow participants; for it is on the basis of this initial information that the individual starts to define the situation and starts to build up lines of responsive action. The individual's initial projection commits him to what he is proposing to be and requires him to drop all pretenses of being other things. As the interaction among the participants progresses, additions and modifications in this initial informational state will of course occur, but it is essential that these later developments be related without contradiction to, and even built up from, the initial positions taken by the several participants. It would seem that an individual can more easily make a choice as to what line of treatment to demand from and extend to the others pres-

ent at the beginning of an encounter than he can alter the line of treatment that is being pursued, once the interaction is under way.

In everyday life, of course, there is a clear understanding that first impressions are important. Thus, the work adjustment of those in service occupations will often hinge upon a capacity to seize and hold the initiative in the service relation, a capacity that will require subtle aggressiveness on the part of the server when he is of lower socioeconomic status than his client. W. F. Whyte suggests the waitress as an example:

> The first point that stands out is that the waitress who bears up under pressure does not simply respond to her customers. She acts with some skill to control their behavior. The first question to ask when we look at the customer relationship is, 'Does the waitress get the jump on the customer, or does the customer get the jump on the waitress?' The skilled waitress realizes the crucial nature of this question. . . .
> The skilled waitress tackles the customer with confidence and without hesitation. For example, she may find that a new customer has seated himself before she could clear off the dirty dishes and change the cloth. He is now leaning on the table studying the menu. She greets him, says, "May I change the cover, please?" and, without waiting for an answer, takes his menu away from him so that he moves back from the table, and she goes about her work. The relationship is handled politely but firmly, and there is never any question as to who is in charge.[3]

When the interaction that is initiated by "first impressions" is itself merely the initial interaction in an extended series of interactions involving the same participants, we speak of "getting off on the right foot" and feel that it is crucial that we do so. Thus, one learns that some teachers take the following view:

> You can't ever let them get the upper hand on you or you're through. So I start

out tough. The first day I get a new class in, I let them know who's boss. . . . You've got to start off tough, then you can ease up as you go along. If you start out easy-going, when you try to get tough, they'll just look at you and laugh.[4]

Similarly, attendants in mental institutions may feel that, if the new patient is sharply put in his place the first day on the ward and made to see who is boss, much future difficulty will be prevented.

Given the fact that the individual effectively projects a definition of the situation when he enters the presence of others, we can assume that events may occur within the interaction which contradict, discredit, or otherwise throw doubt upon this projection. When these disruptive events occur, the interaction itself may come to a confused and embarrassed halt. Some of the assumptions upon which the responses of the participants had been predicated become untenable, and the participants find themselves lodged in an interaction for which the situation has been wrongly defined and is now no longer defined. At such moments the individual whose presentation has been discredited may feel ashamed, while the others present may feel hostile; and all the participants may come to feel ill at ease, nonplussed, out of countenance, embarrassed, experiencing the kind of anomy that is generated when the minute social system of face-to-face interaction breaks down.

In stressing the fact that the initial definition of the situation projected by an individual tends to provide a plan for the co-operative activity that follows—in stressing this action point of view—we must not overlook the crucial fact that any projected definition of the situation also has a distinctive moral character. It is this moral character of projections that will chiefly concern us in this report. Society is organized on the principle that any individual who possesses certain social characteristics has a moral right to expect that others will value and treat him in an appro-

priate way. Connected with this principle is a second, namely that an individual who implicitly or explicitly signifies that he has certain social characteristics ought in fact to be what he claims he is. In consequence, when an individual projects a definition of the situation and thereby makes an implicit or explicit claim to be a person of a particular kind, he automatically exerts a moral demand upon the others, obliging them to value and treat him in the manner that persons of his kind have a right to expect. He also implicitly foregoes all claims to be things he does not appear to be and, hence, foregoes the treatment that would be appropriate for such individuals. The others find, then, that the individual has informed them as to what is and as to what they *ought* to see as the "is."

One cannot judge the importance of definitional disruptions by the frequency with which they occur, for apparently they would occur more frequently, were not constant precautions taken. We find that preventive practices are constantly employed to avoid these embarrassments and that corrective practices are constantly employed to compensate for discrediting occurrences that have not been successfully avoided. When the individual employs these strategies and tactics to protect his own projections, we may refer to them as "defensive practices"; when a participant employs them to save the definition of the situation projected by another, we speak of "protective practices" or "tact." Together, defensive and protective practices comprise the techniques employed to safeguard the impression fostered by an individual during his presence before others. It should be added that, while we may be ready to see that no fostered impression would survive if defensive practices were not employed, we are less ready perhaps to see that few impressions could survive, if those who received the impression did not exert tact in their reception of it.

In addition to the fact that precautions are taken to prevent disruption of projected definitions, we may also note that an intense interest in these disruptions comes to play a significant role in the social life of the group. Practical jokes and social games are played, in which embarrassments which are to be taken unseriously are purposely engineered. Fantasies are created, in which devastating exposures occur. Anecdotes from the past—real, embroidered, or fictitious—are told and retold, detailing disruptions which occurred, almost occurred, or occurred and were admirably resolved. There seems to be no grouping which does not have a ready supply of these games, reveries, and cautionary tales, to be used as a source of humor, a catharsis for anxieties, and a sanction for inducing individuals to be modest in their claims and reasonable in their projected expectations. The individual may tell himself through dreams of getting into impossible positions. Families tell of the time a guest got his dates mixed and arrived when neither the house nor anyone in it was ready for him. Journalists tell of times when an all too meaningful misprint occurred, and the paper's assumption of objectivity or decorum was humorously discredited. Public servants tell of times a client ridiculously misunderstood form instructions, giving answers which implied an unanticipated and bizarre definition of the situation.[5] Seamen, whose home away from home is rigorously he-man, tell stories of coming back home and inadvertently asking mother to "pass the fucking butter."[6] Diplomats tell of the time a near-sighted queen asked a republican ambassador about the health of his king. . . .[7]

For the purpose of this report, interaction (that is, face-to-face interaction) may be roughly defined as the reciprocal influence of individuals upon one another's actions when in one another's immediate physical presence. An interaction may be defined as all the interaction which occurs throughout any one occasion when a given set of individuals are in one another's continuous presence; the term "an encounter" would do as well. A "performance" may be defined as all the activity of a given participant on a given occasion which serves to influence in any way any of the other participants. Taking a particular participant and his performance as a basic point of reference, we may refer to those who contribute the other performances as the audience, observers, or co-participants. The pre-established pattern of action, which is unfolded during a performance and which may be presented or played through on other occasions, may be called a "part" or "routine." . . .

When an individual plays a part, he implicitly requests his observers to take seriously the impression that is fostered before them. They are asked to believe that the character they see actually possesses the attributes he appears to possess, that the task he performs will have the consequences that are implicitly claimed for it, and that, in general, matters are what they appear to be. In line with this, there is the popular view that the individual offers his performance and puts on his show "for the benefit of other people."

It will be convenient to begin a consideration of performances by turning the question around and looking at the individual's own belief in the impression of reality that he attempts to engender in those among whom he finds himself.

At one extreme, one finds that the performer can be fully taken in by his own act; he can be sincerely convinced that the impression of reality which he stages is the real reality. When his audience is also convinced in this way about the show he puts on—and this seems to be the typical case—then, for the moment at least, only the sociologist or the socially disgruntled will have any doubts about the "realness" of what is presented.

At the other extreme, we find that the performer may not be taken in at all by his own routine. This possibility is understandable, since no one is in quite as good an observational position to see through the act as the person who puts it on. Coupled with this, the performer may be moved to guide the conviction of his audience only as a means to other ends, having no ultimate concern in the conception that they have of him or of the situation. When the individual has no belief in his own act and no ultimate concern with the beliefs of his audience, we may call him cynical, reserving the term "sincere" for individuals who believe in the impression fostered by their own performance. It should be understood that the cynic, with all his professional disinvolvement, may obtain unprofessional pleasures from his masquerade, experiencing a kind of gleeful spiritual aggression from the fact that he can toy at will with something his audience must take seriously.

It is not assumed, of course, that all cynical performers are interested in deluding their audiences for purposes of what is called "self-interest" or private gain. A cynical individual may delude his audience for what he considers to be their own good, or for the good of the community, etc. For illustrations of this we need not appeal to sadly enlightened showmen, such as Marcus Aurelius or Hsun Tzu. We know that in service occupations practitioners who may otherwise be sincere are sometimes forced to delude their customers, because their customers show such a heartfelt demand for it. Doctors who are led into giving placebos, filling-station attendants who resignedly check and recheck tire pressures for anxious women motorists, shoe clerks who sell a shoe that fits but tell the customer it is the size she wants to hear—these are cynical performers whose audiences will not allow them to be sincere. . . .

[W]hile the performance offered by impostors and liars is quite flagrantly false and differs in this respect from ordinary performances, both are similar in the care their performers must exert in order to maintain the impression that is fostered. Whether an honest performer wishes to convey the truth or whether a dishonest performer wishes to convey a falsehood, both must take care to enliven their performances with appropriate expressions, exclude from their performances expressions that might discredit the impression being fostered, and take care lest the audience impute unintended meanings. Because of these shared dramatic contingencies, we can profitably study performances that are quite false in order to learn about ones that are quite honest.

In our society, the character one performs and one's self are somewhat equated, and this self-as-character is usually seen as something housed within the body of its possessor, especially the upper parts thereof, being a nodule, somehow, in the psychobiology of personality. I suggest that this view is an implied part of what we are all trying to present, but provides, just because of this, a bad analysis of the presentation. In this report, the performed self was seen as some kind of image, usually creditable, which the individual on stage and in character effectively attempts to induce others to hold in regard to him. While this image is entertained *concerning* the individual, so that a self is imputed to him, this self itself does not derive from its possessor, but from the whole scene of his action, being generated by that attribute of local events which renders them interpretable by witnesses. A correctly staged and performed scene leads the audience to impute a self to a performed character, but this imputation—this self—is a *product* of a scene that comes off, and is not a *cause* of it. The self, then, as a performed character, is not an organic thing that has a specific location, whose fundamental fate is to be born, to mature, and to die; it is a dramatic effect arising diffusely from a scene that is presented, and the characteristic issue, the crucial concern, is whether it will be credited or discredited.

In analyzing the self, then, we are drawn from its possessor, from the person who will profit or lose most by it; for he and his body merely provide the peg on which something of collaborative manufacture will be hung for a time. And the means for producing and maintaining selves do not reside inside the peg; in fact, these means are often bolted down in social establishments. . . .

The whole machinery of self-production is cumbersome, of course, and sometimes breaks down, exposing its separate components. . . . But well oiled, impressions will flow from it fast enough to put us in the grips of one of our types of reality—the performance will come off, and the firm self accorded each performed character will appear to emanate intrinsically from its performer. . . .

In developing the conceptual framework employed in this report, some language of the stage was used. . . . [However], this report is not concerned with aspects of theater that creep into everyday life. It is concerned with the structure of social encounters—the structure of those entities in social life that come into being whenever persons enter one another's immediate physical presence. The key factor in this structure is the maintenance of a single definition of the situation, this definition having to be expressed, and this expression sustained in the face of a multitude of potential disruptions.

A character staged in a theater is not in some ways real, nor does it have the same kind of real consequences as does the thoroughly contrived character performed by a confidence man; but the *successful* staging of either of these types of false figures involves use of *real* techniques—the same techniques by which everyday persons sustain their real social situations. Those who conduct face-to-face interaction on a theater's stage must meet the key requirement of real situations, they must expressively sustain a definition of the situation, but this they do in circumstances that have facilitated their developing an apt terminology for the interactional tasks that all of us share.

Notes

1. Gustav Ichheiser, "Misunderstandings in Human Relations," supplement to *The American Journal of Sociology*, LV (September 1949), pp. 6–7.

2. Willard Waller, "The Rating and Dating Complex," *American Sociological Review*, II, p. 730.

3. W. F. Whyte, "When Workers and Customers Meet," Chap. VII, *Industry and Society*, ed. W. F. Whyte (New York: McGraw-Hill, 1946), pp. 132–33.

4. Teacher interview quoted by Howard S. Becker, "Social Class Variations in the Teacher-Pupil Relationship," *Journal of Educational Sociology*, XXV, p. 459.

5. Peter Blau, "Dynamics of Bureaucracy" (Ph.D. dissertation, Department of Sociology, Columbia University, [1955], University of Chicago Press), pp. 127–29.

6. Walter M. Beattie, Jr., "The Merchant Seamen" (unpublished M.A. Report, Department of Sociology, University of Chicago, 1950), p. 35.

7. Sir Frederick Ponsonby, *Recollections of Three Reigns* (New York: Dutton, 1952), p. 46.

Reprinted from: Erving Goffman, *The Presentation of Self in Everyday Life*, pp. 1–4, 6–18, 66, 252–253. Copyright © 1959 by Erving Goffman. Reprinted by permission of Doubleday, a division of Random House, Inc. ✦

13

Cyberspace and Cyberselves

Dennis D. Waskul

Goffman's "Presentation of Self" suggests that in everyday social life, we do not simply take the attitude of others toward ourselves but actively influence their attitude toward us. We do so by managing their impressions of us. We thereby elicit social validation for the kind of person or self that we want to be and contribute to the social construction of our own selves. Yet, in everyday social life, we cannot be just anything we want to be. Physical characteristics like skin color, secondary sexual characteristics, and bodily markers of age are difficult, although not always impossible, to conceal. The clothes we can afford to buy and places we can afford to frequent constrain our presentations of selves. Moreover, many people whom we encounter in everyday life have prior knowledge of us, either directly or indirectly. The self that we present to them must be at least minimally consistent with that prior knowledge if we hope to avoid being considered a fraud. Although we influence the self that others attribute to us in everyday social life and assume different selves in different situations, our freedom of self-presentation has definite limits.

Contemporary computer technology has expanded our freedom of self-presentation by creating new realms of social interaction and self-construction. In this selection, Dennis Waskul explores how the presentation of self in cyberspace both resembles and differs from the presentation of self in everyday social life. Waskul observed online chat sites for months and con-

ducted online interviews with 59 people who regularly participated in the "chat" on those sites. On the basis of that information, Waskul documents how computer-mediated communication has created a new arena of dislocated and disembodied interaction and self-presentation.

Waskul shows that computer-mediated communication has created a new realm of social being or what he terms *cyberselfhood*. Participants in online interaction are free to choose their screen names and identities. Their physical characteristics need not constrain who or what they claim to be. Although participants in online interaction know that those with whom they are interacting may not "really" be who or what they claim to be, they observe a "working consensus" not to challenge one another's self-claims. They collectively accept that in cyberspace, representation is all you get, and they revel in the freedom that affords. Many assume a number of different and quite distinct selves on different chat sites.

As Waskul notes, many participants in online chat consider it a playful and enjoyable game of self-presentation and multiplicity. Yet, that playfulness does not detract from its seriousness. Many develop meaningful relationships in cyberspace and become committed to one or another of their cyberselves. As newspaper headlines routinely remind us, those relationships and selves sometimes spill over into everyday social life with sometimes tragic consequences. And, it is easy to exaggerate the differences between self-presentation in cyberspace and everyday social life. Our presentations of self in everyday social life may be more constrained than they are in cyberspace, but there too we are continually engaged in a collective process of self-construction. Cyberselfhood merely makes that everyday construction of self more transparent.

W ho are we when online? What can personhood mean when experienced on a computer? When interacting with others on the Internet, what can be attributed to the technology, the person, and interactions be-

119

tween people? Why do some people believe they are "more themselves" online than in "real life," how do they distinguish between these two (or more) selves, and what are the implications of this? What does it mean when disembodied virtual persons have better conversations, make better friends, or have better sex on the Internet than embodied people in everyday life? . . . There are no simple answers to these kinds of questions, yet each suggests the extent to which computer-mediated communications pose new questions to old problems of social interaction and selfhood.

* * *

There is no such *thing* as "cyberspace." The word is a concept; an abstraction to refer to something that isn't a thing at all . . . However, to say there is no such thing as cyberspace is not to say that it is only a hallucination. Instead, cyberspace rightly belongs in a special category of abstractions that have a similar unique basis in reality. This category includes things like society, social institutions, norms and values—for all practical purposes, the "stuff" of social reality. After all, there is no such thing as a society either. We all live lifetimes in society and none of us have ever seen one. Nor is there any such thing as an institution, a norm, or a value. All we "see" are the doings of people, the consequences of what they have done, and the places where these activities occur. Which is to say, in tandem with our definition of cyberspace, these "things" are concepts, abstractions we evoke to make meaningful the virtually incomprehensible and seemingly endless array of innumerable activities that people do. . . .

[T]he problem with most conceptions of cyberspace is an overemphasis on the "cyber" (the technology) and an underemphasis on the "space" (which is something that is socially produced). . . . [T]he Internet is more than the sum of its technological parts; it is a network of unique [media] for communication—"spaces"—where people meet others,

socialize, play, correspond, do business, shop, publish creative works, converse, flirt, have sex, and so on. This is also to say that the social environment of the Internet cannot be explained or reduced to the technological components that comprise the medium. One cannot in any meaningful way understand the nature of online chat . . . by reference to the cables, wires, or binary codes by which these experiences are made possible. As individuals interact in, on, and through computer networks, a socially constructed environment—a "place"—emerges that is greater than the sum of wires, telephone lines, digital cables, and computers that comprise it. . . .

In this way, cyberspace is similar to any other social space. It is a socially constructed reality; its unique feature is that it exists within computer networks and surrounding technologies. Like other constructed realities, cyberspace isn't so much a physical thing as it is a concept that contains shared meanings, understandings, and information. Approaching cyberspace this way magnifies how it is similar to any other constructed reality. For example, one would be foolish to believe they can understand the nature of . . . church or school by examining the buildings, cathedrals, desks, and pews where church and school are experienced. The reality of church and school are emergent from what people think and do—and how these thoughts and doings interact with the thoughts and doings of others—when they are in those buildings, cathedrals, desks, and pews. The reality of cyberspace and the experience of cyberspace are much more like these other social spaces than different.

* * *

When people communicate on the Internet, they interact with others and create personally meaningful identities in electronic space. . . . This is neither surprising nor unusual; selfhood thrives everywhere people communicate and interact . . . [E]xperiences of self and social situation on the Internet share much in common with experiences of self and social situation in everyday life. An online self is, at one level, no different from selfhood in any other context; a self on the Internet is something symbolic, communicated, presented and negotiated. On the other hand . . . alterations in the means by which people communicate will subtly, yet powerfully, transform the boundaries and nature of social interaction and selfhood. When people interact by [media] of communication, they must translate themselves through the conventions of the media, and in that process, selfhood is necessarily transformed. . . .

[C]yberspace is . . . mediated by technologies . . . that dislocate space, time, and personal characteristics of human interaction. Without referent or necessary commitment to the "physically real," online communications allow participants to construct new places, new social roles, and personally meaningful identities. With the click of a mouse, people can interact with diverse others in a multiplicity of socially produced places, providing a context for experience of anonymous yet personally meaningful identities situated in a geographically spaceless context where commitments to any self are as easily disposed of as they are accessed. The key question here, then, is how these fluid selves are constructed, how are they experienced, and what this form of selfhood can tell us about the nature of self in everyday life.

* * *

Cyberselfhood: Writing Self into Existence

Cyberselfhood begins with the creation of a screen name, which is of utmost importance in chat communication. In online chat, participants do not know who they are communicating with, but they do know which other screen names are present in the channel, and all communication is associated with the screen name of the message sender(s). Thus, the whole of a person's online presence must be condensed into a screen name—a single word or phrase. For these reasons, screen names are a critical element in the presentation of an online self; with screen names, chat participants convey important meanings about who and what they claim to be. . . .

Understanding selfhood in online chat requires that we . . . recognize the importance of names, and understand how they convey significant meanings that influence how we interact with others. Although in online chat a screen name may consist of just one or two words, as Haya Bechar-Israeli (1995) has illustrated, these words can evoke complex meanings and images—and this is not unique to the Internet. . . . As anyone with a nickname or anyone who has legally changed their name already knows, one's name is an important part of one's self and how others perceive one—something of which chat participants are acutely aware and actively manipulate.

As chat participants select, change, and manipulate various screen names, they begin a process of toying with their self in what will become a uniquely situated identity game. That is, by selecting a screen name, participants associate themselves with a self-selected label that is intended to convey crafted meanings. As chat participants quickly learn, their screen name is the prominent indicator of who they claim to be, their interests, and motives for interaction.

In many cases, screen names are simple derivatives of a first name. For example, a screen name such as "M1che1e" is presumably based upon the first name Michelle. In some cases, this may be the chat participant's real first name; in other cases it probably isn't. In all cases, we cannot know for sure. After all, a first name will usually indicate a gender and, for various reasons, chat participants may intentionally conceal their gender, or present themselves as the opposite gender.

First names are the easiest way to accomplish either objective. Some screen names indicate location. For example, "MrMaine" presumably indicates the geographic location of the person, although here too we cannot know for sure—perhaps "MrMaine" lives elsewhere but has some special interest in the state or some other reason for suggesting a personal association with Maine. Screen names may also be based on a person's hobbies and interests. For example, "GuitarPickn" would seem to indicate the person's interests in guitars and guitar playing. Other screen names are based on occupations ("TeachMan" is suggestive of a male teacher), while still more are based on life styles ("VegDiet" might indicate that this person is a vegetarian). Not surprisingly, there are a number of screen names that are based on motives for online interaction. Screen names like "PhoneFun4u," "M4Cyber," and "HotChic4Fun" unambiguously communicate sexual interests and motivations for online communication.

What is significant about these screen names is that they provide an important outward cue about who these people claim to be, how we might communicate with them, and what we might expect from those interactions. Chat participants are fully aware of this and actively manipulate these meanings to entice the kind of communications in which they are most interested. For example, if a chat participant were not interested in cybersex, they would be wise to avoid using a screen name like "SexyLady"; such a screen name would surely evoke innumerable invitations for hot chat. Likewise, if a person were interested in finding a partner for cybersex, they would be wise to approach people with screen names like "M4Fun" or "KinkyChick," while also avoiding chat participants with screen names like "Jesus4life." Regardless, screen names frequently indicate how we may communicate with online chat participants. If a person were interested in chatting with "Jesus4life," he or she would already know

where to start a conversation—the screen name is a cue to inquire on matters of faith.

In everyday life, clothing, hairstyles, accessories, and a huge assortment of various other material and contextual cues convey symbolic information about the kind of people we are. Throughout his work, Erving Goffman magnified the importance of these kinds of symbolic cues, brilliantly analyzing how they are used in a twin process by which people both "give" and "give off" crafted impressions of self. Because these cues are not immediately present in online chat, screen names function as a kind of substitute. Without physical presence, screen names become the only initial means by which chat participants can communicate qualities of selfhood that are normally observed (gender, age, geographic location), discerned by social cues (marital status, social status), or acquired through knowledge of the person (hobbies, interests). In this way, screen names are important components of the presentation of an online self. . . .

As important as screen names are, they are just one facet of the presentation of an online self. In the final analysis, a self does not reside solely in a name but emerges in communication and interaction. In online chat, or anywhere else, a self must be presented, negotiated, and validated in a situated context among others. This process can be routinely observed in almost any chatroom at almost any time; it goes on perpetually. For example, consider the following:

RedWines: Let's have an age/sex check

LeFetes: 24/F

EdsFerret: 6 F

RedWines: 20/f

DocNut: 27/m

LeFetes: How about a state check?

RedWines: MD

EdsFerret: OH

DocNut: MI

LeFetes: FL

EdsFerret: What is your occupation Doctor???

DocNut: psychologist. . . . YIKES!!!

EdsFerrett: Oh, no I already feel like I'm being analyzed :)

DocNut: where ya from EdsFerret??

EdsFerrett: Toledo, Ohio

LeFetes: Hey RedWines, what do you do?

RedWines: I work with retarded adults

RedWines: and what do you do?

LeFetes: I'm a secretary?

LeFetes: . . . and I play the guitar

EdsFerrett: Hello, LeFetes. is that a French name?

LeFetes: Actually I'm Italian

LeFetes: . . . But my moms French

Ball 0: Hi everyone!

EdsFerret: That's neat, do you know French?

LeFetes: me oui moin ami

LeFetes: yes

EdsFerrett: moi aussi aujourd hui.

Ball 0: Any college students here?

AndyCapps: Yes, Miami Univ. in OH

EdsFerrett: The University of Toledo

Ball 0: Univ. CA, San Diego

Ball 0: What are you studying, Andy?

AndyCapps: Accounting. and you?

Ball 0: Psych

Ball 0: I'm learning to mess with people's minds. :)

This brief conversation is characteristic of online chat. Conversations typically begin and continue (on and on) as illustrated above. Because chat environments deny physical presence, nothing can be directly observed—everything must be communicated; all elements of selfhood must be presented to others; one must literally write one's self into existence. This process is not especially difficult; in fact, it seems to happen spontaneously. Once participants have stated basic information about themselves (usually age and gender), conversations quickly develop in relationship to that information and participants reveal more about who they claim to be—often with very playful overtures (also illustrated above).

What are explicit in this process are the *self-claims* that are made. That is, participants claim information that pertains to who they are. For example, even in the short excerpt cited above, self-claims proliferate and a considerable amount of information is conveyed. We have learned, for instance, that LeFetes is a twenty-four-year-old female from Florida. She is a secretary and plays guitar. She considers herself an Italian, but her mother is French. She is (at least to some degree) bilingual, able to communicate in English and at least some French. What is important about these self-claims is not that people make them, but rather, that they have no choice but to make them if they wish to participate in online chat to any meaningful degree. In this way, online chat is organized around what is perhaps the most basic tenet of human interaction.

While there is nothing in online chat that requires it, everything about human interaction is linked to a simple rule: We cannot interact, communicate, or even be in the presence of others and fail to communicate something about who we are. So basic is this rule that in everyday life, the Internet, or anywhere else it is most often taken for granted and hardly noticed. Yet, this rule is absolutely central to the experience of life in society, so much so that it represents the foundation of Erving Goffman's (1959, 1) insightful analysis. . . .

Goffman . . . explore[s] the various "sign vehicles" by which . . . information is conveyed, and how this "sets the stage for a kind of information game—a potentially infinite cycle of concealment, discovery, false revelation, and rediscovery" (1959, 8)—not at all unlike online chat. Thus, on the Internet, like anywhere else, people who are in the presence of others acquire information about each other. Self-claims in online chat are not a departure from, but rather an extension of, this basic principle. In online chat, this information is acquired through screen names, but more importantly, through deliberate self-claims that participants communicate to others in text. The difference is that, due to the absence of physical presence and contextual cues, the self-claims of online chat are much more explicit, blatant, and obvious than the kind of subtle symbolic craftiness by which these claims are made in everyday life. Another important difference comes from the fact that self-claims in online chat are much more difficult to verify; the "rules" of the "information game" to which Goffman (1959, 8) refers are ambiguous and ephemeral. For example, because "she" is not physically present, we cannot know for sure if LeFetes is really a woman, twenty-four years old, Italian, or anything else "she" has claimed, although we cannot always be any more sure of these things in everyday face-to-face interaction either. Thus, other chat participants may accept, challenge, or simply ignore these claims but, generally speaking, unless there are gross discontinuities, self-claims are rarely contested to any significant degree—just as they are rarely contested in everyday life. Instead, when chat participants make self-claims, additional information may be asked and given, inquiries may be made, details may be provided, and in this process a cyberself is

interactively crafted through the course of communication.

In crafting a screen name and interacting with others in chat channels, a "cyberself" is established. As already emphasized, cyberselfhood shares all the essential characteristics of any other self: it is something that is symbolic, presented, negotiated, and validated in a process of communication and interaction with others. Which is to say, cyberselfhood is emergent. As one participant said: "I didn't think through the creation of identity, it just evolved. I just make it up as I go along, as I talk to people. I don't change online; I just evolve." Furthermore, like any other self, a cyberself is situated; in this case, it is situated squarely in a computer-mediated communication environment. Thus, a cyberself may be defined as an emergent set of transient meanings that are crafted by individuals in association with others that temporarily refer to a person who is situated in the ether of electronic space. Or, stated differently, a cyberself refers to the meaning of personhood or experience of personal identity emergent within communication technologies and situated in interactions between people in these contexts. Like any other self, a cyberself is presented and negotiated in an ongoing process of communication. As one interacts with others, a cyberself is momentarily validated. Cyberselves are always situated performances that exist at the surface of a communicated present. To state it bluntly, a cyberself is always whatever is passing for a self at the moment in an electronic computer-mediated context.

Anonymity and Disembodiment: Hyperfluidity and Doubt

Anonymity is an important part of online communication and interaction. . . . [I]n the anonymous environment of online chat, presentation of self is everything; with screen names and self-claims, anyone can present themselves as anyone. To compromise anonymity is to compromise the supreme power to construct any self that one desires at any moment. Thus, as many participants have indicated, anonymity is highly valued because it is the means by which dynamic and fluid cyberselves are constructed:

> Online allows much more freedom—it's anonymous—whatever mood you're in you act upon. We all project an image with others—and are pretty consistent in person—online it doesn't have to be consistent.

> The anonymity factor can be intriguing, it gives one the freedom to chose which room to go into, whom to talk to and when, what to say, to lie or be honest while also knowing that every other user has the same freedom.

> It [anonymity] gives me the opportunity to express myself with no one to stare or wonder and not worry about where I was or with what company I was keeping.

As these statements illustrate, the anonymity of online chat allows participants the option to be someone different. So long as no one knows who you are, it is not necessary to be yourself. As one chat participant explained, "I'm constantly changing my alter-egos and identities on this silly system. You think I could get a life or somethin'." However, online chat pushes the envelope of this self-fluidity even further. Online chat is not only anonymous, but also a uniquely disembodied form of real-time communication. Sitting at a computer keyboard typing messages back and forth, selves are communicated but bodies are nowhere to be seen. With the corporeal body hidden behind the scene of interaction, participants are free to be without being; online chat dislocates selfhood from the constraints of the body; self is not contained or affixed to any physical form. Thus, it is anonymity that allows participants to be someone different, but it is disembodiment that transforms all categories of personhood into possibilities for the self that can be instantly realized, altered, and even

deleted. For this reason, in the anonymous and disembodied environment of online chat, selves are not only fluid, they are *hyperfluid*. Properties of selfhood are transformed from nouns to verbs—self-selected, fluid, and dynamic identity utensils that are more or less useful for the purposes of communication and social interaction. All categories of personhood become pure labels: symbols to think and interact with, not within. Many respondents report this to be a liberating experience of free self-expression:

> Sometimes I pretend I'm a woman, I've also invented experiences. It enables me to play out fantasies. It allows me to take dreams one step closer to reality.

> You can be anything. I may stretch truth and be with whoever I want—no inhibitions.

> Online can be fantasy—You can be anyone you want to be. It also allows some to exercise a fantasy existence that they would never dare in real life.

Although many participants value the freedom of hyperfluidity, these conditions pose certain problems to cantankerous issues of legitimacy. To illustrate, consider the Net folk story of Douglas Adams. According to Net folklore, Adams, having acquired celebrity status for his wildly popular *Hitchhiker's Guide to the Galaxy,* paid a visit to his own online fan club. However, upon arrival he was ruthlessly accused of being an impostor, and no amount of biographical trivia or argument could sway the consensus that he was a fraud. Consequently, Adams was not allowed to participate in his own electronic collectivity of enthusiasts. This Net folk story (of unknown authenticity) illustrates one of many ways that the "freedom to be anything" can become a source of frustration and concern. To further illustrate, consider the following responses to the question "What, if anything, do you dislike about online chat?"

I don't know if people are as they claim to be. Many people are not what they claim to be. Men posing as women, etc!

I enjoy the opportunity to meet people anonymously, but people often misrepresent themselves and turn out to be vastly different than their profile and behavior online would indicate.

Because people can take any identity they want, they do. People who are 50 tell you they are 25, males tell you they're females, etc. People lie about who they are.

There are a lot of very very horny guys out there, and so much so that they sometimes pretend they are women to get the bi or lesbian girls to talk to them. I don't know if that's a sexual game they play for their own fantasies, or if they're just lying assholes.

These problems are perennial to online chat; they are endemic to anonymous and disembodied forms of communication and interaction. In everyday life, someone who is not what he or she appears to be occasionally fools us. But on the Internet the art of the con is reduced to such relatively simple techniques that most people can reasonably manage to use them, and we are all made into potential fools. Looking at it pragmatically, on the Internet an "adult" is anyone who clicks a button that says, "Yes, I am over 18"; a "woman" is anyone with a female screen name; an "African" is anyone who says so; and so on. Each presents potential problems of authenticity that make anonymity and hyperfluidity both a value and a source of frustration.

In spite of these problems, interaction persists through what Erving Goffman (1959, 9–10) calls a "working consensus." That is, "together the participants contribute to a single overall definition of the situation which involves not so much a real agreement as to what exists but rather a real agreement as to whose claims concerning what issues will be temporarily honored." As MacKinnon (1995) notes, because participants are denied direct knowledge of one another, they must suspend or "forget" about the person behind the persona and rely on the individual's word as an accurate representation of self. In fact, as Douglas Adams learned, the ultimate challenge to online interaction is the possibility that some participants will *not* suspend doubt. In this way, there is a certain epistemology [or theory of knowledge] at work in online chat, and failure to interact with others on the basis of that epistemology may be the most disruptive thing a chat participant can do. This epistemology is founded on the obvious fact that in computer-mediated environments, representations are all that exist, and since there is no way to conclusively determine if representations adhere to what is true or real in the off-line world all presentations of self are potentially suspicious—there is no way of sifting out the "real" from the "fake." Thus, in order for interaction to proceed, it is necessary for participants to suspend doubt and formulate a "working consensus" which identifies not so much what is "real" but what claims concerning which issues will be temporarily honored. Several participants noted this process:

> Question: *If you don't actually meet the person, how do you know if they are what they claim to be?*
>
> Answer: *You don't! That's part of the appeal! Some u meet some u don't but u get right to the heart of an issue without getting caught up. If u don't meet what difference does it make? As long as you have a good time, who cares!*
>
> Question: *How can you tell if the people you meet are "genuine" or "fake"?*
>
> Answer: *I have yet to be disappointed. I just go on instincts, trust, and faith. Mostly I go on how they treat me and what I pick up along the way.*

By agreeing on a working consensus, whether aware of this agreement or not, chat participants initiate a form of engagement—a willing suspension of disbelief. . . . Chat participants generally understand that cyberselves are dramatic enactments. Or, in other words, participants are acutely aware that in online chat people enact self-performances that, like any other dramatic performance, are not necessarily real. However, to enjoy the drama (the chat), one must at least temporarily suspend knowledge that it's all "pretend"—hence the dramaturgical epistemology of online chat. This suspension of disbelief affords users a certain privilege of engagement where *"pretending that the action is real* affords us the thrill [of the drama], *knowing the action is pretend* saves us from the pain of [reality]" (Laurel 1993, 113, emphasis in original). . . .

Through engagement, participants can experience the representational and dramatic world of online chat directly without disruption or distraction. This requires that participants proceed with interaction under the assumption that what you see is what you get, and the representation is all there is. . . .

Communication Play: Self-Games and the Multiplicity of Cyberselves

Not only can online chat participants present one cyberself, they can also have multiple screen names—each independent of the others—providing an opportunity to construct multiple anonymous cyberselves. As several chat participants explained, multiple screen names allow for multiple cyberselves that are often divided according to various motives for interaction and defining characteristics of selfhood:

> One name . . . is known only to my closest online friends. I use that name when I don't want to be bothered by strangers. The other names are used when I go in to chat rooms or private rooms where I wouldn't normally want my friends to find me.

I actively use four of my five screen names . . . each screen name represents a different persona.

> (Q) *How many screen names do you currently use?*
>
> (A) 3
>
> (Q) *Explain why you use more than one screen name:*
>
> (A) I am curious to see other people's different reactions to various "personalities."

This multiplicity of anonymous self-enactments often results in communications that may be metaphorically called an ongoing "self-game." That is, online chat participants often actively and consciously play with multiple representations of who they are in these . . . online environments. After all, online interaction is a pastime that is usually done for the purposes of leisure and enjoyment, and thus, we should not be surprised that online interaction and cyberself enactments often become a literal form of communication play. As some chat participants explained:

> Some people take this as a total game—I call it Nintendo for adults!!

> I'm sure people modify who they are online, it's part of the game I guess, the mystery and fun of discovery.

> I have a different persona for each moniker. One is very sexy, but I have one who is grouchy and a real bitch. Another sarcastic, and another is very sweet. I know it sounds very schizophrenic, but actually, it is a lot of fun.

As these responses suggest, for many participants online chat is a communication game that is all about "playing with yourself" (in a literal rather than figurative sense). As one chat participant appropriately explained, "Like anything else, online is a game . . . isn't everything a game? Only here, I play with who I am." Furthermore, in the self-games of online chat, there is little commitment to any given self. In online chat, one's self is a fluid horizon of possibilities, and for many participants that is precisely what makes it fun. Each user has the power to create an unlimited self through interaction with others, and toying with these immense possibilities is what the game is all about. Several chat participants indicated this when they said:

> It's kinda like split personalities. Shows that someone is only who they want to be when it's most comfortable. . . .

> I think if a person has a good imagination the skyl's] the limit—you can become anything you want!

As these respondents clearly indicate, online chat often acquires game-like qualities. If, however, we are to adopt a game metaphor for understanding selfhood in online chat, it is important to qualify [that metaphor]. . . . [P]layfulness does not imply that all is fun and games. Persons can (and do) form deeply meaningful interpersonal relationships in the course of playful encounters. Playfulness does not eliminate capacities for such things as commitment and trust but merely makes such qualities playable. . . . [W]e would be wise to avoid a "play" versus "serious" dichotomy. . . . Serious play is a prevailing standard of any gaming activity, and just because some people are "playing" does not mean they may not take the activity seriously. Like all kinds of games, much online interaction can be found to be playfully serious. . . .

In summary, when online, just as in face-to-face situations, a self emerges through interaction with others. The structure of online chat is multiple and simultaneous. Not surprisingly, so too is cyberselfhood. Parallel to the multiple and simultaneous channels of online communication exist a multiplicity of cyberselves. Each cyberself is an anonymous set of meanings associated with a screen name that may be presented as virtually anything. These interactions become a form of dramatic communication play. . . .

Conclusions

Online chat is a unique form of communication and interaction situated in a computer-mediated environment that alters the significance of time, space, physical location, and the corporeal body as interaction variables. It is the *form* of interaction that transforms social spheres into new online environments, with new patterns of social interaction. Furthermore, it is the form of online chat that allows for a fluid multiplicity of cyberselves that may be realized or deleted at any moment. . . .

[O]nline chat reveals two quintessential characteristics that are essential to understanding this form of communication and interaction: it is uniquely *dislocated* and *disembodied*. Online chat and most other forms of computer mediated communication occur in a "place" without geographic "space"; in a real-time communicative environment without corporeal co-presence. Dislocated from the constraints of geographic location and the corporeal body, online chat is an ultimate context for self-multiplicity—a place for the experience of a no-holds-barred orgy of extreme potential self-fluidity. . . .

References

Bechar-Israeli, H. 1995. "From <Bonehead> to <cLoNehEAd>: Nicknames, Play and Identity on Internet Relay Chat." *Journal of Computer-Mediated Communication*, 1 (2), http://shum.huji.ac.il/jcmc/vol1/issue2/vol1no.2.html.

Goffman, Erving. 1959. *The Presentation of Self in Everyday Life*. Garden City, NY: Doubleday Anchor.

Laurel, B. 1993. *Computers as Theater*. Reading, PA: Addison-Wesley.

MacKinnon, R. 1995. "Searching for the Leviathan in Usenet." In *Cybersociety: Computer-Mediated Communication and Community*, (ed. by S. Jones), pp. 112–137. Thousand Oaks, CA: Sage.

14

The Gloried Self

Patricia Adler and
Peter Adler

This selection dramatically illustrates the interrelation between public self-images and individuals' self-concepts or sense of their "true" selves. Patricia and Peter Adler describe how sudden celebrity transformed the self-conceptions of players for a highly successful college basketball program. These players not only saw themselves reflected in others' treatment of them, but also on the television screen and in the pages of newspapers and magazines. The Adlers remind us that others' reactions to an individual are not the only source of self-images today. For celebrities at least, the mass media are also a source of stylized and often exaggerated self-images.

The Adlers also remind us that individuals are not passively molded by socially reflected or media images of themselves. With the encouragement of their coaches, the players attempted to resist the influence of both the hero worship by fans and media hype. Ultimately, however, the glory was too intoxicating and the media portrayals too seductive. What started out as a mere act to give reporters and fans what they expected became a trap. The more effectively the players presented themselves as the media portrayed them, the more the players thought of themselves in those terms.

As the Adlers observe, such celebrity and glory are not without cost. An individual's self-concept is usually multi-dimensional. It consists of an organized complex of social identities and corresponding self-evaluations. We each may think of ourselves as serious students, good friends, insen-

sitive sons or daughters, relatively unattractive romantic partners, mediocre athletes, and so on. We may consider some of these identities more important than others, but we consider all dimensions of who and what we "really" are. It was just such multi-dimensionality that the basketball players sacrificed for glory. Their identity as basketball players engulfed other dimensions of their self-concepts. The Adlers describe how the brilliant glory of socially reflected and media self-images can blind an individual to other prior or possible identities. They leave us to ponder the question, what might happen to such an individual's self-concept when his or her glory fades?

In this paper we describe and analyze a previously unarticulated form of self-identity: the "gloried" self, which arises when individuals become the focus of intense interpersonal and media attention, leading to their achieving celebrity. The articulation of the gloried self not only adds a new concept to our self-repertoire but also furthers our insight into self-concept formation in two ways: it illustrates one process whereby dynamic contradictions between internal and external pressures become resolved, and it highlights the ascendance of an unintended self-identity in the face of considerable resistance.

The development of the gloried self is an outgrowth of individuals becoming imbued with celebrity. . . . Development of a gloried self is caused in part by the treatment of individuals' selves as objects by others. A "public person" is created, usually by the media, which differs from individuals' private personas. These public images are rarely as intricate or as complex as individuals' [personal] selves; often, they draw on stereotypes or portray individuals in extreme fashion to accentuate their point. Yet the power of these media portrayals, reinforced by face-to-face encounters with people who hold these images, often causes individuals to objectify their selves to themselves. Individuals thus become initially alienated from themselves through the separation of their self-concept from the conception of their selves held by others. Ultimately, they resolve this disparity and reduce their alienation by changing their self-images to bridge the gap created by others' perceptions of them, even though they may fight this development as it occurs.

Characteristically, the gloried self is a greedy self, seeking to ascend in importance and to cast aside other self-dimensions as it grows. It is an intoxicating and riveting self, which overpowers other aspects of the individual and seeks increasing reinforcement to fuel its growth. Yet at the same time, its surge and display violate societal mores of modesty in both self-conception and self-presentation. Individuals thus become embroiled in inner conflict between their desire for recognition, flattery, and importance and the inclination to keep feeding this self-affirming element, and the socialization that urges them to fight such feelings and behavioral impulses. That the gloried self succeeds in flourishing, in spite of [the] individuals' struggle against it, testifies to its inherent power and its drive to eclipse other self-dimensions.

Drawing on ethnographic data gathered in a college athletics setting, we discuss the creation and the character of the gloried self, showing its effects on the individuals in whom it develops. . . . Over a five-year period (1980–1985), we conducted a participant-observation study of a major college basketball program. . . . The research was conducted at a medium-sized (6,000 students) private university (hereafter referred to as "the University") in the mid-south central portion of the United States, with a predominantly white, suburban, middle-class student body. The basketball program was ranked in the top 40 of Division I NCAA schools throughout our research, and in the top 20 for most of two seasons. The team played in post-season tournaments every year, and in four complete seasons won approximately four times as many games as it lost. Players

generally were recruited from the surrounding area; they were predominantly black (70 percent) and ranged from lower to middle class. . . . We analyze [these] athletes' experiences and discuss the aggrandizing effects of celebrity in fostering the gloried self's ascent to prominence. Then we look at the consequent changes and diminishments in the self that occur as the price of this self-aggrandizement. . . .

The Experience of Glory

Experiencing glory was exciting, intoxicating, and riveting. Two self-dimensions were either created or expanded in the athletes we studied: the reflected self and the media self. . . .

The Reflected Self

As a result of the face-to-face interactions between team members and people they encountered through their role as college athletes, the athletes' impressions of themselves were modified and changed. As Cooley (1902) and Mead (1934) were the first to propose, individuals engage in role-taking; their self-conceptions are products of social interaction, affected by the reflected impressions of others. According to Cooley (1902), these "looking-glass" selves are formed through a combination of cognitive and affective forces; although individuals react intellectually to the impressions they perceive others are forming about them, they also develop emotional reactions about these judgments. Together, these reactions are instrumental in shaping their self-images. . . .

The forging and modification of reflected selves began as team members perceived how people *treated* them; subsequently, they formed *reactions* to that treatment. One of the first things they all noticed was that they were sought intensely by strangers. Large numbers of people, individually and in groups, wanted to be near them, to get their autographs, to touch them, and to talk to them. People treated them with awe and respect. One day, for example, the head coach walked out of his office and found a woman waiting for him. As he turned towards her, she threw herself in front of him and began to kiss his feet, all the while telling him what a great man he was. More commonly, fans who were curious about team matters approached players, trying to engage them in conversation. These conversations sometimes made the players feel awkward, because, although they wanted to be polite to their fans, they had little to say to them. Carrying on an interaction was often difficult. As one player said:

> People come walking up to you, and whether they're timid or pushy, they still want to talk. It's like, here's their hero talking face-to-face with them, and they want to say anything just so they can have a conversation with them. It's *hero-worshipping*. But what do you actually say to your hero when you see him?

These interactions, then, often took the form of ritualized pseudo-conversations, in which players and their fans offered each other stylized but empty words.

Many fans [identified the players] socially and expect[ed] them to respond in kind. Players found themselves thrust into a "psuedo-intimacy" (Bensman and Lilienfeld 1979) with these fans, who had seen them so often at games and on television. Yet their relationship with the players was one-sided; fans often expected players to reciprocate their feelings of intimacy. As a result of their celebrity, team members . . . were open to engagement in personal interaction with individuals whom they did not know at all.

Players also found themselves highly prized in interacting with boosters (financial supporters of the team). Boosters showered all players with invitations to their houses for team meetings or dinner. They fought jealously to have players seen with them or gossiped about as having been in their houses. It

soon became apparent to players that boosters derived social status from associating with them. . . . This situation caused players to recognize that they were "glory bearers," so filled with glory that they could confer it on anyone by their mere presence. They experienced a sense of the "Midas touch": They had an attribute (fame) that everybody wanted and which could be transmitted. Their ability to cast glory onto others and their desirability to others because of this ability became an important dimension of their new, reflected self-identity.

The Media Self

A second dimension of the self created from the glory experience was influenced largely by media portrayals. . . . Most of the athletes who came to the University had received some media publicity in high school (68 percent); but the national level of the print and video coverage they received after arriving, coupled with the intensity of the constant focus, caused them to develop more compelling and more salient media selves than they had possessed previously.

Radio, television, and newspaper reporters covering the team often sought out athletes for "human interest" stories. These features presented media-framed angles that cast athletes into particular roles and tended to create new dimensions of their selves. Images were created from a combination of individuals' actual behavior and reporters' ideas of what made good copy. Thus, through media coverage, athletes were cast into molds that frequently were distorted or exaggerated reflections of their behavior and self-conceptions.

Team members, for whom the media had created roles, felt as if they had to live up to these portrayals. For instance, two players were depicted as "good students"—shy, quiet, religious, and diligent. Special news features emphasized their outstanding traits, illustrating how they went regularly to class, were humanitarian, and cared about graduating. Yet one of them lamented:

> Other kids our age, they go to the fair and they walk around with a beer in their hand, or a cigarette; but if me and Dan were to do that, then people would talk about that. We can't go over to the clubs, or hang around, without it relaying back to Coach. We can't even do things around our teammates, because they expect us to be a certain way. The media has created this image of us as the "good boys," and now we have to live up to it.

Other players (about 20 percent) were embraced for their charismatic qualities; they had naturally outgoing personalities and the ability to excite a crowd. These players capitalized on the media coverage, exaggerating their antics to gain attention and fame. Yet the more they followed the media portrayal, the more likely it was to turn into a caricature of their selves. One player described how he felt when trapped by his braggart media self:

> I used to like getting in the paper. When reporters came around, I would make those Mohammed Ali type outbursts—I'm gonna do this, I'm gonna do that. And they come around again, stick a microphone in your face, 'cause they figure somewhere Washington will have another outburst. But playing that role died out in me. I think sometimes the paper pulled out a little too much from me that wasn't me. But people seen me as what the paper said, and I had to play that role.

Particular roles notwithstanding, all the players shared the media-conferred sense of self as celebrity. Raised to the status of stars, larger than life, they regularly read their names and statements in the newspaper, saw their faces on television, or heard themselves whispered about on campus. One team member described the consequences of this celebrity:

> We didn't always necessarily agree with the way they wrote about us in the paper, but people who saw us expected us to be like what they read there. A lot of times it made us feel uncomfortable, acting like that, but we had to act like they expected us to, for the team's sake. We had to act like this was what we was really like.

Ironically, however, the more they interacted with people through their dramaturgically induced media selves, the more many of the team members felt familiar and comfortable with those selves ("We know what to do, we don't have to think about it no more"). The media presented the selves and the public believed in them, so the athletes continued to portray them. Even though they attempted to moderate these selves, part of them pressed for their legitimacy and acceptance. Over time, the athletes believed these portrayals increasingly and transformed their behavior into more than mere "impression management" (Goffman 1959). . . . [They] went through a gradual process of . . . becoming more engrossed or more deeply involved in their media selves. The recurrent social situations of their everyday lives served as the foils against which both their public and their private selves developed. The net effect of having these selves placed upon them and of interacting through them with others was that athletes eventually integrated them into their core self.

Self-Aggrandizement

Athletes were affected profoundly by encounters with the self-images reflected onto them by others, both in person and through the media. It was exciting and gratifying to be cast as heroes. Being presented with these images and feeling obligated to interact with people through them, athletes added a new self to their repertoire: a glorified self. This self had a greater degree of aggrandizement than their previous identities. The athletes may have dreamed of glory, but until now they had never formed a structured set of relationships with people who accorded it to them. Yet although they wanted to accept and enjoy this glory, to allow themselves to incorporate it into a full-blown self-identity, they felt hesitant and guilty. They wrestled with the competing forces of their desires for extravagant pleasure and pride and the normative guidelines of society, which inhibited these desires. The athletes' struggle with factors inhibiting and enhancing their self-aggrandizement shows how and why they ultimately developed gloried selves.

Inhibiting Factors

Players knew they had to be careful both about feeling important and about showing these feelings. The norms of our society dictate a more modest, more self-effacing stance. Consequently the players worked hard to suppress their growing feelings of self-aggrandizement in several ways. First, they drew on their own feelings of *fear* and *insecurity*. Although it violated the norms of their peer culture to reveal these feelings, most of the athletes we interviewed (92 percent) had doubts or worries about their playing abilities or futures.

Second, they tried to *discount* the flattery of others as exaggerated or false. . . . Athletes . . . tended to evaluate their behavior less globally than did their audience and to interpret their successes as based less on their own outstanding characteristics than on some complex interaction of circumstances.

Third, the athletes' feelings of importance and superiority were constrained by the actions of the coach and by the norms of their peer subculture. For his part, the coach tried to keep players' self-aggrandizement in check by *puncturing* them whenever he thought they were becoming too "puffed" (conceited). He "dragged" (criticized, mocked) them both in team meetings and in individual sessions, trying to achieve the right balance of confidence and humility.

In addition, players punctured their teammates by ridiculing each other publicly in their informal sessions in the dorms. Each one claimed to be the best player on the team, and had little praise for others. The athletes did not actually think their teammates had no talent; rather, the peer subculture allowed little room for "glory passing." As a result, except for the braggarts (about 20 percent of the group), none of the players expressed in public how good they felt and how much they enjoyed being treated as stars. Instead, they tried largely to suppress the feelings of excitement, intoxication, and aggrandizement, not to let themselves be influenced by the reflected sense of glory. As one player remarked:

> You feel it coming up on you and you know you got to fight it. You can't be letting your head get all out of control.

Fourth, the coach helped to *normalize* the athletes' experiences and reactions by placing them in the occupational perspective. Being adulated was part of the job, he believed, and this job was no more special than any other. . . . He conveyed this sense of occupational duty to his players and assistants. Like him, they had to "get with the program," to play to the public and help support people's sense of involvement with the team. In public, then, players feigned intimacy with total strangers and allowed themselves to be worshiped, meanwhile being told that this was merely a job.

Enhancing Factors

Yet as tired as they were, as repetitive as this behavior became, the athletes knew that this job was unlike any other. The excitement, the centrality, and the secrecy, which did not exist in the everyday world made this arena different. As one assistant coach explained:

> The times were exciting. There was always something going on, something happening, some new event occurring each day. We felt like we were newsmakers, we were important. We touched

so many more lives, were responsible for so many more people, and so many more people cared, wanted to know something from us. It was very intoxicating. Everyone even close felt the excitement, just from elbow-rubbing.

Athletes also were influenced in their developing feelings of self-importance by the concrete results of their behavior. . . . [T]hey were able to observe the outcomes of their behavior and to use them to form and modify assessments of their selves. Thus, when the team was winning, their feelings of importance, grandeur, talent, and invincibility soared; when they lost, they felt comparatively incompetent, powerless, and small. Because the team's record throughout our research period was overwhelmingly successful, team members reviewed the outcomes of their contests and the season records, and concluded that they were fine athletes and local heroes. . . .

One result of receiving such intense personal interest and media attention was that players developed "big heads." They were admired openly by so many people and their exploits were regarded as so important that they began to feel more notable. Although they tried to remain modest, all of the players found that their celebrity caused them to lose control over their sense of self-importance. As one player observed:

> You try not to let it get away from you. You feel it coming all around you. People building you up. You say to yourself that you're the same guy you always were and that nothing has changed. But what's happening to you is so unbelievable. Even when you were sitting at home in high school imagining what college ball would be like, you could not imagine this. All the media, all the fans, all the pressure. And all so suddenly, with no time to prepare or ease into it. Doc, it got to go to your head. You try to fight it, and you think you do, but you got to be affected by it, you got to get a big head.

Although the players fought to normalize and diminish their feelings of self-aggrandizement, they were swept away in spite of themselves by the allure of glory, to varying degrees. Their sense of glory fed their egos, exciting them beyond their ability to manage or control it. They had never before been such glory-generating figures, had never felt the power that was now invested in them by the crowds or worshipful fans. They developed deep, powerful feelings affirming how important they had become and how good it felt.

All the members of the University's basketball program developed gloried selves, although the degree varied according to several factors. To some extent, their aggrandizement and glorification were affected by the level of attention they received. Individuals with more talent, who held central roles as team stars, were the focus of much media and fan attention. Others, who possessed the social and interpersonal attributes that made them good subjects for reporters, fruitful topics of conversation for boosters, and charismatic crowd pleasers, also received considerable notice. In addition, those who were more deeply invested in the athletic role were more likely to develop stronger gloried selves. They looked to this arena for their greatest rewards and were the most susceptible to its aggrandizing influence. Finally, individuals resisted or yielded to the gloried self depending on personal attributes. Those who were . . . more modest and more self-effacing tried harder to neutralize the effects and had more difficulty in forging grandiose self-conceptions than those who were boastful or pretentious.

The Price of Glory

Athletes' self-aggrandizement, as we have seen, was a clear consequence of the glory experience. Self-diminishment was a corresponding and concomitant effect. Athletes paid a price for becoming gloried in the form of self-narrowing or self-erosion. They sacrificed both the multi-dimensionality of their current selves and the potential breadth of their future selves; various dimensions of their identities were either diminished, detached, or somehow changed as a result of their increasing investment in their gloried selves.

Self-Immediacy

One of the first consequences of the ascent of the gloried self was a loss of future orientation. In all their lives, from the most celebrated player to the least, these individuals had never experienced such a level of excitement, adulation, intensity, and importance. These sensations were immediate and real, flooding all team members' daily lives and overwhelming them. As a result, their focus turned toward their present situation and became fixed on it.

This reaction was caused largely by the absorbing quality of the moment. During the intensity of the season (and to a lesser extent during the off-season), their basketball obligations and involvements were prominent. When they were lying exhausted in their hotel rooms, hundreds of miles from campus, or on their beds after a grueling practice, the responsibilities of school seemed remote and distant. One player described his state of preoccupation:

> I've got two finals tomorrow and one the next day. I should be up in the room studying right now. But how can I get my mind on that when I know I've got to guard Michael Jordan tomorrow night?

Their basketball affairs were so much more pressing, not only in the abstract but also because other people made specific demands on them, that it was easy to relegate all other activities to a position of lesser importance.

Many players who had entered college expecting to prepare themselves for professional or business careers were distracted from those plans and relinquished them (71 percent). The demands of the basketball schedule became the central focus of their lives; the associated physical, social, and professional dimensions took precedence over all other concerns. Despite their knowledge that only two percent of major-college players eventually play in the NBA (Coakley 1986; Leonard and Reyman 1988), they all clung to the hope that they would be the ones to succeed. One of the less outstanding athletes on the team expressed the players' commonly held attitude toward their present and their future:

> You have to have two goals, a realistic and an unrealistic. Not really an unrealistic, but a dream. We all have that dream. I know the odds are against it, but I feel realistically that I can make the NBA. I have to be in the gym every day, lift weights, more or less sacrifice my life to basketball. A lot.

To varying degrees, all players ceased to think about their futures other than as a direct continuation of the present. They were distracted from long-term planning and deferment of gratification in favor of the enormous immediate gratification they received from their fans and from celebrity. What emerged was a self that primarily thought about only one source of gratification—athletic fame—and that imagined and planned for little else.

The players imagined vaguely that if they did not succeed as professional athletes, a rich booster would provide them with a job. Although they could observe older players leaving the program without any clear job opportunities, they were too deeply absorbed in the present to recognize the situation. Ironically, they came to college believing that it would expand their range of opportunities . . . yet they sacrificed the potential breadth of their future selves by narrowing their range of vision to encompass only that which fed their immediate hunger for glory.

Diminished Awareness

Locked into a focus on the present and stuck with a vision of themselves that grew from their celebrity status, all team members, to varying degrees, became desensitized to the concerns of their old selves. They experienced a heightened sensitivity and reflectivity toward the gloried self and a loss of awareness of the self-dimensions unrelated to glory. Nearly everyone they encountered interacted with them, at least in part, through their gloried selves. As this self-identity was fed and expanded, their other selves tended to atrophy. At times the athletes seemed to be so blinded by their glory that they would not look beyond it. . . .

This diminished awareness had several consequences. First, in becoming so deeply absorbed in their gloried selves, athletes relegated non-athletic concerns to secondary, tertiary, or even lesser status. These concerns included commitments to friends, relatives, and school. For example, many athletes (54 percent) began each semester vowing that it would be different this time, but each semester they "forgot" to go to class. Reflecting on this occurrence, one player mused:

> You don't think, it's not like you goin' to be a bad boy today, or you goin' to pull the wool over someone's eyes. You just plain ol' forget. You sleep through it.

For a while the athletes could ignore the facts and the consequences of their behavior, but this denial wore thin as the semester progressed, and they fell behind more noticeably. Then they moved into a stage of neutralization, blaming boring professors, stupid courses, exhaustion, coaches' demands, or injury.

Second, their new personas were expanded, even in their interactions with friends. Players referred to this situation as being "puffed," and each accused the others of it:

> Sometimes I can't even talk to Rich no more. He's so puffed in the head you can't get him to talk sense, he's lost touch with reality. It's like it's full of jello in there and he's talking a bunch of hot air.

What the athletes sensed as filling the heads of these puffed players was the self-image created by the glory experience.

Third, some athletes plunged into various acts because these acts fed their gloried selves (60 percent). They distanced themselves from their old values and took potentially career-ending risks. For example, when a player who filled a substitute role was "red-shirted" (excused from play without losing his scholarship or expending a year of eligibility) for the year because of injury, he was willing to give up this desirable and protective status when asked to do so by the coach. He was convinced easily, despite his secondary position, that the team could not function without him; like others, he blocked off the warnings and the caution that stemmed from an awareness of other needs and interests. The same lack of reflectiveness and self-awareness prevented players with chronic injuries, those who were hobbling and could no longer jump, from admitting to themselves that their playing days were over, that their gloried selves had to retire.

Self-Detachment

For some team members and at times for all, the distinction between their gloried selves and their other selves became more than a separation; the distance and the lack of reflectiveness grew into detachment. In the most extreme cases (18 percent), some athletes developed a barrier between this new, exciting, glamorous self and their old, formerly core selves. They found it increasingly difficult to break through that barrier. They experienced a dualism between these selves, as if occasionally they represented discrete individuals and not multiple facets of the same person; at times, they shifted back and forth between them. Ultimately, the different images became so disparate that they could not be fused, or else individuals became so deeply involved in their gloried selves that they lost control over their efforts to constrain and integrate them. The more these individuals interacted with others through this self, the more it developed a life and a destiny of its own.

For instance, one of the most popular players on the team developed a gloried self that was tied to his self-proclaimed nickname "Apollo." Charismatic and enthusiastic whenever he was in public, he generated enormous amounts of attention and adulation through his outgoing personality. On the court he would work the crowd, raising their emotions, exhorting them to cheer, and talking brashly to opposing players. Reporters thronged to him, because he was colorful, lively, and quotable. In public settings, he was always referred to by his nickname.

Yet, although this player deliberately had created the Apollo identity, eventually it began to control him. It led him to associate at times with people who valued him only for that self; it surfaced in interactions with friends when he had not called it forth. It led him to detach himself from responsibility for things he did while in that persona. As he reported:

> I had a summer job working for some booster at a gas station. I figured he wanted to show off that he had Apollo pumping his gas. I'd go into my act for the customers and the other employees, how fine I was, lotta times show up late or not at all. I figured he wouldn't fire me. But he did. Looking back, I can't see how I just up and blew that job. That ain't like me. That was Apollo done that, not me.

Other team members, who did not go so far as to create separate identities for their gloried selves, still experienced feelings of bifurcation. Their former selves were mundane and commonplace compared to their new, vibrant selves. These contrasting selves called forth different kinds of character and behavior. At times, the team members found it difficult to think of themselves as integrated persons, incorporating these divergent identities into one overall self. Feelings of fragmentation haunted them.

Discussion

As we have shown, high school graduates entered the world of college athletics and underwent a fundamental transformation. Thrust into a whirlwind of adulation and celebrity, they reacted to the situation through a process of simultaneous self-aggrandizement and self-diminishment. The gloried self expanded, overpowering all . . . other . . . self-dimensions; it became the aspect of self in which they lived and invested. They immersed themselves single-mindedly in this portion of their selves, and the feedback and gratification they derived from this identity dwarfed their other identities. They had not anticipated this situation, but gradually, as they were drawn into the arena of glory, they were swept away by stardom and fame. Their commitment to the athletic self grew beyond anything they had ever imagined or intended. Once they had experienced the associated power and centrality, they were reluctant to give them up. They discarded their other aspirations, lost touch with other dimensions of their selves (even to the point of detachment), and plunged themselves into the gloried self.

Athletes' gloried selves arose originally as dramaturgical constructions. Other people, through the media or face to face, conferred these identities on athletes through their expectations of them. Athletes responded by playing the corresponding roles because of organizational loyalty, interactional obligations, and enjoyment. Yet in contrast to other roles, which can be played casually and without consequence, athletes' actions in these roles increased their commitment and their self-involvement in them and made the athletes "more or less unavailable for alternative lines of action" (Kornhauser 1962:321). The gloried self not only influenced athletes' future behavior but also transformed their self-conceptions and identities. . . . [This] entire process . . . illustrates the relationship between dramaturgical roles and real selves, showing how the former comes to impinge upon and influence the latter.

References

Bensman, Joseph and Robert Lilienfeld. 1979. *Between Public and Private*. New York: Free Press.

Coakley, Jay J. 1986. *Sport in Society*. 3d ed. St. Louis: Mosby.

Cooley, Charles H. 1902. *Human Nature and Social Order*. New York: Scribners.

Goffman, Erving. 1959. *The Presentation of Self in Everyday Life*. New York: Doubleday.

Kornhauser, William. 1962. "Social Bases of Political Commitment: A Study of Liberals and Radicals." Pp. 321–339 in *Human Behavior and Social Processes*, ed. A. M. Rose. Boston: Houghton Mifflin.

Leonard, Wilbert and Jonathon Reyman. 1988. "The Odds of Attaining Professional Athlete Status: Refining the Computations." *Sociology of Sports Journal* 5, 162–169.

Mead, George Herbert. 1934. *Mind, Self, and Society*. Chicago: University of Chicago Press.

15

Narratives of Self in Codependents Anonymous

Leslie Irvine

In the preceding selection on the presentation of self, Goffman implies that the self must be dramatically realized on each and every occasion of social interaction. Yet, that is not how most individuals in this and many other societies subjectively experience themselves. They believe that they have a true, or core, self that remains fundamentally the same over time, across different social situations, and regardless of the particular social roles they perform. In this selection, Leslie Irvine demonstrates that such consistent and core selves are narrative accomplishments. They are products of stories we tell one another and ourselves that coherently integrate our varied social experiences around common themes. Such narratives of the self are not just about the individuals who tell them. In order to be convincing to ourselves and others, they must be anchored in social relationships or what Irvine calls institutions—organized patterns of collective activities. Social relationships and institutions provide the formulas or coherent themes for our narratives of self, supporting characters, and receptive audiences. The narrative accomplishment of the self is most apparent when individuals' self narratives lose their social moorings, and they must find new relationships and institutions in which to anchor new and revised stories about themselves.

That was the case with the members of Co-dependents Anonymous (CoDA) whom Irvine studied. As she notes, individuals commonly came to CoDA when an important relationship had ended. They had lost the social relational anchor for the stories that had sustained their prior self and needed to repair the narrative damage. CoDA provided them with accounts for their failed relationships, a formula for new narratives of self, and a receptive audience for those revised stories. Members of CoDA were a receptive audience for one another's revised narratives of self as long as a member followed the CoDA narrative formula. Accuracy mattered less than coherently integrating the particular details of the individual's life around the common themes of abusive childhoods, dysfunctional relations, and the like.

Yet, as Irvine argues, it was not enough for members of CoDA merely to tell a story of a codependent self and convince others of that story in order to accomplish a new self. They had to convince themselves of this new narrative of self. It had to become part of their internal conversation. For example, Irvine herself learned how to tell a formula story of a codependent self and convince others of it, but she never defined herself as "codependent" because she did not believe the story that she was telling. She had another story to tell herself that was firmly anchored in her University and with her colleagues there: She was a sociologist conducting research.

The CoDA members' narrative accomplishment of self is particularly obvious because it is so central to the groups' meetings. Yet, like them, we all accomplish consistent and coherent selves through the stories we tell one another and ourselves. We emphasize parts of our past, creatively revise others, and ignore still others when telling the stories about ourselves that we do. And, like the members of Codependents Anonymous, we learn how to tell those stories to others and depend on them to accept or at least not challenge our stories. This is another way that the self is created, maintained, and sometimes changed through social interaction which, in turn, shapes how we interact with ourselves through internal conversations.

Selfhood is a narrative accomplishment. The self is the premise and the result of the stories people tell about themselves—especially those they tell *to* themselves. Numerous ideas compete with this narrative image. Selfhood has been equated with the soul or spirit, versions of which include the "inner child" of contemporary self-help discourses. For Goffman (1959) and those influenced by him, the self is less permanent but equally elusive. It is the product of action, a quality attributed to a social actor after a competent "performance."

This idea may appeal to a small number of academics, but many more people seem to find the possibility incomprehensible, if not terrifying. . . . In opposition to subjective experience, it suggests that nothing remains beyond the performance. . . . Of course, interaction plays a vital part in shaping the self. There is, however, a sense that, at the core of one's overlapping roles, one is more than the sum of one's roles. This is the side of selfhood that I want to understand.

The self is more than the sum of its parts, and narrative is what allows it to *be* more. In speaking of "having" a self or "finding" oneself, people tell themselves a story that there is indeed a self to "have" or to "find." . . . These are not simply stories *about* the self; they are, as Arthur Frank writes, "the self's medium of being" (1995, p. 53). The experience of "having" a self consists of an "internal conversation" (Gagnon 1992) about who one is. Selfhood is inseparable from narrative, and the most powerful narratives—at least in this culture—are those that portray it as "real," an entity or possession.

Insisting that the self is accomplished narratively does not mean that I think that people simply go around making up stories about themselves. Narratives of the self are not free-floating. Neither are they whimsical. Of course, some people *do* invent elaborate lies about themselves, but we call them confidence men or bullshit artists, or we medicate them and avoid them. That is not the kind of storytelling to which I refer. Rather, I am referring to an enduring and convincing (or at least plausible) story about who one is. The story has variations and digressions, but along a core theme that one is, as William James (1910) put it, "in some peculiarly subtle sense the same." One's stories persuade one's audience that one "is" a particular kind of person. When one is one's own audience, the telling amounts to "having" a self.

Good stories must meet several requirements. They must fulfill their audiences' expectations for what counts as convincing. They must be coherent, drawing together disparate elements that end up seeming inherently related. They must make events seem to lead to one another. In addition, they must have satisfying endings—not happy endings, necessarily, but endings that provide resolution while leaving enough ambiguity to enliven listeners' imaginations. Good stories—stories that work—offer a reality that is, to use the words of a U2 song, "even better than the real thing." For listeners, stories make experiences possible that would, in "real life," be impractical, dangerous, time-consuming, costly, or otherwise impossible. When told well, stories offer a vicarious experience that is satisfying in ways that the actual experience would not—or could not—be.

In much the same way, the narrative self is "even better than the real thing." If a "real" self *did* exist, it would be inaccessible and incomprehensible, at moments so painfully intense and so raw as to offer no practical guidance for behavior. But the self-storyteller uses a set of narrative techniques that yield a product that is better than authentic. As a story, the self can be convincing, coherent, and have a satisfying ending. Self-stories can also have sufficient ambiguity to accommodate lives that are in progress and subject to change. It is the unique capacity of human beings to meet both sets of requirements—to tell good stories that can also accommodate uncertainty—and it is the power of institutions that allows them to do so. By "institutions," I mean patterns of activities organized around a common goal. Institutions make self-stories consistent and convincing by providing formulas, supporting characters, and opportunities to tell one's stories. One way to test this claim is to examine instances in which people lose the institutional moorings for their stories. What happens to the experience of selfhood during divorce, for example?

Of all the institutions in which daily life takes place, relationships are especially salient for selfhood. Initially, the other person is an audience for the story-telling that begins during courtship, with the revealing of histories and the discovery of common likes and dislikes. Once two people become a couple, the other continues to act as an audience during the recounting of quotidian events that occurred at home or work. But the other person gradually has a role in those events, and a shared history emerges. Storytelling of this sort has a purpose beyond merely conveying information. In the telling, people reassure themselves that they exist. One's stories enclose narratives of the self within them. As their stories unfold, they reaffirm the existence of the self as audience to themselves. . . . Significant other people are audiences, co-authors, participants, and critics, but one also hears, stars in, critiques, and revises one's own stories. In adulthood, one's stories either feature, refer to, or are prompted by relationships. The level of disclosure that characterizes intimacy means that this is all the more so for couples.

When people become "uncoupled," as Diane Vaughan (1986) aptly puts it, the experience suggests failure. The ability to have a relationship is a major test of adulthood (see Vaughan 1986), and a divorce or a breakup implies that one is deficient in some fundamental way. This may seem unlikely in times when divorce and separation have become commonplace. Yet, even today, "relationships are almost universally viewed in suc-

cess/failure terms," writes McCall (1982). Therefore, "any party to a terminated or even a spoiled relationship is tarred by failure. . . ." (p. 219). Even if one does not take one's *own* divorce as a sign of failure, others often see it in that light. Research suggests that, although divorce *itself* has become more accepted, divorced *people* have not. . . . Because the event is still widely considered indicative of a personal flaw, the stories that people tell afterwards must somehow redeem this experience of failure. To do so, uncoupling stories must take the form of "accounts" (Scott and Lyman 1968). Accounts are "linguistic devices [that] explain unanticipated or untoward behavior" (p. 46). They either mitigate one's responsibility for certain conduct or accept responsibility but neutralize the consequences of doing so. Accounts that accomplish the former are called "excuses"; those that accomplish the latter are known as "justifications." By either relieving or neutralizing personal responsibility, accounts diminish blame and, therefore, reduce the effects of stigma. In addition, accounts do more than convey information to *others*; they also explain one's own conduct to *oneself*. Consequently, they restore one's own sense of self-approval.

To complicate matters further, at the very time that people most need to repair their self-narratives, they have lost the resources with which to do so. Specifically, it is not the self that is lost during uncoupling, although that is how it is experienced. What one loses is an essential institutional context for one's stories. Familiar characters disappear or become altogether evil. Familiar plot lines become meaningless. Even the vocabulary of one's stories must change, since uncoupling means that two people whose language had slowly evolved from "I" to "We" must think and speak of themselves as "I" again. In short, the breakup disrupts a story in which the relationship itself plays a major part.

Accounts of uncoupling must therefore accomplish several things. To be convincing, they have to use vocabulary that is "anchored in the background expectations of the situation" (Scott and Lyman 1968, p. 53). Audiences have standards for what they will find credible. Accounts must be consistent with what "everybody knows" about what they purport to explain—or at least with what "everybody" in a particular setting "knows." In the case of uncoupling, accounts have to convey legitimate reasons for breaking up. In middle-class American culture, it is considered appropriate to emphasize the importance of the individual over the relationship. Although few people would list the sense of obligation to oneself as the sole reason for breaking up, it nonetheless constitutes an appropriate factor in explanations for doing so. Studies suggest that even those who do not initially have this sense of self-obligation eventually come to acquire it as a means of making positive sense of the loss . . . (Vaughan 1986) . . . . People redeem the failure of uncoupling, and, consequently, redeem damaged selves, by constructing accounts that meet the standards set by their audiences—including themselves. The result is a story of the process of uncoupling that encloses a self that is "even better than the real thing." One ends up with a sense of self that is, by virtue of narrative reconstruction, far better than any "real" self could be.

In what follows, I examine this process through ethnographic research in Codependents Anonymous, a popular Twelve Step group known simply as CoDA. During the past decade and a half, a number of peer-support, self-help programs modeled after Alcoholics Anonymous have appeared in response to different troubles attributed to substances and behaviors. CoDA is one such program. It attracts people who believe they have histories of "dysfunctional" relationships. Codependency is described as a psychospiritual "condition" that allegedly causes people to "lose touch with" themselves through their preoccupation with others, sometimes depicted as an "addiction." There is, however, a more sociological explanation available. Most people seek out CoDA after a divorce or the breakup of a serious relationship—or after a series of such events. They come in search of answers to the question "What happened?", but lurking beneath this is a deeper question: "What's wrong with me?" In the group's therapeutic discourse, many people claim to find a way to account for their experience, and, consequently, a new sense of who they are. I took their claims seriously, and aimed at understanding what makes that sense possible. I traced it to the regeneration of self-stories in which a new institutional formula replaced the one lost during uncoupling.

Methods

I attended over 200 CoDA meetings on Long Island and in New York City, which represents more than 400 hours of fieldwork done over the course of 17 months. I attended only meetings that were open to the public. (CoDA has "closed" meetings for gay men and lesbians and for in-depth study of the Twelve Steps in sequence, but I did not attend any of these.) I attended the meetings of one particular group consistently over the course of the research, and attended a second group's meetings for about six months. The rest of the time, I visited other locations to observe 18 different groups. Each meeting drew an average of twenty people, almost all of whom were white baby boomers, and 58 percent of whom were female. CoDA's tradition of anonymity, combined with the lack of any research by CoDA itself, make other demographic data scarce. Using dress, demeanor, and the occasional reference to occupation as very rough gauges, I would place most members in the ambiguous category of the middle class, although more toward the lower than the upper end.

I was particularly interested in the content of the "sharing" that took place during the meetings. Sharing represents a class of situations that Robert Zussman calls "autobiographical occasions" (1996), which require people to give accounts of themselves. After each meeting, I made extensive notes about the sharing I had heard, taking care to disguise identities to respect the anonymity that is a vital tradition of the group. Two kinds of sharing go on in CoDA. In the first, a volunteer talks, or "shares," about his or her codependency and recovery in front of the entire group for 10 to 15 minutes. The text read at every meeting suggests that only those who have had "enough time in the Program to generally qualify" as "recovering" share in front of the entire group. Although this "qualification" is left to individual judgment, the people who shared at the meetings I attended had been working a recovery program for several months before sharing with the group. When the qualified speaker finishes, individual sharing, open to all, begins. For this second kind of sharing, the groups either form smaller groups or allow individuals to request to speak by a show of hands, with each person calling on the next one to share as time allows. Individual sharing often focuses on a theme suggested by the person who has just finished speaking to the groups. These themes usually consist of Twelve Step clichés, such as "Taking care of myself," or "Owning my power." Before this sharing begins, the volunteer leader reads a standard set of instructions from a text provided by CoDA. These remind everyone to talk only about oneself and not to interrupt another's sharing or give advice. Codependents believe that they have put the wants and needs of others before their own, and that they have given advice too freely or taken advice too willingly. The meetings aim to help people overcome behavior of this sort. They are structured to allow everyone who wants to share an opportunity to do so. Occasionally, someone will pass up his or her turn, but doing so regularly would be enacting "codependent" behavior. Depending on the size

of the meeting, the individual sharing goes on for about thirty or forty minutes. Then, the group reconvenes for closing rituals. These vary somewhat among groups. Some recite positive affirmations. Others use a form of prayer, but all meetings end with members joining hands for a traditional Twelve Step cheer: *Keep coming back! It works if you work it, so work it. You're worth it!* The entire meeting lasts sixty to ninety minutes.

Twelve Step traditions of anonymity prohibited me from identifying myself as a researcher at the meetings. Moreover, CoDA's democratic, non-hierarchical structure meant that there were no gatekeepers from whom I could get permission to openly study the group. Newcomers to CoDA are quickly absorbed into the interaction without concern for identities outside the meeting. Indeed, there are strong prohibitions against revealing more than one's first name. Therefore, in most meetings, I participated in the "sharing." I did not have to make up a story about codependency, as I would have if I had tried to "pass" in Alcoholics or Gamblers Anonymous. The meaning of codependency is sufficiently open that it can accommodate the events of any life. In the culture of CoDA, each individual has the freedom, indeed the right, to decide what his or her codependency means. Thus I was able to share without lying about my history. However, this inevitably meant that the members saw me as a fellow codependent, and I did nothing to dissuade them of this. Members who knew about my research usually assumed that I wanted to find the causes of codependency and help other codependents.

After I had attended one group's meetings for about six weeks, I approached some of the members for interviews. . . . I first approached people who had several years of involvement with CoDA, believing that I could learn more—and more quickly—from them. I then approached people whose sharing had raised topics about which I wanted to learn more. I re-interviewed several people a year later. Moreover, I established sufficient rapport with several of the members to talk with them informally before and after meetings. . . .

In the interviews, I asked each person to talk at length about life before and since CoDA. The interviews were unstructured, and began with my asking how long they had attended CoDA and what had prompted them to do so. In many ways, then, the interviews were an extended version of sharing. I analyzed the transcripts and compared them with my fieldnotes from the sharing at meetings and with the popular codependency advice literature. I developed categories of codes for both the chronological unfolding of these recovery narratives and for the predominant themes they contained. I interviewed until my coverage of topics had reached "saturation," or until I began to hear the same things repeatedly and no longer heard anything new.

The analysis revealed a characteristic sequence through which members order the events of their lives. People who find the codependency discourse convincing learn, by listening to others, to fit the events of their lives into this sequence, or "narrative formula." Each meeting reinforces the story or adds a new installment. The narrator and the listeners situate the new information within existing themes. . . . At each meeting, a narrator picks up the story where it left off, taking it in a new direction, and taking the story of the self in a new direction as well. Over the long term, the narrator and the group remember these themes, and, consequently, legitimate them as the narrator's self. . . . For example:

> I have a self now because, in CoDA, I've learned about why my life has taken its particular path. It's like I know who I am. These people here know me, the real me. *(man, age forty-five)*

> All this time, because of codependency, I haven't been able to be myself. I didn't

know it, though, until CoDA. Now I can see that there's been a purpose to that, so that I could find out who I am now. You know what they say at the meetings about becoming who you were meant to be, "precious and free?" Well, through working the Program and through sharing and listening to other people, I've learned who I really am, for the first time in my life. *(man, age thirty-nine)*

This is not to say that everyone in CoDA tells exactly the same story. To the contrary, they tell *unique* stories. They do, however, use the same formula. Much of the appeal of the codependency discourse no doubt comes from its ability to do two things simultaneously: to work at the somewhat "universal" level of a culturally legitimate account of uncoupling *and* at the idiosyncratic level of a unique, personal history. At the "universal" level, codependency's core tenets echo popular beliefs about relationships and uncoupling. "Everybody knows," for example, that no one should have to sacrifice a sense of who one "is" for a relationship. As a discourse, codependency legitimates the belief that relationships fail to work, in a "universal" sense, when people "give away" their "true" selves. Yet, it is not enough to say that one's relationship failed simply because one gave up the sense of who one "is." This may satisfy some audiences, but one must also have a more detailed explanation of the breakup that will answer one's *own* questions. Accounts of uncoupling must, therefore, be specific and idiosyncratic as well as universal. If a universal level of explanation would suffice, then people could attribute divorce to simple probability. However, when the experience strikes home, statistical probability makes for a poor explanation. Divorce rates may be predictable, but one's *own* divorce is unique. Accounts of uncoupling must, therefore, follow cultural standards, but also accommodate individual lives. The "open" quality of the codependency discourse allows people to use it to create accounts that do both. It can accommodate a wide range of problems and circumstances that people bring with them, and it can also recast those problems and circumstances to fit within its confines.

Narratives of Codependency

The Institutional Shaping of the Self

Autobiographical occasions have formulas for what constitutes a "good" story. The medical history given to a doctor would not satisfy a family member who asks how one feels. . . . The "official" story told during a job interview would not work on a first date. Likewise, the audience at CoDA meetings has standards for what constitutes a "good" story of codependency and recovery. By listening to hundreds of people share, I began to understand these standards. This "narrative formula," as I call it, follows a five-part chronology.

Each speaker begins by describing the childhood circumstances that fostered one's codependency. Next comes a recounting of the "dysfunction" that followed from that childhood. A third part gives a depiction of what is known in Twelve Step groups as "hitting bottom," the low point at which the speaker recognized that something was wrong. A fourth part portrays how one is "working a Program," or what one is doing to "recover" from codependency. Fifth, and finally, the speaker redeems the past by describing the positive changes that have transpired since being in recovery. These five elements appeared in all the group sharing I observed and in every interview. Together, they create a "good" story of codependency. The *content* of the narratives differs among individuals, but the *order* is formulaic and provided by the codependency discourse.

The group reproduces the formula through the rule that only those who "qualify" as "recovering" may share in front of the entire group. By restricting this role to more sea-

soned members, the group transmits a set of ideas about how recovery works. Moreover, because the more seasoned members tend to tell more optimistic stories, newcomers learn not only *how* recovery works, but *that* it works. In one particular group, I learned just how important this is. A woman who struck me as developmentally disabled began coming to meetings. She shared in front of the whole group after attending only twice. She did not keep to the chronological formula. She did not have enough time in recovery to inspire the others with tales of improvement. In addition, she volunteered to share two weeks in a row. To avoid embarrassing her and encouraging their own controlling, codependent behavior, no one told her what she was doing wrong. Although the members took no formal steps to correct her, they nevertheless enacted various informal techniques to communicate their disapproval. Once she started speaking, the "glue" that normally held the meeting together would dissolve. The others began quiet side conversations. They rolled their eyes. They glanced impatiently at their watches. Some even left early. Through their behavior, the others told her that the meeting had effectively ended. She eventually stopped coming to meetings, although I cannot say exactly why. While she attended, however, the group had nevertheless made something clear: although there are few explicit rules for sharing, there is a "correct" way of doing so. Let me illustrate it systematically.

"Abusive" Childhoods and the Origins of Codependency

In the first phase of the sharing, each speaker begins to frame the outcome of one's life within the course of an unrecognized "condition." Codependency, as the text read at each meeting explains, "is born out of our sometimes moderately, sometimes extremely dysfunctional family systems." The family is considered the primary mechanism through which society's "dysfunction" is transmitted. In this view, families, *by defini-*

tion, "abuse" their children by denying them the unconditional love that the innocent "inner" self requires for its "healthy" development. The failure to love unconditionally is ubiquitous. Therefore, all families are considered dysfunctional, differing only in degree, and all manner of experience is recast to this end. Any and everyone's family history becomes reconceptualized as "abusive." People who do not come from families of addicts or alcoholics—and this includes most CoDA members—find other sorts of problems. Even in the absence of any obvious family troubles, members went to great lengths to find or invent them. I was struck by the ways that seemingly unexceptional childhoods became "dysfunctional" families. The "abuse" ranged from vague inadequacy, to overwork, and even to Catholicism.

> There's no drug addiction or alcoholism in my immediate family. . . . Just a super codependent, shame-based family. I just never felt good enough. *(woman, age thirty-six)*

> There was so much abuse in my family. Abuse and neglect. There was always food on the table, always a roof over our heads. But my parents were both working all the time and never there for us. It was so abusive emotionally. Really dysfunctional. *(man, age forty-one)*

> Nobody in my family was alcoholic or into drugs. We were just guilt-ridden Catholics. *(woman, age thirty-eight)*

> My father came from the old country, you know, where a man doesn't hug his kids. I never got a hug from my father. That's so abusive to a kid. *(man, age forty-two)*

Granted, some members of CoDA *did* give accounts of authentic-sounding physical and emotional mistreatment they endured as children. For the most part, however, the term "abuse" was used quite indiscriminately. When a person could not recall an instance of "abuse," it did not imply its absence, but its severity. The inability to recall "abuse" allegedly meant that the "victim" had "denied" the experience in order to survive it. The "abuse" must have been so intense that the mind blocked it out as a survival mechanism. For example:

> My upbringing was so dysfunctional that it's hard to remember. I shut down so much. *(woman, age forty-two)*

> I can't remember anything before the age of 21, so I know it must have been pretty bad. My parents must have abused me so bad that I just shut down in order to survive it. *(man, age forty-five)*

As Rice (1992) puts it, "the canon CoDA members tap for their life stories systematically, however inadvertently, alters their lived experiences to fit neatly within its boundaries" (p. 355). . . . Thus, every childhood becomes an "abusive" childhood. Conversely, of course, this means that "to 'explain' their lives [using codependency's rhetoric], members must sacrifice those aspects that lie beyond the outline of a 'good' theory of 'co-dependency'" (p. 356). The possibility of "denial" makes this sacrifice less final.

It also raises the issue of the "truth" of the stories. Narratives of codependency—and narratives in general—do not correspond with any objective reality. That is not their point. Their point is to show how a particular "past came to be, and how, ultimately, it gave birth to the present" (McAdams 1993, p. 102). Audiences have standards for what constitutes a "good" story, and the person who shares in CoDA must adhere to them. The question is not whether any given item is true, but whether it makes for a "good" story. What is interesting about forgotten instances of childhood "abuse" is not their veracity. It is how they make particular kinds of stories possible, and so remake the lives of those who tell them. As Frank has written, "[t]he stories we tell about our lives are not necessarily the lives as they were lived, but these stories become our experiences of those lives" (1995,

p. 22). The person who begins a commitment to CoDA and its discourse enters a world in which all families are considered abusive. Within the group, one can legitimately tell only stories that begin with "abuse." Were it not for the "abuse," one's life would have turned out differently. Since one has ended up in CoDA, the "abuse" *must* have happened. Consequently, members generate stories about "abusive" childhoods, and the stories then become their experience. Their histories gradually resemble what the formula for a "good" story of codependency prescribes. . . .

Excusing "Dysfunction"

As the sharing continues, the narrative describes how the "abusive" childhood set one up for "dysfunction" in later life. It attributes one's recent past or present situation to undiagnosed codependency, which originated in childhood circumstances. By blaming relationship troubles on one's unrecognized codependency in this way, the account reduces individual blame and its accompanying stigma. Moreover, the chronology helps to create a good story by making the present seem like the logical, and even inevitable, outcome of the past (Slavney and McHugh 1984).

As was the case with "abuse," what constitutes "dysfunction" varies widely. Within the discourse, any relationship or situation with a less than satisfactory outcome qualifies as "dysfunctional." To be sure, I heard some members share about appalling emotional and physical situations. Nevertheless, more often, the term described far less dramatic elements of dissatisfaction. Consider these examples from one small group:

> A man described a vague but troubling need to be "in control" of his relationship with his girlfriend. He never explained what he actually *did* to be controlling, but simply repeated stock phrases such as, "I've got to surrender my need to be in control. It's so 'dysfunctional'," and "Hav-

ing to be in control leads to a lot of 'dysfunction' in my life."

> A woman described a falling-out with a friend who disapproved of the amount of money she had spent on landscaping. "We've got it [the money], and seeing the flowers makes me happy," she said. "I like to have my house looking a certain way and she shouldn't have anything to say about it." She "needed" to put in these flowers, she says, to have the kind of environment she wants. Her friend's disapproval allegedly indicates the friendship's "dysfunction," and the speaker wants to avoid that kind of "unhealthiness."

> A woman voiced concern about her resentment over her daughter-in-law's absence from a family gathering. She saw this as an attempt by the younger woman to ruin her day. "She shouldn't be able to control my feelings," the woman said. "This has taught me that I've got to detach. I won't be part of that 'dysfunction'."

> A woman expressed pride in having shown a new ability to "take care of" herself. She had refused to baby-sit for a family member who had asked her to do so on the spur of the moment. To comply with the request would have encouraged "dysfunction."

> A man talked about a recent meal he had eaten at a restaurant. The server had misunderstood his order, and he did not bring it to her attention. He wondered what made him "relate to people in such 'dysfunctional' ways."

> A man described resentment and anger stemming from his "dysfunctional" relation with his mother. She had recently recommended that he see the movie "Nell," and he struggled to figure out why.

I use these illustrations not to question their putative dysfunction, but to highlight its role in the narrative. Each example represents an instance that had not gone the way the speakers had hoped. By calling them dysfunctional, the speakers could attribute the outcome to an inherent flaw in the relationship, thereby relieving themselves of their share of the interactional responsibility. They could acknowledge that they had acted badly, but simultaneously claim that, in light of such "dysfunction," they could not have done otherwise. Things may have gone wrong, but through no fault of their own. In the same way, "dysfunction" can excuse entire relationships. For example:

> I realize now that I picked her because she repeated all that chaos from when I was growing up. It was hell—both the marriage and my childhood. I did some really rotten things, I know, but it's because of the total dysfunction I saw as a kid. What I thought was love was really something else, some toxic stuff that went on at home. I acted the same way I saw my parents act. *(man, age thirty-nine)*

> I married my father. I grew up thinking that he was what a husband should be like. So I went out and married a man just like him. What else did I know? My relationship with my husband brought out all the issues I had with my father. All I knew was dysfunction. *(woman, age thirty-six)*

"Hitting Bottom"

The term speaks for itself. Although the "bottom" differs among speakers, it is always an emotional low point.

> When I was at my bottom, I went and bought a piece of hose, you know, to use in my exhaust pipe. I just wanted to have it around, to keep that option open. I was walking around feeling this dread, this constant feeling of dread. And in my more lucid moments I would say, "geez, I've really got to do something or I'm going to end up dead." *(woman, age thirty-seven)*

The account of the "bottom" is an important aspect of the narrative. It foregrounds a self that has not only endured hardship and conflict, but one that has found an intriguing solution. The "bottom" brings richness and complexity to the self that will emerge from the story. As the narrative progresses, having survived the "bottom" will suggest competence and maturity that redeems the discredited self. More immediately, it introduces an optimistic tone to the narrative. Psychologists suggest that this better allows people to cope with adversity. . . . Sociologically speaking, optimism reveals the narrator's underlying faith in the belief that life can be good and that one is, to some extent, able to direct oneself toward its goodness.

> You really do, you hit bottom and you say, "Look, I'm happy for the air that I'm breathing," and you start from there and everything else is a plus. *(man, age forty-five)*

Working a Program

This segment of the sharing depicts what the speaker is doing to find that good life. Here, the speaker shows how to use a Twelve Step phrase, he or she is not only "talking the talk," but also "walking the walk." One demonstrates to oneself and to the group that one is serious about recovery. It is not merely something that one talks about once a week, but it is something that one "works on" the remaining six days, as well. This indicates that the project of self-recreation through storytelling occurs on a daily basis. For example:

> I'm more in touch with the power in the universe now. I pray and meditate every day. I read meditation books in the morning. I read spiritual books. I've been journaling. I've really been focusing on myself. I have more of a sense of self now, and I have the Program to thank for that. *(man, age forty)*

Since the discourse maintains that each person alone knows best what he or she should do to foster recovery, what constitutes "working a Program" can vary widely. It is difficult to fake this part of the narrative. For this reason, I never spoke in front of the entire group. Because I was not "working a Program," I could not have given the group what they were expecting to hear. In small group sharing, I could talk more generally, saying things like "I'm trying to figure out what's best for me." My experience makes an important point: it is not enough to simply tell a story about oneself; one must also believe in one's own story. Although I understood the formula for a narrative of codependency, I did not "become" codependent because I did not believe that the story represented who I "am." I seem to have managed impressions successfully enough to have others attribute a codependent identity to me; no one ever called it into question, and, on several occasions, my "codependency" was even the subject of friendly teasing. But the impressions of others did not translate into self-identification. Since a self "involves something internally felt as well as socially enacted, it cannot be constructed out of material the actor himself or herself believes to be untrue" (Vinitzky-Seroussi and Zussman 1996, p. 233). Although I could tell a story that convinced others that I belonged in the group, I never convinced myself—or, for that matter, even tried to. For others, however, it was a different matter:

> I recognize that, within me, there's a self—[I] prefer the term "inner child." And this child knows what's right for me to do, and this child has always been with me, but my codependency has boxed it in. In recovery, I'm trying to set that child free so that my life makes sense. I'll keep working the Program, and I'll see who I was supposed to be, and I'll be that person. *(woman, age forty)*

Sometimes, convincing others is an important aspect of convincing oneself. For example, I interviewed a woman who had come to CoDA because her grown son had persistent alcohol and drug problems, which led to chronic unemployment and occasional legal troubles. The son returned home to live from time to time, but each episode ended when he stole money from her purse or pawned the family's television or stereo. The

woman had nursed him through numerous rehabs, and her dedication had caused considerable friction with her husband. She eventually decided to "detach" from her son to preserve her marriage, which meant banning him from the house. She turned to the popular advice literature in her search for a way to cope with her feelings of failure. She had begun to see her problem as one of codependency, but she had never said as much aloud, largely because she lacked a sympathetic audience for her claim. She had withdrawn from friendships because her friends would not understand why she had banned her son from the house. "I felt like a failure," she said. What she claimed to appreciate about CoDA was having an arena in which she could say, "I am codependent. My son has drug and alcohol problems," without fear of a negative reaction from others. "For a long time," she told me, "I couldn't even bring myself to say it at a meeting. But there's no judgment here." Gradually, through practice in front of an audience that had heard it all before, she integrated "My son has drug and alcohol problems" into her narrative of the self. She can now speak of it without embarrassment; indeed, her embarrassment has been replaced by pride at what she has "overcome." It was not enough to be convinced of her codependency in private; saying it aloud among others who believed her was a turning point.

Redeeming the Past

Here, the speaker recounts how codependency, though painful, ultimately led to personal "growth." The hardship is portrayed as all for the best, thereby showing that one has indeed learned something through the misfortune.

> I think the pain was all worth it when I see what's happened for my growth. *(age forty-six)*

> I finally have come to the other side of the anger, the blaming, the bitterness, and finally have been truly able to see the

benefits of it, that the characteristics that developed out of the abuse and dysfunction—I'm realizing that maybe if these things hadn't happened, I might not have the characteristics that I have today. (*age forty-five*)

The redemptive quality of the accounts fits a pattern often observed among people attempting to make sense of loss. For example, Marris (1974) maintains that people demonstrate what he calls a "conservative impulse" in response to significant loss and change. In order to make new experiences manageable, people apply information from one situation to another and consolidate experience into familiar categories. They depend on a "continuity of conceptions and experiences" to make sense of their lives. When an event disrupts one's ability to find meaning in experience, as when an important relationship comes to an end, coming to terms with that experience "depends on restoring a sense that the lost attachment can still give meaning to the present" (p. 149).

The experience of loss arouses contradictory reactions: return to the past, if possible; or forget it completely. Either of these would ultimately prove detrimental, since the former denies the reality of the present, and the latter "den[ies] the experience on which the sense of self rests" (Marris 1974, p. 151). The resolution most people eventually reach reconciles both alternatives. People master grief, Marris claims, "by abstracting what was fundamentally important in the relationship and rehabilitating it" (p. 34). For example, bereaved family members often try to do what the deceased "would have wanted." This abstracts the intimacy once shared with the deceased and rehabilitates it in the lives of those who go on living. The process of abstraction and rehabilitation demonstrates the "conservative impulse." New, confusing information (the absence of the spouse) is integrated into an established framework (the spouse's preferences). In this way, the bereaved can effectively restore the continuity

of purpose that the death of a spouse disrupts. Likewise, codependents manifest a similar "conservative impulse" in their accounts. They abstract what their relationships had provided—a coherent, chronological, reasonably optimistic story about their lives—and rehabilitate it in revised self-stories. Even hardship becomes part of a story about how one's life is progressing for the best.

Good stories need satisfying endings. Since the lives of those telling the stories are still in progress, the endings must keep a number of alternatives open for the future and be flexible enough to change as the tellers change. Yet, they should not be so open that they suggest indecision and a lack of purpose. In sharing, this ambiguity is accomplished through recovery clichés such as "Taking Care of Myself" or "Believing in Myself" and "Getting in Touch with My Feelings." These and other similarly vague phrases convey a positive orientation toward the future without pinning one down to specifics. For instance:

> The biggest help to me has been being honest with myself. CoDA has given me the courage to believe in myself and not believe all the lies from the past, from the way I was raised. (*woman, age forty-five*)

Those whose lives had not yet taken a definite turn for the better still seemed reasonably assured that things would improve in time. They expressed tentative mastery over the future, as in "I'm not sure how this will end up, but I'll be fine as long as I keep doing what I've learned to do." For example:

> I've been in a real crummy spot, and it's been hard to try to do recovery and keep it all together. CoDA has made me realize that I have no control over what my wife decides to do. I can just take care of myself and know that, whatever happens, I'll get through it. (*man, age thirty-seven*)

With endings such as this one—"Whatever happens, I'll get through it"—narrators affirm the "growth" of the self. They convince themselves and others that they now have the ability to reconcile the tough issues of adult life with their own capabilities.

Conclusion: The Self as Continuous Project

The existence of an institutionalized narrative formula of codependency does not reduce the experience of having a self to mastering a story. I do not propose that narrators establish coherent identities simply by using CoDA's rhetorical resources to their own advantage. If this were so, anyone who understood the conventions of a coherent narrative of self could speak one, and, by doing so, could make it happen. . . . Because the narrative of the self is, as Gagnon (1992) put it, an "internal conversation," the experience of selfhood hinges as much—or more—on believing in one's *own* stories than on getting *others* to believe them. The narrative accomplishment of selfhood differs dramatically from the impression management that constitutes selfhood [for] Goffman. . . . Goffman emphasizes the impressions made on others. What I describe here is much more internal; it is impression management *directed at oneself* (see Vinitzky-Seroussi and Zussman 1996). . . .

This research reveals that the desire for integrity—whether phrased as an "internal conversation" or a feeling that we are "in some peculiarly subtle sense the same"—is in no danger of disappearing. Despite scholarly claims about the death of the self, it remains alive and well outside the ivory tower. If CoDA members are indicative of anything, they are indicative of the strength and ubiquity of the belief in the essential self, experienced as continuous and coherent. This continuity and coherence consist of an ongoing story that people tell to themselves, as well as to other people. While the story has integrity, it also leaves room for a great deal of ambiguity, for it is not yet finished.

The particular form of the . . . self that is created in CoDA is of a therapeutic sort distinguished by its articulation in relation to something conceptualized as a condition. Ev-

eryone who comes to CoDA does so during an extremely difficult time. But many people spend three, four, and even five years in the group. They talk about "life in recovery," which raises a question. If people go to CoDA when a relationship ends, but continue to attend long after the sting of uncoupling has subsided, what, then, do they see themselves "recovering" *from*? Quite simply, they are "recovering" from codependency, but they will never get a clean bill of health. The discourse builds in large part on a medical metaphor: it portrays codependency as a *condition*, not an *injury*. One cannot recover from a condition. It causes varying degrees of discomfort and requires varying levels of intervention. But it never completely heals and it forever affects the way one goes about one's life. Once people identify themselves as codependents, they can never fully "recover." The pain of a particular relationship may pass, but the underlying condition that is thought to have fostered the troublesome "dysfunction" does not. One's codependency may go into a remission of sorts as one begins to "take care of" oneself, but it will never go away. As a condition, it requires continuous monitoring, which is best accomplished through continuous participation in CoDA. This subtly but effectively transforms one's purpose for attending. A person comes to the group for support during uncoupling. Along the way, he or she finds (or creates) so many fundamental problems that "recovery" becomes a life-long project. The loss triggers the introspection, but it continues long afterwards. Meanwhile, a more social phenomenon has taken place, in the development of a socio-biography. By the time the crisis period ends, many people feel little need to move on. They become institutionally anchored in the group. They have found friends there—or at least found something that feels like friendship. They have "become" codependent provided, of course, that they see *themselves* that way. . . .

This does not mean that stories of the self are capriciously cobbled together; rather, it drives home the point that they are grounded in institutions, which give them life. Freud once claimed that adults must be able "to love and to work." For adults, selfhood centers on whom one loves and what one does for a living, since adult life transpires largely within these two institutions. Much of the sociological research on the self would suggest that it emerges through the appropriation of social statuses such as "manager," "waitress," "husband," or "wife." But the essential ingredient that the institutions of love and work provide for selfhood has less to do with acquiring particular statuses than it does with the ability to talk about oneself in contexts. Selfhood, I argue, is a narrative accomplishment, made possible by institutions. They are so essential for the experience that even those who, like the members of CoDA, condemn mainstream institutions as sources of "dysfunction" will rely on them for the sake of selfhood, and those who lose one set of institutional anchors will find others.

Some readers might claim that the observations made within such a unique setting cannot be generalized beyond it. I do not want to generalize far beyond CoDA about the substance of the self (although I suspect that the . . . therapeutic self is indeed quite prevalent) but I do want to generalize about process. People working to "recover" from codependency represent unique concerns, and perhaps extreme examples, but their endeavors can still apply to the broader experience of selfhood, more generally. The issues raised and illuminated by codependency have resonance beyond this particular group. Since selfhood can be considered an American entitlement, the quest undertaken by men and women conspicuously in search of the self can reveal what makes this taken-for-granted experience possible. The proper study of this experience is in narrative, but the proper study of narrative is in institutions.

References

Frank, A. W. (1995). *The wounded storyteller: Body, illness, and ethics.* Chicago: University of Chicago Press.

Gagnon, J. (1984, 1992). "The self, its voices, and their discord." In C. Ellis and M. Flaherty (Eds.), *Investigating Subjectivity* (pp. 221–243). Newbury Park: Sage.

Goffman, E. (1959). *The presentation of self in everyday life.* Garden City, NY: Anchor Books.

James, W. (1910). *Psychology: The briefer course.* New York: Henry Holt and Co.

Marris, P. (1974). *Loss and change.* New York: Pantheon.

McAdams, D. P. (1993). *The stories we live by: Personal myths and the making of the self.* New York: Guilford Press.

McCall, G. I. (1982). "Becoming unrelated: The management of bond dissolution." In S. Duck (Ed.), *Personal Relationships.* Vol. 4, *Dissolving Personal Relationships* (pp. 211–232). London: Academic Press.

Rice, J. S. (1992). "Discursive formation, life stories, and the emergence of co-dependency: 'Power/knowledge' and the search for identity." *Sociological Quarterly, 33,* 337–364.

Scott, M. B., & Lyman, S. M. (1968). "Accounts." *American Sociological Review, 33,* 46–62.

Slavney, P. R., & McHugh, P. R. (1984). "Life stories and meaningful connections: Reflections on a clinical method in psychiatry and medicine." *Perspectives in Biology and Medicine, 27,* 279–288.

Vaughan, D. (1986). *Uncoupling: Turning points in intimate relationships.* New York and Oxford: Oxford University Press.

Vinitzky-Seroussi, V., & Zussman, R. (1996). "High school reunions and the management of identity." *Symbolic Interaction, 19,* 225–239.

Zussman, R. (1996). "Autobiographical occasions." *Contemporary Sociology, 25,* 143–148.

Part V

The Organization of Social Interaction

Social interaction has an organization all its own, apart from the participants' particular characteristics and the larger social environments in which it occurs. Indeed, social interaction is meaningful because it is patterned, organized, and orderly. Participants commonly share an implicit understanding of its organization and, therefore, similar expectations of what each is likely to do under different circumstances. This shared but implicit understanding turns both action and inaction, the expected and unexpected, into meaningful events. For example, individuals who are acquainted expect to exchange greetings when they meet. If we walk past those whom we know without greeting them, they will probably consider it a snub. Our failure to greet them is meaningful, because they expect a greeting. Although we may blatantly ignore expected patterns of interaction, we do so at the risk of sending unintended messages to others and often unflattering ones about ourselves.

One of the principal tasks of microsociology is to investigate and describe recurrent patterns of interaction and the principles of their organization. The goal is to understand how individuals achieve mutual understanding and collectively construct meaningful social lives. That is the focus of the selections in this section. They describe the organization of different aspects of social interaction, explain individuals' commitment to sustaining orderly patterns of interaction, and illustrate how such patterns of interaction provide the glue of social life. ✦

16

Face-Work and Interaction Rituals

Erving Goffman

An earlier selection by Erving Goffman examined some of the dramatic or theatrical characteristics of social interaction. It described how individuals enact selves and reach a working consensus concerning the respective parts each will play in the course of their interaction. In this selection, Goffman observes that individuals effectively claim positive social value or "face" through the lines they take or parts they perform during interaction. He also argues that individuals are emotionally invested in claiming and maintaining face. The embarrassment we experience when we stumble, forget our lines, or otherwise bungle a social performance clearly demonstrates his argument.

According to Goffman, the maintenance of face requires that individuals uphold an expressive order. That is, an individual must meet others' expectations of how the type of person that she or he claims to be should act. In turn, others must treat her or him as that type of person. Thus, the maintenance of face depends on an implicit agreement: I will protect your face, if you protect mine. We usually honor this agreement because of our common emotional investment in face, resulting in our self-regulated participation in orderly patterns of social interaction.

Goffman describes two basic kinds of face-work that characterize such orderly interaction. The first is self-explanatory: we attempt to avoid places, people, situations, and topics that might threaten our own or others' face and at-

tempt to ignore events that do. However, we do not always succeed, which necessitates the second kind of face-work, or what Goffman calls the corrective process.

Goffman describes the corrective process as a "ritual" for two reasons. First, it consists of a routine interchange of "moves." When a threat to face occurs, we expect the involved parties to engage in a sequence of familiar acts and interpret the absence of any such moves in terms of that expected pattern. If, for example, an individual who has offended someone fails to offer an apology, we are likely to conclude that he or she is cold and uncaring. This example illustrates how socially expected patterns of interaction turn both action and inaction into meaningful events.

Second, the corrective process is like a religious ritual, expressing individuals' mutual reverence for face. The countless times a day that we say "excuse me," "I'm sorry," and "thank you" indicate just how highly we regard both our own and others' face. Thus, Goffman's characterization of face as "sacred" is at most only a slight exaggeration.

Every person lives in a world of social encounters, involving him either in face-to-face or mediated contact with other participants. In each of these contacts, he tends to act out what is sometimes called a line—that is, a pattern of verbal and nonverbal acts by which he expresses his view of the situation and through this his evaluation of the participants, especially himself. Regardless of whether a person intends to take a line, he will find that he has done so in effect. The other participants will assume that he has more or less willfully taken a stand, so that if he is to deal with their response to him he must take into consideration the impression they have possibly formed of him.

The term *face* may be defined as the positive social value a person effectively claims for himself by the line others assume he has taken during a particular contact. Face is an image of self delineated in terms of approved social attributes—albeit an image that others may share, as when a person makes a good showing for his profession or religion by making a good showing for himself.

A person tends to experience an immediate emotional response to the face which a contact with others allows him; he cathects his face; his "feelings" become attached to it. If the encounter sustains an image of him that he has long taken for granted, he probably will have few feelings about the matter. If events establish a face for him that is better than he might have expected, he is likely to "feel good"; if his ordinary expectations are not fulfilled, one expects that he will "feel bad" or "feel hurt." In general, a person's attachment to a particular face, coupled with the ease with which disconfirming information can be conveyed by himself and others, provides one reason why he finds that participation in any contact with others is a commitment. A person will also have feelings about the face sustained for the other participants; and, while these feelings may differ in quantity and direction from those he has for his own face, they constitute an involvement in the face of others that is as immediate and spontaneous as the involvement he has in his own face. One's own face and the face of others are constructs of the same order; it is the rules of the group and the definition of the situation which determine how much feeling one is to have for face and how this feeling is to be distributed among the faces involved.

A person may be said to *have*, or *be in*, or *maintain* face when the line he effectively takes presents an image of him that is internally consistent, that is supported by judgments and evidence conveyed by other participants, and that is confirmed by evidence conveyed through impersonal agencies in the situation. At such times the person's face clearly is something that is not lodged in or on his body, but rather something that is diffusely located in the flow of events in the en-

counter and becomes manifest only when these events are read and interpreted for the appraisals expressed in them.

The line maintained by and for a person during contact with others tends to be of a legitimate institutionalized kind. During a contact of a particular type, an interactant of known or visible attributes can expect to be sustained in a particular face and can feel that it is morally proper that this should be so. Given his attributes and the conventionalized nature of the encounter, he will find a small choice of lines will be open to him and a small choice of faces will be waiting for him. Further, on the basis of a few known attributes, he is given the responsibility of possessing a vast number of others. His co-participants are not likely to be conscious of the character of many of these attributes until he acts perceptibly in such a way as to discredit his possession of them; then everyone becomes conscious of these attributes and assumes that he willfully gave a false impression of possessing them.

Thus, while concern for face focuses the attention of the person on the current activity, he must, to maintain face in this activity, take into consideration his place in the social world beyond it. A person who can maintain face in the current situation is someone who has abstained from certain actions in the past that would have been difficult to face up to later. In addition, he fears loss of face now partly because the others may take this as a sign that consideration for his feelings need not be shown in the future. There is nevertheless a limitation to this interdependence between the current situation and the wider social world: an encounter with people whom he will not have dealings with again leaves him free to take a high line that the future will discredit, or free to suffer humiliations that would make future dealing with them an embarrassing thing to have to face.

A person may be said to *be in wrong face* when information is brought forth in some way about his social worth which cannot be integrated, even with effort, into the line that is being sustained for him. A person may be said to *be out of face* when he participates in a contact with others without having ready a line of the kind participants in such situations are expected to take. The intent of many pranks is to lead a person into showing a wrong face or no face, but there will also be serious occasions, of course, when he will find himself expressively out of touch with the situation.

When a person senses that he is in face, he typically responds with feelings of confidence and assurance. Firm in the line he is taking, he feels that he can hold his head up and openly present himself to others. He feels some security and some relief—as he also can when the others feel he is in wrong face but successfully hide these feelings from him.

When a person is in wrong face or out of face, expressive events are being contributed to the encounter which cannot be readily woven into the expressive fabric of the occasion. Should he sense that he is in wrong face or out of face, he is likely to feel ashamed and inferior because of what has happened to the activity on his account and because of what may happen to his reputation as a participant. Further, he may feel bad because he had relied upon the encounter to support an image of self to which he has become emotionally attached and which he now finds threatened. Felt lack of judgmental support from the encounter may take him aback, confuse him, and momentarily incapacitate him as an interactant. His manner and bearing may falter, collapse, and crumble. He may become embarrassed and chagrined; he may become shamefaced. The feeling, whether warranted or not, that he is perceived in a flustered state by others, and that he is presenting no usable line, may add further injuries to his feelings, just as his change from being in wrong face or out of face to being shamefaced can add further disorder to the expressive organization of the situation. Following common usage, I shall employ the term *poise* to refer to the capacity to suppress and conceal any tendency to become shamefaced during encounters with others.

In our Anglo-American society, as in some others, the phrase "to lose face" seems to mean to be in wrong face, to be out of face, or to be shame-faced. The phrase "to save one's face" appears to refer to the process by which the person sustains an impression for others that he has not lost face. . . .

As an aspect of the social code of any social circle, one may expect to find an understanding as to how far a person should go to save his face. Once he takes on a self-image expressed through face, he will be expected to live up to it. In different ways in different societies, he will be required to show self-respect, abjuring certain actions because they are above or beneath him, while forcing himself to perform others, even though they cost him dearly. By entering a situation in which he is given a face to maintain, a person takes on the responsibility of standing guard over the flow of events as they pass before him. He must ensure that a particular *expressive order* is sustained—an order that regulates the flow of events, large or small, so that anything that appears to be expressed by them will be consistent with his face. When a person manifests these compunctions primarily from duty to himself, one speaks in our society of pride; when he does so because of duty to wider social units, and receives support from these units in doing so, one speaks of honor. When these compunctions have to do with postural things, with expressive events derived from the way in which the person handles his body, his emotions, and the things with which he has physical contact, one speaks of dignity, this being an aspect of expressive control that is always praised and never studied. In any case, while his social face can be his most personal possession and the center of his security and pleasure, it is only on loan to him from society; it will be withdrawn, unless he conducts himself in a way that is worthy of it. Approved attributes and their relation to face make of every man his own jailer; this is a fundamental social constraint, even though each man may like his cell.

Just as the member of any group is expected to have self-respect, so also he is expected to sustain a standard of considerateness; he is expected to go to certain lengths to save the feelings and the face of others present, and he is expected to do this willingly and spontaneously because of emotional identification with the others and with their feelings. In consequence, he is disinclined to witness the defacement of others. The person who can witness another's humiliation and unfeelingly retain a cool countenance himself is said in our society to be "heartless," just as he who can unfeelingly participate in his own defacement is thought to be "shameless."

The combined effect of the rule of self-respect and the rule of considerateness is that the person tends to conduct himself during an encounter so as to maintain both his own face and the face of the other participants. This means that the line taken by each participant is usually allowed to prevail, and each participant is allowed to carry off the role he appears to have chosen for himself. A state where everyone temporarily accepts everyone else's line is established. This kind of mutual acceptance seems to be a basic structural feature of interaction, especially the interaction of face-to-face talk. It is typically a "working" acceptance, not a "real" one, since it tends to be based not on agreement of candidly expressed heart-felt evaluations, but upon a willingness to give temporary lip service to judgments with which the participants do not really agree.

The mutual acceptance of lines has an important conservative effect upon encounters. Once the person initially presents a line, he and the others tend to build their later responses upon it, and in a sense, become stuck with it. Should the person radically alter his line, or should it become discredited, then confusion results, for the participants will

have prepared and committed themselves for actions that are now unsuitable. . . .

By *face-work* I mean to designate the actions taken by a person to make whatever he is doing consistent with face. Face-work serves to counteract "incidents"—that is, events whose effective symbolic implications threaten face. Thus, poise is one important type of face-work, for through poise the person controls his embarrassment and hence the embarrassment that he and others might have over his embarrassment. Whether or not the full consequences of face-saving actions are known to the person who employs them, they often become habitual and standardized practices; they are like traditional plays in a game or traditional steps in a dance. Each person, subculture, and society seems to have its own characteristic repertoire of face-saving practices. It is to this repertoire that people partly refer when they ask what a person or culture is "really" like. And yet the particular set of practices stressed by particular persons or groups seems to be drawn from a single logically coherent framework of possible practices. It is as if face, by its very nature, can be saved only in a certain number of ways, and as if each social grouping must make its selections from this single matrix of possibilities.

The members of every social circle may be expected to have some knowledge of face-work and some experience in its use. In our society, this kind of capacity is sometimes called tact, *savoir-faire*, diplomacy, or social skill. Variation in social skill pertains more to the efficacy of face-work than to the frequency of its application, for almost all acts involving others are modified, prescriptively or proscriptively, by considerations of face. If a person is to employ his repertoire of face-saving practices, obviously he must first become aware of the interpretation that others may have placed upon his acts and the interpretation that he ought perhaps to place upon theirs. In other words, he must exercise perceptiveness. But even if he is properly alive to symbolically conveyed judgements and is socially skilled, he must yet be willing to exercise his perceptiveness and his skill; he must, in short, be prideful and considerate. Admittedly, of course, the possession of perceptiveness and social skill so often leads to their application in our society that terms such as politeness or tact fail to distinguish between the inclination to exercise such capacities and the capacities themselves.

I have already said that the person will have two points of view—a defensive orientation toward saving his own face and a protective orientation toward saving the others' face. Some practices will be primarily defensive and others primarily protective, although in general, one may expect these two perspectives to be taken at the same time. In trying to save the face of others, the person must choose a tack that will not lead to loss of his own; in trying to save his own face, he must consider the loss of face that his action may entail for others.

In many societies, there is a tendency to distinguish three levels of responsibility that a person may have for a threat to face that his actions have created. First, he may appear to have acted innocently; his offense seems to be unintended and unwitting, and those who perceive his act can feel that he would have attempted to avoid it had he foreseen its offensive consequences. In our society, one calls such threats to face *faux pas, gaffes, boners,* or *bricks.* Secondly, the offending person may appear to have acted maliciously and spitefully, with the intention of causing open insult. Thirdly, there are incidental offenses; these arise as an unplanned but sometimes anticipated by-product of action—action the offender performs in spite of its offensive consequences, although not out of spite. From the point of view of a particular participant, these three types of threat can be introduced by the participant himself against his own face, by himself against the face of the others, by the others against their own face, or by the others against himself. Thus, the person may find himself in many different relations to a threat to face. If he is to handle himself and others well in all contingencies, he will have to have a repertoire of face-saving practices for each of these possible relations to threat.

The Basic Kinds of Face-Work

The Avoidance Process

The surest way for a person to prevent threats to his face is to avoid contacts in which these threats are likely to occur. In all societies, one can observe this in the avoidance relationship and in the tendency for certain delicate transactions to be conducted by go-betweens. Similarly, in many societies, members know the value of voluntarily making a gracious withdrawal before an anticipated threat to face has had a chance to occur.

Once the person does chance an encounter, other kinds of avoidance practices come into play. As defensive measures, he keeps off topics and away from activities that would lead to the expression of information that is inconsistent with the line he is maintaining. At opportune moments he will change the topic of conversation or the direction of activity. He will often present initially a front of diffidence and composure, suppressing any show of feeling, until he has found out what kind of line the others will be ready to support for him. Any claims regarding self may be made with belittling modesty, with strong qualifications, or with a note of unseriousness; by hedging in these ways, he will have prepared a self for himself that will not be discredited by exposure, personal failure, or the unanticipated acts of others. And if he does not hedge his claims about self, he will at least attempt to be realistic about them, knowing that otherwise events may discredit him and make him lose face.

Certain protective maneuvers are as common as these defensive ones. The person shows respect and politeness, making sure to extend to others any ceremonial treatment that might be their due. He employs discretion; he leaves unstated facts that might implicitly or explicitly contradict and embarrass the positive claims made by others. He employs circumlocutions and deceptions, phrasing his replies with careful ambiguity, so that the others' face is preserved even if their welfare is not. He employs courtesies, making slight modifications of his demands on or appraisals of the others, so that they will be able to define the situation as one in which their self-respect is not threatened. In making a belittling demand upon the others, or in imputing uncomplimentary attributes to them, he may employ a joking manner, allowing them to take the lie that they are good sports, able to relax from their ordinary standards of pride and honor. And before engaging in a potentially offensive act, he may provide explanations as to why the others ought not to be affronted by it. For example, if he knows that it will be necessary to withdraw from the encounter before it has terminated, he may tell the others in advance that it is necessary for him to leave, so that they will have faces that are prepared for it. But neutralizing the potentially offensive act need not be done verbally; he may wait for a propitious moment or natural break—for example, in conversation, a momentary lull when no one speaker can be affronted—and then leave, in this way using the context instead of his words as a guarantee of inoffensiveness.

When a person fails to prevent an incident, he can still attempt to maintain the fiction that no threat to face has occurred. The most blatant example of this is found where the person acts as if an event that contains a threatening expression has not occurred at all. He may apply this studied non-observance to his own acts—as when he does not by any outward sign admit that his stomach is rumbling—or to the acts of others, as when he does not "see" that another has stumbled. Social life in mental hospitals owes much to this process; patients employ it in regard to their own peculiarities, and visitors employ it, often with tenuous desperation, in regard to patients. In general, tactful blindness of this kind is applied only to events that, if perceived at all, could be perceived and interpreted only as threats to face.

A more important, less spectacular kind of tactful overlooking is practiced when a person openly acknowledges an incident as an event that has occurred, but not as an event that contains a threatening expression. If he is not the one who is responsible for the incident, then his blindness will have to be supported by his forbearance; if he is the doer of the threatening deed, then his blindness will have to be supported by his willingness to seek a way of dealing with the matter, which leaves him dangerously dependent upon the cooperative forbearance of the others.

Another kind of avoidance occurs when a person loses control of his expressions during an encounter. At such times he may try not so much to overlook the incident as to hide or conceal his activity in some way, thus making it possible for the others to avoid some of the difficulties created by a participant who has not maintained face. Correspondingly, when a person is caught out of face because he had not expected to be thrust into interaction, or because strong feelings have disrupted his expressive mask, the others may protectively turn away from him or his activity for a moment, to give him time to assemble himself.

The Corrective Process

When the participants in an undertaking or encounter fail to prevent the occurrence of an event that is expressively incompatible with the judgments of social worth that are being maintained, and when the event is of the kind that is difficult to overlook, then the participants are likely to give it accredited status as an incident—to ratify it as a threat that deserves direct official attention—and to proceed to try to correct for its effects. At this point, one or more participants find themselves in an established state of ritual disequilibrium or disgrace, and an attempt must be made to re-establish a satisfactory ritual state for them. I use the term *ritual* because I am dealing with acts through whose symbolic component the actor shows how worthy he is of respect or how worthy he feels others are of it. The imagery of equilibrium is apt here, because the length and intensity of the corrective effort is nicely adapted to the persistence and intensity of the threat. One's face, then, is a sacred thing, and the expressive order required to sustain it is, therefore, a ritual one.

The sequence of acts set in motion by an acknowledged threat to face, and terminating in the re-establishment of ritual equilibrium, I shall call an *interchange*. Defining a message or move as everything conveyed by an actor during a turn at taking action, one can say that an interchange will involve two or more moves and two or more participants. Obvious examples in our society may be found in the sequence of "Excuse me" and "Certainly" and in the exchange of presents or visits. The interchange seems to be a basic concrete unit of social activity and provides one natural empirical way to study interaction of all kinds. Face-saving practices can be usefully classified according to their position in the natural sequence of moves that comprise this unit. Aside from the event which introduces the need for a corrective interchange, four classic moves seem to be involved.

There is, first, the challenge, by which participants take on the responsibility of calling attention to the misconduct; by implication, they suggest that the threatened claims are to stand firm and that the threatening event itself will have to be brought back into line.

The second move consists of the offering, whereby a participant, typically the offender, is given a chance to correct for the offense and re-establish the expressive order. Some classic ways of making this move are available. On the one hand, an attempt can be made to show that what admittedly appeared to be a threatening expression is really a meaningless event, or an unintentional act, or a joke not meant to be taken seriously, or an unavoidable, "understandable" product of extenuating circumstances. On the other hand, the meaning of the event may be granted and effort concentrated on the creator of it. Information may be provided to show that the creator was under the influence of something and not himself, or that he was under the command of somebody else and not acting for himself. When a person claims that an act was meant in jest, he may go on and claim that the self that seemed to lie behind the act was also projected as a joke. When a person suddenly finds that he has demonstrably failed in capacities that the others assumed him to have and to claim for himself—such as the capacity to spell, to perform minor tasks, to talk without malapropisms, and so on—he may quickly add, in a serious or unserious way, that he claims these incapacities as part of his self. The meaning of the threatening incident thus stands, but it can now be incorporated smoothly into the flow of expressive events.

As a supplement to or substitute for the strategy of redefining the offensive act or himself, the offender can follow two other procedures: he can provide compensations to the injured—when it is not his own face that he has threatened; or he can provide punishment, penance, and expiation for himself. These are important moves or phases in the ritual interchange. Even though the offender may fail to prove his innocence, he can suggest through these means that he is now a renewed person, a person who has paid for his sin against the expressive order and is once more to be trusted in the judgmental scene. Further, he can show that he does not treat the feelings of the others lightly, and that, if their feelings have been injured by him, however innocently, he is prepared to pay a price for his action. Thus, he assures the others that they can accept his explanations without this acceptance constituting a sign of weakness and a lack of pride on their part. Also, by his treatment of himself, by his self-castigation, he shows that he is clearly aware of the kind of crime he would have committed had the incident been what it first appeared to be, and that he knows the kind of punishment that ought to be accorded to one who would commit such a crime. The suspected person thus shows that he is thoroughly capable of taking the role of the others toward his own activity, that he can still be used as a responsible participant in the ritual process, and that the rules of conduct which he appears to have broken are still sacred, real, and unweakened. An offensive act may arouse anxiety about the ritual code; the offender allays this anxiety by showing that both the code and he as an upholder of it are still in working order.

After the challenge and the offering have been made, the third move can occur; the persons to whom the offering is made can accept it as a satisfactory means of re-establishing the expressive order and the faces supported by this order. Only then can the offender cease the major part of his ritual offering.

In the terminal move of the interchange, the forgiven person conveys a sign of gratitude to those who have given him the indulgence of forgiveness.

The phases of the corrective process—challenge, offering, acceptance, and thanks—provide a model for interpersonal ritual behavior, but a model that may be departed from in significant ways. For example, the offended parties may give the offender a chance to initiate the offering on his own before a challenge is made and before they ratify the offense as an incident. This is a common courtesy, extended on the assumption that the recipient will introduce a self-challenge. Further, when the offended persons accept the corrective offering, the offender may suspect that this has been grudgingly done from tact, and so he may volunteer additional corrective offerings, not allowing the matter to rest until he has received a second or third acceptance of his repeated apology. Or the offended persons may tactfully take over the role of the offender and volunteer excuses for him that will, perforce, be acceptable to the offended persons.

An important departure from the standard corrective cycle occurs when a challenged offender patently refuses to heed the warning and continues with his offending behavior, instead of setting the activity to rights. This move shifts the play back to the challengers. If they countenance the refusal to meet their demands, then it will be plain that their challenge was a bluff and that the bluff has been called. This is an untenable position; a face for themselves cannot be derived from it, and they are left to bluster. To avoid this fate, some classic moves are open to them. For instance, they can resort to tactless, violent retaliation, destroying either themselves or the person who had refused to heed their warning. Or they can withdraw from the undertaking in a visible huff—righteously indignant, outraged, but confident of ultimate vindication. Both tacks provide a way of denying the offender his status as an interactant, and hence denying the reality of the offensive judgment he has made. Both strategies are ways of salvaging face, but for all concerned the costs are usually high. It is partly to forestall such scenes that an offender is usually quick to offer apologies; he does not want the affronted persons to trap themselves into the obligation to resort to desperate measures.

It is plain that emotions play a part in these cycles of response, as when anguish is expressed because of what one has done to another's face, or anger because of what has been done to one's own. I want to stress that these emotions function as moves, and fit so precisely into the logic of the ritual game that it would seem difficult to understand them without it. In fact, spontaneously expressed feelings are likely to fit into the formal pattern of the ritual interchange more elegantly than consciously designed ones.

Making Points– The Aggressive Use of Face-Work

Every face-saving practice which is allowed to neutralize a particular threat opens up the possibility that the threat will be willfully introduced for what can be safely gained by it. If a person knows that this modesty will be answered by others' praise of him, he can fish for compliments. If his own appraisal of self will be checked against incidental events, then he can arrange for favorable incidental events to appear. If others are prepared to overlook an affront to them and act forbearingly, or to accept apologies, then he can rely on this as a basis for safely offending them. He can attempt by sudden withdrawal to force the others into a ritually unsatisfactory state, leaving them to flounder in an interchange that cannot readily be completed. Finally, at some expense to himself, he can arrange for the others to hurt his feelings, thus forcing them to feel guilt, remorse, and sustained ritual disequilibrium.

When a person treats face-work not as something he need be prepared to perform, but rather as something that others can be counted on to perform or to accept, then an encounter or an undertaking becomes less a scene of mutual considerateness than an arena in which a contest or match is held. The purpose of the game is to preserve everyone's line from an inexcusable contradiction, while scoring as many points as possible against one's adversaries and making as many gains as possible for oneself. An audience to the struggle is almost a necessity. The general method is for the person to introduce favorable facts about himself and unfavorable facts about the others in such a way

that the only reply the others will be able to think up will be one that terminates the interchange in a grumble, a meager excuse, a face-saving I-can-take-a-joke laugh, or an empty stereotyped comeback of the "Oh yeah?" or "That's what you think" variety. The losers in such cases will have to cut their losses, tacitly grant the loss of a point, and attempt to do better in the next interchange. . . .

In aggressive interchanges, the winner not only succeeds in introducing information favorable to himself and unfavorable to the others, but also demonstrates that as interactant he can handle himself better than his adversaries. Evidence of this capacity is often more important than all the other information the person conveys in the interchange, so that the introduction of a "crack" in verbal interaction tends to imply that the initiator is better at footwork than those who must suffer his remarks. However, if they succeed in making a successful parry of the thrust and then a successful riposte, the instigator of the play must not only face the disparagement with which the others have answered him but also accept the fact that his assumption of superiority in footwork has proven false. He is made to look foolish; he loses face. Hence, it is always a gamble to "make a remark." The tables can be turned and the aggressor can lose more than he could have gained had his move won the point. . . .

Cooperation in Face-Work

Since each participant in an undertaking is concerned, albeit for differing reasons, with saving his own face and the face of the others, then tacit cooperation will naturally arise so that the participants together can attain their shared but differently motivated objectives.

One common type of tacit cooperation in face-saving is the tact exerted in regard to face-work itself. The person not only defends his own face and protects the face of the others, but also acts so as to make it possible and even easy for the others to employ face-work for themselves and him. He helps them to help themselves and him. Social etiquette, for example, warns men against asking for New Year's Eve dates too early in the season, lest the girl find it difficult to provide a gentle excuse for refusing. This second-order tact can be further illustrated by the wide-spread practice of negative-attribute etiquette. The person who has an unapparent negatively valued attribute often finds it expedient to begin an encounter with an unobtrusive admission of his failing, especially with persons who are uninformed about him. The others are thus warned in advance against making disparaging remarks about his kind of person and are saved from the contradiction of acting in a friendly fashion to a person toward whom they are unwittingly being hostile. This strategy also prevents the others from automatically making assumptions about him which place him in a false position and saves him from painful forbearance or embarrassing remonstrances.

Tact, in regard to face-work, often relies for its operation on a tacit agreement to do business through the language of hint—the language of innuendo, ambiguities, well-placed pauses, carefully worded jokes, and so on. The rule regarding this unofficial kind of communication is that the sender ought not to act as if he had officially conveyed the message he has hinted at, while the recipients have the right and the obligation to act as if they have not officially received the message contained in the hint. Hinted communication, then, is deniable communication; it need not be faced up to. It provides a means by which the person can be warned that his current line or the current situation is leading to loss of face, without this warning itself becoming an incident.

Another form of tacit cooperation, and one that seems to be much used in many societies, is reciprocal self-denial. Often the person does not have a clear idea of what

would be a just or acceptable apportionment of judgments during the occasion, and so he voluntarily deprives or depreciates himself while indulging and complimenting the others, in both cases carrying the judgments safely past what is likely to be just. The favorable judgments about himself he allows to come from others; the unfavorable judgments of himself are his own contributions.

This "after you, Alphonse" technique works, of course, because in depriving himself, he can reliably anticipate that the others will compliment or indulge him. Whatever allocation of favors is eventually established, all participants are first given a chance to show that they are not bound or constrained by their own desires and expectations, that they have a properly modest view of themselves, and that they can be counted upon to support the ritual code. . . .

A person's performance of face-work, extended by his tacit agreement to help others perform theirs, represents his willingness to abide by the ground rules of social interaction. Here is the hallmark of his socialization as an interactant. If he and the others were not socialized in this way, interaction in most societies and most situations would be a much more hazardous thing for feelings and faces. The person would find it impractical to be oriented to symbolically conveyed appraisals of social worth, or to be possessed of feelings—that is, it would be impractical for him to be a ritually delicate object. . . . It is no wonder that trouble is caused by a person who cannot be relied upon to play the face-saving game. . . .

Conclusion

Throughout this paper it has been implied that underneath their differences in culture, people everywhere are the same. If persons have a universal human nature, they themselves are not to be looked to for an explanation of it. One must look rather to the fact that societies everywhere, if they are to be societies, must mobilize their members as self-regulating participants in social encounters. One way of mobilizing the individual for this purpose is through ritual: he is taught to be perceptive; to have feelings attached to self and a self expressed through face; to have pride, honor, and dignity; to have considerateness; to have tact and a certain amount of poise. These are some of the elements of behavior which must be built into the person, if practical use is to be made of him as an interactant, and it is these elements that are referred to in part when one speaks of universal human nature.

Universal human nature is not a very human thing. By acquiring it, the person becomes a kind of construct, built up not from inner psychic propensities but from moral rules that are impressed upon him from without. These rules, when followed, determine the evaluation he will make of himself and of his fellow-participants in the encounter, the distribution of his feelings, and the kinds of practices he will employ to maintain a specified and obligatory kind of ritual equilibrium. The general capacity to be bound by moral rules may well belong to the individual, but the particular set of rules which transforms him into a human being derives from requirements established in the ritual organization of social encounters. . . .

17

The Interaction Order of Public Bathrooms

Spencer E. Cahill

This selection illustrates the dramatic and ritual character of everyday social life that Goffman identified with the example of routine behavior in public bathrooms. From Goffman's dramaturgical perspective, bathrooms are backstage regions where individuals can temporarily retire from their frontstage performances. However, public bathrooms do not insulate individuals from potential audiences. When not concealed in toilet stalls, they must be ready to perform and to uphold what Goffman called "the interaction order." Yet, individuals in public bathrooms routinely engage in acts that are inconsistent with their frontstage performances and undermine the "sacred" face they claim through those performances. Thus, public bathrooms are scenes of many socially delicate situations that reveal just how loyal we are to the commonly understood but unspoken rules that govern everyday social interaction.

First, this selection illustrates that much behavior in public bathrooms consists of what Goffman called "interpersonal rituals." Individuals show respect for one another by honoring one another's right to be left alone and the turn order of queues. They show respect for their relationships with others by acknowledging those with whom they are previously acquainted. Other ritual conduct in public bathrooms addresses the socially delicate situations that occur within them. For example, men using adjacent urinals do not glance at one another and then look away as they might under other circumstances but keep their eyes glued to the wall directly in front of them. Other ritual conduct counteracts the profaning implications of the acts for which public bathrooms are explicitly designed.

Second, this selection illustrates the variety of backstage behaviors that routinely occur in public bathrooms. In addition to the acts for which they are explicitly designed, individuals retreat to bathrooms to inspect and repair their frontstage appearance and costumes or "personal fronts." They retreat to bathrooms when overcome by emotion. And, groups who are acting as an ensemble or "performance team" retreat to bathrooms to boost team morale, rehearse lines, and give one another direction.

Both forms of routine behavior in public bathrooms, ritual and backstage, reveal many of the usually unrecognized standards that govern everyday social interaction and our usually unrecognized commitment to them. Backstage behavior reveals, by way of contrast, the behavioral standards that govern our frontstage performances. And, our ritual conduct in public bathrooms demonstrates just how committed we are to upholding the expressive order that sustains the "sacredness" of our own and others' "face." The usually unnoticed but exquisite orderliness of everyday social interaction clearly does not stop at the bathroom door.

[Some] years ago the anthropologist Horace Miner (1955) suggested, with tongue planted firmly in cheek, that many of the rituals that behaviorally express and sustain the central values of our culture occur in bathrooms. Whether Miner realized it or not . . . there was more to this thesis than his humorous interpretation of bathroom rituals suggests. As Erving Goffman (1959: 112–113) once observed, the vital secrets of our public shows are often visible in those settings that serve as backstage regions relative to our public performances:

> it is here that illusions and impressions are openly constructed. . . . Here the performer can relax; he can drop his front,

165

forego speaking his lines, and step out of character.

Clearly, bathrooms or, as they are often revealingly called, restrooms, are such backstage regions. By implication, therefore, systematic study of bathroom behavior may yield valuable insights into the character and requirements of our routine public performances. . . .

This study is . . . concerned with routine bathroom behavior. Over a nine-month period, five student research assistants and I spent over one hundred hours observing behavior in the bathrooms of such public establishments as shopping malls, student centers on college campuses, and restaurants and bars at various locations in the Northeastern United States. These observations were recorded in fieldnotes and provide the empirical basis for the following analysis.

The Performance Regions of Public Bathrooms

Needless to say, one of the behaviors for which bathrooms are explicitly designed is defecation. In our society, as Goffman (1959: 121) observed, "defecation involves an individual in activity which is defined as inconsistent with the cleanliness and purity standards" that govern our public performances.

Such activity also causes the individual to disarrange his clothing and to "go out of play," that is, to drop from his face the expressive mask that he employs in face-to-face interaction. At the same time it becomes difficult for him to reassemble his personal front should the need to enter into interaction occur.

When engaged in the act of defecation, therefore, individuals seek to insulate themselves from potential audiences in order to avoid discrediting the expressive masks that they publicly employ. . . .

In an apparent attempt to provide such privacy, toilets in many public bathrooms are surrounded by partially walled cubicles with doors that can be secured against potential intrusions. Public bathrooms that do not provide individuals this protection from potential audiences are seldom used for the purpose of defecation. In the course of our research, for example, we never observed an individual using an unenclosed toilet for this purpose. If a bathroom contained both enclosed and unenclosed toilets . . . individuals ignored the unenclosed toilets even when queues had formed outside of the enclosed toilets. In a sense, therefore, the cubicles that typically surround toilets in public bathrooms, commonly called stalls, physically divide such bathrooms into two distinct performance regions.

Indeed, Goffman (1971: 32) has used the term "stall" to refer to any "well-bounded space to which individuals lay temporary claim, possession being on an all-or-nothing basis." . . . [A] toilet stall is clearly a member of this sociological family of ecological arrangements. Sociologically speaking, however, it is not physical boundaries, per se, that define a space as a stall but the behavioral regard given such boundaries. For example, individuals who open or attempt to open the door of an occupied toilet stall typically provide a remedy for this act, in most cases a brief apology such as "Whoops" or "Sorry." By offering such a remedy, the offending individual implicitly defines the attempted intrusion as a [violation] and, thereby, affirms his or her belief in a rule that prohibits such intrusions (Goffman 1971: 113). In this sense, toilet stalls provide occupying individuals not only physical protection against potential audiences but normative protection as well.

In order to receive this protection, however, occupying individuals must clearly inform others of their claim to such a stall. Although individuals sometimes lean down and look under doors of toilet stalls for feet, they typically expect occupying individuals to mark their claim to a toilet stall by securely closing the door. On one occasion, a middle-aged woman began to push open the unlocked door of a toilet stall. Upon discovering that the stall was occupied, she immediately said, "I'm sorry," and closed the door. When a young woman emerged from the stall a couple minutes later, the older woman apologized once again but pointed out that "the door was open." The young woman responded, "it's okay," thereby minimizing the offense and perhaps acknowledging a degree of culpability on her part.

As is the case with many physical barriers to perception (Goffman 1963: 152), the walls and doors of toilet stalls are also treated as if they cut off more communication than they actually do. Under most circumstances, the walls and doors of toilet stalls are treated as if they were barriers to conversation. Although acquainted individuals may sometimes carry on a conversation through the walls of a toilet stall if they believe the bathroom is not otherwise occupied, they seldom do so if they are aware that others are present. Moreover, individuals often attempt to ignore offensive sounds and smells that emanate from occupied toilet stalls, even though the exercise of such "tactful blindness" (Goffman 1955: 219) is sometimes a demanding task. In any case, the walls and doors of toilet stalls provide public actors with both physical and normative shields behind which they can perform potentially discrediting acts.

Toilet stalls in public bathrooms are, therefore, publicly accessible yet private backstage regions. Although same-sexed clients of a public establishment may lay claim to any unoccupied toilet stall in the bathroom designated for use by persons of their sex, once such a claim is laid, once the door to the stall is closed, it is transformed into the occupying individual's private, albeit temporary, retreat from the demands of public life. While occupying the stall, that individual can engage in a variety of potentially discrediting acts with impunity.

When not concealed behind the protective cover of a toilet stall, however, occupants of public bathrooms may be observed by others. . . . Same-sexed clients of a public establishment can enter and exit at will the bathroom designated for their use, and it may be simultaneously occupied by as many individuals as its physical dimensions allow. By implication, occupants of public bathrooms must either perform or be ready to perform for an audience. As a result, the behavior that routinely occurs in the "open region" of a public bathroom, that area that is not enclosed by toilet stalls, resembles, in many important respects, the behavior that routinely occurs in other public settings.

The Ritual of Public Bathrooms

As Goffman (1971) convincingly argued, much of this behavior can best be described as "interpersonal rituals." Emile Durkheim (1965), in his [classic] analysis of religion, defined a ritual as a perfunctory, conventionalized act which expresses respect and regard for some object of "ultimate value." . . . Drawing inspiration from Durkheim, Goffman (1971: 63) pointed out that despite the increasing secularization of our society there remain

> brief rituals one individual performs for and to another, attesting to civility and good will on the performer's part and to the recipient's possession of a small patrimony of sacredness.

Still borrowing from Durkheim . . . Goffman (1971: 62) divided these interpersonal rituals into two classes: positive and negative.

According to Durkheim, negative rituals express respect and regard for objects of ultimate value by protecting them from profanation. According to Goffman (1971: 62), negative interpersonal rituals involve the behavioral honoring of the scared individual's right to private "preserves" and "to be let alone." As previously noted, for example, individuals typically refrain from physically, conversationally, or visually intruding on an occupied toilet stall. In doing so, they implicitly honor the occupying individual's right to be let alone and in this respect perform a negative interpersonal ritual.

Similarly, the queues that typically form in public bathrooms when the demand for sinks, urinals, and toilet stalls exceeds the available supply are also products of individuals' mutual performance of negative interpersonal rituals. Individuals typically honor one another's right to the turn claimed by taking up a position in such a queue, even when "creature releases" (Goffman 1963: 69) threaten to break through their self-control. Young children provide an occasional exception, sometimes ignoring the turn-order of such queues. Yet even then the child's caretaker typically requests, on the child's behalf, the permission of those waiting in the queue. Between performances at a music festival, for example, a preschool-age girl and her mother were observed rapidly walking toward the entrance to a women's bathroom out of which a queue extended for several yards down a nearby sidewalk. As they walked past those waiting in the queue, the mother repeatedly asked "Do you mind? She really has to go."

However, the interpersonal rituals that routinely occur in the open region of public bathrooms are not limited to negative ones. If individuals possess a small patrimony of sacredness, then, as Durkheim (1974: 37) noted, "the greatest good is in communion" with such sacred objects. When previously acquainted individuals come into contact with one another, therefore, they typically perform conventionalized acts, positive interpersonal rituals, that express respect and regard for their previous communion with one another. In a sense, negative and positive interpersonal rituals are two sides of the same expressive coin. Whereas negative interpersonal rituals symbolically protect individuals from profanation by others, positive interpersonal rituals symbolically cleanse communion between individuals of its potentially defiling implications. Although a positive interpersonal ritual may consist of no more than a brief exchange of greetings, failure to at least acknowledge one's previous communion with another is, in effect, to express disregard for the relationship and, by implication, the other individual's small patrimony of sacredness (Goffman 1971: 62–94).

Even when previously acquainted individuals come into contact with one another in a public bathroom, therefore, they typically acknowledge their prior relationship. In fact, the performance of such positive interpersonal rituals sometimes interfered with the conduct of our research. On one occasion, for example, a member of the research team was in the open region of an otherwise unoccupied men's bathroom. While he was writing some notes about an incident that had just occurred, an acquaintance entered.

A: Hey _____! (walks to the urinal and unzips his pants) Nothing like pissin.

O: Yup.

A: Wh'da hell ya doin? (walks over to a sink and washes hands)

O: Writing.

A: Heh, heh, yea. About people pissin. . . . That's for you.

O: Yup.

A: Take care.

O: Mmm. Huh.

As this incident illustrates, individuals must be prepared to perform positive interpersonal rituals when in the open region of public bathrooms, especially those in public establishments with a relatively stable clientele. Whereas some of these may consist of no more than a brief exchange of smiles, others may involve lengthy conversations that reaffirm the participants' shared biography.

In contrast, when unacquainted individuals come into contact with one another in the open regions of public bathrooms, they typically perform a brief, negative interpersonal ritual that Goffman (1963: 84) termed "civil inattention." In its canonical form,

> one gives to another enough visual notice to demonstrate that one appreciates that the other is present . . . while at the next moment withdrawing one's attention from him so as to express that he does not constitute a target of special curiosity or design.

Through this brief pattern of visual interaction, individuals both acknowledge one another's presence and, immediately thereafter, one another's right to be let alone.

A variation on the canonical form of civil attention is also commonly performed in the open region of public bathrooms, most often by men using adjacent urinals. Although masculine clothing permits males to urinate without noticeably disturbing their clothed appearance, they must still partially expose their external genitalia in order to do so. Clearly, the standards of modesty that govern public behavior prohibit even such limited exposure of the external genitalia. Although the sides of some urinals and the urinating individual's back provide partial barriers to perception, they do not provide protection against the glances of someone occupying an adjacent urinal. In our society, however, "when bodies are naked, glances are clothed" (Goffman 1971: 46). What men typically give one another when using adjacent urinals is not, therefore, civil inattention but "non-person treatment" (Goffman 1963: 83–84): that is, they treat one another as if they were part of the setting's physical equipment, as "objects not worthy of a glance." When circumstances allow, of course, unacquainted males typically avoid occupying adjacent urinals and, thereby, this ritually delicate situation.

It is not uncommon, however, for previously acquainted males to engage in conversation while using adjacent urinals. For example, the following interaction was observed in the bathroom of a restaurant.

> A middle-aged man is standing at one of two urinals. Another middle-aged man enters the bathroom and, as he approaches the available urinal, greets the first man by name. The first man quickly casts a side-long glance at the second and returns the greeting. He then asks the second man about his "new granddaughter," and they continue to talk about grandchildren until one of them zips up his pants and walks over to a sink. Throughout the conversation, neither man turned his head so as to look at the other.

As this example illustrates, urinal conversations are often characterized by a lack of visual interaction between the participants. Instead of looking at one another while listening . . . participants in such conversations typically fix their gaze on the wall immediately in front of them, an intriguing combination of the constituent elements of positive and negative interpersonal rituals. Although ritually celebrating their prior communion with one another, they also visually honor one another's right to privacy.

Due to the particular profanations and threats of profanations that characterize public bathrooms, moreover, a number of variations on these general patterns also commonly occur. In our society, as Goffman (1971: 41) observed, bodily excreta are considered "agencies of defilement." Although supported by germ theory, this view involves somewhat more than a concern for hygiene. Once such substances as urine, fecal matter, menstrual discharge and flatus leave individuals' bodies, they acquire the power to profane even though they may not have the power to infect. In any case, many of the activities in which individuals engage when in bathrooms are considered both self-profaning and potentially profaning to others. As a result, a variety of ritually delicate situations often arise in public bathrooms.

For example, after using urinals and toilets, individuals' hands are considered contaminated and, consequently, a source of contamination to others. In order to demonstrate both self-respect and respect for those with whom they might come into contact, individuals are expected to and often do wash their hands after using urinals and toilets. Sinks for this purpose are typically located in the open region of public bathrooms, allowing others to witness the performance of this restorative ritual. Sometimes, however, public bathrooms are not adequately equipped for this purpose. Most commonly, towel dispensers are empty or broken. Although individuals sometimes do not discover this situation until after they have already washed their hands, they often glance at towel dispensers as they walk from urinals and toilet stalls to sinks. If they discover that the towel dispensers are empty or broken, there is typically a moment of indecision. Although they sometimes proceed to wash their hands and then dry them on their clothes, many times they hesitate, facially display disgust, and audibly sigh. By performing these gestures-in-the-round, they express a desire to wash their hands; their hands remain contaminated, but their regard for their own and others' sacredness is established.

Because the profaning power of odor operates over a distance and in all directions, moreover, individuals who defecate in public bathrooms not only temporarily profane themselves but also risk profaning the entire setting. If an individual is clearly responsible for the odor of feces or flatus that fills a bathroom, therefore, he or she must rely on others to identify sympathetically with his or her plight and, consequently, exercise tactful blindness. However, this is seldom left to chance. When other occupants of the bathroom are acquaintances, the offending individual may offer a subtle, self-derogatory display as a defensive, face-saving measure

(Goffman 1955). Upon emerging from toilet stalls, for example, such persons sometimes look at acquaintances and facially display disgust. Self-effacing humor is also occasionally used in this way. On one occasion, for example, an acquaintance of a member of the research team emerged from a toilet stall after having filled the bathroom with a strong fecal odor. He walked over to a sink, smiled at the observer, and remarked: "Something died in there." Through such subtle self-derogation, offending individuals metaphorically split themselves into two parts: a sacred self that assigns blame and a blame-worthy animal self. Because the offending individual assigns blame, moreover, there is no need for others to do so (Goffman 1971: 113).

If other occupants of the bathroom are unfamiliar to the offending individual, however, a somewhat different defensive strategy is commonly employed. Upon emerging from a toilet stall, individuals who are clearly responsible for an offensive odor seldom engage in visual interaction with unacquainted others. In so doing, they avoid visually acknowledging not only the presence of others but others' acknowledgement of their own presence as well. In a sense, therefore, the offending individual temporarily suspends his or her claim to the status of sacred object, an object worthy of such visual regard. The assumption seems to be that by suspending one's claim to this status, others need not challenge it and are, consequently, more likely to exercise tactful blindness in regard to the offense.

Thus, despite Miner's humorous misidentification and interpretation of bathroom rituals, there is something to recommend the view that many of the rituals that behaviorally express and sustain the central values of our culture occur in bathrooms. Although those "central values do but itch a little," as Goffman (1971: 185) noted, "everyone scratches." And, it must be added, they often scratch in public bathrooms. However, routine bathroom behavior consists of more than the interpersonal rituals that are found in other public settings or variations on their general theme.

Backstage Behavior in Public Bathrooms

Clearly, public establishments differ in the degree to which their clients observe generally accepted standards of behavioral propriety. Moreover, the behavior that routinely occurs within an establishment's bathrooms typically reflects the degree of behavioral "tightness or looseness" (Goffman 1963: 200) that characterizes that establishment. For example, bathrooms in neighborhood bars are characterized by considerably more behavioral looseness than are bathrooms in expensive restaurants. Regardless of the degree of tightness or looseness that characterizes the frontstage region of a public establishment, however, somewhat greater behavioral looseness will be found in the establishment's bathrooms. After all, even the open region of a public bathroom is backstage relative to the setting beyond its doors. As such, public bathrooms offer individuals at least some relief from the behavioral harness that the frontstage audience's eyes impose upon them. . . .

Managing Personal Fronts

When in a public setting, as Goffman (1963: 24) pointed out, individuals are expected to have their "faculties in readiness for any face-to-face interaction that might come" their way. One of the most evident means by which individuals express such readiness is "through the disciplined management of personal appearance or 'personal front,' that is, the complex of clothing, make-up, hairdo, and other surface decorations" that they carry about on their person (Goffman 1963: 25). Of course, keeping one's personal front in a state of good repair requires care and effort. . . . However, individuals who are inspecting or repairing their personal fronts in

public encounter difficulties in maintaining the degree of interactional readiness often expected of them; their attention tends to be diverted from the social situations that surround them (Goffman 1963: 66). For the most part, therefore, close [inspection] and major adjustments of personal fronts are confined to backstage regions such as public bathrooms.

Most public bathrooms are equipped for this purpose. Many offer coin-operated dispensers of a variety of "personal care products" . . . and almost all have at least one mirror. The most obvious reason for the presence of mirrors in public bathrooms is that the act of defecation and, for females, urination, requires individuals to literally "drop" their personal fronts. In order to ensure that they have adequately reconstructed their personal front after engaging in such an act, individuals must and typically do perform what Lofland (1972) has termed a "readiness check." For example, the following was observed in the men's bathroom of a neighborhood bar:

> A young man emerges from a toilet stall and, as he passes the mirror, hesitates. He glances side-long at his reflection, gives a nod of approval and then walks out the door.

When such a readiness check reveals flaws in the individual's personal front, he or she typically makes the appropriate repairs: Shirts are often retucked into pants and skirts, skirts are rotated around the waist, and pants are tugged up and down.

Because bodily movement and exposure to the elements can also disturb a disciplined personal front, the post-defecation or urination readiness check sometimes reveals flaws in individuals' personal fronts that are the result of normal wear and tear. Upon emerging from toilet stalls and leaving urinals, therefore, individuals sometimes repair aspects of their personal fronts that are not normally disturbed in the course of defecating or urinating. For example, the following was observed in the women's bathroom of a student center on a college campus.

> A young woman emerges from a toilet stall, approaches a mirror, and inspects her reflection. She then removes a barrette from her hair, places the barrette in her mouth, takes a comb out of her coat pocket, and combs her hair while smoothing it down with her other hand. With the barrette still in her mouth, she stops combing her hair, gazes intently at the mirror and emits an audible "ick." She then places the barrette back in her hair, pinches her cheeks, takes a last look at her reflection and exits.

Interestingly, as both this example and the immediately preceding one illustrate, individuals sometimes offer visible or audible evaluations of their reflections when inspecting and repairing their personal front, a finding that should delight proponents of Meadian sociological psychology. Public bathrooms may protect individuals from the critical reviews of external audiences, but they do not protect them from those of their internal audience.

In any case, public bathrooms are as much "self-service" repair shops for personal fronts as they are socially approved shelters for physiological acts that are inconsistent with the cleanliness and purity standards that govern our public performances. In fact, individuals often enter public bathrooms with no apparent purpose other than the management of their personal front. For example, it is not uncommon for males to enter public bathrooms, walk directly to the nearest available mirror, comb their hair, rearrange their clothing, and then immediately exit. In our society, of course, females are often expected to present publicly a more extensively managed personal front than are males. Consequently, females often undertake extensive repairs in public bathrooms. For example, the following was observed in the women's bathroom of a student center on a college campus:

> Two young women enter, one goes to a toilet stall and the other immediately approaches a mirror. The second woman takes a brush out of her bookbag, throws her hair forward, brushes it, throws her hair back, and brushes it into place. She returns the brush to her bookbag, smoothes down her eyebrows, and wipes underneath her eyes with her fingers. She then removes a tube of lipstick from her bookbag, applies it to her lips, and uses her finger to remove the lipstick that extends beyond the natural outline of her lips. As her friend emerges from the toilet stall, she puts the lipstick tube back into her bookbag, straightens her collar so that it stands up under her sweater and then exits with her friend.

Even though individuals routinely inspect and repair their personal fronts in the open regions of public bathrooms, they often do so furtively. When others enter the bathroom, individuals sometimes suspend inspecting or repairing their personal fronts until the new arrivals enter toilet stalls or approach urinals. In other cases, they hurriedly complete these activities before they can be witnessed. . . . Despite the furtiveness that sometimes characterizes individuals' inspection and repair of their personal fronts, however, the open region of a public bathroom is often the only available setting in which they can engage in these activities without clearly undermining their frontstage performances. As Lofland (1972: 101) observed in a somewhat different context, "it is apparently preferable to be witnessed by a few . . . in a brief episode of backstage behavior than to be caught . . . with one's presentation down" on the frontstage.

Going Out of Play

While a disciplined personal front may serve to express interactional readiness, public actors must also "exert a kind of discipline or tension" in regard to their bodies in order to actually maintain the degree of interactional readiness that is expected of them (Goffman 1963: 24). After all, a variety of bodily processes can drain individuals' attention away from the social world around them, causing them to turn inward and, interactionally speaking, to go out of play. Of course, the ostensive purpose of public bathrooms and their toilet stalls is to provide public actors with socially approved shelters in which to indulge such bodily processes. . . .

In addition to creature releases that threaten to slip through an individual's self-control, emotional reactions may also cause individuals to go out of play. In such cases, individuals may conclude that precipitant leave taking is preferable to going out of play in full view of their frontstage audience. Under these circumstances, therefore, they may quickly retreat to the protective cover of a toilet stall. Although it is difficult for an observer to ascertain if this has taken place, it was the research team's impression that incidents, such as those described by Margaret Atwood (1969: 71) in her novel, *The Edible Woman,* are not uncommon. The narrator, Marian, was sitting with some friends in a bar when she noticed "a large drop of something wet" on the table near her hand.

> I poked it with my finger and smudged it around a little before I realized with horror that it was a tear. I must be crying then . . . I was going to break down and make a scene, and I couldn't. I slid out of my chair, trying to be as inconspicuous as possible, walked across the room avoiding the other tables with great care, and went to the Ladies Powder Room. Checking first to make sure no one else was in there—I couldn't have witnesses—I locked myself into one of the plushy-pink cubicles and wept for several minutes.

Depending on how precipitant such leave-taking is, of course, same-sexed members of the individual's frontstage audience may feel justified in conversationally intruding on this private preserve in order to inquire about his or her well-being. It is probably easier, however, to deflect such questions from behind the protective cover of a toilet stall than it would be if the frontstage audience witnessed such a display of emotion.

Parallel to individuals who retire to toilet stalls when they are overcome with emotion, entire "performance teams" (Goffman 1959: 77–105) sometimes retreat into public bathrooms in order to conceal the paralyzing embarrassment that results when a collective performance [collapses]. . . . For example, the following conversation between three young women was recorded in the bathroom of a student center on a college campus. Although the incident that led to this conversation was not observed, it obviously resulted in such paralyzing embarrassment.

> A: That was sooo embarrassing! I can't believe that just happened. (general laughter)
>
> B: He must think we are the biggest bunch of losers.
>
> A: I can't believe I just screamed loud enough for everyone to hear.
>
> C: It really wasn't all that loud. I'm sure he didn't hear you.
>
> A: How can you say that? He turned around just as I said it. Why didn't you guys tell me he was standing right there?
>
> B: _____, we didn't see him right away, and I did try to tell you but you were so busy talking that I . . .
>
> A: I can't believe that just happened. I feel like such an asshole.
>
> B: Don't worry 'bout it. At least he knows who you are now. Are you ready?
>
> A: I'm so embarrassed. What if he's still out there?
>
> B: You're gonna have to see him at some point.

In addition to concealing a temporary loss of control, these defensive strategies also buy individuals and performance teams time, as this example illustrates, in which to gather themselves together before once again facing the frontstage audience.

However, occupants of public bathrooms and their toilet stalls who use them for purposes other than those for which they were explicitly designed must exercise some caution. Unusual or unusually loud noises and unusually long occupancy, if someone is aware of the duration of the occupancy, may lead others to intrude upon these private preserves. By implication, individuals who use public bathrooms and their toilet stalls in order to conceal autoerotic activities, the usage of illicit drugs, emotional reactions, or other potentially discrediting acts must still exercise a degree of self-control.

Staging Talk

As Goffman (1959: 175) observed, performance teams routinely use backstage regions to gather themselves together [and] discuss . . . problems involved in the staging of their collective performance:

> Here the team can run through its performance, checking for offending expressions when no audience is present to be affronted by them; here poor members of the team . . . can be schooled or dropped from the performance.

In the conversation reproduced above, for example, B and C not only attempt to belittle the discrediting implications of A's earlier actions, but B also schools A in the art of staging collective performances. If, according to B, A had paid more attention to the other team members' directional cues, she could have avoided this embarrassing incident.

In addition to retreating into public bathrooms after the failure of a collective performance, performance teams also retire to public bathrooms in order to take preventive measures against such an occurrence. Here the team may agree upon collusive signals, rehearse their planned performance, and exchange strategic information. In bathrooms in bars, for example, performance teams were sometimes overheard discussing the planned targets of members' erotic overtures, the overtures they had received, the source of such overtures, and their likely responses. By providing other members of a performance team with such strategic information, of course, an individual may prevent them from interfering with his or her personal project and may even enlist their aid in accomplishing it.

Sometimes, moreover, the backstage discussions that occur in public bathrooms are at least partially concerned with a team member's morale or that of the entire team. In the previously discussed conversation between the three young women, for example, B and C attempt to boost A's morale by both belittling the discrediting implications of her earlier actions and encouraging her to "go on with the show." As Goffman (1959: 175) pointed out, backstage derogation of the audience is another strategy that performance teams commonly employ in order to maintain their morale. For example, a young woman was overheard making the following remark to two other young women in the bathroom of a popular nightclub.

> You guys think I'm obnoxious! WELL just take a look at _____, my God!

In any case, both performance teams and individual performers . . . routinely use public bathrooms as staging areas for their public performances. . . .

Conclusion

The behavior that routinely occurs within [public bathrooms] reveals, by way of contrast, some of the requirements that we must meet in order to maintain an unblemished public face. As the preceding analysis indicates, typical bathroom behaviors include the open staging of public performances, the concealment of emotional reactions, the indulgence of creature releases, and the inspection and repair of personal fronts. If, moreover, public bathrooms are backstage regions relative to the public settings beyond their doors, then the behaviors that tend to be confined to public bathrooms are inconsistent with the behavioral standards that govern our public performances. By implication, therefore, these standards would seem to require the presentation of a disciplined personal front, the avoidance of visible concern with its maintenance, the suppression of animal natures, some minimal degree of interactional readiness, and performances that appear "only natural." Without such readily accessible backstage regions as public bathrooms, it becomes increasingly difficult to fulfill these requirements; much of what we do in public bathrooms, then, is what we must not do elsewhere but what we must do somewhere.

In addition to noting such backstage behavior, the preceding analysis indicates that a number of interpersonal rituals found in other public settings are also routinely performed in public bathrooms. Although, at first glance, this finding may seem to contradict the characterization of public bathrooms as backstage regions, even "loosely defined" social situations are, in Goffman's (1963: 241) words, "tight little rooms." In fact, it may be within such loosely defined situations that the central values of our culture itch the most and are, by implication, most in need of scratching. Within public bathrooms, the animal natures behind our expressive masks and the blemishes underneath our disciplined personal fronts are often exposed. When we find ourselves in such ritually delicate situations, we need assurances that we retain our small patrimony of sacredness despite evidence to the contrary. In a sense, interpersonal rituals are routinely performed in public bathrooms because of, rather than in spite of, their backstage character.

In short, systematic study of routine bathroom behavior reveals just how loyal members of this society are to the central values and behavioral standards that hold our collective lives together. Whatever else they may do, users of public bathrooms continue to bear the "cross of personal character" (Goffman 1971: 185), and, as long as they continue to carry this burden, remain self-regulating participants in the "interaction order" (Goffman 1983).

References

Atwood, M. (1969) *The Edible Woman.* Boston: Little, Brown.

Durkheim, E. (1974) *Sociology and Philosophy.* (D. F. Pocock, trans.). New York: Free Press (originally published in 1924).

——. (1965) *The Elementary Forms of the Religious Life.* (J. W. Swain, trans.). New York: Free Press (originally published in 1915).

Goffman, E. (1983) "The interaction order." *Amer. Soc. Rev.* 48 (February): 1–17.

——. (1971) *Relations in Public: Microstudies in Public Order.* New York: Basic Books.

——. (1963) *Behavior in Public Places: Notes on the Social Organization of Gatherings.* New York: Free Press.

——. (1959) *The Presentation of Self in Everyday Life.* Garden City, NY: Doubleday.

——. (1955) "On face-work: An analysis of ritual elements of social interaction." *Psychiatry* 18 (August): 213–231.

Lofland, L. (1972) "Self-management in public settings: Part I." *Urban Life* 1 (April): 93–108.

Miner, H. (1955) "Body ritual among the Nacirema." *Amer. Anthropologist* 58 (June): 503–507.

18

Wheelchair Users' Interpersonal Management of Emotions

*Spencer E. Cahill and
Robin Eggleston*

Everyday interaction is characterized by not only an expressive order, but an emotional order as well. This is nowhere more apparent than in public places where strangers and casual acquaintances routinely meet and sometimes interact. There, calm composure usually prevails and open expressions of intense emotions are rare. Yet, underneath this calm veneer, emotions such as fear, embarrassment, anger, and resentment often boil. This selection illustrates the considerable emotion work required to keep those emotions from boiling over into public interactions with the example of wheelchair users' public experience.

Wheelchair users' public experience is especially emotional. They often find themselves in embarrassing situations. They are treated both rudely and with kindness. They routinely receive needed and unneeded, wanted and unwanted, helpful and harmful assistance from others. All of these circumstances stir their emotions. Yet, as this selection illustrates, wheelchair users usually avoid publicly expressing their embarrassment, anger, and resentment so as to avoid evoking emotions in others. This is only one of the ways that wheelchair users manage both their own and others' emotions in public.

Although unusually demanding, wheelchair users' emotion work in public places illustrates the effort required to sustain the emotional tranquility of everyday public life. Like wheelchair users, we often make humorous remarks to relieve the tension of problematic situations. We suppress our anger so as not to provoke others'. We act graciously toward those who treat us both ungraciously and overgraciously so as not to anger or embarrass them. We manage our own emotions so as to manage others' and thereby sustain the emotional orderliness of everyday social interaction.

Since the 1970s, students of social life have learned many lessons about the social sources and consequences of emotions. Many of us now appreciate that social life is as much an affair of the heart as of the head, but perhaps we do not appreciate this fact deeply enough. We still tend to concentrate on individuals' socially guided management of their own emotions to the neglect of their management of one another's. . . .

Yet, as Goffman (1963a, 1971) demonstrates convincingly, individuals in public places attempt to assure one another of their civility and goodwill so as not to evoke embarrassment, fear, or anger in others or in themselves. Although they often appear emotionally reserved and indifferent, that appearance is a consequence of emotion work rather than its absence. . . . The study of public life has much to teach us about the emotional dynamics of social interaction and life, if only we are willing to learn from those who notice what we usually miss. [And, when it comes to the interpersonal management of emotions], those whose principal mode of mobility is a wheelchair cannot help noticing what the rest of us can overlook more easily. . . .

Our specific focus is the emotional dilemmas faced by wheelchair users when in public places. We begin by briefly describing the inspiration and empirical basis of our analysis. Then we examine three general types of emotional challenges that wheelchair users confront in public places. Our purpose is not only to provide some insight into wheelchair users' public lives but also to draw from their example more general lessons about the emotional dynamics of contemporary public life and the interpersonal dynamics of emotion management. . . .

The Instruction of Wheelchair Use and Users

Our collective interest in wheelchair users' public experiences grew out of conversations between the first author and second author, who has used an electrically powered wheelchair as her principal mode of public mobility [for some time]. At the urging of the first author, she started to make fieldnotes of her daily participant observation of the social life of a wheelchair user. . . . [T]he first author supplemented these with fieldnotes that he made when using a wheelchair in public places for the specific purpose of participant observation. . . . We also collected and read wheelchair users' autobiographical accounts. . . . In addition, we collectively conducted and recorded interviews with seven women and five men who regularly use a wheelchair in public places. . . .

Although initially we did not intend to focus on the emotional challenges of public wheelchair use, emotional dilemmas loomed large in our own and our informants' accounts and in the published accounts of other wheelchair users' public experiences. Gradually we became convinced that those dilemmas contained a revealing story about the place of wheelchair users in public life, about contemporary public life more generally, and about interpersonal processes of

emotion management. The following analysis tells that story.

The Emotional Demands of Public Wheelchair Use

For many wheelchair users, the very decision to venture into public places is emotionally turbulent. The desire for autonomy and for the many pleasures that only public places offer collides with fears—among others, fear of moving past and among much larger vehicles. There is the fear of upsetting others that has kept one of our informants, who recently started using a wheelchair, from using it in restaurants.

> I think it's hard for people to eat food close to people who are ill. There's something about the process of eating that makes people even more uptight about disease. . . . My rolling in probably wouldn't affect people in that way, but in the back of my mind I'm afraid it would. I'll have to get over that.

Wheelchair users also fear, with justification, being an embarrassing and embarrassed public spectacle.

Humoring Embarrassment

Like those whom one of our informants calls "stand-up people," wheelchair users face a variety of embarrassing possibilities whenever they venture into public places. For any number of reasons, they may lose control over self or situation (Gross and Stone 1964), falling short of what is generally expected of public actors. Wheelchair users, however, face a number of uniquely embarrassing contingencies because the physical environment, both natural and constructed, is unfriendly to their mode of mobility. Rain and snow can leave them immobile and embarrassingly in need of rescue. Doorway thresholds, uneven sidewalks, and unanticipated depressions at the bottom of curb cuts may cause a wheelchair to tip over, leaving its occupant embarrassingly sprawled on the ground. Crowded and narrow passageways may make it nearly impossible for wheelchair users to avoid knocking merchandise off shelves, rolling into standing strangers, or struggling to maneuver around tight corners in front of anxiously paralyzed bystanders. Although wheelchair users do not welcome such discomfort, many become quite adept at easing the "dis-ease" (Gross and Stone 1964:2) of potentially embarrassing situations because they face them so often.

Humor is the most common and perhaps most effective strategy that wheelchair users employ for this purpose. . . . [L]aughing at or joking about embarrassing events reduces their seriousness and thereby lessens potentially embarrassing concern about them. Laughter and humor are also means of allaying anxiety (Coser 1959:174), which can serve a dual definitional purpose. A wheelchair user's potentially embarrassing situation often provokes anxiety in witnesses to her or his plight. Defining the situation as laughable can ease everyone's particular "dis-ease," as the second author learned when shopping at a clothing store.

> I wheeled up to the entrance to a dressing room while my friend held a number of garments. I forgot to set the brakes on my chair, so when I started to raise myself up with my crutches the chair went rolling backwards while I went falling forward onto the floor. My friend stood there with this look of alarm until I started laughing. The two of us started laughing, and then a saleswoman came rushing over: "My goodness, are you all right?" I answered "Yes, I'm fine" while still laughing. Her facial expression went from alarm to unconcern in a flash, once she realized we were laughing.

Through incidents like this, wheelchair users acquire the experiential wisdom that a sense of humor is "a tremendous asset."

> . . . if you can laugh at yourself, no matter what. . . . And if it's funny to me first, then my feelings aren't hurt. And you don't feel self-conscious because you can laugh with me.

As this 60-year-old woman had learned from countless falls in public places, laughter can both prevent and relieve hurt feelings, anxious self-consciousness, and the contagious "dis-ease" of embarrassment.

On the other hand, humor sometimes has the opposite effect. A woman who had been using a wheelchair in public for only six months told us of her recent experience in a shopping mall bathroom.

> There was a whole line of people waiting to get into these two stalls. It was packed. And I'm trying to back up and not doing a very good job of it and having to start over again, bumping into the washbasin. I finally get myself around, with all these people obviously watching me. There was dead silence. So I finally got myself out, and I looked up at all these people and I went "Now, I would like a big round of applause, please." Nobody did anything. It was like you can't make a joke about this stuff. I thought "Give me a break."

Like hospital patients who joke with the medical staff about death (Emerson 1969), this woman apparently exceeded the topical limits of her audience's sense of humor. At least they blatantly refused her invitation to laugh at her plight and reduce its definitional seriousness (Coser 1959:172). This incident illustrates one of the emotional dilemmas that wheelchair users face when in public places: they must attempt to remain poised and good-humored in frustrating and potentially embarrassing circumstances without thereby increasing others' already considerable discomfort at those circumstances. In public places they often have the double duty of managing their own and others' emotions (Hochschild 1979). . . .

This is clearly the case when wheelchair users are interrogated by curious children, as often happens, about their unusual mode of mobility and physical condition. All but one of our informants report that they gladly answer such young interrogators' questions. One informant, whose left leg had been amputated, had an uncommon sense of humor, but his openness with young children was not unusual.

> Kids go "Where's your leg?" "It's gone. If you find it, I'll give you fifty cents. I've been looking for that damn thing all week." "Can I see it?" "Sure." I take my pants up, show the stump. "Wow, it's gone. You're not sitting on it." "Yep, it's gone." They're frank. They're very candid.

Inquisitive children's accompanying adult caretakers, however, seldom appreciate their young charges' candor. As the man quoted above reported, "The parents turn blue. They turn shades of pink and red. I have to protect the kids from the parents. They want to jerk them away." Other informants reported similar experiences.

> And children, you find that they come up and ask "How come you're in a chair? You mean you can't walk? Really?" But if there's an adult with them, they tend to pull the child back. "Oh now, don't disturb her." And I say "They're not disturbing me."

If our informants are at all representative, most wheelchair users not only graciously endure and satisfy young children's uncivil curiosity when in public places. They also attempt to manage the embarrassment (and sometimes the wrath) of those curious children's adult caretakers in the interest of child protection. Whatever emotion work (Hochschild 1979:561–563) is done is usually done by them.

Fred Davis (1961:127) once observed that "in our society the visibly handicapped are customarily accorded, save by children, the surface acceptance of democratic manners

guaranteed to nearly all." He may have been right about children, but many wheelchair users probably would find his attribution of democratic manners to children's elders a bit too generous. In both our own and our informants' experience, most adults indeed accord wheelchair users the surface acceptance of civil inattention in public places (Goffman 1963a:84). Yet there are more than a few exceptions. These include walkers, as they are sometimes called by wheelchair users, who proclaim their admiration of a wheelchair user at the expense of his or her right to be let alone in public (Goffman 1971:62). The older the walker and the younger the wheelchair user, the more common this treatment seems. The second author, for example, who is in her early twenties, is routinely approached by considerably older strangers, who cheerfully inform her that they think she "is wonderful." Although clearly complimentary, such unexpected and seemingly groundless public praise is an embarrassment. Simultaneously flattered, embarrassed, and resentful of the intrusion, the wheelchair user faces the dilemma of formulating an appropriate response, and usually settles for a half-hearted "thank you."

Wheelchair users commonly resolve the emotional dilemmas of their public lives in this way. They expressively mask their own emotions so as to manage others'. They cover their embarrassment with good humor, relieving witnesses' emotional discomfort. They hide resentment behind calm graciousness, saving forward strangers the embarrassment that would be caused by expressing such resentment. Even when wheelchair users feel fully justified in their emotional reactions, their public expression often contrasts sharply with their private feelings. The example of righteous anger suggests some reasons why.

Embarrassing Anger

Like children (Cahill 1990), wheelchair users are alternately treated like "open persons" (Goffman 1963a:126) and subjected to "nonperson" treatment in public places (Goffman 1963a:84). Although both forms of treatment betray others' surface acceptance of wheelchair users, the latter is usually the more maddening. Occupants of various service roles are the culprits mentioned most often. Apparently uncomfortable salesclerks may busy themselves folding merchandise as if a potential customer in a wheelchair were invisible. Restaurant personnel may huddle behind a wheelchair user, close enough to let her overhear their discussion of "where to put her." All kinds of service workers may treat a wheelchair user's walking companions as his or her spokespersons and caretakers. Sometimes they return change to such companions after receiving payment from the wheelchair user, or ask her companions "And what would she like?"

Such nonperson treatment often provokes wheelchair users' anger but seldom the expression of that anger. As one of our informants told us, "I just want to reach out and grab a hold of them and shake them for all they're worth. But I just sit back, and I grit my teeth." Our informants report that they usually try to respond to nonperson treatment not with anger but with calm reminders of their presence and ability to speak for themselves. They also report that this strategy is usually effective in eliciting an embarrassed apology and more civil treatment.

Yet no matter how common and how effective such gentle reminders are, wheelchair users sometimes reveal their anger at nonperson treatment through hostile comments and tone. When a waiter asked the wife of one of our informants whether "he will be getting out of the chair," our informant sarcastically replied, "Yes, he will." Such hostile expressions can be even more effective than calm reminders in eliciting embarrassed apologies, but at the expense of leaving the wheelchair user feeling embarrassed and guilty about his or her lack of emotional poise. In this respect and most others, wheelchair users are as much children of their emotional culture

. . . as are most contemporary Americans. To borrow a distinction from Hochschild (1990:122–24), our "feeling rules" sometimes prescribe anger but our "expression rules" proscribe its expression. These contradictions lead to conflicting feelings of justifiable anger and guilt at expressing the anger. Wheelchair users are not alone in experiencing such contradictory feelings in public or elsewhere.

Private guilt and embarrassment are not the only potentially unwelcome consequences of wheelchair users' public expressions of anger. Rather than eliciting embarrassed apologies, their anger may be returned, as one of our informants learned when she protested a robustly walking man's choice of parking places.

> I've had a guy park in a handicapped parking spot and I've gone up and said: "Look, do you realize you're parked in a handicapped parking spot?" And he said "I know it, and I'm sick of you people getting all the good spots. It's reverse discrimination. I'm sick of being discriminated against." "Well," I said, "I'm going to call the police and you can tell your story to them." And he says, "Go ahead. I've had it. It's about time."

Although this man moved his car when our informant wheeled to the nearest public telephone, it was a harder-won moral victory than she had anticipated. . . . [Thus,] wheelchair users who publicly express moral outrage must be prepared to receive what they give. Their angry protest may be met with angry resistance, creating an embarrassing and sometimes alarming public scene that they must then manage or escape.

The angry protests of self-appointed defenders of wheelchair users' public privileges are no less instructive in this regard. One of our informants, who drove a car with hand controls that was otherwise unremarkable, told us of the following public encounter:

> I pull the car into a handicapped place, and this car pulls up alongside me with

two young women in it. One of them leans over and says, "You know you're in a handicapped place." And I said, "Yes, I'm disabled." And then she says, "You don't look disabled." And I don't usually do this kind of thing, but I just said, "What does disabled look like?" And they just drove off. Maybe I shouldn't have done that, but it was one of those days.

The informant's hostile retort and the tinge of guilt he apparently felt as a result illustrate both the possible subjective costs and the interpersonal risks of publicly expressing anger. This is one horn of an emotional dilemma that wheelchair users often face in public. Should they suppress their righteous anger and forgo the satisfaction that its expression often brings, or should they assume the costs and risks of expression? As suggested previously, our informants, like the second author, commonly resolve this dilemma in favor of suppression—if not of their anger, then at least of expression.

That decision, however, does not always save wheelchair users from the embarrassing public scenes that angry protests can create. Their walking companions see to that, as a 34-year-old paraplegic woman explains.

After thirteen and a half years you've heard just about everything, so it's like "Oh, you know." But it's my friends who [say] "Can you imagine the nerve? Let's get out of here." They've actually made me leave. My ex-boyfriend, we got up from the table and walked out . . . it started when they didn't know where to put me, and then the waitress ignored me. And he had just had it. He said "We're out of here." I said "Don't make an issue out of it." "The issue's made." Got my purse, got my coat, and we started to leave. We had the manager on our coattails. I think that's more embarrassing.

As Goffman (1963b:31) observes, "[T]he person with a courtesy stigma can in fact make both the stigmatized and normal uncomfortable" by confronting everyone "with too

much morality." Walkers who befriend and accompany wheelchair users in public are apparently no exception. Their easy susceptibility to moral outrage may lead to public scenes that their wheelchair-using companions would just as soon avoid. As if their occasional nonperson treatment were not painful enough, wheelchair users also must sometimes bear the embarrassment of their defenders' self-righteous zeal.

Wheelchair users' experiences with public anger are not unique. Regardless of our mode of mobility, public expressions of anger are risky: they can provoke angry retaliation and create embarrassing scenes. For most of us, much of the time, those potential costs seem to outweigh whatever personal satisfaction we might gain by expressing our righteous rage. Consequently we "surface act" (Hochschild 1979:558) so as to prevent our anger from reaching the surface. Thus, public appearances of emotional indifference are sometimes just that—appearances. Wheelchair users' experiences in public places remind us of how much emotion work may be invested in maintaining those appearances.

Ingratiating Sympathy

Prevailing expression rules, possible retaliation, and potential embarrassment are not the only deterrents to wheelchair users' public expression of righteous anger. They also know that they cannot afford to alienate the walkers who populate the public places they frequent. Experience has taught them that their uncooperative bodies and, more commonly, the unfriendliness of the physical environment to their mode of mobility sometimes leave them hopelessly dependent on others' sympathetic assistance. They may need waiters to move chairs away from a table so that they can wheel their own under it, or to store their wheelchair after transferring to a chair with legs. Often they must rely on strangers to fetch items from shelves that are either too high or too low for them to reach. They may wheel down a curb cut on one side of a street only to find a curb on the other side, over which anonymous passersby must help them if they are to continue along their intended path. Like one of our informants, they may find themselves in a restaurant or bar without "handicap accessible" toilet facilities and themselves without same-sexed companionship, and thus may require the assistance of total strangers to use those much-needed facilities. Or, like another of our informants, they may need to flag down a passing motorist on a city street to help them replace a foot on the footrest of their wheelchair after it has been dislodged by an involuntary spasm. These are only a few of the circumstances in which wheelchair users find themselves requiring the sympathetic assistance of walkers with whom they are unacquainted. . . .

Whatever its form, that assistance qualifies as sympathetic. According to Clark (1987:296), sympathy consists of "empathy plus sentiment, empathy plus display or all three." The assistance that walkers sometimes provide wheelchair users in public places has at least two of those components. It involves empathetic role-taking and is a culturally recognized expression of sympathy, even if not motivated by sincere "fellow-feeling" or sentiment. Regardless of the motivation, its provision stirs emotions.

Although many wheelchair users do not hesitate to ask for assistance when they need it, they are as aware of, and as strongly committed to, prevailing sympathy etiquette (Clark 1987) as other rules of feeling and expression. Therefore they often find themselves torn between concern about making excessive claims on others' sympathy and their immediate need for sympathetic assistance. Guilt is the typical result.

If I'm in the grocery store, and I need something, and I ask somebody to get it [I say] "Oh, I'm sorry." And I find myself making excuses, saying things like "Oh, it's just not been my day" or "it seems everything I want today is up too high." I feel like I'm putting people out of their

way. I feel like I'm imposing on someone to ask for help.

This informant told us that she did not have to apologize or explain herself because "people would bend over backwards to help you," but she seemed implicitly to know better. Even while she laid claim to others' sympathy, her apologies and accounts demonstrated her awareness of sympathy etiquette and its proscription against excessive claims (Clark 1987:305–307). Her guilty penance of remedial work (Goffman 1971:108–18) may have assured her benefactors that she would claim no more sympathy, time, and attention than necessary.

This wheelchair user's sensitivity to the sacrifices of sympathetically helpful strangers is not unusual. Wheelchair users often are forced to request sympathetic assistance from strangers in order to continue on their daily rounds, but still feel a pang of guilt when doing so. Those who have some choice may feel somewhat more than a guilty pang. . . . For example, one of our informants, who could walk short distances with the aid of a cane, often [felt like a fraud who was exploiting strangers' kindness].

I've had people do double and triple takes when I get up out of my wheelchair. . . . Sometimes when I'm using my chair in the grocery store and I can't reach something, I get up; sometimes I ask people to get it for me. I mean, that's where I feel like a fraud, because I can get up. But if I get up, then I feel like a fraud because people can tell that I'm using a wheelchair but I don't need to—I mean I don't *have* to.

Like this woman, many wheelchair users are aware that they must appear strong, independent, and brave so as to avoid "being perceived as self-pitying" and overdemanding of others' sympathy (Clark 1987:307). To avoid such a perception and the resulting guilt, they may take needless risks and expend needless energy rather than requesting even minor aid from strangers. The micropolitical benefits of such dogged self-reliance may also help to compensate for inefficient expenditures of time, energy, and personal safety.

Even if wheelchair users defiantly refuse to pay the subjective price of guilt when requesting and accepting sympathetic assistance, they pay an interpersonal price. Whatever the benefits, as Clark (1987:299–300) observes, receiving sympathy obligates the recipient to repay the granter with "emotional commodities such as gratitude, deference and future sympathy." And deferential gratitude is the only emotional currency with which wheelchair users can repay strangers whom they are unlikely to encounter in the future. Using such currency to compensate helpful and sympathetic strangers for their sacrifices is not without micropolitical implications: Wheelchair users thereby elevate their benefactors' interactional standing or "place" at the expense of their own (Clark 1990).

Wheelchair users often pay that price cheerfully when they require and request sympathetic assistance, but those are not the only occasions on which they are expected to pay it. Walkers who are unknown to wheelchair users provide sympathetic assistance not only when it is requested, but also when it is not. The first author learned this in the opening moments of his first public appearance in a wheelchair.

> I got the chair unfolded and assembled and started wheeling down the hallway. As I was approaching the door, a woman walked alongside my chair and asked: "Are you going that way?" Assuming that she meant toward the door, I answered "Yes." She gracefully moved in front of me and opened the first of the double doors. I thanked her. She then just as gracefully opened the outer door once I was through the first, and again I thanked her.

From all reports, this is not an unusual experience for wheelchair users. Walkers often

quicken or slow their pace so as to be in a position to open and hold doors for wheelchair users whom they do not know. They offer to push occupied wheelchairs up steep inclines, and sometimes begin to do so without warning. Also, they volunteer to fold and load wheelchairs into users' cars and vans. These are only a few examples of the unsolicited assistance that wheelchair users report receiving from strangers. . . .

[Yet], unsolicited acts of sympathetic assistance place wheelchair users under no less of an obligation than acts that are requested. It is still generally expected that the recipient will repay the granter with "deferential gratitude," and the micropolitical cost of that repayment may be even greater than for requested acts of sympathetic assistance. Simmel offers a theoretical explanation:

> Once we have received something good from another person . . . we no longer can make up for it completely. The reason is that his gift, because it was first, has a voluntary character which no return gift can have (1950:392).

This voluntary character is absent from the provision of sympathetic assistance in response to a request from an apparently "sympathy worthy" (Clark 1987:297–298) wheelchair user. If the provision of the requested assistance is of little moment to the person asked, as is commonly the case, then provision is no less obligatory than repayment. To refuse such a request is to risk being judged hatefully heartless. In contrast, an unsolicited act of sympathetic assistance contains what Simmel (1950:393) calls "the decisive element of . . . freedom," which is absent from the deferential gratitude offered in return. Moreover, as Clark (1990:315) observes, the donor of an emotional gift such as sympathetic assistance "gets to impose his or her definition of what the other wants or needs." To accept such an emotional gift is not only to "contract an irredeemable obligation" (Simmel 1950:393) but also to concede definitional authority over one's own wants and needs to another, thereby doubly diminishing the recipient's interactional standing. Thus the micropolitical implications of the kindness often displayed toward wheelchair users in public places can be quite unkind.

This is not to say that wheelchair users never appreciate unsolicited offers and acts of sympathetic assistance. One of our informants reports that he adjusts the speed of his wheelchair in relation to the reflections of approaching walkers in glass doors so as to ensure that they will reach the door slightly before him and will open and hold it for him voluntarily. At times he is more than willing to absorb the micropolitical losses caused by accepting such a minor expression of sympathetic kindness, and he is not alone.

Yet neither he nor other wheelchair users appreciate all the unsolicited assistance that sympathetic walkers shower on them. Sometimes they resent the costs in definitional authority or in mere time and energy that such acts of kindness impose. In the 1970s, for example, one of our informants was mistaken for a wounded veteran of the Vietnam war by a bouncer at a popular country and western bar. Before our informant could correct the misidentification, the bouncer carried him and his chair past the long queue of people awaiting admittance to the bar, forcibly removed some patrons from a table, and then offered the table to our informant and his companions. When the bouncer left to order "drinks on the house," our informant's wife wisely advised him, "Don't you dare tell him you're not a vet." For the rest of the evening, our informant and his companions were held hostage to the bouncer's definition of the situation, and had to feign knowledge of Vietnamese geography. Another informant reports that bartenders routinely refuse to accept payment for his drinks, insisting that his "money's no good here." A relatively well-paid civil servant, our informant resented the definitional implication that he was unable to pay his own way, but some-

times "let it go because they just wouldn't take my money." At times, too, unsolicited assistance merely makes wheelchair users' lives more difficult, as when walkers insist on helping a wheelchair user disassemble, fold, and load the wheelchair into a car or van, taking twice as long to do so as the user commonly takes and sometimes damaging the wheelchair in the process.

Even more maddening are those occasions on which self-appointed benefactors bear some responsibility for the wheelchair user's plight. One of our informants reported that she called a restaurant to inquire if it was accessible to wheelchair users. After being assured that it was, she made reservations for the following evening.

> [W]e got there to find that they had four or five steps, and there was no way I was going to get up there. So the owner of the restaurant and several of the male kitchen help came out and just picked my chair right up. They made every effort, once I got there, to help, which was really nice, but at the same time I was not happy after what they'd told me. . . . I get embarrassed when people make too much fuss over me.

This embarrassed and unhappy, if not angry, woman never returned to the restaurant in question. Yet on the evening of her first and only visit, she graciously thanked its owner and his employees for helping her over, through, and out of a predicament into which he had lured her. Her apparently insincere expression of seemingly undeserved gratitude is not aberrant among wheelchair users who receive unsolicited and unwelcome acts of sympathetic assistance. Here again, wheelchair users' public expression and their private feelings often contrast sharply.

At least our informants often express gratitude for unsolicited offers and acts of assistance even when they are unneeded, unwelcome, inconvenient, embarrassing, and demeaning. They know all too well the consequences of not doing so: their self-appointed benefactors, as well as those who witness his or her charity, are likely to judge them harshly for any hint of ingratitude. One of our informants learned this on his first trip to a highly recommended barbershop.

> I drove over there and got out of my car and wheeled up to the door. I opened the door and prepared to go in, and one of the two barbers came out and grabbed my handles. Now, as I've said, I like to do and insist on doing things for myself, but this fellow would not let go of the handles. I had my brakes on, preventing him from pushing me, but he insisted that he was going to push me over the threshold. . . . And finally . . . I forget what he said, but I asked for an apology. And he said "Okay, I apologize, but you have a chip on your shoulder, don't you?"

Like recipients of other forms of charity, wheelchair users who refuse or resist unsolicited acts of sympathetic assistance risk being viewed as having . . . "a chip on their shoulders." For many wheelchair users on many occasions, thankful and deferential acceptance of such charitable acts may seem less micropolitically costly than being judged ungrateful, testy, and uncivil.

Even when wheelchair users are willing to pay the price of such harsh judgments rather than cooperating in diminishing their interactional place, another consideration often prevents them from doing so. As Goffman (1963[b]:113) observes, the treatment of those who bear a stigma conveys to them that their "real group," the one whose interests they must champion, "is the aggregate of persons who are likely to suffer the same deprivations as [they suffer] because of having the same stigma." Wheelchair users are no exception, and many take this lesson to heart. Therefore they feel a sense of responsibility toward other wheelchair users and worry that their example might influence how other wheelchair users are treated in the future.

> I have people falling all over themselves trying to help me. It used to bother me, but, God, the older you get the less it does. But I know a lot of people it does. I've got one friend that's at the point of being rude. This is bad because it sets a bad example. That person in the future may not be quite so willing to help the next person who really needs it.

As in this woman's case but not her friend's, the contradiction between the wheelchair user's immediate micropolitical interests and the presumably greater interests of his or her "real group" often blocks the wheelchair user's expression of his or her subjective emotional reactions to unsolicited and unwelcome offers and acts of assistance. He or she consequently sacrifices interactional place for the presumably greater good of those who share the stigma of moving through public places in a sitting position.

The Wages of Public Acceptance

As late as the early 1970s, persons with visible disabilities were legally banned from public places in a number of American cities. . . . Today wheelchair users are a common presence in public places, attracting only occasional stares and many minor acts of [assistance]. Yet, the surface acceptance and assistance that others commonly grant them are not without a price. . . .

[W]heelchair users still must endure being treated like children in public places. Sometimes they are treated as open persons who can be addressed at will about their condition and the technical means of their mobility. At other times they are discussed and talked past as if absent. Robert Murphy (1987:201) suggests that people with disabilities are treated like children in part because "overdependency and nonreciprocity are considered childish traits," but wheelchair users seldom exhibit such traits in public. Although wheelchair users often depend on others' friendly assistance when the physical features of public places prove difficult to negotiate, most take pains to avoid exhausting the goodwill and sympathy of those who move through public places in a standing position.

The above discussion demonstrates that wheelchair users more than reciprocate . . . the public acceptance and assistance that others grant them with considerable emotion work and micropolitical sacrifices. That work and those sacrifices profit the walkers who they encounter in public. As Goffman (1963b:121) suggests, wheelchair users' public poise, even temper, and good humor, ensure that walkers "will not have to admit to themselves how limited their tactfulness and tolerance is." On the contrary, wheelchair users' request for and acceptance of public aid provide walkers an opportunity to demonstrate to themselves, if not others, that they are kind and caring people. The wheelchair users' common expressions of gratitude confirm that self-congratulatory moral identity. . . . [Thus], it is an open question whether walkers help wheelchair users as much in public as wheelchair users help them.

Perhaps wheelchair users who frequent public places are still sometimes treated as children because the attention-attracting assistance they sometimes must request, but more often receive, overshadows all the interactional and identificatory assistance they give others. Yet one can easily discern wheelchair users' efforts and sacrifices on others' behalf by looking beyond the glare of physical feats and into the emotional and micropolitical shadows of public encounters. In those shadows wheelchair users stand tall, supporting the emotional weight of public tranquility and their public benefactors' moral identities.

Public Life and Emotion Management

More general lessons await students of social life in the emotional and micropolitical shadows to which wheelchair users' public experiences lead. Strangers in public places may appear to be acting "almost subliminally, demanding nothing of each other" (Strauss 1961: 63–64), but much is demanded of them. . . . Strangers in public places devote considerable energy to preserving their own and one another's privacy, anonymity, and socially valued identities. . . . Wheelchair users' public experiences suggest that [much of that effort is emotional].

Wheelchair users are not the only ones who manage both their own and others' emotions in public places. Walkers who encounter wheelchair users in public undoubtedly sometimes avoid expressing their own private anxieties, aversion, admiration, or sympathetic concern out of concern for the wheelchair users' feelings. It is also doubtful that public encounters between unacquainted walkers and wheelchair users are unusual in this respect. Our public etiquette would seem to proscribe the public expression of emotions that are prescribed by our feeling rules, and public life is often emotionally provocative. Although strangers in public places may take pains to avoid physical contact with one another, nonetheless they touch one another emotionally in a variety of ways. They are touched embarrassingly by one another's presumed judgments as well as by one another's embarrassment. They are caressed reassuringly by others' averted gaze and pinched by fear by others' stares. Others' slights and impositions touch them with anger, and they feel a touch of guilt over their own anger. They touch one another sympathetically when requesting and providing minor acts of public aid, and repay such gifts touchingly in a variety of emotional currencies.

Yet whatever our mode of public mobility, we commonly appear emotionally reserved in public places. We mask our emotions so as not to excite others'. We manage our own expressions and thereby others' feelings. We surface act so as to sustain the tranquil exterior of public life and to avoid being swept away by its emotionally turbulent undercurrents. As suggested by the example of wheelchair users, this is part of the implicit bargain of contemporary public life. It is the price of public acceptance. . . . It is a special characteristic of public anonymity that the very process of producing it socially gives it the appearance of being not only asocial but unemotional as well. Students of social life must look beyond those appearances in order to fully understand public bonds and the bindings of contemporary society. The example of wheelchair users suggests that these bindings include interpersonal processes of emotion management. . . .

References

Cahill, Spencer. 1990. "Childhood and Public Life: Reaffirming Biographical Divisions." *Social Problems* 37: 390–402.

Clark, Candace. 1987. "Sympathy Biography and Sympathy Margin." *American Journal of Sociology* 93: 290–321.

——. 1990. "Emotions and Micropolitics in Everyday Life: Some Patterns and Paradoxes of Place." Pp. 305–33 in *Research Agendas in the Sociology of Emotions*, edited by Theodore Kemper. Albany: SUNY Press.

Coser, Rose. 1959. "Some Social Functions of Laughter: A Study of Humor in a Hospital Setting." *Human Relations* 12: 171–182.

Davis, Fred. 1961. "Deviance Disavowal: The Management of Strained Interaction by the Visibly Handicapped." *Social Problems* 9: 121–132.

Emerson, Joan. 1969. "Negotiating the Serious Import of Humor." *Sociometry* 32: 169–181.

Goffman, Erving. [1955] 1982. "On Face-Work." Pp. 5–45 in *Interaction Ritual*. New York: Random House.

——. 1963a. *Behavior in Public Places*. New York: Free Press.

——. 1963b. *Stigma*. Englewood Cliffs, NJ: Prentice Hall.

——. 1971. *Relations in Public*. New York: Basic Books.

Gross, Edward and Gregory Stone. 1964. "Embarrassment and the Analysis of Role Requirements." *American Journal of Sociology* 70: 1–15.

Hochschild, Arlie. 1979. "Emotion Work, Feeling Rules, and Social Structure." *American Journal of Sociology* 85: 551–575.

——. 1990. "Ideology and Emotion Management: A Perspective and Path for Future Research." Pp. 117–42 in *Research Agendas in the Sociology of Emotions*, edited by Theodore Kemper. Albany: SUNY Press.

Murphy, Robert. 1987. *The Body Silent*. New York: Holt.

Simmel, Georg. 1950. *The Sociology of Georg Simmel*, edited by Kurt Wolff. Glencoe, IL: Free Press.

Strauss, Anselm. 1961. *Images of the American City*. New York: Free Press.

19

The Conversational Co-Construction of Bad Diagnostic News

Douglas Maynard

In the very first selection, Berger and Luckmann noted that conversation was the most important "vehicle of reality-maintenance." As such, conversation has attracted the attention of many social scientists who have developed a specialized area of study called *conversation analysis,* perhaps the most micro of all microsociologies. Conversation analysts closely examine detailed transcriptions of actual conversations so as to identify their recurrent features and the common-sense practices and understandings that they reveal. They are particularly interested in how particular patterns of conversation serve to accomplish different social actions.

Among other things, conversation analysis has demonstrated that each turn of talk references or shows some appreciation for the prior turn at talk. This allows speakers to monitor how others have understood what they have said and to correct misunderstandings. Hence, the turn-by-turn organization of conversation facilitates the achievement of mutual understanding. Conversationalists may sometimes violently disagree, but they almost always mutually understand that they do disagree.

Conversation analysis has also shown that certain kinds of responses to particular turns-at-talk, such as invitations, offers, and assessments, are preferred in the sense that they are delivered straightforwardly and without delay. In contrast, dispreferred responses tend to be delayed, qualified, or otherwise "marked." For example, acceptances of invitations tend to be immediate and direct, while rejections tend to be delayed, qualified, apologized for, or explained. This *preference format,* in the words of conversation analysts, promotes social affiliation and is closely related to what Goffman calls "face." Refusing an invitation can imply that the issuer of the invitation is not a suitable companion and challenge his or her claim to face or positive social value. Delaying the refusal of an invitation allows the person making it an opportunity to reformulate it and avoid its refusal, while qualifications, explanations, and apologies soften the blow of the refusal.

Conversational analysts initially confined their attention to the study of casual, everyday conversation. More recently, many have analyzed forms of conversation that serve to accomplish institutionally or organizationally specialized tasks. For example, they have studied news interviews, 911 emergency calls, and doctor-patient consultations. This selection concerns another type of organizationally specialized conversation. It examines so-called *informing interviews* at clinics for developmental disabilities during which members of the clinics' professional staff inform parents of their child's diagnosis.

Douglas Maynard, the author of this selection, suggests that clinicians seldom bluntly present a diagnosis to parents but attempt to "co-implicate" them in the diagnosis through the use of what he calls a "perspective-display" series. That is, the clinician first asks the parent or parents for their assessment of their child's problem. If that assessment is more or less consistent with the diagnosis the clinician is about to deliver, he or she presents the diagnosis by building upon the parents' own assessment. If, however, the parents' assessment is inconsistent with the coming diagnosis, the clinician attempts to move the parents' assessment closer to that diagnosis before delivering it. Through the use of such conversational practices, clinicians soften parents' potential resistance to the receipt of bad diagnostic news and present the diagnosis as a collaborative construction rather than an authoritative pronouncement.

They thereby promote mutual understanding and social affiliation.

Conversation analytic transcription attempts to capture the way the conversation actually sounds. Hence, words are written phonetically as they were actually pronounced. Brackets ([ ]) indicate simultaneous speech, and equal signs (=) indicate "latching" or the lack of any break between words. Parentheses indicate silence, and the number inside the parentheses indicates the length of the silence in seconds (a period inside the parentheses indicates a micro-second silence). Colons (:::) indicate a drawn-out pronunciation, and underlining indicates emphasis. These transcribing conventions are used in this selection.

Although some readers are intimidated by the technically detailed character of conversation analysis, the logic is straightforward and clearly illustrated by conversational examples. Those who make the effort to follow the logic of its analyses are rewarded with fascinating insights into the detailed ways we all participate in the everyday construction and maintenance of social reality. Through the turn-by-turn organization of conversation, we routinely achieve and maintain mutual understanding, social affiliation, and a shared or objective reality. Although we are seldom consciously aware that we are doing so, we exhibit considerable practical knowledge, skill, and artfulness in every conversation in which we participate. Conversation analysis helps bring to our conscious awareness what we usually take for granted—our own continual participation in the construction of social reality.

In ordinary conversation, when there is bad news to tell, it can be organized so that the recipient rather than the bearer of the news ends up pronouncing it (Schegloff 1988). By prefacing the bad news, by giving pieces of information from which inferences can be made, and so on, the bearer alludes to the tidings, and thereby induces the recipient to guess at what they are. Schegloff (1988) provides the following telephone-call example . . . Belle conveys news to Fanny about a mutual friend by announcing "something terrible":

(1) [DA:2:10]
```
 1   B:  . . .I, I-I had something (.) terrible t'tell
 2       you. so ⌈u h :        ⌉
 3   F:        ⌊ How t⌋errible ⌈is it
 4   B:                        ⌊·hhhhh
 5       (.)
 6   B:  Uh: ez worse it could be:.
 7       (0.7)
 8   F:  W'y'mean Eva?
 9       (.)
10   B:  Uh uh ·hh=
11   F:  =Wud she do die:?=
12   B:  =Mmhm,
13       (.)
14   F:  When did she die,
```

The announcement and subsequent formulation that the news is "ez worse it could be" (line 6) are ways of clueing Fanny, who guesses at the news (lines 8, 11). Then Belle confirms these guesses (lines 10, 12). . . .

A deliverer's clues . . . engage a recipient's common-sense knowledge of the world, the participants' "recipient-designed" mutual knowledge, and "their orientation to the occasion of the conversation." The practices of clueing, guessing, and confirming are also displayed in institutional settings—particularly medical ones—where professionals must convey bad news. . . . Thus, a mother recalls her experience of finding out that she has given birth to a Down's Syndrome child:

And you know he [the father] was just acting so strangely and by then you get all these apprehensive feelings which I had during the pregnancy anyhow. And then the doctor came in and he drew the curtains around my cubicle and I thought, oh no, you know. And he told me the baby was born completely healthy, but he's not completely normal. And I looked at him and I said, he's mongoloid. And I've never seen a mongoloid baby before in my life, but all of a sudden the flat features, the thrusting of the tongue, you know, just kind of hit me in the face. And that poor doctor couldn't bring himself to say the word. He said, it shouldn't have hap-

pened to you, not to your age bracket.
(Jacobs 1969, 5)

The doctor's clues here include drawing the curtains and then alluding to abnormality. Based on her "feelings" and prior, unthematized noticings, the mother guesses that the baby is "mongoloid," a matter that the doctor, by reciting how unlikely the event was, confirms in an indirect way.

These excerpts demonstrate that a bringer of bad news may have difficulty stating the news outright. By avoiding the pronouncement and simply confirming a recipient's inference, a teller can manage the conveyance as a joint activity. The bearer does not claim completely independent knowledge, and instead elicits a display of what the recipients, through their own knowledge or beliefs, can infer. In medical settings where clinicians must routinely deliver bad diagnostic news, it appears that this pattern of confirming can be actualized more explicitly than by mere reliance on clues and guesses. Clinicians can use a "perspective-display series," a device that operates in an interactionally organized manner to *co-implicate* the recipient's perspective in the presentation of diagnoses. Schematically, the series consists of three turns:

1 clinician's opinion—query, or perspective-display invitation;

2 recipient's reply or assessment;

3 clinician's report and assessment.

Because the clinician, in a manner analogous to the clueing and guessing activity described above, sets up a diagnostic telling to confirm the recipient's own perspective, a consequence of employing this series is to embed that perspective as a constituent feature of the telling.

The Perspective-Display Series

The data for this chapter derive from "informing interviews" recorded in two clinics for developmental disabilities (mental retardation, autism, language and learning disabilities,

etc.). At such clinics, children go through an extensive evaluation process, which may include speech, psychological, psychiatric, pediatric, educational, and other kinds of examinations. When these tests are completed, clinicians meet with parents to tell them about the clinic's findings and diagnoses, and to make recommendations as to how to handle identified problems. This meeting or informing interview may last from 20 minutes to 2 hours as participants discuss a wide variety of concerns. . . .

While this chapter is mostly about turns (2) and (3) in the perspective-display series, some preliminary comments about turns (1) and (2) will be helpful in our later analyses. First, these two turns are similar to what Sacks (1992 [1966]) has called a pre-sequence. Pre-sequences include the summons-answer type, by which participants provide for coordinated entry into conversation; pre-invitations (*Are you busy Friday night?*), by which a speaker can determine whether to solicit someone's coparticipation in a social activity . . . and preannouncements (*Have you heard?*) through which a speaker can discover whether some news-to-be-told is already known by a recipient. . . . Depending on what a speaker finds out by initiating a pre-sequence, the conversation, invitation, or announcement may or may not ensue. Thus, in ordinary conversation, the perspective-display [initiation] and its reply operate like a pre-sequence and seem to have alternative trajectories. . . . However, in the clinical environment, the relationship between the first two turns and the third-turn report in the perspective-display series appears more fixed or *rigid* than in conversation; only one . . . trajector[y] occurs. After asking parents for their view, clinicians unfailingly provide their assessment of the child (for discussion, see Maynard 1991).

A second matter concerning turns one and two in this series: it is here that clinicians and parents may collaboratively establish an alignment regarding two matters on which the delivery of diagnostic news depends: the existence of a child's problem and the expertise of the clinic for dealing with it. Turn 1, the perspective—display invitation, elicits the parents' view of their child, and does so through a variety of forms. A major distinction is between those queries that are *unmarked* and those that are *marked*, depending on whether they initiate reference to a problem as a possession of the queried-about child. When an invitation itself proposes a problem or difficulty, it is marked:

(2) [8.013]

    Dr: What do you see? as- as his difficulty.
           (1.2)
    Mo: Mainly his uhm: (1.2) the fact that he doesn't understand everything (0.6) and also the fact that his speech. (0.7) is very hard to understand what he's saying.

When an invitation does not propose a problem in this way, it is unmarked:

(3) [9.001]

    Dr: Now that you've- we've been through all this I just wanted to know from you:::. (0.4) ˙hh <u>how</u> you see Judy at this time (2.2)
    Mo: The same.
           (0.7)
    Dr: Which is?
           (0.5)
    Mo: Uhm she can't talk . . .

Marked queries presumptively ask parents for their view and occasion, from the parents, an immediate account of the child's difficulty. Unmarked queries are less presumptive but nonetheless also seek an eventual formulation of a child's problem. Once clinicians and parents exhibit accord on the existence of a problem, this also implies an alignment as lay and professional participants with regard to expertise for understanding the problem's exact nature. The very proposing of a "problem," that is, reflexively suggests a course of action in which parents, in one way or another, have sought out the clinic for its specialized knowledge. Establishing these matters sets up a hospitable environment that allows clinicians to present the diagnosis relatively smoothly. Nevertheless, in reply to a perspective—display invitation, a parent may resist a problem formulation. This, as we shall see, necessitates a specific kind of interactive work before the clinician can deliver the diagnostic news.

After parents display their views, then, clinicians regularly deliver diagnostic news as a *confirmation* of what has been said. Depending upon the relation of the elicited perspective to the clinical position, such confirmation can be relatively simple or more complex. If the parents formulate some problematic condition that is perceivedly close to the clinical position, then the confirmation will be accompanied only by a reformulation and technical elaboration of the parent's version. When the clinical diagnosis departs significantly from that version, a diagnostic presentation will be accompanied by work that, while still confirming and reformulating what parents have said, also "upgrades" the severity of a child's condition. Overall, it is the possibility of confirming the parent's view that seems central to the diagnostic news delivery done through a perspective-display series. Furthermore, this confirmation is an *achieved* phenomenon. When parents go along with, or themselves produce, problem proposals, the nature of this achievement is somewhat hidden. But when parents are resistant to problem proposals, we can clearly see that the alignment between clinician and parent is a matter of delicate interactive management.

To demonstrate these matters, I will begin by showing how "simple" confirmations work, and how they are achieved features of using a perspective-display series. Then I will take up progressively more "complex" deliveries that involve "upgrading" the nature of a condition to which parents have alluded. With more complex diagnostic news deliveries, every step in the process of leading towards a diagnosis can involve or invoke the parent's view, such that when some ultimate diagnostic term is produced, it appears as something on which clinician and parent, in a variety of ways, converge. This convergence may include, in addition to their displayed, mutually reinforcing *views*, demonstrations of the parties' shared *reactions* to the condition. In the end, however, convergence and mutuality come to be based on the clinical position, not the parents' version or one that is in between. While clinicians may demonstrate agreement with, and/or understanding of the parents' perspective, a claim is mounted that the parents' view affirms the very diagnosis of which they are now being informed.

Diagnostic News as Confirmation

Simple confirmations occur when a clinician displays agreement and offers to reformulate and elaborate the parent's displayed view along more technical lines:

delivery of diagnosis = confirmation + reformulation + elaboration

The next excerpt shows the pattern; it begins with a perspective-display invitation (line 1) and a reply (lines 3–7):

(4) [8.013]
```
 1  Dr:  What do you see? as- as his (0.5) difficulty.
 2       (1.2)
 3  Mo:  Mainly his uhm: (1.2) the fact that he
 4       doesn't understand everything. (0.6) and
 5       also the fact that his speech (0.7) is very
 6       hard to understand what he's saying (0.3)
 7       lot┌s of ti┐me
 8  Dr:     └right ┘
 9       (0.2)
10  Dr:  Do you have any ideas wh:y it is? are you:
11       d┌o yo┐u? h
12  Mo:   └No ┘
13       (2.1)
14  Dr:  ˙h okay I(0.2) you know I think we basically
15       (.) in some ways agree with you: (0.6) ˙hh
16       insofar as we think that (0.3) Dan's main
17       problem (0.4) ˙h you know does: involve you
18       know language.
19       (0.4)
20  Mo:  Mm hmm
21       (0.3)
22  Dr:  you know both (0.2) you know his- (0.4) being
23       able to understand you know what is said to
24       him (0.4) ˙h and also certainly also to be
25       able to express:: (1.3) you know his uh his
26       thoughts
27       (1.1)
28  Dr:  ˙hh uh:m (0.6)  hhh in general his
29       development . . .
```

In her reply, the mother (Mrs. C) formulates her son's problem, after which the clinician (Dr. E) produces an agreement token (line 8). This token may encourage continuation on the part of Mrs. C, which does not occur (silence at line 9). Next, Dr. E initiates a question-answer sequence concerning "why" there is a problem (lines 10–11), which is unsuccessful in eliciting further material from his recipient. Then, although qualifying himself, Dr. E more fully expresses agreement with Mrs. C's perspective (lines 14–15), and reformulates the parent's complaint about Dan's understanding and speech as involving a "main problem" the child has with "language" (lines 16–18). Dr. E also precedes the reformulation with emphasis on the verb "does," which is a way of tying to the parent's prior assessment and further marking agreement with it. Following Mrs. C's continuer (line 20), Dr. E elaborates on the diagnosis (lines 22–6), incorporating one term ("understand") that repeats what Mrs. C has said (line 4) and also using another ("express his thoughts") that is hearably a close version of Mrs. C's reference to "speech" (lines 5–7). In this series, the clinician's activities of confirmation, reformulation, and elaboration are all present and they severally work to co-implicate the parent's perspective in the diagnostic news.

Not any or all parental replies to a perspective-display invitation will offer an auspicious context for a confirming diagnostic news delivery. For instance, in replying to a perspective-display invitation, parents may take a position that there is no problem. Clinicians with "bad" diagnostic news to deliver are not, then, in a position of being able to confirm. Instead, they may have to work to *achieve* just that conversational environment which is ripe for a confirmatory delivery. Clinicians have a variety of devices for handling the "no problem" reply from parents, such as listening for or encouraging talk in which some diagnosable condition or difficulty is eventually broached (Maynard 1991).

(5) (Simplified)

```
 1  Dr:  How's Bobby doing.
 2  Mo:  Well he's doing uh pretty good you know
 3        especially in the school. I explained the
 4        teacher what you told me that he might be
 5        sent into a special class maybe, that I was
 6        not sure. And he says you know I asks his
 7        opinion, an' he says that he was doing
 8        pretty good in the school, that he was
 9        responding you know in uhm everything that
10        he tells them. Now he thinks that he's not
11        gonna need to be sent to another school.
12  Dr:  He doesn't think that he's gonna need to be
13        sent
14  Mo:  Yeah that he was catching on a little bit uh
15        more you know like I said I-I-I know that
16        he needs a- you know I was 'splaining to her
17        that I'm you know that I know for sure that
18        he needs some special class or something.
19  Dr:  Wu' whatta you think his problem is.
20  Mo:  Speech.
21  Dr:  Yeah. yeah his main problem is a- you know a
22        language problem.
23  Mo:  Yeah language.
```

This excerpt starts with an unmarked invitation, which initially obtains a positive assessment from the mother, Mrs. M (lines 2–3). However, in the course of reporting a conversation with her son's teacher (lines 3–11, 14–18), Mrs. M exhibits a position implying that she sees Bobby as having a problem ("I know for sure that he needs some special

class or something," lines 17–18). Dr. E immediately follows this with a marked invitation (line 19) or one that contains a problem proposal. With this, he takes up what Mrs. M had implied and asks her for an explicit problem formulation, which she provides at line 20. Then Dr. E uses two "yeah" tokens to confirm her perspective, and yet reformulates what she has said by suggesting that the "main problem is . . . a language problem" (lines 21–2).

Also note how the parent receives the diagnosis by changing her terminology to match the clinician's (line 23). Subsequently (in talk not reproduced here), Dr. E elaborates the diagnosis using words that further incorporate Mrs. M's displayed perspective. Overall, then, the way in which the parent's perspective is co-implicated in the delivery of diagnostic news here is similar to the previous example, with the exception that the clinician must strategically deal with an initial positive assessment on the part of [the] recipient. Thus, the confirmation type of delivery is an achievement in that it depends on parents presenting not just anything in reply to a perspective-display invitation, but just that material which allows agreement and confirmation to be done. When that material is not initially produced, clinicians will seek it out, which suggests that their use of the perspective-display series is oriented to developing a hospitable environment for delivering a diagnosis.

Upgrading a Condition

Even when a clinical diagnosis departs significantly from a recipient's position, the delivery still can involve a confirmation. Once that confirmation is performed, clinicians may reformulate and then add the upgraded diagnosis onto what has already been said. It seems, then, that "complex" deliveries have a progressivity to them that is set off by confirming the parents' view:

delivery of diagnosis = confirmation + reformulation
+ upgraded diagnosis + elaboration

What distinguishes the upgraded diagnosis from reformulations or elaborations is evidence internal to the talk between clinician and parent showing that both may be oriented not just to a difference in vocabulary but to a difference in level of seriousness. That is, the distinction between lay and professional terminology in earlier examples appeared to be a technical one. However, in contrast to lay terminology, professional nomenclature can imply a more critical and potentially stigmatizing condition for a child. In this situation, parents may subtly resist a proffered diagnosis, and clinicians will show a sensitivity to this resistance.

For instance, in one interview, a clinician asked a mother how she felt about her daughter's "functioning in the school." The mother replied that the girl was "not right on her level that she should be," that the teachers "don't think she's on her level," and that "she is kinda slow":

(6) [3.047]

```
 1  Mo:  . . . and I have seen no progress, from
 2        September to June. For her learning
 3        ability, she is slow.
 4        (0.6)
 5  Dr:  That's what we uh:: also found on- on
 6        psychological testing, ˙hhhh That she was
 7        per- not performing like a normal (0.2) uh:::
 8        six and a half year old uh (0.4) should.
 9  Mo:  mm hmm
10  Dr:  And that she was performing more uh (0.3)
11        ˙hhhh what we call as a borderline (0.4)
12        rate of retardation ˙hhh uh:::m
13        (2.2)
14  Dr:  For a normal (0.4) kind of might use a
15        number ˙hhhh it's usually about hundred
16        (0.2) or more. (0.6) and anywhere between
17        uh:: (0.3) eighty two and (1.2) uh:::: (0.4)
18        ninety is kind of uh:: (0.4) borderline
19        (0.6) kind of uh:: (0.2)  hhh functioning.
```

Here, the clinician, Dr. H, employs another device for confirming the parent's perspective, suggesting (line 5) that the clinic has "also found" what the mother has just said about the child being slow. Then, the clinician proposes to reformulate this as "not performing like a normal . . . six and a half year old" (lines 7 and 8). This reformulation is met with a continuer at line 9, following which, Dr. H, by way of the "and" (line 10) adds a clinical term, "borderline rate of retardation" (lines 11–12). Note, then, that reformulations may foreshadow the upgraded diagnoses they precede. After this, at line 13, there is a large silence. In systematic fashion . . . this at least shows, on the part of the parent, an unwillingness to endorse the clinic's terminology and can indicate a withheld disagreement (Maynard 1991). Subsequently, while Dr. H appears to explain the diagnosis (lines 14–18), in returning to the diagnostic category, he no longer refers to "retardation," and instead pairs "borderline" with "kind of functioning" (lines 18–19). Thus, Dr. H *retreats* from using a term that was added on to a confirmation and reformulation of the parents' version, which indicates the clinician's understanding that it may not have been as acceptable as the previous reformulation. Indeed, just after line 19 above (in talk not reproduced here), Mrs. B says, "Well I think she will progress later," and suggests that the child will do better in second grade. Then, Dr. H shows a further orientation to the difference in positions, stating, "One of the reasons why we are having this conference is also to make you aware of her limitations, and not to agree with you in everything that you say, saying that she is going to catch up, and she is going to do well in, second grade or third grade and such things like that."

Example (6) show[s] how asking the parents for their view may obtain a problem formulation that indicates a relatively hospitable environment for a confirming type of diagnostic news delivery. However, while being able to confirm and reformulate a parent's view may go smoothly, adding an upgraded diagnosis may not result in felicitous treatment by parents. Anticipating this, clinicians may employ other devices that help prepare the way for an upgraded diagnosis. The result can be long and complex deliveries of diagnostic news. I will examine a complex delivery, which shows that, through the perspective-display series and related devices, it is possible to reduce very stark disparities between parental and clinical perspectives regarding the condition of a child.

Reducing Disparity

If we were to categorize or code the parental and clinical perspectives in the interview from which the next excerpts (7a–f) derive, these perspectives would appear far apart, if not contradictory. Objectively, in fact, the situation would seem to present a high probability of argument and conflict:

Summary codification—Example 7

Parent's Perspective	Clinician's Perspective
the basic condition is hyperactivity	hyperactivity is one condition among several
the problem is temporary	the problems are not temporary
there is no brain damage	there is brain damage, which is the basic condition

We might predict that clinician and parent would dispute the child's symptoms, the duration of his condition, and what the basic condition is. Instead, as the interview proceeds, the distance between the participants narrows and the clinician's informing occurs harmoniously and affirmatively rather than argumentatively or conflictually. In part, this may be because, after confirming and refor-

mulating the parent's perspective, but before moving to present an upgraded diagnosis, the clinician engages in *converting* and *identifying*, which are two other forms of co-implicating the parent's perspective. These forms, along with the perspective-display series and its progressive manner of presenting diagnostic news, help reduce the disparity between parties' perspectives. However, they do not imply compromise between the parties, nor do they involve negotiation over the existence, nature, and duration of problems. By proposing to bring a recipient's perspective in line with the clinical position, these forms are persuasive devices.

The first excerpt from this interview starts with the parent, Mrs. L, attributing to the clinician a particular statement regarding the potential of her son (lines 1–3 below). When, at line 4, Dr. C seems to disaffiliate from this attribution, Mrs. L backs down (line 5). And after Dr. C completes her utterance at line 6, the parent acknowledges Dr. C's position (line 7). Then, the clinician probes (lines 8–9) Mrs. L for her own view on the matter of her son's potential, which she gives in lines 10–11:

(7a) [30.001] (simplified) (The mother, Mo, is referred to in the text as "Mrs. L")
```
 1 Mo:  . . . from what I was told in the beginning
 2       and you told me too, he will outgrow this as
 3       he goes along.
 4 Dr:  Well. Yeah, It's not exactly-
 5 Mo:  more or les⌈s h:::: hhhh      ⌉
 6 Dr:            ⌊important what I⌋said.
 7 Mo:  Yea⌈h      ⌉
 8 Dr:     ⌊Wh⌋at- what do you think, I mean do
         you
 9       think Barry will outgrow his problems?
10 Mo:  Well! I think so, in way- I hope so! in
11       ways. Because you know . . .
```

In a qualified way, then, Mrs. L indicates a belief that her son will outgrow his problems (lines 1–3, 5, 10–11), and goes on (in talk not reproduced here) to list several reasons why: he will get proper preschooling, eventually go into a regular school, take medication, and she had been told that his problems were childhood ones that would only last until puberty.

After this, the clinician introduces a typical perspective-display invitation:

(7b) [30.016]

  Dr: What do you think is wrong with him.
      (0.3)
  Mo: Well:, he's hyperactive child.
  Dr: Mm⌈hmm
  Mo: ⌊ˑhhhh⌋so:::, the definition they said when a baby's born the brain is developed, to that certain point. ˑhhhhhh now with hyperactive child, that brai- the brain hasn't developed, to that certain point . . .

From here, Mrs. L goes on to explain her concept of hyperactivity, and in reply to a question from the clinician, indicates hearing the explanation and diagnosis from a cousin who had seen a pediatric neurologist and psychiatrist because her child seemingly had similar problems. Mrs. L's alluding to this seems to warrant an inference from Dr. C, which, however, is disconfirmed:

(7c) [30.070]

  Dr: So . . . you suspect there's something wrong with Barry's brain then?
  Mo: We:ll::, um (.) uh::::m, not really, I would say (.) learn::ing (.) difficulties. You know, like uh he wasn't grasping.

Mrs. L next describes when problematic behavior first started (at age two) and how she became more suspicious that something was wrong when B was age three because he still was not "talking right" and was resistant to toilet training.

Then, through various displays of agreement, Dr. C confirms Mrs. L's views. Below, at line 5, the clinician uses a formulaic expression ("we agree with you"), although she also qualifies it (lines 6–7). In addition, at line 9, redoing an utterance that was overlapped by Mrs. L's line 8 query, Dr. C emphasizes or accents the verb "is" before repeating the very term ("hyperactive") that Mrs. L has used. At

line 11, the clinician also stresses the verb ("has") which prefaces a gloss ("trouble") of what the parent discussed earlier. As mentioned, such emphasis is a way of both tying to the prior talk and marking agreement with it.

(7d) [30.119]

  1 Mo:⌈(So that's) how I th⌉ought something was
  2 Dr:⌊So that's why we-⌋
  3 Mo: wro⌈ng th⌉ere.
  4 Dr: ⌊right⌋
  5 Dr: And (0.3) you know, we (.) we agree with
  6   you, you know, we- ih- cer- to the certain
  7   degree.⌈We feel that
  8 Mo: ⌊Is he gonna be all⌋right. heh huh
  9 Dr: We- we feel that (0.3) Billy is: hyperactive.
10 Mo: Yeah.=
11 Dr: =y'know:, and he has had trouble, (.) for a
12   long ti:me.⌈ˑhhhh⌉
13 Mo: ⌊Yeah.⌋
14 Dr: But we don't see this as something that's
15   just gonna pass:
16 Mo: Y⌈eah, well I know that,⌉
17 Dr: ⌊and an- go away.   ⌋
18 Mo: Right.

Subsequently, at lines 14–15, Dr. C, using a contrast marker ("but") and contrast stress on the verb "don't" . . . takes up a position that contradicts what the parent has said regarding the child outgrowing his problems, and thus reformulates Mrs. L's version of the problem. Technically, while this is a *disagreement* (Pomerantz 1984; Sacks 1987), it follows the preference *form* in which it is packaged as *agreement*. That is, the disagreement is postpositioned within the turn it occupies by the occurrence of preceding agreements and the contrast marker.

In a sense, the confirmation and reformulation succeed here. That is, after Dr. C produces various terms and characterizations, Mrs. L gives indications of assent (lines 10, 13, 16) and seemingly aligns (at line 18) with the proposed reformulation (lines 14–15, 17) thereby apparently relinquishing her earlier-stated view regarding the temporariness of the problem (see example [7a] above), and also possibly defusing a potential argument. So far, this excerpt is similar to examples (4) and (5) above, wherein the clinician confirms and then suggests a reformulation of what a parent has said. And here, as in (5), the parent clearly accepts the suggestion.

In this instance, however, the confirmation-reformulation is not the end of the line or the immediate prelude to an elaboration; it precedes a move to present more serious diagnostic terminology. Moreover, in contrast to example (6) . . . this move involves other work on the part of the clinician, who proposes *converting* the parent's formulation of the problem to being among items on a list of things. Below (lines 4–5), Dr. C suggests that hyperactivity is "one of the problems" that B has, and then proffers "another" difficulty of the child and details its characteristics (lines 7–8, 10–11, and 13–14).

(7e) [30.119]

```
 1  Dr:  He ha:s serious problems.
 2  Mo:  Hm::
 3  Dr:  A:nd, you know, we don't know:: what kind of
 4       term to apply ta these problems, One of the
 5       problems is that he is hyperactive.⌈h  h h h h⌉
 6  Mo:                                     ⌊Mm hmm⌋
 7  Dr:  another is that he's just sort of
 8       disorganized, in the way he⌈takes  ⌉in the
 9  Mo:                             ⌊ (Mya)⌋
10  Dr:  world, he doesn't take it in the way  hh
11       other children,
12  Mo:  Y⌈eah.⌉
13  Dr:   ⌊his-⌋his age.  hhh He can't put things
14       together in his mi::nd the wa⌈y othe⌉r
15  Mo:                               ⌊Ye::ah⌋
16  Dr:  children would.
```

Mrs. L, in providing continuers (lines 6, 9, 12, 15) that allow the production of these detailings, at least "goes along with" Dr. C's descriptions and, insofar as "yeah" (lines 12, 15) is stronger than "mm hmm" in this regard, may even agree with them.

The activity of converting, in short, involves the parent assenting to the assemblage of a list that incorporates her version of the basic problem as apparently equivalent to other members of that list. It is no longer that hyperactivity is the son's basic problem, as was the parent's initial perspective. Now, that is one item in an inventory, which also includes being "disorganized" in taking in the world, and having difficulty putting "things together in his mind." Such conversion figures in Dr. C's delivery of the core diagnosis, which comes after the two participants go on to discuss how Billy is doing in the "readiness program" at school. Dr. C, upon stating that Billy will "progress and learn, but he will always have a definite problem," reintroduces the issue of something being "wrong with the brain" (lines 1-4 below; cf. [7c] above):

(7f) 30.186

```
 1  Dr:  Now when you say: uh you know, the ter:m
 2       something wrong with the brain, is very
 3       vague, we don't like it (.) you
 4       don⌈'t like it.⌉
 5  Mo:     ⌊Yeah right.⌋
 6  Dr:  But hhhhh when we have to descri:be Barry's
 7       problems, we would have to say that there is
 8       something that⌈is not⌉working right
 9  Mo:               ⌊Yeah ⌋
10  Dr:  in the brain
11  Mo:  Mm
12  Dr:  that's causing these things. It's causing
13       the hyperactivity,  hhhh⌈it's:  ⌉causing him
14  Mo:                          ⌊ Yeah⌋
15  Dr:  ta see the wor::ld, in a different way, from
16       other children,
17  Mo:  Mm yeah
18  Dr:  It's causing him to be:- his (.) thoughts to
19       be maybe a little disorganized, when he
20       tries ta order the world,
21  Mo:  Mm::
22  Dr:  in his mind. And  hhhh if you know, we had
23       ta say, uh if we had ta give a diagnosis
24       (0.2) hh you know when you write away to
25       schools:: or ta other doctors, you have to
26       write something down as a diagnosis. I feel
27       that hyperactivity, just alone, wouldn't be
28       enough.
```

```
29        (0.2)
30 Mo:   Mm ┌hmm┐
31 Dr:      └hhh ┘and that we would have ta say
32        something like brain damage.
33 Mo:   Mm hmm
34 Dr:   in terms of (0.2) of Barry's problems
35 Mo:   Mmm.
36 Dr:   Because it's a kind of thing that's- it's
37        not jus:t hyperactivity that's gonna be
38        helped with a little medicine,  hhhh
          He-he
39        is going to nee:d, (0.5) a s- special
40        education: (.) all the way through.
41 Mo:   Uh ha.
42 Dr:   We feel.
43 Mo:   Yeah.
```

The beginning of this excerpt shows the phenomenon of *identifying*. As evident in numerous interviews, this involves procedures whereby a clinician construes the parents' feelings in regard to hearing projected diagnostic terminology. Here, there are two aspects to the proposed identifying. Firstly, at lines 2–4, Dr. C acknowledges that her own reference to "something wrong with the brain" is "very vague," claims not liking the phrase, and suggests that this attitude is shared by her recipient, who agrees (line 5). Thus, if it is agreed that "we" and "you" do not like something, it exhibits a mutuality in one attitudinal area for the otherwise-partitioned sets of people who are so categorized.

Secondly, in moving to the diagnostic presentation, Dr. C portrays herself as forced to do so. She invokes the phrase "have to" in reference to (a) describing "B's problems" (line 6) and (b) saying the brain is not "working right" (lines 8, 10). Recall that Mrs. L has already shown resistance to characterizations of the severity and nature of the child's problem (she thought the problem would eventually go away, and that it was not brain damage). Being forced to describe problems and to say the brain is not working right, while not disavowing such matters, at least mildly mimics Mrs. L's resistance to these character-

izations. In summary, identifying with a recipient in these ways takes her perspective into account by intimating that the clinician can understand what it is like to confront the bad news that must be delivered. This is a slightly different way of co-implicating the parents' perspective than we have seen so far, for it means that the clinician has incorporated already-displayed and yet anticipated reactions to the diagnosis.

The co-implicating of a parent's perspective is also accomplished here in the more usual sense, when Dr. C reinvokes the converting and detailing from excerpt (7e), which include Mrs. L's view regarding the nature of the problem. At lines 8, 10, and 12, that is, Dr. C suggests that the brain problem may be "causing these things" (line 12), a phrase that ties to the previously named symptoms (hyperactivity, seeing the world in a different way, having disorganized thoughts) that are reassembled within a three-part list (lines 12–13, 15–16, and 18–20), a rhetorical device that implies a sense of coherence, completeness, and unity (Atkinson 1984, 57; cf. Jefferson 1990) to the package of symptoms. Beyond the sheer content of the list, Dr. C thereby appeals for some other condition to be "causing" them. And each part of the list meets with continuers, including two agreement tokens (lines 14 and 17) that permit Dr. C to progress to delivery of the official diagnosis. Thus, as opposed to being some unilateral declaration of Dr. C, the listing is collaboratively produced. Accordingly, to the extent that this listing serves as a warrant for the upcoming diagnosis, the basis for the warrant is in the parent's as well as the clinic's perspective.

Finally, in arriving at the actual term, Dr. C again portrays herself as forced to give it (lines 22–6), and invokes the institutional context—having to "write away" to schools and doctors—as an explanation for such force. The theme of partial resistance is thereby once more salient, and serves as a prelude to Dr. C discounting the parent's term, "hyperactivity" (lines 26–8), before going on to pronounce the diagnosis of brain damage (lines 31–2). This diagnosis, in a variety of ways, is an "upshot" (Heritage and Watson 1979) of what has gone before, and, as Dr. C elaborates (lines 36-40), also projects a specific, recommended treatment (special education as opposed to medication). The proposal for treatment here illustrates how closely therapies are linked to diagnostic terms and may be driving their use. That is, the very careful movement away from the parents' perspective and towards the clinic's position reflects not just an abstract concern with correct terminology, but with concrete remedies for the problems. . . .

In review, this informing interview begins with a query and a perspective-display invitation that succeed in eliciting the parent's view of her child's condition as being temporary and basically involving hyperactivity. The third part of the perspective-display series follows a format in which the clinician confirms, reformulates, and then upgrades the conditions that the parent has named. The confirmation entails the clinician agreeing with the parent's proposal of hyperactivity, while the reformulation contradicts what the parent has said regarding the temporariness of the problem. After the parent gives signs of changing her perspective on this issue, the clinician proposes additional problems to the hyperactivity, *converting* the latter to one among several symptoms. The parent also goes along with these proposals, and then the clinician delivers a term that is "upgraded" with respect to another aspect of the parent's perspective. Whereas Mrs. L had resisted the suggestion that something was "wrong with B's brain" (example 7c above), the clinician subsequently (7f) presents "brain damage" as the basic diagnosis. Dr. C prefaces this delivery by *identifying* with the parent and by invoking the agreed-upon symptomology. Although the interview would objectively exhibit disparities between parent and clinician, the perspective-display series and related strategies of co-implicating parental perspectives in the delivery of diagnostic news permit positional differences between the deliverer and recipient to be publicly overcome. The movement that overcomes such differences is in the direction of the clinical position, and thus the series may be a persuasive way that clinicians ratify and confirm a parent's own perspective even while suggesting, indeed using that perspective to affirm, the alternative.

Conclusion

The perspective-display series is a means by which participants to a clinical informing engage a circuit of talk that displays [the] recipient's view as a prelude to the delivery of diagnostic news. By way of this series, clinicians can deliver, as a product of talk and interaction, a diagnosis that confirms and co-implicates [the] recipient's perspective. In initiating the series, a perspective-display invitation seeks material from parents with which agreement can be formulated, to thereby begin, with a confirmation of what the parents had to say, a progressive delivery of diagnostic news. Upon this confirmation, clinicians can build reformulations, upgraded diagnoses, and technical elaborations. As compared with the clueing, guessing, and confirming strategy identified at the outset of this chapter, the perspective-display series more explicitly engages the recipient's perspective for a bad news delivery, yet still has this confirmatory aspect as a central feature.

Devices such as identifying with the recipient and converting the recipient's formulation of the problem to a symptom of something more basic may be employed in service of a progressive news delivery. In all, these mechanisms allow for diagnostic presentations that contain a parent's perspective as an embedded feature, and may thus persuade a parent to align with the clinical position. A further effect of using the perspective-display series is to portray the clinician not as one whose assessment is an independent discovery, nor the parent as one who must be moved from a state of ignorance to knowledge. Rather, the parent is one who partially knows the truth and the clinician is one who, in modifying or adding to what a parent already knows or believes, proposes to ratify the displayed perspective. . . . By co-implicating their recipients' knowledge or beliefs (and anticipated reactions) in the news they have to deliver, clinicians present assessments in a publicly affirmative and nonconflicting manner.

References

Atkinson, J. M. 1984. *Our Masters' Voices: The Language and Body Language of Politics*. London: Methuen.

Heritage, J., and D. R. Watson. 1979. Formulations as conversational objects. In G. Psathas (ed.), *Everyday Language: Studies in Ethnomethodology*. New York: Irvington, pp. 123–162.

Jacobs, J. 1969. *The Search for Help: A Study of the Retarded Child in the Community*. Washington, DC: University Press of America.

Jefferson, G. 1990. List construction as a task and resource. In G. Psathas (ed.), *Interaction Competence*. Lanham, MD: University Press of America, pp. 63–92.

Maynard, D. 1991. Perspective-display sequences and the delivery and receipt of diagnostic news. In D. Boden and D. H. Zimmerman (eds.), *Talk and Social Structure*. Cambridge: Polity Press, pp. 164–192.

Pomerantz, A. M. 1984. Agreeing and disagreeing with assessments: Some features of preferred/dispreferred turn shapes. In J. M. Atkinson and J. Heritage (eds.), *Structures of Social Action: Studies in Conversation Analysis*. Cambridge: Cambridge University Press, pp. 57–101.

Sacks, H. 1987. On the preference for agreement and contiguity in sequences in conversation. In G. Button and J. R. E. Lee (eds.), *Talk and Social Organization*. Clevedon: Multilingual Matters, pp. 54–69.

——. 1992 [1964–1972]. *Lectures on Conversation*, 2 vols., edited by G. Jefferson. Oxford: Blackwell.

Schegloff, E. A. 1988. On an actual servo-mechanism for guessing bad news: A single case conjecture. *Social Problems* 35(4): 442–457.

Part VI

Social Interaction and Relationships

We often speak of social relationships as if they were things that existed apart from social interaction. This is implied, for example, when we say that we have a certain kind of relationship with someone. Yet social relationships are not so much something we have as something we do. Social interaction is the source and sustenance of social relationships. Their only existence apart from interaction is in memory and imagination. And even there, they tend to wither away without the nourishment of social interaction.

Our understanding of different kinds of relationships clearly influences how we interact with one another. For example, most of us do not tell checkout clerks in supermarkets intimate details about our private lives. However, it is because we do not do so that our relationship with checkout clerks is fleeting and relatively anonymous. If we did share our intimate secrets with a checkout clerk, and she or he reciprocated, then our relationship would be intimate. Relationships are ways individuals relate to one another, which is just another way of referring to patterns of social interaction.

Social relationships provide the immediate context of our social lives and experience. They support and undermine our sense of self. They emotionally tie us to others in bonds of mutual obligation. Our positions in networks of relationship determine our social standing in the neighborhood, at school, and at work. And, how others relate to us shapes our most personal experiences. The selections in this section examine both the interactional dynamics of relationships and how they, in turn, shape our lives and experience. ✦

20

Parents, Kids, and Cars

Amy Best

Most of us think of parent-child relationships as both enduring and continually changing. Even young children try to gain freedom from parental control, and parents often resist those attempts, at least temporarily. As a result, parents and children are constantly negotiating the terms of their relationship in this and other respects. Such parent-child negotiations are probably most intense during young people's long transition from childhood to adulthood, in our society, roughly the teenage years and often into the early twenties. Young people strive for greater autonomy, and parents, often out of concern for their children's safety, try to maintain some control over their lives.

In our society, gaining the ability to drive and car ownership are major steps in young people's growing autonomy. Except in those few cities with extensive and reliable mass transportation, being unable to drive or without a car is to be hopelessly dependent on others to get where you need and want to go. It is hardly surprising, then, that driving privileges and car ownership are major subjects of negotiation between parents and their teenage children in this society.

This selection examines negotiations between parents and children over car privileges from the perspective of the children, and how those negotiations are influenced by social factors external to the family. For example, it shows how young people plead with parents to allow them to drive and for financial assistance in purchasing a car of their own. Despite concerns about their child's safety,

many parents often relent, to some degree, in part because it means that they will no longer have to chauffeur the child here and there. However, parents use car privileges to control their children, restricting or withdrawing them if their newly driving child displeases them. They also often extract promises from the child to assume some of the family's transportation needs in return for driving privileges and assistance in purchasing a car. In these and other ways, parents and their young adult children negotiate the changing terms of their relationship around cars.

Foreshadowing the following section, Amy Best, the author of this selection, also examines how a family's class or income and general social standing influence these negotiations. More affluent parents can clearly contribute more to their child's car ownership—and may even buy them a new car—than can less affluent parents. Hence, young people are reminded of their class standing when negotiating with their parents over car ownership. They also learn something about their parents' approach to money, such as expecting one "to earn their own way."

Although focused on parents and children's negotiations around car privileges, this selection illustrates some more general sociological lessons. Even enduring social relationships, such as those between parents and children, husbands and wives, and long-standing friends, are subject to negotiation and change. Those negotiations, in turn, do not occur in a social vacuum but are influenced by various social influences that originate outside the relationship. Social relationships are never defined once and for all but are ongoing social constructions.

Jorge, a bright young 17-year-old Latino, is a senior at Bernards, a prestigious all boys school in the Northern California city where this research was conducted. Jorge is a lot like the other young men who attend Bernards: His priorities are academic, he is actively involved in a host of extracurricular activities intended to boost his college applications, and he feels assured that his dreams of a bright future will be realized. But every day after school, after he has finished football practice or one of the many other school-based extracurricular activities he pursues, Jorge boards two buses for the 2-hour ride that brings him across town to the Eastside where he lives with his mother and father. To outsiders, the city's Eastside is viewed as a hotbed for gang activity. But a more complex depiction is one that reveals the Eastside as one of the largest ethnic enclaves for the Vietnamese and Latino communities in the county. And although it has more than its share of rundown houses, overcrowded apartments, and families living on the edge, the Eastside is also home to many middle-class families. Jorge comes from one such family. His mother and father travel each morning the 40-plus miles to their jobs to guarantee they stay that way. From their combined income, his parents pay a mortgage on a modest home, his mother drives an Infiniti, a midpriced luxury sedan, and they are able to finance the cost of a private school education with the hope of a secured future for their only child. It is their dual income that allowed them to surprise Jorge with a 1998 Ford Explorer last Christmas. The impetus—"They don't have time to drive me, so they got me my own car," Jorge explains. Like most kids at this prestigious all boys school, Jorge doesn't work. "School is my job," he offers, yet adding, "I want to get a job and try to lift that burden off my parents." But Jorge is simply too busy to find the time. For now, he is just happy he no longer has to ride the two buses each afternoon to get home.

When asked if he'd ever lost his car privileges, he answers with a matter-of-fact tone, "It's not worth taking away the keys. I do a lot of stuff. They feel bad taking away my extracurriculars," adding a few moments later, "my curriculars are more than just hanging out with friends. I do a lot of stuff at school." By just about anybody's standards, Jorge is a good kid: earning high marks in school, getting along with fellow classmates, and being

involved in school athletics and several academic clubs. For many middle-class parents such as Jorge's, it is a matter of good practical sense to give their child a car once he or she is able to legally drive. As Jorge's narrative suggests, driving their child to and from the endless stream of organized activities, in addition to managing two busy professional schedules of their own, is almost impossible. This is the "time bind" Arlie Hochschild (1997) so cogently described in her book by the same name. For middle- and upper-middle-class children struggling to gain an edge in what could only be described as the ever increasing[ly] competitive marketplace of high stakes education, all of this is a matter of course. . . .

Jorge's story about how he came to have his own car is an interesting one because it provides important clues not only about the decisions parents and teens make concerning teens' changing roles and responsibilities inside and outside family as teens move into adulthood, but also something about how these decisions are made and the social forces that deeply influence them. Whereas Jorge's story seems to reveal something about the inadvertent gains of greater independence for children of working parents and the intense academic demands for college-bound kids, it also points to the central role of class and the demands of work in structuring these family decisions. This article examines how young adult children collaboratively negotiate for greater freedom and independence while also fulfilling increasing family responsibilities as they transition to adulthood by focusing on how teens negotiate with parents around driving and the car.

"Yes, No, Maybe So": Framing Co-Collaborative Negotiations Between Parents and Teens

For adolescents, getting "the license" usually results in more time spent away from family. But for many, the license is also accompanied by greater responsibility to the family. Young adults are often expected by their parents to share more of the work that maintains modern family life once they are able to drive. Highlighting the interactional dynamics as they are narrated by teens themselves, I identify the ways in which the car serves as cultural object around which parents and kids negotiate kids' independence from the world of family, arguing that this process is not without some struggle. Gripped by a very concrete concern for their children's safety, parents often award greater freedoms to their kids reluctantly (Kurz, 2002). Parents exercise considerable control over their young adult children, placing limits on how they may drive, when they may drive, and where they may drive. However, the conventional characterization of parent-youth relationships as one of warring positions, although at times apt, in the end fails to explain the complexities and contradictions that emerge as parents and kids struggle together and apart to make sense of a variety of changes in family structures, family responsibilities and family roles in contemporary America. . . .

I highlight the perspectives of young adults, keeping in mind that the accounts provided by parents would likely look quite different from those provided here. Family sociologists and life course scholars have long overlooked the active role children and youth play in socialization in family contexts. . . . [Today] [f]amily studies scholars increasingly see children as fully participating family members . . . active in the complex negotiations of family practices and relationships and contributing in significant ways to the everyday construction of family life (Larson & Richards, 1994; Smart, Neale, & Wade, 2001). . . . [Here] I examine how parents and their young adult children negotiate around driving and having a car, drawing attention to the collaborative nature of these negotiations and the active role teens, themselves, play in them. I examine how these negotiations si-

multaneously express and construct class for these teens by drawing teens into the economic contexts of their families. . . . [Then] I examine how teens perform the work of family life as they manage the increasing responsibilities to family that accompany learning to drive, also considering what this emerging responsibility means for their independence from family. . . .

Background to the Study

Data for this article were drawn from a larger multimethod study focusing on how cars operate as cultural objects through which kids make sense of what it means to be young in culture today, engage the process of cultural production, and solidify their social identities. How young adults interactionally manage the "push and pull" of freedom from and responsibility to family . . . is the particular focus of this analysis. This article primarily draws from materials gathered through focus groups and in-depth interviews with slightly less than 100 young men and young women. . . . All interviews were conducted in a Northern California city and its surrounding suburbs. Like other California cities, this city is sprawling, lacking a comprehensive public transportation system. For this reason, a significant portion of the population relies on automobiles as their primary ground transportation. As a result, cars are a central part of the landscape and car culture is firmly embedded in everyday life. . . .

Begging, Pleading, and Granting Permission: Parents and Kids Collaboratively Negotiate the Car

For many kids, perched at the threshold of adulthood, getting a driver's license offers the promise of greater freedom, independence, and autonomy. In the words of one young woman, "you feel kind of liberated." Freedom, as it is articulated by youth around driving, carries several meanings. First, freedom is defined directly in connection with parental ties. That is, it is largely understood as a freedom *from* the constant presence of parents. Freedom is also defined in terms of young adults' changing relationships and greater access to a number of public settings beyond family. In short, youth gain freedom *to* spaces previously closed off to them. In very concrete terms, the license represents greater freedom of movement, as one European American young woman explained,

> When I got my driver's license, I looked at it as freedom, getting out from my parents, going places you couldn't get to before because you had to have your parent's permission . . . not having to be worried about being dropped off and being picked up. Going to the library even or a dance club or a party and not having to worry about, I don't know, your parents having to come pick you up. Not necessarily, it wasn't embarrassment for me, it was more, just like okay, I make my own choices I can leave when I want to you know, I made this decision to come here you know I'll drop you off. I felt more like an adult but um, I don't know, I went to the beach, to people's houses, friends' houses, the movies.

In addition to the most obvious gains, the most cherished aspect of this new freedom is her greater ability to exercise control of her life, where she goes and when. Although she alludes to her concern for her appearance within youth cultural worlds (parents are rarely seen as social capital in youth peer groups), for this young woman, what seems most important is her ability to be self-determining, something few adolescents regularly enjoy. As this woman notes, it is not just freedom from parents that is gained but also greater control over self in different social settings. . . .

The struggle to claim greater freedom over self and setting, in short over one's life, in-volves a series of negotiations and ongoing interactions with parents. Hortencia, a young Latina who participated in one of the focus groups, explains,

> My parents I don't think they were strict, but then again they weren't maybe because I challenged them on it, I mean, it wasn't, when they would say no to something I would say, but why?, here are my reasons why I can do this, what are your reasons? So I kind of engaged them in a conversation and because like I was always totally involved in school when I was, it was just like by chance if I went somewhere, like I didn't, I didn't, for me like, I was never into drinking, I was never into, so I knew what I was doing was fine. After I talked to them they would let me go.

With the exception of a few, most teens, like Hortencia, saw these as negotiations where parents were at the very least willing to listen to their child. Sarah and Christina, both European American and female, seem to be the exceptions to the rule.

AB: Do you have a car?

Sarah: I'm gonna get a car when I have money. Yeah my parents don't like me and they don't like the fact that I would ever get a car because I'm a B-I, B with an itch and I would probably run people off the road, trust me PMS straight out . . . I'll get my driver's license but no car.

AB: Will your parents let you drive their car?

Sarah: I don't think they trust me.

Christina: I got my permit when I was fifteen and I had kept wanting to go get my license. I took all the driving lessons and everything. My mom finally decided you know "we'll just put this off, put this off." So when I was eighteen I got my license on my own. Since they [parents] don't have to sign anything. She'd used it as a punishment because I wanted to drive myself to school and work and every thing else . . . umm . . . she would say "no, no, no you have to do things my way" and if they weren't done the right way "you can't get your license."

But as much as young adults play an active role in these negotiations with parents, they do so under particular conditions of constraint. For those kids who must drive a parent's car . . . asking permission to borrow their parents' car also often means having to manage their parents' work and leisure schedules. Consider the comments from one South Asian young woman:

> I needed the car and my mom needed a car for work and it was kind of getting difficult where you know if she needed the car on her days off and I would have to revolve my schedule around her and stuff . . . I was sharing it. It was like between me, my mom and my sister and like, the way it was set up was my sister would carpool with her friend to school and that would be the days that my mom would take it to work and then a couple of days it would be home because my mom needed to run errands or whatnot.

A young Latina explained how this worked in her household.

> AR: I've always had their cars, they've always let me borrow their cars, my dad, yeah, always, like I mean, he would give me the one he didn't like.
>
> AB: Now, does he still do that or do, do you have your own car?
>
> AR: No, now, 3 years ago I got my own car.
>
> AB: So when driving the back-up car, before you got your car did you have to ask or?
>
> AR: I had to ask, of course.

For this young woman, it is simply a matter of course that she would seek permission to drive her father's car. Although family cars are essentially shared resources in many fam-

ilies, in the end, few kids see these cars as their own or themselves [as] having equal negotiating power in decisions over them. The car ultimately belongs to a parent and not them. This is reinforced by the fact that young adults are typically expected to satisfy a number of questions pertaining to their upcoming activities before permission to borrow the car is granted. The consequence is that their freedom to then travel beyond their immediate setting is contingent. After all, a parent has the power to say no. When asking to borrow her mother's car, Lucena explains that sometimes, "they would be like; no you can't take the car, but it wouldn't be like for punishment it's just that they didn't want me to. They didn't feel like it [laughs]."

Usually, it is the parents' busy work schedule that curtails young adult children's freedom to easily move between the world of family and beyond. I listened to many young adults as they identified the difficulty in trying to resolve scheduling conflicts. Marisol explains, "I started driving because I needed a ride to go to school and they can't take me to school, so that's why I started driving. [But] um I can only go to school and back home and they, if they wanted me to do some like, run some errands or something they will give me the car." This struggle to gain access to the family car is perhaps particularly acute at this historical moment. Time spent away from family, at work and school or involved in a variety of extracurricular and leisure activities, for both parents and their children is considerable (Kincheloe, 1997). Jorge explains, "All of us are so busy. Since I got my own car, we're like three units. Cause we have our own work. My mom works in Oakland now. I do all my stuff at school like I said, so I don't get home until 5 or 6. My dad doesn't get home until 6 or 7. We all arrive home at different times; we do our own things on the weekend." Jorge's scenario, discussed earlier, is all too common. His parents both work full-time, each commuting far more than an 80-mile stretch each day, and Jorge's life is swamped by the demands of school and extracurricular activities as Jorge struggles to maintain an edge over his peers in the context of "high stakes" education.

It is not surprising, then, that many young adults experience these negotiations as both tiresome and involving too many constraints [and] that they work to initiate a new set of negotiations revolving around getting their own car. The same South Asian young woman who eventually was given a new Honda Civic during her sophomore [year] in college remarked, "I remember I started telling my parents I want a new car, I want a new car, I totally initiated it. So now all of us, all my friends I can remember we all had an old car and now all of us, you know, have gotten new cars within like a year, a year and a half." But many young adults exercise very little power in these negotiations. Consider the following remarks from one European American young woman,

> My parents bought me a car. I used my dad's car for a good year and a half and then my parents bought me a car and um, we went and looked at cars together and I was trying to pick the right color and the right style because I wanted to look good. And then um, then they just decided to get a car and show up with it one morning and um they just showed up with it . . . they ended up getting me a Mazda Protégé, four-door sedan, you know, beige, nice and neutral . . . I was all excited and just the idea that I had my own car. . . . But um, after a while of driving it I was kind of bummed out, I would see my friends get cars and they got cars they wanted and cars that were cooler . . . I didn't get what I wanted.

This young woman, although recognizing the privilege of being given her own car by her parents, also recognizes the lack of choice she was able to exercise in the decision-making process. She wanted something stylish and good looking, and her parents wanted a practical "neutral" car. Her parents' preferences won

out over her own. Pam, an African American junior in high school, described a similar scenario during one of the focus groups:

> Pam: My mom's buying me my own [car] right now.
>
> AB: What's she buying you?
>
> Pam: I don't know.
>
> AB: Do you have a say in it, like what you get?
>
> Pam: No. Whatever she picks that's what I get. I don't care if both of the bumpers is falling off she's gonna get it for me.

In another focus group, Lenore, a Latina sophomore, explains,

> AB: He's gonna give a car for your birthday?
>
> Lenore: No [not for my birthday but], just because I asked him to.
>
> Jeanie: Can I borrow your dad?
>
> Patti: Spoiled.
>
> Lenore: I am not cause I have to beg him before he lets me get one.
>
> AB: Anyone else, get a car?
>
> Patti: I wish . . .

Patti and Jeannie regard Lenore's position as an enviable one. She is getting a car, which is something they are without. But Lenore is quick to remind them that the car was not simply awarded but eventually promised after considerable energy on her part. Begging, a term teens commonly use to characterize how their objectives are achieved as they negotiate with parents, is one that suggests work in the absence of equal power. The decision largely rests on the parent.

Parents often decide to give a car to their child as a gift celebrating what are essentially defined as meaningful milestones, usually educational, for their young adult children. Graduation from high school, graduation from college, and the start of college, although socially defined as special occasions in their own right, are elevated in importance as is the parent's role in these events when such an expensive gift is given.

Car Privileges, Class Privilege: Grades and Gas Money

Class structures these negotiations in meaningful ways. In an immediate sense, class plays a role in whether or not parents will be able to buy a car and, more important, the kind of car they are able to buy for their child. Class also organizes how kids talk about these decisions. Most middle- and upper-middle-class kids who were given cars as gifts took for granted that such a gift was a consequence of their parents' economic resources. One young woman who was given a brand new red Pontiac Firebird for her 16th birthday explained,

> They paid [for the car and related expenses] because I was in high school and I didn't have a job, you know my parents wanted me to focus on school and sports and I didn't have time to do a job after that. So that was my job, basically . . . my parents just never like, you know, said don't worry about it.

This young woman gets a car, a meaningful object in youth cultural worlds, but doesn't have to compromise her free time or time dedicated to studies or sports to do so because of her privilege and affluence.

Yet, it is also through these negotiations that kids are drawn into the economic contexts of their family lives. Decisions over whether to buy a car, what kind of car, and its intended uses reveal to kids, although not likely for the first time, how their parents think about spending money and perhaps provide occasion for them to formulate their own ideas about financial spending. This seemed evident when talking with a number of kids, all squarely middle class, about having an expensive car. When talking about other kids they knew who were given what

were seen as unreasonably expensive cars as gifts by a parent, a number of them were critical of this decision and objected on moral grounds. Invoking the importance of cultivating a work ethic, one biracial young man who drove a used Ford Taurus wagon, which he almost entirely financed himself from money his parents had put aside from his modeling as a child, remarked, "They're not going to appreciate their car because they didn't work for it, they just kind of got it." . . . Another European American young man who was given his grandfather's relatively new Jeep Grand Cherokee (because he was no longer able to drive it himself) offered,

> I find it kind of funny when you know someone who like got a brand new car, Amanda Wilton, and totaled it. Then, like, her mom gets her a brand new car, I mean you know, it's fine because, that's what her mom chose to do and everything but I, I don't, maybe she'll get the impression that cars can be, you know just tossed away and you'll get a new one for free.

Countering prevailing perceptions of teens as irresponsible and immature, this young man adopts an "adult" attitude that assumes that there is something to be learned through buying a car, whether that is the value of money or hard work. Different [values] get knotted as this young man struggles to resolve the contradictions inherent in buying a teenage child a high priced luxury car. Debating the freedom of (parental) choice, a high premium value in American culture on one hand, and a parent shamelessly indulging a child's every want on the other, also reveals some . . . cultural contradictions . . . namely, the opposing American ideals of deferred gratification and conspicuous consumption that inflect how kids (and parents) make sense not just of this cultural object but of work to articulate their own parental values, their values around having "stuff," and their desire to display their class membership through this status-conferring object.

Whereas some parents were willing and able to buy a car for their young adult child, other parents expect their kids to also contribute. "They were paying the payments under their name and I was paying them cash every month for my car. I would pay like $200 and it was like $350 so they would like pay [the remaining amount], you know what I mean," one European American young woman who was given a new Volkswagen Jetta explained. The ability to financially contribute was often critical to the move toward purchasing a car and was generally seen by young adults as a sign of their growing maturity and movement into adulthood. For this South Asian young woman, her ability to cover monthly payments was seen as a key negotiating strategy, enabling her to cleverly persuade her father to agree to the car.

> I was like, I think I have enough money where if you guys put the down payment maybe I could make the monthly payments, you know. And then they were just like, hmmm, we'll see, we'll see, don't worry about it . . . coming around. So I used that as an excuse. I was like, come on you know and then I think either my brother got a raise or something, something happened where he, I asked him to help me out. So then we came up with a plan, okay if my dad put the down payment then we would both pay half of the monthly. And so but they were still kind of like, yeah we'll see, we'll see and then my dad got a new car so I kind of laid a guilt trip on him. I was like, well you got a car and my sister got a car when she went to State, so did my brother and now I'm starting and my birthday's coming up, you know that kind of a thing and so they ended up getting me a car and now I have to pay half the monthly installments.

Although some parents partly or fully finance the cost of buying a new or used car for their child, it is often with the expectation that the child will contribute to other car-related expenses. Expenses related to traffic violations,

such as car accidents or speeding tickets, insurance payments or surcharges, gas, and repairs were commonly seen as the responsibility of the young adult child. One young woman was given a gas allowance with the understanding that if she exceeded the allowance, she had to pay for it. Although one could argue that these are lessons in financial responsibility for young adults, and no doubt they are, one also can argue that this is also about parental control and monitoring. Parents indirectly, although perhaps not always effectively, are able to exercise control over their kids, regulating and monitoring their whereabouts and how they spend their own money. This is because kids must often find part-time employment to cover these expenses, consuming much of their free time outside of school; the money they generate from these jobs often goes directly to cover these costs rather than being spent on other items or activities.

Because parents play such a meaningful financial role in purchasing and maintaining their young adult child's car, the car often is used as a means of control by many parents. The loss of car privileges is common among teen drivers, often resulting from activities and behaviors entirely unrelated to driving. "My dad's actually gonna give me a car this summer but I can't drive it until next year cause I kind of got in trouble," one young woman explained in a focus group interview. Referring to the car, Andrea, a European American young woman, offers,

> AR: It was basically kind of like held over my head a lot, you clean your room or you don't get the car this weekend. Always, you know, the car was always taken away if I didn't do what they wanted.
>
> AB: Did you lose your car a lot?
>
> AR: Yeah. I was pretty good but my dad was big on keeping the car clean, keeping your room clean, it was mostly household chores, it was a way to get me to do things and I didn't do them all the time so I would get my car taken away a lot.

This strategy of control was especially common for parents who partially and fully financed cars for their kids. It is interesting that those kids whose parents did not buy them a car rarely mentioned the use of the car as a resource of parental control. I interpret this particular strategy of control as a class-based strategy insofar as only parents with disposable income will be able to finance a car for their kids. For young adults who purchase their own car and pay for their own insurance, parents are less able to use this strategy as a means of control, as was the case for this European American young man, Jay, who fully financed his car, a fully-loaded Mustang GT:

AB: So did your mom help you with?

KA: No. She didn't know about it, she almost disowned me for it actually.

AB: Tell me about that, what happened?

KA: She just didn't think I needed it and I didn't need it but I wanted it and I normally do whatever I want. It sounds weird but I normally don't listen to my mother very much, so. She didn't have any say in what I did really. She just didn't talk to me for a week and then she got over it. . . .

Whereas some parents take the car away as a punishment, parents also use the promise of a car as incentive to cull a desired behavior. "I want to get a sports utility . . . my parents said they would help me buy a new car if I move back in so that's another reason I want to move back into my parents' house," one young Latino explained. Lots of parents use the car as leverage in arguments over performance in school and decisions over future career and educational plans. In fact, some kids even identified their parents' attempts as outward bribes. Consider Mike, for example. Mike, who is Iranian and Filipino, spoke repeatedly about the control his parents exerted over him, although with astonishing resignation. "Yeah they're strict. They're still trying to be strict but I'm kind of like hard to control." In the course of the interview, I learned that his relationship with his folks had been turbulent in the past. Mike had been kicked out of his parents' house a few times, on one occasion being left with little choice but to live in his car temporarily. Direct attempts to punish Mike rarely worked according to Mike. In a desperate attempt to bring Mike under control, his parents offered to buy him a very expensive car if he agreed to commit himself to his college studies.

They'll probably buy the next car, half of it or most of it. They're talking about getting me a new car, and getting me the one I want if I do well in college. There's the ultimatum. But I'm totally ready for that and I hella want to. Six years of suffering for an Audi s4. It's like a $41,000 car, that's really nice.

Again, class plays a role here in a few ways. First, given that this strategy requires some degree of financial flexibility on the part of the parents, I argue that this is a strategy of control [that is] used largely (although not exclusively) by middle- and upper-middle-class parents. This particular strategy also seems to be tied to the middle-class value placed on education. . . . [T]hese decisions [also] work to define and construct class for these teens. The fact that parents are able or not able to buy a $40,000 car for their child reveals something about the economic context of their lives to their children that in turn embeds class . . . in the lives of their children. It is through these decisions that teens come to think of themselves and their families in terms of class. As a status-conferring object, the car serves as a meaningful symbol of class membership and belonging. . . .

* * *

Teens' Care Work: Sharing Resources, Constructing Family Life

Whereas getting a car and getting a driver's license usually are accompanied by more time spent away from family as young adult children and parents collaboratively negotiate over gradual gains in freedom, for many youth, getting a driver's license is also accompanied by greater responsibility to various family members and "the family" as an acting unit. Mothers and fathers separately and together often expect that kids take on more responsibilities normally reserved for adult family members. These responsibilities include driving other family members around: younger brothers and sisters to school, grandparents to the doctor, and running errands for the family such as picking up groceries. "I have to pick up the laundry and pick up groceries and stuff," Crystal offered during an interview. Maria, a Latina, explains,

AR: My dad wanted me to take my mom out shopping and take the responsibilities that he didn't want to do anymore.

AB: Did your mom not drive?

AR: She never learned.

AB: So when you had that responsibility what were some of the things that you did?

AR: Oh, just take her to the store, grocery shopping mostly, yeah, doctor's appointments and all that.

Nan, a European American young woman, offered,

AB: Your parents let you drive to school?

HE: Yeah. I dropped my sister, my sister didn't go to the same school as me at that time, she was in junior high, so I would drop her off.

Hortencia, a young Latina whose mother was collecting disability from a work-related injury and whose father was getting "too old" to drive, conceptualized these responsibilities in terms of her duties as a daughter. She offers,

Well, the thing is in my situation I kinda had to learn how to drive. My parents are

older, my mom is like fifty something, 55 and my dad's 66, so they're older and my dad's sick too, and huh, in case of an emergency, I need to know how to drive cause my sisters are way older than me. I'm like 10 years younger than my older sister. So, I'm like really young so I kinda had to learn just in case of an emergency if something happens, you need to learn to get yourself out of a situation or take somebody somewhere.

What is also meaningful to her story is that she had yet to get her license. The driving she did—mostly local driving, running errands, and helping her parents out "in case of an emergency"—was done at a considerable risk. . . .

Often, parents are willing to cover car expenses in exchange for their children providing this family care work. Mike explains,

They paid for everything. They still pay for my insurance. They're covering all that stuff. I just have to pick up my sister here and there. I really don't mind because my sister's like totally cool.

For many parents, the license means greater freedom for them. Ken, another young man, offers,

My mom is glad that I have my license because then she doesn't have to come and pick me up at twelve o'clock and she's not too thrilled about doing that. So, she was counting the days of when I would get my license, I would always say.

The new-found freedom parents experience combined with the need for kids to fulfill these responsibilities often has consequences for the driving rules they establish and enforce for their young adult children. Mena, a South Asian woman, elaborates,

In high school, my parents were very strict so we didn't really get to go out much, so that was another thing about me taking out the car or anything . . . I never had the car when, I was in high school, so he never restricted us and then he, I don't think he had much of a choice to restrict because when we used to go to college, we had to commute so if he took the car away from us then.

To impose restrictions would mean additional work for this parent. Mike further elaborates,

> They really couldn't take their car away from me for a while because of like the fact that my sister needed a ride to school and I was her ride to and from school. It was a necessity for me to be driving so I always pretty much have my car. Maybe if I were to do something really bad they'd take it away for like a week. No big deal. . . .

[Although] teens are primarily seen as economic drains on families rather than as contributors, this research demonstrates that teenagers engage in significant family care work and, in doing so, support family well-being.

The negotiations [in which] parents and their young adult children engage as young adults meaningfully contribute to family life need to be understood within the context of broader social forces and shifts in family. As has been well documented . . . more family members [now] must work to secure a livable family wage (M. Fine & Weis, 1998; Rank, 2001). This is increasingly the case for a larger number of families, particularly those at the lower end of the wage continuum. . . . These families, as they struggle to adapt to changing economic and social circumstances such as declining wages and the subsequent demand for longer hours at work, must often rely on the family care work and wage work their teenage children provide to survive as families. In these family situations, it often makes economic sense to impose fewer driving restrictions and to even contribute a nominal sum to purchasing an inexpensive used car for their young adult children as was the case for a number of interview participants. In doing so, parents are in essence providing the resources so that their young adult children can more meaningfully contribute to ongoing family life, helping to secure its economic and social well-being.

Middle-class and upper-middle-class parents also rely on their teen children to run errands and shuttle younger siblings around. In fact, one young man with whom I spoke remarked that his parents, his father a successful surgeon and mother a stay-at-home mom, would never dare take his car away, even though they regularly threatened to do so if he did not improve his grades. When I asked why, he said that his mother hates having to run out to the store to get milk when they are out. Recall for a moment Jorge's story told in the beginning of this article about managing the busy schedule required to succeed in high stakes education and the economic and time demands such a schedule requires from the parents of these children. The difference, then, between these family groups seems to be one of material need. The work teens do for those families concentrated on the lower end of the economic ladder is usually not optional. This work often is necessary for their parents to create income, especially because these families are unable to rely on outside sources to care for elderly extended kin or to pay for various car or delivery services, on which middle- and upper-middle-class families increasingly rely (Hertz, 1986). Working poor families often live in communities with families in like economic situations, where all adult family members work and, thus, are unable to benefit from neighborhood carpools that usually require that one parent have enough free time away from work. For upper-middle-class families, buying a car for their teen makes good sense because it results in additional time for the parents to dedicate to work and leisure activities. These parents, then, are less reliant on the family care work completed by their teen children, although they certainly benefit from it.

Conclusion

Studying cars tells us much about how young adults negotiate everyday life. . . . This analysis demonstrates how young men and young women, as they talk about cars, negotiate the perimeters of daily family life. . . . What is clear is that as young men and women articulate their relationships to cars, they are also articulating their own understandings of their connection to the world of family and the public world beyond. Focusing in on the interactional work of parents and their young adult children as they collaboratively negotiate around driving, this article has explored how young adults struggle for freedom from the family setting, while also drawing attention to the demand for greater responsibility to family that arises for these young men and women. . . .

References

Fine, M., & Weis, L. (1998). *The unknown city: The lives of poor and working class young adults.* Boston: Beacon.

Hertz, R. (1986). *More equal than other: Women and men in dual-career marriages.* Chicago: University of Chicago Press.

Hochschild, A. R. (1997). *The time bind: When work becomes home and home becomes work.* New York: Metropolitan Books.

Kincheloe, J. (1997). Home alone and "bad to the bone": The advent of postmodern childhood. In S. R. Steinberg & J. L. Kincheloe (Eds.), *Kinder culture: The corporate construction of childhood* (pp. 30–48). Boulder, CO: Westview.

Kurz. D. (2002). Caring for teenage children. *Journal of Family Issues, 23*(6), 748–767.

Larson, R., & Richards, M. H. (1994). *Divergent realities: The emotional lives of mothers, fathers and adolescents.* New York: Basic Books.

Rank, M. (2001). The effect of poverty on America's families: Assessing our research knowledge. *Journal of Family Issues, 22*(7), 882–903.

Smart, C., Neale, B., & Wade, A. (2001). *The changing experience of childhood: Families and divorce.* New York: Blackwell.

21

A Personal Story of Doing Family

Nancy Naples

The interactional construction and maintenance of social relationships is most apparent
when problems occur within them that disrupt
the routine patterns of interaction that have
sustained them. This selection tells an intensely
personal story of the author's struggle to "do"
family even though those family relationships
challenged her own sense of personal identity.
As the author, Nancy Naples, reports, she dated
boys for a number of years, married once, and
lived with another man before adopting a lesbian identity as an adult. When she announced
that identity, or "came out," to her siblings, her
relationships with them were forever changed.
They either did not know how or refused to relate to her on those terms. They convinced her
to conceal her lesbianism from their parents
and tried to ignore it themselves. They objected
when she proposed bringing her lesbian lover
to family gatherings and begged her to conceal
the nature of their relationship if she did. Although Naples resented their rejection and denial of her own sense of self, her understanding
of what it meant to be a family prevented her
from acting on that resentment. She buried her
lesbian identity when around her siblings, often
neglecting and damaging her significant relationship with her lover.

Eventually, her inability to "do" family the way
that she had understood it and still sustain her self-
affirming relationships with her lover and friends
caused Naples to reassess the meaning of family.

She concluded that family had less to do with biological kinship and marital connection than with
sharing, acceptance, and mutual support. She decided to quit doing family unthinkingly on the basis
of unquestioned cultural understandings and do
so self-reflectively. She decided to devote her efforts to constructing a family of choice rather than
of origin. In addition to her lover and friends, that
family of choice included some of her biological siblings, but only those who could accept her lesbianism, and other chosen family members.

Naples' story reveals some of the relational
difficulties that lesbian, gay, and bisexual people
face in a society that considers heterosexuality
normal and deviations from it abnormal. Her
story also has a more general lesson. It illustrates that we do relationships and particular
forms of them whether we fully realize what we
are doing or not. Naples performed the family
role her siblings assigned her, dutifully keeping
her lesbianism to herself. She consequently neglected her loving relationship with her partner
at the time, undoing their relationship. Like her,
the way we relate to particular others is often
guided by unquestioned cultural understandings
of what different kinds of relationships should
be. However, different kinds of relationships are
what they are because we interactionally make
them that way. If they are not what we think
they should be, it is because we are not "doing"
them that way. Patterns of relating make relationships and make them what they are.

Standing at my father's freshly dug grave
holding the American flag the funeral director had just handed to me, I had the feeling I
was in a bad made-for-TV movie. Since my
mother was too sick with Alzheimer's to attend and I was the oldest of the six siblings, I
was given the "honor." I thought it was especially odd since, given my left-leaning politics,
I would be the least likely member of my
family to fly the flag on the major military
and other national holidays. As I watched my
three sisters, two brothers, their spouses, and

my fifteen nieces and nephews slowly make their way back to the cars with other members of my large "heteronormal" extended family, I at once ached to be accepted as a part of their world and longed for my "real" family.

I flashed back to the last time I stood by this graveside. It was also a somewhat dreary fall day. My brother Donald, who was the nearest in age to me (born less than a year and a half after me) and who was closest to me in other ways as well, had died in a car crash. At this time, my father decided to buy a plot in the local cemetery in their suburban community just north of New York City that would fit eight family members—less than needed if all of us wanted to be buried there, more if everyone else was buried with their own nuclear family. So now two of the plots are inhabited. I wondered who besides my mother would join them. I presumed that all the other siblings would be buried with their nuclear families. Maybe my father thought that since I was "single," namely had no "family" of my own, it would make sense for me to join them when the time came.

The significance of my singleness in the context of all the two-parent male and female families who made up the funeral procession was not lost on my two aunts. Earlier at the funeral parlor I overheard one of my aunts say to another aunt, "You know, the one I feel the most sorry for is Nancy. She has nobody." Their hushed and worried exchange amused me somewhat, although I also felt a great deal of sadness since, as many gays and lesbians, I am rich with loving and intimate friends whom I consider my "real" family. Yet in fact I was indeed alone at my father's funeral. Where was everybody?

When my brother Donald died in 1985, two of my most treasured "real" family were there for me. My lover Nina, who died in 1987 of breast cancer, and Peter, my brother-in-spirit who died of AIDS in 1996, were with me and were important witnesses over the years to the difficulties I had negotiating

relationships with my family. Nina and Peter most assuredly would have been by my side had they been alive. Yet since neither Nina nor Peter were my legal or biological relations, their presence would have done little to shake the perception of my aloneness in the heteronormative world of my family.

Nina was my first female lover. We met in graduate school and I fell madly in love with her. When I "came out" to a lesbian friend about our relationship, she expressed great pleasure at my "coming to consciousness" or something to that effect. She made me feel that my more than fifteen years as a practicing heterosexual was something akin to false sexual consciousness. I resisted the revised grand narrative she attempted to impose on my sexual identity. I asserted that my relationships with men, as troubled as they were, were authentic expressions of my sexual desire. However, as I made this statement I remember feeling uncomfortable about laying claim to some authentic self.

Maybe my long heterosexual history has made it difficult for my siblings to accept my claim to a lesbian identity. Nina was incorporated into my family as my "best friend." No questions were asked about why I was no longer seeing my boyfriend Mark, nor did anyone ever ask why I never had another boyfriend after him. This seemed like an obvious question since I had dated boys since eighth grade, been married once, and lived with another man for several years. Nor did I take the initiative to explain. I just believed deep in my bones that coming out to my parents and siblings at the time would only strain my already conflict-ridden relationship with them. I did not feel that I had anything to gain from doing so and had much more to lose. I remember having drinks with Donald one Christmas eve. When he said he wanted to ask me something important about Nina, I held my breath for what I thought would be the inevitable question: Are you and Nina lovers? I remember how perversely relieved I was when he asked me a very different question: Had I ever thought about her dying?—she was in the first of several rounds of chemotherapy treatment for breast cancer.

Not surprisingly, the unspoken but palpable homophobia I felt from my family was deeply woven into my own psyche. I colluded in the silence about it while Nina was alive. However, after she died I desperately wanted them to acknowledge who she was in my life and what her loss meant for me. I remember my mother commenting on what a good friend and social worker (my previous career) I was, given my central role in Nina's care, which included taking her to doctors' appointments and chemo treatments, sleeping over at the hospital during the last months of her life, and acting as executor of her will. Not even the fact that she left me all her worldly possessions, the money from the successful lawsuit against the breast surgeon who misdiagnosed the cancer, and her precious dog, Lucy, could shake my family's construction of my "friendship" with Nina.

Given the diversity among my siblings, coming out to them was much easier as well as much harder than I anticipated. The reactions ranged from downright hostility and rejection to ambivalent acceptance (the subtle message was that as long as I did not speak too much about my life as a lesbian, they could accept it). My brother John, the most hostile one, was violently angry and said in an attacking tone that having a sister who was a lesbian was a great embarrassment for him and that he would surely lose friends because of it. My brother Paul refused to hear it at all. Lisa and Melissa, the youngest of the clan, were mildly accepting, although over the years it became clear that, as Lisa put it, they would rather "not think about it." Karen, the remaining sister, was the most profoundly disturbed by it. Karen became a born-again Christian in her early twenties and was very invested in the antihomosexual position her church promulgated. Her comments about how homosexuality was a sin against God and that gays were sexually promiscuous,

carriers of diseases, and a basic threat to the moral fabric of society greatly distressed me even though I was well versed in the religious right's view of what they disparagingly call the "homosexual lifestyle." Once, I tried to explain the epidemiology of the AIDS virus to her. I dispassionately noted that the majority of those infected throughout the world are practicing heterosexuals and that lesbians are not at especially high risk of HIV. Karen responded, "Well you have your opinion and I have mine." I realized in this brief attempt to present another view that I was forced to sell out gay men who did have AIDS. I knew better. After all, I teach about homosexuality, compulsory heterosexuality, and the social construction of gender to large classes of undergraduates and have had to find that careful balance between encouraging a critical consciousness and directly challenging their worldviews.

Religion also served as a main wedge between my other siblings and me. We were brought up by a devout Catholic mother, and all of my siblings—with the exception of my sister Karen, who became a member of a conservative Christian church—continued to attend mass regularly and participate in all the Catholic sacraments. They baptized each of their children in the Catholic Church. I attended most of the baptisms but became increasingly pained by the way this ritual further marginalized me in the family. My lack of religious affiliation and unmarried status made me unfit, in my siblings' eyes, to be godparent to any of my fifteen nieces and nephews.

Regardless of their individual responses to my coming out as a lesbian, each sibling strongly warned me against telling my parents. I think they all firmly believed that, as my brother John said, "it would kill daddy"—a projection of their own fears and a threat that is frequently used to keep gays and lesbians in the closet. Of course I did not really believe that the simple statement about my sexual orientation would kill my father or mother. However, on one level I felt I had nothing to gain by taking the risk and, on another level, I figured my father already knew. After all, he was a firefighter in the West Village for twenty-five years, even helping to put out the fires of Stonewall. I rationalized that if he wanted to deal with my lesbian identity, he would bring it up himself. So we developed an unspoken contract. I would not name my relationships with women as lesbian and he would accept my girlfriends into his home, no questions asked. I thought that was fair for the most part. In retrospect, I realize that I somehow bought into the fear that my lesbian self was a shameful secret that might have the power if not to kill, at least to deeply harm others.

Over the more than ten years since I came out as a lesbian to my siblings, I tried to find a way to be a part of the family while also trying to protect myself from their rejection of my lesbian self. I maintained normalized relationships with all but my brother John and related to the other brother Paul through my sister-in-law, who seemed to be more open. I stopped celebrating Christmas and Thanksgiving with them. I would limit my visits to one or two days, staying over no more than one or two nights. Since my parents had moved from my childhood home on Staten Island to a small town just an hour and a half north of Manhattan, I could stay with my friends and drive up for the day. I did not discuss my relationships with my family and showed up unaccompanied, even when in a relationship, for most events such as christenings, weddings, baby showers, and physical and mental health crises. I sent money or gifts for birthdays and Christmas, but generally kept my worlds separate. When I moved to California, just forty miles south of my sister Lisa, I expected some challenge in balancing the different worlds, but she happened to be one of the two supportive sisters so I was not too concerned about it.

Yet in some ways the geographic closeness did pose some additional dilemmas. I recall the Christmas of 1994 right after my nephew James was born. Wanting to be helpful, I offered to make Christmas dinner for Lisa and her husband, Michael. But Melinda, my lover at the time, did not want to do the holiday thing in this way. What she wanted was a quiet dinner with me at home. Caught between my different families, I decided to make dinner for us at home and later to bring dinner to Lisa and Michael. This seemed doable at the time. The first snag, however, occurred after I described the Santa-Fe-inspired meal I planned to make. Lisa explained that her husband would not eat what Melinda and I had decided on for the main course and that since she was breast-feeding James, she would have to pass on the jalapeno corn bread. Okay, I thought, I need a fall-back plan. I decided to make two dinners, one for Melinda and me, plus one for Lisa and Michael. I made two corn breads, one with and one without the jalapenos. After completing our main course, I put a chicken in the oven to roast. Naturally, all of this took extra time so Melinda and I sat down to eat later than I intended. With the fireplace burning brightly and the candles nicely lit on the table, Melinda was anticipating a very relaxed meal. I, on the other hand, was anxious that we were running late so I could not really enjoy the meal, which was also interrupted several times while I checked the chicken. Then the phone rang. It was my sister wondering where we were. She told me that Michael loved my cooking so that he skipped lunch and was starving. I explained that things were taking a bit longer but that I would be there soon. Melinda, however, did not want to join me on the trip up to my sister's and I struggled with her for a while until the phone rang.

It was Peter wishing me a Merry Christmas. I explained the dilemma to him and complained that Melinda would not come with me to my sister's. Having met many of my family members, he not-so-diplomatically said, "Why should she? Let her stay home if she wants." It did seem such an obvious solution but I now realized how much I wanted to merge my different worlds for that holiday. So out the door I went, telling Melinda I would be back as soon as I could to share desert with her. Arriving at my sister's, I went into a flurry of activity heating up and then serving the food. I felt like a volunteer for Meals-on-Wheels. And, of course, I could not relax with them much since I felt I needed to get back home or Melinda would start feeling abandoned. I can laugh at the scene now, but it more than symbolized the absurdity and frustration in my attempts to navigate between different family forms.

So, for the most part, my siblings did not have to see me in a relationship with a woman. My long history as a practicing heterosexual was enough to negate my claims to a lesbian identity. How could someone who was involved with men for so long really be a lesbian? I fit none of their stereotypes. My sister Karen rationalized my claim to a lesbian identity as follows: "Well, after all you had such bad relationships with men." The obvious implication was that if I met the right man, I would change my mind. Again I was faced with proving my authentic identity, this time foregrounding my lesbian self. Another cliché I recognized in my family's response was the one that links having a career with my not needing men. Here the traditional gender division of labor, which assigns women to the private sphere of the home and men to the public breadwinner role, was upset by the fact that I had a career and therefore did not need the male breadwinner. Of course, what logically follows that particular assumption is that women's full-time employment is a basic threat to the heterosexual family form—an old but persistent concern.

My family is more traditional than many, I suppose. During the 1950s and 1960s, we even had a girl's side and a boy's side of the dinner table. If you tried to cross over to the wrong side, you suffered great insults. The boys were taught auto mechanics and electronics among other technical skills. The girls learned child care and cooking among other homemaking skills. I always resisted. Fortunately my sister Karen, who was three years younger than me, took to these activities, and I put up such a stink about performing them that I was off the hook.

My siblings have all followed the traditional route. The women have taken their husbands' names and have, for the most part, placed their own careers on hold until all their children are in school. My life as an unmarried college professor of sociology and women's studies was so far from their own lives that they could hardly comprehend it except that they knew I attended a lot of conferences. Furthermore, they never wanted to learn more about it so I rarely discuss what I do with them. I do not think my experience here differs much from other academics who come from the working class. However, I fear that part of my family's reluctance to ask more about my life's work is that for them women's studies equals feminist equals lesbian—and therefore something about my lesbian world might come up. So it is best not to even start down that road.

I continued to keep my worlds relatively separate with a few moments of overlap until 1997 when my mother's Alzheimer's escalated and we had to put her in a nursing home. This precipitated more intense and regular contact with my family. This difficult event overlapped with the start of a new relationship with Sharon, a woman who said that she would not mind being integrated into my family. In fact, she said, "I'm good with lover's families. They like me." I was so pleased to finally have the opportunity to merge my worlds. I neglected to warn her, however, that I had never successfully done so before. She did wonder why I became increasingly anxious as we drove closer to my father's house a week before Christmas. I even passed the turnoff and drove her around the town and several of the surrounding towns before returning to complete the drive to the house. When we arrived at my father's home, my sister Melissa with her son and my hostile brother, John, were there.

My plan was to spend the night and go visit my other brother, Paul's family before making the four-hour drive to Sharon's home the next afternoon. However, shortly after our arrival, as I was wrapping presents in one of the bedrooms, John comes in and asks me in a very accusatory tone: "you're not going to make some big announcement that we should know about? Paul is afraid to come over because he thinks you are planning some big surprise." I was speechless with fury. I now wish I had thought of some clever rejoinder such as: "Oh, you must be watching too many episodes of *Ellen*. If so, you'd know I would only do it in an airport over a loudspeaker." But instead, I was paralyzed with anger and fear. I emerged from the room, didn't say a word to Sharon, went to play with my nephew, and left her to interact with my father and brothers—the second of whom had shown up by this time. Paul proceeded to glare at her from the kitchen. He never spoke to her. It was as though Sharon had a neon sign on her chest that read in bold scarlet letters: BEWARE, LESBIAN IN THE HOUSE. Later she explained that she felt I had taken her to some anonymous suburban family and dropped her off where she had to introduce herself and be subjected to the critical gaze of the residents. I disappeared emotionally under the homophobic gaze of my brothers. Sharon was angry that I had left her with these "strangers." I tried to explain that I could not have anticipated my reaction since it was the first time I ever really allowed the two worlds to collide so directly. She said that I should have at least warned her that she was the first female lover that I had introduced into the family. I had mistakenly assumed that Nina was the first lover they had met. Since I came out to them after she died, I had wishfully thought that would count and so my introducing them to Sharon should be no big deal.

The Christmas visit would send me on a very difficult soul-searching journey to confront and effectively eject much of the self-hate I had internalized. This was indeed a very good thing for me in the long run. Unfortunately, in the short run, I was to face a series of painful internal and external crises before I felt purged of some of my own internalized homophobia.

So now fast forward to the week of my father's death, which was quite unexpected. He had problems with his lungs, emphysema, a series of bouts with pneumonia, but until this last week or so no one thought his illness was life-threatening. I won't go into the unfortunate series of medical events that contributed to his death but state simply that I did not have much time to prepare for how I would balance my conflicting worlds while all this was going on.

As a consequence of the previous Christmas I had decided not to stay over with my family if I could avoid it. When I got the call from my youngest sister, Melissa, that I better get "home" I did not even think about what it would be like to stay with my siblings during the emotionally painful days leading up to my father's death. Since it involved coming to a collective decision about removing the breathing tube, I assumed it best to stay with them. I also thought I would be criticized harshly if I chose to stay in Manhattan with my friends Jen and Terry, whose apartment was in fact closer to the hospital. I rented a car at the airport and drove to Melissa's home in New Jersey.

The first couple of days were difficult but manageable. All six of us seemed to be getting along pretty well. I remember calling one of my aunts to give her an update and saying how good our communication was as we were debating the pros and cons of removing the ventilator. Each day I spoke to my soon-to-be ex-lover, Sharon (we were in the process of breaking up), who was trying to be supportive. She had initiated the break-up a few weeks earlier. I was resisting vehemently. I had some crazy idea in the back of my mind that this crisis might bring us closer together. Little did I know how wrong I was. Each day Sharon offered to come. I so wanted to take her up on her offer. After all, my siblings all had their spouses and children with them. I had neither lover nor friend. But I also knew, given the view of homosexuality held by my sister Karen, that it would be difficult to have my ex-lover with me, although I had no idea how messy it would become.

When Karen and her children began discussing the possibility of moving up to my father's house so they could be closer to the other cousins, I finally saw an opportunity to invite Sharon to join me. When I mentioned that she was coming, Karen threw a fit. She ranted, "How could you bring this into the family at such a time? What about the children? This is a time for the family to be together. It's not a time for us to have to deal with this." I tried to explain that Sharon was my family and that I needed the support. And, further, I was a lesbian whether my lover was with me or not. She refused to calm down and, in a huff, went up to pack her and her children's bags.

Melissa, the youngest sibling, came to me pleading, "Nancy, do something!" So I took a deep breath, went to my sister Karen and said, "Fine, I'll tell my lover not to come." I thought that this was the only way we could get through the next couple of days. I felt defeated and so alone but I was, after all, the older sister, a role that I performed uncritically for much of my life. After this incident, I could no longer stay with them. I quietly packed my bags and said that I would go stay with my friends in Manhattan. I drove away thinking what a fool I was for forgetting where I really belonged. When I arrived at the airport, I should have gone directly to Jen and Terry's apartment for they were part of my "real" family. How could I have gotten it so wrong?

To make matters worse, Sharon was profoundly offended by my decision to acqui-esce to Karen's tantrum. She resented that I placed my need to keep peace in the family over our relationship and told me that if I had discussed my fear of merging the two worlds with her, she might have helped me come up with the solution that eventually I had to turn to anyway—staying with my friends in the city. Further, she painfully exclaimed, how did I think this made her feel as the one defined as a dreaded threat to the moral integrity of my family? I could not find the words to explain what it had been like for me the day before with my sisters.

This conversation took place over the phone. I had just left my father's bed in intensive care when I called her. When I asked her if she would be willing to come after my father died, she initially said, "Why should I? After all, one goes to a funeral to be supportive of the family and your family doesn't want me there." Well, I was devastated to say the least. I called another dear friend and sobbed for an hour. When I returned to my father's bedside, he was dead. So you can see now why I increasingly felt as though the bad TV-movie kept getting worse. Here I was, the only family member left at the hospital, staying through the night to be with my father so that he wouldn't be alone when he died, only to get caught up in a competing drama down the hall. I hope the guilt I feel over this dreadful episode will diminish with time.

After my father died, the nurse contacted my other siblings and they all returned to the hospital. We each said goodbye in our own way and left. It was after 2 A.M. I drove back to Manhattan, exhausted and traumatized by what had just occurred, and I collapsed into bed.

The following day I spent a long time describing the events to Jen and Terry and called some of my other close friends. I also contacted Sharon and asked her once again if she would come to be with me. She finally agreed but we did not decide whether or not she would attend the wake and funeral. I felt a bit aimless that day and thought that, even though it would have been easier to avoid it, I should drive to my father's house and together with my siblings confront the reality of his death. I also resented letting Karen's fear of my lesbian existence keep me away. I did not want her to have that much power over my choices at this point. Anyway, very quickly after I arrived it became clear to me that my lesbianism and the fear that my lover would come to the wake and funeral was the central topic of conversation. I went into the living room and all but my brother Paul were sitting there. John turned to me and said, on behalf of my siblings, that they wanted to talk to me, that they wanted to know what it was going to be like. At first I did not understand what they wanted to know. I thought that maybe since I had experienced so much loss, they wanted me to explain what it would be like at the funeral or the wake. I asked what they meant.

My sister Lisa then turned to me and said, "We want to know what it is going to be like when your lover comes. Are you two going to be touching or whatever?" At this point, I chose not to let them know that Sharon was, in fact, my ex-lover. I thought if I said, "Oh, you don't have to worry. We broke up," it would only feed into their self-righteousness and belief that there was something dangerous about lesbian love. As John and my two youngest sisters tried to explain their concerns, I painfully noted the smug look on my sister Karen's face. Now she was not the sole voice, the religious fanatic with some extreme view, but, rather, just another of my siblings, who all felt that it was an awful thing for me to be a lesbian. I wondered what they thought Sharon and I would do at the funeral parlor. Everyone but Karen had met her the previous Christmas, but paranoia had overtaken them and they clearly were not thinking rationally.

I, of course, felt attacked, horrified and desperately alone in my father's house. I knew that my siblings only felt free to express their hatred and fear of my lesbian self because he was dead. It made me miss him even more. I got up and started packing my things to leave. Lisa came in and tried to explain why she thought it was a good thing for us to have this discussion, that my lesbianism was no longer a taboo subject, that she loved me, and that my lover would always be welcome in her house. I was appalled at the thought that there should have to be any question about this. I replied that they should deal with their own irrational fears about my sexuality but to leave me out of their conversations in the future. How unloving and hateful could a group of people be—people who are supposed to love me and want the best for me! I understood then that I was tolerated as part of the family as long as they thought I was alone, had no one to love me, to hold me, to comfort me. As I drove back to Manhattan, I understood even more deeply that the precious intimate friendships I had constructed over the years were truer expressions of "real" family than my biological family ever had been.

I missed Nina and Peter more than ever. How different the energy that surrounded Nina's last weeks and her memorial service. Right after Nina died, Peter told me that he had asked her what he was supposed to do with me—since we weren't really "friends," not like he was with Nina. I inherited Peter from Nina, and, I guess, he inherited me as well. He replaced Donald as the brother I could talk to. There was so much I couldn't tell Donald. His own homophobia made him less than the best confidante for me when Nina was first diagnosed with cancer. I am so grateful to Nina for leaving Peter to me and me to him. We were "real" family for each other, Peter with no other kinfolk, me with lots of related kin but none I felt close to or who loved me as freely. Peter was there for me from the time Nina died until his own untimely death.

I so much prefer the version of family I learned from Nina and Peter to the one my biological family embraces. For my biological family, the effort to "do family" takes the form of boundary maintenance—controlling who and what can enter for fear that the family constellation is so fragile any slight disruption will cause permanent damage. Ironically, in their efforts to patrol the borders, the illusive ties that kept me linked to my family have been irrevocably severed.

I don't expect to have any future contact with my two brothers or my sister Karen. For Karen, I would have to confess my "sin," repent, and renounce my "homosexual lifestyle." Equally unlikely, she would have to forsake the treasured religious beliefs that have provided an anchor for her since her early twenties. Recently her ten-year-old son sent a letter to all his aunts and uncles seeking money for a bike-athon to support a missionary for his church. I could no longer ignore my negative feelings about this church in order to fulfill my familial obligations as his aunt. And I do not expect to have any meaningful contact with Sharon. This also saddens me greatly for despite the fact that we could not negotiate my family nor build toward our own version of family, we did love each other.

Yet despite all the losses I have suffered over the years in both my families, I am an incurable romantic. I deeply long to create daily life with someone—to swap stories of the day, to perform mundane household tasks together, to share meals, and to regularly experience the pleasures of physical touch. Fortunately, I find myself in a new relationship, this time with someone who wants to "do" family in much the same way I envision. The process of negotiating my two families continues, however. My new lover is coming to visit soon. In order to miss the Los Angeles traffic the morning she returns home, it would be most convenient for us to stay with my sister Lisa, who lives ten minutes from the airport. Recall that she was the one who said that my lover would always be welcome in her home. Yet does this offer extend to an overnight stay? I fear calling her on

it and bumping up once again against the razor-sharp boundary of my biological family. I also want to protect my new lover from any hurt or rejection, to do a better job than I did for Sharon. I am torn. Should I just give up my desire to merge my worlds and book a room in a hotel by the airport or should I give my sister a chance to show up for me? It is a hard call.

Well, after my father's funeral everyone returned to his house for a luncheon. I returned with them, flag in hand, and spent my remaining hours in his house talking to my aunts and several of my favorite cousins. After they left, I wasn't sure what to do. I wandered from room to room, looked in closets, found the hardcover copy of my book that I had recently given my father, and took one of his flannel shirts off a hanger. I decided to call my ex-lover. But she was neither at her home nor her work phone. She and my friend Jen had, in fact, made it to the first night of the wake. Need I add that, not surprisingly, nothing dramatic happened. None of my siblings' fears about how our presence together might disrupt the dignified nature of the wake were realized. I did feel compelled to keep my physical distance from her. Sharon decided to leave the next morning. We both agreed that was best. But I was glad she came, even for the one night. The only surprising and touching moment occurred when my sister Melissa introduced herself to Jen and thanked her for taking care of me, her big sister.

When I decided I needed to leave my father's house after the funeral luncheon and return to my "real" family in Manhattan, I put on the flannel shirt and went looking for my brother John, who had been so outraged by my lesbian self. I gave him the flag and my book and told him I didn't expect him to read it but he could have it if he wanted. I drove away while he stood motionless in the driveway. I knew he would miss my father more than anyone since he lived the closest and had followed closely in his footsteps as a

New York City firefighter. The house was recently sold and even though I never lived there, I felt the loss of the "family homestead." I also mourned the fantasy that one day I would be an accepted member of my biological family. Yet letting go of the need to keep my heteronormal self alive, I have come to more fully embrace and gain sustenance from my "real" family who have been there all along. . . .

The story I tell about my father's funeral emphasizes the emotional work involved in "doing family."[1] Family is not merely a natural constellation of individuals connected by biology and the state with some set of behaviors that everyone knows and willingly performs. Family must be achieved and constructed on a daily basis. Bisexuals, gays, lesbians, and all of us who do not fit into the normative heterosexual-family model understand this well. But all of us, regardless of the family form we inherit or create, must work to sustain these relationships.

I draw on the *symbolic-constructionist* perspective for my analysis of "doing family." Candice West and Don Zimmerman (1987) argue that "gender is fundamental, institutionalized, and enduring; yet, because members of social groups must constantly (whether they realize it or not) 'do' gender to maintain their proper status, the seeds of change are ever present" (Lorber 1987: 124). . . . As Barrie Thorne (1995:498) points out, "'Doing gender' is a compelling concept because it jolts the assumption of gender as an innate condition and replaces it with a sense of ongoing process and activity." Yet gender, and family, are more than performances. They are structured in ways that are not always visible to the performers. As Thorne (1995:499) argues, "gender extends beyond daily cultural performance, and it will take much more than doing drag and mocking naturalized conceptions to transform it. Gender—and race, class, and compulsory heterosexuality—extend deep into the unconscious and the shaping of emotions . . . and outward

into social structure and material interests." In much the same way, I argue, how we perform "family" is shaped by material as well as cultural practices that are often invisible to us as we interact with family, friends, lovers, coworkers. However, the practice of ongoing self-reflection provides one strategy to make visible how daily interactions are shaped by dominant constructions and structures of family. Self-reflective practice is a collective activity that involves ongoing dialogue, behaviors, and political activities that serve to challenge the more oppressive features of patriarchal families.

We first learn to do family and relationships more generally in the families in which we grow up, whether biological, adopted, or otherwise constituted. Since many of these families adhere to some version of compulsory heterosexuality (Rich 1980), our models for performing family are constrained by prescriptions of the "family ethic."[2] Consequently, developing alternative models of "doing family" forms a central task for gays and lesbians and others who do not fit into the normative heterosexual-family form. . . . We are also challenged by the complex negotiations and contradictions between the performance of family, gender, and sexuality expected by our families and the relationships we form as lesbians, gay men, bisexuals, or transgendered people. Unfortunately, we often find ourselves repeating behaviors and imposing expectations that were developed through our early family experiences, thus limiting relational expression to patriarchal patterns of interaction. The process of telling, retelling, writing, and rewriting this story provided me with the distance to see how my attempts to construct my own family form were circumscribed by the limited vision of family I brought into this activity. . . .

In the midst of my family's exaggerated performance of heteronormativity, I often felt my lesbian self rendered invisible despite "coming out" to all my siblings. For much of my adult life I could not break through their denial. The events leading up to and surrounding my father's death served to thrust my lesbian self into the center of their consciousness in such a way that it symbolized a threat to the integrity of the family unit. Of course, it was my father's death that fundamentally unraveled the tightly bound net that held us together. In many ways, I was unprepared for the rejection; in other ways, I had been preparing for it most of my conscious life. The crisis led to a reevaluation of my relationship to my family as well as an opportunity to develop a new interpretive framework through which I might be able to construct a family that does not replicate the negative aspects of the earlier formation. However, I recognize the challenge posed by the legacy of doing family unreflectively for so many years. . . .

While I expect that I will gain more from this exercise than my readers, I hope that I have demonstrated the challenges we all face and the benefits that ensue when we do family self-reflectively, rather than treat family as a taken-for-granted institution outside of our own making. This lesson is one I have learned from my many lesbian, gay, bisexual, and heterosexual family and friends. The family form I recommend is one built on respect for differences and openness to the diversity of expressions of intimacy. . . .

While the story I tell is particular to my own coming to consciousness about the dilemmas of doing family, I believe it illustrates some of the conflicts between different constructions of family that many of us encounter. The features of my own story include the ways in which religion, class differences, as well as gender and sexuality increasingly widened the emotional and physical divide that ultimately severed me from my family as a complex unitary form. The struggle to negotiate my lived experiences as a lesbian within my family has helped me differentiate among the family members, distancing me from some siblings while drawing me closer to others. In this way, I can now integrate these particular members of my childhood family as chosen members of my family of choice, creating a much more affirming and flexible relational structure. For me, the challenge of doing family had always meant choosing between one form or the other, rather than finding a way to include different family members from my different families together. Given the very bounded way my family did familial relationships, however, it is not surprising that I encountered such difficulty. . . .

[W]hy [did] my family have such significance for me[?] Others might have distanced themselves more quickly than I did in response to the homophobia I encountered from it. I believe in retrospect that part of the answer can be found in the intense emotional and practical hold that my large working-class family had over me. As the oldest child in an Irish-Catholic working-class family, the pressure I felt to show up for the family in a variety of ways formed part of my earliest memories. As we grew older, I listened to my parents' great disappointment when one sibling, then a second, moved away. (I was the third to "leave.") We were expected to stay close, to be there for each other, in what was a fairly tightly bounded family constellation. . . .

My long history as a practicing heterosexual provided a convenient back-drop for my family's denial of my lesbian existence. But today I can also see how internalized homophobia played a role in my willingness to remain silent and to continue to perform a version of my heteronormative self into my forties. My need to maintain this role within my family had particular consequences for my women lovers, who were not as invested in performing such roles. Although it took me many years and the death of my father to fully acknowledge the shame that kept me silent, I also gained much strength from my lovers and others in my family of choice who taught me how to trust my heart, find my voice, and construct a new vision for doing family. I dedicate this essay to them.

Notes

1. The names of all but those who have died have been changed.
2. Mimi Abramovitz (1988: 2) defines the "family ethic" as a "preoccupation with the nuclear family unit featuring a male breadwinner and an economically dependent female homemaker." The family ethic also privileges the white middle-class family over working-class and nonwhite racial-ethnic families.

References

Abramovitz, Mimi. 1988. *Regulating the Lives of Women: Social Welfare Policy from Colonial Times to the Present.* Boston: South End Press.

Lorber, Judith. 1987. "From the Editor." *Gender & Society* 1(2): 123–124.

Rich, Adrienne. 1980. "Compulsory Heterosexuality and Lesbian Existence." *Signs* 5: 631–660.

Thorne, Barrie. 1995. "Symposium: On West and Fenstermaker's 'Doing Difference.'" *Gender & Society* 9(4): 497–499.

West, Candice, and Sarah Fenstermaker. 1995. "Doing Difference." *Gender & Society* 9: 8–37.

West, Candice, and Don H. Zimmerman. 1987. "Doing Gender." *Gender & Society,* I: 125–151.

22

Caring For and About the Mentally Ill

David A. Karp

Social relationships are products of patterns of social interaction, but once they have arisen they entail a sense of mutual obligation. This is commonly what we mean when we say we have a particular kind of relationship with someone. We are referring to the fact that we feel we owe him or her our time, sympathy, support, or the like and that we count on her or him for similar things. However, there are limits or boundaries to our felt obligations even within close and intimate relationships. Relationships become strained when their demands exceed one or another party's sense of obligation to the other parties. Mental illness places even the closest relationships under such strain, as the sociologist David Karp illustrates in this selection.

According to Karp, relationships between the mentally ill and the loved ones who care for them provide insights into the moral and social foundations of all relationships. Mental illness tests the boundaries of our sense of obligation and responsibility to each other. Caregivers of the mentally ill speak about "drawing the line" between what they owe their mentally ill child, parent, or spouse and their obligations to themselves. Where they draw that line probably depends on how deeply committed they are to the identity that the relationship sustains. For example, Karp notes that mothers tend to feel more deeply responsible for and obligated to help mentally ill children than do fathers, in part, perhaps, because mothers tend to invest more of themselves in their parental iden-

tity than do fathers. However narrowly or widely drawn, the character and unpredictability of mental illness test the boundaries of caregivers' sense of obligation to mentally ill loved ones.

As Karp recounts, caregivers of the mentally ill do not draw those boundaries once and for all but continually reassess and revise them. The initial diagnosis of mental illness often strengthens caregivers' sense of obligation to their loved ones. Although they sometimes resist the diagnosis, it implies that their loved one's troublesome and often hurtful conduct is beyond her or his control. Caregivers determine to learn all they can about their loved one's mental illness and help her or him over it. Yet, in most cases, caregivers come to recognize that their loved one will never get over her or his mental illness and will need continual care. That recognition clearly tests the boundary of their sense of obligation and leads them to reassess where to draw the line. They begin to ask themselves what their loved one's obligations are to care for him- or herself. They expect their loved one to try and get better, but the mentally ill often refuse to cooperate in their treatment. The caretakers sometimes think that the ill loved one is using his or her condition to manipulate them, and feel like giving up on him or her. Yet, caregivers often feel embarrassed by and guilty over those very feelings.

In some cases, those feelings are not enough to prevent them from breaking their bonds to their ill loved one. They feel that they are being engulfed by their relationship and losing their self to it. As Karp explains, contemporary Americans feel a deep ambivalence about attachment and individual freedom. They want the security and satisfactions of close personal attachments but also to maintain a separate individual identity. The staggering demands of caring for a mentally ill loved one can threaten a caregiver's ability to sustain an identity separate from the caregiving relationship. That is where many ultimately draw the line on their obligations to their ill loved one. Torn between their sense of obligation to their loved one and to themselves, they decide to protect the self from being totally engulfed by their relationship to her or him.

Although a particularly dramatic illustration, relationships between the mentally ill and the loved ones who care for them reveal the nature of our obligations and responsibilities to each other. They depend on how much of ourselves we invest in our relationships with others. As Karp suggests, people in other societies may invest more in relationships with family members than do most Americans and feel a much deeper sense of obligation and responsibility to them than we generally do. Also, we draw different boundaries around different kinds of relationships, depending on how much of our self we invest in them. Relationships sustain our sense of self but can also engulf it if they interfere with relationships that sustain other aspects of who and what we think we really are or could be. It is a delicate balance that is easily upset.

. . . Over a three-year period I listened to many parents . . . talk about the heartache associated with a child's mental illness. I have also interviewed children of emotionally sick parents, spouses with a mentally ill partner, and siblings of those suffering from depression, manic-depression, or schizophrenia. . . . [E]ach has a unique story to tell about what it is like to care for a sick family member. Every relationship poses distinctive challenges as individuals struggle to understand the pain of another's illness and its consequences. At the same time, my lengthy conversations with the family members of people with a major mental illness reveal strong regularities. Caregivers must negotiate the boundaries of their involvement with the sick, and, in their efforts to do this, there are striking similarities that transcend the particularities of each circumstance. My central purpose [here] is to illuminate these commonalties. I am most primarily interested in how family members construct obligations to someone with a serious emotional illness and then deal with the inevitable difficulties in honoring their commitment.

Substantively, this [chapter] is about the social tango between emotionally ill people and those who try to help them. In an even more encompassing way, the difficult task of caring for a sick person provides a conceptual space for examining the essential nature of people's obligations and responsibilities to each other. Nearly every general theory concerned with understanding social order assumes that expectations of reciprocity and exchange constitute the essential foundation of organized society. "Obligation," the theorist Georg Simmel wrote, "belongs among those 'microscopic,' but infinitely tough threads which tie one element of society to another, and thus eventually all of them together in a stable collective life."[1] In this way, the relationship between sick people and their caregivers exposes the limits of obligation, responsibility, empathy, understanding, and sympathy in *all* relationships. This study of family caregivers, therefore, speaks to no less a question than "What do we owe each other?"

The relationship between sick people and those close to them may be the quintessential case for thinking about the moral and social foundations of all human relationships. Severe illness, because it so thoroughly disrupts family life, calls attention to the taken-for-granted, normally invisible boundaries of social relationships. Prolonged illness makes demands on a child, parent, spouse or sibling that test the relative strength of the ties that bind us together. In a beautifully written book, based on her experience with "chronic fatigue syndrome," Kat Duff wisely advises that "Not only is it better for the sick to be left alone at times, it is also better for the well to leave them at times. Healthy people can be contaminated by the gloom and depression of the ailing if they come too close or have too much sympathy."[2] The [following] accounts . . . will show that sustaining an appropriate level of involvement with a mentally ill child, parent, sibling, or spouse is extraordinarily difficult. . . .

My analysis throughout this chapter is directed at understanding what family members take into account as they try to set obligation boundaries between themselves and the mentally ill person in their lives. . . . [C]aregivers' assessments about proper involvement with a mentally ill person [is] *a process over time*. It is a process characterized by intense efforts to make sense of another's illness and to negotiate how best to help them without becoming engulfed by their misery. I will show that the kinds of boundaries that seem appropriate at the outset of an illness are quite different from those established at later points in a caregiver's evolving "joint career" with an ill person.[3]

As is so frequently the case when analyzing qualitative data, the central metaphor that animates my thinking comes from the words of the respondents themselves. With extraordinary regularity, the people interviewed spoke about their difficulty in *drawing the line* between themselves and an ill spouse, child, brother, or parent. We learn from their comments that decisions about how and where to draw responsibility lines are surrounded by intense emotions, equivocation, uncertainty, and ambivalence. Along with the kind of bewilderment and consternation intrinsic to relationships with mentally ill people, decisions about how to draw boundaries are compounded by a widely held cultural prescription that over-involvement with dependent people might properly be considered a disease. The existence of a whole social movement in America dedicated to avoiding "enabling" and "codependence" is striking evidence of Americans' confusion about the permissible limits of human closeness. Codependency can arise as a pathological condition only in a society that fosters deep ambivalence about the value of extensive ties.

This chapter, then, is primarily about how sixty people draw and then redraw appropriate boundaries between themselves and a sick family member. Their stories attest to the near impossibility of arriving at a line that makes sense and is workable over time. Eventually, respondents reluctantly realize

that whatever line they draw, like the proverbial line in the sand, is transitory and easily blown away by the shifting and wholly unpredictable winds of mental illness. Still, unless they abandon the relationship altogether, family members have no alternative in the face of another's emotional illness except to try over and again to find a balance between the requirements of care and the maintenance of their own well-being. My goal is to reveal regularities in caretakers' thinking, feeling, and behaving as they try to determine an appropriate level of commitment to an ill person. The question directing my analysis in the following pages asks, "What features of the situation do family members take into account as they try to construct boundaries of obligation between themselves and the mentally ill person in their lives?"

The interview materials suggest four overlapping dimensions that frame the relationship between caregivers and family members. While each of these four experiential moments generally occurs sequentially, it would be a mistake to understand them as operating in an absolutely stage-like fashion. Rather, I view these interpretive junctures in family members' illness careers as bearing a simultaneous, dialectical, and mutually transformative relationship with each other. I offer them as a framework for economically presenting the data and, thus, for looking at key elements of consciousness shared by nearly all the respondents in this study. They are:

1. HOPING AND LEARNING—Those new to mental illness and the caregiver role rely heavily on medicine to solve what they hope will be a limited and curable problem in the life of a loved one.

2. REVISING EXPECTATIONS—Most caregivers must eventually confront the reality that a loved one's mental illness will not disappear. This recognition, in turn, generates new expectations for both the sick family member and themselves.

3. ASSESSING RESPONSIBILITY—A critical factor in determining their degree of obligation is caregivers' ongoing assessment of how much responsibility a sick person can and ought to take in solving [his or her] own problem.

4. PRESERVING ONESELF—At critical junctures during the course of caregiving, respondents grapple with having to decide whether their own health and identities are so compromised that they can no longer maintain a commitment to care.

Drawing the Line

Eventually, as later sections will show, caregivers do withdraw support under certain predictable circumstances. However, as they recount their histories of caring when a family member becomes mentally ill, they nearly uniformly felt a strong obligation to care at the outset of the "trouble." Here's a sampling of the way they saw their obligations early in their caregiving careers:

I don't really see what I am doing as duty. . . . I mean, I know that I have a duty to make it through the snow storm to work on a bad day. I see that as duty. I see that as being a good soldier . . . I won't let you down, and that kind of thing. I don't think any of those thoughts in relation to being here for him [son]. I just feel that it is very much an unfinished job. . . . Responsibility is deeper [than duty]. Duty—you know exactly the limits of it. . . . Responsibility, it's your essence. I mean, could you sleep? Could your soul rest? Would your dreams be troubled if you really didn't meet your responsibility?

> RETIRED BOOK EDITOR, *age fifty-one, mother*

My mother looks at it that I should take care of her. . . . You know . . . "I gave birth to her, so she owes me this life (of hers)." . . . So, you know, it's one of those things. You make the decision. I guess you allow yourself to feel the obligation. Because I

could walk away from it . . . but I look at it that when I go to meet my God, I don't want to have any feeling . . . like I didn't do everything that I could have.

> ACCOUNTANT, *age thirty-five, daughter*

. . . I should note here that the cultural mandate to care for an ill family member is not felt equally by everyone. The sociologist Candace Clark has made important observations about the connection between the social statuses of persons and the "width" of their respective sympathy margins.[4] Spouses, for example, are expected to honor sympathy requests for problems that would seem too trivial in another relationship. Husbands and wives can complain to each other at length about a bad day at work, for example, and feel wronged if their partner does not pay close attention and extend considerable sympathy. The relationships between parents and children are bounded by quite different rules. In this case, the margins are asymmetrical since parents are expected to freely extend far more sympathy to their children (especially, of course, young children) than they can legitimately expect in return. In particular, mothers of sick children clearly expressed the greatest obligation to care.

We bring these children into the world. We give them life. We're responsible. Until the day God takes them, we are their parents, we are responsible, and no matter what. If there is an illness there, you have an extra responsibility. I really believe that and I feel that with all my heart.

> REAL ESTATE BROKER, *age forty-five, mother*

It has got to be heartbreaking to see your kid in a mental hospital.

I wanted to kill myself, David, I wanted to kill myself. Do you understand that? It wasn't just because I was depressed. It was because I felt responsible and helpless to do anything and no one loved him but me in the whole wide world and my love wasn't enough. I couldn't put my arms around him and give him what he needed. I wanted to die. . . . I mean, I tried to bargain with God, "Take my life, fix my kid's." To this day, if God said to me, "Will you come with me now if I make them all happy and straightened out and productive and they will be all right?" I'll go, "Yes! Gladly!" You know, "[If I] never have another moment's happiness. Fine! I'll go with you!"

UNEMPLOYED, age fifty, mother

Although it is utterly devastating to have a child become mentally ill, several mothers nevertheless acknowledged that it would be difficult to give up the caregiving role. In one case, a mother of a child who recently became eighteen explained that she was about to experience a deep identity loss because her daughter, in the throes of a manic episode, planned to leave home against her wishes.

Oh my God, how do I be her mother [now]? How do I be her mother when she is not living in my house? And now that she's hit the road, it's a real crisis for me. . . . I had to give up the last piece of managing her life. She's eighteen and I have no more to say. And she hit the road. And . . . she's not safe. . . . As long as she was in my sphere . . . I was going to manage it. . . . I can't do it anymore. I don't know what to do with myself. I don't know how to be her mother [now]. From the day she was born she didn't eat and didn't sleep and she needed fifteen casts and had diarrhea, and all that stuff. I've been doing that (caring for her) since the day she was born, eighteen years plus three weeks.

PHYSICAL THERAPY TEACHER,
age forty-nine, mother

Men appear to have a different perspective on caregiving. This "finding" fits with the frequently made observation that women have always been socialized to be caregivers and feel far more comfortable with that role than men. . . . Men sometimes quickly "burn out" as caregivers. Women, on the other hand, who do not typically approach their commitment to a sick family member in solution terms, are, compared to men, normally more tolerant caregivers. Women, in other words, are often more involved caregivers than men because they are trained for that role and because their commitment to caregiving is not contingent on the eradication of the problem. Women's words about obligation sometimes contrast sharply with those of men, many of whom seem far more pragmatic in determining the boundaries of their responsibilities. Two men, for example, independently talked about how the travel demanded by their work was a welcome respite from a home dominated by a mentally ill partner or child.

I travel and that allows me some time alone with my thoughts. I think it helps. I enjoy . . . business trips. . . . I enjoyed it before I really understood the full extent of my wife's disease, but it certainly helps now. . . . My opinion [is that] this [mental illness] is something guys handle better than women. . . . Guys are better at rationalizing . . . [and] saying, "Yuh, I did do as good a job as I can. It wasn't a great experience, but there wasn't anything else I could do about it and I've learned from it and then moved on."

SALESMAN, age forty-two, husband

When I'm not around to take care of day-by-day issues, she's [wife] much stronger and much more able to do things on her own. I find when I'm away from home that I'm not worried because she seems to get her stuff together. So, I don't know to that extent whether my being there . . . helps her or gets in her way. I know when I travel for work—I tend to work eighteen-hour days—and, you know, go back to the hotel room when all the restaurants are closed and eat a box of crackers and peanut butter. So it's not a glamorous travel life but my mind tends to be at ease.

ELECTRONICS DESIGNER, age sixty, husband

. . . As Christena Nippert-Eng maintains in her provocative and insightful book about the linkages between work and home life, "All boundaries are socially constructed. . . . Over the natural non-order of things, we impose boundaries on everything, including our daily activities and the places and people with whom we pursue them."[5] Illness is surely a social occasion that sets in motion active efforts at "boundary work." Although any boundaries that human beings construct are subject to change and renegotiation over time, illness, because of its capacity to so thoroughly disrupt the coherence of daily life, demands ongoing assessments about the proper boundaries between family caregivers and patients. Family members confronted with the reality of mental illness quickly learn that without constructing appropriate boundaries they risk becoming engulfed and potentially consumed by the other's illness. The inevitable task that "well" family members face is to honor the obligation and commitment they feel toward their sick spouse, parent, child, or sibling without losing their own health and self.

As the following accounts will show, sustaining an appropriate level of involvement with a mentally ill person is extraordinarily difficult. Partly this is so because of the intrinsic nature of "mental" illness. Not only is the course of the illness unpredictable, but the ailing person may also act unpredictably. It is hard enough for a healthy person to imagine the pain of a person who suffers from a physical illness they themselves have never experienced. It is quite another thing to understand a person who thinks and feels in ways that seem totally incomprehensible. One respondent tried to draw the contrast between the caregiving contingencies of physical and mental illness this way:

> What do words mean? Words don't mean the same thing [to a mentally ill person]. Reality is not the same. You are not dealing in the same dimension. You have to understand . . . what that person's illness is and what the words really

mean. . . . What frightens me about it is that reality is different. . . . Mentally ill people see things that are not there, or that I don't see, [that] other people don't see, and I don't know what they are seeing. I don't know what they are going to do. . . . Like my mother-in-law now has cancer [and] is having chemotherapy. She is a remarkable person. But there is like no problem. She is sick, she is tired. With the chemotherapy she is getting better. She is tired, she goes to sleep. She tells you, "I feel tired now" or "I don't feel like eating" or "I am sad I lost my hair." But we are all talking in the same place. She doesn't say, "I am sad that I lost my hair" and really means that "I want to kill you and God is going to come down and strike everyone dead in this house tonight." With a mentally ill person, you don't know. . . . I don't really feel like mentally ill people can hurt me. But . . . it's like you are just not in the same place and it makes me nervous. Like I really have no control.

> INSURANCE ADMINISTRATOR,
> *age forty-six, daughter/sister*

The very unpredictability of the course of mental illness ensures that the lines established between caregiver and patient at one moment may not work shortly thereafter. Ill family members may, depending on their particular problem, alternate between episodes of deep depression, mania, florid psychosis, and wellness. Moreover, each discrete episode of illness may be different from those that preceded it. In the middle of an illness episode individuals may not comprehend their problem, may create huge difficulties in their own and caregivers' lives (such as spending money wildly, getting into automobile accidents, running away from home), and certainly may be incapable of expressing the sort of gratitude other ill people ordinarily extend to their caregivers. As a result, the central interpretive problem and practical dilemma for caregivers, heightened in the case of mental illness, is how to draw appropriate boundaries between themselves and a sick family member. The confusion, bewilderment, and consternation about "drawing the line" with someone suffering from depression, manic-depression, or schizophrenia is clear in the following comment:

> The one [thing] that I think is the trickiest and is very emotional and very stressful is walking that line of "What do I do for this person, and what do I not do?" Because you constantly have to reevaluate that one. You know, you can hear yourself tell yourself [that] . . . you just have to do the best you can for this person, but it's sad and you try to accept that. But having to always say, "Now, what should I be doing for this person, and what should I not be doing? You know, they're disrupting my life. How much should I give?" It's a constant struggle. That's the one that's the toughest, and it just really gets wearing and very difficult. Like, right now my mother's very ill, so it's going to be even more difficult. . . . And I'll tell you, the few times that I have walked away, I get just an incredible feeling. When you've drawn the line and you're not doing this reevaluating, and you're not having any contact, and you're living a normal life, it's just incredible. It's a wonderful feeling. You know, it's just wonderful. You go out with friends. I mean, you don't think about it. It's just great. . . . But it's always constantly reevaluation. That's the most difficult thing.
>
> ACCOUNTANT, *age thirty-five, daughter*

. . . The choice of caregivers can, of course, be as stark as staying or leaving. One woman, caring for a sick daughter, has not been in touch with her mentally ill mother for nearly fifteen years. Yet another interview centered on a young man's painful decision to finally leave his wife. However, the more usual concerns of the interviewees is how constantly to shuttle between distance and closeness in their efforts to provide ongoing support. The remainder of this chapter details the factors caregivers take into account as they try to solve the most vexing caregiving equation—calculating the appropriate levels of involvement necessary to help another in trouble without jeopardizing their own life, liberty, and pursuit of happiness.

Caregiving in Context

Human troubles are often characterized by moments of epiphany or revelation when, after long periods experienced as utter chaos and confusion, the nature of the problem suddenly *seems* clear. In the case of illness, one such moment is receiving a diagnosis. Of course, a person's behaviors are sometimes so beyond the norms of civility and acceptability that the label *mental illness* is quickly attached to them. Flips into psychotic mania, attempts at suicide, or having robust hallucinations rarely go unnoticed or are passed off as being within the bounds of normalcy. Still, large numbers of people who are eventually deemed mentally ill go for months, even years, without an "official" diagnosis. Family members, therefore, sometimes equally go for months or years feeling anger, fear, confusion, and concern about a loved one's oppressive behaviors without being able to name them as illness. The point at which a person's troublesome behavior is transformed into a disease, via the pronouncements of medical experts, is typically a moment of epiphany for caregivers (and sometimes for patients). Such an epiphany is, however, only the beginning of an ongoing interpretive process aimed at establishing comfortable caregiving boundaries.

Hoping and Learning

It is difficult to overestimate the power of receiving a medical diagnosis. Since a diagnosis of mental illness remains deeply stigmatizing, it is not surprising that "patients" often reject it. Sometimes family members are similarly shocked by the mental illness diagnosis and their first impulse is also to reject it.

One woman told me that "when I heard those words [mental illness] from a doctor, it scared the life out of me." When the doctor explained "you have a serious problem on your hands. This boy is absolutely manic-depressive, if not schizophrenic," her response was to think "Oh my, don't say that. . . . It's just emotion. He needs to talk to a counselor." Another mother confessed that she was "scared by everything that was happening. I didn't know what was going on with my son. My son wouldn't even talk to me. He was out of his mind. . . . You know, [I was thinking] things like is he going to be in this hospital for the rest of his life?" For most family members, though, a diagnosis clarifies a history of problems and generates hope that a deeply disruptive family member will finally be "cured."

> I loved getting the diagnosis. That was the best day of my life.
>
> PHYSICAL THERAPIST, *age forty-nine, mother*

> I'll tell you one of the best days of my life was when I got a phone call from the hospital telling me what they decided was wrong with him [husband] and they couldn't understand why I was so excited or happy.
>
> DAY CARE ATTENDANT, *age fifty-five, wife*

> Well, before she was diagnosed as being bipolar, I was seriously thinking about getting a divorce because she was just so argumentative. You know, after she was diagnosed *it was something*. It was not a character or a personality issue. . . . It was something that . . . she had no obvious control over and could be treated with medication. That put a different light on it.
>
> ELECTRONICS DESIGNER, *age sixty, husband*

. . . Once it becomes clear that the problem is mental illness—usually after a dramatic crisis—family members often go through a period of actively learning about it. This may involve conversations with medical people and sometimes extensive reading. This learning process is typically accompanied by heroic efforts to save or cure the sick person. Heroic measures are more easily undertaken at the outset of a catastrophic illness because sympathy margins remain wide and caregivers often believe that once an emotionally ill person realizes how much he or she is cared about, they will get better. Heroic measures also display strong commitment, something that individuals are expected to show when someone close is in a crisis. At this point in a family member's illness career the caregiving role is normally embraced fully, enthusiastically, and optimistically. In effect, there is no constructed boundary between the ill person and family member during the early stages of what is now openly a "caring" role. If there has been any change, it is that boundaries between well and sick family members become even more porous than previously.

> Several of his sisters had said to me, "Don't feel you have to stick around for him because you feel sorry for him." But it never occurred to me [to leave]. I felt that I ought to help him get through it. I always believed he could get through it, although there were times right in the middle of it when I thought, "My God."
>
> CUSTOMER SERVICE REPRESENTATIVE, *age thirty-five, wife*

> I felt that if I worked hard enough and fast enough I could make her [daughter] better. Anything [the doctors] suggested I jumped on with great enthusiasm.
>
> NURSE, *age fifty, mother*

Such efforts might continue for some time, even years but with growing doubts about their efficacy. Unfortunately, in virtually every interview, respondents eventually had to come to the reluctant conclusion that initial hopes for a solution to the problem were an illusion. Those who thought the right combination of love and care, medication, and counseling would heal a sick spouse, child, sibling, or parent slowly came to the recognition that the problem was far more complex than they initially imaged. The imagery that an episode of mental illness could be fixed in the way doctors might help a broken bone to mend gave way to a consciousness of mental illness as a permanent condition. Unlike receiving a diagnosis, the recognition of mental illness' permanence seeps into caregivers' consciousness over time. Still, there must be a moment somewhere along the line when a caregiver finally acknowledges the idea that the problem is unlikely ever fully to disappear. That moment no doubt also constitutes an epiphany, albeit a negative one, that sets in motion a wholly new view of their relationship with the ill person in their lives.

While every respondent grappled with the concept of permanence, Angela, a forty-six-year-old woman whose life is bounded by a daughter, a sister, and mother with mental illness, as well as another child with cerebral palsy, summed up with great precision the changes in consciousness generated by having to admit that a mental illness may never go away. The matter of permanence came up in our conversation as we were talking about feelings of chronic loss and sorrow generated by her children's illnesses. Here, in some detail, is what she said:

> I guess I didn't feel her loss that much until after she [sister] tried to commit suicide. I mean I didn't feel like it would be permanent. . . . You know, she did have these periods of getting better and so I didn't feel it as permanent. . . . I always thought that maybe she would get better or she'd go to a different doctor. . . . I still didn't see it as permanent. It was later.

> *So, are you saying that the loss becomes more profound at the moment of recognition of permanence?*

> Oh definitely, for her [mother] and for my daughter. That [recognition] is just devastating. Well, if it is not permanent it is like

having a cold or something. I mean you go through this period and the person is really unhappy. . . . [For example], you go through labor and you have a child. They'll be an end to it. And at the end, you know, all of your efforts and suffering will have been for something, you feel. But when you finally realize that there is no end, then you have a whole different mind-set so you have to change. . . . First of all, a lot of your sympathy and support will dry up because people are going to get sick of doing that [caretaking]. . . . So you'll be out there alone, sort of trekking along, trying to support them because . . . whatever happens to that person, no matter how bad they get, whatever happens, you are not going to desert them. That is how I feel with my . . . mother and my daughter. . . . I will try to offer some level of support and be there for them.

> So if it is permanent, then my whole life has changed and I have to offer this kind of support that I don't really want to offer, but I feel like I have to. And I wouldn't feel like a decent person if I didn't. . . . You know, my mother may die in a few years. My sister may be alive for all of my life, but she has her husband. . . . But with all of them, it is to some extent that you feel like that. But with my daughter I felt it most profoundly. When it's not permanent you can withstand almost anything. When it's permanent, it's completely different.

> INSURANCE ADMINISTRATOR, *age forty-six, daughter/sister*

Revising Expectations

. . . [E]ven when the recognition of mental illness's permanence settles into their consciousness and seriously erodes the belief that a resolution of the problem is possible, respondents rarely lose hope altogether. At the point in our conversation when we discuss the chronic nature of mental illness and the likelihood that it will be a lifelong problem, caregivers sometimes follow their realistic assessment of things with the nearly apologetic statement, "But I still can't help but to feel hope." In [a] self-help group [for caregivers of the mentally ill], a repeating theme of the talk, often invoked after someone has detailed a particularly difficult situation, is the observation that the medications for mental illness are getting better all the time and that medical science might even one day solve the problem. Nevertheless, nearly everyone interviewed described how they felt obliged to ratchet down their expectations for the person in their care.

> I gave up the future. . . . She is really lost to us as the kid that we knew and the relationship that we had. This is gone. We are grieving the final loss. And they [doctors] said to me, "She might come back." And I said, "I can't do that. I have to grieve that she is totally gone and that she's not coming back in any sense that we knew her." Not that we will never see her again, but that she is not coming back in any sense that we knew her. . . . Anything that I get from this point forward is a gift and not a disappointment. . . . Oh, I sob my guts out. But I'm not sorry for me. I mean, once in a while I say, "This sucks. This is awful. Why do I feel so terrible?" But that's like really rare. I lost this kid. I lost the last piece of this kid. I sob for my loss. I don't sob for me. Does that make sense to you?
>
> PHYSICAL THERAPIST, *age forty-nine, mother*

You have to realize that the person is not going to be what you want them to be or not going to have the life you would like for them.

> ACCOUNTANT, *age thirty-five, daughter*

Caregivers also ratchet down expectations for their own lives.

> We almost had to put our life on hold. I find we're five years behind all of our friends. We just bought a house. Most of our friends bought a house when they were in their late twenties. And . . . last

March, about kids, I finally got up the guts, and said "Okay, I want to start talking about kids. It's really on my mind. It's bothering me. All of our friends have kids. All of our friends are now on their second kid by this point. And . . . it's hitting me." Up until then, it hadn't even hit me. And so we talked about it. And, you know, I said to Tom, "I'm not talking about getting pregnant tomorrow. I just want you to know this is what's going through my mind." The kids thing came up again around Christmas time . . . and we said we'll talk about it in a little bit. And then, when Tom went through this depression a couple of weeks ago, I thought to myself, "My God, what would happen if I had a child? All this energy for years I've put into Tom, I'm not going to have anymore." So, that's a big case scenario. Everything I do I have to think about how's this going to affect Tom. . . . So, I mean, we're at the point now where we still put off the decision. God help me when I turn forty [*laughing*], but we still have a couple more years.

> CUSTOMER SERVICE REPRESENTATIVE, *age thirty-five, wife*

In order not to leave you with the mistaken impression that all caregivers eventually feel utterly fatalistic about the future, I should say that some also describe feelings of efficacy and progress in their efforts to help. Although admitting that it is still difficult for them to figure out exactly what they might realistically expect for their son's future, Eileen and Bill are optimistic. From the time [their son] Ray suffered a severe psychotic episode, the trajectory of his illness has been toward greater health. He has returned to school and recently began a new job. Eileen observed that "he's thinking really clearly and pacing himself and monitoring himself. I think most of our work with him is over really." And Bill added, "I guess one of the things we've learned is . . . about taking time. These things do not just flip into the next phase just like that. It just keeps evolving [in a positive directionl. Progress is being made and . . . we've learned stuff and Ray has learned stuff and we have a relationship with the doctor and we have some sense of what to do and what not to do."

Even among those who report progress, the dominant theme of the interviews is an increasing recognition that, despite their best efforts at caretaking, the problem will remain. At a point, everyone also realizes that they truly cannot control the course of another's mental illness and must surrender to that reality. Perceiving their inability to control things is exceedingly important because once that becomes a caretaker's prevailing view, it calls forth renewed efforts to recast the boundaries of obligation. The realization that intractable illness thwarts their earlier goal of control is an "identity turning point" in the careers of caregivers.[6] Now, they feel more disposed to accept the inevitability of the problem, to define it more thoroughly in disease terms, and, consequently, to feel less responsible for the unfortunate consequences of their family member's illness.

> I was tired. I was fed up. I was really angry at her. . . . I was furious at her for two months. . . . One of the things that I kept saying was, "I think what I'm going through is the last stage of acceptance." . . . I mean, part of it was [that] in order to accept her illness I had to let go of my responsibility. . . . My feeling, where I sit right now is that . . . I have absolutely no control over her. She can go off her medication. She can totally, excuse me, fuck up her life and I have no control over that. I can't stop it. . . . I think that is the acceptance I got to last December.
>
> PHYSICAL THERAPIST, *age forty-nine, mother*

And by that point he had pulled away from everybody. He wouldn't see anybody. So I mean, it was just a train heading [toward a crash]. There was nothing I could do. . . . Every time I thought I was helping, it was making things worse. So, I guess I must have at some point just sat back and said, "I'm doing all I can and if something else happens, I know I've done my best."

> CUSTOMER SERVICE REPRESENTATIVE, *age thirty-five, wife*

. . . A caregiver's dual recognition that (1) mental illness is unlikely ever to be resolved and (2) that they cannot control it, leads to a fundamental reassessment of their felt obligations. At this juncture in their relationship with an ill family member, caregivers begin to ask themselves with increasing frequency the question "What are my spouse's (or my child's, my sibling's, my parent's) obligations to care for themselves?" Once that question seriously arises in their consciousness, wholly new perceptions and emotions about their role in an ill person's life become possible.

Assessing Responsibility

. . . Within the last ten to fifteen years, biological explanations of human behavior have [dominated America's thinking]. The prevailing wisdom in American psychiatry seems to be that affective disorders are brain diseases. Advocate groups such as NAMI (National Alliance for the Mentally Ill) fully embrace the view that people suffering from depression, manic-depression, and schizophrenia have "broken brains," in effect. . . . [N]early everyone interviewed for this book, although willing to speculate about the social or situational factors that might kick off an illness episode, ultimately saw their loved one's problem as a product of bad brain chemistry.

My purpose here certainly is not to unravel how nature and nurture might combine in the case of mental illness. Whatever might be the cause(s) of mental illness, I understand the appeal of biological explanations, both for caregivers and those afflicted. If the problem is essentially biological, caregivers and their loved ones are largely absolved from responsibility—caregivers from the responsibility of somehow having caused a family member's anguish and ill persons from responsibility for their unacceptable behavior. Biological explanations, by understanding mental illness as somehow rooted in neurotransmitters gone awry, significantly insulate caregivers and patients from moral blame. However, despite generally embracing biological explanations, caregivers who routinely deal with a family member's difficult, hurtful, and unreasonable behaviors inevitably navigate a difficult explanatory course between determinism and personal responsibility. It is a caregiving paradox that while speaking the language of biological determinism, caregivers still invoke personal responsibility as a criterion for assessing the extent of their obligations.

Once again, the case of mental illness raises distinctive puzzles for caregivers. I have already discussed how perceptions of permanence and an inability to control the ill person's behavior shape feelings of duty and responsibility over time. To these socially rooted caregiving contingencies let me now add another—the relative willingness of patients to comply with medical treatment. Because of the stigma attached to the mental illness label, the debilitating side effects of powerful psychotropic medications, and often the inability of mentally ill people to appreciate how strange their behaviors seem to others, many ill family members simply deny that they are sick and, thus, refuse any form of treatment.

In those families where an ill person does not comply with medical treatment, the reservoir of caregiving sympathy quickly evaporates. Among support group members, conversations often center on strategies for getting family members to accept that they have a disease and to comply with medical protocols. Whether or not their ill spouse, child, parent, or sibling undergoes therapeutic treatments, everyone interviewed agreed that they must bear significant responsibility for getting well. Exhibiting such responsibility becomes, at a certain point, the *sine qua non* of their willingness to continue as caregivers. Rachel, who has been caring for two siblings, captures sentiments expressed repeatedly in the interviews:

It is a complicated thing with mental illness because, on the one hand, if you buy the idea people really do have . . . a brain disorder, [that] there's something wrong with the serotonin levels or something in [their] head, well then you really can't hold people . . . responsible for their behavior. . . . But it's also got to be pretty hard to hear from somebody who is saying, "[There is] nothing I can do. I am just sick and that is it." . . . I mean, it is hard to hear that and I guess the difference between my brother and sister is that when he first got sick, he pretty much almost immediately assumed a major part of the responsibility for his illness. I mean, he has worked. He has gone to school. He has read books. He has gone to support groups. He has had regular medical appointments. For the most part he has been compliant with medicine for the better portion of the time he has been sick. He has listened to people [and] gotten advice. I mean, he is not perfect at dealing with it, but that [compliance] really is what has to happen. I would say the same thing about my sister's illness or my mother's alcoholism. The sin isn't in being sick. The real sin is people who simply don't accept [their illness] and [don't] get the help that they need so that they can at least attempt to help themselves. . . . Until they get to the point of helping themselves, you know, the best psychiatrists in the world and pills are just no magic potion because there is a lot of work that has to be done. And you know, I suppose some people just say, "It's too much work. I am not going to bother to get better. It's too painful." And I think that is where my sister is at. She just sees it as too daunting a job. Better to be sick than [to] crack away at some of the things that have shaped her whole life—her identity of depression. I mean, that is how she identifies herself—with depression and a depressed life; not being able to go anywhere and not having any goals or aspirations.

TECHNOLOGY LICENSER, *age thirty-three, sister*

... [C]aregivers nearly always came to feel that they should continue to extend themselves only if their family member seemed to be making a good faith effort to help themselves.

> Until it got down to the essence of him having to be responsible for his own actions [our marriage was in trouble]. . . . Now I feel that it's a much more healthy [situation] . . . because he really is responding. . . . Joe is willing to work hard at this [staying well]. . . . I keep saying to him, "you have only one soul to save and that's your own." If you are saving your soul you won't be a burden to anyone else. . . . I am very fortunate that he is so motivated, that he wants to figure this out. He wants to have a good life.
>
> NURSE, *age fifty, wife*

> I feel that even if they have a mental illness, there are responsibilities that go along with the mental illness. . . . You see your doctor when you're supposed to. You take your medication as you're supposed to. You live as healthy a lifestyle that you can. If it means that there are people in your life that contribute to your mental illness, then you avoid those people. You absolutely have some control over your own mental illness. . . . With mental illness, yes, it's something that's going on in the body that you don't have any control over. But if it means you avoid alcohol to keep it controlled, then you don't drink. If it means you need to walk a half-hour every day to get the serotonin levels up, then you walk that half-hour every day. Take charge!!! Don't think that it's somebody else's responsibilities.
>
> RETIRED SECRETARY, *age fifty-eight, mother*

The interpretive problem of deciding just how strenuously to draw caregiving boundaries is additionally complicated by the perceived difficulty in determining whether someone's behaviors truly arise from that person's mental illness. As the previous comments indicate, caregivers invariably wonder whether a mentally ill person can, in fact, exercise control over many of their problematic behaviors. Consequently, caregivers routinely face the dilemma of deciding whether to hold the *person* or the *disease* responsible for objectionable behaviors. Although those sick with physical illnesses may sometimes be accused of abusing the "sick role," caregivers ordinarily feel able to determine the authenticity of their complaints and the propriety of their inability to fulfill social obligations.[7] The matter is more opaque in the case of mental illness. As a result, respondents in this study often described how caregiving boundaries were frayed by the suspicion that the ill person in their life sometimes manipulates them. . . .

> I also got angry because I really view a lot of it as being manipulative and the older I got, the angrier I got at him [father] because I could see that he could control it when he wanted to. . . . When I was growing up he could control it around who he wanted to. Maybe there were a couple of isolated incidents where he really couldn't, but for the majority of it he would switch like that [*snaps fingers*] when somebody else came around. . . . There was a tremendous amount of control there that he was not exerting and so I got angry because he would manipulate. He would manipulate in the sense that he would want everybody's pity, but he wouldn't do anything anybody suggested.
>
> LAWYER, *age thirty-three, daughter*

> I think the illness breeds a certain form of manipulation. Some of it is that you know the person is manipulating you and some of it is, you know, they really aren't well and this is their survival skill.
>
> TECHNOLOGY LICENSER, *age thirty-three, sister*

The emotions surrounding caregiving become especially complicated when people have feelings that they consider illegitimate. That is, the problems of managing emotions are compounded when people feel a second order of emotions, emotions about their emotions. The interviews are replete with expressions of embarrassment, shame, and guilt for feeling anger, resentment, or even hate toward a person you are supposed to love.

A growing body of literature on the sociology of emotions centers on the idea that we do not simply feel emotions; we also create, intensify, suppress, and transform them. One relevant question to ask, therefore, is "How do people deal with emotions when culturally given 'feeling rules' are not well-developed?"[8] I can say with clarity right now that, in the case of mental illness, feelings about caregiving evolve to the point where individuals are forced to entertain these questions: "What are the circumstances under which I would have to leave? What are my limits as a caregiver?" The final data section of this chapter focuses on their answers.

Preserving Oneself

There is a . . . bias in the sample of people assembled for this study. Because many of them were recruited from a "Family and Friends" self-help group, they are people who are sufficiently invested in the caregiving role to participate weekly at the meetings. This is, therefore, primarily a study of how people who have elected to stay in a caregiving relationship bear responsibility. My generalizations cannot extend to those who have given up and exited from the lives of mentally ill relatives. However, several respondents certainly have a perspective on family members who either are not doing their fair share of caregiving or have left altogether. One of my interviews was with the eldest daughter in a large family who was faced with virtually the sole responsibility of caring for her schizophrenic mother. Ordinarily, Joanna simply assumed that it was her duty to be The Caregiver, saying at one point, "I was born with the obligation." However, feelings of resentment toward family members who were literally "hiding out" from her mother (by having unlisted telephone numbers and not revealing their home addresses) surfaced on the occasion of a funeral. Here's the scene Joanna described:

> Her brothers and sisters, yes, they're hiding out. She does have contact with one sister. This sister has a lot of problems too. It's not a good situation for them to be together. But yes. . . . I'm really angry at the fact that they did that. Absolutely. I still can't comprehend how somebody could do that. I really haven't given it much thought until I went to my grandmother's funeral back in January. And I realized that everybody was so uncomfortable, and everybody was so concerned with my mother's being there, and the fact that I brought her. I realized that, you know, "She's your sister as much as she's my mother, and she's sick." And they were looking at me like, "Can't you take her somewhere or do something with her?" And I'm thinking, "You know, you're not here [for her] now. You should have been there years ago, too." I try to forget about it, because confronting them about it or expressing how I feel about it just doesn't seem to have achieved anything. But I absolutely had some resentment for that toward her siblings and her parents.
>
> ACCOUNTANT, *age thirty-five, daughter*

Interestingly, when people talk about family members who have opted out of any caregiving, they rarely express rancor toward them. While upset by their own caregiving burden, they seem to understand the motives of those who have left. Their understanding, even compassion, for relatives who do not help them with an ill family member is possible in a culture that deifies personal freedom and the obligation of individuals to achieve self-fulfillment. Indeed, as one of my graduate students from Thailand periodically reminds me, the obligation issues that so confound the people interviewed for this study do not exist in her country. She reports that the question "Shall I subordinate my own needs and desires to the task of caring for a sick spouse, child, parent, or sibling?" cannot even arise in the consciousness of a Thai family member. There simply is no competing expectation to the cultural demand that one be a devoted caregiver.

Although the sociological analysis of individualism extends to the origins of the discipline, the conversation about its significance in understanding American character and social structure was reinvigorated through the writings of Robert Bellah and his colleagues. *Habits of the Heart* details how the ethic of individualism in the United States fosters self-absorption and guarantees a collective sense of strangeness, isolation, and loneliness. At one point, the authors discuss the deep ambivalence Americans have about freedom and attachment. The dilemma posed by the need both for attachment and freedom is beautifully captured in Bellah's analysis of romantic love in America. On the one side, Americans believe deeply in romantic love as a necessary requirement for self-satisfaction. At the same time, love and marriage, which are based on the free giving of self to another, pose the problem that in sharing too completely with another one might lose oneself. The difficulties that Americans have in maintaining intimate relationships stem in part from the uneasy balance between sharing and being separate.[9]

. . . Certainly, as the quotes throughout this chapter suggest, the task of caregiving is often deeply connected with the privilege of loving. That being so, the ambivalence felt by caregivers as they search for the proper balance of attachment and separation arises from precisely the same cultural confusions that compromise our capacity to love. My data affirm Bellah's theoretical observations that the fear of losing oneself is what ultimately motivates people to leave relationships that threaten to engulf them. When asked what might persuade them to exit from their caregiving situation, most of the respondents first declared that they were un-

likely ever to back away completely from their caring obligations. When pressed further, though, they commonly articulated three fundamental criteria that might require exiting—the realization that their efforts to care are ineffective, feeling that their own health is seriously jeopardized by caring, and believing that their self or identity is in danger of obliteration because of their relationship with a mentally ill person.

I know . . . my limit is reached [when] all I think about is . . . getting her [mother] in the car and driving off a cliff because I can't stand to be with her and I feel she can't do this to people anymore. . . . In a way my identity disappeared because I was just sucked into that blackness and weirdness. . . . For me, this is my parent and I felt like she was destroying me and I hated her for that. But then I thought this is my mother and she loves me . . . I have very little sympathy, which is sort of cruel of me.

INSURANCE ADMINISTRATOR, *age forty-six, daughter/sister*

I reach some limit in terms of support. . . . I had stood by him through a number of drunk episodes and situations where he was suicidally depressed. . . . I've seen him fuck up his relationships over and over again, and I was there for him. . . . I did not cut this person off easily. But I reach the point with my own mental health [where] I could not take his abusiveness anymore. I just felt like I had to take care of myself and I couldn't [help him] anymore.

RESEARCH PROFESSOR, *age forty-seven, sister*

The breaking point that I am referring to is where I just . . . am not going anywhere with this and I think that I am not going to be able to help her, and the marriage is probably going down the drain. . . . I have tried every venue to help my wife and I am not helping her and at the same time I am destroying myself.

SHOP MANAGER, *age twenty-six, husband*

The data and analysis presented in this chapter . . . suggest that different illnesses generate distinctive caregiving contingencies. I have maintained that mental illness poses its own unique interpretive dilemmas for caregivers. With greater frequency than for most physical illnesses, mentally ill persons will reject medical diagnoses, will refuse to participate in efforts to become well, will be angry and hostile toward caregivers, and will be unable to express gratitude for the care they receive. Because these dimensions of mental illness may not be wholly apparent at the outset of caregiving efforts, perspectives on caring shift over time. Initial definitions of appropriate responsibility boundaries prove inadequate as a caregiver's consciousness about a family member's mental illness evolves. Although I am hesitant to describe caregivers' perspectival shifts in terms of predictable stages, I have identified four interpretive "junctures" in an individual's efforts to care for a mentally ill family member. Early in a patient's illness career, caregiving boundaries are expansively drawn and extensive efforts are often made to "cure" an afflicted person's illness. At some point, caregivers realize that while there may be periods of remission, mental illness is likely to be a lifelong condition. This causes caregivers to revise life expectations both for themselves and the ill person in their care. An understanding that the problem may be permanent, along with an eventual awareness of their inability to control the ill person's behaviors, moves caregivers to yet again reassess their responsibilities. In particular, they gauge their own obligation by the ill person's willingness to comply with medical treatment. Such thinking about joint responsibility often requires delicately balancing biological views of mental illness's cause with ideologies of personal responsibility. Finally, caregivers may, at some point, discontinue care. Such a decision is related to the unhappy realization that nothing they try is effective in ameliorating the problem and that continued caring will fundamentally undermine their own health and the integrity of their identity.

Throughout I have avoided such descriptors as "the caregiving role" or "the caregiving burden." Certainly, the words of respondents imply the existence of broadly held cultural scripts about the obligation to care. However, the notion of a singular caregiving role implies a consistency and uniformity of experience that does not adequately address the contextual factors that shape caregiving. The notion of a caregiving role does not sufficiently attend to how a caregiver's [experience] shifts as clarity about the character of mental illness emerges over time. Put in slightly different terms, the interview materials highlight the dialectical, processual, and emergent relationship between sufferers of any illness and those who care for them. The data illustrate that the moral boundaries of caregiving are constantly "under construction," dependent as they are on the meanings generated through the ongoing interactions of caregivers and patients.

Arthur Frank writes, "Caregivers are the other halves of illness experiences. The care they give begins by doing things for ill persons, but turns into sharing the life they lead." And later, "Eventually a balance must be worked but between what the ill person needs and what the caregivers are able to provide."[10] This chapter has been directed at learning how the lives of caregivers and mentally ill family members become intertwined and how caregivers try to sustain workable levels of responsibility. . . .

Notes

1. K. Wolff (ed.), *The Sociology of Georg Simmel* (Glencoe, IL: The Free Press, 1950), p. 395.

2. L. Duff, *The Alchemy of Illness* (New York: Bell Tower, 1993), p. 83.

3. The idea of "joint career" comes from H. Blumer, *Symbolic Interaction: Perspective and Method* (Englewood Cliffs, NJ: Prentice-Hall, 1969).

4. C. Clark, *Misery and Company: Sympathy in Everyday Life* (Chicago: University of Chicago Press, 1997).

5. C. Nippert-Eng, *Work and Home* (Chicago: University of Chicago Press, 1996), p. xi.

6. A. Strauss, "Turning points in identity." In C. Clark and H. Robboy (eds.), *Social Interaction* (New York: St. Martin's Press, 1992).

7. See T. Parsons, *Essays in Sociological Theory* (Glencoe, IL: The Free Press, 1954).

8. A. Hochschild, *The Managed Heart: Commercialization of Human Feeling* (Berkeley: University of California Press, 1983).

9. R. Bellah et al., *Habits of the Heart: Individualism and Commitment in American Life* (Berkeley: University of California, 1985).

10. A. Frank, *At The Will of the Body* (Boston: Houghton Mifflin, 1991), pp. 6, 47.

23

The Social Contexts of Illness

Arthur W. Frank

We live our lives within webs of more and less intimate and more and less equal social relationships. Those relationships shape our personal experiences and our responses to them. In turn, those relationships change in response to our shifting circumstances and reactions to them. Probably no experience better illustrates this interconnection between social relationships and personal experience than that of critical illness. The preceding selection considered how mental illness alters intimate relationships from the perspective of caregivers of the ill. This selection examines the social relational contexts of physical illness from the perspective of the ill person. In it, Arthur Frank reflects upon his own experiences with life-threatening illness and others' responses to him when he was ill. Frank draws general lessons from those reflections about the social shaping of the experience of illness and about the life-affirming importance of sharing and listening to stories of illness.

As Frank notes, when we seek treatment for illness, we become enmeshed in impersonal and subordinating relationships with medical personnel. Physicians and nurses colonize our bodies and reduce us to a disease. They are not interested in what the ill person's experiences mean to her or him but translate those experiences into generalized symptoms of a disease. Medical personnel do not treat the patient as an individual with a rich social life and history but as a carrier of disease. And, according to Frank, the more serious the illness, the more distant physicians and others seem

to become. In Frank's words, physicians also dominate the drama of illness. The patient must patiently await physicians' verdicts. The patient is continually reminded of how little they know about their own condition. The physician determines what is wrong with the patient and what the patient must do or what must be done to her or him if she or he is to get well. Physicians thereby take control over patients' bodies and, at least temporarily, over their lives.

The particular disease that physicians diagnose also affects both how others respond to the ill person and how the ill person views herself or himself. Frank contrasts his experience of a heart attack with that of cancer. Unlike the heart attack, cancer was stigmatizing both because of the visible signs of its treatment and our collective fear of the disease. The stigma of cancer can lead many friends and family members to deny the illness and the ill person, as did some of Frank's friends and family. However, others, usually those who had also experienced their own or a loved one's critical illness, acknowledged Frank's illness and affirmed their relationship with him. In either case, illnesses such as cancer change how others treat an individual and often how she or he responds to them, changing, undermining, and sometimes strengthening their relationships. It seldom leaves them untouched.

As Frank suggests, the experience of illness is not just bodily but social. How individuals respond to illness depends on how others respond to the illness, to the ill person, and how they have responded to him or her in the past. The response does not come from inside the ill person but from the web of social relationships in which she or he is and has been embedded. Frank urges the ill to share the experience of illness with others and urges the rest of us to listen so as to learn to value life for itself. He also implicitly urges us to recognize how profoundly social relationships shape our lives and experience, including the experience of our frail bodies.

I have experienced life-threatening illness twice. I had a heart attack when I was thirty-nine and cancer at age forty. Now that these illnesses are in remission, why go back and write about them? Because illness is an opportunity, though a dangerous one. To seize this opportunity I need to remain with illness a little longer and share what I have learned through it. . . .

I am not an inspiring case, only a writer. By profession I am a university professor, a sociologist with additional training and experience in philosophy, communications, and psychotherapy. These resources helped me put my experiences into words. But I do not write as any kind of expert; I present myself only as a fellow sufferer, trying to make sense of my own illnesses. . . .

Critical illness leaves no aspect of life untouched. The hospitals and other special places we have constructed for critically ill persons have created the illusion that by sealing off the ill person from those who are healthy, we can also seal off the illness in that ill person's life. This illusion is dangerous. Your relationships, your work, your sense of who you are and who you might become, your sense of what life is and ought to be—these all change, and the change is terrifying. Twice, as I realized how ill I was, I saw these changes coming and was overwhelmed by them. . . .

I have put my body in the hands of physicians off and on since I was born. But until I was critically ill I never felt I was putting my life in their hands. Life-threatening illness gave doctors a new dimension of importance for me. I had never expected so much from them or been so sensitive to their shortcomings. . . .

After [an] ultrasound a physician said, "This will have to be investigated." Hearing this phrase, I was both relieved and offended. The relief was that someone was assuming part of the burden of worrying about what was happening to me. But I was also offended by his language, which made my body into medicine's field of investigation. "I" had become medicine's "this." The physician

did not even say, "We'll have to find out what's wrong with you," which would have been a team of real people ("we") speaking to another person ("you").

"This will have to be investigated" was not addressed to me at all. The physician was speaking as if to himself, allowing me, the patient, to overhear.

"This will have to be investigated" assumes that physicians will do the investigation, but they too are left out of the phrase, anonymous. "Will have to be" suggests the investigation happens of its own necessity. Why should a physician speak this way? Because if in the course of this investigation mistakes are made (as the physician who spoke had already mistaken my diagnosis), no individual physician is responsible. The mistakes are just part of a process; they too "have to be." I imagine he spoke out of fear as well as uncertainty. He responded by making himself and other physicians anonymous. And I had to be made anonymous.

I, my body, became the passive object of this necessity, the investigation. I could imagine how native people felt when European explorers arrived on their shores, planted a flag, and claimed their land on behalf of a foreign monarch who would bring civilization to the savages. To get medicine's help, I had to cede the territory of my body to the investigation of doctors who were as yet anonymous. I had to be colonized.

The investigation required me to enter the hospital. Fluids were extracted, specialists' opinions accumulated, machines produced images of the insides of my body, but the diagnosis remained uncertain. One day I returned to my room and [found] a new sign below my name on the door. It said "Lymphoma," a form of cancer I was suspected of having. No one had told me that this diagnosis, which later proved to be wrong, had been confirmed. Finding it written there was like the joke about the guy who learns he has been fired when he finds someone else's name on his office door. In this case, my name had not been changed, it had been defined. "Lymphoma" was a medical flag, planted as a claim on the territory of my body.

This colonization only became worse. During chemotherapy a nurse, speaking to [my wife] Cathie, referred to me as "the seminoma in 53" (my room number). By then the diagnosis was correct, but it had crowded out my name entirely. The hospital had created its own version of my identity. I became the disease, the passive object of investigation and later of treatment. Nameless, how could I be a person who experiences?

The ill person actively tries to make sense of what is happening to her body. She tries to maintain a relationship between what is happening to her body and what is going on in the rest of her life. When a person becomes a patient, physicians take over her body, and their understanding of the body separates it from the rest of her life. Medicine's understanding of pain, for instance, has little to do with the ill person's experience. For the person, pain is about incoherence and the disruption of relations with other people and things; it is about losing one sense of place and finding another. Medicine has no interest in what pain means in a life; it can see pain only as a symptom of a possible disease. Medicine cannot enter into the experience; it seeks only cure or management. It does offer relief to a body that is suffering, but in doing so it colonizes the body. This is the trade-off we make in seeking medical help.

If the treatment works, the passivity is worth it. When I am ill, I want to become a patient. It is dangerous to avoid doctors, but it is equally dangerous to allow them to hog center stage in the drama of illness. The danger of avoiding doctors is immediate and physical, but if we allow them to dominate the drama, they will script it to include only disease. By saying "This will have to be investigated," my physician claimed center stage and scripted the drama to follow; the person within my body was sent out into the audience to watch passively. . . .

Relationships between patients and medical staff, whether physicians or nurses, involve people who are intimate with each other but rarely become intimates of each other. For a truly intimate relationship people need a sharing of time and personal history and a recognition of each other's differences. Medical intimacy categorizes rather than recognizes, and it is one-sided. The patient's life and body are an open book, or chart, to the medical staff. The staff sometimes share their experiences with patients, but in my memory these moments are the exceptions. More important, physicians and nurses can choose what they will tell a patient about themselves, and whether they will say anything at all. There is the real asymmetry, which becomes more complicated during moments that are critical in the patient's life but represent just another day's work for the staff. . . .

I always assumed that if I became seriously ill, physicians, no matter how overworked, would somehow recognize what I was living through. I did not know what form this recognition would take, but I assumed it would happen. What I experienced was the opposite. The more critical my diagnosis became, the more reluctant physicians were to talk to me. I had trouble getting them to make eye contact; most came only to see my disease. This "it" within the body was their field of investigation; "I" seemed to exist beyond the horizon of their interest.

Medical staff often believe they are involved in the patient's personal life. When I was admitted to the hospital, the resident doing my intake physical made a point of saying he was now getting the "social history." Cathie and I were curious to know what the hospital considered important as social history. The resident then asked what my job was. I answered and waited for the next question; he closed the chart. That was it, nothing more. What bothered us was the illusion that he had found out something. The resident took his inquiry into my social history seriously and seemed to have no sense of how little he learned. The irony of there being only one question completely escaped him. He was filling in a category, employment, to give himself the illusion of having recognized me as a "social" being.

The night before I had surgery, I was visited by an anesthesiologist who represented the culmination of my annoyance with this nonrecognition. He refused to look at me, and he even had the facts of the planned operation wrong. When he was leaving I did the worst thing to him I could think of: I made him shake hands. A hand held out to be shaken cannot be refused without direct insult, but to shake a hand is to acknowledge the other as an equal. The anesthesiologist trembled visibly as he brushed his hand over mine, and I allowed myself to enjoy his discomfort. But that was only a token of what I really wanted. I wanted him to recognize that the operation I was having and the disease it was part of were no small thing.

The kind of recognition I wanted changed over the course of my illness. While seeking diagnosis I felt that I was in a struggle just to get physicians to recognize the disease; once I got them onto the stage of my illness, the problem was to keep it my drama, not theirs. The active roles in the drama of illness all go to physicians. Being a patient means, quite literally, being patient. Daily life in the hospital is spent waiting for physicians. Hospitals are organized so that physicians can see a maximum number of patients, which means patients spend maximum time waiting. You have to be patient. Maybe the doctor will come this morning; if not, maybe this afternoon. Decisions about treatment are stalled until the doctor's arrival; nurses and residents don't know what's happening. Hopes, fears, and uncertainty mount.

When the physician does arrive, he commands center stage. I write "he" because this performance is so stereotypically masculine, although women physicians learn to play it

well enough. The patient hangs on what brief words are said, what parts of the body are examined or left unattended. When the physician has gone, the patient recounts to visitors everything he did and said, and together they repeatedly consider and interpret his visit. The patient wonders what the physician meant by this joke or that frown. In hospitals, where the patient is constantly reminded of how little he knows, the physician is assumed not only to know all but to know more than he says.

In becoming a patient—being colonized as medical territory and becoming a spectator to your own drama—you lose yourself. First you may find that the lab results rather than your body's responses are determining how you feel. Then, in the rush to treatment, you may lose your capacity to make choices, to decide how you want your body to be used. Finally, in the blandness of the medical setting, in its routines and their discipline, you may forget your tastes and preferences. Life turns to beige. It is difficult to accept the realities of what physicians can do for you without subordinating yourself to their power. The power is real, but it need not be total. . . .

Whenever I told someone I had cancer I felt myself tighten as I said it. Saying the word "cancer," my body began to defend itself. This did not happen when I told people I was having heart problems. A heart attack was simply bad news. But I never stopped thinking that cancer said something about my worth as a person. This difference between heart attack and cancer is stigma. A stigma is, literally, a sign on the surface of the body marking it as dangerous, guilty, and unclean. Stigmas began as judicial punishments in the form of notched ears, brandings, and other visible mutilations of the body. These marks allowed those who came into contact with the stigmatized person to see whom they were dealing with. The stigmatized were expected to go to the margins of society and hide their spoiled bodies. The causes of stigmatization have changed, but the hiding has not.

My heart attack damaged my body but did not stigmatize it. I became short of breath while doing tasks that were normal for a man my age. This was inconvenient and embarrassing but not stigmatizing. The damaged body only fails to perform properly; the stigmatized body contaminates its surroundings. During my heart problems I could no longer participate in certain activities; during cancer I felt I had no right to be among others. As much as I disliked being in the hospital, at least there I felt I belonged. I knew this was foolish. I didn't belong in the hospital; I was hiding there. Ill persons hide in many ways. Some begin to call cancer "c.a.," "the big C," or other euphemisms. I called it cancer, but as I said it I felt that tightness.

Heart attacks are invisible on the body's surface. To myself and to others, I looked no different. One wears cancer. My own visible stigmas were hair loss and my intravenous line. The line created a bulge over my chest, but I could conceal it. Getting dressed each day became an exercise in concealment. I wore shirts that were heavy and loose fitting and equally loose sweaters. A tie under the sweater added some bulk, and a sport coat further obscured the contours of my body. The question, of course, is why I wanted to hide the line from others. The sad answer is that I experienced the visible signs of cancer as defects not just in my appearance, but in myself.

The visible sign most closely associated with cancer is hair loss. Alopecia, or baldness, is caused not by cancer itself but by its treatment. Chemotherapy is not very discriminating. Cancer cells divide rapidly, but so do the cells of hair follicles, the intestinal lining, and gums. The drugs destroy cells in all these areas, creating their particular side effects. Thus there is truth to the folk wisdom that baldness indicates chemotherapy is working. Even knowing this, my enthusiasm for losing my hair was qualified.

My hair fell out several days after my first chemotherapy treatment. First it lost its tex-

ture and became thin, then the hair on the sides of my head rubbed off while I was washing it. I was left with a patchy-looking mohawk. It was almost Halloween, but I resisted the temptation to turn my appearance into a punk costume.

Some people try to preserve what hair they have for as long as they can. I thought I looked stranger with some hair than I would with none. Also we got tired of cleaning out the tub and drain every time I took a shower; hot water speeds up the hair loss. So Cathie helped me shave off the rest of my hair, which was truly a labor of love. That shaving marked my full passage into another stage of illness, and it was a sad thing. The loss of hair has to be mourned; it is another break with the younger self you no longer are. . . .

Cancer can do terrible things to the body, but so can other diseases. Cultural historians tell us that for at least a century cancer has been North Americans' most feared disease. This fear is explained only partially by either actual rates of cancer incidence and mortality or by the physical suffering it causes. Society, not the disease itself, makes cancer as dreaded as it is. A culture in which people are unwilling to speak the name of the disease obviously has a special fear. We do not call heart attack "h.a." Cancer alone is mythologized as some savage god, whose very name will invoke its presence. If the name of cancer is unspeakable, what evil does the person with cancer believe can be brought by its presence? Newspaper stories and political speeches use cancer as the metaphor for all the worst that can happen. The ill person then becomes the bearer of these horrors. Just as I tried to hide my intravenous line under my coat, persons with cancer want to hide their disease. Never have I tried so hard to be invisible. . . .

. . . Cathie and I had always hoped that if the worst happened, friends and relatives would respond with care and involvement. Then the worst did happened, and we no longer expected what others would do, we knew. Some came through; others disappeared. We now find it hard to resume relationships with those who could not acknowledge the illness that was happening, not just to me but to us. Those relationships were a loss. . . .

People did not act differently toward me while I had cancer, they only exaggerated how they had always acted. The compassionate ones became more loving, the generous more giving, the ill at ease more defensive. The bullies were peskier than usual, and the ones who were always too busy remained busy. Some people whom I expected to be supportive denied that I was ill at all; medical staff denied that I was anything but the disease. Others affirmed that although I was ill and illness counted, we still had a relationship. These denials and affirmations were not always easy to recognize as they happened. Denials can be subtle; after being with someone I would feel bad and not be sure why.

But illness also exaggerated the ways I acted toward others. I needed other people desperately but, feeling stigmatized, I was cautious of them. One day I would express closeness, the next day distance. My behavior caused others to exaggerate their responses to me, and in my perception of them I exaggerated their actions still further. Even the strongest relationships came under stress. This is how the ill person experiences others during illness: subtle denials, strained affirmations. . . .

The ultimate denial is by friends and loved ones who simply disappear from the ill person's life. In disappearing, they deny that anything special is happening or, alternatively, that the ill person exists at all. Either form of denial can be truly devastating. If I asked these people why they disappeared from Cathie's life and mine during cancer, they would probably say they were busy, they did not want to bother us, and they "knew" we would call if we needed anything. But what we needed was to hear they cared. Such people can't see what their behavior looks like to the ill person and those who are caring for

him or her. At Christmas, just after chemotherapy treatment, I was at a small family gathering but was still too weak to get up and circulate among the guests. Someone I had felt close to arrived, a man I had not heard from during my illness. He did not come to the end of the room where I was sitting and did his best not to look in my direction. Perhaps I was too vulnerable to go to him or just too tired, or perhaps I felt, as I do now, that it was his responsibility to come to me.

A relative tried to excuse the behavior of the people who disappeared from Cathie's and my life during cancer by saying that they "cared silently at a distance." We know cancer is hard for people to confront, but from the perspective of the ill person and caregivers, "caring silently" might as well not be happening. Their distance looks like another denial of the illness. Just as I had expected that physicians would behave differently if I became critically ill, I also expected something more from family and friends. My expectations weren't always met; although the generous became more giving, the busy were still too busy.

Those who best affirmed my experience were often people who had been through critical illness themselves or with someone close. We did not necessarily talk a great deal about specific experiences, but these friends seemed able to look at me clearly and to accept what they saw. They rarely tried to cheer me up, but being with them usually did cheer me. Human suffering becomes bearable when we share it. When we know that someone recognizes our pain, we can let go of it. The power of recognition to reduce suffering cannot be explained, but it seems fundamental to our humanity. . . .

Illness excuses people from their normal responsibilities, but the cost of being excused is greater than it appears at first. An excuse is also an exclusion. When an ill person is told, "All you can do is get well," he is also being told that all he *can* do is be ill. Telling someone he doesn't have to do anything but get well turns into a message that he has no right to do anything until he can return to his normal tasks. Again, just being ill has no value; on the contrary, the ill person is culpable.

People can't give up the idea that the ill person is responsible for the disease. If the ill person has a responsibility to get well, then presumably he is responsible for having become ill in the first place. The ideal of getting well also excludes and devalues those who will not get well.

If we reject the notion that the ill are responsible for getting well, then what is their responsibility? It is to witness their own suffering and to express this experience so that the rest of us can learn from it. Of course others must be willing to learn; society's reciprocal responsibility is to see and hear what ill people express.

A recent newspaper story suggests how little we understand about the expression of experience as both a right and a responsibility. The story's theme is the need for cancer patients to "talk openly" about their illness. This need is defined as exclusively the patient's; the story does not mention society's need to hear such talk or whether others are willing to listen. The story, a medical-psychological moral fable, contrasts two teenagers with leukemia. One teenager exemplifies openness. When a stranger in a supermarket asks her if she is ill, she raises her wig and says that she is being treated for leukemia. The other teenager withdraws from friends and physicians and refuses further treatment. Without saying so, the article implies that the "open" child will survive and the "withdrawn" child will not.

Stories like this perform a sleight of hand; they make the social context of each child's life disappear. Each teenager has a history of relationships with other people, and it is this history that produces the different behaviors. Their responses to leukemia do not just happen, the way some of us just happen to get leukemia. Whatever causes the disease, the response to it is learned. The teenagers' openness and withdrawal are responses to their experiences with family, friends, schools, and medi-

cal staff. The "open" one has been lucky enough to feel valued regardless of being ill. Her sense of stigma at home, at school, and in the hospital has been minimized. She has been allowed to feel that whatever problems her disease creates, illness is not a personal failure. She takes a risk when she shows her bald head to a stranger, but her willingness to do so results from how those around her have already responded to her baldness. The people she has met have acted in ways that allow her to anticipate support from those she now meets; at least she knows she has people to fall back on.

An ill child withdraws when he senses that people do not like what he represents. To his parents he embodies their failure to have a healthy child. He sees them being sad and guilty, and he feels guilty for having made them feel this way. To his siblings he may represent a drain on family time and financial resources. To other children his presence brings a fear of something they understand only enough to worry that it will happen to them. All adolescents experience their bodies changing, and his peers may see in the leukemic their fears of these changes going wrong. To medical staff he represents their failure to cure him. I imagine physicians evaluate their professional self-image in terms of the success of their treatments. They see themselves in a contest with the disease, and when disease persists, they have lost. They cannot think in terms of care that goes beyond treatment.

The child withdraws because he believes others would be happier if they did not have to see him. They may not reject him in any overt way, but he senses from their expressions that he is causing them pain. His withdrawal is no more the result of his "personality" (much less the lack of what some call "fighting spirit") than the other child's openness is. Each child is only looking around, assessing what support is available, and making what seems to be the best deal.

The newspaper story does not talk about the children's circumstances; instead it discusses withdrawal as "psychologically damaging" and openness as being "better adjusted." But the children are not damaged or adjusted; society is. The social group around each child has either helped her adjust or has damaged him, and those groups in turn find support or denial in other groups. The newspaper story makes these groups disappear through its use of the word "psychological," creating the illusion that each child's behavior comes out of that child, the way the leukemia comes from within the child's physiology. Healthy people comfortably accept the social myth that illness behavior is inside the person. We want to enclose the ill person in a psychological language that turns his reality inward, closing off external influence. Then we hand the whole thing to medicine.

The ultimate moral of the story is medical compliance. The open child is the good medical citizen who stays in treatment. The withdrawn child plays his sick role badly. He does not try to get well. As soon as we think of the child's withdrawal as "his" and not a response learned from others, we cannot avoid the implication that he does not deserve to get well. Although the story quotes physicians and passes itself off as "scientific," the science only dresses up the moral fable beneath. The disease is depicted as a fall from grace of a normal childhood. One child redeems herself through the courage of her openness, and the other continues falling. By making disease an issue of the ill person's morality, the story perpetuates a language of stigma.

Where is responsibility in this story? The newspaper account carries a clear implication that the ill person's responsibility is to be a good medical citizen. But the matter is not so simple. I see the children as equally responsible, though only one is happily so. The happy child lifts her wig and proclaims she is a leukemia patient. She performs a significant act of public education, and I have no wish to detract from the honor she deserves. I hope the person she spoke to came away recognizing the ill person's strength as a person, not just a patient. When she perpetuates the openness she has experienced from others, the child widens the circle of public recognition. She has fulfilled her responsibility.

But the withdrawn child is no less responsible, no less a witness to his experience. Like the open child, he reflects the attitudes of those around him. He too acts according to others' cues of what they want of him, which is to disappear. His withdrawal may result in psychological damage, but again the initial damage is not the child's. The damage is caused by those who cannot value the ill.

We may talk about the heroic individual who puts aside society's script for illness, but this is mostly talk. Even the ill person who refuses to let her actions be determined by the way she is treated bases this response on resources developed earlier. Adolescents are more susceptible to the way they are treated at the moment because their personal history is shorter. We who are older are no less creatures of the ways we have been treated; we just have a longer history against which to evaluate our present circumstances.

The responsibility of the ill, then, is not to get well but to express their illness well. And the two have nothing to do with each other. I wish I could believe that those who express their illness well have a greater chance of recovery, but I cannot. Perhaps someday we will understand more of how the mind affects the body. For now I only believe that those who express their illness live their lives fully to the end of the illness. For me this is enough—it has to be enough. If we cannot value life for itself, then we see ill persons only in terms of what they could be doing if they were well, and we see children only as what they will do when they become adults. We fail to value life as a frail bit of good luck in a world based on chance. . . .

Part VII

Structures of Social Life

S ocial life is neither random nor constantly changing. It is generally orderly, and its organization more or less enduring. It is, in other words,
structured. Individuals interactionally create and sustain social order,
structuring their social lives, but they seldom experience the resulting social structures as their own creation.

The individual is born into a world already populated by different categories of people who engage in particular kinds of activities and participate in established networks of social relationships. For the individual,
those social identities, roles, and organizations are simply there. They constitute a massive social structure that seems as inflexible, inescapable, and
constraining as the physical environment. For example, contemporary
Americans confront a world populated by blacks and whites, the admired
and the disdained, waitresses and customers, rich and poor, and the like.
Those social identities and roles largely determine with whom particular
individuals interact, how, and under what circumstances. They consequently decide in which networks of social relationships different types of
people participate. They structure individuals' experiences, how they interpret those experiences, and thereby shape their lives. Sociologists have
long been interested in the interrelationships among social structure, interpersonal interaction, and subjective experience. The selections in this
section address various aspects of those complex interrelationships. ✦

24

Preadolescent Cliques, Friendships, and Identity

Patricia Adler and
Peter Adler

Perhaps the most fundamental dimension of so-cial structure is stratification, or the relative dis-tribution of material and symbolic resources, social prestige, and power among individuals. Although a product of patterns of interaction, once stratified hierarchies are established they tend to perpetuate themselves by reproducing the patterns of interaction that sustain them. They are consequently experienced as inevita-ble and profoundly influence individuals' lives and sense of self. However, they do not shape in-dividuals' lives and selves directly but indirectly through the patterns of interaction they pro-mote. That is most apparent when stratification hierarchies are one-dimensional and the people involved are in direct contact with one another.

Clique stratification among older elemen-tary-school-age children is such a case, as Patricia and Peter Adler report in this selection. A single popular crowd tends to dominate each grade, and those below tend to recognize their lower rank. Moreover, children's confinement together at school makes it impossible for them to avoid one another, so they are constantly reminded of where they stand on the stratification hierarchy by how other children treat them. Patricia and Peter Adler describe the hierarchy of children's

cliques and the characteristic patterns of interac-tion within and between cliques that define and sustain that hierarchy. The popular group was highly exclusive and internally stratified into lead-ers and various ranks of followers. Immediately below them were the "wannabes" who imitated popular clique members and hung around them in hopes of inclusion. The large middle group showed little interest in being popular and sepa-rated themselves into small, inclusive, and inter-nally equitable friendship groups. Finally, the iso-lates were disdained by everyone, including one another, and were friendless at school.

According to the Adlers, characteristic pat-terns of interaction among and between mem-bers of the various cliques profoundly influenced the children's self-concepts, resulting in a "hierar-chy of identity" but one that did not simply repli-cate the clique hierarchy. Leaders of the popular clique thought quite highly of themselves be-cause of the attention and regard others gave them, but their followers were not so fortunate. They tended to be insecure and worried about their ranking within the clique, the possibility of losing the leaders' favor, and exclusion from the popular group. Wannabes' self-concept suffered from constantly aspiring for something that they never or only temporarily and grudgingly re-ceived. Members of the middle group tended to have more positive self-concepts because, al-though they endured the ridicule of the popular group, they had the support and affirmation of close friends. Needless to say, the isolates ques-tioned what was wrong with them even though they tried to ignore their constant exclusion and degradation at the hands of other children.

As the Adlers propose, this example illustrates the complex and indirect ways that social struc-tures influence subjective experience. Lower-ranking people in stratified hierarchies do not necessarily have lower self-esteem or more nega-tive self-concepts than those ranking above them. What and how they think about themselves de-pends on their interactional experience and rela-tionships. Social structures influence individuals' self-concepts only indirectly through the crystal-lized patterns of interaction that characterize and sustain them. Those patterns of interaction may bind lower-ranking people together in networks of mutual support and affirmation and pit higher-ranking people against one another in competitive struggles that breed insecurity and self-doubt. Those are only a couple of possibilities, but they illustrate that high social position is not necessarily a psychological blessing or lower social position a psychological curse. What the Adlers call the structural-relational foundations of identity are more complex than that. The influence of social structures on individuals cannot be assumed. It must be determined through study of the crystallized patterns of interaction that characterize and sustain particular social structures.

Preadolescents' peer friendship groups constitute one of the most profound and meaningful elements of their lives. Having a circle of close and loyal friends can signify the difference between an active, exciting, and secure social life, and one that is filled with uncertainty, insecurity, and degradation. While [there is much] research on adolescents' friendship groups . . . this topic remains underaddressed with respect to the lives of elementary school children. Yet elementary school friendship groups are not only organized, but highly differentiated and stratified. . . .

Social psychologists have identified people's self-concept or identity as the location of their feelings about themselves, the image they hold as experiencing beings interacting with the world. . . . A central theme in the literature on the self-concept is that the content and organization of identities reflect the content and organization of society (Gecas 1982). . . . Identities symbolize self meanings, and are acquired in particular situations based on people's comparison of their roles to others and others' counter-roles (Lindesmith and Strauss 1956; Turner 1956). At the same time identities form the core of our self-esteem, the emotional dimension of our selves. Identities thus specify the content and evaluation of our selves, and guide

and regulate our subsequent thoughts, feelings, and behavior, operating cybernetically to reciprocally relate the individual and the social structure (Stryker 1980).

Scholars have explored numerous sources that contribute to the foundation of identity. . . . [O]ur research highlights the role of friendship groups in affecting the formation of children's conceptions of self. Children learn, in interacting both within and between friendship groups, what kind of social competence, currency, and charisma they possess. Their efforts locate them in clearly identifiable positions along the peer status hierarchy. This analysis posits a *structural-relational* base to identity. . . . It conceives people's friendship group affiliation as forged and maintained through situational, negotiated interaction, yet crystallized into symbolic clusters of stratified roles that influence the character and interpretation of their subsequent interaction. The processual, micro perspective meets the structural perspective . . . in the crystallized interactions that are recurrent between members of these groups.

In this article we directly address the status and relational dimension as basis for inter- and intragroup stratification, showing the powerful hierarchies among preadolescent children. Drawing on seven years of participant-observation research, we outline the typologies of social groups commonly found among preadolescents. In contrast to teenagers' diverse and loosely arranged groups, preadolescent social groups tend to be smaller, less eclectic, and more socially restricted by their encapsulation in homerooms. As a result, their status stratification tends to be more unidimensional, a single popular crowd dominating over the grade and other groups lining up beneath it. We look at variations in the character, composition, and social experience associated with membership in groups at different positions, and at the consequences of friendship group membership for a social-relational hierarchy of identity. We conclude by addressing the foundations of this identity hierarchy in relation to theories of identity. . . .

Methods

This research draws on data gathered through longitudinal participant observation and interviews with students in the upper grades (third through sixth) of elementary schools. Over the course of seven years (1987–1994) we observed and interacted with children both inside and outside of their schools. The children we studied came from seven large public and five small private schools that drew from middle- and upper-middle-class neighborhoods (with a smattering of children from lower-socioeconomic areas) in a large, predominantly white university community with a population of around 85,000. As is consistent with the demographics of the community, the majority of children we observed attended public schools. The data we present describe and analyze the concerns and ideologies of this overwhelmingly middle- and upper-middle-class population. While doing our research, we occupied several roles: parent, friend, counselor, coach, volunteer, and carpooler. . . . We undertook these diverse roles as they naturally presented themselves and as deliberate research strategies, sometimes combining the two as opportunities for interacting with children became available through familial obligations or work/school requirements. As a research team, we were diverse in gender, which enabled us to interact well with both boys and girls and to employ a range of roles and perspectives.

In interacting with children we tried to develop and expand on the "parental" research role by observing, casually conversing and interacting with, and interviewing children, children's friends, other parents, and teachers. This built upon our natural parenting activities, contacts, interests, and style, taking us into locations and events populated by chil-dren. We did much of our research outside of school settings. We followed our daughter and son, their friends and enemies, the children of our neighbors and friends, and other children we met through our involvement in youth leisure activities through their school and out-of-school experiences. . . . We also gathered data inside of school settings, conducting individual and group interviews with children outside of and in their classrooms.

Though most studies of children focus on institutionalized educational settings, we gathered data in both school and out-of-school recreational settings, becoming actively involved in a variety of "afterschool" arenas such as organized youth sports, extra-curricular academic activities, and neighborhood play. While our main understanding of the setting and the behavior of the participants was derived from our years of participant-observation with nearly a hundred children of each gender, we augmented these data with more focused conversations with children. We conducted in-depth, unstructured interviews with approximately forty boys and girls from a variety of ages and social groups, culling individuals from the popular inner clique, the wannabes, the nonpopular middle circles, and isolates. . . . We then conducted selected interviews with seven teachers at three different public elementary schools to get a broader overview of social cliques and their dynamics from individuals whose experiences were more comparatively rooted in working with many different groups of children over the years. . . .

The Status Hierarchy

Children from all the schools we studied described the arrangement of members of their grade into a hierarchy based on peer status. . . . For every age level, within each gender group, and in every school with a population of more than eighty students per grade, the social system was composed of four main strata: the high, wannabe, middle, and low ranks. At the high end was the popular clique, comprising the exclusive crowd. Below them were the wannabes, the group of people who hung around the popular clique hoping for inclusion. Next was the middle group, composed of smaller, independent friendship circles. At the bottom were the social isolates who found playmates only occasionally, spending most of their time by themselves.

The Popular Clique

At the top of every grade was the popular clique. Members of this group were often referred to by themselves and others as "the cool kids." . . . Several features distinguished the makeup of this group.

The popular clique formed the largest friendship circle in the grade. In some grades it was an integrated whole, in others it was composed of interrelated and overlapping subgroups. The size of this clique grew as children advanced through the elementary grades, starting out small and incorporating new members each year. By the fourth and fifth grades it usually encompassed around one-third of the entire population. Taylor, a fifth-grade boy, outlined the relative size of the four social groups he saw in his grade:

> The cool group is at the top, say 35 percent of the kids. Then you've got the cool followers [wannabes], the ones that follow the cool kids around, they're around 10 percent. The medium group is the biggest, around 45 percent. They're all divided up into little groups, but there's a lot of them. Then the rest are in the outcast group, maybe 10 percent there, too.

Members of the popular clique had the most active social lives, both during school and outside of it, had the largest number of friends, appeared to have the most fun, and . . . commanded the most attention in the grade. They spent their time talking and whispering, running from one activity to the other, busying themselves with friends, and having dates and parties after school and on weekends. The greatest amount of crossgender interaction occurred within this group, as boys and girls talked on the phone after school, socialized at parties and movies, and "went" (steady) with each other. . . . Their activities, social liaisons, and breakups were known about not only within their own circle, but by the rest of the grade as well.

This group of people set the tone for, and in many ways influenced, the behavior of the entire grade. Miss Moran, a fourth-grade teacher, offered her observations of the popular clique's dominance:

> I see the popular clique as controlling the rest of the class, so the middle group, although they're not part of it, depending on the agenda of the powerful clique, they will respond in a certain way or they will act in a certain way. They're not totally separate. The popular clique controls everything, classroom climate, as far as who feels comfortable blurting out an answer to a question. They just have a lot of power. So that even the people who are not popular but relatively comfortable will always keep an eye on the popular clique.

Although nonmembers did not directly engage with the popular people in their activities, jokes, or games, they were aware of them and set their attitudes and behavior in relation to them.

Another feature that differentiated the popular crowd from the others in the grade was its exclusivity. Cliques are closed friendship groups, guarding their borders from undesirable interlopers. Located at the top of the status hierarchy, popular clique members accepted as friends only those judged worthy. They might dangle membership in front of others . . . but this did not mean that they would let them into the clique. Joe, a sixth-grade nonpopular boy, offered his view on the exclusionary behavior of clique leaders:

Joe: I've noticed a lot of things called clubs, and they usually have enrollment tests, and I've seen these be very demanding, and I've seen these be kind of trivial and stupid, but always it's something for the leader to laugh at the other one, and, for instance, give the leader control of the other person. But I still think that by doing that, and the other people doing that, they're kind of telling the leader, okay, I'll do whatever you want. And so then that goes into a cycle, so the leaders ask for more, they do it, they ask for more, they do it, and on and on and on.

The more individuals could be manipulated into self-debasing actions, the slimmer their chances of being accepted into the group, and the more they were taunted with futile opportunities for membership just to amuse the leaders and reinforce their influence. Most cliques admitted new members only when an existing member sponsored them and the leader approved, when people moved into the school system or neighborhood who looked highly desirable, or when power plays or fights broke out, motivating conflicting members to include and elevate newcomers who would support them. . . .

As fundamental to cliques as their exclusivity was the internal hierarchy of their role structure. Although the movement of people within a clique might be fluid and shifting, people moved among a cluster of positions that were characterized by certain regular features. Differences in popularity, power, and control separated members in positions more central to the group from those at the periphery.

The most powerful and pivotal role in the clique was the leader's. Cliques usually took the single-leader mode, with one person serving as the most forceful of the group, dominating over all the others. The leader had the power to set the clique boundaries, include or exclude potential members, raise or lower people in favor, and set the collective trends and opinions. Single-leader cliques co-

alesced around this central person and had an undisputed pyramid structure with different layers of subordinate strata arranged below.

A second form that cliques less commonly took involved two leaders. Two leaders could operate in tandem, as friends, or more independently, often with an element of competition. When two friends ran a clique together, they tended to be best friends, to operate in a unified manner on issues, and to use their combined power to dominate over others. In other cases, two powerful leaders might belong to a clique and not align themselves so completely. Ben, a fourth-grade boy, explained how his broader clique was divided into two subgroups independently led by Todd and Steven:

Todd had people who liked him more than Steven, but still liked Steven. Steven had others who liked him more than Todd, but still liked Todd. They formed together into one group and played together. But Steven had more followers than Todd, and so he was the most powerful. But he couldn't always get Todd and his friends to follow him all the time.

Just below the leaders were the second-tier clique members. This notch was usually occupied by one or two people at a time. Individuals in this position were close to the top, the next tier falling a significant step below them. Melanie, a fifth-grade girl who occupied the second tier with a friend, described the structure of her fourth-grade clique:

We had three levels, kind of. There was Denise in the center, and then me and Kristy kind of just close to the center, and then there was another level beyond us, way beyond us. But we were pretty much scared of Denise.

Individuals could attain second-tier status in one of two ways. Some came to this highly placed position because they were best friends with the leader. This type of relational status was dependent, however, on the favor of the clique leader. If friendships and alliances shifted, as they were apt to do, the person(s) in the second-tier position could be replaced with a new status occupant. Melanie discussed how she was ejected from the role she had occupied in her fourth-grade clique when her best friend, the leader, abandoned her:

> Yeah. Denise liked me best for a while, and she and I were real close. So, even though she was the leader, I was up there too. But then the boys started liking Kristy because she was a blonde. And my boyfriend dumped me and went off with Kristy. And then Denise was best friends with Kristy and was just a bitch to me: I went way down, way.

The other way people attained a position close to the top was through their own power. They might have followers who liked and supported them, they might have had high ranking before the current leader assumed prominence, or they may have contributed to unseating a previous leader.

The third clique role was occupied by the followers, who formed the bulk of the people in the group. Although less visible than the leaders, followers formed an indispensable part of the clique, as their unhesitant acceptance of leaders' actions and authority legitimated the leaders' role. They were connected to the group by their relation to one or more central members, and occupied positions that varied in status. Blake, a fifth-grade boy, described the hierarchy of members in his clique, carefully noting the gap between the two higher tiers and the followers:

> Bob was at the top, number one, and Max was number two. They were pretty much the most popular people. Then there was a jump between them and the rest of the group. Nobody was at three, but Marcus was a three and a half, and so were three other guys. A few people were at three and three-quarters, then Josh was a four and John was a four. Everyone else moved between three and a half and four, including me. It could shift a lot.

The composition of the followers, while marked by subtle shadings, was fluid and mobile, with members moving up and down as they were targeted for ridicule or favor by more leading members. Some people were secure followers, while others held a more precarious position. Yet while different followers had their own clump of immediate friends, the leaders were sought by all of the clumps.

Relationships within the popular group were significantly affected by its exclusivity, prestige, and power. . . . Popular clique members were sensitive to their social position, both within the grade and within the clique. Maintaining their membership in the popular crowd and at the highest rank within it took concerted effort. Friendships were strongly influenced by underlying status concerns. Less-popular people tried to curry favor with more-popular people in order to improve their standing in the group. They imitated leaders' behavior and supported leaders' opinions to enhance their acceptance and approval. In turn, leaders acted to maintain their own popularity and control by seeking the continuing endorsement of other group members. Actions and friendships, then, were always subtly influenced by the consequences they might have on power and position, making them more self-consciously manipulative.

Several factors undercut the strength of the loyalty bonds that might have developed among members of the popular clique, giving their relationships a fragile quality. First . . . the underlying preoccupation with rank and status created an atmosphere of competition, setting members against each other in their quest to remain accepted and well-regarded. Second, the dynamics through which leaders carved out and maintained their power undercut loyalty. One of the primary ways leaders held dominance was by alternately gracing followers with their favor and then swinging the other clique members against them. Over time, everyone had the opportunity to experience the vicissitudes of this treatment, with its thrill of popularity and its pain of derogation. This shifting treatment prevented potential rival leaders from gaining a toehold of influence at the same time as it reinforced leaders' control over clique followers. Clique members liked and admired, but also feared, their leaders and these people's power to make their lives miserable. Few had the courage to defy the leaders and stand up against them when they or their friends became the butt of teasing and exclusion. They knew that alliance with stigmatized clique members would cast them into the painful position these others occupied. As a result, they learned that the price of loyalty was severe, and that it was safer not to stick up for their friends but to look out for themselves instead. They thus joined with leaders in ridiculing other group members. A third factor weakening the loyalty bond within popular clique relations lay in the means by which clique members were chosen. Inclusion in the clique was determined by group leaders rather than by the general membership, and followers often embraced new members because they were popular with leaders rather than because they, themselves, liked them. As a result, when these individuals were cast into disfavor . . . other clique members did not jump to their defense. Tracy, a fourth-grade girl from the middle level, offered her view of the fickleness of the relationships that characterized the popular people:

> Some of the popular group, they just hang out with those people to be popular and they are not their friends; and if someone is being teased, they will just say in some instances, like, "I don't really care," since she was only in there to be popular, not really to be my friend. And for the popular group, some of the people who are really mean, they don't have that many people to help them out when other people are doing the same thing to them, since they have been so mean to others.

Members of the popular clique might thus find themselves in a group with people that they liked only slightly or not at all.

Some members of the popular clique held long-lasting relationships. Constancy among best-friend pairs existed, and connections within smaller subgroups often endured. Like status and position, however, individuals, relationships and membership within the popular clique integrated flux and insecurity with this stability. Popular people changed their friends from time to time, getting sick of hanging out with some people and moving on to others within the group. As one popular fifth-grader noted in reflecting on the fluidity of people's friendship patterns, "They move around a lot. Some of them are friends with most of the same people, but most of them are friends with different people." In addition, people moved into and out of the group. Of those exiting, some left to join with new friends, while others were expelled. Any clique member could be thrown out of the group, and this awareness was widespread, although some were more vulnerable than others. Followers were the most easily dislodged, as they had the weakest base of support and least power. They could be cast out if the leaders turned against them and turned everybody else against them. . . . But leaders, too, could be dumped if they acted bad enough. Mark, a popular fifth-grader, recalled the expulsion of one clique leader:

> Mark: Preston used to be the most popular kid in school but he got too lazy and he took advantage of kids. So kids dumped him.
>
> Q: *That's not so easy, to dump the most popular kid, is it?*
>
> Mark: Yeah. When everybody doesn't like him, it's like, See ya.
>
> Q: *And what makes everyone turn against someone?*

Mark: If they take advantage of you. Like, say, Preston used to always say, like, "Go get me that piece of paper," and if you didn't get that piece of paper you were *uncool* (inflects with overdramatic flair). People didn't like being *uncool* for not serving somebody. So he got kicked out.

Preston's expulsion was consequential and enduring. By six months later, none of his former friends had taken him back. He had fallen hard, tumbling down past the followers and wannabes into a threesome in the middle ranks. More common than these permanent actions, however, were temporary expulsions. Individuals could be kicked out by their friends and readmitted shortly thereafter. Ryan, a fourth-grade boy, talked about the vicissitudes of people's exits from and reentries into relationships with the popular clique:

It's happened to me before. I've been kicked out, and some other people. You have to watch what you wear, what you say. It's hard, but you get over it. Like just some days people are in bad moods. Other days, they let you in. So it kind of depends on mood.

Membership in the popular clique, because of its exclusive character, was thus fragile and uncertain.

The Wannabes

The cool people and their accepted followers constituted the ranks of the popular clique. Surrounding them and striving, less successfully, for acceptance were the wannabes to the popular clique. . . . Wannabes were the people referred to by Taylor, earlier, when he fairly accurately noted that the "cool followers" comprised around 10 percent of the grade. Clique members occasionally included individuals outside of their strict borders into their games or activities. In so doing, they usually invited participation from individuals with a peripheral, or borderline, status. These were people who were not explicitly members of the clique but who hung around the group hoping to be incorporated into activities. They fell below the clique followers, even those who had some friends outside the group, on the stratification hierarchy because the followers were fully accepted group members. Wannabes usually had most of their friends outside of the group, but were partly accepted by some people on the inside. Mr. Clark, a fifth-grade teacher, described their configuration:

I think a lot of those kids want to be liked by the popular kids, so therefore they are willing to hang out until they are accepted. And then when the group accepts them and lets them in, even if it's for just a while, then they feel good because all of a sudden these popular kids are now their friends. They feel good because they are getting acknowledged by somebody from that top group. If they are going to widen the group, these are the people they will turn to. They're not really in, but they're not altogether out.

In short, wannabes held the lowest status of any near-clique members.

In most instances when clique members deigned to play with outsiders, these marginals were readily available. Stacy, a fourth-grade popular girl, described why the pool of borderline people waited to be included:

The wannabes try to hang around, and try to be in, and try to do stuff that is cool, but they aren't . . . really cool. But they think they are, and if we play with them, they think they'll get cooler, so they're always ready if we want them.

In making efforts to be included, wannabes copied the behavior of the popular people. They imitated their clothing and hair styles, bought the same kind of music, and tried to use the same vocabulary. According to fifth-graders, they'd use remarks like, "Hey, man, what's up?" instead of "Hello," or they'd say they were "hanging out" instead of "playing." The thrust of these linguistic efforts was to assert their coolness through a pseudo-maturity, to act like teenagers. Several middle-rank third-grade girls secretly mocked the cool wannabe girls because they all adopted a particular mannerism of the leader, that of running her fingers through her hair and shaking her head in a distinctive manner. Every time one of them did this, these other girls would look at each other and try not to laugh, often unsuccessfully. Wannabes also tried to lure popular people into friendship with what Rizzo (1989) has called "friendship bids": overnight or party invitations, material possessions such as sport cards to trade or clothes to borrow, and trips with their family to movies or other entertainment events. For these offerings they received some attention, but it was often short-lived.

Their efforts to be included also resulted in their exhibiting some extreme behavior. They would run and fetch things for popular people, carry their messages to others, and threaten to beat up people who were out of favor with the crowd. Even when they were not being belittled, they acted out and made fools of themselves. In the children's peer culture, such vulnerability was quickly noticed and regarded as a sign of insecurity and weakness. Rather than helping them become accepted, it was taken as a sign of desperation, thrusting them further outside of the group. . . .

People around the periphery might be called upon by popular people to join their clique activities for a variety of reasons. Boys' play, which usually involved sports, commonly occurred within moderately large groups. . . . If their clique was too small to accommodate a particular sport, boys often invited outsiders to participate. Ryan, the fourth-grade boy quoted earlier, explained who participated in his clique's activities:

The more people that you have playing football or basketball or something the better, because then you have more people to pass to, and more people to block, or whatever, so they like to include, if we are playing sports, they like to include more people. But if we're just kind of hanging out, just kind of sitting around and talking, it's just the main people and no borderline ones.

In addition to simply having larger and more differentiated teams, boys often invited marginals to play with them because it was easier to play aggressively against people who were less close friends. In fact, poor treatment of the people who occupied the borderline status seemed fairly common. This involved a complex combination of acceptance and rejection: On the one hand they were more accepted than the total rejects, yet they experienced the bulk of the rejection behavior, as they were the ones who tried to be included, and were alternately welcomed and shunned. Laura, a sixth-grade girl looking back at fifth grade, tried to explain the relation of the borderline tier and their treatment by the rest of the clique:

Laura: We would pretty much treat them like shit, but they were our friends. We would treat them like shit, but we would be nice to them, and they would always just come back.

Q: *They were in the crowd but they were on the margins?*

Laura: Yeah. It kind of just depended on what we wanted. We kind of used them in a way. But we were friends with them, but sometimes we were just like "Pffft" (gestures condescendingly, like she is blowing them off). . . . Just to have somebody to be mean to; that's who we'd be mean to.

Individuals who stood outside the main circle of the group's membership thus filled the important function of defining clique boundaries, as shifting as they were, and of making all fully accepted clique members, no matter what their ranking, appreciate the benefits of their insider status. Clique members usually recognized the positive role these people filled, and although they derided wannabes, they worked to retain their attention.

When they were not playing with the cool kids, the wannabes formed smaller friendship groups of their own. They hung out alone or congregated with each other in circles of two, three, or four people. These were not strong friendship groups, however, as each person thought he or she was better than the rest and belonged with the popular clique. Wannabes also served as a buffer zone, accepting rejects from the top group. Individuals [who] were discarded by their popular friends could find inclusion there. . . .

Wannabes accepted the popular rejects to improve their own status. Most popular rejects maintained at least a few ties to people who were still popular, and connecting themselves to semi-popular people might result in their gaining more popularity. Popular people saw right through this transparent strategy. In scoffing at the wannabes, Lauren, a popular third-grader, noted, "People that we dump go into the middle, and the wannabes down there all think they are cool because they used to be cool and they are talking to them, but what really happened is they got booted." Accepting rejects diminished wannabes' status further with the people whose acceptance they sought. Yet even though the popular people scoffed at the wannabes from their high perch, when they became the object of exclusion, they valued wannabes' intermediate status. Holding some ties into the popular clique, wannabes were not as far removed from the upper echelons as were members of the middle circles. Mark, the popular fifth-grade boy, discussed the role of the wannabes in his fall from and reentry into popularity:

Q: When you got kicked out of the cool group, who did you hang out with?

Mark: I hung out with, like, the wanna-bes of the cool kids. For, like, a couple of weeks. And then my old friends said, This guy's okay, and they let me back in. And then I was back in the cool group.

Q: So you didn't go down to the medium kids?

Mark: No. I knew that if I hung out with the medium kids for too long I was never going to get back into the cool group.

Q: So the wannabes of the cool kids are higher up than the medium kids?

Mark: Yeah. Because they're like risking it, they're just enough trying to be cool that they are noticed. And sometimes the cool kids let them in. So they're kind of on the map, the edges.

Middle-Level Friendship Circles

After the popular group and its hangers-on, the main body of each grade fell into the middle rank. . . . These were the people who were considered non-popular, who didn't try to be cool or to be accepted by the cool people.

Constituting approximately half of each grade, this group was large and fairly amorphous, made up of many different subgroups and subtypes. Mrs. Perkins, a fifth-grade teacher, offered her observations of the composition of the middle group:

They're not all one group; they're very diverse. On the strong end, they're very well-adjusted kids, who may be above the popular games, who may not want to get into the teasing; they may not want to get into the power struggles, and sometimes are very stable kids. Then I've got some kids who are just not as socially astute, who don't wear the right clothes, but still [are] well-rounded kids, healthy. And then I'd say you have some computer nerd types who seem to be very socially inept, but not in a bad sense. Just in a kind of dorky sense.

People in the middle rank clustered into small groups of friendship circles. This could range anywhere from pairs of best friends or threesomes, to slightly larger groups. Middle friendship circles rarely got too large, or they tended to develop cliquish tendencies. Nicole, a fourth-grade girl from the middle stratum, described the social clumpings surrounding her:

They're the people that mind their own business, sort of people that get in a group, maybe three to five people. They just stick to that group, don't even attempt to make other friends, and nobody attempts to penetrate into the group, except for just a few exceptions.

Others corroborated this assessment, referring to the middle friendship circles as "just a slop of two or three-person groups," or as "a couple of people in a parking lot, just all standing together, talking in little groups of three, couple of them are friends."

In contrast to the popular clique's strongly tiered ranking, middle friendship circles had only a weak hierarchical system, operating between the different friendship circles rather than within them. The higher-status aggregations might accept and be considered acceptable by the popular group's rejects, such as by Preston, the formerly popular clique leader who tumbled down into the middle range. The intermediate circles minded their own business and played among themselves. The lower middle circles might be just one step above the social isolates. Mark, the popular fifth-grader, characterized these latter groups by saying, "These are the kids who have the guts not to just hang out in the sandbox, but are still pretty far down."

Most nonpopular people recognized their middle-level status and accepted it. They shared the realization that they were not the type to be included in the elite circles, offering various accounts to explain this. Some described themselves as too quiet or too shy to be the "popular type," while others described themselves as "the type that other people don't like." If they were ever unsure about this, the popular people made sure to reinforce these perceptions by picking on them and deriding them, both individually and in groups.

One of the strongest features that differentiated middle friendship circles from the cliques found at the upper end of the status hierarchy, apart from their size, was their willingness to accept people. Whereas popular groups were exclusive, maintaining tight control over their boundaries and keeping important members in and undesirables out, middle friendship groups more readily welcomed people who wanted to join in or play with them. Timmy, a third-grade boy from a middle circle, described how his group accepted outsiders to play:

Sometimes, a lot of people who really aren't in will get together and form a big game of basketball and they will let anyone come in because they are a lot nicer, so if someone gets ejected from a group, they usually come over. We've had a lot of people from the popular group come over to the unpopular people because they want to play a game and the popular people usually cheat or don't treat them fairly.

Another characteristic that differentiated middle friendship circles from cliques was their democratic leadership structure. While cliques had clearly defined leaders and a strongly articulated hierarchy of internal stratification, friendship circles were much more egalitarian. They were not identified by a single core person, no one person led the decisions about what they should do or think, and no leader dominated the delineations of the borders. Mary, a fifth-grade nonpopular girl, talked about the democratic nature of the leadership structure in the middle circles:

> Usually, someone would just suggest something, and usually we either like it or we, if we don't like it, then somebody else would suggest something else. We don't usually have a person that chooses what we're gonna do. We just all of a sudden choose something and we see if everybody else likes that idea.

The friendship bonds in the middle circles were also distinctive from those of the popular clique. . . . Relationships in these circles were often more intimate and intense than those in the popular or wannabe groups. This was partly due to the small size of these friendship circles and the frequency of members' interactions. Popular people had many more people with whom they regularly socialized, and they tended to regard all members of the clique as their friends. Wannabes had a weak and diffused group that never coalesced, being focused instead around the popular clique. In contrast, members of middle circles had many fewer individuals with whom they interacted. Marty, a fifth-grade nonpopular boy, offered his observations about the difference in friendship relationships between the middle and popular levels:

> I would probably say that if you were a member of the smaller groups that you would have more one-on-one experience, and you would probably get even closer and closer. And if you're in the more popular groups, you probably wouldn't stay with one person for very long, and you'd keep on moving from subgroup to subgroup, because the whole group is larger. They're like groups of twenty or thirty kids.

The lack of competition for status stratification within the nonpopular circles also affected the character of their relationships.

People did not have to be as conscious about who was in better favor, about losing favor, or about getting picked on by their own friends as they did in the popular clique. Consequently, they had a greater degree of loyalty and trust among their friends and felt freer to discuss sensitive issues. Ariana, a nonpopular fourth-grader, talked about the nature of the relationships in her circle:

> I have lots of friends that are not in the popular group, that are in the middle, so I always knew that there was someone to turn to. With my friends you can always express your feelings and say that this person is really hurting my feelings, and then maybe we will all talk it over. There's no one who is mean in our group, who thinks she's better than the rest of us or who lords it over all of us. So we know we can really count on each other, like if anyone makes fun of us, we know that our friends will always stick up for us.

Like the popular cliques, middle friendship circles exhibited both turnover and constancy in their relationships and membership. Some people remained in their groups or friendships over long periods. They bonded tightly with friends, spent considerable time at school, home, and recreational activities together, and developed close relational ties. Others developed an orbit surrounding a certain group that they moved into and out of over a period of time. Adam, a fifth-grade boy, described the ebb and flow of his relationship with his core middle friendship group:

> *Q: So would you say that these groups are fairly stable, or that this kind of breaking off and re-forming is more common?*
>
> Adam: I would say it's in between. I have gone from together for two years, broken up for a week, together for two days, broken up for three weeks, over and over.

Q: And when you get back together, do you go back to the same people or do you go into another group?

Adam: Same people.

. . . Individuals had a greater degree of social security, however, because there were not the kind of capricious, demanding leaders ready to expel them from the group. People left middle circles because they got into fights with other people in the group, or because they did not want to do what others wanted to do. Sometimes two people would gang up on one, leaving that person isolated. Other times a larger group would get fed up with someone. Nick, a fifth-grade boy from a middle circle, described the collective group dynamics associated with people's exit from such groups:

Q: So one could get kicked out of a group like that?

Nick: Right, but only if most of the people got agreement from each other. They could use persuasion, they could use insults, they could use reasons why the other people would want that person kicked out. They could make up stories, which I've seen a lot, about the other person, they could spread rumors, and so forth. But what they can't do, which the popular people do, is to have one person decide that you're uncool and just kick you out on his own.

Social Isolates

Past the ranks of the middle circles, the small groups of people who had two or three friends, were those individuals who had no real friends. These loners, drifters, "dweebs," and "nerds" occupied the bottom stratum of the grade, and stuck out in everyone's view. . . . Other kids noticed the social isolates and clearly differentiated them from the middle people at the low end of the ac-

ceptable realm. These were the people who wandered around the playground at recess, making up a game by themselves, talking to an adult playground aide, or just hanging around the sidelines. At lunch they ate by themselves, as nobody wanted to sit with them. When it came time to form into groups they were chronically left out. When asked to reflect on the reasons for people's isolation, Tracy, a middle-rank fourth-grade girl, and Adam, a middle-rank fifth-grade boy, offered these independent observations:

Tracy: There are some kids who just go outside and try to hang around people, but they don't really fit in with them, so they just stay there but not talk.

Adam: They're different. It's a lot like segregation. If you're different, you go off and sit alone.

Tracy's and Adam's remarks indicate that people perceived these individuals as apart from the rest of the grade, mostly because of something inherent in their own nature. They were different; they did not fit in with the others. Something about the way they looked or the way they acted deviated from the norm. . . .

Although they spent considerable time alone, social isolates longed to be included in the interaction and play of their classmates. From time to time they would make attempts to join in various conversations and games. These efforts occasionally yielded some success, they [were] being taken into activities, tolerated or somewhat included in the lunchroom, or made part of a collective action strategy. Ryan, the popular fourth-grade boy discussed earlier, explained the way people without friends could get included in the activities of the popular group:

There are some people who have no friends, or maybe sometimes one or two, and sometimes they just sit down and read in the classroom or sit outside and kind of don't do much. But sometimes even if we don't like the person, sometimes the really unpopular kids get included just because they're needed in a game, and say six people are needed and maybe we have five people. They want one more people to make teams even, then they can ask someone who is just sitting around if they want to do something.

In a case like this, the added people would feel included for the duration of the game. Timmy, the middle-rank third grader, talked about a friend of his who was very isolated. He discussed his friend's attempts to be included in interaction with others:

Q: *Does he try to be included in groups?*

Timmy: Yeah, he does that a lot, and he usually gets included, except he's not really part of it, like if someone's having a conversation with someone, he tries to be a part of it, but he doesn't really know anything about it, so he's not part of the whole thing. I think that's what makes him feel lonely because he's not part of [being] with anyone, he's not part of, like, the group of kids, really.

More often, however, isolates' attempts at inclusion were unsuccessful. When they summoned the nerve to ask other people if they could join them in play, they would be laughed at and treated poorly. People made sport out of teasing them and picking on them. While popular leaders degraded their followers, followers degraded the wannabes, and wannabes degraded the middle people, everyone could safely offset their own humiliation by passing it on to individuals at the lowest stratum. No one came to these individuals' defense, and everyone could unite in feeling superior to them. People called them names, started fights with them, made fun of their clothing and appearance, and talked

about them as having "cooties." . . . People rebuffed those labeled as losers from play with hardly a care for their feelings. Terry, the fourth-grade middle-level boy, discussed the way loners were rejected cruelly by groups of people, particularly those at the popular rank:

At recess they [isolates] maybe just go out and talk or something to other people, but they don't really play games or anything. They try to, but some people don't let 'em. Sometimes people say, just to be mean, that the game is full, when there's only five people or ten people, but then they let other people in after.

After a series of such encounters, the potential benefit of social interaction tended to no longer seem worth the risk of degradation and humiliation. Mary, the middle-level fifth-grade girl discussed earlier, offered her observation of what frequently happened when social isolates made repeated unsuccessful attempts to be included with others:

Q: *And do people at the bottom ever try to get in with other friendship groups?*

Mary: Once or twice, and then the people shatter their self-confidence so they don't try again.

Such encounters often led loners to retire further into seclusion and cease interacting with people. They ate lunch by themselves every day, often stayed inside at recess, and went home right after school. People who experienced prolonged or severe isolation sometimes invoked the ultimate recourse: They transferred to another school.

While isolates spent much of their time alone, they drifted in and out of some relationships and sought out people in lesser positions they could more safely befriend. . . . Most of the people in the bottom stratum were aware of the presence of other social isolates. These individuals could be found drifting by themselves in the playground or being taunted and teased by more socially successful people. When people clumped together into groups for play, the loners were left hanging around the edges. In many cases, however, rather than forming their own groups, isolates' reaction to others in similar situations was mutual rejection. They were no more eager to befriend these outcasts than were others in the class. Meredith, a third-grade social isolate, expressed her lack of interest in her social peers:

> Q: *So what might you do then at recess?*
>
> Meredith: Well, sometimes I look at how people are playing, it makes me feel good. Sometimes I just play a simple game by myself. Just games by myself that I make up.
>
> Q: *Are there other kids that are also playing by themselves?*
>
> Meredith: Well, I have to say there're sure to be, but very little. A very little group of them.
>
> Q: *So, do you ever play with any of them?*
>
> Meredith: No, not really.
>
> Q: *How come? You don't like them?*
>
> Meredith: Sort of that. There's different reasons.

Miss Moran, [a] fourth-grade teacher, explained why she thought social outcasts shunned each other:

> Q: *Is it a stigma to be friends with another person down there?*
>
> Miss M: Yeah. Well, for instance, if I were to say, "Okay, make groups," and there's two or three of them standing around, and they have to be in a group with each other, it's obvious to everyone that those are the leftovers. And some of

them are knowledgeable enough to not want to be in that situation, although a few seem so out of it that they are oblivious.

Despite the potential stigma, there came a time when social isolates got desperate and made friends. They could no longer stand the loneliness and boredom, and they overcame their feelings of distaste for other pariahs. They managed to put up with annoying behavior and overlook the teasing of high-status people, even if it increased when they joined with other isolates. Tracy, the fourth-grade middle-level girl, described how some loners joined together:

> Tracy: Eventually some of them will meet someone else that they kind of like, and then they will start hanging out with them, and then after about half the year it will become a little group of two or three people.
>
> Q: *So people don't always stay by themselves forever?*
>
> Tracy: Right, eventually some of them find someone, or they just get so lonely they force themselves to be with someone.

Despite their stigmatized status in the peer social hierarchy, most individuals were able to turn somewhere, even if it was not in their school or in their grade, to find companionship. Having some friend, even if that person was of lower status, was critical. Otherwise isolates spent all their time after school and on weekends watching television, playing video games, reading books, participating in organized afterschool activities, and hanging around with their parents. Forming friendships with younger people was easier for social isolates, because they were often able to leave the stigma of their outcast status behind and adopt a high status in a new school or neighborhood crowd on the basis of their advanced age and grade. Roger, a severely isolated third-grader, described his most steady companion:

> Mostly I play with my next door neighbor, Eric; he's two years old. I really help out with him, 'cause his dad's usually at work, and his mom has arthritis. So when I come over it's a big help for them. They go run errands. Mostly Eric wants me to come along. They say it's okay because they could get more done when they're doing errands when I'm around. Like, I take care of Eric, tell him not to take the things off the shelf, it helps them a lot. 'Cause if he sees something when they're not looking, then they have to go there and put it back, and then they have to find the area again, and he does it again, a lot of junk. So I help out a lot.

Roger was able to find a regular playmate by going outside of both his school's status system and his age system. When pariahs made inroads into new crowds, their acceptance was sometimes short-lived, however, as news travelled, and their outside friends discovered their pariah status. This often resulted in their being dropped.

The Identity Hierarchy

People's location at the various levels of the social stratification hierarchy led them to vastly dissimilar interactional experiences. The size of their group, the type and intensity of its activities, the nature of the relationships within it, and its relative super/subordination to other groups were all colored by this ranking system. These features led people to develop feelings about themselves, or self-concepts, that were anchored in their social-relational placement. This resulted in a second form of stratification: the identity hierarchy.

Individuals in the elite, leader stratum of the popular clique sat atop the identity hierarchy. They compared other people unfavor-

ably with themselves, regarded their own activities as the most exciting and fun, and believed that everybody was envious of them. They basked in the attention they received from the rest of the grade, and were proud to think that they could convince anyone they wanted to follow them or to join their group. They considered their interest a prize bestowed on those lower than them, to be received with eagerness. Some people believed that cool leaders had the most positive self-identity merely by virtue of their position. . . . Mary, the fifth-grade middle-level girl, expressed this relational viewpoint:

> Well, I think that with the leaders of the big group, they usually have the most self-esteem because there's no one else to make fun of them; there's no one else for them to be competing with unless there's another person that's a leader, and they can really do anything that they want, so I think they have the most self-esteem.

Yet other members of the group did not share this positive identity. Followers suffered through their subordination to the leaders, by being bossed around, derided, and stigmatized, and by frequently worrying about losing their position in the group. Despite how they presented themselves to outsiders, Blake, the popular fifth-grade boy, noted that "the people in the top group are insecure also, especially the followers, because you get made fun of, then your self-esteem goes." Mr. Clark, the fifth-grade teacher, explained why this came back to affect the self-concepts of all members of the popular group:

> Your self-esteem, the day-to-day worries about self-esteem, are going to be much more pronounced with the popular group, even if you're on the top. You're going to have setbacks, and your popularity's such a big issue that you're always feeling either attacked or you're feeling on top of things.

After those in the popular clique, members of the middle friendship circles had the most positive self-identities, lacking both the social pretensions and the status insecurities plaguing the popular clique members. Individuals in the middle group generally felt good about themselves. While they had to endure status derogation from popular clique members, they derived significant security from the loyalty of their friends. They did not have to worry about coming in to school and finding that all their friends had been on the phone the night before and had decided that they were out of favor. They could trust their friends to stick up for them and not betray them. They knew that fights might occur, but that they would be over, and that their friends would still be faithful to them. Mary, the fifth-grade middle-level girl, talked about the feelings of confidence she derived from the relationships within her group:

I would rather be in my own circle of friends and be, everyone's nice and everything, instead of having to deal with what the leader says and being bossed around, having to do what they say and do to be in that group. It makes me feel like I am worth something, instead of always having to sell myself to be popular.

People in the middle level held many shared views about members of the other strata. There was some degree of envy towards the popular clique, both for the abundance of their friends and the excitement of their activities, yet their feelings towards them were predominantly negative. They often noted the way the cool people acted as though they were superior, and referred to them as having "swelled heads" and "big egos," and as being "full of themselves." . . . [T]hey rejected the popular people's attitude of superiority toward them. Terry, a fourth-grade middle-rank boy, offered his views of the popular crowd:

Q: *What do you think of the kids that think they're cool?*

Terry: Mostly they're just jerks.

Q: *Why is that?*

Terry: 'Cause they treat other kids a lot more mean, they pick on kids, pick on little kids, they screw up loads. They spray paint on the walls and stuff. They like to get in trouble.

Middle people reserved their harsher criticism for the wannabes, however. As did the popular people, they regarded the wannabes as weak and insecure. They watched as the wannabes unsuccessfully imitated the popular people. Ariana, the fourth-grade girl noted earlier, offered a commonly held negative view of the wannabes:

Q: *What do the middle people tend to think about the wannabes?*

Ariana: Well, from my experience, we'd just laugh. We'd laugh at how they are being dragged around by other people.

Q: *They are making fools of themselves for people?*

Ariana: Right. How they will go to any extent to be with those people. What makes them happy? All they want is to be with those people. But they never get the job, 'cause they always get shoved out. There's no sense of, there's nobody being themselves.

Thus, while members of middle friendship circles suffered from being ridiculed by the popular people, they enjoyed an autonomy that the status-seeking wannabes lacked. Individuals at the middle rank derived a great deal of security and self-esteem from the loyalty of their friends. They might not have had the status and excitement of the large popular group membership and the most privileged activities, but their relationships flourished because they were internally focused and supportive, and their identities were strong.

Although the wannabes ranked higher on the status hierarchy than the people from the middle rank, they paid a high price for it in self-esteem. The wannabes' position in the social status system was unique. They were defined not by their own social group, but by their relation to a group to which they only marginally belonged. They were not members of the popular clique, yet neither were they independent of it. They forged their behavior, attitudes, and relationships by fervently looking up to the clique above them, hoping for a trickle-down of attention that would draw them into greater favor. They desperately aspired to be accepted by people who toyed with them, using them for their own benefit. They suffered by always desiring something that they never really attained, enduring the frustration of experiencing it temporarily only to lose it again. They knew that the people they wanted as friends did not want them, and mocked, teased, and derided them. Scott, a fourth-grade wannabe, explained the contradictory treatment he experienced from the popular people:

> With the popular group you get to do more stuff, you get to have more play, you get to have more fun at recess, you get to play with all the people that are kind of up on theirselves, have big egos, and really think they're great. You play with them but they don't—in football they never pass to you, and in basketball they never really pass to you, so there're advantages to being in the popular group but there's a lot of disadvantages to being in the popular group.

But the wannabes did not have secure membership in their own friendship circles to use as a safety net. If they were to let go of their clutch onto the popular crowd, they knew that they might tumble into the isolate rank. They therefore clung to the liminality of the in-between, striving for acceptance but never fitting in. Mr. Goodwin, the fourth-

grade teacher, analyzed the way this made them feel:

> The ones who are really feeling the pain are the ones who're hanging onto this popular group, but I think they're the ones who are really low in self-esteem. They don't seem to enjoy anything for the sake of it, they're just kind of analyzing things from the outside. And therefore, if they're not part of the group, they're trying to figure out what's wrong with them. . . . I guess the point I'm really trying to make is that there's that small group of kids who don't fit in either group; they're not happy. They're not happy with themselves, they're not happy with where they are, and they try so hard. . . . I would say they have some social problems, identification problems. They don't know who they are really yet, or where they want to be.

Wannabes' intense status aspirations thus yielded them intense status insecurity. They suffered the continual anguish of domination and exclusion at the hands of the popular clique. They lacked the loyalty and trust of the true friendships found in the middle circles. Their identities were stronger than that of an isolate only by virtue of the companionship and social activities in which they were able to engage, which gave them some feeling of self-worth.

At the bottom of the status hierarchy, isolates were also at the bottom of the identity hierarchy. Most isolates recognized the effects of their low social status on their ability to form relationships and be included in social activities. Although they tried not to think that there was something wrong with them, their wonder about themselves sometimes surfaced. Mr. Clark, the fifth-grade teacher, expressed his concerns about the feelings and identities of the social isolates:

> I think some who are down there, who are kind of nice kids, are feeling quite a bit of pain. They probably sit there now and then and say, What's wrong with me?

Why does no one . . . I know where I am,
I'm way down here with these weird kids.
And I think there's some pain there. I've
asked myself this question, Why are these
kids down there, and I'm sure that they
probably do too.

Unlike people in the other three strata,
who all had some group that they disdained,
whether higher or lower, the pariahs held
contempt for no group. Their feelings about
the people in the other groups fell into one
of two categories: envy and dislike. Many isolates envied the social standing and relationships accompanying location in the higher
strata. They looked longingly at the activities
of the popular crowd and wished they were a
part of it. Rudy, the third-grade isolate, expressed his feelings about the cool kids:

> Rudy: They do a lot of cool things at re-
> cess. They dig in the sandbox,
> they always get in a long group of,
> like a lot of bunch of kids, like in
> different grade classes, but then
> they break up to another group
> of kids.
>
> Q: *So you think that would be better to
> be in a bigger group of kids?*
>
> Rudy: Well, it would be more comfort-
> able, for me anyways.

Social isolates' exclusion from nearly all
social activities, coupled with the extreme
degradation they suffered at the hands of the
popular and wannabe crowds, left them with
the lowest sense of self-worth. Social isolates'
exclusion, rejection, ostracism, and limited
scope of activities carried a heavy toll on their
feelings about themselves. They tried to de-
ceive themselves into thinking they had
friends or that they were accepted, but they
could only sustain this image for so long.
They occasionally tried to manage their
stigma by ignoring it, but they ultimately had
a hard time disguising their pariah status, and
had to accept their disvalued identity.

Conclusion

Elementary school children's social experiences are strongly affected by the location of
their friendship group along the continuum
of status and popularity. Those who attain
membership in the elite popular clique enjoy
the benefits of a more expansive social life
and a superior position relative to other
crowds, but they pay for this with a greater
anxiety about their place within the group.
Wannabes, forming the periphery around the
popular crowd, have the opportunity to participate in some popular-group activities and
thus derive a measure of reflected status, but
they never attain membership in the group
that they fervently seek. Most people fall into
the largest category, composed of smaller,
mid-level friendship circles that garner low
prestige and suffer degradation from the
popular people, but whose members care
less about their social ranking and enjoy secure relationships with friends. At the bottom of the grade are the social isolates, combining pariah social status with a virtual lack
of viable peer friendships. The identity stratification of the groups is thus somewhat different from the hierarchical arrangement
based on status; the top and bottom strata
remain constant but the positions of the middle rank and wannabes are reversed. Members of middle circles, by virtue of the loyalty
and support they derive from their strong
friendship relations with their peers, hold more
positive self-concepts than the higher-status
wannabes, despite the latters' circulation within
the broader confines of the popular clique. . . .
[T]he stratification of [girls' and boys'] peer societies into typological groups and the interactional dynamics both within and among
these groups appear to be fairly consistent for
members of both genders. Preadolescent boys'
and girls' social worlds are thus different in
some ways and similar in others. While we
have noted that boys and girls stratify themselves in popularity according to different factors (Adler, Kless, and Adler 1992), there is

more similarity to the friendship structures and interactions across gender than up and down the status hierarchy. Boys and girls are thus both competitive and cooperative, hierarchical and leveling, and they compose their peer societies into stratified groups that are fundamentally comparable.

This research asserts the importance of social position to identity. A question raised, however, concerns the precise nature of the relationship between social position and identity. Our data suggest that the hierarchical ordering based on popularity and status is not strictly replicated in the identity arena. This varies from the direct stratification of status ranking and self-esteem found by sociologists who have studied the prestige hierarchy of occupations (Hodge, Siegel, and Rossi 1964) and the prestige hierarchy of ethnic and racial groups (Bogardus 1959). In addition, most social psychologists, as Rosenberg (1981, p. 603) has noted, have "tended to take it for granted that those ranking lower in the various status hierarchies would have lower self-esteem than the more favored members of society."

The structural-relational hierarchy of identity inferred by our data is more complex than this, as it is grounded in two complementary elements, status and relationship. . . . Together, these two elements combine to stratify groups and their members along the identity hierarchy, as Table 24.1 illustrates.

Table 24.1 **A Hierarchy of Group Identity**		
	Status	**Relationship**
Popular	+	− +
Middle	−	+
Wannabe	− +	−
Isolate	− −	− −

. . . The importance of status elements to identity [reflects] . . . structuralists' concern with individuals' self-conceptions as based on social position and connected to social structure. The relational elements of identity are rooted in the emergence and negotiation of individuals' reciprocal friendship relations, thus evoking an interactional base in the social situation. Yet children's definitions and evaluations of self do not arise out of a combined patchwork of structural and processual influences, but are firmly grounded in a more integrated *structural-relational* foundation. This foundation is rooted in . . . the crystallized interactions that bind groups of people together and at the same time distinguish them from each other. The crystallized interactions that repeatedly characterize children's interactions both within and between groups are what mark the groups' character, distinguish them in relation to one another, and set the members' identities. These include such patterned interactions as the repeated exclusion of wannabes by the popular clique members, the failures by the social isolates to find acceptance with any group, and the non-hierarchical, leaderless character of the middle friendship circles. . . .

References

Adler, Patricia A., Steven J. Kless, and Peter Adler. 1992. "Socialization to Gender Roles: Popularity Among Elementary School Boys and Girls." *Sociology of Education* 65: 169–187.

Bogardus, E. S. 1959. "Race Reactions by Sexes." *Sociology and Social Research* 43: 439–441.

Gecas, Victor. 1982. "The Self-Concept." *Annual Review of Sociology* 8: 1–33.

Hodge, R. W., P. M. Siegel, and P. H. Rossi. 1964. "Occupational Prestige in the U.S." *American Journal of Sociology* 70: 286–302.

Lindesmith, Alfred R., and Anselm L. Strauss. 1956. *Social Psychology.* New York: Holt, Rinehart and Winston.

Rizzo, Thomas A. 1989. *Friendship Development Among Children in School.* Norwood, NJ: Ablex.

Rosenberg, Morris. 1981. "The Self-Concept: Social Product and Social Force." Pp. 591–624 in *Social Psychology,* edited by Morris Rosenberg and Ralph H. Turner. New York: Basic.

Stryker, Sheldon. 1980. *Symbolic Interaction: A Social Structural Version.* Menlo Park, CA: Cummings.

Turner, Ralph H. 1956. "Role Taking, Role Standpoint, and Reference Group Behavior." *American Journal of Sociology* 61: 316–328.

25

The Contrasting Agendas of Black and White Sororities

Alexandra Berkowitz and Irene Padavic

Individuals' actions are guided by their definitions of situations in which they act, but those situations are not of their own choosing. Their social structural positions largely determine the circumstances under which they must act. Also, their interpretations of those circumstances are not of their own invention but are based on cultural and subcultural meanings borrowed from the social groups to which they belong. Cultural and subcultural understandings historically emerge, in turn, from particular groups' collective attempts to cope with the circumstances that they face. Social structures thereby influence individuals' actions both directly and indirectly. They historically shape the cultural and subcultural meanings individuals use to interpret their current circumstances and largely determine what those current circumstances are. This selection illustrates both the historical and more direct influence of social structures on individuals' interpretations of situations and actions with the contrasting examples of black and white sororities in the southeastern United States.

For some time, as this selection points out, varied sources informed young, middle-class white women that their future depended on "getting a man" who would support them. Few African-American women had that luxury. Racial discrimi-

nation made it impossible for most African-American men to earn the income necessary to support a wife and family. Marriage was not as economically significant to African-American women as it was to more advantaged white women. Most African-American women, whether married or unmarried, worked and learned to rely on female kin and friends for support. The image of the strong, self-sufficient black woman consequently became widespread in the African-American subculture, an image many young African-American women were encouraged to and attempted to emulate.

Today, most young American women, whether black or white, expect to work during much of their adult lives and recognize the importance of economic self-reliance. Although that expectation and recognition is consistent with long-standing understandings in the African-American subculture, young white women tend to be caught between the conflicting cultural scripts of economic self-reliance and dependence upon a man. Those different cultural understandings, shaped by the different social structural circumstances of white and black American women, are reflected in the different organization and agendas of the black and white sororities described in this selection. The members of the white sororities devote much of their efforts to organizing social events that encourage dating or pairing with a man. They also ritualistically celebrate milestones in romantic relationships. In contrast, members of the African-American sororities devote far more of their energy to community service and building social networks that might support them in their future careers. In the authors' words, white sororities emphasize "getting a man," and black sororities, "getting ahead." As the authors argue, those different emphases reflect the different structural positions of young black and white women in America, even though the distance between those positions may have shrunk in recent years. Members of these black and white sororities continue to bring different historical frames of reference to their current circumstances—frames of reference that were shaped by the past social structural divide between the lives of black and white American women. This is but one illustration of how social structures shape individuals' lives and the cultural meanings that guide how they live them.

Young women on the threshold of adulthood must pass through a maze of conflicting expectations about how a woman should organize her life. For white women, traditional societal expectations encourage her to devise a plan that relies on men for financial support, and thus, even at young ages, many concentrate significant amounts of energy in the pursuit of a man. . . . Yet, these young women receive a concurrent message about the importance of economic self-reliance in an era of rising rates of divorce and single-parent families. More glamorous versions of this message emphasize the joys to be found in careers.

Young black women also receive the cultural injunction that feminine success entails marriage to a man, but such messages are tempered to a greater extent than they are for white women by admonitions for independence. As Collins (1991, 42) discovered when asking African American women students about lessons their mothers taught them about men, most answers stressed self-reliance and resourcefulness: "Go to school first and get a good education—don't get too serious too young"; "Make sure that you can take care of yourself before you settle down"; and "Want more for yourself than just a man." Higginbotham and Weber's (1992) quantitative analyses led them to similar conclusions. Whereas between 18 and 22 percent of white parents stressed marriage as a primary goal for their daughters in the sample, the corresponding figures for black parents were only between 4 and 6 percent. Even more tellingly, whereas between 56 and 70 percent of white parents stressed the need for an occupation to their daughters, 94 percent of black parents stressed this, leading the researchers to conclude that, "Unlike white women, black women are typically so-

cialized to view marriage separately from economic security, because it is not expected that marriage will ever remove them from the labor market" (Higginbotham and Weber 1992, 429). . . .

In this article, we examine one arena in which young women collectively try to make sense of these conflicting scripts and shape their biographical trajectories: college sororities. We would be wrong to assume that young sorority women are simply passive recipients who internalize messages promoted by their communities. College life offers young people on the brink of adulthood their first extended brush with extrafamily life and the opportunity to develop alternative orientations to social scripts (Sanday 1990). Corsaro's (1997) . . . theory of interpretive reproduction, although concerned with children's sense-making processes, applies to sorority members as well: These young people collectively interpret, negotiate, and often refine and transform the information they receive from the adult world rather than passively internalize it. Sorority women's impetus for making such interpretations and refinements is to create sense out of conflicting messages they receive. On one hand they are taught that finding a man is the key to organizing life, and on the other they are taught that having a career is the key. To interpret and respond to this conflicting information, they draw on historical frames of reference, which are based on their understandings of the past experiences of people they define as similar to them. Each sorority member actively contributes to the group's ideology according to her own historical frame of reference, and thus sorority culture is produced and reproduced.

Our interview data show that the results of this process of interpretive reproduction have led to sorority structures that vary dramatically by race: While white sororities are structured to largely ignore the career message and concentrate on the more traditional goal of pairing ("getting a man"), black sororities are organized to facilitate economic self-sufficiency ("getting ahead," in the words of these women) and to contribute to the betterment of the black community. We attribute these variations to the different historical and structural realities that have shaped black and white women's lives and the way these young women interpret and incorporate these orientations into their sororities. . . .

This article shows that sorority membership has different meanings for black and white members. In turn, these meanings stem from current marriage and labor force realities and from historical differences in the races' orientations to family, work, and community. These current and historical factors appear in the sorority structures that these young women help to create as they respond to differing emphases on how a woman should organize her life.

Background

Historically, black women did not have the option afforded middle-class white women of following the dictates of the dominant gender ideology that called for female passivity, domesticity, and reliance on men for their livelihood. As a result of racial discrimination, black men often could not provide the sole support for a household, thus leading to married black women's much higher rates of labor force participation compared to white women's (Amott and Matthaei 1991; Dill 1986). Due in part to the scarcity of good jobs at good wages for men, African American culture came to rely on an extended family system in which women provided material help to one another (Cherlin 1992). This emphasis on familial ties with women has lessened the economic basis of the husband-wife bond that is so salient in the white culture (Cherlin 1992). These factors—men's marginality to the family's economy and women's high labor force participation—allowed the image of strong, self-sufficient

black women to become a culturally available category for young black women to emulate today.

The history of work and family life is not the only heritage that valorizes strength in black women: Political examples can be found in the civil rights struggle. . . . According to Jones (1985), general grass roots support for the movement came from ordinary women, many of whom were "militant . . . in the community, outspoken, understanding and willing to catch hell, having already caught [their] share" (p. 280). Here, again, the notion of "strong, black womanhood" was a culturally available category for young women within the black community.

Modern structural conditions further encourage black women's greater reliance on paid work over marriage as a means of support. Black women are less likely than white women to marry, stay married, or remarry (Cherlin 1992). In fact, black women spend a total of 22 percent of their lives in marriage, compared to 43 percent for white women (Cherlin 1992). The chances of marriage for highly educated black women are even . . . slim[mer]: The ratio of single, black college-educated women to men is two to one (Strong and DeVault 1994). African American college women's own observations of family life, added to the media's popularization of these facts (along with those about black, female, single parenthood) probably further encourage self-sufficiency.

Turning to college women in particular, Holland and Eisenhart (1990) found that black college women anticipated being the most viable economic contributors to their future families and that they believed it was unwise to rely on men too much. While women of both races at the campuses they studied spent a great deal of time on thoughts of romantic relationships, the black women were less focused on finding a man. Holland and Eisenhart speculated that, like the white women, black women may have desired a male-centered life but were forced to adjust their aspirations to accommodate a reality that offered fewer marriageable men.

African American sororities were founded to provide an avenue for engaging in community service and general racial uplift (Davis 1982, 93; Giddings 1988). Their direct precursor was the black women's club movement, which flourished at the end of the eighteenth and beginning of the nineteenth centuries (Glover 1993, 8–9). . . . These clubs, which led to the founding of the first black sorority in 1908 (Davis 1982), sought to improve the lives of vulnerable members of the community by creating leaders to be involved in black community development. Giddings's (1988) history of Delta Sigma Theta described how the sorority's founders sought to provide a training ground for women leaders who could then influence the political and social issues of the day. . . . Indeed, the sorority's first activity was participating in the women's suffrage march on the eve of President Wilson's inauguration in 1913. In the 1930s, the Deltas established traveling libraries in the South, where libraries were forbidden to blacks. In the 1960s, many chapters participated in freedom rides and sit-ins, where their involvement was so great that it inspired a new project: fund-raisers to obtain bail money for members. More recently, the sorority has helped create housing for elderly and handicapped African Americans. The community action orientation of this and other African American sororities (Davis 1982, 93) is congruent with the cultural image described above of black women as the strong, vocal center of the African American family and community. Finally, African American sororities have been instrumental in furthering members' careers (Glover 1993), an attribute that our interviews show is highly salient to current members.

Historically, the cultural dictates, desirable attributes, and structural conditions that white women faced have been very different. The cultural model that society has favored for them has promoted passivity, subservience, and domesticity—attributes that are a far cry from a model of strong womanhood. A white woman's worth traditionally has been tied very closely to having a man, and, until recently, middle-class white women have expected to rely on men, rather than the labor market, for financial support (Cancian 1989, 19). Economic dependency gave rise to the cultural correlate that women who could afford to do so should shape their lives based on intimate relationships (Blumstein and Schwartz 1989, 125). . . .

The second wave of the feminist movement in the 1970s allowed young women to experience greater educational opportunities and some freedom from oppressive gender expectations. These cultural trends were paired with changing economic and social conditions, such as a rising divorce rate and a stronger financial need for married women's income. As a result, more white women have entered the labor force, and fewer are relying on men for financial support. A new message that encouraged independence was now available to college women.

Despite these major changes in the social and economic world that young white women face, a preference for the gender relations of the 1950s seems to hold for some college women.

Holland and Eisenhart (1990) claimed that for the white college women in their sample, "the business of being attractive and maintaining relationships with men was as salient to them as it was for their mothers and grandmothers." The peer groups they analyzed valued neither academics nor female friendship bonds but instead concentrated on male-female romantic relationships. Most of the white women in their study considered other women to be peripheral; they turned to them to conduct the main activity of finding a man, and these friendships were at the mercy of the demands of boyfriends and romantic pursuits (Holland and Eisenhart 1990).

The tendency to concentrate on men is even more pronounced in white sororities, which encourage an ideology about gender arrangements that is based on the woman-homemaker, male-breadwinner cultural model described above. Predominantly white sororities were founded for many reasons: to guarantee an exclusive dating and mating pool (Fass 1977, 201), to provide supervised housing (Treichler 1985), and to offer access to campus political power (Horowitz 1987).

Risman (1982) noted that, ultimately, sorority life helped to socialize members to be male centered rather than career oriented. These organizations have maintained some 1950s ideals well past that decade, even though on graduation many sorority women will be working in the labor force and coping with career demands, underemployment, single parenting, and possibly poverty (Risman 1982). While it is unsurprising that in 1964 sorority members were found to have a greater "need" for heterosexual relationships than did "independents" (women unaffiliated with sororities) (Jackson and Winkler 1964, 380), it is surprising that in 1991 sorority women were still far more likely than independents to endorse male-dominant-female-submissive attitudes (Kalof and Cargill 1991). Risman (1982) similarly found that sororities encouraged traditional orientations by teaching members that "their success depends not upon their personal achievement in school or sports, but upon their relationship to boys" (p. 240).

Despite their endorsement of traditional gender arrangements, modern sorority women . . . are not planning lives that are exclusively family centered. Handler (1995) pointed out that larger structural changes are not lost on white sorority women and that sororities are changing with the times, for example by offering workshops on career networking. Moreover, sorority women tend to support positions associated with feminism, such as abortion rights and equal pay (Handler 1995). Clearly, white sorority women do not simply accept a traditional set of sorority ideals and incorporate them in an undiluted way into lives that will, for most, include labor force participation. Their task of reconciling these two competing orientations is more difficult. Nevertheless, we argue that, just as black sorority members' cultural legacy affects their current orientations to men and careers, white sorority members' cultural legacy of relying on men as a way of organizing life after graduation still affects theirs.

Data and Method

[Our] data consist of twenty-six open-ended, in-depth interviews that the first author conducted with sorority members at two state universities (one predominantly black and one predominantly white) in the Southeast. Interviews were divided evenly between white and black sorority sisters. The white women represented eleven different national sororities (out of sixteen on campus), and the black women represented four (which comprise the total number of black sororities on both campuses). . . .

Members of all four black sororities on the two campuses were interviewed. (These four represent the four national sororities; we interviewed five members from one sorority, four from another, and two each from two more sororities.) However, the large number of white sororities necessitated selecting a sample. To ensure representativeness, our sample consisted of four women from high-status sororities, five from medium-status, and four from low-status ones. The sorority-ranking scale is one that is understood by members of the Greek system (Risman 1982), who use the terms, *strong, moderate,* and *weak.* . . .

Comparisons between the white and black sororities in this study are more complex than is perhaps immediately apparent. The issues that enhance this complexity include membership size, sorority location, and the presence of sorority houses. The white sororities had between 100 and 150 members, compared to between 10 and 45 members of the black sororities. In addition to their larger membership, the white sororities occupied residential houses, which did not exist for the black sororities on either campus. Finally, the white sororities were located on only one of the campuses identified in the study, while the black sororities are represented on both campuses. Due to the variation in responses that could result from such differences, we consider the implications of these issues in the analysis.

Because this study is confined to campuses in the southern United States, our results might have been different if other areas of the country had been included. . . . [W]e cannot make claims about the national representativeness of our study, but we note that while geographically limited . . . research cannot be considered definitive, it can add to our understanding by illustrating the processes by which sororities encourage romantic or career orientations.

Finding Men

While reporting percentages based on such small sample sizes ($n = 13$ for both black and white women) has the potential to be misleading, we find some differences dramatic enough to merit reporting. When we asked women, "How important is it to have a man in your life?" 54 percent of the white women (seven women) compared to only 15 percent of black women (two women) reported that it was very important. One white woman spoke for many interviewees:

My roommates and I are constantly going on about why guys aren't calling us. . . . I feel weird if no guys call me during the week, whether it be a friend or a guy that I don't even like, but just to have a male call me. I need that.

Another spoke strongly of her need for her current boyfriend:

It is the most stable thing that I have ever had in my life. . . . I don't seem to get along well with female friends; I don't know why. Having a boyfriend is something that I know is stable and I feel like I always have something and it is probably the only thing that keeps me sane.

These women's emphasis on relationships with men may reflect the ideology still current with many middle-class, white women in our society that, to some extent, women's worth rests on having a man.

Most black women in our sample did not share this orientation, perhaps because of the lack of eligible black men or because of the cultural proclivities laid out above. Fifty-four percent of the black sorority women (seven women) reported that men were not very important to them. For many, what was important was exploring other avenues for achievement, particularly being strong and independent. As one said,

A man falls after my religion, my sorority, and definitely after my school work. It is something that I would like to have but it isn't that important because I am all into this woman's lib thing and I feel that I can do things by myself. . . . So, if I have a man and he is bringing me down I would just rather be by myself.

In fact, for some black women, the sorority provided an alternative to a dating relationship:

Having a boyfriend is not really that important. That is another reason why I joined the organization because I am not one of those types that always has a man on her arm every day. I knew that by joining the organization, regardless of whether I had a boyfriend or not, I could go to any city and have a bond with most of the sisters that I would contact and be a part of activities with.

As these quotations illustrate, these women are not repudiating the idea of relationships with men; indeed, 15 percent (two women) claimed that having a man was very important. . . . Holland and Eisenhart (1990) found that college women of both races were obsessed with romance, emphasizing that notions of romantic fulfillment are probably not identical for white and black women, however. . . . While we cannot shed light on the *meaning* that romance holds for them, we do argue that young black women do not look to sororities as the place to pursue that life goal.

We found sharp differences in the extent to which white and black sororities set up events to encourage male-female pairing. All white interviewees reported the existence of formal ceremonies for a sister who reaches a milestone in a romantic relationship. The most common milestone is being "laveliered," whereby a fraternity man gives the sorority woman a charm to wear as a necklace that signifies the strength of their romantic involvement. Increasingly serious milestones are "pinnings" (when a fraternity man gives his fraternity pin to a sorority woman), getting "promised" (when a woman receives a promise ring as a symbol of an impending engagement), and engagements. Sorority members announce these events at an emotionally charged ceremony known as "the candlelight." In this ritual, each woman keeps secret her laveliering or other new status until the night of the ceremony. The sorority members form a circle and pass around a candle while singing a special sorority song. The candle passes once for sisterhood, again for a lavaliere, a third time for a pin, then again for a promise ring and a final time for an engagement. A woman who has achieved a milestone blows out the candle at the appropriate time, announcing to the chapter the relationship event. Sorority women highly value and eagerly anticipate the ceremony. Clearly, candlelights are a formal, structured event wherein a woman can be publicly praised for

her attainment of a man. One sister explained, "It is considered an honor in our sorority to [participate in] a candlelight ceremony. It is considered a very happy and lucky thing to have found a man." In contrast, she described academic achievement as far less important an honor in her sorority. In another sorority with an elaborate candlelight ceremony, the award to the woman with the highest grade point average was significantly less emotionally charged: She was awarded a bag of potato chips.

Indeed, women described the candlelight ceremony as a major highlight of sorority experience, something that many strove to obtain. One woman engineered her boyfriend's joining a fraternity for this express purpose:

> The whole thing was that I wanted my boyfriend to join a fraternity so that I could be laveliered. I finally got to have a candlelight and it was the neatest thing. Everyone was so proud of me. I got thrown into the middle of the circle and jumped on and hugged. I had been waiting for a long time and everyone knew that, so when it finally came, it felt really good.

In contrast, the concept of laveliering does not even exist in the African American Greek system; other romantic milestones receive little commemoration. Only five of the African American sorority women reported any ceremonial acknowledgment of romantic relationships, and these ceremonies were only small add-ons to weddings, where the bride "gets chanted by the sorority with a special hymn." The African American interviewees said that romantic milestones mattered only insofar as they contributed to the happiness of a sister, and they saw no reason to have a ritual response to various romantic events.

The emphasis on a social life centering on interactions with men is further exemplified through the high number of date functions that the white sororities sponsored. All but one sponsored four or more a year, usually events like a formal, a semiformal, a hay ride, a grab-a-guy (where women must find a date within a few hours for a party), and a crush (where each woman invites two men to a sorority party). While a date is not mandatory for crushes, they are mandatory for the other events. According to one member, "the idea is that you bring a date or you do not go."

Informal parties that do not require a date are held in conjunction with a fraternity and are usually at the fraternity house. All "socials" of this nature are open only to the participating Greek organizations. The atmosphere is bar-like: The music is loud and there is little to do but mingle and dance. This format emphasizes pairing with a man for the evening and perhaps for the night. To help facilitate this, women and men drink a great deal to "relax and interact better with each others." Because most sororities do not allow underage members to drink at fraternity houses, they usually stage a "pre-party" that allows all members to drink. According to one sorority member, "Everyone goes to the pre-party, gets drunk and then goes to the social. At the social, there is music and dancing. A lot of people hook up with a guy or at least try to."

These parties facilitate pairing partly because that is what sorority members want: About half reported that access to parties with fraternity men was their prime reason for joining, and many said that meeting men was the best part of their overall sorority experience. In the words of one woman, "It is necessary for us to have so many social events because it is the expectation of a lot of girls to come into a sorority for the social life. They want to meet guys." Another woman reported, "I wanted to see what it was like with the fraternities and all the socials. I knew a lot of people that went to them and I wanted to have that fun also."

Again in sharp contrast, African American sororities did not actively encourage heterosexual unions. Two women reported that their sororities had no date functions at all,

and the remaining eleven reported only one formal "ball" a year. These balls are part of the sorority's "week," a time dedicated to several events centered on sorority unity, including step-dance shows and seminars. These events do not require dates. One woman explained, "No, you do not need a date [for the ball]; a lot of my sorors [sisters] have gone stag. You can come with your best girlfriend if you want to."

African American sororities' informal social functions (functions that do not require a date) are also quite different from their white counterparts'. The sororities, in conjunction with another sorority or a fraternity, sponsor parties held at a nightclub and open to the public. The goal is to raise funds for the sponsoring organizations. Sororities discourage or forbid drinking at these events because they believe that excessive drinking will impede the goal of fund-raising. Other informal gatherings—some with fraternities and some without—range from board-game tournaments to pot-luck dinners. One woman described her sorority's social events as follows: "Some are done in conjunction with a fraternity but most of them we do on our own. We do things like picnics, bowling or spades tournaments." Another described a typical social with a fraternity: "We might have a pizza party or something to get to know each other better and have a closer relationship. It would be at someone's house and we would just chill out and have a good time."

This evidence implies that black sororities place less emphasis on coupling. Many of the activities, such as game tournaments, actually discourage breaking off into pairs and instead promote group dynamics. The wide variety of social activities that the sorority engages in gives the women a chance to interact and bond with women as well as men. We note, however, that the small size of the black organizations as compared to the white ones may account for some of the above differences. For example, the small size of black sororities may have necessitated nondate social gatherings such as bowling parties or card tournaments. If half the sisters of a small, twenty-person sorority do not have dates, a formal party requiring dates would be doomed, unlike a one-hundred-member sorority. Similarly, black sororities' small size (along with the lack of black sorority houses on these campuses) may have been a factor in their hosting open parties at public clubs rather than events that were members-and-guests only. Thus, black sororities' small size may have exacerbated their tendency to downplay man hunting.

This section has shown that the white sororities had a stronger commitment to activities that facilitate romantic relationships. The high number of date functions creates a situation in which women are continuously searching for eligible dating partners. This puts pressure on women to find a steady partner to alleviate the anxiety of finding a different man for each event. The informal social functions do not require dates, but their format and high rate of alcohol use encourage coupling. The candlelight ritual offers women a status-oriented and tangible reason to strive for a romantic relationship. Sorority events for the African American women are usually more than ways to meet men, as exemplified by the fund-raising open parties and by the informal social functions that are more group oriented.

Engaging in Community Service

In keeping with their founding principles, African American sororities were much more community service oriented than their white counterparts. The black women described community service as a central and meaningful part of their sorority experience, while white women generally viewed it as a way to facilitate their social lives.

About half of the African American women cited community service as one of their main reasons for joining, while none of the white women reported it as a motivation. The African American women saw their sorority membership as a means to "give back to the community," a way of "uplifting" themselves and their black brothers and sisters:

> I joined because I saw the women as strong black women in the community and I saw their purpose as being a way to uplift the black community. I just wanted to help contribute to that because some of the characteristics that I saw in them, I saw in myself. I consider myself a strong black woman and I am always willing to help someone.

Moreover, all of the black women identified community service as the activity that took up most sorority time. This dedication to social improvement went beyond peripheral involvement in a high number of service projects. The women celebrated the idea that their sororities were originally founded to serve the community, and prior community service experience was a membership prerequisite: "If you do not have community service coming in . . . you are showing them that you are not a dedicated person."

All interviewees were able to give detailed descriptions of the local projects their sorority was involved in, ranging from tutoring children in underprivileged areas or serving dinner at the local homeless shelter to sponsoring blood drives and community cleanups. In addition, the national chapters have designated community service projects that they require local chapters to be involved in: "we have a national project . . . which is geared towards unwed mothers. We go to schools and have centers that teach prenatal care, help educate them as well as give them some career training." As these examples make clear, most projects centered on direct participation with the groups they seek to help—often in the black community—rather than on raising funds to send to charity.

In contrast, the white sororities were far less focused on community service. Most had one philanthropic event a year, usually a fund-raiser. Fund-raisers were first and foremost social events, such as dance contests or sports tournaments, that brought many Greek organizations together. Sororities sent the money to a charity designated by the national chapter, a format that does not allow for direct involvement with the people receiving the money. Beyond this main yearly activity, some sororities conducted smaller fund-raisers and projects, but interviewees did not talk about community service with anything approaching the enthusiasm that was typical for the black interviewees nor was community service experience a prerequisite for membership. One sister described her group's involvement:

> We donate money to a pediatric ward. It is not a big part of the sorority life. It happens once a spring. It's a lip-synch contest. . . . The social part is big, but as far as helping the children, we basically send the money away. The purpose of the philanthropy is not a big part but the way to get the money is a big deal.

In sum, the black sororities were far more deeply involved in community service at the practical and ideological levels than were the white sororities.

Enhancing Careers

Sorority membership tends to be a life-long commitment for African American women; graduation signals a woman's transfer to the graduate alumnae chapter where participation is often more intensive. The African American women we interviewed said that their sorority affiliation was part of their identity and would remain with them throughout the course of their lives as "a source of help and support." In contrast, white women's sorority membership was limited to their college years; although opportunities to continue involvement after college graduation existed, no woman planned to do so. Besides

valuing the sister relationship in its own right, black women expected to realize a career payoff for their membership. White women had no such expectation. We examine these themes below.

Relationships with other women were the *sine qua non* of black sororities, and the organizations ensured continuity with programs that span the phases of the life course. Auxiliary groups of the sororities are made up of junior high and high school girls who participate in many of the collegiate chapters' activities and attend seminars that the graduate chapters host on study skills, etiquette, or on the sorority itself. Girls involved in auxiliary chapters usually seek to join the sorority when they reach college. One college woman said of her membership, "I was in the [adolescent group] for eight years so I knew that when I came to college what sorority I was going to pledge."

Graduating from college was by no means an end to sorority involvement; in fact, many anticipated that participation on the graduate level would be the most fruitful portion of their sorority experience. Graduate chapters sponsor the adolescent groups, are active in the collegiate chapter by donating funds for seminars, and sponsor their own community service projects and social functions. Yet, it is the career connections that these groups offer that our African American interviewees felt to be the most significant part of sorority life after college. All thirteen anticipated that the sorority would be crucial in career networking:

> It will open doors. . . . The unwritten rule is that you are supposed to help that person [a sorority sister]. They are to come first. If she is a member, I should be able to get that position regardless of my credentials but my credentials should be up to standards before I come to her.

The idea of seeking strong, professional black women as role models and possible mentors was a recurrent theme for these college women, who spoke of ties with graduate chapters as a way to gain access to successful African Americans:

> When I came here [to college], I looked at the women who were already members and they were perfect. They had an aura about them and I wanted to be like them. The women in the graduate chapter are mostly professionals, a lot of teachers, administrative women. My pediatrician is a member.

White women's sorority involvement is almost exclusively at the collegiate level; white sororities do not sponsor adolescent auxiliary groups, and graduate chapters are inconsequential to career building. Because white members view sorority membership primarily as a means to a productive social life centering on men, few women planned to participate in alumnae chapters. Indeed, "too much" involvement indicates that a woman is still living in the past:

> After college, I would not mind going to rush a few times but I do not want to be one of those ladies that is like the chapter advisor and is always hanging around the house like they are still in college.

Another concurred:

> I think it is important that when you are young that you do things to get them out of your system. I don't want to be thirty and feel like I have to go dancing and drinking at a bar with my girlfriends.

As for career connections, few white women believed that the sorority would benefit their careers. One woman described why she joined:

> I don't think it will help me get ahead. . . . I think that the main thing that it will do for me is that I will be able to look back and say that at least I tried it and I did not miss out. I don't think I will have any contact with it when I graduate.

We do not mean to imply that white sorority women were not career oriented; they were. In describing their futures, the majority of both black and white women presented plans that included a husband, children, and a career for at least some period of their lives. Unlike the black women, however, the white women did not regard sorority membership as a means to that goal. It would help only remotely, by increasing a woman's chance of being selected for positions in high-status, Greek-dominated campus organizations that "look good on a resume."

Both white and African American sorority women claimed that sisterhood was an important reason for joining the sorority, but the meaning of sisterhood set the two groups apart. For the black women, sorority sisterhood entailed a lifelong commitment that they expected would remain salient to their identities even after their collegiate years. In contrast, the white women regarded sorority sisterhood as part of the college experience rather than part of their lifelong identity. Moreover, unlike their black counterparts, they did not expect a career payoff for membership. In sum, for both groups, sororities were the key group for facilitating important relationships that are difficult to forge alone. For white women, these relationships are with men; for black women, they are with other women and with black communities.

Summary and Conclusion

White sorority women in this sample regarded sorority membership as a way to lead a productive social life that they hoped would enable them to get a man. The structure of their sororities encouraged this pursuit of romantic relationships by sponsoring candlelighting ceremonies, frequent formal date events, and informal functions whose barlike ambiance and high rate of alcohol consumption facilitated coupling. Despite this emphasis, these women are not living in a time warp, and most had career aspirations: Ten of the thirteen mentioned careers as figuring in their future, although they acknowledged that sorority life will do little to further that goal. In contrast, African American women's sorority participation centered on community service and career advancement. Community service was the largest activity that the sororities engaged in and was a meaningful part of all phases of participation (adolescent, collegiate, and graduate). Interviewees described the role of sorority graduates in career networking as perhaps the most beneficial aspect of sorority life. Moreover, black sororities did not offer much institutional support for romantic relationships: They offered virtually nothing akin to candlelightings, sponsored few date functions, and centered informal social functions on group activities. Not surprisingly, most of the black women in this sample did not feel that having a romantic relationship was a necessity.

These different orientations affected women's sense of sisterhood and levels of commitment to the sorority. African American women's more intense involvement was fostered by opportunities to participate throughout the life course; in comparison, white women's orientation toward the sorority was much more phase oriented, limited to their college years, although their feelings toward it were strong during those years. The two types of sorority appear to be structured to facilitate different agendas: for white women, short-term participation geared to meeting men, and for black women, long-term participation geared to furthering both individual careers and the uplifting of the race through community projects.

We argue that the key to understanding the differences between the groups in their orientation to sorority life lies in their differing current structural positions and historical frames of reference. For the black sororities, historic images of strong, independent, black women and the modern statistical reality of black female marriage and poverty rates have shaped the sorority structure as well as the ideology and activities of their members. In the same way, the white sororities are responding to their cultural heritage, which has emphasized relying on a man for support and remaining within the domestic sphere. These differences influence the current structures of the sororities and the way that individual women interpret their own experiences.

Yet, white sorority women are in an odd position because this model no longer fits the modern social reality that prescribes labor force attachment for women (Risman 1982). The attempts of white sororities to put "new wine into old bottles"—to offer modern young women the man-centered solution to the question of how to organize a life—still seem to be successful: Sorority membership has been on the rise for the past two decades (Lord 1987). The conflict with sorority ideology that would seem to be inevitable as white sorority women become more independent and career oriented may have been averted by cosmetic changes such as sorority seminars on careers. We speculate, however, that white sorority women compartmentalize their career and their romantic goals and use sororities to further only the latter. This is not to say that the women themselves are not career oriented; it is to say that their sororities are not structured to offer ways to help them achieve that goal.

In sum, both sorority systems grew from different socio-historical roots. They stemmed from an earlier era and reflect those traditions today. We do not mean to glamorize the black sorority structure, because it has its own set of problems, especially in the area of hazing. Yet, it seems that the black sorority structure is more in tune with the probable labor force and family prospects of modern college women. Many features of black and white women's lives are converging. For the first time in history, the labor force participation of white women is equal to that of black women (Reskin and Padavic 1994), signifying the reality that most women—including white sorority alumnae—will be part of the workforce. White family patterns are also coming to more closely resemble African Americans' as white women are increasingly likely to be single parents (Saluter 1992). It seems that African American sororities' orientation toward career building is more in step with the reality of the modern college woman. The historical frame of reference that young black women bring to sorority life is more consistent with the demands of contemporary society. To ensure its survival, the white sorority structure will probably shift to accommodate the larger social changes that increasingly manifest themselves in individual members' lives.

This study . . . furthers the project specified by West and Fenstermaker (1995, 13) of understanding the workings of race and gender in situated contexts. As they note, to capture what it actually means for a person to simultaneously experience these categories, research must focus on the particular mechanisms and situations that produce or mitigate inequality. In this study, we have identified mechanisms that perpetuate or mitigate the inequality that stems from women's dependence on men: Candlelightings, formal date functions, and alcohol consumption encourage it; multigenerational membership, career networking, and an absence of date functions mitigate it. Drawing on Corsaro (1997), we note that sorority women have participated in the creation of these practices, and they have brought to that enterprise their understandings of the past experiences of their mothers, grandmothers, and other people of their own gender and race. Because of different historical frames of reference, black and white women create very different understandings. In showing how black and white sorority members collectively attempt to make sense of given scripts and arrive at interpretations and strategies for dealing with them, we have documented how these different understandings play out in one small setting. . . .

References

Amott, T., and J. Matthaei. 1991. *Race, gender and work: A multicultural economic history of women in the United States.* Boston: South End.

Blumstein, P., and P. Schwartz. 1989. "Intimate relationships and the creation of sexuality." In *Gender in intimate relationships: A microstructural approach,* edited by B. J. Risman and P. Schwartz, 120–129. Belmont CA: Wadsworth.

Cancian, F. M. 1989. "Love and the rise of capitalism." In *Gender in intimate relationships: A microstructural approach,* edited by B. J. Risman and P. Schwartz, 12–25. Belmont CA: Wadsworth.

Cherlin, A. S. 1992. *Marriage, divorce, remarriage.* Cambridge, MA: Harvard University Press.

Collins, P. H. 1991. "The meaning of motherhood in black culture and black mother-daughter relationships." In *Double stitch: Black women write about mothers and daughters,* edited by P. Bell-Scott, B. Guy-Sheftall, J. J. Royster, J. Sims-Wood, M. DeCosta-Willis, and L. P. Fultz, 42–60. New York: Harper Perennial.

Corsaro, W. A. 1997. *The sociology of childhood.* Thousand Oaks, CA: Pine Forge.

Davis, M. 1982. *Contributions of black women to America,* vol. 2. Columbia, SC: Kenday Press.

Dill, B. T. 1986. "Our mothers' grief: Racial ethnic women and the maintenance of families." *Journal of Family History* 13: 425–431.

Fass, P. 1977. *The damned and the beautiful: American youth in the 1920s.* New York: Oxford University Press.

Giddings, P. 1988. *In search of sisterhood: The history of Delta Sigma Theta Sorority, Inc.* New York: Morrow.

Glover, C. C. 1993. Sister Greeks: African-American sororities and the dynamics of institutionalized sisterhood at an Ivy League university. Paper presented at the Eastern Sociological Society Meeting, Boston.

Handler, L. 1995. "In the fraternal sisterhood: Sororities as gender strategy." *Gender & Society* 9: 236–255.

Higginbotham, E., and L. Weber. 1992. "Moving up with kin and community: Upward social mobility for black and white women." *Gender & Society* 6: 416–440.

Holland, D. C., and M. A. Eisenhart. 1990. *Educated in romance: Women, achievement, and college culture.* Chicago: University of Chicago Press.

Horowitz, H. L. 1987. *Campus life: Undergraduate cultures from the end of the eighteenth century to the present.* New York: Knopf.

Jackson, R., and R. C. Winkler. 1964. "A comparison of pledges and independents." *Personnel and Guidance Journal* (December): 379–382.

Jones, J. 1985. *Labor of love, labor of sorrow: Black women, work, and the family from slavery to the present.* New York: Basic Books.

Kalof, L., and T. Cargill. 1991. "Fraternity and sorority membership and gender dominance attitudes." *Sex Roles* 25: 417–423.

Lord, M. J. 1987. "The Greek rites of exclusion." *The Nation* (4 July): 10–13.

Reskin, B. F., and I. Padavic. 1994. *Women and men at work.* Newbury Park, CA: Pine Forge Press.

Risman, B. J. 1982. "College women and sororities: The social construction and reaffirmation of gender roles." *Urban Life* 11: 231–252.

Saluter, A. 1992. "Marital status and living arrangements: March 1992." *Current Population Reports,* Series P-20-468 (December), p. xiii.

Sanday, P. R. 1990. *Fraternity gang rape: Sex, brotherhood, and privilege on campus.* New York: New York University Press.

Strong, B., and C. DeVault. 1994. *Human sexuality.* Mountain View, CA: Mayfield.

Treichler, P. 1985. "Alma mater's sorority: Women and the University of Illinois 1890–1925." In *For alma mater: Theory and practice in feminist scholarship,* edited by P. A. Treichler, C. Kramarae, and B. Stafford, 5–61. Champaign: University of Illinois Press.

West, C., and S. Fenstermaker. 1995. "Doing difference." *Gender & Society* 9: 8–37.

26

Working and Resisting at Route Restaurant

Greta Foff Paules

People in social structural positions of power can impose systems of meaning and action on others. Administrators, executives, and managers of varied organizations impose systems of meaning and action on their employees, clients, and, often, customers. For example, executives and managers of chain restaurants commonly mandate how tasks will be divided and performed in minute detail, what employees can and cannot wear to work, and how they should interact with customers. Yet, such social structural power has its limits. Those who are subject to it seldom passively accept its dictates and definitions of situations. Rather, they subtly, and sometimes not so subtly, resist the efforts of those in more structurally powerful positions to shape their conduct and thinking. They draw upon local sources of power in those efforts and protect their sense of self from organizational definitions of who and what they should be.

In this selection, Greta Foff Paules illustrates such resistance among waitresses at a chain restaurant that she calls "Kendelport Route." As with most chain restaurants, executives at corporate headquarters attempt to organize and standardize operations at each restaurant. They determine how the restaurants will be designed, equipped, and divided into "stations." They decide what dishes will be offered and how they are prepared. They dictate what employees can and cannot

wear at work and how they perform their respective tasks. As Paules notes, they also attempt to promote an image of food service work as servitude. Waitresses are forbidden from eating, drinking, or merely sitting in the presence of customers. They require waitresses to wear plain uniforms that set them apart from customers. They encourage the unilateral use of first names in interactions between customers and waitresses by requiring waitresses to wear name tags or introduce themselves by first name. These and other conventions are symbols of servitude that encourage customers to treat waitresses as mere servants, and as Paules observes, many customers do.

However, waitresses at Route reject this symbolism of service and refuse to think of themselves as servants. Rather, they see themselves as soldiers locked in battle with a rude public. They see themselves as private entrepreneurs earning tips through their own skill and savvy. They feel little loyalty to the company because of the minimal wages they earn. Rather, they believe it is the company's responsibility to provide them with a favorable environment for their business enterprise—earning tips. Most of the waitresses' earnings come from "their" customers rather than the company, limiting its perceived power over them. Waitresses at Kendelport Route also benefit from the severe labor shortage in the area. Managers need experienced, skilled waitresses more than the waitresses need a job at Kendelport Route. They can simply take their business of earning tips elsewhere.

Waitresses draw upon these sources of local power and effectively resist the company's implicit definition of them as servants. Although they often beguile and defer to customers in attempts to earn handsome tips, waitresses are not taken in by their own performances. Rather, they take pride in their ability to "get" tips from customers. They also combat customers' blatant attempts to belittle and intimidate them. They refuse to be treated as submissive servants.

The example of the Route waitresses illustrates both the power of social structure to shape our everyday social lives and its limits. Like the Route waitresses, those in social structural positions of greater power often pressure us to feel, think, and act as they see fit. They often determine the circumstances under which we must act. However, we seldom passively accept their dictates or our circumstances. Rather, we respond to them, sometimes resisting them, sometimes reluctantly bending to them, and often doing a bit of both. Social structural arrangements clearly shape our everyday lives, but they do not determine them because they are, at least in part, of our own making.

This is a study of a small group of women who wait tables in a family-style restaurant in New Jersey. It is a study of women who are neither organized nor upwardly mobile yet actively and effectively strive to protect and enhance their position at work. It is about women who refuse to submit unquestioningly to the dictates of management, to absorb the abuses of a hurried and often hostile public, or to internalize a negative image of self promoted by the symbols of servitude, which pervade their work. It is about women who "don't take no junk."

The restaurant where this study was conducted, referred to here as Route, or Kendelport Route, is located on a busy interstate highway in an area undergoing rapid residential and commercial development. It is surrounded by malls, business parks, research campuses, and housing complexes in various stages of completion. Great expanses of bulldozed forest and billboards announcing forthcoming construction portend continued development in years to come. The entire region, however, suffers from an intense shortage of labor that may temper its growth in the future. Help-wanted signs promising an enjoyable working environment, flexible hours, and good pay and benefits adorn the front windows and doors of many stores and restaurants. Some are never removed. This climate of desperation has far reaching implications for employer-employee relations and for the quality of work life within the restaurant.

Route belongs to a well-known restaurant chain, which developed from a donut stand founded in the early fifties. The chain has more than twelve hundred units or "stores" located throughout the United States and several abroad. The caliber of the chain's food, service, and decor places it in the mid to lower range of the restaurant spectrum. Bon vivant urban professionals do not condescend to dine at Route, which is not greasy enough to be camp. The restaurant does appeal to budget-conscious families, senior citizens on fixed incomes, athletic teams, and church groups. In the predawn hours, Route absorbs the night life that has been dispelled from nearby bars at closing, as well as teenagers who congregate in packs over coffee and fries, and drug dealers who ostentatiously stack fifty- and hundred-dollar bills on booth tables, then stiff their waitresses. Like many roadside restaurants, Route is also the occasional resting place of the homeless, who find refuge on a stool at the counter from the cold, the heat, and the loneliness outside.

Route waitresses include teenagers and women in their sixties; mothers-to-be (three waitresses were pregnant when the research ended), teen-mothers, grandmothers, and women with no children; full-time workers who have been waiting tables for decades, and women who also hold jobs as telephone operators, cleaning women, cashiers, or companions for the ill. There is a Route waitress who picked cotton and peanuts alongside sharecropper parents when she was six and wore bleached flour sacks for slips, and another whose father is rumored by her co-workers to own "a big, fine mansion . . . with a maid and everything. . . . A girl who was brought up with nannies." In contrast to some restaurants in the area, Route attracts few college students to its waitressing staff. This may be due to the intensely serious work atmosphere or to the stigma attached to Route waitresses. A sense of how the public perceives the restaurant was suggested by a comedian on the "Tonight Show," who hypothesized that Route purposefully hired the ugliest women it could find in order to make the food appear more appetizing.

Approximately thirty waitresses work at Kendelport Route. One to eight waitresses may be on the floor at a given time. The restaurant employs dishwashers or "service assistants," who are often referred to as busboys though they do not bus tables, which is the waitress's job. It employs cooks and prep cooks, and on busy shifts hostesses are scheduled to work the register and seat incoming parties. The managerial staff consists of two managers and a general manager. There are also *PICs* and *SCs* (person-in-charge and service coordinators): employees, usually waitresses, who act as managers for one or two nights a week, allowing managers an occasional night off. Because there are no regular persons-in-charge or service coordinators, *PIC* and *SC* is generally understood as something one does, not is. This is reflected in the language of the restaurant: a waitress is rarely referred to as a *PIC* or *SC*; rather she is said to be *PICing* or *SCing*. . . .

Job categories at Route are segregated along gender lines. During the research period, all managers at Kendelport Route were male, but there were female managers at other units in the district, and women had managed at Kendelport in the past. All but one to two cooks and dishwashers were male. By contrast, virtually all servers were women. Of the few waiters who worked at the restaurant, two were dating waitresses. One, a rugged college student, reported being addressed as "waitress" by inattentive customers: an indication that the public is not accustomed to seeing waiters at Route. Hostesses also tended to be women. . . .

[The Symbolism of Service]

Employees of service industries are encouraged to treat customers with unflinching reverence and solicitude; to regard their con-

cerns and needs as paramount; to look upon them as masters and kings. But to accept this image of the other requires that one adopt a particular image of self. If the customer is king (or queen), the employee by extension is subject, or servant. In the restaurant, a complex system of symbolism encourages customer and worker alike to approach service as an encounter between beings of vastly different social standing, with unequal claims to courtesy, consideration, and respect. Though the customer accepts the imagery of servitude and adopts an interactive posture appropriate to the role of master, the waitress rejects the role of servant in favor of images of self in which she is an active and controlling force in the service encounter. Perhaps because of this, she is able to control the feelings she experiences and expresses toward her customers, and she is neither disoriented nor self-alienated by the emotional demands of her work. . . .

Waitress as Servant

The image of waitress as servant is fostered above all by the conventions that govern interaction between server and served. Much as domestic servants in the nineteenth century did not dine with or in the presence of masters, so today waitresses are forbidden to take breaks, sit, smoke, eat, or drink in the presence of customers. At Route, employees are not allowed to consume so much as a glass of water on the floor, though they are welcome to imbibe unlimited quantities of soda and coffee out of sight of customers. The prohibition against engaging in such physically necessary acts as eating, drinking, and resting in the customer's presence functions to limit contact between server and served and fortify status lines. It is, in addition, a means of concealing the humanness of those whom one would like to deny the courtesies of personhood. When indications of the server's personhood inadvertently obtrude into the service encounter, customers may be forced to modify their interactive stance. One Route waitress commented that when her parents ate at the restaurant her customers treated her with greater respect.

> They look at me like, "Oh my God. They have *parents*?" It's sometimes like we're not human. It's like they become more friendly when my parents are there and I get better tips off them. And I've never gotten stiffed when my parents have been sitting there. . . . They see that outside of this place I am a person and I have relationships with other people. . . .

[T]he waitress is discouraged from adorning herself in a way that might appear cheap. She is also discouraged from dressing above her station. . . . The aggressively plain uniform of the waitress underscores status distinctions between those who render and those who receive service in the same way that the black dress and white cap of the nineteenth-century domestic acted as a "public announcement of subservience" (Rothman 1987: 169; Sutherland 1981: 29–30). . . . In the modern service encounter, the need to underscore the server's inferiority may be especially strong as the status differential between server and served is intrinsically tenuous. The superiority of customer to waitress is limited temporally to the duration of the encounter and spatially to the boundaries of the restaurant. Rigidly defined dress codes, which eliminate all clues of the server's nonwork status, may serve to put the customer at ease in issuing orders to one whose subordination is so narrowly defined. . . .

The linguistic conventions of the restaurant and, in particular, the unilateral use of first names, further emphasize status differences between customer and waitress. . . . [T]he unilateral use of first names signals the subordinate status of the addressee; thus, African Americans, children, and household domestics have traditionally been addressed by first names by those whom they in turn address as *sir, ma'am, Mr.* or *Mrs.*

Restaurants perpetuate this practice by requiring servers to wear name tags which, regardless of the worker's age, bear only her first name, and by requiring servers to introduce themselves by first name to each party they wait on. Waitresses generally have no access to the customer's first or last name (the customer's larger "information preserve" prohibits inquiry) and are constrained to resort to the polite address forms *sir* and *ma'am* when addressing their parties. . . .

[M]odern service organizations must be charged with actively perpetuating the conventions of servitude and, in some cases, inventing new conventions. . . . The restaurant requires the waitress to dress as a maid and introduce herself by first name . . . and the restaurant promotes the degrading term *server*. In preserving the conventions of servitude the company encourages the waitress to internalize an image of self as servant and to adopt an interactive stance consistent with this image. In promoting an image of server as servant to the public, the restaurant encourages customers to treat, or mistreat, the waitress as they would a member of a historically degraded class.

That customers embrace the service-as-servitude metaphor is evidenced by the way they speak to and about service workers. Virtually every rule of etiquette is violated by customers in their interaction with the waitress: the waitress can be interrupted; she can be addressed with the mouth full; she can be ignored and stared at; and she can be subjected to unrestrained anger. Lacking the status of a person she, like the servant, is refused the most basic considerations of polite interaction. . . .

The imagery of servitude is the most insidious and perhaps, therefore, the most dangerous of hazards the waitress encounters. It pervades every aspect of her work, pressuring her to internalize a negative perception of self and assume a corresponding posture of submission; yet, because it is symbolically conveyed and not, for the most part, explicitly advocated, it cannot be directly confronted and may not even be consciously recognized. Nevertheless, the Route waitress successfully resists the symbolism of service, counterpoising company-supported understandings of her role as servant with her own images of self as a soldier confronting enemy forces, or alternatively, as an independent businessperson, working in her own interests, on her own territory.

Waitress as Soldier

If asked, a waitress would certainly agree that waiting tables is much like doing battle, but waitresses do not voluntarily make the comparison explicit. Rather, the perception of waiting tables as waging war and accordingly, the self-perception of waitress as soldier, is expressed implicitly in the waitress's war-oriented terminology: groups of tables under the control of individual waitresses are referred to as *stations*; the cooks' work area is referred to as the *line*; simultaneously adding several checks to the cooks' wheel is *sandbagging*; to receive many customers at once is to get *hit*; a full station or busy line is *bombed out*; old food and empty restaurants are *dead*; customers who leave no tips, *stiff*; abbreviations used by the waitress to communicate orders to the cook are *codes*; to get angry at someone is to *go off* on or *blow up at her*; to be short an item of food on an order is to *drag* the item; the number of customers served is a *customer count*; the late shift is *graveyard* or *grave*; to provide assistance to a co-worker (especially a cook) is to *bail him out*. Waitresses occasionally devise new uses of the war idiom. One waitress commented that when she was pregnant she had her friend *run* the eggs while she went to throw up. Later, when the manager refused to let her go home, the waitress responded by handing him her book and walking out: "I walked off—I abandoned ship," she recalled. Explaining why she objected to a manager having

an affair with a waitress, another waitress commented that managers "don't supposed to infiltrate the treaty."

Though much of this is official company terminology, it assumes the connotations of battle only in connection with the waitress's informal, and more blatantly war oriented language. To refer to the nucleus of the kitchen as the *line* does not in itself convey a sense of combat; there are assembly lines and bus lines as well as lines of fire and battle. Only when the cooks' line is regularly said to be *bombed out*, or when stations are repeatedly referred to as *getting hit*, does the battle-oriented meaning of these terms become apparent.

Several of the war idioms used by waitresses are not specific to restaurant work but are used in other occupations, or are common slang. The point here is not that the waitress's view of her work is unique, but that it is a view very different from that promoted by the physical props and interactive conventions of the restaurant. Like many people, and seemingly to a greater degree, the waitress views her work as something of a battle and those with whom her work brings her into contact as the enemy. More important, she views herself, not as a servant who peacefully surrenders to the commands of her master, but as a soldier actively returning fire on hostile forces. The waitress's capacity to sustain this self-image while donning the costume of a maid and complying with the interpersonal conventions of servitude, attests to her strength of will and power of resistance. The same may be said of all subordinate persons who are forced to resist without openly violating the symbolic order (Scott 1985: 33).

Waitress as Private Entrepreneur

During a rush, when the restaurant looks and sounds like a battle zone, the metaphor of service as war and waitress as soldier is most salient. During more peaceful periods, a different image of self assumes prominence: that of waitress as private entrepreneur. While these perceptions of self can be viewed as divergent and even opposed, both convey a sense of power and action.

Evidence that the waitress perceives herself as a private entrepreneur is found in her conceptual isolation of herself from the company and in her possessiveness toward people and things under her jurisdiction. The waitress's self-isolation may be expressed relatively directly, as in the following comments of a Route waitress:

> When she [a dissatisfied customer] was getting ready to pay her check, I was ringing it up and she was asking me my name, she was asking my manager's name, she was writing down the regional office's number. So I said, "Look. Do you have a problem? I'm a grown woman. If you have a problem with me, talk to me. If you have problem with Route, call the region. Fine. If you have problem with me, talk to me."

It is also expressed in the waitress's ambivalence toward performing tasks not directly related to the business of making tips. As an independent businessperson, the waitress views her responsibilities to the company as extremely limited. The company pays her a minor retainer, but it is felt to cover few duties beyond those immediately related to waiting tables. Accordingly, *sidework* (stocking supplies and cleaning other than that involved in bussing tables) is performed by the waitress with an air of forbearance as though it were understood that such work was above the call of duty.

The term *sidework* fosters the view that these tasks are peripheral to the waitress's work, but in fact, the thorough completion of sidework duties is critical to the smooth functioning of each shift and to peaceful relations between shifts. The failure of swing waitresses to stock chocolate fudge spells disaster

for grave waitresses faced with twenty orders for sundaes and no supplies. Likewise, the neglect of grave waitresses to fill the syrup dispensers and stock butter creates chaos for the day shift. There is rarely time to stock the necessary items while waiting tables; supplies are often packed in boxes under other boxes on shelves in locked rooms or freezers; they are packaged in jumbo cans and jars, which are heavy and difficult to open; and they sometimes require heating or defrosting before they can be used. Still, stocking and cleaning for the next shift are peripheral to the waitress's work in the sense that they do not directly enhance her tip earnings, and this is the sense that is most significant for the waitress as entrepreneur.

The waitress may, in addition, consider it beyond the call of duty to intervene on the company's behalf to prevent theft of restaurant property.

> I constantly tell Hollinger [a manager] he's a jerk. Constantly. Cause he's an ass. Because, people came in and ripped off place mats on graveyard, and he came in giving me heck. . . . And I said, "Let me tell you something, Hollinger. I don't *care* if they rip off the place mats. If you want somebody to stand by the door, and by the register, then you'd better hire somebody just to do that. Cause that's not my job. I'm here to wait on the people. I take the cash. I can't be babysitting grown adults."

The place mats referred to here were being sold by Route as part of a promotional campaign; waitresses do not use place mats to set tables. The point is significant because . . . waitresses are extremely possessive of, and so likely to protect, restaurant property that they use in their work.

The waitress's tendency to isolate herself from the company, which she perceives as neither liable for her faults nor warranted in requiring her to do more than wait tables, indicates that she does not see herself as an employee in the conventional sense. . . .

[H]er sense of independence is fostered by the tipping system, which releases her from financial dependence on the company, and by the circumscription of managerial authority, which indirectly augments the scope of her autonomy. At the same time, the waitress's perception that she is in business for herself may prompt her to assert her independence more strongly.

In keeping with her self-image as entrepreneur, the waitress refers to restaurant property as though it belonged to her. She speaks of *my* salt and peppers, *my* coffee, *my* napkins, *my* silverware, *my* booths, *my* catsups, *my* sugars. Linguistically, people too belong to the waitress who talks of *my* customers, *my* district manager, and *my* manager. The inclusion of managers among the waitress's possessions reflects her view of managers as individuals hired by the company to maintain satisfactory working conditions so she can conduct her business efficiently. . . .

The waitress also exhibits possessiveness in the way she treats her belongings and the belongings of others. Though she is unwilling to discourage customers from stealing company place mats, she may protect items she uses, and so regards as her own. . . . If waitresses are adamantly protective of their own property, they are equally respectful of the property of others. In the restaurant, ownership is determined by location: supplies located in a waitress's station belong to her for the duration of the shift. . . . A waitress who wishes to borrow a cowaitress's catsups, silverware, napkins, or coffee must ask to do so. If she cannot locate the owner and is in desperate and immediate need of an item, she may take it but will apologetically inform the owner as soon as possible that she "stole" the needed article. Borrowing or stealing customers is never acceptable. Apart from those rare occasions when she has obtained her co-worker's consent beforehand, a waitress will not take the order of a party seated in a co-worker's station no matter how frantically the customers wave menus, or how impatiently they glare at passing employees. If, as frequently happens, the "owner" of the party has disappeared, or if there is some confusion concerning the party's ownership, a waitress will search the corners of the restaurant and question every employee in an effort to locate or identify the rightful owner, rather than take the order herself and risk being accused of theft. Indeed, waitresses avoid becoming involved with their co-workers' customers, even in the interest in lending assistance. One waitress recalled that a cowaitress and friend had been caught in the cross fire of a customer food fight and had been doused with orange soda. Asked if she had intervened on behalf of her friend and reprimanded the customers, the waitress responded, "No. I didn't say nothing. Cause that's Mary's people." . . .

Freedom of Emotion

As she resists company efforts to influence her perception of self, so the waitress maintains control over the emotions she experiences and, to some degree, expresses in the service encounter. The waitress may adopt a submissive or energetically friendly manner toward those she serves, but she recognizes this manipulation of self as a means of manipulating the other. The boundary between front and backstage, between manufactured and spontaneous emotion, remains distinct; even in the midst of a performance the waitress does not lose herself in her role or lose sight of her objective.

This is my motto: "You sit in my station at Route, I'll sell you the world. I'll tell you anything you want to hear." Last night I had this guy, wanted my phone number. He was driving me nuts. And I wasn't interested. . . . He goes, "Well, how come you and your husband broke up?" I said, "Well, he found out about my boyfriend and got mad. I don't know. I don't understand it myself." And he started laughing. And I'm thinking, "*This is my money.* I'll tell you anything." . . . I got five bucks out of him. He didn't get my phone number but *I got my five-dollar tip*. I'll sell you the world if you're in my station. (emphasis added)

The waitress does not sell her customer the world, only a moment of cheerful banter and an illusion of friendship. For this sale she is adequately compensated: "I got my five-dollar tip"—as though she had settled beforehand on a fair price for her illusion.

The success of such an encounter is not measured by monetary rewards alone, however. For the waitress as for all social actors, skillful dissimulation may be an exercise in autonomy, an expression of control. . . . The degree of control the waitress maintains over her inner state is suggested by the ease with which she turns on and off the facade of subservience or conviviality: a smile becomes a sneer even as she turns away from the table; "yes, ma'am, yes sir" become vehement expletives as soon as she disappears behind the lines.

> I can cuss like a wizard now. Because when they get on your nerves you go in the back and before you know it you saying, "You motherfucker, you God damn bastard, you blue-eyed faggot" . . . I came out with some names I ain't never thought I knew.

Many servers commented that waitressing had made them tougher and had, in addition, altered their perception of the public.

> It's changed me a lot. I have less patience with the public. I found out how rude and cruel people today are . . . I seen two faces of the public, and I don't like it. I don't like their evil side. . . . After you been working with the public for X amount of years, you start seeing the good and the bad in people, and the bad outweighs the good. . . .

As the waitress comes to see the public in an increasingly negative light, she comes to interpret her customers' rudeness and impa-

tience, like their low tips, as evidence of their "evil side," and not a reflection on her waitressing or social skill. In turn, she becomes less willing to tolerate impatience and irritation which she no longer accepts responsibility for provoking. In terms of her own idiom of war, the waitress claims the right to return fire on what she has come to regard as inherently aggressive, hostile forces.

> The worst experience I had as far as customer was when I worked graveyard and a family came in . . . two girls and a man and a woman. She obviously was a foreigner, cause she spoke broken English. . . . And she was very rude, very nasty to me. . . . First thing that she did when she sat down was complain. From the time she sat down to the time they ended up walking out, she complained left and right. And she embarrassed me. She tried to embarrass me. She tried everything in the book. She degraded me. But I stood up to her, and I wouldn't let that happen. I stood up to her regardless of whether they were customers, regardless of whether I lost my job. Nobody's going to degrade me like that because I'm a waitress. . . . And then she started getting loud. And boisterous . . . I said, "Look." And then I put my book down. I slammed my book down. I put my pen on the table . . . I said, "Look. If you can do a better job than me, then you write your damn order down yourself and I'll bring it back to the kitchen. When it's ready I'll let you know, and you go back and pick it up." *Then* she called me a foreigner. And that's when the shit hit the fan. I said, "How dare you have the gall to call me a foreigner? *You're* the one that's in America. *You're* the foreigner. The problem with you foreigners, is *you* come in this country and *you* try to boot Americans out of their *own* jobs, their *own* homes, and you try and take over this country." I said, "Don't you *ever* call me a foreigner, lady. Because I'll take you right by your collar now. I don't care whether I lose my job or not." *Then* she started curs-

ing at me, and then I cursed right back at her. . . . Then she started arguing with her husband. . . . Called him a MF, bad, bad, vulgar language, right?. . . . And he said, "If you call me that one more time . . . I'm going to knock you right in your MFing mouth. And I'll put you on the ground in front of everybody." And she deserved it, and when he said it, I applauded him. I said, "Boy, I'll tell you. If I was married to a bitch like her, I would have knocked her out a long time ago." And he just smiled at me and turned around and walked out.

The waitress slams down her book immediately before releasing her anger on the woman, thereby signaling that she is no longer willing to play the role of compliant servant; she is going to take a stand as a person. In breaking character and expressing her anger she defies company- and customer-supported conceptions of the waitress as one obligated to endure mistreatment at the hands of her supposed social betters. . . .

Another waitress recounted the following episode . . .

I had brought out this lady's chicken fried steak and the middle wasn't cooked enough for her. . . . Instead of her saying, "Ma'am, would you please take this back to the kitchen and have it cooked a little bit more?" she slide that shit over to me and said, "You take this shit back in the kitchen cause it ain't cooked." I turn around to her, I said, "Who the Hell you think you're talking to?" I said, "Do you know who you're talking to?" I said, "Do I look like one of your children? Cause if I do, you better take another look. Now I can understand that you upset cause the middle of your chicken ain't done. . . . But. In the same token, I think you better learn to tone that voice of yours down. Cause you don't talk to me or nobody else like that." "Well" [the woman said], "I don't have to take this. I talk to the mana"—I said, "Damn you, lady, you talk to any damn person you want to talk to." Cause

by that time I'd about had it. She [could] kiss my ass far as I was concerned.

[This comment] illustrate[s] the waitress's concern with contesting the belief that a server who is rude to a customer will lose her job. The waitress who related the incident above described the customer's view as follows:

They figure they say what they want and do what they want; figure you might be afraid to say anything. . . . You know, "She ain't going to say nothing because . . . I go to the boss and tell her boss and she'll lose her job, so she ain't going to say nothing to me.

When assumptions like these surface, in the form of rudeness or threats to contact supervisors, the waitress responds by informing the customer or demonstrating by her actions that she is confident no action will be taken against her.

The following exchange concluded a heated interchange between a waitress and customer regarding the waitress's failure to remember that the customer's boyfriend had not ordered sausage with his breakfast. Note that the waitress volunteers her name to the customer underscoring her lack of concern with being reported. . . .

She [the customer] said, "Well, I would like to call in the morning and talk to your manager." I said, "Fine. My name is Mae Merrin. You can call him. I been here seven years. I ain't going nowhere. Especially over a couple pieces of meat."

Regardless of whether the waitress directly confronts the issue of her own expendability, her decision to retaliate against an offensive customer challenges the view that she, like a servant, is constrained to submit to abuse as part of her job. The promptness and intensity of her reaction indicate the degree to which this conception diverges from her own perception of self as an independent, but to the company indispensable, businessperson.

Hazards of Personality Control

. . . While interpersonal activity may always and everywhere have demanded maintenance of a facade, individuals are increasingly pressured to experience, rather than merely express appropriate emotions. In *The Managed Heart*, Hochschild (1983) proposes that organizations are no longer content that their workers engage in surface acting, which relies on technical maneuvers to portray feelings, and in which "the body, not the soul, is the main tool of the trade" (1983: 37). Today, workers are encouraged to engage in deep or method acting, in which the worker draws on a reservoir of "emotion memories" to produce an appropriate response (empathy, cheerfulness) for a given role and scene. Toward this end, workers are urged to adopt a view of the service encounter and of the consumer that will evoke a suitable interactive stance. Flight attendants are counseled to look upon the cabin as a living room and passengers as guests, and to regard difficult passengers as children who need attention. The assumption is that flight attendants will feel sincerely sympathetic with passengers they perceive as guests or children and will not be inclined to reciprocate their anger or impatience (Hochschild 1983).

By furnishing the waitress with the script, costume, and backdrop of a servant, the restaurant encourages her to become absorbed in her role or, in Hochschild's terms, to engage in deep acting. In so doing, the company may hope to enhance the authenticity of the performance and reduce the possibility that the server will break character and express emotions incongruous with the role she is expected to play. As one perceives herself as a servant, the waitress should willingly abdicate her claim to the courtesies of interaction between equals; she should absorb abuse with no thought of retaliation; she should fulfill requests however trivial and unreasonable, and accept blame however mis-

directed, because as a servant it is her job to do so. . . .

More than anything else, the waitress's ability to withstand the symbolic machinery of her work without suffering emotional estrangement testifies to her power of resistance. Though constrained to comply with the interactive conventions of master and servant, while clad in a domestic's uniform, the waitress does not internalize an image of service as servitude and self as servant. In times of stress she sees her work as war and herself as soldier. In times of peace she sees her work as a private enterprise and herself as entrepreneur. Like all social actors, the waitress monitors her projected personality and manipulates her feelings in the course of social interaction, but she does so knowingly and in her own interests. This manipulation of self does not induce self-alienation or emotional disorientation. The waitress distinguishes clearly between emotions expressed in order to please or appease a potential tipper, and emotions that arise spontaneously and are genuine. With experience her ability to separate front and backstage expressions of subservience and conviviality increases and she may silently applaud her powers of deception even as she stands before her audience of customers. To some extent, too, the waitress determines the degree to which she is willing to put up with rudeness in the interests of protecting a potential tip. . . .

Here . . . the intention has not been to deny that waitressing and other direct-service jobs are emotionally taxing and exploitive. Work that regularly provokes outbursts of anger and engenders an embittered view of those with whom one must daily interact, off and on the job, is both injurious and in the strictest sense, coercive. It has also not been the purpose of this discussion to exonerate organizations that perpetuate rituals of deference that threaten the dignity and deny the personhood of those who serve. Though the waitress rejects the symbolic implications of these rituals, her customers do not. The symbolism of service encourages the customer to assume the posture of master to servant, with all accompanying rights of irrationality, condescension, and unrestrained anger. The resulting conflict of perspectives is a constant source of friction between server and served, friction that diminishes the quality of the waitress's work environment and periodically erupts into open fire.

The aim of this discussion has been to explore the ways in which the waitress confronts the emotionally coercive demands of her work. . . . Route waitresses demonstrate that women may respond to the adverse conditions of their work not merely in the passive sense of suffering injuries, but in actively resisting, reformulating, or rejecting the coercive forces they encounter. Like the flight attendant, the waitress is pressured to see and feel about her work in company-endorsed ways; and like the flight attendant, she has little influence over the setting of the stage on which she must act out her work role. And yet the waitress does not overextend herself into her work, and when she distances herself from her job she does not "feel bad about it." . . .

This investigation has sought to avoid the view that women are resigned to their subjection by examining structure and strategy as interlocking systems, adopting a more comprehensive understanding of action, and reformulating conventional questions about women and work. . . . Rather than ask, *Why are women passive?* we have asked, *How are they active?* In adopting this approach the intent has not been to downplay the difficulties of the waitress's position or deny the need for structural reform that would ensure her greater financial security and eliminate the coercive symbolism of service. Rather, the goal has been to balance pervasive images of female submission and passivity with a glimpse of defiance. . . .

References

Hochschild, Arlie. 1983. *The Managed Heart: Commercialization of Human Feeling.* Berkeley: University of California Press.

Rothman, Robert A. 1987. "Direct-Service Work and Housework." In *Working: Sociological Perspectives.* Englewood, Cliffs, NJ: Prentice Hall.

Scott, James C. 1985. *Weapons of the Weak: Everyday Forms of Peasant Resistance.* New Haven, CT: Yale University Press.

Sutherland, Daniel E. 1981. *Americans and Their Servants: Domestic Service in the United States from 1800 to 1920.* Baton Rouge: Louisiana State University Press.

Excerpted and reprinted from: Greta Foff Paules, *Dishing It Out: Power and Resistance Among Waitresses in a New Jersey Restaurant,* pp. 1–4, 6, 131–138, 140–147, 150–154, 156–158, 160–164, 182. Copyright © 1991 by Temple University. Reprinted by permission of Temple University Press. All rights reserved. ✦

27

Making It "Decent" on the Streets

Elijah Anderson

Nowhere in America are the powerful constraints of social structure more obvious than in many of our impoverished, inner-city neighborhoods. Over the past few decades, relatively well-paid manufacturing jobs have largely disappeared from these neighborhoods, leaving only menial service jobs that often pay less than a living wage. As legitimate economic opportunities have shrunk, an underground economy of drug dealing and street crime has flourished. Those who could afford to leave have largely done so. Many governmental agencies, including the police, have largely given up on these neighborhoods, leaving residents to their own devices. Financially strapped local schools largely fail to educate. Because many of these neighborhoods are predominately African American, their residents also routinely experience the insults of racism, such as being stalked by security guards in retail stores. For those born into these social structural conditions, there is little basis for hope and every reason to believe that the surrounding society has abandoned them.

This selection is excerpted from a larger study of such impoverished, predominately African-American neighborhoods in Philadelphia, where the author, Elijah Anderson, has lived for many years. Anderson has spent countless hours frequenting these neighborhoods and talking with their residents. He provides an intimate portrait of everyday life in these neighborhoods and the struggles of their residents to overcome the social structural circumstances that shape their lives.

In the larger study, Anderson observes that most residents of these neighborhoods describe themselves as "decent" in the sense of being law-abiding, hardworking, and family oriented. However, residents who are more deeply alienated from the values of the surrounding society largely control the public places of these neighborhoods. These residents live by what is known as the code of the street. This code of conduct places a premium on demanding personal respect and taking care of oneself. Even the most minor slight or "diss" requires a quick, often violent response so as to maintain one's street reputation. According to the "code," establishing and maintaining a reputation on the street is necessary to deter exploitation and victimization. Convinced, often with good reason, that no one else will look out for them, including the police, these "street-oriented" residents believe that they must defend and protect their reputation and, thereby, themselves by whatever means possible.

Although so-called decent residents of these neighborhoods do not share the values of their more street-oriented neighbors, they must still honor the *code of the street* when in public places. They must give the impression that they too demand respect and will meet any challenge, with violence if necessary. If they do not do so, they leave themselves vulnerable to harassment and criminal victimization. Hence, they must constantly engage in what Anderson calls "code switching" between their more conventional personal values and those of the code that governs much of the public life of their neighborhood.

This selection recounts the story of one former drug dealer, Robert, who, after spending time in prison, returns to his impoverished neighborhood and attempts to make a "decent" living and improve the neighborhood. It documents the many challenges that he faces. From the beginning, he is torn between his old street reputation and his newfound sense of purpose. He must deal with seemingly uncaring and sometimes hostile governmental authorities. And, he must battle his former street-oriented friends for control of the corner where he runs his small businesses. This requires perilous code-switching. He must trade on his former reputation and threats of retaliation in order to claim a place on the street while avoiding any actions that might incur the wrath of governmental authorities or, being that he remains on parole, even send him back to prison. For now, Robert has succeeded, but his story is far from over. He will continue to face the challenges that he currently does, and despite the strong support of many other decent residents of his neighborhood, he will have to do so by his own wits and street savvy.

Robert's story is exemplary of the challenges faced by those who reside in our impoverished, inner-city neighborhoods. Social structural conditions such as the deindustrialization of American inner cities, residential segregation, governmental neglect, and lingering racism breed contempt for the surrounding society and often self-defeating styles of life. Yet, as Anderson notes, it would be unfair to blame the residents of these neighborhoods for their circumstances. They had no control over the social structural forces that have shaped their lives, and are simply doing their best to adapt to them. Some, like Robert, still heroically attempt to make it "decent" and improve their communities, while others have all but given up on legitimate avenues to success and simply try to survive on the streets. Who is to say which is the more reasonable response to the social structural conditions that they must face every day?

Ten years ago, at age seventeen, Robert was arrested and sentenced for the aggravated assault of a rival drug dealer. Having been convicted as a juvenile, he has now served his time. When he returned to the old neighborhood from prison, many people who had known him before his conviction believed that he would settle some old scores and revive his old drug gang, that things would get hot in the 'hood. Some of his old friends approached him with gifts, welcoming him back into the fold. Among these offerings was a pistol, ostensibly for his protection, which Robert flatly refused. He had decided

in prison that he did not want to go that route again. He simply wanted some space, to catch up on "the haps" and to spend time with his girlfriend, Thomasina. He wished to find a way to earn money legitimately. Nevertheless, from the moment he set foot on his old turf, the people there expected to see some action.

When Robert was arrested, charged, and convicted, he had already developed a strong name on the street. Many considered him a big-time drug dealer, and he was one of the most feared people on the streets of the community. It was assumed that he would "get" anyone who crossed him. This reputation allowed him to go about the neighborhood unmolested. To be sure, people sometimes tested him, but this only made Robert stronger, for he took great delight in meeting the tests people set for him. He was a man, and in this environment nothing was more important than his manhood. Nevertheless, when he was incarcerated, his status and identity underwent a fundamental change. On the street his status remained high, but in prison in rural Pennsylvania he encountered white prison guards who treated him very badly. They called him "nigger" on an almost daily basis, planned Ku Klux Klan meetings in his presence, assigned him to "shit" work, and in other ways rode and harassed him all the while, hoping he "would strike out at one of them so they could extend [his] time." Robert says, "I was smart enough to avoid their traps, but many other black guys fell for it."

For the most part, he maintains, prison was "good for me. It made me think and reassess my life." In prison he became aware of his inability to read and the deficiencies of his vocabulary and decided he had an opportunity to rectify these problems. He had his friends and relatives send him books. He read and studied the dictionary, the Koran, the Bible, and other works, all from cover to cover. By the time he was released, he had gained a new attitude. He could see that a "game was being run" on the community. In prison most of the inmates were black or Hispanic, while most of the guards were white men from the surrounding rural areas. He felt that the guards and prison staff were being supported, if not subsidized, by "people like me." The streets in his neighborhood fueled the prison engine by providing young men who actively played their roles in a grand scheme. He knew he had to change himself and his community, and he committed himself to this end.

Since his release from prison Robert has shunned his previous materialism and become a somewhat ascetic individual—more calm, more thoughtful. Many of his former friends looked at him strangely, because they do not see the Ruck (his street name) they knew. He was always intelligent and motivated—this is what made him an upcoming leader in the drug trade—but now he was applying these traits not to living out the code of the street but to making the transition to a life of decency. This confused his old friends, because prison usually enhances one's prestige on the street, particularly in terms of code values like toughness, nerve, and willingness to retaliate for transgressions.

Yet Robert returned from prison to put his old street way of being behind him. Over the past months he has joined with three other young men—David, Tyrone, and Marvin, all desiring to change—to do what they can to support one another in turning their lives around. The young men grew up together in the local neighborhood, where they had their share of fights and run-ins with the law. Each of them has his own history, but there are common threads. They have all survived grinding urban poverty. They have endured the gamut of problems—welfare, single-parent households, emotionally and physically abusive fathers—and, like Robert, gravitated initially to the street, which provided them with family of a sort. On the street and in the gangs, they experienced a certain cohesion, bravado, and coming of age. Obtaining a

high level of street knowledge from all of this, they understood the code very well. Nevertheless, something was missing from their lives. Their awareness of this prompted them to raise searching questions about their futures—where they would be in five, ten, or fifteen years. Would they be simply more casualties of the street? Could they really attain the "good life"? What were the impediments to such a goal? Whenever they would get together, they would discuss such issues. Robert was usually the main catalyst for this kind of talk.

After a few months of sitting around on one another's stoops discussing and critiquing the system and their roles in it, they decided to begin to take some concrete steps toward change. . . . They worked to move away from the lives of petty criminal activity, including hustling and drug dealing. They wanted to see themselves one day as solid pillars in their community. But how could they get on the road to that end? They decided to approach a well-known community activist named Herman Wrice.

For many years Herman has been a very active old head in the impoverished inner-city community. He has worked hard to close down crack houses and to frustrate drug dealers. Having lived in this community for so long, he is deeply invested in cleaning it up. He feels strongly that the drug trade and the lack of jobs are the bane of the community's existence. Herman is highly visible in the community and has gone the extra mile in fighting drug dealing, to such an extent that from time to time his life has been threatened. But he has great courage, which is highly respected on the street, and strong motivation . . . [Herman] has known many of the neighborhood's young men for years. He knows many of their mothers and fathers and other family members well. So Robert and the other young men viewed Herman as approachable; they reasoned, correctly, that he would lend them a sympathetic ear.

On a Tuesday afternoon in July 1997, the four of them went to Herman with their plan for turning their lives around. They simply requested some time to talk. Herman listened. They told him, essentially, "We'd like to change. Can you to help us?" Their approach was so unusual that Herman was at first incredulous and somewhat suspicious. After so many years of working with young people in the community, of harassing drug dealers and closing them down, was he now seeing some real success for his efforts? He speculated that the drug trade was becoming increasingly dangerous and competitive and that this was why these young men wanted out. Yet he remained uncertain and perplexed. The young men's request "blew my mind," he says. Were they on the level?

"If you're serious about wanting to improve the neighborhood, you can start by cleaning up this lot," he said, pointing to an overgrown and trash-filled vacant lot. His command was a test, and the young men may have known this, but they agreed to clean up the lot. The task required a couple of days' work, but the boys accomplished what they started. Herman was impressed, though still not totally convinced that they were serious. He therefore showed them another, bigger lot to clean up as well. This task took them even longer, but they did finish it.

Again they returned to Herman, who was more impressed though still not fully convinced. He knew they had been drug dealers, whom he sees as businessmen "but with a terrible product," and wondered whether they might become entrepreneurs. Could they sell fruit on a local street corner instead of drugs? Could this then grow into a larger market, contributing eventually to revitalizing the community? If so, Robert and the others might be visible role models of hard work, an example to younger people.

With this in mind he said to them, "OK, meet me down at the [food distribution] docks at five tomorrow morning." He was testing and probing, for he did not want to be taken in. His knowledge and understanding were that committed drug dealers don't just get up at five in the morning and present themselves for honest work. But these young men surprised him; they appeared promptly at five, and Herman presented his plan for them to become fruit sellers, pointing out how this effort, while small, could grow into something much larger. The boys listened intently. Herman can be a very persuasive person. They hung on his words. They appeared hungry for an opportunity to go legitimate, to make a difference in their own community.

Once Herman decided to help them, he gave them about $800 for materials and lumber to construct a fruit stand, which had to be built in compliance with the Philadelphia Licenses and Inspections (L&I) codes. Given the young men's inexperience, their first attempt was not very successful; in fact, the stand blew over in the wind. But Herman took them to the Italian Market, an open-air market full of wooden stands, and had them get the advice of people who knew about building stands. Robert and the other young men then went back and built another stand and painted it white as mandated by L&I. L&I also required them to bring the whole thing downtown for inspection. Herman intervened again and arranged through the district police captain to have the inspector come to them.

At first the young men purchased fruit from the docks, took it back to their community, and set up shop on a busy thoroughfare. People did begin purchasing fruit and vegetables from them. The boys were heartened by how easy it seemed to start up something legitimate. But Herman also told them about other important requirements of becoming small businessmen: issues like licenses and inspections, bookkeeping, and taxes. The young men were undaunted and attempted to rise to the occasion. At this point Herman approached various professors at the University of Pennsylvania, including myself. One professor at the Wharton School invited the young men to attend one of his seminars, making them the focus of a class on small-time entrepreneurship.

The class involved the nuts and bolts of starting up a small business. In the classroom Robert and the others encountered young white and black students of the Wharton School, not to mention a professor who was interested in them and their future. They were all ears, listening attentively and taking copious notes. The students and the professor provided them with much needed advice, but they also gave them accounting and tax books. The young men took it all in and left the class with their minds brimming with ideas about business. . . .

Ever since the young men have had the stand up and operating, Robert has been the most consistent worker. He is serious and focused, the one who gets the fruit every day, stocks the shelves, and sells it in all kinds of weather. Having also acquired an aluminum hot dog stand that he began operating across the street, he literally runs back and forth between the two stands. In addition, he is what people in the community would call "free-hearted," sometimes giving away food when people ask for it, telling them to pay him when they get the money. His generosity cuts down on profits, but he still clears one to two hundred dollars a day. Now just a shadow of his former large-living, materialistic self, Robert is resigned to making do with relatively little. At the stand he calls passersby over and enjoins them to buy something or, if they can't do that, simply to contribute something "to the cause." And people do.

Robert's popularity and reputation in the community account in part for the group's success. His neighbors, friends, and relatives generally want to see him succeed. But the group has its detractors, most often among old friends who are still involved in the drug trade. When these people see Robert standing on the corner selling fruit, they mock him and the others. At times they flash their considerable wads of cash, or "cheese," as they call it, and laugh, putting Robert and his partners down as "little Hermans." While a term of derision in the minds of street toughs and hoodlums, "little Hermans" is a complimentary term in the minds of many . . . men of the community. . . . Robert and the others pretend to be unfazed, but they are in fact challenged and encouraged to settle on their new identity, trying out the role of "upstanding young men" of their community and, in fits and starts, learning to appreciate the positive connotations of the term "little Hermans." But serious as they are about turning their lives around and serving the community and its children as positive role models, the boys are beginning to confront the truth that this is not an easy or simple process.

For instance, as Robert and the boys experience success, they face the problem of how to make the transition from underground hustling activities to legal entrepreneurship—or, as Robert puts it, from "underground ghettonomics to above-ground economics"—and attain a semblance of organization. While Robert takes his role very seriously and usually does exactly what is required, he cannot always motivate the others to be as consistent in doing their parts. Still, he rarely complains. The group seldom engages in casting blame or trading recriminations. One major operating principle the group has developed is that people do "what they are strong at." Robert knows he is strong at selling and at public relations. The others have their strengths as well. Two are still in high school. It may on the surface look as though the others are simply using Robert getting over on him—but he does not see things this way. He contends that they are all working together toward the common goal of improving their lives and, by extension, their community. . . .

Of course, their old ideology of alienation from mainstream society is a complicating factor in their transition. To be sure, many decent people may work two or three jobs to make ends meet or pick up some kind of more or less legal hustle, join forces with their relatives, or barter and trade favors and services with their neighbors and friends. People associated with the criminal element, on the other hand, tend to justify their criminal behavior by reference to racism, which they and their friends and neighbors face daily. Some of them remember the racism they have endured from whites and from the black "system operators," who are seen as standing in and acting as proxies for the white power structure.

Accordingly, many of those who remain part of the underground economy are quite embittered, if not profoundly alienated from the wider system, believing that this system is absolutely unfair to black people. Rather than feeling connected to the wider society and emulating it, they suspect and distrust anyone associated with mainstream institutions. They often demand that other blacks show solidarity with them. This orientation can—and does to some extent for Robert—inhibit a full conversion to participation in the world of L&I, Wharton, and legitimate, visible forms of entrepreneurship.

Robert's ambivalence became apparent one afternoon in early January 1998, while I was standing with him at his hot dog stand, watching him sell hot dogs. A customer approached once every ten or fifteen minutes. In between customers Robert was also manning the fruit stand across the street and engaging in conversation with friends who happened by there as well. Because of his status on the street, younger and older fellows alike would often come by for advice.

Suddenly, a city L&I truck pulled up. Out hopped a black man of about fifty in the company of a forty-five-year-old black woman. They demanded to see Robert's license for the hot dog stand. Now, Robert had acquired the 1998 license, but had neglected to carry it on his person. In fact, he had misplaced the paperwork for the 1998 license and only had the sticker for 1997, which was displayed on his stand. He pointed out the sticker to the man, but the inspector insisted, "I need the current license."

When Robert could not produce the license, the inspector, clearly not inclined to give him a break, became gruff. Robert tried to explain that he had been there for a while and that he did in fact have his license but had lost it. The man was unmoved; he simply said, "This will be a lesson to you to get your license." I tried to intervene, explaining the situation, and asked if he could not just give Robert a warning. "This *is* a warning," he snapped, and I said nothing more. After a little more tense conversation between the two, Robert turned to me and said, "See how hard it is to fit into this system?" Then he muttered under his breath, "System operator," referring to the black man. The inspector overheard the comment, and the tension escalated.

Robert next invoked the name of the district police captain, who had been quite supportive of him and is a strong advocate of community policing. But this apparently carried no weight with the inspector, who proceeded to lecture Robert some more on the need for paperwork. Finally, he filled out a report form, which he wanted Robert to sign immediately. "Here, sign this," he said. "I got to read it first," said Robert. After a few seconds, the inspector became impatient, and said, "All right, all right," taking the clipboard and form and writing at the bottom where Robert's signature was to go, "Refused to sign." Robert then became outright angry, complaining about not having had enough time to read the form. People passing by looked over at what appeared to be the beginning of a commotion. A crowd was beginning to form. The inspector would not discuss the matter further, telling Robert he would have to go downtown now to deal with the matter. In the meantime, the inspector said, "You must cease operations right now, and if I see you operating, I'll confiscate it [the stand]. I've got a hook on this truck," he added, pointing to the back of his truck.

Robert stood fuming and frustrated. Clearly, he saw the inspector as picking on him—a young black man trying to abide by the system, trying to go straight, but getting no support from people he thought should be helping him the most: other black people who should know all about the racism of the system and so should collude with him against it. He could not understand why this man would not give him a break.

This alienation from "the system" and the belief that blacks have to mobilize against it helps to legitimate—for its participants—the code of the street, settling scores personally, going for oneself. The inspector sees himself as just doing his job. But Robert has his doubts. He feels that, because of politics and racism, the inspector would never go to the Italian Market and "pick on them, because he'd lose his job in two seconds. You don't see him coming after the Koreans either. He just gon' pick on another black man." Robert wants the inspector to be what is often called a "race man," but the inspector wants to see himself as a "professional." So he goes by the book and demands that Robert obey the rules and hold to the notion "that race doesn't enter into it." Robert views it very differently, though; he thinks the inspector is betraying his race.

Most people like Robert who are trying to make the transition from street to decent, to negotiate the wider system, eventually run up against this problem. Robert wants the system to be racially particularistic, to recognize him as an individual with his own problems and needs for special treatment and collusion against the system, but the system does not always cooperate.

On the street, in his old life as a drug dealer, a person like Robert could, and did, demand that others "make way" for him. In his street world he had a particular reputation, or name, and a history of resorting to violence to make sure that they did. He carried a gun. In giving all that up, he has stepped into a world where he has no particular sta-

tus—where L&I doesn't fear him or want to please him. And because he carries no gun, his old friends on the street do not need to make way for him either. He has thus entered a kind of limbo with regard to his status and the rules that govern the management and outcome of conflicts involving him.

An illustration of his loss of power on the street came up recently when Robert was putting away his hot dog stand for the evening, locking it up in a fenced lot. While he was doing this, his backpack, which contained his licenses and other paperwork, was lying on the ground. While his back was turned, someone took the backpack. When he finished, Robert noticed the theft and became livid. Nobody would rob a drug dealer, he felt, for fear of being shot in retaliation, but "they" robbed him. In Robert's analysis, the people who took the bag knew they had a guardian angel in Herman because "they knew Herman would talk Robert out of doing something foolish to retaliate."

As Robert told me the story, I pointed out that the thief could simply have been a crack addict who made no such calculations. Robert admitted that he didn't know, but he said, "Even crack addicts have sense [know how far they can go with whom]. It makes you wonder, Is it better to be loved or feared?" In this comment Robert seemed to question his new orientation.

Yet his analysis is revealing in that it shows his awareness that as he makes his transition to a decent life he is losing something very important on the street—credibility, props (deference), and, ultimately, protection. The whole point of the street posture is to let people know, "If you mess with me, there will be consequences. Don't count on the law. Don't count on the cops. It's me and you." That's the essence of the street code. Robert's experience can be held up and studied as an example in microcosm of the difficulty of making the transition from the street to the decent world of law-abiding people. . . .

The problem for Robert is that as he leaves his old life and moves toward his new life, he is . . . becoming somewhat marginal to both groups. In this sense he also becomes weakened as a player in the neighborhood. Furthermore, the fact that Robert is now on parole means there are certain rules he absolutely must follow. If he engages in any form of violence, he risks returning to jail. He knows this, and the others know it as well. To survive in this community, one must be able to wield the credible threat of violence. It is not that the person must always engage in violent acts; rather, he must be able to threaten violence at some point to keep the "knuckleheads" in line. Clearly, Robert cannot credibly threaten violence without jeopardizing his own freedom. Assuming this, some of the young men will try and test Robert, probing to see just what they can get away with in their dealings with him.

Over the months since his release from jail, Robert has been tested a number of times, from both sides of the fence. A probation officer recently placed him in handcuffs, only to let him go and apologize. Robert was provoked and very disturbed, for he could see no reason for such treatment, and later the officer could not give a good reason for it either. But the incident allowed Robert to see just how vulnerable he now was to the whims of individuals charged with upholding the system.

More recently, Robert has been forced to confront the tension between the street and the decent world even more directly. He has accepted a business proposition from a woman in the neighborhood, Ms. Newbill. For many years Ms. Newbill has been operating a carryout restaurant on the corner across from Robert's fruit stand. Lately, however, drug dealers have taken to hanging around, intercepting Ms. Newbill's customers. Part of what makes the carryout attractive for the drug dealers is that people hang out there: it is busy with traffic, and the dealers can blend in with the young people who are simply standing on the corner, and even sell drugs to some of them.

While Ms. Newbill was there alone, this is what they did. Police driving by couldn't always distinguish between the drug dealers and the kids just hanging out. In fact, adapting to the code, otherwise law-abiding and decent youths at times develop an interest in being confused with those who are hardcore street, because such a posture makes them feel strong and affords them an aura of protection, even allowing them to "go for bad"—or pretend they too are tough.

Because of the presence of drug dealers, Ms. Newbill's business declined, since few people wanted to run an obstacle course to buy sodas and hamburgers. When she complained about this to the dealers, their response was to rob her store at gunpoint. They also vandalized her automobile, which she parked outside the store. Wanting no further trouble, she had an inspiration. She offered to lease the deli section of the business to Robert for $800 per month in the hope that his presence, as a person with respect and props, could deter the drug dealers. Robert has accepted the challenge. He feels it's a good deal, just the opportunity he's been looking for to become a legitimate businessman and not just a street vendor. On his first day he made $91. If he can maintain that level of profit, he thinks, he can make a go of the business.

This involvement has given Robert an even bigger stake in the corner the store occupies, across the street from the fruit stand. He, Ms. Newbill, and the drug dealers all know this. One of the many ironies here is that in his previous life Robert established himself as a drug dealer on this very corner and, to this day, feels he can claim some "ownership" rights to it. In fact, he introduced to the drug trade the young dealers with whom he is now competing for the corner. And, invoking his "rights," he has told them that they must take their drugs off his corner, because they harm his legitimate business, that by continuing to sell, they are disrespecting him, or dissing him. Yet they still want to sell drugs on the corner and say they are entitled to do so because "this is where [they] grew up." Robert answers that they must be responsible young men and not defile their neighborhood. He also points out to them that such "defilement" hurts his own business, and thus must cease.

Before Robert was incarcerated, his was a big name in the neighborhood. He was an enforcer for a drug-dealing gang. This role gave him great props on the streets, indicating that he was not to be messed with. But now, as was pointed out above, he can be only a shadow of his former self, because such displays of violent behavior could get him arrested and reincarcerated. Having publicly come out as a little Herman, and a legitimate businessperson, he finds himself in a dilemma: Does he revert to his street self in pursuit of decent goals?

It's a predicament that Robert must confront on his own. He knows it, and his antagonists know it. They all know that the police are not the main players here, the ones to "get cool" with; rather, the "beef" is between Robert and the drug dealers. These are the people with whom he must now achieve a new understanding. They are testing his mettle, probing for weakness, to see if he is the same old Ruck. Much suggests to them that he is not. Above all, he is now on parole and thus must watch his step in dealing with people the way he would have dealt with them "back in the day," or the old days; moreover, his close association with Herman is something of a liability on the street.

Robert has been going through a gradual transformation, shedding his "old skin" and identity of Ruck and taking on his new identity of Robert, or Rob. His former street cronies constantly address him by his street name of Ruck, while the decent people of the community, people he is getting to know better, address him more consistently as Robert.

If Rob resolves the current tension and passes the test, he will be much stronger than he was before, garnering juice, or respect, and credibility from others he meets on the street. Bear in mind, Rob already has credibility and respect from many of the decent people who know him and what he has been up against; many are cheering for him, the celebrity of the neighborhood. It is the street element, specifically the local drug gang, that he must now impress. For his part, Herman understands that he must not fight this battle for Rob, that Rob must fight it for himself. After all, he will not always be with Rob. Choc is Rob's main opponent in the contest for the corner in front of Ms. Newbill's. He grew up and has been living in the area for a long time, and, as was indicated earlier, Rob helped raise him and introduce him to the drug trade. Choc's mother still lives in the area, just a few doors away from Rob's store.

Soon after taking control of the store, Rob confronted Choc about his drug-dealing activities. He said, "Listen, Choc, this has to stop. If you want to sell drugs, go somewhere else. You not gon' do it here. Go sit on your mother's step and sell. Don't sell in front of my business." Choc responded, "Why you want to do that [keep us from selling drugs here]? You know how it is. I got to eat. I got to make a living, too. Why you want to be so hard?" Rob answered that he also had to make a living and that the drug dealers were hurting his business. They could sell somewhere else; they did not have to sell on his corner. Choc responded that this is where his mother lives: "I grew up here, so I can do what I want. I'll die for this [corner], 'cause I got to eat. And ain't nobody gon' stop me from eating." Rob asked, "Is that how you feel?" Choc bellowed, "Yeah!" "All right, I'm gon' talk to your mama about it and see if she feel the same way."

Many people in the neighborhood are aware of the present tension around the corner by Ms. Newbill's. A beef has been created and infused with a certain social significance.

People want to know what is going to happen next. Will Rob back down? Or will the boys back down? Either way, the result carries implications for the community and the local status order. Core elements of the code of the street are heavily in play: Can I take care of myself without going to the authorities? Do I have enough juice or personal power to do what I want? The metaphor of a chess game is not lost, as both Rob and Choc consider their next moves, with everyone anxiously looking on. Ostensibly, it is between them and nobody else. In fact, it is over who is going to rule the community in the long run—the decent folks or the street element. The struggle over the corner may be viewed as simply one battle in a war.

In trying out strategies for winning, Rob offered a scenario of what he might do in regard to Choc. He said, "I'm gon' go tell his mother, that if I crack him in his head he won't be selling drugs there. Now, there are three corners that he can't sell on: where I got the fruit stand, where Ms. Newbill's place is, and in front of the library or gym. He can go over to the vacant lot where the gas station used to be. I'll tell him, 'You can sell over there because my customers don't come that way,' but he knows that place is in the open, and Captain Perez [leader of local district] will get him if he do that. 'You can't sell on any other corner. But since you are gonna sell anyway, go over and sell on the vacant gas station lot.'" Rob knew that setting up business there would put Choc in the open so the captain could see him, and everyone knew that the captain was not to be trifled with.

Choc then sent five others of the local community to warn Rob, as a way both of getting the message back to Rob and of obtaining feedback on the situation and drumming up support: "Rob is gonna find himself with some problems" was a common sentiment. These five people, one by one, came back to Rob his first day on the job at Ms. Newbill's and told him what Choc had said—"that he will find himself in some problems." And they would inquire of Rob, "What's going on?" or "You closing down drug corners, now?" or "Choc feels some type o' way about all this [he's mad]."

Herman and I were at Ms. Newbill's on Rob's first day as the proprietor of his new business there. Rob made us cheesesteaks and then came and sat with us. It was clear that he was not himself. He was somewhat agitated, and his street antennae were on high alert, as he glanced back and forth at the front door, studying everyone who entered. Suddenly he said, "Did you see that? Did you see that?" Herman asked, "What?" "She nodded her head, gave a signal to somebody," replied Rob. We looked up and saw an older woman standing in line to pay for some soap: She was facing the street. We noticed nothing out of the ordinary. But Rob was very concerned. He seems to have thought the woman might be alerting someone outside that we were here: if they wanted us, here we were. This turned out to be nothing. . . .

Soon we received our food and soft drinks. People continued to enter and leave. It was clear that our presence was the support Rob needed. He relaxed, and we had easy talk for the next hour and a half, at which point we left. Every minute we were there, we were putting the word out that drug dealing would not be tolerated on this corner. Herman felt strongly that the young men who were coming and going were letting others know that we were there and that we were committed to being there. And that was what Rob needed on his first day at Ms. Newbill's.

After one man left, Herman said of him confidently, "Yeah, he know Rob will hurt that boy [Choc], so why mess up Rob's future by sending Rob back to jail for killing this nut? He's putting Rob's word out that Rob is here to stay." The man was a crack addict named Johnny Brown, a mechanic—"the best there is when he can stay off that stuff." Brown is like a neighborhood courier who knows the latest about the neighborhood: "He know everything, including the shooting last night." He will also get the word to the neighborhood that another day has passed and that Rob has not been chased out. Everyone is watching, expectantly, taking in the drama. The atmosphere is something like that of *High Noon*, in part because there were shootouts on this busy, lucrative corner in the past. The stakes, financial and social, are high.

Moments later Maurice's brother Tip (a crack addict) comes in, approaches Rob, and asks, "Do you want me to get rid of him, old head? I know you, old head." In conversation the use of the term "old head" is most often an address of respect, but may also be slightly derisive, depending on the social context. Although the address does not always go by age, anyone over forty years old is considered to be past his prime and generally not as tough as the younger men. Reverent younger men may gently put such people in their place by calling them "old head." Rob says of Tip, "I didn't need his help. 'Cause then Tip would have been on the corner. In other words, you can't 'ask a devil to get rid of a devil, because then all you get is another devil.'"

The code of the street says, in certain circumstances, that each person will test the next person, probing to take his measure, in order to know how to behave toward that person. The people who survive respond by showing their tough sides. If they can do that, they deserve to be left alone. Herman comments, "Rob is like a test tube baby. He is an ongoing experiment, and we got to save this one." Herman's role, as it has been all along, is to help Rob through the obstacle course toward . . . decency. Herman can often be heard from the sidelines, coaching, "Now, don't go and bust the man in his face. There is always a better way [than violence]"—this is his constant message.

Because of his relationship with Herman—and Herman's relationship with the police—Rob now and then converses with the local police, who recognize him when they see him on the streets. On one recent afternoon Rob encountered a policeman, who said, "How you doing, Rob?" The local drug dealers see this, too, and their reaction might be "Aw, he's rattin' to the cops." This relationship with the police brings Rob respect and derision at the same time. His goal is to be completely on his own, to establish himself as a decent person in the community with the props of such a person, along with the props of the street life: toughness and decency, which are not easy to manage and to combine. But Rob must do so if he is to exist in the community with the status he would like. Without his knowledge of the code of the street, he would be in more peril. Possessing it is knowing to some degree what to do in what circumstances, and what not to do.

At this point Rob has figured out his next move with the drug dealers, but he does not know how it will work out. He is reluctant to bring Captain Perez into it, for doing so would hurt his long term status and reputation on the street. Perez might come in with too much police power and authority, and that would lead the others on the street to say, "Aw, he had to bring in the police. Aw, he's just a pussy, he went and got them to help him." Not to involve the police will give Rob more "heart" on the corner, on the street, where standoffs like this must be settled "man to man."

According to the code, the man goes for himself, takes up for himself, and calls on no one else to fight his battles. Whether he is successful or not in dealing with the situation man to man, the outcome will become known around the neighborhood, and his status on the street will be affected. To have to resort to the cops or anyone else is to be judged a chump, to have lost heart. He loses "stripes," or respect, because he cannot deal with the threat by the street code. Practically speaking, the police cannot be present all the time. Hence real and enduring protection depends on having a name, a reputation, and credibility for being able to defend what is rightfully one's own, even to the point of engaging in physicality; in a word, the person must get with the challenger, get in his face, and deal with him.

What Rob did was to go see Choc's mother and threaten Choc through her. Standing at the Little League field that evening, he explained to me that he told her that her son's drug dealing in front of the store was hurting his business and that if it did not stop, he would be forced to "handle his business." "So I'm just lettin' you know." "Don't worry about [it], Ruck, I'm gon' talk to him," responded Choc's mother, Mrs. Harmon. "I'm just lettin' you know," Rob repeated, " 'cause I been knowin' y'all for a long time. And I didn't want to just move out like that, without talking to you first. He said he's 'willing to die for the corner.' " Unlike some other mothers, Mrs. Harmon did not deny her son's involvement in the drug trade. She owned up to his dealing drugs in front of the store, expressed her own exasperation with it, and indicated she would handle it.

Telling Choc's mother has turned out to be a deft move on Rob's part because it increases the number of people who can work to defuse the situation. Choc's mother has strong emotional reasons to prevail on her son. It also gives Choc an excuse for capitulating, for, even though he may feel manly and able enough to overcome Rob, he knows he is disturbing his mother. Now he can give in but still save face by telling his boys, "I did it for my mother." For the time being, Rob's strategy seems to have worked. The boys have stopped selling drugs on Ms. Newbill's and Rob's corner. Things have cooled down. . . .

Rob still confronts major challenges. The test he went through is only one among many he will face in the future. He resides and operates in a community in which most of the residents are decent or trying to be. But there is also a street element that is less decent, poorly educated, alienated, and to

some extent angry; finally, there is a criminal element that is not only street-oriented but often also in the business of street hustling and drug-related crime.

Rob has to navigate this environment, not simply as an ordinary person, not as a drug dealer, but as a legitimate businessman operating a carryout. That means that from time to time he has to meet with all kinds of people, some of whom are involved in scams, trying to shoplift, to sell him stolen goods. Every day will bring another test. He'll be tried by drug dealers because his corner is so valuable; it represents capital. As an issue of urban turf, somebody must run that corner: either the police or the drug dealers. In this case, for the time being, Rob is running it. But a new drug gang could come to town, make dibs on this corner, and challenge him. And this time he may not know the man's mother.

Thus far Rob is surviving, and his capital has grown. His business is expanding. Word has gotten around that he's serving food at a decent price and declaring that he's not putting up with the drug activity on the corner. The neighborhood has breathed a sigh of relief, and now people visit the store in large numbers. One man likened the situation to "sunshine after the rain, and now that the sun is out, the people have returned." Rob likens it to there being "a new sheriff in town," and his presence signals a new day for the "Stop and Go." Before the standoff between Rob and the drug dealers, many community residents, particularly the decent people, stayed away. But since he has won—at least for the time being—they have returned. The whole situation is public. Rob has in effect retaken the corner, and his accomplishment affects not just that corner but the whole neighborhood as well. For several blocks around, a sphere of influence has been created that Rob controls and the drug dealers are keeping out of. . . .

The task is difficult because Rob is navigating an environment of so many alienated people, some of them without hope, some of them ready to try to pull him down—for as he rises, they may feel a sharp drop in their own self-esteem. As he gains more legitimate clout, however, his influence spreads through the neighborhood and he becomes a role model for those who lack direction or have fallen into the street life: he has visibly pulled himself up and thus offers them a profoundly different way out of the street. His example shows this way can work.

Yet it is a fine understanding of the code of the street that enables Rob to survive the many physical standoffs that characterize ghetto street life. It is by deftly interpreting and abiding by the rules of the code that he is able to get through his days and nights, to manage the respect necessary to keep the drug dealers, scam artists and others at bay, or in line. At the same time he must function in the decent world as well, in the world of legitimate business practice—licenses, tax laws, and the like. The inner-city success story therefore requires the ability to code-switch, to play by the code of the street with the street element and by the code of decency with others. . . .

Rob is caught up in a subculture that is a function of alienation and the social isolation that results from it—a culture rife with bad schooling, racism, poverty, and devastations of drugs and violence. Crime is rampant there, but the police tolerate a good deal of it. Captain Perez is more engaged, but most officers basically try to maintain order without hurting themselves. In addition, the community is composed of working-class and very poor people since those with the means to move away have done so. . . . The result of all this is that the inner-city community has become a kind of urban village, apart from the wider society and limited in terms of resources and human capital. Young people growing up here often receive only the truncated version of mainstream society that comes from television and the perceptions of their peers. . . .

The condition of these communities was produced not by moral turpitude but by economic forces that have undermined black, urban, working-class life and by a neglect of their consequences on the part of the public. Although it is true that persistent welfare dependency, teenage pregnancy, drug abuse, drug dealing, violence, and crime reinforce economic marginality, many of these . . . problems originated in frustration and the inability to thrive under conditions of economic dislocation. . . . Any effort to place the blame solely on individuals in urban ghettos is seriously misguided. The focus should be on the socioeconomic structure, because it was structural change that caused jobs to decline and joblessness to increase in many of these communities. . . . [W]hen jobs disappear and people are left poor, highly concentrated and hopeless, the way is paved for the underground economy to become a way of life, an unforgiving way of life organized around a code of violence and predatory activity. Only by reestablishing a viable [legitimate] economy in the inner city, particularly one that provides access to jobs for young inner-city men and women, can we encourage a positive sense of the future. . . .

Part VIII

The Construction of Social Structures

The selections in the previous section examined various ways that social structures profoundly influence individuals' subjective experiences, interactions, relationships, and fates. However, the authors also implied that social structures endure because they are interactionally reproduced. Although social structures often seem self-perpetuating, they are perpetuated by individuals who engage in recurrent patterns of interaction. Individuals may experience social structures as an external environment as powerfully constraining as the physical environment, but social structures are quite unlike the physical environment. Their power does not come from nature but from human definition and collective action. They are humanly created and re-created. The selections in this section examine the interactional creation, accomplishment, perpetuation, and redefinition of different types and dimensions of social structure. They remind us that we humans organize and structure our own social lives. Some of us may influence those processes more than others, but we all participate. ✦

28

Society in Action

Herbert Blumer

Herbert Blumer was an important proponent and contributor to the sociological perspective of "symbolic interactionism," a name that he himself gave to it. This approach to the study of social life grew out of George Herbert Mead's ideas about the human self, thought, and interaction. As you may recall, Mead argued that individuals interact with themselves much as they interact with one another. They continually engage in an inner conversation. Rather than blindly responding, they define and interpret their experience. Their action and interaction is symbolic and meaningful.

Blumer argues that the study of social life must start from Mead's basic insights. Human social life is a continual process of individual and collective definition and interpretation. Society, culture, and social structure are not static things but are derived from what people do. And what people do is engage in symbolic interaction, both with one another and with themselves. Through processes of definition and interpretation, humans fit their individual lines of action together and construct joint actions. As Blumer further argues, students of social life cannot afford to ignore the fact that even the action of such human collectivities as societies, nations, and organizations are based on processes of definition, interpretation, and symbolic interaction.

Blumer draws three lessons about the study of social life from this basic insight. First, no matter how stable and orderly, social life is always subject to the "play and fate of meaning." Recurrent patterns of interaction and collective action are based on definitions and interpretations that may change unpredictably. Second, the networks of joint action that are often called "social institutions" are not self-governing and self-sustaining entities, but rather are sustained by human interaction and are governed by human definition and interpretation. Third, the construction of joint action is based on understandings and meanings that emerge from prior interaction. No matter how new they may seem, they have a history. These are the specifications of Blumer's more general lesson: social structures, cultures, institutions, and societies exist only in human action and interaction. Thus, human action and interaction are what students of social life must ultimately study.

Human groups . . . [consist] of human beings who are engaging in action. The action consists of the multitudinous activities that the individuals perform in their lives as they encounter one another and as they deal with the succession of situations confronting them. The individuals may act singly, they may act collectively, and they may act on behalf of, or as representatives of, some organization or group of others. The activities belong to the acting individuals and are carried on by them always with regard to the situations in which they have to act. The import of this simple and essentially redundant characterization is that fundamentally human groups or society *exists in action* and must be seen in terms of action. This picture of human society as action must be the starting point (and the point of return) for any scheme that purports to treat and analyze human society empirically. Conceptual schemes that depict society in some other fashion can only be derivations from the complex of ongoing activity that constitutes group life. This is true of the two dominant conceptions of society in contemporary sociology—that of culture and that of social structure. Culture as a conception, whether defined as custom, tradition, norm, value, rules, or such like, is clearly derived from what people do. Similarly, social structure in any of its aspects, as represented by such terms as social position, status, role, authority, and prestige, refers to relationships derived from how people act toward each other. The life of any human society consists necessarily of an ongoing process of fitting together the activities of its members. It is this complex of ongoing activity that establishes and portrays structure or organization. . . .

The central place and importance of symbolic interaction in human group life and conduct should be apparent. A human society or group consists of people in association. Such association exists necessarily in the form of people acting toward one another and thus engaging in social interaction. Such interaction in human society is characteristically and predominantly on the symbolic level; as individuals acting individually, collectively, or as agents of some organization encounter one another, they are necessarily required to take account of the actions of one another as they form their own action. They do this by a dual process of indicating to others how to act and of interpreting the indications made by others. Human group life is a vast process of such defining to others what to do and of interpreting their definitions; through this process, people come to fit their activities to one another and to form their own individual conduct. Both such joint activity and individual conduct are formed *in* and *through* this ongoing process; they are not mere expressions or products of what people bring to their interaction or of conditions that are antecedent to their interaction. The failure to accommodate to this vital point constitutes the fundamental deficiency of schemes that seek to account for human society in terms of social organization or psychological factors, or of any combination of the two. By virtue of symbolic interaction, human group life is necessarily a formative process and not a mere arena for the expression of pre-existing factors.

[H]uman beings must have a makeup that fits the nature of social interaction. The hu-

man being is . . . an organism that not only responds to others on the non-symbolic level but as one that makes indications to others and interprets their indications. He can do this, as Mead has shown so emphatically, only by virtue of possessing a "self." Nothing esoteric is meant by this expression. It means merely that a human being can be an object of his own action. Thus, he can recognize himself, for instance, as being a man, young in age, a student, in debt, trying to become a doctor, coming from an undistinguished family, and so forth. In all such instances, he is an object to himself; and he acts toward himself and guides himself in his actions toward others on the basis of the kind of object he is to himself. . . .

[T]he fact that the human being has a self . . . enables him to interact with himself. This interaction is not in the form of interaction between two or more parts of a psychological system, as between needs, or between emotions, or between ideas, or between the id and the ego in the Freudian scheme. Instead, the interaction is social—a form of communication, with the person addressing himself as a person and responding thereto. We can clearly recognize such interaction in ourselves, as each of us notes that he is angry with himself, or that he has to spur himself on in his tasks, or that he reminds himself to do this or that, or that he is talking to himself in working out some plan of action. As such instances suggest, self-interaction exists fundamentally as a process of making indications to oneself. . . .

The capacity of the human being to make indications to himself gives a distinctive character to human action. It means that the human individual confronts a world that he must interpret in order to act instead of an environment to which he responds because of his organization. He has to cope with the situations in which he is called on to act, ascertaining the meaning of the actions of others and mapping out his own line of action in the light of such interpretation. He has to construct and guide his action instead of merely releasing it in response to factors playing on him or operating through him. He may do a miserable job in constructing his action, but he has to construct it. . . .

This view of human action applies equally well to joint or collective action, in which numbers of individuals are implicated. Joint or collective action constitutes the domain of sociological concern, as exemplified in the behavior of groups, institutions, organizations, and social classes. Such instances of societal behavior, whatever they may be, consist of individuals fitting their lines of action to one another. It is both proper and possible to view and study such behavior in its joint or collective character instead of in its individual components. Such joint behavior does not lose its character of being constructed through an interpretive process in meeting the situations in which the collectivity is called on to act. Whether the collectivity be an army engaged in a campaign, a corporation seeking to expand its operations, or a nation trying to correct an unfavorable balance of trade, it needs to construct its action through an interpretation of what is happening in its area of operation. The interpretive process takes place by participants making indications to one another, not merely each to himself. Joint or collective action is an outcome of such a process of interpretative interaction.

As stated earlier, human group life consists of, and exists in, the fitting of lines of action to each other by the members of the group. Such articulation of lines of action gives rise to and constitutes "joint action"—a societal organization of conduct of different acts of diverse participants. A joint action, while made up of diverse component acts that enter into its formation, is different from any one of them and from their mere aggregation. The joint action has a distinctive character in its own right, a character that lies in the articulation or linkage as apart from what may be articulated or linked. Thus, the joint action may be identified as such and may be

spoken of and handled without having to break it down into the separate acts that comprise it. This is what we do when we speak of such things as marriage, a trading transaction, war, a parliamentary discussion, or a church service. Similarly, we can speak of the collectivity that engages in joint action without having to identify the individual members of that collectivity, as we do in speaking of a family, a business corporation, a church, a university, or a nation. . . .

In dealing with collectivities and with joint action, one can easily be trapped in an erroneous position by failing to recognize that the joint action of the collectivity is an interlinkage of the separate acts of the participants. This failure leads one to overlook the fact that a joint action always has to undergo a process of formation; even though it may be a well-established and repetitive form of social action, each instance of it has to be formed anew. Further, this career of formation through which it comes into being necessarily takes place through the dual process of designation and interpretation that was discussed above. The participants still have to guide their respective acts by forming and using meanings.

With these remarks as a background, I wish to make three observations on the implications of the interlinkage that constitutes joint action. I wish to consider first those instances of joint action that are repetitive and stable. The preponderant portion of social action in a human society, particularly in a settled society, exists in the form of recurrent patterns of joint action. In most situations in which people act toward one another, they have in advance a firm understanding of how to act and of how other people will act. They share common and pre-established meanings of what is expected in the action of the participants, and accordingly each participant is able to guide his own behavior by such meanings. Instances of repetitive and pre-established forms of joint action are so frequent and common that it is easy to understand why scholars have viewed them as the essence or natural form of human group life. Such a view is especially apparent in the concepts of "culture" and "social order" that are so dominant in social-science literature. Most sociological schemes rest on the belief that a human society exists in the form of an established order of living, with that order resolvable into adherence to sets of rules, norms, values, and sanctions that specify to people how they are to act in their different situations.

Several comments are in order with regard to this neat scheme. First, it is just not true that the full expanse of life in a human society, any human society, is but an expression of pre-established forms of joint action. New situations are constantly arising within the scope of group life that are problematic and for which existing rules are inadequate. I have never heard of any society that was free of problems nor any society in which members did not have to engage in discussion to work out ways of action. Such areas of unprescribed conduct are just as natural, indigenous, and recurrent in human group life as are those areas covered by pre-established and faithfully followed prescriptions of joint action. Second, we have to recognize that even in the case of pre-established and repetitive joint action, each instance of such joint action has to be formed anew. The participants still have to build up their lines of action and fit them to one another through the dual process of designation and interpretation. They do this in the case of repetitive joint action, of course, by using the same recurrent and constant meanings. If we recognize this, we are forced to realize that the play and fate of meanings are what is important, not the joint action in its established form. Repetitive and stable joint action is just as much a result of an interpretative process as is a new form of joint action that is being developed for the first time. This is not an idle or pedantic point; the meanings that underlie established and recurrent joint action

are themselves subject to pressure as well as to reinforcement, to incipient dissatisfaction as well as to indifference; they may be challenged as well as affirmed, allowed to slip along without concern as well as subjected to infusions of new vigor. Behind the facade of the objectively perceived joint action, the set of meanings that sustains that joint action has a life that the social scientists can ill afford to ignore. A gratuitous acceptance of the concepts of norms, values, social rules, and the like should not blind [us] to the fact that any one of them is subtended by a process of social interaction—a process that is necessary not only for their change but equally well for their retention in a fixed form. It is the social process in group life that creates and upholds the rules, not the rules that create and uphold group life.

The second observation on the interlinkage that constitutes joint action refers to the extended connection of actions that make up so much of human group life. We are familiar with these large complex networks of action involving an interlinkage and interdependency of diverse actions of diverse people—as in the division of labor extending from the growing of grain by the farmer to an eventual sale of bread in a store, or in the elaborate chain extending from the arrest of a suspect to his eventual release from a penitentiary. These networks with their regularized participation of diverse people by diverse action at diverse points yields a picture of institutions that have been appropriately a major concern of sociologists. They also give substance to the idea that human group life has the character of a system. In seeing such a large complex of diversified activities, all hanging together in a regularized operation, and in seeing the complementary organization of participants in well-knit interdependent relationships, it is easy to understand why so many scholars view such networks or institutions as self-operating entities, following their own dynamics and not requiring that attention be given to the participants within the network. Most of the sociological analyses of institutions and social organization adhere to this view. Such adherence, in my judgment, is a serious mistake. One should recognize what is true, namely, that the diverse array of participants, occupying different points in the network, engage in their actions at those points on the basis of using given sets of meanings. A network or an institution does not function automatically because of some inner dynamics or system requirements; it functions because people at different points do something, and what they do is a result of how they define the situation in which they are called on to act. A limited appreciation of this point is reflected today in some of the work on decision-making, but on the whole the point is grossly ignored. It is necessary to recognize that the sets of meanings that lead participants to act as they do at their stationed points in the network have their own setting in a localized process of social interaction—and that these meanings are formed, sustained, weakened, strengthened, or transformed, as the case may be, through a socially defining process. Both the functioning and the fate of institutions are set by this process of interpretation as it takes place among the diverse sets of participants.

A third important observation needs to be made, namely, that any instance of joint action, whether newly formed or long established, has necessarily arisen out of a background of previous actions of the participants. A new kind of joint action never comes into existence apart from such a background. The participants in-volved in the formation of the new joint action always bring to that formation the world of objects, the sets of meanings, and the schemes of interpretation that they already possess. Thus, the new form of joint action always emerges out of and is connected with a context of previous joint action. . . .

[H]uman society [is] people engaged in living. Such living is a process of ongoing activity in which participants are developing lines of action in the multitudinous situations they encounter. They are caught up in a vast process of interaction in which they have to fit their developing actions to one another. This process of interaction consists in making indications to others of what to do and in interpreting the indications as made by others. . . . This general process should be seen, of course, in the differentiated character which it necessarily has by virtue of the fact that people cluster in different groups, belong to different associations, and occupy different positions. They accordingly approach each other differently, live in different worlds, and guide themselves by different sets of meanings. Nevertheless, whether one is dealing with a family, a boy's gang, an industrial corporation, or a political party, one must see the activities of the collectivity as being formed through a process of designation and interpretation.

Reprinted from: Herbert Blumer, *Symbolic Interactionism: Perspective and Method*, pp. 6–7, 10, 12–13, 15, 16–20. Copyright © 1998. Reprinted by permission of Pearson Education, Inc., Upper Saddle River, NJ. ✦

29

Borderwork Among Girls and Boys

Barrie Thorne

Gender is one of the most fundamental dimensions of the social structure of all known human societies. Yet gender is as much a human creation as any other dimension of social structure. Anatomical sex may be a natural fact of human life, but its meanings are not. It is these meanings, rather than reproductive biology, that constitute gender. Femininity and masculinity are as much products of human definition, interpretation, and interaction as any other human meanings. In this selection, Barrie Thorne examines the construction and reproduction of gender among elementary-school children. She concentrates on a recurrent pattern of interaction that she calls "borderwork."

Most children define themselves as either a boy or girl during the preschool-age years. Once they do, they tend to prefer the company of "their own kind." The result is a kind of self-imposed segregation between girls and boys. Boys tend to play with other boys and girls tend to play with other girls. Although girls and boys do continue to interact with one another, much of that interaction serves to erect, rather than break down, the invisible symbolic barrier between them. This kind of interaction is what constitutes the borderwork pattern.

Thorne examines three varieties of borderwork: chasing games, such as "chase-and-kiss"; rituals of pollution, such as "cooties"; and invasions, usually of girls' activities and territories by boys. As she demonstrates, these familiar and memorable forms of interaction create gender divisions and perpetuate prevailing gender stereo-types. When engaged in borderwork, girls and boys treat each other as members of opposing, if not antagonistic, teams. Their gender identities take priority over their personal identities. For example, a boy who is being chased by a girl is much more likely to exclaim, "Help, a girl's chasing me!" than "Help, Susie's chasing me!" They also tend to lump all boys and all girls together. "Boys are mean." "Girls have cooties." They thereby exaggerate gender difference and perpetuate gender stereotypes.

Thorne suggests that interaction between men and women often resembles the borderwork of school-age children, in that adults also enact gender stereotypes and exaggerate gender difference. Like boys and girls, men and women interactionally produce and reproduce their gender and the often rocky relations between the sexes. And what is interactionally produced can be interactionally changed. Gender—the meanings of anatomical sex—is not imposed on us by nature or social structure. To borrow from Blumer, our femininity and masculinity are derived from what we do, not from what we are.

My husband, Peter, and I became parents several years after I had . . . started to teach and do research on gender. . . . Parenting returned me to the sites of childhood—the Lilliputian worlds of sandboxes, neighborhood hideouts, playgrounds, elementary-school lunchrooms. I found that these sites, that the sheer presence of groups of children, evoked memories of my own childhood. . . . Those memories, and my experiences as a parent, whetted my interest in learning, more systematically, about girls' and boys' daily experiences of gender. I decided to hang out in an elementary school, keeping regular notes on my observations, especially of boys' and girls' relationships with one another. . . .

During the 1976-77 school year, I observed for eight months in a public elementary school in a small city on the coast of California. I gained initial access to this school, which I will call Oceanside (all names of places and people have been changed), through the teacher of a combined fourth-fifth-grade class. I regularly observed in Miss Bailey's classroom and accompanied the students into the lunchroom and onto the playground, where I roamed freely and got to know other kids as well.

In 1980, when I was living in Michigan, I did another stint of fieldwork, observing for three months in Ashton School, my pseudonym for a public elementary school on the outskirts of a large city. . . . In addition to observing in an Ashton kindergarten and a second-grade classroom, I roamed around the lunchroom, hallways, and playground. This experience helped me broaden and gain perspective on the more focused and in-depth observations from the California school. . . .

Borderwork

Walking across a school playground from the paved areas where kids play jump rope and hopscotch to the grassy playing field and games of soccer and baseball, one moves from groups of girls to groups of boys. The spatial separation of boys and girls constitutes a kind of boundary, perhaps felt most strongly by individuals who want to join an activity controlled by the other gender. When girls and boys are together in a relaxed and integrated way, playing a game of handball or eating and talking together at a table in the lunchroom, the sense of gender as boundary often dissolves. But sometimes girls and boys come together in ways that emphasize their opposition; boundaries may be created through contact as well as avoidance.

The term "borderwork" helps conceptualize interaction across—yet, interaction based on and even strengthening—gender boundaries. This notion comes from Fredrik Barth's

[1969] analysis of social relations that are maintained across ethnic boundaries (e.g., between the Saami, or Lapps, and Norwegians) without diminishing the participants' sense of cultural difference and of dichotomized ethnic status. Barth focuses on more macro, ecological arrangements, whereas I emphasize face-to-face behavior. But the insight is similar: *although contact sometimes undermines and reduces an active sense of difference, groups may also interact with one another in ways that strengthen their borders.* One can gain insight into the maintenance of ethnic (and gender) groups by examining the boundary that defines them rather than by looking at what Barth calls "the cultural stuff that it encloses" [Barth 1969, p. 15].

When gender boundaries are activated, the loose aggregation "boys and girls" consolidates into "the boys" and "the girls" as separate and reified groups. In the process, categories of identity, that on other occasions have minimal relevance for interaction, become the basis of separate collectivities. Other social definitions get squeezed out by heightened awareness of gender as a dichotomy and of "the girls" and "the boys" as opposite and even antagonistic sides. Several times I watched this process of transformation, which felt like a heating up of the encounter because of the heightened sense of opposition and conflict.

On a paved area of the Oceanside playground, a game of team handball took shape (team handball resembles doubles tennis, with clenched fists used to serve and return a rubber ball). Kevin arrived with the ball, and, seeing potential action, Tony walked over with interest on his face. Rita and Neera already stood on the other side of the yellow painted line that designated the center of a playing court. Neera called out, "Okay, me and Rita against you two," as Kevin and Tony moved into position. The game began in earnest with serves and returns punctuated by game-related talk—challenges between the opposing teams ("You're out!" "No, exactly on the line") and supportive comments between team members ("Sorry, Kevin," Tony said, when he missed a shot; "That's okay," Kevin replied). The game proceeded for about five minutes, and then the ball went out of bounds. Neera ran after it, and Tony ran after her, as if to begin a chase. As he ran, Rita shouted with annoyance, "C'mon, let's play." Tony and Neera returned to their positions, and the game continued.

Then Tony slammed the ball, hard, at Rita's feet. She became angry at the shift from the ongoing, more cooperative mode of play, and she flashed her middle finger at the other team, calling to Sheila to join their side. The game continued in a serious vein until John ran over and joined Kevin and Tony, who cheered; then Bill arrived, and there was more cheering. Kevin called out, "C'mon Ben," to draw in another passing boy; then Kevin added up the numbers on each side, looked across the yellow line, and triumphantly announced, "We got five and you got three." The game continued, more noisy than before, with the boys yelling "wee haw" each time they made a shot. The girls—and that's how they now seemed, since the sides were increasingly defined in terms of gender—called out, "Bratty boys! Sissy boys!" When the ball flew out of bounds, the game dissolved, as Tony and Kevin began to chase after Sheila. Annoyed by all these changes, Rita had already stomped off.

In this sequence, an earnest game, with no commentary on the fact that boys and girls happened to be on different sides, gradually transformed into a charged sense of girls-against-boys/boys-against-the-girls. Initially, one definition of the situation prevailed: a game of team handball, with each side trying to best the other. Rita, who wanted to play a serious game, objected to the first hint of other possibilities, which emerged when Tony chased Neera. The frame of a team handball game continued but was altered and eventually overwhelmed when the kids began to evoke gender boundaries. These boundaries brought in other possibilities—piling on players to out-

number the other gender, yelling gender-based insults, shifting from handball to cross-gender chasing—which finally broke up the game.

Gender boundaries have a shifting presence, but when evoked, they are accompanied by stylized forms of action, a sense of performance, mixed and ambiguous meanings . . . and by an array of intense emotions—excitement, playful elation, anger, desire, shame, and fear. . . . These stylized moments evoke recurring themes that are deeply rooted in our cultural conceptions of gender, and they suppress awareness of patterns that contradict and qualify them. . . .

Chasing

Cross-gender chasing dramatically affirms boundaries between boys and girls. The basic elements of chase and elude, capture and rescue are found in various kinds of tag with formal rules, as well as in more casual episodes of chasing that punctuate life on playgrounds. These episodes begin with a provocation, such as taunts ("You creep!" "You can't get me!"), bodily pokes, or the grabbing of a hat or other possession. A provocation may be ignored, protested ("Leave me alone!"), or responded to by chasing. Chaser and chased may then alternate roles. Christine Finnan (1982), who also observed schoolyard chasing sequences, notes that chases vary in the ratio of chasers to chased (e.g., one chasing one, or five chasing two), the form of provocation (a taunt or a poke); the outcome (an episode may end when the chased outdistances the chaser, with a brief touch, wrestling to the ground, or the recapturing of a hat or a ball); and in use of space (there may or may not be safety zones). Kids sometimes weave chasing with elaborate shared fantasies, as when a group of Ashton first- and second-grade boys played "jail," with "cops" chasing after "robbers," or when several third-grade girls designated a "kissing dungeon" beneath the playground slide and chased after boys to try to throw them in. When they captured a boy and put him in the dungeon under the slide, two girls would guard him while other boys pushed through the guards to help the captured boy escape.

Chasing has a gendered structure. Boys frequently chase one another, an activity that often ends in wrestling and mock fights. When girls chase girls, they are usually less physically aggressive; for example, they less often wrestle one another to the ground or try to bodily overpower the person being chased. Unless organized as a formal game like "freeze tag," same-gender chasing goes unnamed and usually undiscussed. But children set apart cross-gender chasing with special names. Students at both Oceanside and Ashton most often talked about "girls-chase-the-boys" and "boys-chase-the-girls"; the names are largely interchangeable, although boys tend to use the former and girls the latter, each claiming a kind of innocence. At Oceanside, I also heard both boys and girls refer to "catch-and-kiss"; and, at Ashton, older boys talked about "kiss-or-kill," younger girls invited one another to "catch boys," and younger girls and boys described the game of "kissin'." In addition to these terms, I have heard reports from other U.S. schools of "the chase," "chasers," "chase-and-kiss," "kiss-chase," and "kissers-and-chasers." The names vary by region and school but always contain both gender and sexual meanings.

Most informal within-gender chasing does not live on in talk unless something unusual happens, like an injury. But cross-gender chasing, especially when it takes the form of extended sequences with more than a few participants, is often surrounded by lively discussion. Several parents have told me about their kindergarten or first-grade children coming home from school to excitedly, or sometimes disgustedly, describe "girls-chase-the-boys" (my children also did this when they entered elementary school). Verbal retellings and assessments take place not only at home but also on the playground. For example, three Ashton fourth-grade girls who claimed

time-out from boys-chase-the-girls by running to a declared safety zone, excitedly talked about the ongoing game: "That guy is mean, he hits everybody." "I kicked him in the butt."

In girls-chase-the-boys, girls and boys become, by definition, separate teams. Gender terms blatantly override individual identities, especially in references to the other team ("Help, a girl's chasin' me!" "C'mon Sarah, let's get that boy!" "Tony, help save me from the girls!"). Individuals may call for help from, or offer help to, others of their gender. And in acts of treason, they may grab someone from their team and turn them over to the other side. For example, in an elaborate chasing scene among a group of Ashton third-graders, Ryan grabbed Billy from behind, wrestling him to the ground. "Hey girls, get 'im," Ryan called.

Boys more often mix episodes of cross-gender with same-gender chasing, a pattern strikingly evident in the large chasing scenes or melees that recurred on the segment of the Ashton playground designated for third- and fourth-graders. Of the three age-divided playground areas, this was the most bereft of fixed equipment; it had only a handball court and, as a boy angrily observed to me, "two stinkin' monkey bars." Movable play equipment was also in scarce supply; the balls were often lodged on the school roof, and, for a time, the playground aides refused to hand out jump ropes because they said the kids just wanted to use them to "strangle and give ropeburns." With little to do, many of the students spent recesses and the lunch hour milling and chasing around on the grassy field. Boys ran after, tackled, and wrestled one another on the ground, sometimes so fiercely that injuries occurred. Girls also chased girls, although less frequently and with far less bodily engagement than among boys. Cross-gender chases, in every sort of numeric combination, were also less physically rough than chasing among boys; girls were quick to complain, and the adult aides intervened more quickly when a boy and a girl wrestled on the ground. Cross-gender chasing was full of verbal hostility, from both sides, and it was marked by stalking postures and girls' screams and retreats to spots of safety and talk.

In cross-gender and same-gender chasing, girls often create safety zones, a designated space that they can enter to become exempt from the fray. After a period of respite, often spent discussing what has just happened, they return to the game. The safety zone is sometimes a moving area around an adult; more than once, as I stood watching, my bubble of personal space housed several girls. Or the zone may be more fixed, like the pretend steel house that the first- and second-grade Ashton girls designated next to the school building. In the Oceanside layout, the door to the girls' restroom faced one end of the playground, and girls often ran into it for safety. I could hear squeals from within as boys tried to open the door and peek in. During one of these scenarios, eight girls emerged from the restroom with dripping clumps of wet paper towels, which they threw at the three boys who had been peeking in, and then another burst of chasing ensued. . . .

'Cooties' and Other Pollution Rituals

Episodes of chasing sometimes entwine with rituals of pollution, as in "cooties" or "cootie tag" where specific individuals or groups are treated as contaminating or carrying "germs." Cooties, of course, are invisible; they make their initial appearance through announcements like "Rochelle has cooties!" Kids have rituals for transferring cooties (usually touching someone else, often after a chase, and shouting "You've got cooties!"), for immunization (writing "CV"—for "cootie vaccination"—on their arms, or shaping their fingers to push out a pretend-immunizing "cootie spray"), and for eliminating cooties (saying "no gives" or using "cootie catchers" made of folded paper). While girls and boys may transfer cooties to one another, and girls may

give cooties to girls, boys do not generally give cooties to other boys. Girls, in short, are central to the game.

Either girls or boys may be defined as having cooties, but girls give cooties to boys more often than vice versa. In Michigan, one version of cooties was called "girl stain." . . . And in a further shift from acts to imputing the moral character of actors, individuals may be designated as "cootie queens" or "cootie girls." Cootie queens or cootie girls (I have never heard or read about "cootie kings" or "cootie boys") are female pariahs, the ultimate school untouchables, seen as contaminating not only by virtue of gender, but also through some added stigma such as being overweight or poor. And according to one report, in a racially mixed playground in Fresno, California, "Mexican" (Chicano/Latino) but not Anglo children give cooties; thus, inequalities of race, as well as gender and social class, may be expressed through pollution games. In situations like this, different sources of oppression may compound one another.

I did not learn of any cootie queens at Ashton or Oceanside, but in the daily life of schools, *individual* boys and girls may be stigmatized and treated as contaminating. For example, a third-grade Ashton girl refused to sit by a particular boy, whom other boys routinely pushed away from the thick of all-male seating, because he was "stinky" and "peed in his bed." A teacher in another school told me that her fifth-grade students said to newcomers, "Don't touch Phillip's desk; he picks his nose and makes booger balls." Phillip had problems with motor coordination, which, the teacher thought, contributed to his marginalization.

But there is also a notable gender asymmetry, evident in the skewed patterning of cooties; *girls as a group are treated as an ultimate source of contamination*, while boys *as* boys—although maybe not, as Chicanos or individuals with a physical disability—are exempt. Boys sometimes mark hierarchies among themselves by using "girl" as a label for low-status boys and by pushing subordinated boys next to the contaminating space of girls. In Miss Bailey's fourth-fifth-grade class, other boys routinely forced or maneuvered the lowest-status boys (Miguel and Alejandro, the recent immigrants from Mexico, and Joel, who was overweight and afraid of sports) into sitting "by the girls," a space treated as contaminating. In this context, boys drew on gender meanings to convey racial subordination. In contrast, when there was gender-divided seating in the classroom, lunchroom, music room, or auditorium, which girls sat at the boundary between groups of girls and groups of boys had no apparent relationship to social status.

Boys sometimes treat objects associated with girls as polluting; once again, the reverse does not occur. Bradley, a college student, told me about a classroom incident he remembered from third grade. Some girls gave Valentine's Day cards with pictures of Strawberry Shortcake, a feminine-stereotyped image, to everyone in the class, including boys. Erik dumped all his Strawberry Shortcake valentines into Bradley's box; Bradley one-upped the insult by adding his own Strawberry Shortcake valentines to the pile and sneaking them back into Erik's box.

Recoiling from physical proximity with another person and their belongings because they are perceived as contaminating is a powerful statement of social distance and claimed superiority. Pollution beliefs and practices draw on the emotion-laden feeling of repugnance that accompanies unwanted touch or smell. Kids often act out pollution beliefs in a spirit of playful teasing, but the whimsical frame of "play" slides in and out of the serious, and some games of cooties clearly cause emotional pain. When pollution rituals appear, even in play, they frequently express and enact larger patterns of inequality, by gender, by social class and race, and by bodily characteristics like weight and motor coordination. When several of these

characteristics are found in the same person, the result may be extreme rituals of shaming, as in the case of cootie queens. Aware of the cruelty and pain bound up in games of pollution, teachers and aides often try to intervene, especially when a given individual becomes the repeated target. . . .

Invasions

. . . [I]n chasing, groups of girls and groups of boys confront one another as separate "sides," which makes for a kind of symmetry, as does the alternation of chasing and being chased. But rituals of pollution tip the symmetry, defining girls as more contaminating. Invasions, a final type of borderwork, also take asymmetric form; boys invade girls' groups and activities much more often than the reverse. When asked about what they do on the playground, boys list "teasing the girls" as a named activity, but girls do not talk so routinely about "teasing boys." As in other kinds of borderwork, gendered language ("Let's spy on the girls" "Those boys are messing up our jump-rope game") accompanies invasions, as do stylized interactions that highlight a sense of gender as an antagonistic social division.

On the playgrounds of both schools, I repeatedly saw boys, individually or in groups, deliberately disrupt the activities of groups of girls. Boys ruin ongoing games of jump rope by dashing under the twirling rope and disrupting the flow of the jumpers or by sticking a foot into the rope and stopping its momentum. On the Ashton playground, seven fourth-grade girls engaged in an intense game of four-square; it was a warm October day, and the girls had piled their coats on the cement next to the painted court. Two boys, mischief enlivening their faces, came to the edge of the court. One swung his arm into the game's bouncing space; in annoyed response, one of the female players pushed back at him. He ran off for a few feet, while the other boy circled in to take a swipe, trying to knock the ball out of play. Meanwhile, the first boy kneeled behind the pile of coats and leaned around to watch the girls. One of the girls yelled angrily, "Get out. My glasses are in one of those, and I don't want 'em busted." A playground aide called the boys over and told them to "leave the girls alone," and the boys ran off.

Some boys more or less specialize in invading girls, coming back again and again to disrupt; the majority of boys are not drawn to the activity. Even if only a few boys do most of the invading, disruptions are so frequent that girls develop ritualized responses. Girls verbally protest ("Leave us alone!" "Stop it, Keith!"), and they chase boys away. The disruption of a girls' game may provoke a cross-gender chasing sequence, but if girls are annoyed, they chase in order to drive the boy out of the space, a purpose far removed from playful shifting between the roles of chaser and chased. Girls may guard their play with informal lookouts who try to head off trouble; they are often wary about letting boys into their activities. . . .

Why Is Borderwork so Memorable?

The imagery of "border" may wrongly suggest an unyielding fence that divides social relations into two parts. The image should rather be one of many short fences that are quickly built and as quickly dismantled. . . . [Earlier] I described a team handball game in which gender meanings heated up. Heated events also cool down. After the team handball game transmuted into a brief scene of chasing, the recess bell rang and the participants went back to their shared classroom. Ten minutes later the same girls and boys interacted in reading groups where gender was of minimal significance. . . . [W]hy [then] are the occasions of gender borderwork so compelling? Why do episodes of girls-chase-the-boys and boys-against-the-girls *seem* like the heart of what "gender" is all about? Why do kids regard those situations as especially

newsworthy and turn them into stories that they tell afterward and bring home from school? And why do adults, when invited to muse back upon gender relations in their elementary school years, so often spontaneously recall "girls-chase-the-boys," "teasing girls," and "cooties," but less often mention occasions when boys and girls were together in less gender-marked ways? (The latter kinds of occasions may be recalled under other rubrics, like "when we did classroom projects.")

The occasions of borderwork may carry extra-perceptual weight because they are marked by conflict, intense emotions, and the expression of forbidden desires. These group activities may also rivet attention because they are created by kids themselves, and because they are ritualized, not as high ceremony, but by virtue of being stylized, repeated, and enacted with a sense of performance. . . . [For example,] cross-gender chasing has a name ("chase and kiss"), a scripted format (the repertoire of provocations and forms of response), and takes shape through stylized motions and talk. The ritual form focuses attention and evokes dominant beliefs about the "nature" of boys and girls and relationships between them.

Erving Goffman [1977, p. 321] coined the term "genderism" to refer to moments in social life, such as borderwork situations, that evoke stereotypic beliefs. During these ritually foregrounded encounters, men and women "play out the differential human nature claimed for them." Many social environments don't lend themselves to this bifurcated and stylized display, and they may even undermine the stereotypes. But when men engage in horseplay (pushing, shoving) and mock contests like Indian wrestling, they dramatize themes of physical strength and violence that are central to [prevailing] constructions of masculinity. And, in various kinds of cross-gender play, as when a man chases after and pins down a woman, he pretends to throw her off a cliff, or threatens her with a snake, the man again claims physical dominance and encourages the woman to "provide a full-voiced rendition [shrinking back, hiding her eyes, screaming] of the plight to which her sex is presumably prone" [Goffman 1977, p. 323]. In short, men and women—and girls and boys—sometimes become caricatures of themselves, enacting and perpetuating stereotypes.

Games of girls-against-the-boys [and] scenes of cross-gender chasing and invasion . . . evoke stereotyped images of gender relations. Deeply rooted in the dominant culture . . . of our society, these images infuse the ways adults talk about girls and boys and relations between them; the content of movies, television, advertising, and children's books; and even the wisdom of experts. . . . This [prevailing] view of gender—acted out, reinforced, and evoked through the various forms of borderwork—has two key components:

1. *Emphasis on gender as an oppositional dualism.* Terms like "the opposite sex" and "the war between the sexes" come readily to mind when one watches a group of boys invade a jump-rope game and the girls angrily respond, or a group of girls and a group of boys hurling insults at one another across a lunchroom. In all forms of borderwork, boys and girls are defined as rival teams with a socially distant, wary, and even hostile relationship; heterosexual meanings add to the sense of polarization. Hierarchy tilts the theme of opposition, with boys asserting spatial, physical, and evaluative dominance over girls.

2. *Exaggeration of gender difference and disregard for the presence of crosscutting variation and sources of commonality.* Social psychologists have identified a continuum that ranges from what Henri Tajfel [1982] calls the "interpersonal extreme," when interaction is largely determined by *individual* characteristics, to the "intergroup extreme," when interaction is largely determined by the *group member-*

ship or social categories of participants. Borderwork lies at the intergroup extreme. When girls and boys are defined as opposite sides caught up in rivalry and competition, group stereotyping and antagonism flourish. Members of "the other side" become "that boy" or "that girl." Individual identities get submerged, and participants hurl gender insults ("sissy boys," "dumb girls"), talk about the other gender as "yuck," and make stereotyped assertions ("girls are cry-babies," "boys are frogs; I don't like boys").

Extensive gender separation and organizing mixed-gender encounters as girls-against-the-boys set off contrastive thinking and feed an assumption of gender as dichotomous and antagonistic difference. These social practices seem to express core truths: that boys and girls are separate and fundamentally different, as individuals and as groups. Other social practices that challenge this portrayal—drawing boys and girls together in relaxed and extended ways, emphasizing individual identities or social categories that cut across gender, acknowledging variation in the activities and interests of girls and boys—carry less perceptual weight. . . .

The frames of "play" and "ritual" set the various forms of borderwork a bit apart from ongoing "ordinary" life. As previously argued, this may enhance the perceptual weight of borderwork situations in the eyes of both participants and observers, highlighting a gender-as-antagonistic-dualism portrayal of social relations. But the framing of ritualized play may also give leeway for participants to gain perspective on dominant cultural images. Play and ritual can comment on and challenge, as well as sustain, a given ordering of reality. . . . I [once] watched and later heard an aide describe a game the Oceanside students played on the school lunchroom floor. The floor was made up of large alternating squares of white and green linoleum, rather like a checkerboard. One day during the chaotic transition from lunch to noontime recess, [a boy named] Don . . . jumped, with much gestural and verbal fanfare, from one green square to another. Pointing to a white square, Don loudly announced, "That's girls' territory. Stay on the green square, or you'll change into a girl. Yuck!"

It occurred to me that Don was playing with gender dualisms, with a basic structure of two oppositely arranged parts whose boundaries are charged with risk. From one vantage point, the square-jumping game, as a kind of magical borderwork, may express and dramatically reaffirm structures basic to . . . the gender relations of the school. In the dichotomous world of either green or white, boy or girl, one misstep could spell transformative disaster. But from another vantage point, Don called up that structure to detached view, playing with, commenting on, and even, perhaps, mocking its assumptions.

References

Barth, Fredrik. 1969. "Introduction." Pp. 9–38 in *Ethnic Groups and Boundaries*, edited by F. Barth. Boston: Little, Brown.

Finnan, Christine. 1982. "The Ethnography of Children's Spontaneous Play." Pp. 358–380 in *Doing the Ethnography of Schooling*, edited by George Spindler. New York: Holt, Rinehart, and Winston.

Goffman, Erving. 1977. "The Arrangement between the Sexes." *Theory and Society* 4: 301–336.

Tajfel, Henri. 1982. "Social Psychology of Intergroup Relations." *Annual Review of Psychology*, 33: 1–39.

30

The Black Male in Public

Elijah Anderson

This selection by Elijah Anderson illustrates how social structural divisions influence interaction and, in turn, how patterns of interaction perpetuate those divisions. It focuses on interactions, involving young black men on the streets of two adjoining neighborhoods in an American city. Of course, race has long been an important dimension of the American social structure that has profoundly influenced interaction both between and among blacks and whites. Although many of the social structural barriers separating blacks from whites have been lowered in recent years, the influence of racial identification on patterns of interaction is still profound. Anderson suggests that recent increases in poverty and crime in the black ghettos of many American cities have even magnified the influence of the overlapping identities of young, black, male, and poor on public interaction in American cities.

According to Anderson, being a young black man from the ghetto is what many sociologists call a "master status." That is, others give that status or identity priority over all other characteristics in defining and deciding what to expect from such an individual. As far as many Americans are concerned, the master status or identity of young black man from the ghetto clearly implies that the individual is potentially dangerous and untrustworthy. Newspapers, television, and often personal experience confirm and perpetuate that stereotype, even among young black men themselves. As Anderson describes

it, those who encounter such an individual in public places react accordingly.

On the other hand, Anderson argues, young black men often confirm others' typification of them as potential predators. They often do so inadvertently and sometimes do so quite purposefully. Young black men are hardly immune to the dangers of city streets and protect themselves by assuming a cool and aggressive pose. Yet that very pose may scare not only potential assailants but everyone else they encounter as well. According to Anderson, young black men sometimes also exploit others' fear of them, so as to claim public places as their exclusive turf. They apparently consider this just compensation for others' public treatment of them.

Anderson does suggest that whites may be more indiscriminate in their fear of young black men than other blacks. He observes that blacks, including young black men, often greet one another in an apparent attempt to allay fears and establish mutual trust. Whites who have little contact with blacks are unaware of this custom. They fearfully avoid even glancing at young black men on city streets, treating them all similarly. The result, in Anderson's words, is a vicious circle of suspicion and mistrust that perpetuates long-standing racial divisions in the American social structure. Public interaction between blacks and whites becomes a form of what Thorne calls "borderwork." Rather than breaking down barriers between blacks and whites, it reinforces them. This is only one example of the many subtle ways that individuals interactionally reproduce the very social structures that shape their experience and lives.

From summer 1975 through summer 1989, I did fieldwork in the general area I call the Village-Northton, which encompasses two communities—one black and low income to very poor (with an extremely high infant mortality rate), the other racially mixed but becoming increasingly middle to upper income and white. When my wife Nancy and I moved to the Village in 1975, I had not planned to study the area; but this changed as I encountered the local community and discovered what seemed an ideal urban laboratory. . . .

Particularly during the 1980s, the problems of United States cities grew more and more insistent, if not intractable to many. With rising unemployment, brought on in part by increasing "deindustrialization" and the exodus of major corporations, the local black community suffered. The employment lives of its members are further complicated by continuing racial prejudice and discrimination, which often frustrate efforts to make effective adjustments to these changes and the emerging reality. Many who have difficulty finding work in the regular economy become ever poorer and may join the criminal underground, which promises them huge financial rewards, a certain degree of "coolness," and happiness—that seems never to fully materialize. Yet in hot pursuit, many alienated young people commit themselves to this way of life, adopting its morality and norms and serving as role models for other youths. In this way the drug economy has become elaborated, and drug use has grown widespread among the local poor. As the black community of Northton has undergone social deterioration, the adjacent Village has experienced "spillover" crime and public incivility.

These developments had profound consequences for the more general area I was studying, requiring further refinement of my research plans from a limited ethnographic representation of the gentrifying neighborhood of the Village to a more inclusive study of the relationship between it and the adjacent black ghetto of Northton. I found that I could not truly understand the Village independent of Northton, and vice versa, particularly where the two communities met, and that realization posed insistent sociological . . . questions. How do these diverse peoples get it on? How are their everyday public lives shaped and affected by the workings of local social institutions? What is the culture of the local public spaces? What is the public social order? Is there one? How are the social changes in the two communities affecting the residents of both?

From the mid-1970s through the 1980s, moving to the city and refurbishing inner-city areas seemed to young professionals like a brilliant idea, and a good investment to boot. They could afford an inner-city home that they could treat as a starter house, and the antique bargains held a special allure. Many were alienated from the life-styles of their suburban parents and sour on what the suburbs represented to them—social and cultural homogeneity—and they saw the city as a place where they might define their own lives in a different manner, close to work and play. This group contributed to the process we know today as gentrification. Yet commitment to such projects had its costs and brought some uncertainty. Crime in the street and wariness about strangers have always been recognized as costs of living in the city, but today many feel such realities have become worse. With looming municipal budget deficits, higher local taxes, a decline in city services, and growing inner-city poverty, drug use, and crime, many gentrifiers have come to see their own fortunes as inextricably linked to those of the nearby ghetto. They realize that changes in the neighboring black community directly and indirectly affect not only their sense of well-being but also their property values. This acknowledgement has slowed down—but not yet reversed—the process of gentrification.

I mean my descriptions and analysis to convey . . . how individuals come to interpret and negotiate the public spaces in the community I have been studying. Much of what I learned came through informal interviews and direct ethnographic observation over an extended period, and it draws on my experiences in the Village-Northton and in nearby communities that share some of the area's more prominent features. . . .

An overwhelming number of young black males in the Village are committed to civility and law-abiding behavior. They often have a hard time convincing others of this, however, because of the stigma attached to their skin color, age, gender, appearance, and general style of self-presentation. Moreover, most residents ascribe criminality, incivility, toughness, and street smartness to the anonymous black male, who must work hard to make others trust his common decency. . . .

Anonymous black males occupy a peculiar position in the social fabric of the Village. The fear and circumspection surrounding people's reactions to their presence constitute one of the hinges that public race relations turn on. Although the black male is a provocative figure to most others he encounters, his role is far from simple. It involves a complex set of relationships to be negotiated and renegotiated with all those sharing the streets. Where the Village meets Northton, black males exercise a peculiar hegemony over the public spaces, particularly at night or when two or more are together. This influence often is checked by the presence of the local police, which in turn has consequences for other public relationships in the Village.

The residents of the area, including black men themselves, are likely to defer to unknown black males, who move convincingly through the area as though they "run it," exuding a sense of ownership. They are easily perceived as symbolically inserting themselves into any available social space, pressing against those who might challenge them. The young black males, the "big winners" of these little competitions, seem to feel very comfortable as they swagger confidently along. Their looks, their easy smiles, and their spontaneous laughter, singing, cursing, and talk about the intimate details of their lives, which can be followed from across the street, all convey the impression of little concern for other pedestrians. The other pedestrians, however, are very concerned about them.

When young black men appear, women (especially white women) sometimes clutch their pocketbooks. They may edge up against their companions or begin to walk stiffly and deliberately. On spotting black males from a distance, other pedestrians often cross the street or give them a wide berth as they pass. When black males deign to pay attention to passersby, they tend to do so directly, giving them a deliberate once-over; their eyes may linger longer than the others consider appropriate to the etiquette of "strangers in the streets." Thus the black males take in all the others and dismiss them as a lion might dismiss a mouse. Fellow pedestrians in turn avert their eyes from the black males, deferring to figures who are seen as unpredictable, menacing, and not to be provoked—predators.

People, black or white, who are more familiar with the black street culture are less troubled by sharing the streets with young black males. Older black men, for instance, frequently adopt a refined set of criteria. In negotiating the streets, they watch out particularly for a certain *kind* of young black male; "jitterbugs" or those who might belong to "wolf packs," small bands of black teenage boys believed to travel about the urban areas accosting and robbing people.

Many members of the Village community, however, both black and white, lack these more sophisticated insights. Incapable of making distinctions between law-abiding black males and others, they rely for protection on broad stereotypes based on color and gender, if not outright racism. They are likely to misread many of the signs displayed by law-abiding black men, thus becoming apprehensive of almost any black male they spot in public. . . .

Two general sociological factors underlie the situation in which the black man in the Village finds himself. The first, the "master status-determining characteristic" of race (Hughes 1945), is at work in the most casual street encounter. . . . In the minds of many Village residents, black and white, the master status of the young black male is determined by his youth, his blackness, his maleness, and what these attributes have come to stand for in the shadow of the ghetto. In the context of racism, he is easily labeled "deviant." . . . In public, fellow pedestrians are thus uncertain about his purpose and have a strong desire to make sense of him quickly, so that they can get on with their own business. Many simply conclude that he is dangerous and act accordingly. Thus in social encounters in the public spaces of the Village, before he can be taken for anything as an individual . . . he is perceived first and foremost as a young black man from the ghetto. . . . Here the second element comes into play. An assessment like this is really a *social definition*, normally something to be negotiated between labeler and labeled. . . .

In a city one has many encounters with anonymous figures who are initially viewed as strangers, about whom little is known or understood. As Goffman (1959) suggests, there are ways strangers can rapidly become known or seen as less strange. In negotiating public spaces, people receive and display a wide range of behavioral cues and signs that make up the vocabulary of public interaction. Skin color, gender, age, companions, clothing, jewelry, and the objects people carry help identify them, so that assumptions are formed and communication can occur. Movements (quick or slow, false or sincere, comprehensible or incomprehensible) further refine this public communication. Factors like time of day or an activity that "explains" a person's presence can also affect in what way and how quickly the image of "stranger" is neutralized. . . .

If a stranger cannot pass inspection and be assessed as "safe" (either by identity or by purpose), the image of predator may arise, and fellow pedestrians may try to maintain a distance consistent with that image. In the more worrisome situations—for example, encountering a number of strangers on a dark street—the

image may persist and trigger some form of defensive action.

In the street environment, it seems, children readily pass inspection, white women and white men do so more slowly, black women, black men, and black male teenagers most slowly of all. The master status assigned to black males undermines their ability to be taken for granted as law-abiding and civil participants in public places: young black males, particularly those who don the urban uniform (sneakers, athletic suits, gold chains, "gangster caps," sunglasses, and large portable radios or "boom boxes"), may be taken as the embodiment of the predator. In this uniform, which suggests to many the "dangerous underclass," these young men are presumed to be troublemakers or criminals. Thus, in the local milieu, the identity of predator is usually "given" to the young black male and made to stick until he demonstrates otherwise, something not easy to do in circumstances that work to cut off communication. . . .

In the Village a third, concrete factor comes into play. The immediate source of much of the distrust the black male faces is the nearness of Northton. White newcomers in particular continue to view the ghetto as a mysterious and unfathomable place that breeds drugs, crime, prostitution, unwed mothers, ignorance, and mental illness. It symbolizes persistent poverty and imminent danger, personified in the young black men who walk the Village streets (see Katz 1988, 195–273). The following narrative of a young black indicates one response of Villagers to the stereotype they fear so much:

> A white lady walkin' down the street with a pocketbook. She start walkin' fast. She get so paranoid she break into a little stride. Me and my friends comin' from a party about 12:00. She stops and goes up on the porch of a house, but you could tell she didn't live there. I stop and say, 'Miss, you didn't have to do that. I thought you might think we're some wolf pack. I'm twenty-eight, he's twenty-six,

he's twenty-nine. You ain't gonna run from us.' She said, 'Well, I'm sorry.' I said, 'You can come down. I know you don't live there. We just comin' from a party.' We just walked down the street and she came back down, walked across the street where she really wanted to go. So she tried to act as though she lived there. And she didn't. After we said, 'You ain't gotta run from us,' she said, 'No, I was really in a hurry.' My boy said, 'No you wasn't. You thought we was gon' snatch yo' pocketbook.' We pulled money out. 'See this, we work.' I said, 'We grown men, now. You gotta worry about them fifteen-, sixteen-, seventeen-year-old boys. That's what you worry about. But we're grown men.' I told her all this. 'They the ones ain't got no jobs; they're too young to really work. They're the ones you worry about, not us.' She understood that. You could tell she was relieved and she gave a sigh. She came back down the steps, even went across the street. We stopped in the middle of the street. 'You all right, now?' And she smiled. We just laughed and went on to a neighborhood bar.

Experiences like this may help modify the way individual white residents view black males in public by establishing conditions under which blacks pass inspection by disavowing the image of the predator, but they do little to change the prevailing public relationship between blacks and whites in the community. Common racist stereotypes persist, and black men who successfully make such disavowals are often seen not as the norm but as the exception—as "different from the rest"—thereby confirming the status of the "rest."

In the interest of security and defense, residents adopt the facile but practical perspective that informs and supports the prevailing view of public community relations: whites are law-abiding and trustworthy; anonymous young black males are crime-prone and dangerous. Ironically, this perceived dangerous-

ness has become important to the public self-identity of many local black men. . . .

[B]oth blacks and whites are cautious with strangers and take special care in dealing with anonymous young blacks. This caution is encouraged by a certain style of self-presentation that is common on the street. Many black youths, law-abiding or otherwise, exude an offensive/defensive aura because they themselves regard the streets as a jungle. A young black man said:

> A friend of mine got rolled. He was visiting this girl up near Mercer Street. He come out of this house, and somebody smacked him in the head with a baseball bat. He had all these gold chains on. Had a brand new $200 thick leather jacket, $100 pair of Michael Jordan sneakers, and they were brand new, first time he had them on his feet. He had leather pants on too. And I'm surprised they didn't take his leather pants. I mean, he had a gold chain this thick [shows quarter-inch with his fingers]. I mean pure gold—$800 worth of gold. He came out this girl's house, after visiting his baby. Cats hit him in the head with a baseball bat, and they took everything. Took his sneaks, his coat, everything. When the paramedics got there he had no coat, no sneaks on. They took his belt, took his Gucci belt, the junkies did. I went to visit him in the hospital, and I'm sorry I went in there. I seen him. The boy had stitches . . . they shaved his head, stitches from here to all the way back of his head. Beat him in the head with a baseball bat. They say it was two guys. They was young boys, typical stupid young boys. Now my boy's life is messed up. He home now, but poor guy has seizures and everything. It's a jungle out here, man. But he sold drugs; the cops found cocaine in his underwear. They [the muggers] got what they wanted.

The young black males' pose is generally intended for people they perceive as potentially aggressive toward them. But at the same time it may engender circumspection and anxiety in law-abiding residents, both black and white, whose primary concern is safe passage on the streets.

In this public environment, pedestrians readily defer to young black males, who accept their public position. They walk confidently, heads up and gazes straight. Spontaneous and boisterous, they play their radios as loud as they please, telling everyone within earshot that this is their turf, like it or not. It may be that this is one of the few arenas were they can assert themselves and be taken seriously, and perhaps this is why they are so insistent.

Other pedestrians withdraw, perhaps with a defensive scowl, but nothing more. For the Village is not defended in the way many working-class neighborhoods are. As the black youths walk through late at night with their radios turned up, they meet little or no resistance. This lack of challenge shows how "tame," weak, or undefended the neighborhood is, except in certain areas where white college students predominate and fraternity boys succeed in harassing apparently defenseless blacks such as women with children, lone women, and an occasional single black man. Black youths tend to avoid such areas of the Village unless they are in groups.

The same black youths might hesitate before playing a radio loud in the well-defended territories of Northton, however. There they would likely be met by two or three "interceptors" who would promptly question their business, possibly taking the radio and punching one of the boys, or worse, in the process. No such defending force exists within the Village. . . .

Another aspect of claiming turf rights is public talk—its idiom, duration, intensity, and volume. At times the language of young black males, even those who are completely law-abiding, is harsh and profane. This language is used in many public spaces, but especially at trolley stops and on trolleys and buses. Like the rap music played loudly on boom boxes, it puts others on the defensive.

The "others" tend not to say much to the offenders; rather, they complain to one another (though some residents have in fact come to appreciate the young males and enjoy the music).

On public transportation young blacks, including some girls, may display raucous behavior, including cursing and loud talk and play. Because most people encounter the youths as strangers, they understand them through the available stereotypes. Law-abiding black youths often don the special urban uniform and emulate this self-presentation, a practice known as "going for bad" and used to intimidate others. As one young black man said:

> You see the guys sometimes on the bus having this air about them. They know that the grown people on the bus hope that these guys are not problems. The boys play on that. I'm talking about with women old enough to be their mothers. Now, they wouldn't be doing this at home. But they'll do it on that bus. They'll carry on to such an extent. . . . Now, I know, especially the young boys. I know they [older people] be scared. They really wondering, 'cause all they know is the headlines, "Juvenile Crime . . ." "Problems of Youth Kids," or "Chain Snatchers." This is what they know. And these people are much more uncertain than I am, 'cause I know.

In some cases black males capitalize on the fear they know they can evoke. They may "put on a swagger" and intimidate those who must momentarily share a small space on the sidewalk. When passing such a "loud" dark-skinned person, whites usually anticipate danger, though they hope for a peaceful pass. Whites and middle-income blacks are often more than ready to cross the street to avoid passing a "strange" black person at close range. Young blacks understand this behavior and sometimes exploit the fear, as illustrated in the following narrative by a young white woman:

I went out for something at the store at about 9:00, after it was already dark. When I came back, there was no place to park in front of my house anymore. So I had to park around the corner, which I generally don't do because there's a greater chance of getting your car broken into or stolen over there, since a lot of foot traffic goes by at night. So I parked the car, turned out the lights, and got out. I began walking across the street, but I got into a situation I don't like to get into—of having there be some ominous-looking stranger between me and my house. So I have to go around or something. And he was a black fellow between twenty and thirty, on the youngish side. He certainly wasn't anybody I knew. So I decided not really to run, just sort of double-time, so I wouldn't meet him at close distance at the corner. I kind of ran diagonally, keeping the maximum distance between him and me. And it must have been obvious to him that I was running out of fear, being alone at night out in the street. He started chuckling, not trying to hide it. He just laughed at what I was doing. He could tell what he meant to me, the two of us being the only people out there.

At times even civil and law-abiding youths enjoy this confusion. They have an interest in going for bad, for it is a way to keep other youths at bay. The right look, moves, and general behavior ensure safe passage. However, this image is also a source of subtle but enduring racial and class distinctions, if not overt hostility, within the community.

Some black youths confront others with behavior they refer to as "gritting," "looking mean," "looking hard," and "bumping." Youths have a saying, "His jaws got tight." Such actions could easily be compared to threatening animal behavior, particularly dogs warning other dogs away from their territory or food. Gritting is a way of warning peers against "messing with me." To grit is to be ready to defend one's interests, in this case one's physical self. It conveys alertness to the prospect of harmful intent, communicating and defining personal boundaries. As one black man said concerning strategies for negotiating the Northton streets near the Village:

> When I walk the streets, I put this expression on my face that tells the next person I'm not to be messed with. That 'You messing with the wrong fellow. You just try it.' And I know when cats are behind me. I be just lookin' in the air, letting them know I'm checkin' them out. Then I'll put my hand in my pocket, even if I ain't got no gun. Nobody wants to get shot, that shit burns, man. That shit hurt. Some guys go to singing. They try to let people know they crazy. 'Cause if you crazy [capable of anything], they'll leave you alone. And I have looked in they face [muggers] and said, 'Yo, I'm not the one.' Give 'em that crazy look, then walk away. 'Cause I know what they into. They catch your drift quick. . . .

The youth is caught up here in a cultural catch-22: to appear harmless to others might make him seem weak or square to those he feels a need to impress. If he does not dress the part of a young black man on the streets, it is difficult for him to "act right." If he is unable to "act right," then he may be victimized by strangers in his general peer group. The uniform—radio, sneakers, gold chain, athletic suit—and the selective use of the "grit," the quasi-military swagger to the beat of "rap" songs in public places, are all part of the young man's pose.

Law-abiding and crime-prone youths alike adopt such poses in effect camouflaging themselves and making it difficult for more conventional people to know how to behave around them, since those for whom they may not be performing directly may see them as threatening. By connecting culturally with the ghetto, a young black may avoid compromising his public presentation of self, but at the cost of further alienating law-abiding whites and blacks.

In general, the black male is assumed to be streetwise. He also comes to think of himself as such, and this helps him negotiate public spaces. In this sense others collectively assist him in being who he is. With a simple move one way or the other, he can be taken as a "dangerous dude." He is then left alone, whereas whites may have more trouble.

Civility and law-abidingness are stereotypically ascribed to the white male, particularly in the public context of so many "dangerous" and "predatory" young blacks. (In fact, white men must campaign to achieve the status of being seen as dangerous in public places.) The white male is not taken seriously on the streets, particularly by black men, who resist seeing him as a significant threat. They think that most white men view conflict in terms of "limited warfare," amounting to little more than scowls and harsh words. It is generally understood that blacks from Northton do not assume this but are open to unlimited warfare, including the use of sticks, stones, knives, and guns, perhaps even a fight to the death.

Most conventional people learn to fear black youths from reading about crimes in the local papers and seeing reports of violence on television, but also by living so near and having the chance to observe them. Every time there is a violent crime, this image of young blacks gains credibility. Such public relations attribute to blacks control over the means and use of violence in public encounters, thus contributing to dominant stereotypes and fear. As is clear from the following interview, black men pick up on that fear:

They [white men] look at you strange, they be paranoid. Especially if you walkin' behind 'em. They slow down and let you walk in front or they walk on the other side. You know they got their eye on you. I walk past one one time. My mother live on Fortieth and Calvary and I did that. I said, 'You ain't gotta slow down, brother. I ain't gonna do nothin' to you, I ain't like that.' He looked at me and laughed. He

knew what I meant, and I knew what he was thinkin'. He had a little smile. It was late at night, about 1:00 A.M. He let me get in front of him. He was comin' from a bar, and he had a six-pack. I'm a fast walker anyway; you can hear my shoes clickin'. I see him slowing down. I said, 'I ain't gonna do nothin' to you, I ain't like that.' He just laughed; I kept on walking and I laughed. That's the way it went.

Whereas street interactions between black strangers tend to be highly refined, greetings of whites toward blacks are usually ambiguous or have limited effectiveness. This general communication gap between blacks and whites is exacerbated by the influx of white newcomers. In contrast to the longtime residents, the newcomers are unaccustomed to and frequently intolerant of neighboring blacks and have not learned a visible street etiquette. The run-ins such new people have with blacks contribute to a general black view of "the whites" of the Village as prejudiced, thus undermining the positive race relations promoted over many years by egalitarian-minded residents.

The result is that the white and black communities become collapsed into social monoliths. For instance, although blacks tend to relate cautiously to unknown black youths, they are inclined to look at them longer, inspecting them and noting their business to see whether they deserve to be trusted. Whites, on the other hand, look at blacks, see their skin color, and dismiss them quickly as potential acquaintances; then they furtively avert their gaze, hoping not to send the wrong message, for they desire distance and very limited involvement. Any follow-up by black youths is considered highly suspect unless there are strong mitigating factors, such as an emergency where help is needed.

A common testimonial from young blacks reflects the way whites encounter them. They speak about the defensiveness of whites in general. White women are said to plant broad grins on their faces in hopes of not being accosted. The smile may appear to be a sign of trust, but it is more likely to show a deference, especially when the woman looks back as soon as she is at a safe distance. When the black stranger and the perceived danger have passed, the putative social ties suggested by the smile are no longer binding and the woman may attempt to keep the "dangerous" person in view, for a sudden move could signal an "attempted robbery" or "rape." . . .

A young black man who often walks through the Village reports this reaction from white women:

> They give the eye. You can see 'em lookin' right at you. They look at you and turn back this way, and keep on walkin'. Like you don't exist, but they be paranoid as hell. Won't say hello. But some of 'em do. Some of 'em say hi. Some of 'em smile. But they always scared.

One young white woman confirmed this: "I must admit, I look at a black [male] on the street just for a few seconds. Just long enough to let him know I know of his presence, then I look away." . . .

Out of a sense of frustration, many young blacks mock or otherwise insult the whites they see in public spaces, trying to "get even" with them for being part of the "monolithic" group of whites. When they encounter whites who display fear, they may laugh at them or harass them. They think, "What do I have to lose?" and may purposely create discomfort in those they see as "ignorant" enough to be afraid of them. Of course the whites of the Village are anything but a monolithic group. But it is convenient for certain blacks to see things this way, placing all whites, whom they see as the source of their troubles, into an easily manageable bag. In this way blacks as well as whites become victims of simplistic thinking.

Black men's resentment, coupled with peer-group pressure to act tough, may cause them to shift unpredictably from being cour-teous to whites to "fulfilling the prophecy" of those who are afraid and uncomfortable around blacks. When confronting a white woman on the streets some youths may make lewd or suggestive comments, reminding her that she is vulnerable and under surveillance. The following account describes such an encounter:

> On a Wednesday afternoon in June at about 2:00, Sandra Norris pushed her nine-month-old daughter down Cherry Street. The gray stone facades of the Victorian buildings sparkled in the sun. The streets seemed deserted, as the Village usually is at this time. Suddenly three black youths appeared. They looked in their late teens. As they approached her, one of the young men yelled to the others, 'Let's get her! Get her!' Making sexual gestures, two of the youths reached for her menacingly. She cringed and pulled the stroller toward her. At that the boys laughed loudly. They were playing with her, but the feigned attack was no fun for Mrs. Norris. It left her shaking.

As indicated above, an aggressive presentation—though certainly not usually so extreme—is often accepted as necessary for black youths to maintain regard with their peers. They must "act right" by the toughest ghetto standards or risk being ridiculed or even victimized by their own peers. Feeling a certain power in numbers, some groups will readily engage in such games, noisily swooping down on their supposed "prey" or fanning out in a menacing formation. Children, white and black, sometimes are intimidated and form fearful and negative feelings about teenage "black boys."

Such demeanor may be a way of identifying with the ghetto streets, but it is also a way of exhibiting "toughness" toward figures who represent the "overclass," which many view as deeply implicated in the misfortunes of their communities. Such conduct is easily confused with and incorporated into ordinary male adolescent behavior, but the result is complicated by race and gender and the generalized powerlessness of the black community. Understandably, middle-class residents, black and white, become even more likely to place social distance between themselves and such youths, conceptually lumping anonymous black males together for self-defense.

Of course not everyone is victimized by crime, but many people take incivility as an indication of what could happen if they did not keep up their guard. When representatives of Northton walking through the Village intimidate residents either verbally or physically, many middle-class people—whites in particular—become afraid of black males in general. They may have second thoughts about "open" and to some degree friendly displays they may previously have made toward blacks in public. Blacks and whites thus become increasingly estranged. In fact there is a vicious circle of suspicion and distrust between the two groups and an overwhelming tendency for public relations between them to remain superficial and guarded.

It is not surprising that the law-abiding black man often feels at a disadvantage in his interactions with whites. Most whites, except possibly those who are streetwise . . . and empathic about the plight of inner-city blacks, are conditioned to consider all black male strangers potential muggers. The average black, because of his own socialization on the streets and his understanding of the psychology of whites, understands this position very well and knows what whites are thinking.

Many blacks and whites seem alarmed when a black youth approaches them for any reason, even to ask the time. Such overtures may simply be the youth's attempt to disavow criminal intent or to neutralize the social distance generally displayed on the streets. But these attempts are easily interpreted as a setup for a mugging, causing the other person to flee or to cut off the interaction. The public stigma is so powerful that black strangers are seldom allowed to be civil or even helpful without some suspicion of their motives. . . .

Even law-abiding black men who befriend whites and belong to biracial primary groups face "outsider" status. For example, when a black visits a white friend's house, knocks on the door or rings the bell and waits, he risks being taken by the neighbors as someone whose business on the stoop is questionable. Some people will keep an eye on him, watching every move until their neighbor comes to the door. It may not matter how well the visitor is dressed. His skin color indicates his "stranger" status, which persists until he passes inspection when the white person answers the door. The white man with the same self-presentation would pass much sooner.

Although they do not usually articulate the problem in just this manner, many black middle-income Villagers feel somewhat bitter about the prejudice of their white neighbors, who are caught up in a kind of symbolic racism. Dark skin has a special meaning, which Village residents have come to associate with crime. Though white Villagers may not have contempt for blacks in general, they do experience anxiety over the prospect of being victimized. So, since blacks are believed to make up a large proportion of the criminals, pedestrians tend to be defensive and short with strange black males. The same people may have intimate black friends and may pride themselves on their racial tolerance. Yet, concerned with safety, they regard blacks as an anonymous mass through which they must negotiate their way to their destination. They may pass right by black "friends" and simply fail to see them because they are concentrating not on the friend but on the social context. Such reactions frustrate many black-white friendships before they have a chance to begin. Blacks generally complain more than whites about such shortcomings of friendly relations. But as blacks make their way around the streets, they too may miss a "friend" of the other color. Such events may have more to do with the ambiguous nature of public race relations than with racial feeling itself. But whatever the cause, these problems are an impediment to spontaneous and biracial interactions. . . .

References

Goffman, Erving. 1959. *The Presentation of Self in Everyday Life.* Garden City, NY: Doubleday.

Hughes, Everett. 1945. "Dilemmas and Contradictions of Status." *American Journal of Sociology*, 50: 353–359.

Katz, Jack. 1988. *Seductions of Crime: Moral and Sensual Attraction in Doing Evil.* New York: Basic Books.

31

Managing Emotions in an Animal Shelter

Arnold Arluke

Social structures endure because one generation transmits to the next the symbols, classification systems, meanings, and rules that structure action, interaction, and social life. Each subsequent generation consequently engages in recurrent patterns of action and interaction that reproduce those social structures. They seldom perfectly replicate social structures, but alter them in various ways that sometimes lead to profound restructuring over time. Even such imperfect replication of social structures is not guaranteed but subject to what Herbert Blumer called "the play and fate of meaning." Yet, social structures are more or less enduring thanks to processes of socialization.

For example, the medical students discussed by Smith and Kleinman in an earlier selection eventually reproduced the affectively neutral culture and social structure of modern medicine. Their teachers and training at medical school subtly but effectively transmitted feeling rules and emotion management strategies that encouraged them to do so. They learned how to control their emotions and, thereby, how to control and distance themselves from their patients. That is, they learned how to reproduce physicians' authority over patients and the conventional structure of the physician-patient relationship.

This selection examines another instance of how emotional socialization promotes the reproduction of social structure, in this case a specific social institution. It concerns a Humane Society shelter where euthanasia of animals was and is

routine. As Arluke observes, people in Western societies have inconsistent and often conflicting attitudes toward animals. On the one hand, we believe that at least some sentient creatures deserve affection and care. On the other hand, we regard others, even of the same species, as utilitarian objects to be used as we see fit. Arluke shows how such conflicting meanings caused new workers at the shelter emotional difficulties. Kinds of animals that they had previously learned to love, care for, and protect were being routinely killed, often with their involvement. Yet, similar to medical students, they learned emotion management and interpretive strategies that relieved their emotional discomfort and convinced them of the nobility of their gruesome tasks. This socialization process produced a new generation of workers who would reproduce the social institution of the animal "kill shelter."

We may be more similar to these kill shelter workers than we might first recognize. Our work often requires us to do things that we find morally troubling and emotionally disturbing. However, we usually learn ways of excusing what we do that calm our emotions. Like the "kill shelter" workers, we learn how to live with all the little murders that we commit as part of our jobs, convincing ourselves that they are necessary and perhaps even noble. The reproduction of social structures requires sacrifices, and most of us learn to make them with hardly a thought and only a twinge of emotion.

From the sociologist's perspective, what is most interesting in the study of conflicts in the contemporary treatment of animals is not to point out that such conflicts exist or to debate the assumptions that underlie them—a task more ably served by philosophers—but to better understand what it is about modern society that makes it possible to shower animals with affection as sentient creatures while simultaneously maltreating or killing them as utilitarian objects. How is it that a conflict that should require a very difficult balancing of significant values has become something that many people live with comfortably? Indeed, they may not even be aware that others may perceive their actions as inconsistent. How is it that instead of questioning the propriety of their conflicts, many don ethical blindfolds?

As with any cultural contradiction, these attitudes are built into the normative order, itself perpetuated by institutions that provide ways out of contradictions by supplying myths to bridge them and techniques to assuage troubled feelings. . . .

Humane and scientific institutions, for example, must teach newcomers in shelters and laboratories to suspend their prior, ordinary or commonsense thinking about the use and meaning of animals and adopt a different set of assumptions that may be inconsistent with these prior views. The assumptions are not themselves proved but rather structure and form the field upon which the activity plays out its life. Typically, these assumptions are transmitted to nascent practitioners of a discipline, along with relevant empirical facts and skills, as indisputable truths, not as debatable assumptions. They must come to accept the premise of the institution—often that it is necessary to kill animals—and get on with the business of the institution. But exactly how do they get on with this business?

In addition to learning to think differently about the proper fate of animals in institutions, workers must also learn to feel differently about them in that situation. Uncomfortable feelings may be experienced by newcomers even if the premise of the institution is accepted at an intellectual level. Although institutions will, no doubt, equip newcomers with rules and resources for managing unwanted emotions, researchers have not examined how such emotion management strategies actually work and the extent to which they eliminate uncomfortable feelings. In the absence of such research, it is generally assumed that newcomers learn

ways to distance themselves from their acts and lessen their guilt. These devices are thought to prevent any attachment to and empathy for animals (Schleifer 1985) and to make killing "a reflex, virtually devoid of emotional content" (Serpell 1986:152).

To examine these assumptions, I conducted ethnographic research over a seven-month period in a "kill-shelter" serving a major metropolitan area. Such a case study seemed warranted, given the sensitivity of the topic under study. I became immersed in this site, spending approximately 75 hours in direct observation of all facets of shelter work and life, including euthanasia of animals and the training of workers to do it. Also, interviews were conducted with the entire staff of sixteen people, many formally and at length on tape, about euthanasia and related aspects of shelter work. . . .

The Newcomer's Problem

Euthanasia posed a substantial emotional challenge to most novice shelter workers. People seeking work at the shelter typically regarded themselves as "animal people" or "animal lovers" and recounted lifelong histories of keeping pets, collecting animals, nursing strays, and working in zoos, pet stores, veterinarian practices, and even animal research laboratories. They came wanting to "work with animals" and expecting to spend much of their time having hands-on contact with animals in a setting where others shared the same high priority they placed on human-animal interaction. The prospect of having to kill animals seemed incompatible with this self-conception.

When first applying for their jobs, some shelter workers did not even know that euthanasia was carried out at the shelter. To address this possible misconception, applicants were asked how they would feel when it was their turn to euthanize. Most reported that they did not really think through this question at this time, simply replying that they thought it was "Okay" in order to get the job. One worker, for instance, said she "just put this thought out of [her] mind," while another worker said that she had hope to "sleaze out" of (or avoid) doing it. Many said that having to do euthanasia did not fully sink in until they "looked the animal in its eyes." Clearly, newcomers were emotionally unprepared to actually kill animals.

Once on the job, newcomers quickly formed strong attachments to particular animals. In fact, it was customary to caution newcomers against adopting animals right away. Several factors encouraged these attachments. At first, workers found themselves relating to shelter animals as though they were their own pets because many of the animals were healthy and appealing to workers, and since most of the animals had been pets, they sometimes initiated interaction with the workers. Newcomers also saw more senior people interacting with animals in a pet-like fashion. Shelter animals, for example, were all named, and everyone used these names when referring to the animals. While newcomers followed suit, they did not realize that more experienced workers could interact in this way with animals and not become attached to them. Moreover, newcomers found that their work required them to know the individual personalities of shelter animals in order to make the best decisions regarding euthanasia and adoption, but this knowledge easily fostered attachments. Not surprisingly, the prospect of having to kill animals with whom they had become attached was a major concern for newcomers. This anticipated relationship with shelter animals made newcomers agonize when they imagined selecting animals for euthanasia and seeing "trusting looks" in the faces of those killed. They also worried about having to cope with the "losses" they expected to feel from killing these animals.

Further aggravating the novices' trepidation was the fact that they had to kill animals for no higher purpose. Many felt grieved and frustrated by what they saw as the "senseless" killing of healthy animals. Several newcomers flinched at the shelter's willingness to kill animals if suitable homes were not found instead of "fostering out" the animals. In their opinion, putting animals in less than "ideal" homes for a few years was better than death.

The clash between the feelings of newcomers for shelter animals and the institution's practice of euthanasia led newcomers to experience a caring-killing "paradox." On the one hand, they tried to understand and embrace the institutional rationale for euthanasia, but on the other hand, they wanted to nurture and tend to shelter animals. Doing both seemed impossible to many newcomers. Acceptance of the need to euthanize did not remove the apprehension that workers felt about having to kill animals themselves or to be part of this process. Their everyday selves were still paramount and made them feel for shelter animals as they might toward their own pets—the thought of killing them was troubling. They even feared getting to the point where they would no longer be upset killing animals, commonly asking those more senior, "Do you still care?" or "Doesn't it still bother you?" Experienced shelter workers acknowledged the "paradox" of newcomers, telling and reassuring them that:

> There is a terrible paradox in what you will have to do—you want to care for animals, but will have to kill some of them. It is a painful process of killing animals when you don't want to. It seems so bad, but we'll make it good in your head. You will find yourself in a complex emotional state. Euthanizing is not just technical skills. You have to believe it is right to make it matter of fact.

Emotion Management Strategies

How did shelter workers manage their uncomfortable feelings? Workers learned different emotion management strategies to distance themselves enough to kill, but not so much as to abandon a sense of themselves as animal people. These strategies enabled workers at least to hold in abeyance their prior, everyday sensibilities regarding animals and to apply a different emotional perspective while in the shelter.

Transforming Shelter Animals Into Virtual Pets

New workers often had trouble distinguishing between shelter animals and their own pets. Failure to make this distinction could result in emotionally jarring situations, especially when animals were euthanized. However, they soon came to see shelter animals as virtual pets—liminal animals lying somewhere between the two categories of pet and object. In such a liminal status workers could maintain a safe distance from animals while not entirely detaching themselves from them.

One way they accomplished this transformation was to lessen the intensity of their emotional attachments to individual animals. Almost as a rite of passage, newcomers were emotionally scarred by the euthanasia of a favorite animal, leaving them distraught over the loss. They also heard cautionary tales about workers who were very upset by the loss of animals with whom they had grown "too close" as well as workers whose "excessive" or "crazy" attachments resulted in harm to animals—such as the person who was fired after she released all the dogs from the shelter because she could no longer stand to see them caged or put to death. Newcomers soon began consciously to restrict the depth of their attachments. As one worker observed: "I don't let myself get that attached to them."

On the other hand, certain mottoes or ideals were part of the shelter culture, and these underscored the importance of not becoming detached from their charges or becoming desensitized to euthanasia. One worker, for instance, told me that you "learn to turn your feelings off when you do this work, but you

can't completely. They say if you can, you shouldn't be on the job." Another worker noted: "If you get to the point where killing doesn't bother you, then you shouldn't be working here."

While they stopped themselves from "loving" individual shelter animals, because of their likely fate, workers learned that they could become more safely attached by maintaining a generalized caring feeling for shelter animals as a group. As workers became more seasoned, individual bonding became less frequent, interest in adopting subsided and a sense emerged of corporate attachment to shelter animals as a population of refugees rather than as individual pets.

Workers also came to see shelter animals differently from everyday pets by assuming professional roles with their charges. One role was that of "caretaker" rather than pet owner. As a worker noted: "You don't set yourself up by seeing them as pets. You'd kill yourself; I'd cut my wrists. I'm a caretaker, so I make them feel better while they are here. They won't be forgotten so quickly. I feel I get to know them. I'm their last hope." Comparing her own pet to shelter animals, another worker noted: "No bell goes off in your head with your own pet as it would with a shelter animal, where the bell says you can't love this animal because you have to euthanize it." If not caretakers, they could become social workers trying to place these animals in homes of other people.

New workers came to view their charges as having a type of market value within the larger population of shelter animals. Their value was not to be personal and individual from the worker's perspective. Rather, they were to be assessed in the light of their competitive attractiveness to potential adopters. This view was nowhere more apparent than in the selection of healthy and well behaved animals to be euthanized in order to make room for incoming animals. An experienced shelter worker described these "tough choices" and the difficulty newcomers had in viewing animals this way:

> When you go through and pull [i.e., remove an animal for euthanasia]—that's when you have to make some real tough choices. If they've all been here an equal amount of time, then if you've got eighteen cages and six are filled with black cats, and you have a variety in here waiting for cages, you're going to pull the black ones so you can have more of a variety. It's hard for a new employee to understand that I'm going to pull a black cat to make room for a white one. After they've been here through a cat season, they know exactly what I'm doing, and you don't have to say anything when you have old staff around you.

In addition, newcomers learned to think differently when spending money for the medical care of shelter animals than they would when spending on their own pets. Although an occasional animal might receive some medical attention, many animals were killed because it was not considered economically feasible to treat them even though they had reversible problems and the cost might be insubstantial. For example, while two newcomers observed the euthanizing of several kittens, an experienced worker pointed to a viral infection in their mouths as the reason behind their deaths. One newcomer asked why the kittens could not be treated medically so they could be put up for adoption. The reply was that the virus could be treated, but "given the volume, it is not economical to treat them."

Keeping shelter mascots further helped workers separate everyday pets from their charges, with mascots serving as surrogate pets in contrast to the rest of the shelter's animals. Cats and dogs were occasionally singled out to become the group mascots, the former because workers took a special interest in them, the latter because workers hoped to increase their adoptability. Unlike other shelter animals, mascots were permitted to run free in areas reserved for workers, such as their private office and front desk, where they were played with and talked about by workers. Importantly, they were never euthanized, either remaining indefinitely in the shelter or going home as someone's pet. Although most shelter workers interacted with the mascots as though they were pets, one shelter worker, akin to an owner, often took a special interest in the animal and let it be known that she would eventually adopt the animal if a good home could not be found. Some of their actions toward these mascots were in clear contrast to the way they would have acted toward regular shelter animals. In one case, for example, a cat mascot was found to have a stomach ailment requiring expensive surgery. In normal circumstances this animal would have been killed, but one of the workers used her own money to pay for the operation.

Using the Animal

By taking the feelings of animals into account, workers distracted themselves from their own discomfort when euthanizing. Workers tried to make this experience as "good" as possible for the animals and, in so doing, felt better themselves. Some workers, in fact, openly admitted that "it makes me feel better making it [euthanasia] better for the animal." Even more seasoned workers were more at ease with euthanasia if they focused on making animals feel secure and calm as they were killed. A worker with twenty years' experience remarked that "it still bothers you after you're here for a long time, but not as much. Compassion and tenderness are there when I euthanize, so it doesn't eat away at me."

One way workers did this was to empathize with animals in order to figure out how to reduce each animal's stress during euthanasia. By seeing things from the animals' perspective, workers sought to make the process of dying "peaceful and easy." As a worker pointed out: "You make the animal comfortable and happy and secure, so when the time to euthanize comes, it will not be under stress and scared—the dog will lick your face, the cats will purr." In the words of another worker: "They get more love in the last few seconds than they ever did." Workers were encouraged to "think of all the little things that might stress the animal—if you sense that some are afraid of men, then keep men away." For example, one worker said that she decided not to have cats and dogs in the euthanasia room at the same time. Observation of euthanasia confirmed that workers considered animals' states of mind. In one instance, where a cat and her kittens had to be euthanized, the mother was killed first because the worker thought she would become very upset if she sensed her kittens were dying. And in another case a worker refused to be interviewed during euthanasia because she felt that our talking made the animals more anxious.

Another way that taking animals into consideration helped workers distract themselves from their own concerns was to concentrate on the methodology of killing and to become technically proficient at it. By focusing on the technique of killing—and not on why it needed to be done or how they felt about doing it—workers could reassure themselves that they were making death quick and painless for animals. Workers, called "shooters," who injected the euthanasia drug were told to "focus not on the euthanasia, but on the needle. Concentrate on technical skills if you are the shooter." Even those people, known as "holders," who merely held animals steady during the injection, were taught to view their participation as a technical act as opposed to a demonstration of affection. In the words of a worker:

The holder is the one who controls the dog. You have your arm around her. You're the one who has got a hold of that vein. When they get the blood in the syringe, you let go. But you have to hold that dog and try and keep him steady and not let him pull away. That's my job.

Bad killing technique, whether shooting or holding, was bemoaned by senior workers. As one noted: "I get really pissed off if someone blows a vein if it is due to an improper hold."

Since euthanasia was regarded more as technical than as a moral or emotional issue, it was not surprising that workers could acquire reputations within the shelter for being "good shots," and animals came to be seen as either easy or hard "putdowns"—a division reflecting technical difficulty and increased physical discomfort for animals. If the animal was a "hard putdown," workers became all the more absorbed in the mechanics of euthanasia, knowing that the sharpness of their technical skills would affect the extent of an animal's distress. . . .

Workers could also take animals into consideration, rather than focus on their own feelings, by seeing their death as the alleviation of suffering. This was easy to do with animals who were very sick and old—known as "automatic kills"—but it was much harder to see suffering in "healthy and happy" animals that were killed. They too had to be seen as having lives not worth living. Workers were aware that the breadth of their definition of suffering made euthanasia easier for them. One worker acknowledged that: "Sometimes you want to find any reason, like it has a runny nose." Newcomers often flinched at what was deemed sufficient medical or psychological reason to euthanize an animal, as did veterinary technicians working in the adjoining animal hospital who sometimes sarcastically said to shelter workers and their animals: "If you cough, they will kill you. If you sneeze, they will kill you."

Workers learned to see euthanasia as a way to prevent suffering. For example, it was thought that it was better to euthanize healthy strays than to let them "suffer" on the streets. One senior worker told newcomers:

I'd rather kill than see suffering. I've seen dogs hung in alleys, cats with firecrackers in their mouths or caught in fan belts. This helps me to cope with euthanizing—to prevent this suffering through euthanasia. Am I sick if I can do this for fifteen years? No. I still cry when I see a sick pigeon on the streets, but I believe in what I am doing.

Once in a shelter, healthy strays, along with abandoned and surrendered animals, were also thought better dead than "fostered out." A worker noted: "I'd rather kill it now than let it live three years and die a horrible death. No life is better than a temporary life." Even having a potential adopter was not enough; the animal's future home, if deemed "inappropriate," would only cause the animal more "suffering." One worker elaborated:

> Finding an appropriate home for the animal is the only way the animal is going to get out of here alive. The inappropriate home prolongs the suffering, prolongs the agony, prolongs the neglect, prolongs the abuse of an animal. The animal was abused or neglected in the first place or it wouldn't be here.

This thinking was a problem for newcomers who believed that almost any home, even if temporary, was better than killing animals. Particularly troubling were those people denied an animal for adoption even though their resources and attitudes seemed acceptable to workers. Some potential adopters were rejected because it was thought that they were not home often enough, even though by all other standards they seemed likely to become good owners. In one case, a veterinary hospital technician wanted to adopt a four-month-old puppy, but was rejected because she had full-time employment. Although she retorted that she had a roommate who was at home most of the time, her request was still denied.

But newcomers soon learned to scrutinize potential adopters carefully by screening them for certain warning flags, such as not wanting to spay or neuter, not wanting to fence in or leash animals, not being home enough with animals, and so on, in addition to such basics as not having a landlord's approval or adopting the pet as a gift for someone else. Most workers came to see certain groups of people as risky adopters requiring even greater scrutiny before approval. For some workers, this meant welfare recipients because they were unwilling to spay or neuter, or policemen because they might be too rough with animals.

Although workers accepted the applications of most potential owners, they did reject some. But even in their acceptances, they reaffirmed their concern for suffering and their desire to find perfect homes; they certainly did so with their rejections, admonishing those turned down for whatever their presumed problems were toward animals. Occasionally, rejected applicants became irate and made angry comments such as "You'd rather kill it than give it to me!" These moments were uncomfortable for newcomers to watch since, to some extent, they shared the rejected applicant's sentiment—any home was better than death. More experienced workers would try to cool down the applicant but also remind newcomers that some homes were worse than death. In one such case, the shelter manager said to the rejected applicant, but for all to hear, "It is my intention to find a good home where the animal's needs can be met."

Resisting and Avoiding Euthanasia

New workers, in particular, sometimes managed their discomfort with euthanasia by trying to prevent or delay the death of animals. Although there were generally understood euthanasia guidelines, they were rather vague, and workers could exert mild pressure to make exceptions to the rules. Certainly, not all animals scheduled or "pink-slipped" to be killed were "automatic kills." As a worker noted: "If a 12-year-old stray with hip dysplasia comes in, yes, you know as soon as it walks in the door that at the end of the stray holding period it's going to be euthanized, but not all of them are like this." A worker described such an instance:

> Four weeks is really young. Five weeks, you're really pushing it. Six weeks, we can take it, but it depends on its overall health and condition. But sometimes we'll keep one or two younger ones, depending on the animal itself. We just had an animal last week—it was a dachshund. She is a really nice and friendly dog. In this case, we just decided to keep her.

Sometimes a worker took a special liking to a particular animal, but it was to be euthanized because the cage was needed for new animals, or it was too young, too old, somewhat sick, or had a behavior problem. The worker might let it be known among colleagues that they were very attached to the animal, or they might go directly to the person making the euthanasia selection with a plea for the animal's date of death to be delayed in the hopes of adoption. One worker had a favorite cat that was to be euthanized, but succeeded in blocking its euthanasia, at least for a while, by personally taking financial responsibility for its shelter costs.

However, opposing euthanasia had to be done in a way that did not make such decisions too difficult for those making them. Workers could not object repeatedly to euthanasia or oppose it too aggressively without making the selector feel uncomfortable. One worker felt "guilty" when this happened to her:

> There was one technician—Marie—who used to make me feel guilty. I have to make room for new animals because we have so few cages. I must decide which old ones to kill to make room for new ones. Marie would get upset when I would choose certain cats to be killed. She would come to me with her runny, snotty nose, complaining that certain cats

were picked to be killed. This made me feel guilty.

If opposing euthanasia failed, workers were able to avoid the discomfort of doing it. One worker said that he would not "be around" if his favorite cat was killed, and noted:

> There's not an animal I'm not attached to here, but there's a cat here now that I like a lot. There's a good chance that she'll be euthanized. She's got a heart murmur. I guess. It's a mild one, but . . . any type of heart murmur with a cat is bad. She's also got a lump right here. They've already tested her for leukemia and it's negative, so they are testing her for something else. But she's just got an adorable face and everything else with her is fine. I like her personality. But I have two cats at home. I can't have a third. I won't be around when they euthanize her. I'll let somebody else do it. I would rather it be done when I'm not here.

Although workers could be exempted from killing animals with whom they had closely bonded, there was a strong feeling that such persons should be there for the animal's sake. Yet if present, they could indicate to others that they did not want to be the "shooter" and instead be the "holder," allowing them to feel more removed from the actual killing. A worker said:

> Especially if it's one I like a lot, I would rather be the one holding instead of injecting. If you don't want to inject, you just back up and somebody else does it. Everybody here does that. I just look at it, I don't want to be the one to do it. Even though people say that holding is the harder of the two, I would look at it as, well, I am the one who is doing this. And sometimes, I don't want to be the one to do it.

Customizing the division of labor of euthanasia to fit their own emotional limits, other workers preferred not to do the holding. One worker observed:

One of the ways that I detach myself from euthanasia is that I do the shooting rather than the holding so that I don't feel the animal dying. I'm concentrating on the technical skill behind the actual injection. And with a dog, you literally feel the animal's life go out of it in your arms, instead of giving the injection and letting it drop.

Using the Owner

Shelter workers could also displace some of their own discomfort with euthanasia into anger and frustration with pet owners. Rather than questioning the morality of their own acts and feeling guilty about euthanasia, workers came to regard owners, and not themselves, as behaving wrongly toward animals. As workers transferred the blame for killing animals to the public, they concentrated their energies on educating and changing public attitudes to pets and making successful adoptions through the shelter.

The public was seen as treating animals as "property to be thrown away like trash" rather than as something having intrinsic value. One worker bemoaned:

A lot of people who want to leave their pets have bullshit reasons for this—like they just bought new furniture for their living room and their cat shed all over it.

This lack of commitment resulted in many of the surrendered animals being euthanized because they were not adoptable and/or space was needed. Speaking about these owners, one worker candidly acknowledged:

I would love to be rude once to some of these people who come in. I'd like to say to these people, "Cut this bullshit out!"

Another worker concluded: "You do want to strangle these people."

Even if pet owners did not surrender their animals to the shelter, they became tainted as a group in the eyes of workers, who saw many of them as negligent or irresponsible. A common charge against owners was that

their pets were allowed to run free and be hurt, lost or stolen. One senior worker admitted: "A bias does get built in. We're called if a cat gets caught in a fan belt. We're the ones that have to scrape cats off the streets." Owners were also seen as selfish and misguided when it came to their pets, thoughtlessly allowing them to breed, instead of spaying or neutering them. Workers often repeated the shelter's pithy wish: "Parents will let their pets have puppies or kittens so they can show their children the miracle of birth—well, maybe they should come in here to see the miracle of death!" Workers could be heard among themselves admonishing the public's "irresponsibility" toward breeding and the deaths that such an attitude caused. A worker explained: "The only reason why it has been killed is that no one took the time to be a responsible pet owner. They felt the cat deserved to run free or they didn't want to pay the money to have it spayed or neutered, or that she should have one litter. Well great, what are you to do with her six offspring?" Even owners who declared great love and affection for their pets sometimes came across in the shelter environment as cruel to their animals. These were owners who let their animals suffer because they could not bear to kill them. A worker noted:

I'll get a 22-year-old cat. And the owner is crying out there. I tell her, "You know, twenty-two years is great. You have nothing to be ashamed of. Nothing." But you get some others that come in and they [the animals] look absolutely like shit. You feel like taking hold of them and saying "What in the hell are you doing? He should have been put to sleep two years ago."

According to shelter workers, owners should have to suffer pangs of conscience about their treatment of animals, but did not. Some owners seemed not to want their pets, and this shocked workers, as one noted: "You'd be surprised at how many people come right out and say they don't want it any more. They are usually the ones who call us to pick it up, otherwise they'll dump it on the street. And of course, we're going to come and get it. I feel like saying 'It's your conscience, not mine, go ahead, do it.' Of course, I don't do that." Many surrenderers, in the eyes of shelter workers, just did not care whether their animals lived or died. At the same time that surrenderers were seen as lacking a conscience, shelter workers were afforded the opportunity to reaffirm their own dedication to and feelings for animals. A worker commented:

> Some surrenderers take them back after we tell them we can't guarantee placement. Most say, "Well that's fine." Like the owner of this cat, he called this morning and said, "I've got to get rid of it, I'm allergic to it." Of course, he didn't seem at all bothered. He goes, "That's fine." Or somebody is going to surrender a pet because they're moving, well, if it was me, and I'm sure quite a few other people here feel the same way, I'd look for a place where pets were allowed. People are just looking out for themselves and not anything else.

In the opinion of the workers, it was important for newcomers to learn not to bear the "guilt" that owners should have felt. To do this, they had to see owners as the real killers of shelter animals. As one worker put it, "People think we are murderers, but they are the ones that have put us in this position. We are morally offended by the fact that we have to carry out an execution that we didn't necessarily order." A senior shelter worker recounted how she came to terms with guilt:

> Every night I had a recurring dream that I had died, and I was standing in line to go to heaven. And St. Peter says to me, "I know you, you're the one that killed all those little animals." And I'd sit up in the bed in a cold sweat. Finally, I realized it wasn't my fault, my dreams changed. After St. Peter said, "I know you, you're the

one that killed all those little animals," I turned to the 999,000 people behind me and said, "I know you, you made me kill all these animals." You grow into the fact that you are the executioner, but you weren't the judge and jury.

Shelter workers redirected their emotions and resources into changing public attitudes about pets in order to curtail the never-ending flow of animals—often called a "flood"—that always far exceeded what was possible to adopt out. Overwhelmed by this problem, workers wanted to do something about it other than killing animals. By putting effort into adoption or public education, they felt they were making a dent in the overpopulation problem instead of feeling hopeless about it. For many, combating pet overpopulation became addictive and missionary. Rather than chew over the morality of their own participation in euthanasia, they felt part of a serious campaign—often described as a "battle"—against the formidable foe of the pet owner and in defense of helpless animals.

Owners were used in ways other than as objects of blame. Successful adoptions helped to accentuate the positive in a setting where there were few opportunities to feel good about what workers were doing. Finding homes for animals came close to the original motivation that brought many workers to the shelter seeking employment. One worker commented: "For every one euthanized, you have to think about the one placed, or the one case where you placed in a perfect family." Another worker said that "you get a good feeling when you see an empty cage." She explained that she did not think that it was empty because an animal had just been killed, but because an animal had just been adopted. Indeed, out of self-protection, when the cage of someone's "favorite" was empty, workers did not ask what happened to the animals so they could assume that it was adopted rather than killed. They talked about how all of their animals were "either PWP or PWG—placed with people or placed with God." Shelter workers felt particularly satisfied when they heard from people who had satisfactorily adopted animals. Sometimes these owners came into the shelter and talked informally with workers; at other times, they wrote letters of thanks for their animals. Besides taping this mail on the walls for all to see, workers mounted snapshots of adopters and their animals in the shelter's lobby.

Dealing With Others

For workers to manage their emotions successfully, they had to learn to suspend asking hard ethical questions. While this was easy to do within the confines of the shelter, it was more difficult outside. Many reported feeling badly when outsiders learned they killed animals and challenged them about the morality of euthanasia. Workers dealt with these unwanted feelings in two ways.

Outside work, they could try to avoid the kinds of contact that give rise to unwanted emotions and difficult questions. Workers claimed that roommates, spouses, family members, and strangers sometimes made them feel "guilty" because they were seen as "villains" or "murderers." As one worker said, "You expect your spouse, your parents, your sister, your brother, or your significant other to understand. And they don't. And your friends don't. People make stupid remarks like, 'Gee, I would never do your job because I love animals too much.'" Workers claimed that they had become "paranoid" about being asked if they killed animals, waiting for questions such as, "How can you kill them if you care about animals so much?" Sometimes people would simply tell workers: "I love animals, I couldn't do that." One worker claimed that these questions and comments "make me feel like I've done something wrong." Another said, "So what does it mean—I don't love animals?" If workers were not explicitly criticized or misunderstood, they still encountered people who made them feel reluctant to talk about their work. One worker noted

that "I'm proud that I'm a 90 per cent shot, and that I'm not putting the animals through stress, but people don't want to hear this."

In anticipation of these negative reactions, many workers hesitated to divulge what they did. One worker said that she had learned to tell people that she "drives an animal ambulance." If workers revealed that they carried out euthanasia, they often presented arguments to support their caring for animals and the need for euthanasia. As one worker noted, "I throw numbers at them, like the fact that we get 12,000 animals a year but can only place 2,000." While concealing their work and educating others about it were by far the most common strategies used with outsiders, some workers would occasionally take a blunter approach and use sarcasm or black humor. The following worker talked about all these approaches:

> People give me a lot of grief. You know, you tell them where you work, and you tell them it's an animal shelter. And they say, "Well, you don't put them to sleep, do you?" And I always love to say, "Well actually I give classes on how to do that," just for the shock value of it. Or it's the old, "I could never do what you do, I love animals too much." "Oh, I don't love them at all. That's why I work here. I kill them. I enjoy it." But sometimes you don't even mention where you work because you don't want to deal with that. It depends on the social situation I am in as to whether I want to go in to it or not, and it also depends on how I feel at a given time. Some people are interested, and then I talk about spaying and neutering their pets.

Another way workers dealt with outsiders was to neutralize their criticism of euthanasia. The only credible opinions about euthanasia were seen as coming from those people who actually did such killing as part of the shelter community. Humor was one device that helped workers feel part of this community. It gave them a special language to talk about death and their concerns about it. As with gallows humor in other settings, it was not particularly funny out of context, and workers knew this, but learning to use it and find it humorous became a rite of passage. For instance, people telephoning the shelter might be greeted with the salutation, "Heaven." Referring to the euthanasia room and the euthanasia drug also took on a light, funny side with the room being called "downtown" or the "lavender lounge" (its walls were this color) and the drug being called "sleepaway" or "go-go juice" (its brand name was "Fatal Plus").

But no ritual practice gave more of a sense of "we-ness" then actually killing animals. No single act admitted them more into the shelter institution or more clearly demarcated the transition of shelter workers out of the novice role. As they gained increasing experience with euthanasia, workers developed a firmer sense of being in the same boat with peers who also did what they did. They shared an unarticulated belief that others could not understand what it was like to kill unless they had also done so. Even within the shelter, kennel workers often felt misunderstood by the front-desk people. As one worker reflected, "It does feel like you can't understand what I do if you can't understand that I don't like to kill, but that I have to kill. You'd have to see what I see. Maybe then." Since outsiders did not share this experience, workers tended to give them little credibility and to discount their opinions. By curtailing the possibility of understanding what they did and communicating with others about it, workers furthered their solidarity and created boundaries between themselves and outsiders that served to shield them from external criticism and diminish any uncomfortable feelings easily raised by the "unin- formed" or "naive."

The Imperfection of Emotion Management

Certainly, the killing of animals by shelter workers was facilitated by the kinds of emotion management strategies that have been discussed. Yet it would be wrong to characterize these people, including those with many years' experience, as completely detached. These strategies were far from perfect. It would be more accurate to say that their institutional socialization was incomplete. All workers, including those with many years of experience, felt uneasy about euthanasia at certain times.

For the few who continued to experience sharp and disturbing feelings, quitting became a way to manage emotions. For example, one worker felt "plagued" by a conflict between her own feelings for the animals which made killing hard to accept and the shelter's euthanasia policy with which she intellectually agreed. She said it was "like having two people in my head, one good and the other evil, that argue about me destroying these animals." This conflict left her feeling "guilty" about deaths she found "hard to justify." After nine months on the job, she quit.

For most workers this conflict was neither intense nor constant, but instead manifested itself as episodic uneasiness. From time to time euthanasia provoked modest but clearly discernible levels of emotional distress. There was no consensus, however, on what kind of euthanasia would rattle people and make them feel uncomfortable, but everyone had at least one type that roused their feelings.

The most obvious discomfort with euthanasia occurred when workers had to kill animals to which they were attached or that they could easily see as pets. While newcomers were more likely to have formed these attachments, seasoned workers could still be troubled by euthanasia when animals reminded them of other attachments. As one veteran worker reflected:

> I haven't been emotionally attached to a dog, except for one, for quite a while. I know my limit. But there are times when I'll look at a dog when I'm euthanizing it and go, "You've got Rex's eyes." Or it's an

Irish setter—I have a natural attachment to Irish setters. Or black cats—I hate to euthanize black cats. It's real hard for me to euthanize a black cat.

Even without attachments, many workers found it "heartbreaking" to euthanize young, healthy and well-behaved animals merely for space because they could have become pets. Without a medical or psychological reason, euthanasia seemed a "waste."

For many, euthanasia became unsettling if it appeared that animals suffered physically or psychologically. This happened, for example, when injections of the euthanasia drug caused animals to "scream," "cry," or become very disoriented and move about frantically. But it also happened when animals seemed to "know" they were about to be killed or sensed that "death was in the air." "Cats aren't dumb. They know what's going on. Whenever you take them to the room, they always get this stance where their head goes up, and they know," observed one worker. Another said that many animals could "smell" death. These workers became uneasy because they assumed that the animals were "scared." "What is hard for me," said one worker, "is when they are crying and they are very, very scared." Another said that she could "feel their tension and anxiety" in the euthanasia room. "They seem to know what's happening—that something is going to happen," she added to explain her discomfort.

Ironically, for some workers the opposite situation left them feeling unsettled. They found it eerie when animals were not scared and instead behaved "as though they were co-operating." According to one worker, certain breeds were likely to act this way as they were being killed: "Greyhounds and Dobermans will either give you their paw or willingly give you their leg, and look right past you. It's as though they are co-operating. The other dogs will look right at you."

Killing large numbers of animals in a single day was disconcerting for nearly everyone.

This happened to one worker when the number of animals killed was so great she could not conceptualize the quantity until she picked up a thick pile of "yellow slips" (surrender forms), or when she looked at the drug log and saw how many animals had been given euthanasia injections. The flow of animals into the shelter was seasonal, and workers grew to loathe those months when many animals were brought in and euthanized. The summer was a particularly bad time, because so many cats came in and were killed. As one worker said, "They are constantly coming in. On a bad day, you might have to do it [euthanasia] fifty times. There are straight months of killing." Another observed, "After three hours of killing, you come out a mess. It drains me completely. I'll turn around and see all these dead animals on the floor around me—and it's "What have I done?" And yet another worker noted:

> It's very difficult when we are inundated from spring until fall. Every single person who walks through the door has either a pillow case, a box, a laundry basket or whatever—one more litter of kittens. And you only have X number of cages in your facility and they are already full. So the animal may come in the front door and go out the back door in a barrel. It's very difficult if that animal never had a chance at life, or has had a very short life.

Even seasoned workers said that it did "not feel right" to spend so much time killing, particularly when so many of the animals they killed were young and never had a chance to become a pet.

All workers, then, experienced at least some uneasiness when facing certain types of euthanasia, despite their socialization into the shelter's culture. The emotions generated by these situations overruled attempts by the shelter to help them manage their emotions and objectify their charges. When emotion management and objectification failed, workers felt some degree of connection and identification with the animals which in turn elicited feelings of sadness, worry, and even remorse.

Conclusion

The initial conflict faced by newcomers to an animal shelter was extreme—because of their prior, everyday perspective toward animals, killing them generated emotions that caused workers to balk at carrying out euthanasia. However, on closer inspection, this tension was replaced by a more moderate and manageable version of the same conflict. The conflict was repackaged and softened, but it was there, nonetheless. Shelter workers could more easily live with this version, and their emotion management strategies got them to this point. These strategies embodied an underlying inconsistency or dilemma between the simultaneous pulls toward objectifying the animals and seeing the animals in pet-related terms—a conflict between rational necessity and sentimentality, between head and heart, between everyday perspective and that of the institution. . . .

A final look at these strategies reveals this underlying tension. By transforming shelter animals into virtual pets, the workers could objectify the animals to some degree, while also categorizing them as something like, yet different from, everyday pets. When it came to actually killing them, workers could play the role of highly skilled technicians efficiently dispatching animal lives seen as not worth living, simultaneously trying to take the emotional and physical feelings of animals into account. Being able to avoid or postpone killing was itself viewed as a struggle between emotion and rationality; importantly, this was allowed, thereby acknowledging some degree of emotion but within limits that reaffirmed a more rational approach. When it came to their view of owners (perhaps a collective projection of a sort), it was the public, and not themselves, that objectified animals; whatever they did, including the killing, paled by comparison and was done out of sentiment and caring. Indeed, outsiders came to be suspected, one-dimensionally, as a distant and alien group, while workers increasingly cultivated a strong sense of we-ness among themselves—humans, too, seem to have two fundamentally different kinds of relations with each other. . . .

It is . . . not surprising that these strategies were sometimes imperfect, failing to prevent penetration of the everyday perspective toward animals into the shelter. Even the most effective programs of organizational socialization are likely to be fallible when workers face situations that trigger their prior feelings and concerns. Many shelter workers may have felt uneasy because at certain times their personal, everyday thinking and feeling about animals in general may have taken precedence over the institutional "rules" for thinking and feeling about animals. . . .

Yet, in the end, by relying on these strategies workers reproduced the institution (e.g., Smith and Kleinman 1989), thereby creating a new generation of workers who would support the humane society model and the kind of human-animal relationship in which people could believe they were killing with a conscience. Far from being a unique situation, the shelter worker's relationship with animals is but our general culture's response to animals writ small. It is not likely that we ourselves are altogether exempt from this inconsistency, as our individual ways of managing our thought and feelings may similarly dull the conflict just enough for it to become a familiar uneasiness. For shelter workers, the conflict is merely heightened and their struggle to make peace with their acts is more deliberate and collective.

References

Schleifer, H. (1985) "Images of death and life: Food animal production and the vegetarian option," in P. Singer (ed.) *In Defense of Animals,* New York: Harper & Row, pp. 63–74.

Serpell, J. (1986) *In the Company of Animals,* Oxford: Basil Blackwell.

Smith, A., and Kleinman, S. (1989) "Managing emotions in medical school: Students' contacts with the living and the dead." *Social Psychology Quarterly* 52: 56–68.

Part IX

The Politics of Social Reality

One of the central themes of this volume is that humans inhabit socially constructed realities. Through interaction with one another, we endow the world of brute physical facts with meaning and create symbolic universes that transcend that world. We interpret and structure our subjective experience in terms of social symbols and meanings. Thus, our reality is socially constructed and decided.

However, individuals' definitions of their subjective experience, themselves, one another, social situations, their society and its past, and the surrounding environment do not always coincide. When such definitional contests occur, power usually decides whose definition will prevail. In our society, for example, the medical profession's authoritative definitions of illness commonly prevail over the Christian Scientists' definitions, and psychiatrists' definitions of subjective experience prevail over their patients'. The politics of reality decide who will participate in the social construction of reality and how much they will contribute.

The more familiar form of politics also involves contested definitions of reality. The social problems that policymakers are urged to address are particular constructions of reality. People and groups make different claims about what social conditions are problems, what kind of problems they are, and how they should be addressed. The politics of reality decide what conditions get defined as problems, how they get defined, and what actions are taken to address them. History, too, is a product of the politics of reality. The past that is transmitted to us is never an unfiltered report of events but involves selection and interpretation. Different views of the past vie to decide what events and historical figures will be remembered and how they will be remembered. Which view of the past prevails depends on the power and influence of their proponents at the time—upon the politics of reality. These politics of reality are the most fundamental politics of human social life that decide what reality everyone in a given social circle will inhabit, and, in some cases, whether they will live at all. The selections in this section examine various aspects of the politics of social reality and their consequences. ✦

32

The Moral Career of the Mental Patient

Erving Goffman

The politics of reality are perhaps most obvious in mental hospitals. Yet students of social life paid little attention to the political struggles of reality construction in mental hospitals before the publication of Goffman's widely read study *Asylums*. They simply assumed the perspective of mental health professionals and did not take seriously their patients' often clashing views of reality. Goffman took a different tack. He attempted to learn about the social life of a mental hospital from the perspective of its patients. This selection, taken from *Asylums*, reveals the politics of reality at that hospital and how they shaped patients' moral careers.

What is at stake in the politics of reality that brings individuals to a mental hospital and keeps them there is their very definition of self. In this selection, Goffman reports that family members, friends, and mental health professionals commonly form a political coalition against patients even before they get to the mental hospital. Once there, the patients' past lives and current circumstances are interpreted so as to justify admittance. From that point forward, patients' definitions of self are hostages to the definitional power of the institution and its staff.

Like those outside the walls of the mental hospital, patients attempt to maintain "face" or effective claims to positive social value. Yet their very presence in the institution indicates that they have fallen from social grace. As Goffman observes, the mental hospital is a mirror that continually reflects unflattering self-images to patients. Although patients attempt to counter these mortifying definitions of self with what Goffman calls "sad tales," they are challenged by everything around them and by everyone in the hospital. Their misdeeds are recorded in case records, reported at staff meetings, and discussed informally. Patients' own presentations of self cannot counter the weight of information that the hospital's staff possesses about them. They consequently have little influence over how others define and treat them. In the politics of reality of the mental institution, patients are virtually powerless.

The goal of the mental institution and its staff is to convince patients to internalize the psychiatric view of reality and themselves. Yet, as Goffman observes, the constant assaults upon patients' definitions of self may have a quite different effect, at least temporarily. Unable to claim or maintain face, patients may conclude that they have nothing to lose by acting shamelessly and do so. Thus, the very institution that is supposed to entice deviant individuals back to the official social reality may sometimes drive them further away. Therein lies a more general sociological lesson. Those who have no power to wield over the politics of reality may simply choose not to participate.

In 1955-56, I did a year's field work at St. Elizabeth's Hospital, Washington, D.C., a federal institution of somewhat over 7000 inmates that draws three quarters of its patients from the District of Columbia. . . . My immediate object in doing field work at St. Elizabeth's was to try to learn about the social world of the hospital inmate, as this world is subjectively experienced by him. . . .

It was then and still is my belief that any group of persons—prisoners, primitives, pilots, or patients—develop a life of their own that becomes meaningful, reasonable, and normal once you get close to it, and that a good way to learn about any of these worlds is to submit oneself in the company of the members to the daily round of petty contingencies to which they are subject. . . .

The world view of a group functions to sustain its members and expectedly provides them with a self-justifying definition of their own situation and a prejudiced view of non-members, in this case, doctors, nurses, attendants, and relatives. To describe the patient's situation faithfully is necessarily to present a partisan view. (For this last bias, I partly excuse myself by arguing that the imbalance is at least on the right side of the scale, since almost all professional literature on mental patients is written from the point of view of the psychiatrist, and he, socially speaking, is on the other side). . . .

Traditionally the term *career* has been reserved for those who expect to enjoy the rises laid out within a respectable profession. The term is coming to be used, however, in a broadened sense to refer to any social strand of any person's course through life. The perspective of natural history is taken: unique outcomes are neglected in favor of such changes over time as are basic and common to the members of a social category, although occurring independently to each of them. Such a career is not a thing that can be brilliant or disappointing; it can no more be a success than a failure. In this light, I want to consider the mental patient. . . .

The category "mental patient" itself will be understood in one strictly sociological sense. In this perspective, the psychiatric view of a person becomes significant only in so far as this view itself alters his social fate—an alteration which seems to become fundamental in our society when, and only when, the person is put through the process of hospitalization. I, therefore, exclude certain neighboring categories: the undiscovered candidates who would be judged "sick" by psychiatric standards but who never come to be viewed as such by themselves or others, although they may cause everyone a great deal of trouble; the office patient whom a psychiatrist feels he can handle with drugs or shock on the outside; the mental client who engages in psychotherapeutic relationships. And I include anyone, however robust in temperament, who somehow gets caught up in the heavy machinery of mental-hospital servicing. In this way, the effects of being treated as a mental patient can be kept quite distant from the effects upon a person's life of traits a clinician would view as psychopathological. . . .

The career of the mental patient falls popularly and naturalistically into three main phases: the period prior to entering the hospital, which I shall call the prepatient phase; the period in the hospital, the inpatient phase; the period after discharge from the hospital, should this occur, namely, the ex-patient phase. This paper will deal only with the first two phases. . . .

The Prepatient Phase

The prepatient's career may be seen in terms of an extrusory model; he starts out with relationships and rights, and ends up, at the beginning of his hospital stay, with hardly any of either. The moral aspects of this career, then, typically begin with the experience of abandonment, disloyalty, and embitterment. This is the case even though to others it may be obvious that he was in need of treatment, and even though in the hospital he may soon come to agree. . . .

In the prepatient's progress from home to the hospital, he may participate as a third person in what he may come to experience as a kind of alienative coalition. His next-of-relation presses him into coming to "talk things over" with a medical practitioner, an office psychiatrist, or some other counselor. Disinclination on his part may be met by threatening him with desertion, disownment, or other legal action, or by stressing the joint and exploratory nature of the interview. But typically the next-of-relation will have set the interview up, in the sense of selecting the professional, arranging for time, telling the professional something about the case, and so on. This move effectively tends to establish the next-of-relation as the responsible person to whom pertinent findings can be divulged, while effectively establishing the other as the patient. The prepatient often goes to the interview with the understanding that he is going as an equal of someone who is so bound together with him that a third person could not come between them in fundamental matters; this, after all, is one way in which close relationships are defined in our society. Upon arrival at the office, the prepatient suddenly finds that he and his next-of-relation have not been accorded the same roles, and apparently that a prior understanding between the professional and the next-of-relation has been put in operation against him. In the extreme but common case, the professional first sees the prepatient alone, in the role of examiner and diagnostician, and then sees the next-of-relation alone, in the role of adviser, while carefully avoiding talking things over seriously with them both together. And even in those non-consultative cases where public officials must forcibly extract a person from a family that wants to tolerate him, the next-of-relation is likely to be induced to "go along" with the official action, so that even here the prepatient may feel that an alienative coalition has been formed against him. . . .

The final point I want to consider about the prepatient's moral career is its peculiarly retroactive character. Until a person actually arrives at the hospital, there usually seems no way of knowing for sure that he is destined to do so, given the determinative role of career contingencies. And, until the point of hospitalization is reached, he or others may not conceive of him as a person who is becoming a mental patient. However, since he will be held against his will in the hospital, his next-of-relation and the hospital staff will be in great need of a rationale for the hardships they are sponsoring. The medical elements of the staff will also need evidence that they are still in the trade they were trained for. These problems are eased, no doubt unintentionally, by the case-history construction that is placed on the patient's past life, this having the effect of demonstrating that all along he had been becoming sick, that he finally became very sick, and that if he had not been hospitalized much worse things would have happened to him—all of which, of course, may be true. Incidentally, if the patient wants to make sense out of his stay in the hospital, and, as already suggested, keep alive the possibility of once again conceiving of his next-of-relation as a decent, well-meaning person, then he, too, will have reason to believe some of this psychiatric work-up of his past. . . .

The Inpatient Phase

The last step in the prepatient's career can involve his realization—justified or not—that he has been deserted by society and turned out of relationships by those closest to him. Interestingly enough, the patient, especially a first admission, may manage to keep himself from coming to the end of this trail, even though, in fact, he is now in a locked mental-hospital ward. On entering the hospital, he may very strongly feel the desire not to be known to anyone as a person who could possibly be reduced to these present circumstances, or as a person who conducted himself in the way he did prior to commitment. Consequently, he may avoid talking to anyone, may stay by himself when possible, and may even be "out of contact" or "manic" so as to avoid ratifying any interaction that presses a politely reciprocal role upon him and opens him up to what he has become in the eyes of others. When the next-of-relation makes an effort to visit, he may be rejected by mutism, or by the patient's refusal to enter the visiting room, these strategies sometimes suggesting that the patient still clings to a remnant of relatedness to those who made up his past, and is protecting this remnant from the final destructiveness of dealing with the new people that they have become. . . .

Once the prepatient begins to settle down, the main outlines of his fate tend to follow those of a whole class of segregated establishments—jails, concentration camps, monasteries, work camps, and so on—in which the inmate spends the whole round of life on the grounds, and marches through his regimented day in the immediate company of a group of persons of his own institutional status.

Like the neophyte in many of these total institutions, the new inpatient finds himself cleanly stripped of many of his accustomed affirmations, satisfactions, and defenses, and is subjected to a rather full set of mortifying experiences: restriction of free movement, communal living, diffuse authority of a whole echelon of people, and so on. Here one begins to learn about the limited extent to which a conception of oneself can be sustained when the usual setting of supports for it are suddenly removed. . . .

Once lodged on a given ward, the patient is firmly instructed that the restrictions and deprivations he encounters are not due to such blind forces as tradition or economy—and hence dissociable from self—but are intentional parts of his treatment, part of his need at the time, and, therefore, an expression of the state that his self has fallen to. Having every reason to initiate requests for better conditions, he is told that when the staff feel he is "able to manage" or will be "comfortable with" a higher ward level, then appropriate action will be taken. In short, assignment to a given ward is presented not as a reward or punishment, but as an expression of his general level of social functioning, his status as a person. Given the fact that the worst ward levels provide a round of life that inpatients with organic brain damage can easily manage, and that these quite limited human beings are present to prove it, one

can appreciate some of the mirroring effects of the hospital.

The ward system, then, is an extreme instance of how the physical facts of an establishment can be explicitly employed to frame the conception a person takes of himself. In addition, the official psychiatric mandate of mental hospitals gives rise to even more direct, even more blatant, attacks upon the inmate's view of himself. The more "medical" and the more progressive a mental hospital is—the more it attempts to be therapeutic and not merely custodial—the more he may be confronted by high-ranking staff arguing that his past has been a failure, that the cause of this has been within himself, that his attitude to life is wrong, and that if he wants to be a person he will have to change his way of dealing with people and his conceptions of himself. Often the moral value of these verbal assaults will be brought home to him by requiring him to practice taking this psychiatric view of himself in arranged confessional periods, whether in private sessions or group psychotherapy.

Now a general point may be made about the moral career of inpatients which has bearing on many moral careers. Given the stage that any person has reached in a career, one typically finds that he constructs an image of his life course—past, present, and future—which selects, abstracts, and distorts in such a way as to provide him with a view of himself that he can usefully expound in current situations. Quite generally, the person's line concerning self defensively brings him into appropriate alignment with the basic values of his society, and so may be called an apologia. If the person can manage to present a view of his current situation which shows the operation of favorable personal qualities in the past and a favorable destiny awaiting him, it may be called a success story. If the facts of a person's past and present are extremely dismal, then about the best he can do is to show that he is not responsible for what has become of him, and the term "sad tale" is appropriate. Interestingly enough, the more the person's past forces him out of apparent alignment with central moral values, the more often he seems compelled to tell his sad tale in any company in which he finds himself. Perhaps the party responds to the need he feels in others of not having their sense of proper life courses affronted. In any case, it is among convicts, "winos," and prostitutes that one seems to obtain sad tales the most readily. It is the vicissitudes of the mental patient's sad tale that I want to consider now.

In the mental hospital, the setting and the house rules press home to the patient that he is, after all, a mental case who has suffered some kind of social collapse on the outside, having failed in some over-all way, and that here he is of little social weight, being hardly capable of acting like a full-fledged person at all. These humiliations are likely to be most keenly felt by middle-class patients, since their previous condition of life little immunizes them against such affronts, but all patients feel some downgrading. Just as any normal member of his outside subculture would do, the patient often responds to this situation by attempting to assert a sad tale proving that he is not "sick," that the "little trouble" he did get into was really somebody else's fault, that his past life course had some honor and rectitude, and that the hospital is, therefore, unjust in forcing the status of mental patient upon him. This self-respecting tendency is heavily institutionalized within the patient society where opening social contacts typically involve the participants' volunteering information about their current ward location and length of stay so far, but not the reasons for their stay—such interaction being conducted in the manner of small talk on the outside. With greater familiarity, each patient usually volunteers relatively acceptable reasons for his hospitalization, at the same time accepting without open, immediate question the lines offered by other patients. Such stories as the following are given and overtly accepted:

> I was going to night school to get a M.A. degree, and holding down a job in addition, and the load got too much for me.

> The others here are sick mentally, but I'm suffering from a bad nervous system and that is what is giving me these phobias.

> I got here by mistake because of a diabetes diagnosis, and I'll leave in a couple of days. [The patient had been in seven weeks.]

> I failed as a child, and later with my wife I reached out for dependency.

> My trouble is that I can't work. That's what I'm in for. I had two jobs with a good home and all the money I wanted.

The patient sometimes reinforces these stories by an optimistic definition of his occupational status. A man who managed to obtain an audition as a radio announcer styles himself a radio announcer; another who worked for some months as a copy boy and was then given a job as a reporter on a large trade journal, but fired after three weeks, defines himself as a reporter.

A whole social role in the patient community may be constructed on the basis of these reciprocally sustained fictions. For these face-to-face niceties tend to be qualified by behind-the-back gossip that comes only a degree closer to the "objective" facts. Here, of course, one can see a classic social function of informal networks of equals: they serve as one another's audience for self-supporting tales—tales that are somewhat more solid than pure fantasy and somewhat thinner than the facts.

But the patient's apologia is called forth in a unique setting, for few settings could be so destructive of self-stories except, of course, those stories already constructed along psychiatric lines. And this destructiveness rests on more than the official sheet of paper which attests that the patient is of unsound mind, a danger to himself and others—an attestation, incidentally, which seems to cut deeply into the patient's pride, and into the possibility of his having any.

Certainly, the degrading conditions of the hospital setting belie many of the self-stories that are presented by patients, and the very fact of being in the mental hospital is evidence against these tales. And, of course, there is not always sufficient patient solidarity to prevent patient discrediting patient, just as there is not always a sufficient number of "professionalized" attendants to prevent attendant discrediting patient. As one patient informant repeatedly suggested to a fellow patient:

> If you're so smart, how come you got your ass in here?

The mental-hospital setting, however, is more treacherous still. Staff have much to gain through discreditings of the patient's story—whatever the felt reason for such discreditings. If the custodial faction in the hospital is to succeed in managing his daily round without complaint or trouble from him, then it will prove useful to be able to point out to him that the claims about himself upon which he rationalizes his demands are false, that he is not what he is claiming to be, and that in fact he is a failure as a person. If the psychiatric faction is to impress upon him its views about his personal make-up, then they must be able to show in detail how their version of his past and their version of his character hold up much better than his own. If both the custodial and psychiatric factions are to get him to co-operate in the various psychiatric treatments, then it will prove useful to disabuse him of his view of their purposes, and cause him to appreciate that they know what they are doing, and are doing what is best for him. In brief, the difficulties caused by a patient are closely tied to his version of what has been happening to him, and if co-operation is to be secured, it helps if

this version is discredited. The patient must "insightfully" come to take, or affect to take, the hospital's view of himself.

The staff also have ideal means—in addition to the mirroring effect of the setting—for denying the inmate's rationalizations. Current psychiatric doctrine defines mental disorder as something that can have its roots in the patient's earliest years, show its signs throughout the course of his life, and invade almost every sector of his current activity. No segment of his past or present need be defined, then, as beyond the jurisdiction and mandate of psychiatric assessment. Mental hospitals bureaucratically institutionalize this extremely wide mandate by formally basing their treatment of the patient upon his diagnosis and hence upon the psychiatric view of his past.

The case record is an important expression of this mandate. This dossier is apparently not regularly used, however, to record occasions when the patient showed capacity to cope honorably and effectively with difficult life situations. Nor is the case record typically used to provide a rough average or sampling of his past conduct. One of its purposes is to show the ways in which the patient is "sick" and the reasons why it was right to commit him and is right currently to keep him committed; and this is done by extracting from his whole life course a list of those incidents that have or might have had "symptomatic" significance. The misadventures of his parents or siblings that might suggest a "taint" may be cited. Early acts in which the patient appeared to have shown bad judgment or emotional disturbance will be recorded. Occasions when he acted in a way which the layman would consider immoral, sexually perverted, weak-willed, childish, ill-considered, impulsive, and crazy may be described. Misbehaviors which someone saw as the last straw, as cause for immediate action, are likely to be reported in detail. In addition, the record will describe his state on arrival at the hospital—and this is not likely to be a time of tranquility and ease for him. The record may also report the false line taken by the patient in answering embarrassing questions, showing him as someone who makes claims that are obviously contrary to the facts:

> Claims she lives with oldest daughter or with sisters only when sick and in need of care; otherwise with husband, he himself says not for twelve years.

> Contrary to the reports from the personnel, he says he no longer bangs on the floor or cries in the morning.

> . . . conceals fact that she had her organs removed, claims she is still menstruating.

> At first, she denied having had premarital sexual experience; but when asked about Jim, she said she had forgotten about it 'cause it had been unpleasant.

Where contrary facts are not known by the recorder, their presence is often left scrupulously an open question:

> The patient denied any heterosexual experiences, nor could one trick her into admitting that she had ever been pregnant or into any kind of sexual indulgence, denying masturbation as well.

> Even with considerable pressure, she was unwilling to engage in any projection of paranoid mechanisms.

> No psychotic content could be elicited at this time.

And, if in no more factual way, discrediting statements often appear in descriptions given of the patient's general social manner in the hospital:

> When interviewed, he was bland, apparently self-assured, and sprinkles high-sounding generalizations freely throughout his verbal productions.

> Armed with a rather neat appearance and natty little Hitlerian mustache, this 45-year-old man, who has spent the last five or more years of his life in the hospital, is making a very successful adjustment living within the role of a rather gay liver and jim-dandy type of fellow who is not only quite superior to his fellow patients in intellectual respects, but who is also quite a man with women. His speech is sprayed with many multi-syllabled words which he generally uses in good context, but if he talks long enough on any subject it soon becomes apparent that he is so completely lost in this verbal diarrhea as to make what he says almost completely worthless.

The events recorded in the case history are, then, just the sort that a layman would consider scandalous, defamatory, and discrediting. I think it is fair to say that all levels of mental-hospital staff fail, in general, to deal with this material with the moral neutrality claimed for medical statements and psychiatric diagnosis, but instead participate, by intonation and gesture, if by no other means, in the lay reaction to these acts. This will occur in staff-patient encounters as well as in staff encounters at which no patient is present.

In some mental hospitals, access to the case record is technically restricted to medical and higher nursing levels, but even here, informal access or relayed information is often available to lower-staff levels. In addition, ward personnel are felt to have a right to know those aspects of the patient's past conduct which, embedded in the reputation he develops, purportedly make it possible to manage him with greater benefit to himself and less risk to others. Further, all staff levels typically have access to the nursing notes kept on the ward, which chart the daily course of each patient's disease, and hence his conduct, providing for the near present the sort of information the case record supplies for his past. . . .

The formal and informal patterns of communication linking staff members tend to amplify the disclosive work done by the case record. A discreditable act that the patient performs during one part of the day's routine in one part of the hospital community is likely to be reported back to those who supervise other areas of his life where he implicitly takes that stand that he is not the sort of person who could act that way.

Of significance here, as in some other social establishments, is the increasingly common practice of all-level staff conferences, where staff air their views of patients and develop collective agreement concerning the line that the patient is trying to take and the line that should be taken to him. A patient who develops a "personal" relation with an attendant, or manages to make an attendant anxious by eloquent and persistent accusations of malpractice, can be put back into his place by means of the staff meeting, where the attendant is given warning or assurance that the patient is "sick." Since the differential image of himself that a person usually meets from those of various levels around him comes here to be unified behind the scenes into a common approach, the patient may find himself faced with a kind of collusion against him—albeit one sincerely thought to be for his own ultimate welfare.

In addition, the formal transfer of the patient from one ward or service to another is likely to be accompanied by an informal description of his characteristics, this being felt to facilitate the work of the employee who is newly responsible for him.

Finally, at the most informal of levels, the lunch-time and coffee-break small talk of staff often turns upon the latest doings of the patient, the gossip level of any social establishment being here intensified by the assumption that everything about him is in some way the proper business of the hospital employee. Theoretically, there seems to be no reason why such gossip should not build up the subject instead of tear him down, unless one claims that talk about those not present will always tend to be critical in order to maintain the integrity and prestige of the circle in which the talking occurs. And so, even when the impulse of the speakers seems

kindly and generous, the implication of their talk is typically that the patient is not a complete person. For example, a conscientious group therapist, sympathetic with patients, once admitted to his coffee companions:

> I've had about three group disrupters, one man in particular—a lawyer [*sotto voce*] James Wilson—very bright—who just made things miserable for me, but I would always tell him to get on the stage and do something. Well, I was getting desperate and then I bumped into his therapist, who said that right now behind the man's bluff and front he needed the group very much and that it probably meant more to him than anything else he was getting out of the hospital—he just needed the support. Well, that made me feel altogether different about him. He's out now.

In general, then, mental hospitals systematically provide for circulation about each patient the kind of information that the patient is likely to try to hide. And, in various degrees of detail, this information is used daily to puncture his claims. At the admission and diagnostic conferences, he will be asked questions to which he must give wrong answers in order to maintain his self-respect, and then the true answer may be shot back at him. An attendant whom he tells a version of his past and his reason for being in the hospital may smile disbelievingly, or say, "That's not the way I heard it," in line with the practical psychiatry of bringing the patient down to reality. When he accosts a physician or nurse on the ward and presents his claims for more privileges or for discharge, this may be countered by a question which he cannot answer truthfully, without calling up a time in his past when he acted disgracefully. When he gives his view of his situation during group psychotherapy, the therapist, taking the role of interrogator, may attempt to disabuse him of his face-saving interpretations and encourage an interpretation suggesting that it is he himself who is to blame and who must change. When he claims to staff or fellow patients that he is well and has never been really sick, someone may give him graphic details of how, only one month ago, he was prancing around like a girl, or claiming that he was God, or declining to talk or eat, or putting gum in his hair.

Each time the staff deflates that patient's claims, his sense of what a person ought to be and the rules of peer-group social intercourse press him to reconstruct his stories; and each time he does this, the custodial and psychiatric interests of the staff may lead them to discredit these tales again. . . .

Learning to live under conditions of imminent exposure and wide fluctuation in regard, with little control over the granting or withholding of this regard, is an important step in the socialization of the patient, a step that tells something important about what it is like to be an inmate in a mental hospital. Having one's past mistakes and present progress under constant moral review seems to make for a special adaptation consisting of a less than moral attitude to ego ideals. One's shortcomings and successes become too central and fluctuating an issue in life to allow the usual commitment of concern for other persons' views of them. It is not very practicable to try to sustain solid claims about oneself. The inmate tends to learn that degradations and reconstructions of the self need not be given too much weight, at the same time learning that staff and inmates are ready to view an inflation or deflation of a self with some indifference. He learns that a defensible picture of self can be seen as something outside oneself that can be constructed, lost, and rebuilt, all with great speed and some equanimity. He learns about the viability of taking up a standpoint—and hence a self—that is outside the one which the hospital can give and take away from him.

The setting, then, seems to engender a kind of cosmopolitan sophistication, a kind of civic apathy. In this unserious yet oddly exaggerated moral context, building up a self or having it destroyed becomes something of a shameless game, and learning to view this process as a game seems to make for some demoralization, the game being such a fundamental one. In the hospital, then, the inmate can learn that the self is not a fortress, but rather a small open city; he can become weary of having to show pleasure when held by troops of his own, and weary of having to show displeasure when held by the enemy. Once he learns what it is like to be defined by society as not having a viable self, this threatening definition—the threat that helps attach people to the self society accords them—is weakened. . . .

In the usual cycle of adult socialization, one expects to find alienation and mortification followed by a new set of beliefs about the world and a new way of conceiving of selves. In the case of the mental-hospital patient, this rebirth does sometimes occur, taking the form of a strong belief in the psychiatric perspective, or, briefly at least, a devotion to the social cause of better treatment for mental patients. The moral career of the mental patient has unique interest, however; it can illustrate the possibility that, in casting off the raiments of the old self—or in having this cover torn away—the person need not seek a new robe and a new audience before which to cower. Instead he can learn, at least for a time, to practice before all groups the amoral arts of shamelessness.

Reprinted from: Erving Goffman, *Asylums*. Copyright © 1961 by Erving Goffman. Reprinted by permission of Doubleday, a division of Random House, Inc. ◆

33

Self Change and Resistance in Prison

Kathryn J. Fox

The previous selection describes how life in a mental hospital was designed to break down patients' existing views of themselves and to encourage their internalization of a psychiatric view of reality and themselves. Over the years, the techniques of self-change or "rehabilitation" that developed in asylums have spread to other institutions of social control, social service agencies, and into the social world at large in the form of self-help groups and the like. Those techniques for changing people's definitions of self are based on psychologistic theories of troublesome behavior and feelings. Psychologistic theories argue that the causes of problematic behavior and feelings lie almost entirely within the individual and generally ignore social conditions and circumstances that might have provoked or encouraged her or his behavior and feelings. The goal of programs based on such theories is to change the individuals, not the social conditions or circumstances of their lives.

That was clearly the case with the "Cognitive Self-Change" (CSC) program in a Vermont prison described in this selection. Prisons in many parts of the world today are expected not only to punish inmates for their criminal acts but also to rehabilitate them—to make them want to give up their criminal ways. The CSC program was designed to rehabilitate violent criminals. Through a variety of exercises, the CSC attempted to get inmates to "talk" a new self into being, much as the members of Codependents Anonymous did

through the stories they told one another at their meetings, as described in Chapter 15. However, while attendance at meetings of Codependents Anonymous is voluntary, inmates' attendance at the CSC meetings was voluntary in name only. Those who successfully completed the CSC program could qualify for early release while those who refused served their full sentence. Feeling coerced into participation, many inmates resisted the program facilitators' definitions of their actions and thinking. CSC meetings often became obvious political battles over inmates' very definitions of self, with facilitators wielding the power of potential early release.

Like other programs of self-change, facilitators of the CSC program first had to convince participants that they had a faulty self that was in need of changing. The program was based on the theory that criminal acts were those of an essentially defective criminal personality. The rehabilitation of criminals requires that they recognize their erroneous ways of thinking—their criminal personalities—and set about changing themselves. Hence, facilitators challenged participants' attempts to explain or justify violent acts or thoughts as reasonable responses to provocations and attributed such acts and thought to "thinking errors"—to defects in their personalities or self. That interpretation ignored the personal costs and potential dangers of not "sticking up for oneself" in prison or the social worlds in which many of the inmates lived before coming to prison. It was a hard sell.

Although the inmates often argued with the facilitators, most tried to give them what they wanted in the hope of early release. The facilitators sometimes challenged inmates' claims that they had changed their ways of thinking but also encouraged them to go through the motions in the belief that they would convince themselves into self-reform by doing so. Some of the inmates simply played the game, becoming "expedient confessors" who feigned self-reform while privately believing that they were decent people who responded reasonably to obvious provocations. Others simply got more angry and violent in response to the continual dismissal of their interpretations of situations and events. Still others may well have adopted the right-thinking, nonviolent self the facilitators demanded.

The problematic character of the CSC program makes transparent the politics of reality involved in all programs of self-reform or rehabilitation. Their purpose is to impose a definition of self on people designated as defective in one way or another. Those with institutional or social structural power use threatened punishments and promised rewards to coerce participants into accepting that they have a faulty self or personality that requires some prescribed repair. The political spoils are individuals' definitions of self. Some valiantly defend their existing definitions of self while others tire of the struggle and remake themselves, transforming the social control imposed upon them into self-control. As this case illustrates, the politics of reality is often a struggle for control of individuals' hearts and minds.

Institutions play vital roles in defining the boundaries within which troubled individuals can be reformed. According to Erving Goffman (1961), total institutions such as prisons strip away the self through a process of coercive "degradation" or "mortification," dismantling the signifying aspects of one's previous life. In total institutions, the erosion of liberty and privacy contribute dramatically to the reconstruction of identity. Relatedly, coercive programmatic practices, such as sentence-contingent therapies and rehabilitation, can virtually "bribe" new selves into being.

This chapter explores the process of self-construction in a "Cognitive Self-Change" (CSC) treatment program for violent offenders in prison. The concept of "self-change" implies a regimen wherein inmates cooperate in their reform. But, although the program emphasizes self-knowledge and self-regulation, the conditions of possibility for self-knowledge are set by the institution. In CSC, prison treatment facilitators insist that violent offenders suffer from "cognitive distortions"—so-called thinking errors associated with a criminal personality. The construction of these thinking errors reflects the interpretive work [in which] participating inmates must engage in order to produce locally viable identities. Concurrently, successful participation in the program affects the length of one's prison sentence. The chapter will focus on the ways in which the institutional discourse of CSC coercively constructs new selves for inmates and the inmates' responses to these constructions.

The Cognitive Self-Change Program

I began observing CSC group meetings in the summer of 1997 with the permission and full cooperation of the Vermont Department of Corrections, as well as the group facilitators and members. My role has been that of a passive observer. Although I interact with other participants, most of the time I take notes quietly. . . .

The groups take place in a regional correctional facility that houses both men and women of all levels of security. There are introductory groups and a second phase for those returned to prison. All participants have been classified as violent offenders. Each group consists of between six to eight inmates and two co-facilitators, most of whom are correctional case workers or probation officers. Each group meets twice a week for an hour and a half. Members are required to begin each session with a "check-in" relating recent situations that had put them "at risk" for violent behavior. In addition, inmates identify the thoughts, feelings, and attitudes that accompanied the incidents and describe the interventions, or "new ways of thinking," they used to defuse them. Check-ins are viewed as practice in the art of self-reflection and reformation.

The rest of the sessions consist of discussions of inmates' criminal histories (called a "Fearless Criminal Inventory"), their patterns of cognitive distortions, and the analysis of homework assignments. Much session time is filled with facilitators and inmates arguing over the criteria for prison release, about the conditions in prison, and the legitimacy and effectiveness of the CSC program. Inmates are required to complete the program satisfactorily in order to be eligible for early release. Thus, a fair amount of time and energy is spent debating the finer points of matters related to "choice" and "force." The Department of Corrections and CSC facilitators view the program as voluntary, while inmates insist it is not. Facilitators repeat that there is no "passing and failing" and that they are not "grading" the thoughts that inmates report. Yet inmates must demonstrate competency in self-reflection in order to be recommended for release.

A body of knowledge about the nature of the criminal self is essential to support correctional rehabilitation and discipline. Individual pathology must be assumed in order to justify incarceration; it is taken for granted that the inmates' personal selves are pathologically violent. Inmates' situations, the contexts for their violent acts, and the nature of their true "selves" are interpreted in a way that supports this assumption and its related institutional practices. Not only have such professional understandings slipped into the public mind and persuaded citizens of the need for self-reflection and rehabilitation (Margolin 1997; Rose 1996a, 1996b), but correctional personnel wield the cultural authority of psychological concepts like a nightstick, reinforcing the power to say who stays inside the prison and who is freed.

The group process of CSC is an effort to instill in inmates a sense of their own responsibility and criminality. The program is based upon the work of Samuel Yochelson and Stanton Samenow (1976) and their assessment of the "criminal personality." In their psychologistic model, criminal violence is the result of poor choices stemming from "cognitive distortions." Rose (1996b, p. 33) has doc-

umented the prevalence of such constructions of the self in disciplinary programs that rely upon notions of "selves with autonomy, choice, and self-responsibility." CSC relies on the same "intellectual machinery" (Rose and Miller 1992, p. 182) to drive home its emphasis on self-regulation, the outcome being the integral construction of criminal selves. The program represents an interesting mix of formulations: a self that is at the same time rational, capable of change, and yet one that is essentially cognitively distorted and in some ways innately criminal. . . . Within this discourse, confession is essential as it shows self-reflection and, hence, rational thought. In CSC, inmates are required to ". . . accept responsibility for crimes for which they have been convicted" and demonstrate a "willingness to report one's [risky] thinking." This reinforces the institution's disciplinary regimes. Selves that are enmeshed in criminal thoughts can easily be regarded as criminal; they are at risk of recidivating. As such, the institution not only specifies the nature and presence of "risky" thoughts, but simultaneously differentiates these criminal selves from their healthier counterparts.

Although participation in CSC is technically voluntary, inmates in the program are eligible for early release whereas those who opt not to participate serve their maximum sentence. In this way, coercion is evident; as a program designer said, "authority is the keystone piece." The paradoxical position of being coerced to volunteer generates anger and resentment among inmates, many of whom refer to the program as "jumping through hoops." Nonetheless, most violent offenders choose to participate.

In each meeting, inmates are asked to report their recent "risky" situations "objectively." For example, an inmate phrased her situation as "not getting my mail on time" and was informed that her phrasing was not objective: "late for you maybe, but not for them." Once inmates have mastered the objective phrasing of situations, they are required to list the thoughts, feeling, attitudes, and beliefs that accompanied the situation. When inmates assert that they just "reacted" in a situation and that there were no thoughts involved, the facilitators insist that they are simply unaware of their underlying thoughts. In this respect, CSC discourse dissects the self as one that has hidden thoughts and feelings—and there are particular ones that motivate violence. Once inmates have properly dissected the thoughts in their heads, they can actively construct new selves.

Inmates are generally adept at describing the feelings they experienced in these risky situations, although they are given a list to consult. Often inmates enumerate dozens of feelings, such as being angry, frustrated, irritated, or disrespected. "Good" check-ins identify the risk for violence or anger, and associate thoughts with feelings. They implicate erroneous thoughts as the culprit for escalating anger and "intervention" thoughts as the reason for de-escalation. Acknowledging the role of these thoughts and choices leads to positive evaluation by facilitators.

According to CSC program literature, fundamental change in inmates is unnecessary; rather inmates are required to demonstrate that they know *how* to change. This means that they must use the discourse of the program effectively. Inmates need to reconstruct their crimes—their lives—within the approved interpretive and linguistic framework. . . . For example, inmates must identify their own criminal patterns from a list of "thinking errors characteristic of the criminal." Among the most popular are "victim stance" (an erroneous perception of victimization), "justification," "anger," and "failure to consider others." Intervention plans for averting future crimes are based upon an understanding of one's own cognitive patterns.

CSC facilitators enforce standards for measuring program competency in inmates by assessing inmates' responses. While facilitators note repeatedly that they do not "judge" or "grade" inmates' thoughts and beliefs, they acknowledge that inmates have to change their beliefs—their selves—at least superficially to meet competency requirements. In this respect, the program establishes the conditions of possibility within which inmates can reconstruct themselves.

Competency is evaluated on the basis of performance in the group, written journal assignments, and relapse prevention plans. Each offers opportunities to demonstrate an ability to curb risky thoughts and attitudes. While behavior in prison matters insofar as assaults would count as evidence of incompetence, language is more essential. Competency is gauged by the use of appropriate concepts and terminology. An inmate who refuses to accept that his thoughts are errors is suspended from the group indefinitely for "not buying it," according to the facilitators. A facilitator explained, "There are no wrong beliefs—there are wrong ones for making it through the program." Acceptance of a criminal identity is essential for success in CSC. Notions of pathological selves are reproduced discursively by recontextualizing inmates' acts and motivations, and reconfiguring their true selves, a language game that inmates must play to reduce their sentences, but one which they ultimately cannot win (Fox 1999).

The persuasive talk of CSC functions to impose particular kinds of criminal selves on inmates. These selves are reproduced by the institution in order to effectively carry out its work. Prison rehabilitation cannot begin until a criminal subject is created. Likewise, incarceration cannot end until inmates' identity work has reconstituted a pathological self. In effect, inmates must first construct criminal selves, which are then reconfigured into reformed identities. . . .

Producing Criminal Selves

Because CSC draws heavily from research on criminal personalities, the program relies upon ideal-typical characterizations of criminal thought patterns. In practice, facilitators interpret inmates' actions and thoughts according to a discourse of criminality. Inmates are asked to construct a biography consistent with this discourse. . . . This sets the parameters for the potential meanings of criminal acts. Inmates reflect upon their "core patterns" of thinking that preceded violent actions, and are instructed to devise "new thinking." In effect, inmates are persuaded that their thought processes were fundamentally inferior. This construction of the criminal mind is the foundation of CSC and offers a basis for possible self-reconstruction in the group meetings.

Inmates' reports on recent risky situations focus on the "mindsets" that fuel violence. The self viewed by facilitators as underlying violence is one that is in the habit of seeing the world incorrectly. In opposition to this, inmates can convey thoughts about how deserving their victims were or about how vindictive and mean correctional personnel are. The purpose of the groups is not to solve problems associated with living in prison, although facilitators occasionally acknowledge that overcrowding, say, is a problem. Rather, facilitators use inmates' complaints about the conditions in prison or their treatment by the guards as evidence of their "mindsets" in connection with violent conduct. For example, in one session, inmates complained about harassment by prison guards and the facilitator suggested that this was an example of a "mindset." One inmate asked how it could be a mindset when so many inmates experienced the [thing]. He was told that criminals share similar mindsets, implying that it was no coincidence that they all ended up in prison. The inmate joked, "I guess the mind is a terrible thing," playing on the television advertisement that "a mind is a terrible thing to waste."

On another occasion, an inmate was told he needed to reflect on his past behavior to discover what patterns of thought he exhibited. He denied there was any pattern because his few acts of violence were situational. He and the facilitators argued for a long time about this, which at one point prompted the following exchange:

FACILITATOR: We're just going through a loop. Unless we're going forward [trails off]

TODD: Forward? Forward to what? What do you want from me? It was bad judgment. It [his story] ain't never gonna change.

FACILITATOR: We'll keep trying to break you down.

Todd refused to grant that his thought patterns were responsible for his actions. Although his claim to poor judgment could be construed as an admission of poor thoughts, it is interesting to note that he was required to construct his biography according to a specific vocabulary. The vocabulary was expected to reflect an institutionally sanctioned view of the criminal mind. Todd needed to accept the global identity of a criminal self, not just admit that he used poor judgment in one instance. Todd would not or could not frame his thoughts as those typical of *criminal thinking* and was eventually given a negative evaluation for program performance, which resulted in suspension. In general, counterclaims deemed illegitimate by facilitators were regarded as "distorted concrete thinking." In the struggle to construct criminally violent selves, conflicting biographies could not be entertained.

Group work functions to detach inmates' actions from biographical particulars and to re-contextualize them in a framework of essential criminality. . . . Yet as one facilitator bemoaned: "[CSC] doesn't consider the forces outside the person; it assumes that thinking alone causes behavior. There's more to it than that!" Nonetheless, reducing explanations of inmates' biographies to the connection between thoughts and risk for violence has programmatically useful consequences.

The simple "underlying pathology" argument actively disables other explanations for inmates' criminal behavior, sustaining criminal selves and advancing program goals.

Merging Criminal Acts Into Criminal Selves

Inmate explanations that provide a mediating context for their violence sound like "justification" to facilitators. As an administrator explained: "There's a difference between the *reason* for what they did and what they did." CSC is only interested in what the inmates did; their reasons are simply thinking errors that explain poor choices. Reasons offered by inmates that try to place the act within a situational context are considered illegitimate. . . .

In order for CSC rhetoric to function as intended, criminal acts have to be viewed in a social vacuum. A facilitator once confided that "when he told me about what happened, I thought his actions were understandable but I couldn't tell him that. I gotta be careful not to feed into that." Thus, an important function of the group process is to decontextualize inmates' behaviors. This has the effect of making their actions seem irrational and unregulated. When, on one occasion, an inmate described his part in a situation as, "I was provoked and hit someone with a baseball bat," a facilitator told him to remove the part about being provoked. This brings the inmate's violent act into focus, telegraphing his motives as problematic.

A more extended example comes from another group meeting. Here, an inmate (Alice) suggested that she was justified in defending herself by cutting someone with a broken bottle. This is eventually transformed into the actions of a violent offender:

FACILITATOR: But the fact is that you cut this [guy].

COFACILITATOR: You kinda minimize by saying you didn't cut him: "I didn't do it" because you didn't mean for it to hap-

pen. But you're responsible because you had the bottle.

ALICE: But if he hadn't come after me . . .

FACILITATOR: That's justification.

ALICE: But it was justified!

FACILITATOR: You're saying "it wasn't my fault."

ALICE: But I think I got screwed. The charges are wrong because they say I went in with intent to do bodily harm.

SECOND INMATE: You're still justifying what you did. You're still saying it wasn't wrong.

FACILITATOR: It doesn't matter what the charge is; it's taking responsibility for what you did.

In this instance, the inmate's attempts to justify or minimize her violence are thwarted. Alice is supposed to describe the situation "objectively," which means she is expected to decontextualize it, to exclude from her narrative all causal references to anything but herself. Alice is reluctant to omit information about the context in which her violence erupted because, the facilitators imply, she is making a subtle attempt to "minimize" her violence. . . . Such a contextual explanation would undermine the program's effort to make offenders individually accountable for their crimes.

Alice was asked to simply refer to her own actions, not those of others. In this sense, the only aspect of the situation of interest in the group process is the act, in and of itself, of cutting someone with a bottle. Insofar as the act is discussed and analyzed out of context, the actor figures as the sole agent of violence. Out of context, it appears that Alice cut someone with a bottle for no apparent reason—other than that she is a violent person.

Inmates contextualize their violent acts in various ways, from talking about individuals who provoked them to stating that poverty causes violent outbursts. This constructs social accounts of their actions. Interestingly, this very discourse is a target for treatment in CSC and serves as proof of extreme criminal thinking. The very reasoning that inmates use to justify their actions is taken to be a part of their problem by the program. The institutional setting for CSC relies upon a construction of inmates as individually pathological; incarceration could not be justified and rehabilitation would make no sense without such a construction. The program enforces a discourse of criminality that validates itself and is impervious to challenge (Fox 1999).

Manufacturing Thinking Errors

Criminals are deemed to be suffering from thinking errors; indeed, such faulty thinking constitutes the criminal mind. Errors in thinking are the cornerstone of interpretations of inmates' actions. Consistent with correctional rhetoric and ideology, cognitive distortions are tied to notions of free will and autonomy. CSC discourse regards as distortions inmates' claims that other people compelled their actions. As a facilitator explained, "Bare bones, you gotta take responsibility for [your] offense." In addition, regardless of others' conduct, inmates need to fit their own actions and thoughts into a pattern suggestive of individual pathology. For example, an inmate named Alicia described a situation in which she was "wrongly accused of stealing" cigarettes. When the facilitator tried to identify Alicia's typical violent pattern, the following exchange developed:

FACILITATOR: What about victim stance?

ALICIA: Is that where someone wrongly accuses you?

FACILITATOR: It's where you *feel* like a victim.

ALICIA: Yeah then.

In the discussion that ensued, the facilitator explained to Alicia that these feelings were evidence of a criminal way of thinking. In general, interactions between facilitators and inmates are designed to reorient inmates' interpretations to focus the blame on themselves.

Inmates' counterclaims are regarded as indicative of how entrenched violent thought patterns can be. CSC presumes that criminal thinking determines the full range of inmates' actions, from extreme resistance to ready capitulation. Indeed, claiming to be a "changed" or renewed person often reinforces facilitators' views. Because distorted thinking is the subject for intervention, some resistance is expected, and this is targeted as well. This is illustrated by an exchange between inmate Todd and two facilitators:

TODD: I have a dilemma because my way[s] of thinking's changed and I know I gotta show you that but I don't get into beefs anymore—I'm above all that.

FACILITATOR: Don't show us that you've changed your thinking, show us that you have interventions.

COFACILITATOR: [incredulously] Yeah, how did you change your thinking?

TODD: You're saying someone can't change their thinking?

COFACILITATOR: Well, we think you may *respond* differently now.

If the essence of a criminal self is distorted thinking, then new and different thinking patterns should reflect a self-transformation. Clearly the object of rehabilitation in CSC is thought processes, yet in the preceding extract, Todd's suggestion that he thinks "differently" than he did before was greeted with skepticism. The suspicion is that Todd may not have changed his real self at all. Thus, the program's discourse reifies the deeply criminal self.

In manufacturing thinking errors, even signs of right thinking may be dismissed. In another exchange, inmates were discussing various intervention thoughts that might prevent violence or anger when an inmate had been waiting for two weeks to be seen in the prison medical facility. One inmate, Lee, spoke to another, Alice, and the following exchange unfolded:

> LEE: Two wrongs don't make a right—that's one I use. [And] no matter what someone else does, they don't deserve to be hit.
>
> FACILITATOR: Doesn't that justify why she's mad? They *made* her mad? How did you justify?
>
> ALICE: My being mad? That I've got a right to be mad because of the way they're [correctional personnel] horsing me around. I'm waiting for two weeks!

This answer was met by a sort of knowing smile by the facilitator. Even intervention thoughts that ostensibly help to prevent violent behavior can serve as evidence of justification. Implicit in this exchange is the presumption that when inmates believe they are devising "real" interventions—and even when the intervention "works" in averting violence—their intervening behaviors emanate from the criminal thought patterns that are so much a part of them.

In another instance, an inmate was upset over a meeting with his caseworker and he intervened in his anger by working on his relapse plan, to which the facilitators responded.

> FACILITATOR: Intervention should be working on the angry part. It's supposed to help you deal with the anger, not the caseworker. It's about *you.*
>
> COFACILITATOR: "Cognitive" means thinking, changing your thinking so you're less risky. It's not a problem-solving course, it's about how can you change your thinking.

Regardless of others' actions toward participants, the "problem" and target of intervention is their angry thoughts. Anger is never justified for inmates because it emerges from a set of faulty thought patterns. In the interpretive schema of CSC, inmate anger is evidence of faulty, pathological thinking rather than legitimate complaints. This, of course, sustains and reproduces angry criminal selves.

Constructing Angry Criminals

In CSC rhetoric, individuals are constructed globally as either victims or victimizers (Best 1997; Young 1996). . . . In the cultural imagination, as well as in social scientific research on criminal minds, criminal selves are deemed essentially distinct from those of law-abiders. CSC was adapted from research and public understandings that erect and sustain the dichotomies of normal thinking/criminal thinking and rationality/anger. As these dichotomies are put into practice, they become part of the disciplining repertoire of social control . . . serving to clearly distinguish those incarcerated and in treatment from those who are not.

Let us briefly examine the use of anger in constructing the violent offender. In a group meeting, a recently returned inmate, Doug, complained about being forced to complete CSC again even though his recent offense was nonviolent. In an exchange with a facilitator, Doug was reminded that CSC was designed to treat rule-breaking behavior generally:

> DOUG: But if it's all that, why would I have to take a separate drug and alcohol program?
>
> FACILITATOR: Did you recently get some bad news?
>
> DOUG: No, it's just that . . .
>
> FACILITATOR: Did you recently get some bad news?
>
> DOUG: [Angrily] No! I see what you're getting at!

In this exchange, Doug's complaints are interpreted as evidence of his anger. As he becomes angry at the suggestion that his resistance was "about" something else, he is characterized as an angry person by the facilitators. In this example, the self-reproductive capabilities of CSC are clear: based upon assumptions of violent offenders as essentially angry, any angry resistance simply reinforces the case for what the inmate is "deep down."

Changing Criminal Selves

Ironically, rehabilitation calls on "essentially" pathological selves to do the work of self-recovery. The goal of producing nonviolent individuals seems to clash with the vital premise that inmates' deeply personal selves are criminal and violent. The resolution of this contradiction unfolds in the interactional practice of reconstructing inmate selves. When facilitators and inmates are dealing in criminal identities, the self that is talked into being is essentially violent and criminal. When the same people engage in transforming these criminal selves, however, their identity work focuses on producing selves capable of rehabilitation and change. The contradiction is kept under control because the discursive acts of constructing troubled selves and reformed selves are managed separately. In effect, different selves are "done with words" when criminals are produced [rather] than when these selves are rehabilitated.

While CSC attempts to change criminal selves by insisting on self-reflection and reform, with captive audiences like incarcerated inmates, institutional rhetoric also draws significantly from an outside world brought into relief. Release from prison is dangled like a carrot and is forceful in additionally fashioning the new selves that, if successful, will see the outside world sooner than expected.

Coercing Changed Selves

Facilitators coerce changed selves by subtly demanding that inmates embrace the representation of themselves as angry; in other words, inmates have to confess to their [hidden] anger. In an exchange with a facilitator, for example, Alice explained her thoughts about a situation in which a prison official reneged on a promise to let her daughter visit her in prison:

> ALICE: I did my end of the bargain; [she's] not doing hers.
>
> FACILITATOR: Something else is going on in that head of yours—those are awfully tame [thoughts].

When Alice then confessed that she was thinking more angry thoughts, the facilitator seemed satisfied. Alice was concerned that feeling angry would be counted against her in the program, but she was assured that it was "normal" for them to have "risk." In this instance, the facilitator rewarded the inmate for having risky thoughts, because anger in inmates is normalized and expected, yet reducing them or intervening in them is also required. Inmates are coerced into "being" angry selves in the context of self-construction. Subsequently, in the context of change, they are coerced into trying to change that aspect of their nature.

Facilitators often asked inmates to find themselves in a "thinking errors list." The list includes various distortions considered typical of criminals, such as "victim stance" and "justification" for criminal acts. Insistence that they had "no patterns" was sanctioned negatively. To complete the program, inmates were required to identify patterns of criminal thought that applied to their ways of thinking. In one instance, when a facilitator persuaded an inmate, Todd, to see himself in the thinking errors list, Todd identified the thinking error that states "the criminal believes that he is a good and decent person. He rejects the thought that he is a criminal." He said that a criminal is "a thief who steals for drugs." He was then told that he misunderstood the point of the assignment; that he should have reflected upon "hurtful, destructive" things he'd done. Todd became frustrated because he was trying to do what he understood to be the assignment, as the following exchange indicated:

TODD: What do you want me to put here?

FACILITATOR: Whatever you want.

TODD: Obviously not. [They discussed the crime for which he was convicted.]

FACILITATOR: Do you think that's criminal?

TODD: Yeah, I guess. But what do you want [for the assignment]?

FACILITATOR: "A thief" is someone else, it's not you. It's supposed to be about you.

COFACILITATOR: How are *you* criminal?

TODD: I reject the thought of being a criminal. That's what it says [on "the thinking errors list"]. That's what I do.

In this instance, the inmate thought he was supposed to write down the patterns that apply to his thoughts—he believes he is a good person. However, he did not perceive this to be an error. Later, when he reiterated that he was not a criminal because he had only one conviction, a facilitator replied, "It does make it difficult when your view is that you're innocent." In effect, he is asked to internalize a "criminal" identity, to accept that his thoughts are merely "typical" criminal ones, thereby adopting his essential criminality as a "master status" (Becker 1963). Acknowledging the criminality of his act is the first step in the process of talking him into being a criminal person—a criminal self. Clinging to the belief that he is essentially a decent person is deemed erroneous and further evidence of how deeply ingrained his criminal thinking is.

Although the target of intervention is the inmate's "mind," the only resources available for making change in group sessions are interactional devices such as writing and speaking. . . . As one facilitator said, "You gotta fake it till you make it," meaning that inmates have to use discursive techniques to demonstrate that they "know *how* to change." Because this interpretive lens shapes the interactions between facilitators

and inmates and is built into the rhetoric of "thinking errors," resistance is regarded as extreme criminal thinking. An exchange in a group meeting demonstrates this point:

FACILITATOR: You gotta get past this, "This isn't gonna work" stuff.

LEE: So what you're saying is that I shouldn't be honest. I should tell you what you wanna hear?

FACILITATOR: Well, by telling us what we want to hear, you're gonna know what we want. . . .

LEE: I don't have a clue what you want!

In this example, the facilitator suggests that giving the facilitators "what they want to hear" would show competency in understanding the program. Resistance, or a reluctance to "try," is perceived as extreme willfulness, a typical criminal pattern. "Trying" is measured by attempts to use the appropriate vocabulary and complete the assignments properly. Whenever inmates would ask about the possibility of failing the program, they were told that "it's not like school, no pass or fail." As one inmate responded: "You say it's not like school, but why does our RP [relapse prevention plan] have to be accepted by you, by whoever? What standard do you use? If it's our thinking, there's no way you can grade it." At times like these, when arguments between inmates and facilitators became circular, facilitators would refer to "the program" and its requirements. Occasionally when inmates objected to the language of "thinking errors" or "criminal personalities," a facilitator would say something like "it's from a book by some psychologists!" in order to reify the program's stance.

Becoming Disciplined

Rose (1996a, p. 46) suggests that decisions about self-conduct and self-presentation are often institutionally embedded in "a web of vocabularies, injunctions, promises, dire warnings, and threats of intervention." In

CSC, some inmates adopt the language of the facilitators and even interject programmatic thinking in exchanges with other inmates. For example, a group member named Doug did a thinking report on his frustration over the fact that he was not being released. The thoughts he mentioned evinced the theme of "why in the hell are they fucking with me?" Another inmate responded that Doug put himself in this predicament by disobeying the stipulations of his release in the first place, thus being returned to jail, after which the following exchange unfolded:

> DOUG: . . . I can relate because Department of Corrections didn't put me here. I put myself here.
>
> FACILITATOR: Then how did you get to these thoughts?
>
> SECOND INMATE: If you knew you were out of place, then are they really fucking with you? . . . If you did all this to get back inside, how can you maintain the belief that they want to keep you in here?

This example illustrates how CSC enforces a discourse of personal responsibility. Denying responsibility for one's criminal actions is the subtext of several of the "thinking errors."

Inmate Resistance

Resistance among inmates is part of the process expected by CSC, but it is assumed also to be worn down with time, persistence, and threats. Inmates resist in a variety of ways. Some may oppose the characterizations of their violence entirely and may suffer the consequences, such as suspension from the group and a stalled release date. Others may confess as required, adopt the rhetoric of CSC, and manifest changed selves. Inmates joke among themselves about how simple it is to perform for the facilitators, to become "expedient confessors" (Scott 1969). This is not to suggest that inmates never change through the group process or that all

evidence of reform is false, but that many inmates do resist the power of correctional personnel by "faking" their transformation.

Resisting Victimizing Narratives

In meetings, inmates are asked to reconstruct the narratives of their criminal impulses and narratives of victimization. They are asked to forsake being victims and to take responsibility as agents of their own criminal actions. As inmates persist in their claims, attempting to excuse their criminal behavior as mitigated, such language is stifled. For example, in the retread group, in the following exchange, Pete explained how he ended up back in jail.

> PETE: I had three domestic assault priors . . . and she stuck me with a fourth one.
>
> FACILITATOR: She stuck you with it?
>
> PETE: Yeah, she did.
>
> FACILITATOR: What was the charge for?
>
> PETE: She said I had her on the ground by the throat.
>
> FACILITATOR: And it didn't happen?
>
> PETE: Yeah, I had her on the ground by the throat. . . .

Note that the facilitator continued to push Pete to accept that his ex-wife did not "do" anything to him, but Pete vehemently disagreed. Subsequently, the other alumni in the group laughed and shook their heads, acknowledging that Pete's story of his own victimization would not succeed by the program facilitators' standards. Claims to victimization are subject to interpretation and negotiation. . . . Again, though, the dichotomy of victimizer/victimized is not challenged, and in this sense, the larger discourse shapes the context of resistance.

CSC's emphasis on self-regulation is evident in group meetings. For instance, a facilitator reported an inmate saying: "What you're asking me to do is be my own [parole officer]!" The facilitator responded, "Exactly! You want me [to be]?" Facilitators stress that one can only control one's own behavior, not the actions of others. For example, when an inmate said his wife "made" him feel guilty, he was told that no one could make him feel anything. Similarly, once in the introductory group, an inmate was complaining about harassment by other inmates, saying:

> They've agitated and provoked me all week, man. . . . Let me tell you something. It's kinda hard to deal with this shit. . . . On the street, you can get away from that situation, but in here, you only have three choices: get off the unit, grab the mop wringer and smash his head, or endure that stuff.

The facilitator told the inmate that the group's function is not to solve the problems of life inside prison; rather it is to focus on "what am I thinking and feeling?" and "how can I think and feel a little differently?" The inmate responded angrily that he could write "five or six thinking reports a day on this one issue!" indicating that thinking reports would not make the trouble disappear. Then he added, "You want us to allow ourselves to be victimized by this guy for months on end. . . . I am *not* a victim!" In this interesting twist on the meaning of victimization, the inmate suggested that the program's insistence on non-violence sabotaged inmates' survival.

In this regard, the inmate complained that the program asked him to place himself at risk for victimization in prison. As a guard told me, the program asks inmates to change "all their beliefs, their associations, everything they've developed to feel safe on this planet." Therefore, a clash between inmate discourse and CSC discourse seems inevitable. As another facilitator despaired: "We're saying 'we want you to live the way we think you should, like our lives.'" In other words, simply typifying people as good or criminal is per-

haps an inadequate interpretation of the complexity of inmates' situations.

Sometimes, the categories of deviant and victim are challenged as acts of resistance. For example, an inmate claimed that he "got shafted" by the juvenile justice system. In another example, he explained that a charge he received for domestic assault was his girlfriend's fault:

> . . . I pushed my girlfriend. She deserved it; she should have gotten more, but I'm a nice guy. If someone is touching me, I'm gonna defend myself. I don't care what society says about it. . . . I don't see why you can't understand where I'm coming from.

He continued that he felt "justified" when his safety was threatened:

> ANGEL: She was hitting me.
>
> FACILITATOR: How did it get to that point?
>
> ANGEL: Oh I see, so it's my fault.
>
> FACILITATOR: It might be—who knows?
>
> ANGEL: No, it wasn't.
>
> FACILITATOR: So victim stance?
>
> ANGEL: Yeah, most definitely. I don't think that's a thinking error. I mean look at the situation. I shoulda fucking smashed her head in. . . .

Here, the inmate is using the concept of "victim stance" quite differently than the program intended. Angel's explanation of the situation rests on understanding his position as a victim; he thoroughly rejects the assertion that this stance represents an erroneous assumption. Thus, he takes the program's language and subverts it to reinforce his construction of events. In this way, then, the process of shaping subjectivity may not always work as planned; CSC concepts can be co-opted, if not overtly rejected.

Resisting Willful Selves

CSC's rhetoric casts individuals as autonomous actors making willful decisions about what they do and how they behave. It stresses that adopting a victim stance allows offenders to choose anti-social behavior. The inmates, however, argue that certain behaviors are not the result of choice. Insofar as inmates maintain a "victimized" self-image, they portray their choices as constrained. By contrast, if actions are the result of individual agency and personal choice, as the program insists, then violence is never justified.

Inmates reported experiencing violence not by choice, but as either a response to victimization, an outgrowth of masculine values, or simply as a matter of pleasure. For example, in an exchange with a facilitator, two inmates, Ian and Angel, argued that sometimes people (in this case, a female offender) react after "putting up with abuse":

> ANGEL: . . . After a while, it pushes you mentally over the edge.
>
> FACILITATOR: Well, maybe she can't do anything about how people treat her, but she has a choice in how she reacts to it.
>
> IAN: But they can aggravate and provoke you to do it [to commit violence].
>
> FACILITATOR: But that's a choice.
>
> IAN: [Angrily] No, it's not a choice. I'd fucking kick all their asses.

Although the inmates believe that their aggression is a response to being victimized by others, in another sense, they refuse to be victimized. Thus, violence is in order to avert victimization.

As John Irwin (1987) points out, hypermasculinity and aggression are features of prison culture, in part, because of identification with subcultures outside prison, but also as adaptations to prison life. It makes sense, then, that male inmates' resistance to the CSC program emerges from their values associated with masculinity. Some of this stems

from their socialization (mainly by their fathers) that taught them that aggression was indicated in certain situations. Indeed, some women reported that their fathers encouraged them to fight as well. Several times, inmates countered the program leaders by saying that "I was brought up to defend myself," and many had difficulty believing that they should respond otherwise. As Matt explained, "It makes me feel weak." Inmates saw some violence as wholly consistent with their subcultural and/or familial value system.

When I suggested to a facilitator that the program might be stripping inmates of their sense of identity without offering an alternative means of achieving status within the prison (or their family) context, he responded: "We aren't trying to take anything away from them. They can keep their values; we are just asking them to modify them." Yet it was clear at times that the goal of value-modification was difficult to reconcile with the life experiences and sanctions of significant others in inmates' lives. A facilitator told me that offenders have said to her: "If I give up these things you say are risky, then who am I? What do I stand for?" From the inmates' points of view, the models proposed in prison treatment programs "are undignified and at times unfeasible" (Irwin 1987, p. 37).

CSC privileges a particular brand of reasoning in its suggestion that conflicts should be resolved nonviolently. On the one hand, the program claims to want only to modify values, yet as correctional personnel, the CSC program leaders and facilitators convey an absolutist ideology—backed by psychological expertise—of right versus wrong, good thinking versus bad thinking, and acceptable behavior versus unacceptable behavior. And all of these aspects—morals, thoughts, and actions—are bound together through the rhetoric of cognitive self-change. In this sense, CSC extends correctional power beyond the discipline of the body that restricts inmates' physical freedom. Inmates' selves—their sensibilities, actions, feelings, and values—are targets for evaluation, intervention, confession and reconstruction. But, at the same time, by fighting back against institutional power, inmates rhetorically resist institutional "rehabilitation" in an attempt to preserve the very selves the institution tries to mortify.

The Complexities of Social Control

Overt social control, such as incarceration and physical discipline, is relatively straightforward in its application. In contrast, cognitive social control, as exercised by CSC, is more subtle, yet pervasive, addressing inmates' minds, choices, talk, and identity. On the dynamic terrain of everyday talk and interaction, selves are contested and reconstructed as the prison asserts its institutional will in intricate and penetrating ways.

As Michel Foucault (1983) pointed out, power dynamics are characterized by the coercion that prompts resistance. Prison inmates resist, in part, because they are constantly confronted by institutional force. They steal bits of freedom by flouting rules and defying definitions. In the process, they bring coercion into relief. In CSC, the interplay between institutional efforts at rehabilitation and inmates' resistance to personal change creates a constantly shifting landscape of self-construction. Some selves are constructed to suit the institutional preference of right-thinking, nonviolent individuals. Some resist to the point of becoming more angry and violent. And some—the "expedient confessors," for example—may superficially comply, while trying to sustain their sense of an unchanged, inner self that they have lived by all along.

In each scenario, the institution sets the parameters for interactions and conditions of possibility for accountable self-construction. But, as imposing as these conditions may be, selves cannot be institutionally dictated or determined. While the prison prescribes formal procedures for rehabilitation and reform, it can't specify the final product because its control of the discursive environment of self-construction is far from complete. CSC certainly operates from a position of discursive advantage; it stipulates the rules and motivations for engaging in the discourse of cognitive self-change. But inmates are neither institutional puppets nor discursive dopes. Institutional discourses can be appropriated for unsanctioned claims. Rules can be bent, interpreted to account for unanticipated acts of resistance. Such resistance embodies more than simply the repudiation of institutional will. It also involves the creation of alternate possibilities for self-preservation. The feigning of self-reform is but one manifestation of these possibilities. The prison may strive for self-mortification, but it can never fully determine the selves that will be produced to fill that vacant space for identity.

References

Becker, Howard. 1963. *Outsiders: Studies in the Sociology of Deviance.* New York: Free Press.

Best, Joel. 1997. "Victimization and the Victim Industry." *Society* 34: 9–17.

Foucault, Michel. 1983. "The Subject and Power." In *Michel Foucault,* 2nd ed., ed. Hubert L. Dreyfus and Paul Rabinow, 208–226. Chicago: University of Chicago Press.

Fox, Kathryn J. 1999. "Changing Violent Minds: Discursive Correction and Resistance in the Cognitive Treatment of Violent Offenders in Prison." *Social Problems* 46: 88–103.

Goffman, Erving. 1961. *Asylums.* Garden City, NY: Anchor Books.

Irwin, John. 1987. *The Felon.* Berkeley: University of California Press.

Margolin, Leslie. 1997. *Under the Cover of Kindness: The Invention of Social Work.* Charlottesville: University Press of Virginia.

Rose, Nikolas. 1996a. "Governing Advanced Liberal Democracies." In *Foucault and Political Reason,* ed. Andrew Barry, Thomas Osborne, and

Nikolas Rose, 37–64. Chicago: University of Chicago Press.

—. 1996b. *Inventing Our Selves: Psychology, Power, and Personhood.* Cambridge: Cambridge University Press.

Rose, Nikolas, and Peter Miller. 1992. "Political Power Beyond the State: Problematics of Government." *British Journal of Sociology* 43: 173–205.

Scott, Robert A. 1969. *The Making of Blind Men: A Study of Adult Socialization.* New York: Russell Sage Foundation.

Yochelson, Samuel, and Stanton E. Samenow. 1976. *The Criminal Personality.* New York: J. Aronson.

Young, Alison. 1996. *Imagining Crime: Textual Outlaws and Criminal Conversations.* London: Sage.

34

The Evolution of Road Rage

Joel Best and Frank Furedi

Social problems are as much a matter of definition as other aspects of human reality. Many social conditions have negative consequences for someone. Some are simply not recognized by most people; others are considered personal rather than social problems; and still others are considered an unfortunate but inevitable fact of human life. Such social conditions only become social problems when they gain the attention of the public and policymakers as a particular kind of problem that can and must be addressed. In most cases, activists, such as Mothers Against Drunk Driving, or professionals, such as physicians and psychologists, make claims that a certain social condition, such as alcohol-related traffic accidents or some forms of adults' treatment of children, are serious problems requiring public concern and intervention. These "claimsmakers" also define the characteristics of the problem or just what kind of problem it is, such as "drunk driving" or "child abuse." In some cases, the media then publicize those claims with print and broadcast stories about the problem. The media then become "secondary claimsmakers," promoting public concern about the problem and increasing pressure on policymakers to address it.

The politics of social problems claims making is often complex. Sometimes there are competing claims about the nature of the problem and, by implication, how it should best be addressed. For example, are the recent incidents of school shootings in the United States a problem of inadequate parenting, media violence, or the ready availability of guns? There is also competition among claimsmakers for different social problems as they vie for public attention and that of policymakers. When claimsmakers for a particular social problem are successful in gaining public attention and concern for the problem, other claimsmakers often try to "piggyback" their pet problem onto the more publicly visible one. For example, claimsmakers for the problem of underage drinking attempted to piggyback that problem onto to the largely successful drunk driving problem by arguing that many drunk drivers were underage drinkers and that reducing underage drinking would greatly reduce drunk driving. Successful social problems claims can also provide a claims-making formula, or "frame," that other claimsmakers can successfully exploit. For example, successful claims about the social problem of child abuse led to claims about a whole series of "abuse" problems, such as wife abuse, elder abuse, and peer abuse. Those conditions we consider social problems are products of such politics of reality. The study of social problems construction helps us better understand the political processes that shape the social realities we inhabit.

In this selection, Joel Best and Frank Furedi examine the related but very different evolution of the social problem of "road rage" in Britain and the United States. Although the British claimed that road rage originated in the United States, the expression was first used in Britain in response to a particularly dramatic assault resulting from a traffic dispute. As is often the case in the emergence of social problems, that incident was treated as an instance of a growing trend and looming social problem of "road rage." Varied claimsmakers, including automobile association officials, psychologists, and political activists, seized the problem of road rage as their own to define and promote. Some attempted to piggyback other social problems onto the attention-grabbing issue of road rage, including environmentalists who argued that road rage was merely one symptom of Britain's destructive "car culture." Other "rage problems," such as "trolley rage" and "air rage," soon spun off the "road rage" social problem. Social problems claims about "road rage" were largely successful in Britain because they resonated with a more general cultural anxiety that the British were losing their characteristic stiff-upper-lip emotional reserve as a result of foreign influences, especially American influences.

Claims about the social problem of road rage in the United States were less successful in generating public concern. The expression "road rage" started to spread in the United States two years after it was first used in Britain. A year later the American Automobile Association published a report on road rage that attracted media attention and led to a Congressional hearing on the "problem." That hearing brought together a variety of claimsmakers for the "road rage" problem, including, again, psychologists, traffic safety advocates, and those who favored increased spending on highway construction. However, the media in the United States were more skeptical of the "road rage" claims than the British media. Newspaper articles questioned the statistical evidence of increasing violence on the road, and cartoonists and humor columnists poked fun at claims that road rage was a serious social problem. Humorists implied that anger on the road was a relatively benign symptom of the many frustrations that were an inevitable part of contemporary life. Although the media skepticism and humor did not silence claimsmakers for the social problem of road rage, they undermined the effectiveness of their claims. Although road rage and the related issue of aggressive driving still occasionally grab a headline or the attention of policymakers in the United States, it is not the kind of taken-for-granted social problem that claimsmakers can piggyback other problems onto or that has spun off imitators, with the possible exception of "air rage."

The contrasting examples of the social construction of road rage in Britain and the United States illustrate the politics of reality involved in the collective definition of social conditions and events as social problems. Social problem claims that receive media exposure and resonate with widespread cultural understandings or concerns tend to be successful and become part of the socially taken-for-granted reality. For example, few Americans question whether drunk driving or child abuse are social problems, as few British question whether road rage is a serious social problem. Yet, these social problems are not mere reflections of harmful social behaviors, but products of effective claimsmaking, media exposure, public perceptions, and public policies. Many other social problem claims have been and are less successful in what might be called the marketplace of social problems claimsmaking, as would seem to be the case with the social problem claims about road rage in the United States. The effective construction of social problems, and unsuccessful claims regarding others, can reveal much about the politics involved in the social construction of reality.

The term "road rage" began to spread in the United States in the summer of 1996, although it took another year to achieve widespread currency. In early June 1997, road rage became a fairly prominent U.S. social problem: the American Automobile Association (AAA) released a report on road rage that attracted coverage in two of the major newsweeklies—*Newsweek* carried a full-page story (Adler 1997), while *U.S. News & World Report* presented five pages on the topic and made road rage its cover story (Vest, Cohen, and Tharp 1997); the following month, there was a congressional hearing on the subject (U.S. House 1997). However, virtually none of the American commentators who pontificated about road rage's significance acknowledged that road rage had first become a celebrated social problem in Great Britain.

This chapter traces the somewhat tangled history of road rage, first in Britain, and then in the United States. Road rage offers a particularly clear—albeit complex and somewhat atypical—example of the . . . diffusion and evolution of a social problem.

Road Rage in Britain

British newspapers first used the term "road rage" in 1994—two years before it would be widely applied in the United States. The first article to use the term appeared in the June 5, 1994, *Sunday Times*; it linked a dramatic news story (an elder of the United Synagogue had been convicted and fined for leaping from his gold Mercedes and punching a Buddhist monk sitting in his Nissan Micra) to other incidents, and argued that these cases revealed a new social problem—road rage. However, this article noted: "Other observers say that 'road rage' is a phenomenon that has spread to Britain from abroad. In the United States the problem has reached epidemic proportions, with 1,500 being killed and injured as a result of traffic disputes last year." (Burrell 1994)

*   *   *

British commentators offered an array of explanations for the new problem. One psychologist writing in the *Police Journal* suggested: "The improvement in driving conditions concerning safety engineering and comfort may have the unforeseen consequence of worsening driver behaviour" (Reinhardt-Rutland 1996: 287). Another psychologist "believes there are too many cars competing for too little road space which means we grow as agitated as rats in an over-populated cage" (Gwyther 1995). A psychotherapist claimed: "There is an idealization of self expression to the extent that almost anything goes. We are encouraged to express ourselves physically" (Spillious 1995). . . . These explanations were embedded in a widely held assumption about growing violence; according to two road-rage experts: "People perceive that society as a whole is becoming more violent, and our behavior behind the wheel is no exception" (Connell and Joint 1996: 1).

Other stories identified additional "rages," [such as] "trolley rage"—conflicts between shoppers maneuvering supermarket shopping carts (called trolleys in Britain), . . . "computer rage"—frustrated workers battering computing equipment . . . [and] "air rage"—disorderly passengers in airliners. . . . Commentators took these "rage" problems seriously; they worried that these phenomena revealed a change in British culture, a decline in traditional civility. Again, there was a general assumption that these problems originated in the United States. . . . [H]aving cultivated and nurtured the term, the British continued to insist that they had imported road rage from the United States.

*   *   *

Two leading competitors—the [Royal Automobile Club] or RAC and the Automobile Association (AA)—in the car-breakdown recovery business were early proponents of the danger of road rage. Most experts quoted in the media were linked to these organizations: Edmund King, RAC campaign spokesperson, emerged as a road rage expert in November 1994; a month later, the AA's Rayner Peet began providing regular comments to the media. In March 1995, the AA scored a major triumph in its publicity battle with the RAC when it published a survey, by Matthew Joint, on the incidence of road rage (Joint 1995). This report, which claimed that nine out of ten drivers experienced road rage, was seized by the British media and frequently cited.

*   *   *

An unusually broad assortment of other claimsmakers sought to link their agendas to the new, highly visible problem. The Suzy Lamplugh Trust (one of the most visible organizations involved in highlighting problems associated with personal safety) jumped on the road-rage bandwagon at the outset. Psychologists, such as David Lewis, Conrad King, and Geoff Scobie, provided the expert authority needed to transform road rage into a social problem (Gwyther 1995; *Independent* 1994; Perry 1995). Conservative politicians regarded road rage as confirmation of their apprehensions about the breakdown of law and order. The Conservative MP Cheryl Gillian played a leading role in raising the issue in Parliament, and expressed concern about the erosion of civility. In May, 1996, Michael Howard (a former Conservative Home Secretary) promised to crack down on road rage.

Environmentalists portrayed road rage as symptomatic of Britain's unhealthy love affair with the car. British road-safety advocacy is animated by an intense hostility to what is disparagingly termed "car culture." Opponents of car culture object to the individualistic ethos associated with car ownership; as one critic puts it: "Driving is quick, private and selfish in the 1990's" (Fowler 1996). Hostility to car culture became a theme of the anti-Thatcherite reaction of the nineties; it was often linked to an environmentalist critique of a materialistic society driven by individual greed. Daniel McCarthy, Devon County Council's road safety officer, who taught courses to help road ragers involved in accidents, pointed to a "growing awareness that cars are bad for the environment and that roads are wrecking the countryside" (Harrison 1996). The environmentalist lobbying group Friends of the Earth argued that the growing incidence of road rage demonstrated that driving was a threat to people's security, that within the broad problem of antisocial behavior on the highways, "Road rage is the tip of the iceberg in that it is merely the unacceptable form of behavior by motorists" (Wolmar 1997). During the nineties, the environmentalist critique of car culture gained strength. Opponents of car culture argued that one benefit of curbing driving was that it would contain road rage. Ben Plowden, the director of the Pedestrian Association and a vociferous critic of car culture, claimed: "With a little imagination we can be free of traffic jams and road rage" (Plowden 1998). . . .

In Britain, then, no single group assumed ownership of the road-rage problem. Al-

though industry initially used it as an advertising gimmick, road rage became integrated into a critique of car culture and, more broadly, anti-Thatcherite criticism of the selfish, uncaring, materialistic 1980s. The rapidly growing therapeutic industry became a major beneficiary of attention to road rage, and expanding the concern about rage from the road to other aspects of social life provided a compelling argument for therapeutic intervention.

Road Rage in the United States

Unlike the British, who invented road rage but claimed it came from the United States, Americans borrowed the term from the British—but never acknowledged its foreign origins. The American press covered road rage as though it was a new, all-American problem. Although a few early stories used the term in 1996, it was not until 1997—three years after the problem emerged in Britain—that road rage attracted extensive, prominent coverage.

A month after the AAA released its report and *U.S. News & World Report* made road rage its cover story, the Congressional Subcommittee on Surface Transportation held a July 17, 1997, hearing on road rage (U.S. House 1997). The hearing featured testimony from various traffic-safety experts, law enforcement officers, anti-speeding activists, and psychologists. While road rage never became the predominant focus of media attention (the major television news programs devoted only two stories totaling less than three minutes to the topic in 1997) . . . it began receiving considerable attention in many of the standard media—*People* magazine (1997), newspaper columns, specialty magazines aimed at business executives, women, and automobile hobbyists, comic strips, and so on.

Part of road rage's attraction may have been its vague definition. It was not clear precisely which driving behaviors counted as road rage. As in the construction of other new crimes, extreme examples of criminal violence typified the problem (Best 1999). Consider these examples from the opening paragraphs of major newsmagazine stories:

> Alfieri . . . attempted to pass [Andrews] on the right shoulder, then pulled around Andrews' car on the left, cut in front and hit the brakes—causing Andrews to swerve into a stopped tractor-trailer, resulting in multiple injuries and the loss of the 6-month-old fetus she was carrying. [Alfieri was] convicted on May 2 of aggravated vehicular homicide (against the fetus). (Adler 1997: 70)

> In Colorado Springs, 55-year-old Vern Smalley persuaded a 17-year-old boy who had been tailgating him to pull over; Smalley decided that, rather than merely scold the lad, he would shoot him. (Vest et al. 1997: 24)

Some claims restricted the term to such violent incidents: "where actual physical assaults take place. . . . The vigilante further escalates abuse and punishment of another combative driver by seeking to physically injure the other driver's vehicle, person, or passengers" (Larson 1999: 26, 28). However, most definitions of road rage were far broader. Some equated it with expressing anger:

> It's where one driver lets another know that he or she is angry because of something that the other driver did. In expressing that anger, the driver might make obscene gestures, scream, honk, put on the brakes, cut in front or brandish a weapon. Or even use the weapon. (*People* 1997:59)

Others equated road rage with "aggressive driving"; thus, the congressional hearing transcript's title was: "Road Rage: Causes and Dangers of Aggressive Driving" (U.S. House 1997). Still other claims focused on problematic driving that might lead others to experience road rage: "Troopers are especially looking for drivers engaged in the kind of activities that anger fellow motorists and spur what has come to be known as 'road rage,' such offenses as speeding, tailgating, driving while under the influence and improper lane use" (Wuerz 1998: 3A). Thus, some claimants equated road rage with "aggressive driving," while others defined it as hostile reactions to others' driving. . . .

Compared to Britain, road rage had fewer advocates in the United States. The July 17, 1997, congressional hearing brought together a constellation of advocates involved in promoting road rage as a social problem. The hearing was intended to generate support for two pending bills: the National Economic Crossroads Transportation Efficiency Act of 1997 (NEXTEA); and the 1997 reauthorization of the Intermodal Surface Transportation Efficiency Act (ISTEA). Like other earlier campaigns against drunk driving and speeding, road rage offered an attention-grabbing issue to which a variety of traffic safety proposals could be appended. Several congressional representatives and federal bureaucrats spoke to the importance of safety issues, although some offered variant interpretations: "Vehicle miles traveled in America have increased 35 percent, but the road capacity has increased by 1 percent. . . . There are solutions to ameliorate this problem, and that is [sic] to . . . build more modern and safer highways" (Representative Bud Shuster in U.S. House 1997: 3).

Representatives of groups with interests in traffic safety also testified. These included Advocates for Highway and Auto Safety (affiliated with the American Insurance Association), the Insurance Institute for Highway Safety, and the American Automobile Association Foundation for Traffic Safety. The AAA presented results of three studies assessing the extent and nature of aggressive driving and road rage: one of these—the so-called Mizell study discussed below—used American data; the other two were British studies. Also represented at the hearing were members of a social movement organization—Citizens Against Speeding and Aggressive Driving—local (Fairfax County, Virginia) law enforcement officers who reported on the effectiveness of an enforcement program, and two psychologists.

The psychologists confirmed that road rage was a serious problem. Leon James, a professor at the University of Hawaii (who billed himself as "Dr. Driving") reported that: "Road rage is ubiquitous in America today. . . . Driving and habitual road rage have become virtually inseparable" (U.S. House 1997: 92, 95). James argued for a broad array of solutions, including establishing QDCs (Quality Driving Circles) and CARR (Children Against Road Rage). Arnold Nereberg, a clinical psychologist, testified: "I consider road rage to be a mental disorder of the 'adjustment reaction type.' It involves clearly expressing the anger directly to other drivers at least twice per year. . . . Fifty-three percent of all drivers have a road rage disorder" (U.S. House 1997: 113–114). James, Nerenberg, and a third psychologist—John Larson (1999)—gave frequent interviews to the press; in 1998, Nerenberg announced formation of the International Association of Road Rage Experts.

For most of these advocates, road rage offered a newsworthy hook, a way to make the familiar, mundane issue of traffic safety seem fresh and compelling. The label "road rage" had succeeded where other, rival terms for the same behavior such as "motormania, predatory driving, and highway madness" had failed to catch the public imagination. Road rage offered an opening for promoting other safety issues; claims about improving drivers' training, lowering blood alcohol content standards, or increasing seat-belt usage could be piggybacked onto warnings about road rage. A Chicago Transit Authority billboard promoted mass transit: "Stop Road Rage Before It Starts." Even routine traffic enforcement efforts became newsworthy when reporters characterized them as campaigns in the war against road rage (Wuerz 1998). In 1997 and into 1998, road rage followed the trajectory taken by many contemporary new crimes (Best 1999): advocates presented a package of terrible examples and frightening statistics; the news media covered these claims; and as road rage became widely recognized, popular culture began to exploit the theme. The AAA and other organizations with a commitment to traffic safety assumed ownership of the problem and continued to keep the issue alive.

Skeptics and Statistics

One potentially awkward problem for claims about road rage was that official statistics gave little evidence that aggressive driving was causing terrible, increasing harm. Britain had "one of the world's lowest accident rates; 3,621 people died here in traffic accidents in 1995, the lowest toll since 1926" (Montalbano 1996: A1). The British crusade against road rage came under continuous questioning by skeptical officials and commentators. Police officials who specialized in traffic safety argued that road rage was just another name for "bad manners and bad driving" (Coren 1994). Jeremy Clarkson (1995), Britain's best-known media commentator on cars, launched a one-man campaign to deride the problem of road rage. The journalist Emma Cook (1995) accused road rage's proponents of opportunistically trying to scare women into purchasing safety-related products. Numerous other journalists concluded that road rage was a media creation. One leading transport editor called road rage a "convenient myth" used to describe routine, road-related violence; he noted that, in October 1996, one of Britain's largest insurance brokers had forced 52,000 customers to buy road-rage coverage, yet a year later, there had not been a single related claim (Moore 1997).

Briefly in 1996, road rage seemed to have the potential to inspire a major crime panic in Britain. Two separate road-related murders—the killings of Stephen Cameron and Lee Harvey—were heavily publicized and viewed as symptoms of escalating road rage. However, it soon became clear that neither killing involved road rage. . . . Yet, in spite of these doubts, road rage became well established in British public discourse, and both therapeutic entrepreneurs and critics of a transportation policy based on private cars and car culture continued to refer to road rage as symptomatic of an emotional malaise afflicting British society.

Skepticism took a somewhat different form in the United States. U.S. figures showed that fatality rates fell substantially during the 1990s to a level that the administrator of the National Highway Traffic Safety Administration conceded was "an all-time low" (Ricardo Martinez in U.S. House 1997: 103). While some skeptics . . . considered these statistics proof that the road-rage crisis was unfounded, other apparently skeptical commentators hedged their bets. A *USA Today* feature story based on an analysis of "more than 500,000 accidents over the past decade shows that aggressive driving imperils the average driver no more today than it did 10 years ago. . . . Aggressive driving is neither a new nor a worsening problem." Yet, the story added "it may be on the verge of becoming worse" (Bowles and Overberg 1998: 17A). The *Washington Post's* story calling the claims into question also noted that: "aggression could be on the rise even though it hasn't shown up in statistics [because] . . . improved safety features such as air bags and better roads could be causing such a drop in injuries and crashes that they mask any other trend"; the story went on to quote an AAA official: "Is there more aggressive driving on the road? There has to be. We have more drivers. We have more congestion" (Davis and Smith 1998: B1).

One possibility was that road rage came to public attention precisely because fatality rates had fallen so markedly. The National Highway Traffic Safety Administration's Ricardo Martinez testified:

Highway fatalities have decreased from 50,984 in 1966 to 41,907 in 1996, despite an enormous increase in travel. The fatality rate—fatalities per mile of travel—decreased by 69 percent during this period, from 5.5 fatalities per hundred million miles traveled to 1.7, an all-time low. Alcohol involvement in fatal crashes has dropped from 57 percent to 41 percent over this same [sic] 15-year period. Seat belt use has grown from 11 percent in 1982 to 68 percent in 1996. (U.S. House 1997: 103)

In other words, as a result of a variety of reforms—improving roadways, designing safer vehicles, reducing the national maximum speed limit to 55 mph in 1974 (Congress did not return the right to set speed limits to the states until 1995), cracking down on drunk drivers, and mandating seat-belt use—there had been great improvements in traffic-safety statistics. However, these reforms could not be expected to continue to reduce death rates. For example, with a growing proportion of cars equipped with air bags and most people in cars using seat belts, fatalities of unrestrained drivers and passengers must approach their lower limit. Further improvements will require focusing on previously neglected causes of traffic deaths—such as road rage and aggressive driving. This is an example of a familiar paradox: solving major social problems invites the recognition of many minor social problems; problems once easy to overlook seem larger, more visible.

Still, road rage's proponents argued that it was a large and growing problem. There were two primary sources for these claims. First, NHTSA Administrator Ricardo Martinez testified:

In 1996, 41,907 people died and over 3 million were injured in police-reported crashes. . . . We estimate that about one-third of these crashes and two-thirds of the resulting fatalities can be attributed to behavior associated with aggressive driving. The more serious the crash, the more likely aggressive behavior is involved. (U.S. House 1997: 10)

Calculating that 28,000 was two-thirds of 41,907, the press began repeating the figure. Critics later commented that the two-thirds estimate was just an estimate; NHTSA was not reporting research results. Moreover, Martinez relied on a broad definition:

> He defined aggressive drivers as individuals who are more likely to: "speed, tailgate, fail to yield, weave in and out of traffic, pass on the right, make improper and unsafe lane changes, run stop signs and red lights, make hand and facial gestures, scream, honk, flash their lights, be impaired by alcohol or drugs, drive unbelted, or take other unsafe actions." Given the kitchen-sink inclusiveness of this list, whatever in the world causes the 13,000 or so traffic deaths that Dr. Martinez does not attribute to aggressive drivers? (Csaba 1997: 43) . . .

The second source for American claims was an AAA-commissioned study by Louis Mizell, Inc., "a Bethesda, Maryland-based firm which specializes in tracking crime and terrorism trends" using a "proprietary database of newspaper and police reports on all kinds of crime dating back to January, 1990" (U.S. House 1997: 153—the Mizell report is reprinted on pp. 167–178). The Mizell study defined "aggressive driving" narrowly: "An incident in which an angry or impatient motorist or passenger intentionally injures or kills another motorist, passenger, or pedestrian, or attempts to injure or kill another motorist, passenger, or pedestrian, in response to a traffic dispute, altercation, or grievance. It is also considered 'aggressive driving' when an angry or vengeful motorist intentionally

drives his or her vehicle into a building or other structure or property" (U.S. House 1997: 170). The study "consulted 30 major newspapers, reports from 16 police departments, and insurance company claim reports to construct the database" (U.S. House 1997: 170). The study identified 10,037 incidents, involving 218 deaths, over a period of nearly seven years; the number of incidents grew each year, suggesting that the problem was growing worse. . . . However, critics generally ignored the Mizell study's unusual definition, and remarked instead that the 218 deaths were a tiny fraction of all traffic-related deaths during the same period. . . . Others argued that the study misidentified the problem: "Coverage of road rage . . . shamelessly disregarded the import of firearms, even though the AAA study found that offenders in road rage incidents often use guns to kill or injure their victims" (Glassner 1999: 8); and although alcohol continued to be involved in nearly half of traffic fatalities, "by the mid-1990s groups like MADD were finding it difficult to be heard in the media over the noise about road rage" (Glassner 1999: 9).

In other words, the American response to road rage was inconsistent. On the one hand, the media promoted the problem as a serious, growing problem—an epidemic. At the same time, critics in the press were sophisticated enough to realize that the evidence supporting these claims was thin. This led to subversive, humorous interpretations of the road-rage campaign.

The Rage Motif and the Problems of Emotion

Contemporary social-problems claims often build upon a core notion, such as abuse or rights. Early claims about child abuse not only subdivided into categories of physical abuse, sexual abuse, emotional abuse, ritual abuse, and so on, but they spun off chains of claims about wife abuse, elder abuse, peer abuse, work abuse, and other forms of abuse experienced by victims who were not children. Similarly, the civil rights movement inspired campaigns for women's rights, gay and lesbian rights, children's rights, disability rights, prisoners' rights, victims' rights, animal rights, and rights for other populations that could articulate their grievances in terms of interference with their rights. Scholars of social movements speak of "master frames"—generic ways of articulating social issues that can be used to mobilize different social movements (Snow and Benford 1992). . . . Notions of abuse or rights can be seen as influential contemporary master frames that can both mobilize adherents around new causes, and that also attract critical analyses. . . .

While the notion of a master frame implies that claims about different social problems will share some fairly elaborate underlying theory of political and social relationships, social problems can share little more than similar names. This was the case with the "rage" family of problems. As noted earlier, once road rage became a familiar concept, British commentators began labeling other displays of inappropriate anger as "____ rage."

In the United States, air rage was the only other rage problem to attract substantial serious press coverage. Instead, the prospect of identifying other rage problems attracted humorists. A September 21, 1997, Sunday comic strip, "Dave," asked: "Road rage . . . an isolated case of aggressive driving gone too far *or* part of a growing national media-induced trend? Is no one safe? Are we on the verge of a 'rage epidemic'?" It then showed frames with people experiencing old rage, reader rage, web rage, smoker's rage, nonsmoker's rage, and rhetoric rage (frustration at a televised politician proposing "more freedom-limiting legislation to make all America safe from this dreaded 'road rage'!"). A similar February 28, 1998, strip for "Troubletown" (syndicated to alternative weekly papers) began "Everybody knows about road rage, but what other kinds of rage

are equally serious?", then featured fifteen frames showing other forms of rage (e.g., rejection rage, bad cellular reception rage). And the popular syndicated humorist Dave Barry wrote a February 1998 column noting that "opinion-makers in the news media have decided that [road rage] is a serious problem, currently ranking just behind global warming and several points ahead of Asia"; he went on to describe "parking lot rage" (waiting for other cars to vacate parking spots) and "shopping cart rage" (caused by supermarket congestion) (Barry 1998).

The responses of these humorists are revealing. First, they obviously recognized the possibilities for constructing claims about new forms of rage ("Are we on the verge of a 'rage epidemic'?"); part of their jokes depended on their audience understanding that rage, like abuse or rights, was a motif or frame that could be used to construct other social problems. Naming problems "____ rage" offered a formula for claimsmaking—and that formula's possibilities presented a recognizable target for humor. This was not an inevitable response. Recall that British commentators treated trolley rage as a genuine problem, whereas Americans found the notion of shopping-cart rage funny. Second, the humorists were implicitly skeptical about the claimsmaking process; they mocked the way politicians and "opinion-makers in the news media" brought new problems to public attention and ranked their seriousness ("all the other kinds of rage that are equally serious," "currently ranking just behind global warming"). Third—and least obvious—it is important to note that the humorists recognized that frustration and anger were at the core of all "rage" problems, and their humor acknowledged that frustration and anger were, after all, common experiences.

Even apparently serious discussions of road rage hinted that the problem had a comic side. Both *Time* and *U.S. News & World Report* printed lengthy, five-page feature articles on road rage: neither story included photographs; rather, both featured large car-toon-like illustrations of outsized, grimacing drivers looming from their vehicles. . . . Although the stories' text treated road rage as a serious problem, the pictures belied that message (Ferguson 1998; Vest et al. 1997).

Road rage and its attendant rages (created in both serious and comic claims) resemble the contemporary concern with hate crimes. Both hate crimes and road rage have names that suggest that inappropriate emotion—particularly anger—is central to these problems. These are problems of emotion—troubling feelings that need to be brought under social control. Most hate-crime laws address behavior (e.g., assault) that is already criminal; they add additional penalties for acts motivated by hatred of some racial or other category to which the victim belongs. It is the evidence of hatred as a motivation that makes the crime a *hate* crime. Similarly, claims about road rage adopt a traditional frustration-aggression model of psychology: drivers become enraged when frustrated by roadway congestion, or by the actions of other drivers. Road rage is bad driving and other acts of hostility—acts already, remember, prohibited under existing traffic and criminal codes—motivated by anger.

The experts that Congress and the media asked to interpret road rage were psychiatrists and clinical psychologists who medicalized road rage by defining inappropriate anger as symptomatic of psychological disorder, a problem of emotion management. They medicalized bad driving: in their view, the flawed emotional reactions of individuals caused the problem, and the solution was treatment that taught anger management:

> We regard aggressive driving behaviors as symptoms of the underlying problem. . . . Most of the individuals I treat have a stress disorder. . . . Stress hormones race through the blood of every driver who holds strongly to any of the five stressful driving attitudes. . . . We introduce aggressive drivers to five alternative attitudes that they

find more appealing than the stressful ones, and convince them to adopt the new attitudes. (Larson 1999: 73–74)

Such therapies turned troubling social behavior into manifestations of psychological problems, deviant actions caused by rogue emotions (Glassner 1999). Almost completely absent was any sort of sociological imagination; through 1998, there was only a single scholarly study—by a team of criminologists in West Australia—exploring the social patterns in road rage (Harding et al. 1998).

In Britain, road rage—and the extended family of rage problems—were less often subjects of humor. Critics worried that the construction of rage as a social problem reflected the ascendancy of a culture of emotionalism. They pointed to the shift from the traditional approval of keeping a "stiff upper lip" to a new emotionalism. . . . In Britain, the problems of rage buil[t] upon a cultural foundation that views social problems as rooted in psychologically destructive behavior. Proponents of the therapeutic ethos contend that British society needs to confront its emotional deficit if it is to avoid a major crisis; one prominent psychologist warns: "The materialist aspirations of today's youth condemn them to an emotional holocaust" (James 1999). From this perspective, road rage is only one of the traumatic experiences inflicted on people by a materialistic society, insensitive to the needs of human emotion.

British critics view this culture of emotionalism as a reflection of foreign influence. The decline of stiff-upper-lip reserve in favor of public displays of emotion (e.g., the grieving surrounding the death of Princess Diana) is part of the Americanization of Britain. According to the journalist Philip Norman (1999), a road-rage incident "rightfully belongs to the New York streets in summertime when scorching heat melts brains along with the Tarmac." The new emotionalism . . . is imported. No wonder the British found it easy to believe that road rage—a crime of emotion—had been transplanted from the United States (Burrell 1994).

Discussion

The different reactions to road rage in Britain and the United States are revealing. The problem first achieved notoriety in Britain, yet British commentators insisted that road rage had originated in the United States, that it had arrived in Britain via diffusion. The British were also quick to identify several other rage problems—trolley rage, air rage, and the like—and the commentators who invented these terms were generally serious. British commentators saw road rage and the larger family of rage problems as evidence of a foreign, corrupting influence—in particular, the spread of American emotionalism and its violence and materialistic car culture. Thus, traditional British civility seemed threatened by an invasion of foreign impropriety. Yet the concept of road rage also expressed a very distinct British perception regarding the negative consequences of car culture. At least for a section of British society, road rage symbolized all that was wrong with private car transportation. This link to the politicalization of car driving suggests that references to road rage are likely to continue as part of the ongoing British debate over car culture.

In contrast, the United States imported the notion of road rage, yet never acknowledged the term's British origins. For example, when the AAA presented three studies of road rage to Congress, it glossed over the fact that two of the three were from Britain. This reluctance to mention foreign influences may reflect Americans' notions of their nation's preeminence. At the same time, Americans responded to claims about road rage in two distinct ways. On the one hand, concerns about road rage (and air rage) received serious attention from Congress, law enforcement, the press, the AAA and various

other organizations concerned with traffic safety, and some psychological experts. On the other hand, there were competing attempts to discount the road-rage problem, either by debunking the claims or by treating rage problems humorously. For Americans, the essence of road rage was not a decline in manners, but *anger*. Treated seriously, anger—like hate—was a negative emotion that reformers believed needed to be brought under control. Anger had destructive consequences, not only for society, but for the individual. But for humorists, anger had a comic quality: they pointed to the myriad frustrations of contemporary life, and viewed the resulting anger—and road-rage proponents' concern with that anger—as at least somewhat funny. [Whether or not] . . . the problem [of "road rage"] . . . endure[s] as a focus for public attention in the United States [remains an open question].

References

Adler, Jerry. 1997. "'Road Rage': We're Driven to Destruction." *Newsweek* 129 (June 2): 70.

Barry, Dave. 1998. "Our Next Epidemic: Get Set for Shopping Cart Rage." *St. Louis Post-Dispatch* (February 8): D2.

Best, Joel. 1999. *Random Violence: How We Talk about New Crimes and New Victims.* Berkeley: University of California Press.

Bowles, Scott, and Paul Overberg. 1998. "Aggressive Driving: A Road Well-Traveled." *USA Today* (November 23): 17A.

Burrell, Ian. 1994. "Motorists Go Armed for War on the Roads." *Sunday Times* (June 5): 1,5.

Clarkson, Jeremy. 1995. "Raging Bulls One, Mad Cows Zero." *Sunday Times* (March 5).

Connell, Dominic, and Matthew Joint. 1996. *Driver Aggression.* London: Road Safety Unit Group Public Policy.

Cook, Emma. 1995. "Motor Hype That Plays on Fear." *Independent on Sunday* (August 6): Real Life 20.

Coren, Giles. 1994. "When Rage Has Wheels." *Times* (December 30).

Csaba, Csere. 1997. "Ravings about Road Rage." *Car and Driver* 43 (October): 43.

Davis, Patricia, and Leef Smith. 1998. "A Crisis That May Not Exist Is All the Rage." *Washington Post* (November 29): B1.

Ferguson, Andrew. 1998. "Road Rage." *Time* 151 (January 12): 64–68.

Fowler, Rebecca. 1996. "End of Our Love Affair with the Car?" *Independent* (May 25).

Glassner, Barry. 1999. *The Culture of Fear: Why Americans Are Afraid of the Wrong Things.* New York: Basic Books.

Gwyther, Matthew. 1995. "Motoring: The Car in Front Is Driving Me Mad." *Independent* (May 7).

Harding, Richard W., Frank H. Morgan, David Indermaur, Anna M. Ferrante, and Harry Blagg. 1998. "Road Rage and the Epidemiology of Violence: Something Old, Something New." *Studies on Crime and Crime Prevention* 7: 221–238.

Harrison, David. 1996. "Driving Toward Desperation." *Observer* (December 8).

Independent. 1994. "Motorway Massage to Combat 'Road Rage'" (August 18).

James, Oliver. 1999. "Up to Nothing." *Guardian* (December 11).

Joint, Matthew. 1995. *What Is "Road Rage"?* London: Automobile Association.

Larson, John. 1999. *Road Rage to Road-Wise.* New York: Forge.

Montalbano, William D. 1996. "Britain Reels from a Rise in Bad Manners." *Los Angeles Times* (June 3): A1.

Moore, Toby. 1997. "Why Road Rage Is Just a Convenient Modern Myth." *Express* (July 31).

Norman, Philip. 1999. "Why John Bull Has Exchanged a Stiff Upper Lip for a Stiff Upper Cut." *Sunday Times* (February 13).

People. 1997. "Make Their Day." 48 (September 1): 59–60.

Perry, Simon. 1995. "RAC's Nervous Breakdown Service." *Daily Telegraph* (December 20).

Plowden, Ben. 1998. "The Car Can Be Curbed." *Independent on Sunday* (November 29).

Reinhardt-Rutland, Tony. 1996. "Road-Rage: Have Cars Become Too Safe and Comfortable?" *Police Journal* 69: 285–288.

Snow, David A., and Robert D. Benford. 1992. "Master Frames and Cycles of Protest." Pp. 133–155 in *Frontiers in Social Movement Theory*, edited by Aldon D. Morris and Carol McClurg Mueller. New Haven: Yale University Press.

Spillious, Alex. 1995. "Why Do We Flip Our Ids?" *Guardian* (October 28): 22.

U.S. House. 1997. Subcommittee on Surface Transportation, Committee on Transportation and Infrastructure. *Road Rage: Causes and Dangers of Aggressive Driving: Hearings.* 105th Congress, lst sess., July 17.

Vest, Jason, Warren Cohen, and Mike Tharp. 1997. "Road Rage." *U.S. News & World Report* (June 2): 24–25, 28–30.

Wolmar, C. 1997. *Unlocking the Gridlock: The Key to a New Transport Policy.* London: Friends of the Earth.

Wuerz, Scott. 1998. "State Police 'See Everything'." *Southern Illinoisan* (February 15): 3A.

35

Commemorating America's Involvement in Vietnam

Robin Wagner-Pacifici and Barry Schwartz

Humans socially construct not only their current reality but also their past. Even our personal or autobiographical memory is not a simple recording of past experience. We tend to remember events that family members and long-term friends retell about us. We contribute to this construction of personal memory by telling stories about ourselves, but these too are socially influenced. Social conventions influence what experiences we recall and what experiences we forget. For example, social convention suggests that even a brief episode of parental abandonment is memorable but that spilling milk is not. Our interpretations of past events are also influenced by our current circumstances. We may interpret past experiences as consistent with who we currently are, or we may interpret those events as things we have to overcome in our struggle to discover ourselves. We do not simply remember but construct personal memories in socially guided ways.

The social construction of collective memory or history is even more apparent. Collective memory supports collective identities, such as national identities, and a sense of common pur-

pose. It gives legitimacy to currently prevailing values and ways of life by suggesting that they have long been fought for and defended. Yet, collective identities, common purposes, values, and ways of life are subject to dispute, and the construction of collective memory or history often reflects those disputes. History is the product of the politics of reality and is subject to revision when political fortunes shift. Recent controversies over whether or not the contributions of racial minorities and women should be more prominently included in American history textbooks are but one example of these continuing politics of reality over the collective past.

A people's collective memory is preserved not only in stories, written texts, and, more recently, on film but also in physical objects. These material manifestations of the collective past are meant to evoke a sense of common identity and purpose with both our contemporaries and predecessors. For example, Americans who gaze upon the glass-encased, original version of the Declaration of Independence or U.S. Constitution are reminded of how their current lives have been shaped by the purported courage and wisdom of our Founding Fathers. Similarly, the statue of Lincoln in his memorial in Washington, D.C., is meant to evoke awe at this representation of a leading personification of our national values.

Monumental commemoration of the collective past is often uncontroversial. Few disputed that George Washington, Abraham Lincoln, or Thomas Jefferson deserved such commemoration in our nation's capital. Similarly, few disputed that the Memorial for the Battle of Saratoga during the War for Independence should be preserved. However, this is not always the case. Some inescapable historical events were and are matters of continuing controversy. Some did not end in collective triumph but in defeat. These events and their commemoration, if any, are subject to definitional disputes over their meaning. As such, debates over whether or not and how to commemorate such events expose the politics of reality that shape our collective memory. This was clearly the case with America's military involvement in Vietnam.

This selection, written by the sociologists Robin Wagner-Pacifici and Barry Schwartz, recounts the controversies and compromises that resulted in the construction of the Vietnam Veterans Memorial. Although American military involvement in Vietnam was politically divisive and eventually ended in defeat, thousands of Americans had died in the conflict fighting for what they thought was the national interest. Initially there was little interest in commemorating the event itself, but pressure mounted to somehow acknowledge the sacrifice of those who perished in the conflict. That resulted in the original design of the Memorial, a black wall of names. However, that design reignited the controversy over the meaning of the conflict and demands for modifications. A flag and statue of three soldiers were added as a compromise, but, as Wagner-Pacifici and Schwartz observe, that memorial continued to reflect Americans' collective ambivalence about the Vietnam conflict.

Yet, despite or perhaps because of the Memorial's unusual design, it evoked stronger emotional reactions than more traditional and monumental memorials. It became a site for continuing debate, both implicit and explicit, about the meaning of American involvement in Vietnam. It seemed to embody the national controversy and ambivalence about that involvement. Rather than resolve the definitional contests over the meaning of America's involvement in Vietnam, it preserved them, perhaps insuring that this is how this tumultuous period of American history will be collectively remembered. In this case, no particular side in the political struggle over the reality of the past decisively won. Instead, it may long be remembered as a divisive and ambiguous event. Although unusual in this regard, the story of the Vietnam Veterans Memorial illustrates the politics of reality that shape our collective memory—our history.

In this article, we address two problems, one general and one particular. . . . The first, general, problem is that of discovering the processes by which culture and cultural meaning are produced. . . . The second, particular, problem is the Vietnam Veterans Memorial. This unusual monument grew out of a delayed realization that some public symbol was needed to recognize the men and women who died in the Vietnam War. But its makers faced a task for which American history furnished no precedent—the task of commemorating a divisive defeat. . . .

We take up our subject by tracing the social, political, and cultural trajectories of the negotiation process that resulted in the Vietnam Veterans Memorial. That process confronted several distinct, but related problems: (1) the social problems of fixing painful parts of the past (a military defeat, a generation of unredeemed veterans) in the public consciousness, (2) the political problem of commemorating an event for which there is no national consensus, and (3) the cultural problem of working through and against traditional expectations about the war memorial genre.

Dedication

On November 11, 1982, seven years after the last American died in Vietnam, the Vietnam Veterans Memorial was dedicated. Immediately before the dedication ceremony, 150,000 spectators watched and applauded as 15,000 veterans passed before them. Elaborate floats and flyovers by fighter planes and helicopters embellished the three-hour parade. The more solemn aspects of this colorful Veterans Day had been established by the reading out of the names of all 57,939 Americans killed in Vietnam in an earlier 56-hour candlelight vigil at the National Cathedral. The president of the United States participated in the observance, lighting a candle for the dead and listening to part of the long roster of names.

From the very beginning of these commemorative rites, the themes of recovery and solidarity were repeated. The motto of the Veterans Day parade, "Marching along Together," reflected these themes and prefaced the dedication day invocation: "Let the Memorial begin the healing process and forever stand as a symbol of our national unity." The rhetoric, however, expressed an ideal, not a reality. If official spokesmen defined the Memorial as a way "to unite our beloved America with her bravest and best," the bravest and best were inclined to ask what took so long. As one veteran put it: "They should have had this when we first came back in 1971." Secretary of Defense Casper Weinberger conceded the delay, but added, "We have finally come to appreciate your sacrifice." Likewise, President [Ronald] Reagan announced that everyone is now "beginning to appreciate that they were fighting for a just cause," as he contemplated the list of those who died for it (*Washington Post*, November 14, 1982, Sec. A, pp. 1, 18, 20; *New York Times*, November 11, 1982, Sec. A, p. 1).

Many people disagreed with the president's assessment. The dedication ceremony itself began with words of contrition rather than unequivocal appreciation: "We ask for grace to face our past." And at the solemn wreath-laying ceremony—the emotional highpoint of the dedication—a bitter voice arose from the crowd: "What were we fighting for?" (*U.S. News and World Report*, November 22, 1982, p. 66). No one can claim that Americans have reached a unified answer to that question.

Dilemmas of Commemoration

. . . The succession of events that led to the Memorial's creation and public reception was a culture-producing process. In that process, contrasting moral evaluations of the Vietnam War and its participants were affirmed. The process itself consisted of [a number of] stages, each defined by the activity of different individuals and different insti-

tutions: (1) the Pentagon's decision to mark the war by an inconspicuous plaque in Arlington Cemetery; (2) congressional activity culminating in a Vietnam Veterans Week and a series of veterans' support programs; (3) a former Vietnam soldier's conception and promotion of a tangible monument; (4) intense controversy over the nontraditional monument design selected by the United States Commission of Fine Arts; (5) modification of this original design by the incorporation of traditional symbols; and (6) the public's extraordinary and unexpected reaction to the Memorial. . . . Our analysis will pass through these stages as we chart the Vietnam Veterans Memorial's development. . . .

Controversies over the merits of a war are expressed at some point in debates over measures taken to commemorate it. The stages in the Vietnam Memorial's construction reveal, on the one hand, the desire for a design that reflects the uniqueness of the Vietnam War and, on the other, the desire for a design that recognizes the sense in which the Vietnam War was similar to previous wars. The Vietnam War differed from other wars because it was controversial, morally questionable, and unsuccessful. It resembled other wars because it called forth in its participants the traditional virtues of self-sacrifice, courage, loyalty, and honor. Tension between alternative commemorative designs centers on the problem of incorporating these contrasting features into a single monument. . . .

Method

When the realities of a particular social experience, such as the Vietnam War, thrust themselves against previously formed assumptions, individual and institutional discourses must realign their terms or remain incapable of making that war understandable. This adaptation is expressed in every aspect of the Vietnam Veterans Memorial's development. Our focus on this development prompted us to examine the discourses of such relevant institutions and individuals as Congress, the Commission of Fine Arts, the mass media, the Memorial's designers and visitors, among others. We found much of this discourse in the *Congressional Record*, dedication speeches, Veterans Day oratory, and commentaries appearing in newspapers and magazines. In addition, many written messages addressed to the dead soldiers are being left at the Memorial by friends and relatives. A sample of 250 of these documents includes statements about the significance of the Memorial itself. A different layer of the Memorial's meaning was the object of observations we made at the site and of similar observations reported by informants. Also, we obtained from the Department of the Interior a partial inventory of objects left at the Memorial since its completion. Typically presented in memory of the dead by family and friends, these objects range from national symbols, like flags, to private possessions, like toys or articles of clothing that once belonged to the deceased. All such tokens are gathered up from the Memorial site by the National Park Service at the end of each day and, along with the written correspondence, are cataloged and stored at the Museum and Archaeological Regional Storage Facility in Lanham, Maryland, where we inspected them.

No one segment of this material provides much useful information. It takes the total body of material, duly combined and arrayed in proper sequence, to reveal the unfolding of commemorative meaning.

A Nation's Gratitude: Search for a Genre

The first official recognition of the Vietnam veteran was not bestowed until 1978, three years after the last American was flown out of Saigon. The recognition itself was hesitant and uncertain. A Vietnam War crypt had already been prepared in the Tomb of the Unknown Soldier, but the Army determined that neither of its two unidentified bodies (only 30% of the remains in either case) made for a decent corpse. Instead of honoring its Vietnam battle dead by symbolically joining them through entombment of unknown soldiers' remains with men fallen in earlier wars, the army recommended that a plaque and display of medals be set apart behind the tomb, along with the following inscription: "Let all know that the United States of America pays tribute to the members of the Armed Forces who answered their country's call." This strange declaration bears no reference at all to the Vietnam War, and it required an act of the Veterans Affairs subcommittee to make it more specific: "Let all people know that the United States pays tribute to those members of the Armed Forces who served honorably in Southeast Asia during the Vietnam era" (*The Nation*, April 8, 1978, p. 389). In even this second, stronger statement, three things are noteworthy: (1) although revised in Congress, the statement was initiated by the military; (2) it received little publicity; and (3) it designated the conflict in Vietnam by the word "era" rather than "war." Thus the recognition came from only a small part of the society for whose interests and values the war was fought; it was communicated to that society without conspicuous ceremony; and it betrayed confusion about the meaning of the war by its failure to find a word to describe it. This last point is the most noteworthy of all. Although a war had not been officially declared, many congressional resolutions during the 1980s referred to the hostilities in Vietnam as "the Vietnam War." Touchiness during the late 1970s about what to call the conflict stemmed from social, not legal, concerns. To name an event is to categorize it morally and to provide an identity for its participants. Anomalous names betray ambiguity about an event's nature and uncertainty about how to react to the men who take part in it.

The first solution to the war's commemorative genre problem was thus halting and uncertain. The fighters were honored but not by an imposing monument. They were honored by a plaque, inconspicuously placed, whose inscription was, itself, indirect and muted. Undeclared wars are usually fought with restraint, however violent they might be. The Vietnam War's first official commemoration mirrored this restraint, marking the cause without really drawing attention to it.

Official ambivalence toward the Vietnam War showed up next in the activities of Congress. It was in Congress, in fall 1978, that the work culminating in the Veterans Memorial began. The plan then discussed, however, was not to commemorate those who had died in the war, but to set aside a special "Vietnam Veterans Week" for its survivors. Thus evolved a second solution to the problem of finding a genre to commemorate the Vietnam War. Time, rather than granite, the dedication of a week rather than the dedication of a tangible monument, sufficed to honor the Vietnam fighting man. This plan's principal entrepreneurs were the members of the Vietnam-Era Caucus, 19 U.S. representatives and senators who had served in the military during the Vietnam War years. They meant to achieve two goals: to unify a nation divided by war and to induce Congress to recognize that many war veterans were suffering from unmet needs. Before anything could actually be accomplished, however, certain obstacles had to be overcome, obstacles inherent in the object of commemoration itself.

To promote unity by separating the event from its men was Congress's first concern. In Congressman Grisham's words, "We may still have differing opinions about our involvement in the Vietnam War, but we are no longer divided in our attitudes toward those who served in Vietnam" (U.S. House of Representatives 1979, p. 12588). At one time, however, the division was deep. Grisham

himself acknowledged that the veterans were stigmatized or, at best, ignored on their return from the battlefront. No ceremony dramatized and ennobled their sacrifices. Most of the other congressmen knew this, and they wanted to upgrade the veterans' status. Transforming the Vietnam soldier from an Ugly American into a patriot who innocently carried out the policy of elected leaders, Congress tried to create a positive image that all Americans could accept.

However, the very attempt to improve the veterans' status raised unsettling questions. Congressmen openly recognized that America's lower-income minorities were disproportionately represented in the armed forces and that the trauma of war bore more heavily on them, economically and psychologically, than it would have on a middle-class army. An uncomplimentary view of the returning soldier accompanied this recognition. The congressmen made no mention of the crimes allegedly committed by American soldiers in Vietnam; however, they did recognize publicly "statistics such as the fact that 25 percent of the persons incarcerated in correctional institutions in America are veterans of the Vietnam War," along with the veterans' need for "an expanded drug and alcohol abuse treatment and rehabilitation program." Family counseling needs were also described: "Of those veterans married before going to Vietnam almost 40 percent were divorced within six months of their return" (U.S. House of Representatives 1979, pp. 12589, 12593, 12584; for details, see Johnson [1976, 1980]; U.S. House Committee on Veterans' Affairs 1981). Congresswoman [Barbara] Mikulski recognized the veterans' social marginality by pleading for the government to "be responsive to the unique problems which they face . . . so that they will be better able to fill their roles in society." Congressman [Abner] Mikva spoke to the same point. Existing veterans' programs, he explained, are not enough for this group. "We must back up this symbolic recognition of their efforts for our country with . . . educational and rehabilitative programs geared to their special needs" (U.S. House of Representatives 1979, pp. 12583, 12588). Here, as elsewhere, the emphasis is on the veterans' shortcomings, and this emphasis reflects society's desire to reconstitute them morally.

It is in this last aspect of congressional discussion that we gain access to the deeper layers of the text being written about the veterans. This text, as presented in the *Congressional Record*, both reveals and participates in a moment of transition in the official assessment of the Vietnam veteran. Our reading of the text locates a residual suspicion about the veterans' psychological and moral status. When one notes all the negative references to the veterans—their employment problems, their physical problems, their psychological problems, their sense of alienation, their inclination toward drugs and crime—it becomes evident that an idiom more relevant to social deviants than to returning soldiers dominated congressional discourse. And this discourse cuts deeper and seemingly truer insofar as its topic included men who had been the agents, if not the architects, of America's first military defeat.

Never during the progress of this discussion did its participants express the desire to memorialize the heroic side of the Vietnam War. They felt that war memories could be expressed suitably in a Vietnam Veterans Week and in a series of veteran rehabilitation programs. A marked utilitarianism became a key part of this commemorative project.

Entrepreneurs and Sponsors

Negative characterizations of the Vietnam veteran might have eventually undermined his positive recognition were it not for a new development, one that was oriented less to the living than to the dead. During the time that the Vietnam-Era Caucus worked on its legislation, a former army corporal from a working-class family, Jan Scruggs, had independently decided on a plan of his own. As noted above, one of the premises of Vietnam Veterans Week was that the soldier must be separated from the cause. This separation is precisely what Scruggs aimed to celebrate publicly. At first, his idea attracted little notice, but it eventually overshadowed Vietnam Veterans Week in commemorative significance. He would build a memorial to the men who served in Vietnam and would inscribe on it the names of all the war dead. The plan represented a different solution to the commemorative genre problem than those previously proposed. It was different in that it combined the traditional idea of a stone monument to the war dead with the radical idea of excluding from it any prominent symbol of national honor and glory. In place of such a symbol would appear a list of the dead soldiers' names—58,000 of them. On May 28, 1979, Scruggs announced the formation of the Vietnam Veterans Memorial Fund to raise money to build the monument.

The accumulation of money to build the Veterans Memorial did not automatically follow from the desire to build it. What needed to be overcome was not only opposition from the still vocal critics of the war, but more important, a sense of uncertainty in the public at large as to what the monument would look like and what it would represent. These suspicions and uncertainties were relieved when the Memorial's original framing rule—"Honor the soldier, not the cause"—was reiterated in the very selection of its sponsors. Chosen were men and women who differed visibly and widely on many political questions but shared the desire to honor the Vietnam veterans. . . . These individuals represented many sectors of society: blacks, Hispanics, women, religious and academic figures, entertainment and sports celebrities, and military men. With the support of this noncontroversial coalition of sponsors, funds were quickly raised to pay for design and construction costs and, by July 4, 1980, a few days after the proclamation of Vietnam Veterans' Week, President [Jimmy] Carter signed a joint resolution that reserved a two-acre site in Constitution Gardens, between the Washington Monument and Lincoln Memorial, for the Veterans Memorial's placement. . . .

The Case of Jan Scruggs

Most accounts of Jan Scruggs's memorial-making efforts began with a phrase like: "Ten years after he was seriously wounded by an enemy grenade. . . ." The fact that Scruggs was recognized as a wounded veteran is very important. Wounds in general play a significant role in the discourse about the Vietnam veterans and their memorial. That Scruggs's wounds are invariably noted means that he is understood to speak authoritatively for the needs of the veterans. Wounds here are legitimating marks. The body of the veteran is, itself, the proof of intimate experience with war, of courage and manhood. Scruggs's wounds make him a generalizable veteran, a collective representation in his own right. This characterization of Scruggs as, first and foremost, a wounded veteran has the effect of invoking the traditional notion of war hero. With that invocation, the traditional notion of a war memorial becomes more plausible.

Scruggs's wounds also resonate with and help to resolve the negative image of the generic Vietnam veteran. The most redeemable veterans were those who had, quite literally, died from their wounds. It is their names alone, after all, that appear on the Memorial wall. The least likely candidates for commemoration were those who had escaped the war unscathed. However, Jan Scruggs, the veteran who carries 11 pieces of a grenade in his body, acts as a perfect mediator between the living and the dead. He is so perfect because he shares something with both. He has suffered for his participation in a bad war and has lived to redeem his fellows. . . .

From the start, [Scruggs] was the sympathetic subject of popular media representations. For Congress he was a representative man, a living symbol of America's hard-working, law-abiding veterans. The 1987 television movie *To Heal a Nation* (based on Scruggs's book of the same title) shows that this perception [was] as plausible [then] as it was 10 years [earlier]. In this movie, Scruggs and the Memorial get equal billing. Scruggs embodies the Memorial. He embodies it now, as he did then, in a multivocal way. Conceding that the Vietnam War would never be deemed justifiable, he appealed to those who opposed it. Having fought himself, and knowing how his comrades thought and felt about the war, he appealed to the veterans and their supporters. The Scruggs image was instrumental, not in preventing or ending the debate over the Veterans Memorial, but in reflecting it. In this way, Scruggs enlisted the patronage of men and women of differing and even opposing points of view. A less attractive man would have been less able to capitalize on Congress's sense of its debt to the veterans.

It was the redemptive qualities of Scruggs's project—precisely, its embodiment of gratitude, the only currency for paying off a moral debt—that congressional supporters emphasized. As President Carter approved Congress's resolution, he expressed his belief that the formal honoring of the veteran would also promote the healing of a nation divided by war. To this end, the Memorial fund's directors continued to avoid political statements in both fund-raising efforts and in contemplation of the Memorial design. The universal support of the Senate and strong support of the House were based on this same requirement: that the Memorial make no reference to the war, only to the men who fought it. Political neutrality was the condition for the support of other sponsoring organizations, including the Reserve Officers Association, Veterans of Foreign Wars, Marine Corps League, Retired Officers Association, and American Gold Star Mothers. These organizations had been assured by Scruggs that the Memorial "will stand as a symbol of our unity as a nation and as a focal point of all Americans regardless of their views on Vietnam" (U.S. House of Representatives 1980, p. 4805). Indeed, its very name would be noncontroversial: it would be a "Veterans Memorial" rather than a "War Memorial." The federal agencies responsible for approving the final design and placement of the Memorial, particularly the Commission of Fine Arts and the Department of Interior, were guided by this same principle.

An apolitical monument was thus supported by the apolitical makeup of its sponsoring agencies. For popular wars the makeup of such groups is less important, since consensus on the object of commemoration already exists. The range of political support for a Vietnam Memorial was stressed precisely because political consensus on the Vietnam cause was minimal. Scruggs's solution to the genre problem was not implemented until it attracted the support of a political spectrum wide enough to make his solution credible, or so it seemed.

Vision and Revision: From Pure to Mixed Genre

Recreating the context and process out of which the Vietnam Veterans Memorial developed, we came to see it not as a monument that ignores political meanings, but as . . . an agency that brings these opposed meanings together without resolving them. In this regard, the first and most fundamental point to emphasize is the nation's failure to reach an agreement on the Vietnam War's purposes and consequences. Hence there is a "genre problem": how to create a memorial that celebrates the virtues of the individual

veteran without reference to his cause. As this criterion was set beside the attitude of the Congress toward the Vietnam veteran, an attitude that combined anxiety about his moral shortcomings (crime, drugs, and alcohol) with gratitude for his sacrifices, there arose pressures in the government to specify the Memorial's essential contours before it invited artists to submit their own designs. Informed by ambivalence about both the cause and its participants, these specifications pushed the Memorial in the direction of the muted and unobtrusive. Thus, in a formal letter approving the design competition, Department of Interior official Bill Whalen explained to the chairman of the Subcommittee on Parks, Dale Bumpers: "Since the proposed memorial is of great significance, and does not memorialize a single person or event, but rather a 10-year period of our Nation's history and is envisioned as a landscaped solution emphasizing horizontal rather than vertical elements, we concur with the report which indicates that a site in Constitution Gardens is preferable" (U.S. Senate 1980, p. 9434). Whalen clearly views the Memorial as significant and noteworthy, yet he understands that a problem inheres in the design of any monument to commemorate this particular "10-year period." As significant as it might be, the Memorial cannot be grand, vertical, or heroic. Like any "landscaped solution," it must hug the ground. It must be modest, horizontal, and nonheroic.

The memorial chosen by the Commission of Fine Arts from the more than 1,400 designs submitted was, indeed, the simplest and least imposing: two unadorned black walls, each about 250 feet in length, composed of 70 granite panels increasing in height from several inches at the end of each wall to 10 feet where they come together at a 125 degree angle. Although this angle aligns the two walls with the Lincoln Memorial and Washington Monument, the walls themselves are placed below ground level, invisible from most vantage points on or near the

Mall. The Vietnam War is thus defined as a national event, but in a spatial context that brackets off that event from those commemorated by neighboring monuments. The walls add to this sense of detachment by their internal format, which draws the viewer into a separate warp of time and space. As one moves from the edge of one wall to the point where it joins the other, one experiences a descending movement in space and a circular movement in time, for the 57,939 soldiers' names appear in the chronological order of the dates of their deaths, such that the war's first and last fatalities are joined at the walls' conjunction.

The commission's preference for this design was unanimous. However, for every layman who approved that choice, another seemed to be enraged by it. Those who shared the designer's goals were inclined to believe she had achieved them. Maya Ying Lin declared that her design was not meant to convey a particular political message but to evoke "feelings, thoughts, and emotions" of a variant and private nature: "What people see or don't see is their own projection." Jan Scruggs concurred: "The Memorial says exactly what we wanted to say about Vietnam—absolutely nothing." Indeed, on the original design the word, Vietnam, did not even appear (a statement indicating that the names on the wall belong to dead soldiers, and identifying the war in which they fought, was added later). This minimalist response to the commemorative task impressed one of the jurors as being "reverential"; another called it "a simple solution for a confused age"; a third saw "no escape from its power." Ellsworth Bunker, former ambassador to South Vietnam, found it to be "a distinguished and fitting mark of respect." Likewise, the *New York Times* applauded the design's "extreme dignity and restraint." It "seems to capture all the feelings of ambiguity and anguish that the Vietnam War evoked [and] conveys the only point about the war on which people may agree: that those who

died should be remembered" (Hess 1983, p. 125; Scruggs and Swerdlow 1985, pp. 63, 68, 69, 97; *New York Times*, May 18, 1981).

It is difficult to tell whether Maya Lin's supporters admired her design because it was an appropriately novel war memorial or because it was not a war memorial at all. The detractors, on the other hand, made frequent comparison between Lin's design and traditional war monuments, highlighting the confrontation between two commemorative styles—a heroic style traditionally associated with noble causes fought for and won, and what could be called an aheroic style, newly conceived for the tasteful recognition of those who had died for a useless and less than noble cause. Most veterans, however, did see something noble, if not useful, in the Vietnam War, and for them the Commission of Fine Arts had gone too far. One veteran, a member of the Memorial fund, described the design chosen by the commission as "the most insulting and demeaning memorial to our experience that was possible . . . a degrading ditch." As to its color: "Black is the universal color of shame, sorrow and degradation in all races, all societies worldwide." For another dissenting fund member, the sinking of the monument into the earth was an admission that the United States committed crimes in Vietnam. (Here are enlargements of the criminality theme that marked congressional discussions about the veterans.) The wall was also condemned as "an open urinal," "a wailing wall for anti-draft demonstrators," "a tribute to Jane Fonda," and a "perverse prank" that would baffle the general public. Another critic, who happened to be the Memorial's biggest financial backer, called the art commission's choice a "slap in the face," a "tombstone," "something for New York intellectuals," a kind of 21st-century art that few would appreciate. To make matters worse, the proposed order of names for the wall presents "a random scattering" that can only confound loved ones. Other critics, including the editors of

National Review, complained about the names themselves. Since the Memorial focuses on individuals, not the war, "it makes death in war a private matter rather than a sacrifice for a collective cause" (Hess 1983, pp. 122–125; Scruggs and Swerdlow 1985, pp. 68, 71, 82–83).

Opposition to the memorial wall was expressed by attacks on details like color, shape, and location, but underlying all specific objections was a disdain for the style itself. Many believed that that style violated the limits of the war-memorial genre. Designed to be apolitical, this memorial struck critics as nonpatriotic and nonheroic. It conveyed a conception of the war and a conception of the soldier that ran counter to those of many Americans. These Americans, responded Jan Scruggs, "wanted the Memorial to make Vietnam what it had never been in reality: a good, clean, glorious war seen as necessary and supported by the united country." One leading opponent of the design conceded that the nation had not looked back favorably on the Vietnam War; however, he believed that "history can be re-evaluated" and "a piece of art remains, as a testimony to a particular moment in history, and we are under a solemn obligation to get that moment down as correctly as possible" (quoted in Scruggs and Swerdlow 1985, p. 94).

Most critics believed that only a "real" memorial could correctly represent the Vietnam War, but since that was politically impossible, they sought an addition to the present design in order to offset the "national humiliation" it perpetuated. At length, a compromise was conceived. An American flag, and next to that, a realistic statue of three soldiers, identifiable as white, black, and Hispanic, portrayed returning from patrol and gazing toward the names on the wall, would bring the original design closer to the traditional genre—would make it look more like a real war memorial. . . .

Flags and Effigies in the Marking of a Lost War

The combination of flag, statue, and name-filled wall reflected profound disagreement as to how the Vietnam War should be remembered and conveyed this disagreement by an apparent binary opposition. The wall was believed to elevate the participant and ignore the cause; the flag and statue were believed to elevate the nation and its causes above the participant. However, the qualities and the relationship between these two patterns of meaning turned out to be more complex than anyone anticipated.

Public discourse about the addition of the flag and statue reveal deep anxieties evoked by the Memorial's original conception. Primary among these was the anxiety about masculinity and its representation. Tradition links masculinity with heroism and strength, but this linkage is weakened by defeat in war. Such concern was rarely if ever openly discussed, but it showed up in the identities of the artists, [in] the artists' attitudes toward the war and their respective contributions to the Memorial, and in their supporters' and critics' own understanding of the war and its soldiers.

Maya Ying Lin was a young, Yale University student when her design was chosen as the winner of the Memorial competition. Lin was an articulate spokesperson for her design and was able to reflect on the way it embodied her intentions (which necessarily coincided with those of the Commission of Fine Arts). When asked, in an interview for *Art in America,* whether she thought the Memorial had a female sensibility, she responded: "In a world of phallic memorials that rise upward it certainly does. I didn't set out to conquer the earth, or overpower it the way Western man usually does. I don't think I've made a passive piece, but neither is it a memorial to the idea of war" (Hess 1983, p. 121). Lin distinguishes her design from the "masculine" memorials by referring to its horizontal positioning and its refusal to dominate the landscape. She does not, however, associate such a design with passivity or weakness. She is articulating an alternative notion of strength. But, intentional fallacy caveats aside for the moment, is this indeed an adequate symbol for the commemoration of anything having to do with war? Is not war, after all, always and everywhere, about the kind of masculine strength associated with conquest and domination?

Referring to the sense of responsibility soldiers have for each other during war, John Wheeler, one of the Vietnam Veterans Memorial project's organizers, and a veteran himself, wrote: "I consider my commitment as a statement that there are things worth dying for. It is a masculine statement. This is why war has tended to be viewed as a masculine enterprise" (1984, p. 140). Clearly the question of masculinity and its meaning was in the air, and the peculiar nature of the Vietnam War made it all the more confusing. The very raising of this question had broad implications for the resolution of the Vietnam Veterans Memorial's genre problem.

A strictly semiotic reading of the wall would highlight its "femininity." It is an opening in nature. It is womblike in its embrace of the visitor. The wall also reflects the visitor in its stone, thus eliciting a form of empathy, a trait traditionally considered more available to women than to men. What, then, remains of war, an archetypically masculine endeavor, in this Memorial? If critics of the Memorial's initial design were occupied by this question, they did not ask it directly. The unconscious strategy was to deflect and displace. Rather than make an issue of the threat to masculinity by feminine forms, the problem was linked to the Memorial's blackness, its placement within rather than upon the earth, its suggestion of weakness and shame rather than pride and strength. Accordingly, Maya Lin's critics made a list of demands that would draw out the Memorial from the inferior realm of darkness and earth into the superior realm of light and sky. They wanted the black granite changed to white; they wanted the walls moved above ground; they wanted a flag. National honor would thus be restored. The masculine (or "phallic," as Maya Lin would put it) would also be asserted and, in the flag, find its patriotic representation.

In addition, a decision was made to "erect" a statue that would serve as a counterpoint to the "establishment" of the wall. Here, Congress had turned away from its own unconscious assertion of masculinity by revising the wording of the Congressional Joint Resolution authorizing the Vietnam Veterans Memorial Fund. The resolution was passed with the original phrase "erect a memorial" changed to read "establish a memorial" (U.S. Senate 1980, p. 9433). However, once the new decision to erect a statue was made, and the sculptor Frederick Hart chosen to implement it, the masculine purview in matters of representing the veterans was overtly acknowledged. The sculptor himself certainly saw it this way. Drawing an explicit comparison between himself and Maya Lin, Hart claimed a special understanding of the veterans: he had studied them for three years. In this connection, he put one of our society's masculine traditions to the service of his craft: "I became close friends with many vets, drank with them in bars." While this experience converts directly into artistic privilege, "Lin's piece is a serene exercise in contemporary art done in a vacuum with no knowledge of the subject" (Hess 1983, p. 124). But how could a young, university-sheltered woman, or any woman, know this subject? In *Time's* assessment of the statue, we are told that the three soldiers "suggest the wordless fellowship that is forged only in combat." In our society, as Wheeler claimed, only men can comprehend that wordless "fellowship."

Even if we grant this claim, the anxious response of the Memorial's critics had, as noted above, another source: the fact of defeat. Since few things threaten traditional concepts of manhood more than defeat in battle, the symbolic burden must be very great indeed on any memorial that seeks to elevate the losing protagonists. As one military officer put it, "Why build a memorial to losers?" (*National Geographic*, May 1985, p. 558). If both the losers and the loss were ignored and the emphasis placed on the transcendent values of the cause, then perhaps no one's masculinity would be threatened. But since the military defeat could not be ignored, the flag and statue can be read as palliatives to doubts about the toughness of America's fighting men. Perhaps this is why the statue was so important to Maya Lin's critics: it drew attention away from the individual men who fought and lost in Vietnam and shifted that attention onto generic, that is, timeless, heroic soldiers. A neat idea, but it was not a convincing one. Its originators did not even convince themselves.

Let us take a closer look at the statue of the three soldiers. It is of a greenish-golden hue. The soldiers, seemingly disoriented, and garbed in finely wrought but distressed uniforms, gaze at the wall. Weapons hang uselessly from two of the soldiers' lowered arms and rest across the other soldier's back. Here, then, is the realism that critics of the wall's abstraction desired. Here is life as opposed to the wall's expression of death but it is life exhausted and confused. These men are of the war, but not at the moment in it. And since the soldiers are placed on only a modest pedestal, visitors cannot even figuratively look up to them; instead, they confront the soldiers almost at eye level. The [feel] of this statue is not heroic.

Considering the Memorial complex as a whole, we find an even broader pattern of assertion and qualification. The wall embodied a controversial assertion: that individuals should be remembered and their cause ignored; the qualifications came with the flag and statue. These, in turn, were beset by their own internal tensions. The statue was conceived as a reactive assertion of pride, hero-

ism, and masculinity, but, through the particular form it took, it emerged as a tempering of all these things. The flag seems to be unconditionally assertive because it is the only part of the Memorial site that draws our eyes upward, but we notice in the peculiar dedication inscribed on its base a kind of backing off: "This flag affirms the principles of freedom for which [the Vietnam veterans] fought and their pride in having served under difficult circumstances." The euphemism is transparent enough. By "difficult circumstances" we are to understand not the power of our enemy but the feebleness of our cause. In this light, the similarities among the three parts of the Memorial become more salient than their differences, despite the realism of the statue's figures and the vertical prominence of the flag. Whether we look down, across, or up, we find ambivalence about the meaning of this war and its protagonists refracted throughout.

While the addition of the flag and statue made the Vietnam Memorial look more like a traditional war monument, it also amplified the tensions and ambivalence that induced the original departure from a traditional war monument design. The vehicle for that departure, the wall of names, admits of its own internal qualifications, but these are more subtle than the ones built into the Memorial's two other parts and are perhaps more important as clues to its sociological significance.

The Political Significance of Names

After reflecting on the criteria for the Memorial competition, Maya Lin expressed her personal agreement with what they were meant to accomplish. "Many earlier memorials," she said, "were propagandized statements about the victory, the issues, the politics, and not about the people who served and died. I felt a memorial should be honest about the reality of war and be for the people who gave their lives" (*National Geographic,* May 1985, p. 557). Such a memorial, Lin also agreed, must contain the name of every soldier who died.

The partial list of war dead is a familiar memorial device, typically found on plaques in schools, churches, city halls, and town squares to mark local sacrifices made on behalf of national causes. Such a list is also found on larger memorial complexes, like the wall of the missing at the national cemeteries in Honolulu and Manila. Lin's conception is different. She presents a national list, a complete inventory of war dead, but she does not make it part of a recognizable monument. She presents nothing but a list, without even a label to identify its contents. She thus defines the war memorial genre as broadly as it has ever been defined before.

To list the names of every fallen soldier, with no symbolic reference to the cause or country for which they died, immediately highlights the individual. But, once it has been determined that the individual will overshadow cause and country, the task of constructing that individual becomes the primary concern. Precisely what, and how much, is to be said? Since Maya Lin's response to the question is to take the naming criterion and make it her dominant motif, there is no identifying of rank, nor any other individualizing markers, such as membership in a specific military service (army, navy, etc.) or place of civilian residence. With the individual's uniqueness thus dissolved into a homogenizing sequence of death dates, how can one claim that the names on the wall personify anything that American society values?

The Memorial's failure to dignify the names of the war dead was lamented by many. The *National Review,* for example, compared the names engraved on the unembellished Memorial wall to a list of traffic accidents (September 18, 1981, p. 106). The magazine *USA Today* (March 1983, p. 70) observed that "nowhere on the Memorial was there to be any

reference to where or why these people died, and no flag or patriotic symbol of any kind would indicate that honor or dedication to duty were involved in their deaths." More frequently, however, the Memorial's naming scheme was regarded as a singularly American tribute to such values as pluralism, egalitarianism, and respect for the individual. In other words, the very fact that Americans can honor a name, regardless of rank and, one might hazard to say, regardless of mission, reveals the respect that American society gives to the individual. . . .

Uses of Genre: The Enshrinement Process

The meaning of the Vietnam Veterans Memorial is defined by the way people behave in reference to it. Some monuments are rarely talked about or visited and never put to ceremonial use. Other monuments, like the Tomb of the Unknown Soldier, are used often as formal ceremonial sites and visited year after year by large numbers of people. Between the Vietnam Veterans Memorial and its visitors, a very different relationship obtains. Not only is the Memorial an object of frequent ceremony and frequent visitation (more than 2.5 million visitors and 1,100–1,500 reunions per year), it is also an object with which visitors enter into active and affective relationships. These relationships have thwarted all original intentions as to what the Memorial should be and represent.

Conceived as something to be passively looked at and contemplated, the Vietnam Memorial has become an object of emotion. This is not the case for the Memorial site as a whole, just the wall and its names. The names on the wall are touched, their letters traced by the moving finger. The names are caressed. The names are reproduced on paper by pencil rubbing and taken home. And something is left from home itself—a material object bearing special significance to the deceased or a written statement by the visitor or mourner.

The dedications of the aggrieved are a spectacle that to many is more moving than the Memorial wall itself. More goes into spectators' reactions, however, than morbid curiosity, for the scenes of mourning are not altogether private affairs. These scenes make palpable a collective loss known to all. Not only, therefore, do friends and family bring their personal grief to the Memorial wall, but society exercises a moral pressure over those not directly affected by loss to add their presence to the situation and to align their sentiments with it.

This moral pressure produces the large gatherings from which much of the Memorial's dramatic impact derives. By contrast, when the Memorial's grounds are deserted, its wall appears less magnetic, less moving, less memorable. Durkheim was referring to such a contrast when he declared that the experience of being in a sacred shrine "is only the sentiment inspired by the *group* in its members, but projected out of the consciousnesses that experience them, and objectified. To be objectified they are fixed upon some object which thus becomes sacred. . . . Therefore the sacred character assumed by an object is not implied in the intrinsic properties of this latter: it is added to them" (1965, p. 261). Just so, the Veterans Memorial is properly designated a sacred shrine because it is the object of solemn assemblies in which moral sentiments arise and reinforce one another.

Since assembly and arousal cannot in themselves account for the Memorial's sacred character, we must not follow Durkheim too closely. Durkheim believed that the sacredness of an object like the Memorial wall obtains exclusively from the way people react to it. Yet, the wall is more than just a convenient screen on which the Memorial's visitors project their sentiments. The wall itself is an evoker of these sentiments. If this were not the case, if any object would do to embody collective feeling, as Durkheim believed,

then we would be hard pressed to understand why other parts of the Memorial—the flag and the statue—do not evoke the same reactions as does the wall. Material tokens are placed much less frequently at the flag and statue than at the wall; expressions of strong emotion occur almost exclusively at the wall; the demeanor of visitors is more solemn, by far, in the vicinity of the wall; the traveling or portable shrine consists of the wall alone. It is the design of the wall specifically, its list of names, that induces these reactions. The names are the objects of a ritual relation that no other part of the Memorial site can sustain. Withal, the ideals and memory of the cause, lacking comparable symbolic and social supports, fade into the background.

However, there is another side to this relationship, one that highlights a different aspect of the tension between national causes and their participants. To the original dilemma of how to honor the participant without reference to the cause, there is a corresponding reciprocal problem of how to ignore the cause without denying the participant. That problem did not occur to the art commissioners who wanted to protect the wall's artistic (ideological?) serenity from "corny patriotic claptrap" (U.S. House of Representatives 1982, p. E5108). But what kind of protection could they give? The corniness arose not from the addition of a flag and statue but from the way visitors conducted themselves in the vicinity of the wall. The impulses and sentiments motivating this conduct, however, were varied and complicated.

Uses of Genre: The Representation of Ambivalence

All nonperishable articles left at the Vietnam Veterans Memorial are collected each day and kept at the Museum and Archeological Regional Storage Facility. Row after row of airtight shelters preserve these "gifts" for the future, thus extending the Memorial in space and in time. This part of the Veterans Memorial complex is the most populist, for its contents, in accordance with Interior Department policy, are determined by the people who visit the Memorial and not by professional curators. It is difficult to tell whether or not the idea for such a museum was part of the Interior Department's struggle against the elitism of the Commission of Fine Arts. That the museum collection negates the complaints of the Memorial's early detractors as well as the praise of its early defenders is more certain. An assessment of the objects themselves shows this to be so.

The most colorful objects left by visitors are flowers, taped to the wall or placed on the ground beneath a loved one's name. Nothing of a political nature is embodied in these floral displays; however, the Park Service's inventory of other (nonperishable) items does convey a coherent political message. This inventory shows that the one object most frequently left by the wall is a small American flag attached to a stick and set in the ground below the name that the visitor desired to mark. Through this offering, visitors uttered a political statement that was not supposed to be made. They asserted their patriotism, their loyalty to a nation. Whether they got the idea themselves or copied it from one another, they could think of no better way to dignify their loved one's memory than to associate his name with his country's emblem.

These assertions are amplified by other objects. The largest category of objects, almost a third of everything that has been deposited by the visitors, consists of military items, mostly patches and insignias marking military-unit membership, as well as parts of uniforms, dog tags, identification bracelets, medals, awards, and certificates. The memorial site was thus decorated by symbols of the roles through which living veterans once enacted their commitment to the nation. These symbols began to appear in great profusion as soon as the Memorial was dedicated and continued to appear two years later when the statue of the three soldiers was unveiled. Designed to draw attention to the individual and away from the nation and its cause, the Memorial's wall turns out to be a most dramatic locus of patriotic feeling. The wall's use moved it toward that traditional war monument genre that opponents and supporters alike once believed it deviated from.

When profusely decorated with patriotic emblems, the wall alone may enhance our idea of the traditional war monument, but it cannot embody that idea. This is because patriotism is not the only response that the wall excites. The Memorial wall has in fact become a kind of debating forum—a repository of diverse opinions about the very war that occasioned its construction. Traditional war monuments serve no such reflexive function.

From its very inception, the Memorial's sponsors insisted that it would make no statement about the war—a promise predicated on the assumption that political silence could somehow be ensured by the Memorial's design. An ordinance that expressly prohibits political demonstrations on Memorial grounds supplemented this assumption. Thus deprived of a traditional public forum, political opinions were, instead, inserted into many of the written statements brought to the wall. Letters, poems, and memos, often accompanied by photographs, can be viewed analytically as publicly accessible private sentiments or as privatized public opinion. Either way, they articulate the public's diverse visions of Vietnam. . . .

Contexts, Constituencies, and Meaning

Effective commemorative tools check ambivalence. The ambivalence attending the Vietnam War, as we have seen, is not suppressed but summarized by the several parts of the Vietnam Memorial's physical makeup.

This ambivalence is not necessarily something the individual feels. It is a social fact, an outcome of the incompatible commemorative viewpoints that were held and the measures that were taken by different constituencies. The Memorial is thus a ritual symbol that expresses the contradictions of society.

The Memorial's contradictions not only betray the state's inability to effect a uniform interpretation of the past; they also affirm the nation as a reality whose salience transcends the state. These affirmations are most apparent to those who regard the Memorial naively, who possess no knowledge of the issues that attended its creation. Our reading of the letters suggests that the people who came to see the names of their loved ones and comrades on the Memorial's wall pay no attention to its color or placement or to its vertical or horizontal lines. Approaching it from the front, they only see the Lincoln Memorial looming before them, and behind, the Washington Monument. Although Maya Lin deliberately aligned these shrines to the Memorial's wall, she and her admirers hardly mentioned, let alone discussed, them in their efforts to defend her original design. For this reason, and because walls that point nowhere make for aesthetic awkwardness, our impression that this alignment was effected for artistic rather than ideological purposes may be justified. However, it is also our impression that for two years following the Memorial's dedication, the Lincoln and Washington monuments (enveloped by the national atmosphere of the Mall . . .) were functional surrogates for the statue and flag, and in later years were supplements to them, eliciting a moral awareness that a memorial wall alone might have been incapable of inspiring. It is, in fact, the capacity to evoke the surpassing presence of the nation itself (a capacity that the Commission of Fine Arts wanted to see the Vietnam Memorial deprived of) that defines the ultimate, nonnegotiable aspect of the war monument genre. Divested of this national presence, as it

would be if placed permanently outside its existing monumental surroundings, the Memorial wall would be experienced differently. It would remain a solemn and affecting monument (as is the wall's portable replica), but against a background of high rises or rolling meadows, against symbols of locality rather than the transcendent reality of the nation, it would become less stirring and magnetic, less sacred. Of this reality the Vietnam Memorial's flag and statue are merely external supports. In a more mundane setting, however, these would be more critical additions to the Memorial than they are in the nation's capital. . . .

Discussion

This study of the Vietnam Veterans Memorial highlights the broad range of variation presently possible within the war monument genre. Unlike the kinds of monuments that mark popular wars, the Vietnam Memorial underwent frequent changes that both affirmed and modified the traditional conception of the war monument. Starting as a modest plaque, it became a politically sanitized wall sculpture, then a more differentiated memorial that included a flag and a realistic statue. These changes resulted from a political process involving competing claims on how the Vietnam War should be remembered. The process was itself a reflection of contradictory assessments of the war in American society as a whole. . . .

In the end, contexts and meanings change. A day will come when the names that appear on the Vietnam Memorial's wall are known to few living persons. On this day, the intensity of feeling evoked by the wall will be less acute; the flags and objects that decorate the wall will be less dense; the solemnity that now grips those who visit the Memorial site will be diluted by an air of casualness; the ritual relation that now links shrine and pilgrim will become a mundane relation that links attraction and tourist. On this day, the Vietnam War will have become a less fitful part of American history. But the Vietnam Veterans Memorial, its several parts continuing to reflect different aspects of the beliefs about the war, will echo the ambivalence with which that war was first commemorated.

References

Durkheim, Emile. 1965. *The Elementary Forms of the Religious Life*. New York: Free Press.

Hess, Elizabeth. 1983. "A Tale of Two Memorials." *Art in America* (April): 121–26.

Johnson, Loch. 1976. "Political Alienation among Vietnam Veterans." *Western Political Quarterly* 29: 398–410.

——. 1980. "Scars of War: Alienation and Estrangement among Wounded Vietnam Veterans." Pp. 213–27 in *Strangers at Home*, edited by Charles R. Figley and Seymour Leventman. New York: Praeger.

Scruggs, Jan C., and Joel L. Swerdlow. 1985. *To Heal a Nation: The Vietnam Veterans Memorial*. New York: Harper & Row.

U.S. House Committee on Veterans' Affairs. 1981. *Legacies of Vietnam: Comparative Adjustment of Veterans and Their Peers*. Report no. 14. March 9. Washington, D.C.: Government Printing Office.

U.S. House of Representatives. 1979. *Congressional Record*. May 24. Washington, D.C.: Government Printing Office.

——. 1982. *Congressional Record*. December 13. Washington, D.C.: Government Printing Office.

U.S. Senate. 1980. *Congressional Record*. April 30. Washington, D.C.: Government Printing Office.

Wheeler, John. 1984. *Touched with Fire: The Future of the Vietnam Generation*. New York: Avon.

Part X

Postmodern Social Reality

Some students of contemporary social life maintain that we have entered a new epoch of human history and experience. Current modes of transportation and electronic means of communication have profoundly altered social life. We may now watch television programs on Kenya in the morning, telephone someone in Japan that afternoon, send a computer message to someone in Israel later, and fly to the Bahamas for the weekend that evening. Such travel and communication expands and multiplies networks of social interaction and relationships. It exposes us to numerous and often clashing versions of reality. Moreover, the diverse array of goods and services sold in the marketplace enable us to create collages of such diverse realities. We may dress like a New England woodsman, courtesy of L. L. Bean, in our Chicago apartment with Southwestern décor, while listening to rap music and feasting on Thai food. We see a kaleidoscope of realities on television, on city streets, and during our travels. Under these conditions, it is difficult to believe that any human reality is inevitable. Even supposedly authoritative experts are suspect. They often disagree and quickly change their minds. Nothing seems certain. This is what many students of social life call the postmodern condition.

The following selections offer contrasting interpretations of the effects of postmodern social life on our experience of self. Is the cascade of increasingly varied social experiences saturating and dissolving the self in a swirling sea of conflicting meanings? Or do we cling to the idea of a "real self" and choose, or are forced to choose, from the varied smorgasbord of possibilities for self-expression that postmodern social life offers? In either case, unlike our ancestors, few of us experience an unquestioned core self firmly rooted in familial and communal roles. Human social life and experience have been and are changing right before our eyes. Students of social life who ignore those changes will be left behind. Although clearly open to different interpretations, understanding contemporary social life and experience requires that they be acknowledged and addressed. ✦

36

The Dissolution of the Self

Kenneth J. Gergen

Many of the selections in this volume explain and illustrate how the self is formed and shaped by social experience. This most basic principle of sociological psychology clearly implies that the character of the self would change as the character of social life historically changes. That, in turn, suggests that our inner lives and selves are quite different from those of all but our most immediate ancestors. There seems to be little doubt that the character of social life in most human communities has undergone profound changes during the twentieth century. Kenneth Gergen examines some of the psychological consequences of these changes in this selection.

In an earlier selection, George Herbert Mead observed that the individual's adoption of the attitude of an organized community, or generalized other, unifies her or his self. Today, however, such a unification of self is more difficult. Contemporary modes of travel and communication expose us to the often inconsistent attitudes of countless people and communities. They allow us to maintain relationships, despite physical separation, and to participate in communities spread over great distances. Television and movies, not to mention newspapers, magazines, and books, bring us into contact with numerous other actual and fictional people and communities. This is what Gergen calls *social saturation*, and it leads to an increasingly dense population of the self. The voices of countless significant and general-

ized others fill our heads, and those voices are seldom in unison or even in harmony.

Our adoption of the attitudes of such countless and contentious significant and generalized others does not unify our selves but pulls them apart. Gergen calls this new pattern of self-consciousness *multiphrenia*, which literally means many minds. We are many different things to many different people and to ourselves. We interpret our experiences and define ourselves in many different and often incompatible ways and evaluate ourselves according to many different and incompatible standards. According to Gergen, that is why we often feel overwhelmed, inadequate, and uncertain. Neither our hearts nor our minds speak with a single voice or for a unified self. Consequently, Gergen argues, the belief that we possess a single true or real self begins to erode. We become increasingly aware that it is our connections to others that make us what we are. We no longer ask ourselves "Who am I?" We ask others "Who can I be with you?" This is what Gergen calls *postmodern being*—a new kind of human being living a new kind of social life.

. . . Cultural life in the twentieth century has been dominated by two major vocabularies of the self. Largely from the nineteenth century, we have inherited a *romanticist* view of the self, one that attributes to each person characteristics of personal depth: passion, soul, creativity, and moral fiber. This vocabulary is essential to the formation of deeply committed relations, dedicated friendships, and life purposes. But since the rise of the *modernist* world-view beginning in the early twentieth century, the romantic vocabulary has been threatened. For modernists, the chief characteristics of the self reside not in the domain of depth, but rather in our ability to reason—in our beliefs, opinions, and conscious intentions. In the modernist idiom, normal persons are predictable, honest, and sincere. Modernists believe in educational systems, a stable family life, moral training, and rational choice of marriage partners.

Yet, as I shall argue, both the romantic and the modern beliefs about the self are falling into disuse, and the social arrangements that they support are eroding. This is largely a result of the forces of social saturation. Emerging technologies saturate us with the voices of humankind—both harmonious and alien. As we absorb their varied rhymes and reasons, they become part of us and we of them. Social saturation furnishes us with a multiplicity of incoherent and unrelated languages of the self. For everything we "know to be true" about ourselves, other voices within respond with doubt and even derision. This fragmentation of self-conceptions corresponds to a multiplicity of incoherent and disconnected relationships. These relationships pull us in myriad directions, inviting us to play such a variety of roles that the very concept of an "authentic self" with knowable characteristics recedes from view. The fully saturated self becomes no self at all. . . .

I . . . equate the saturating of self with the condition of postmodernism. As we enter the postmodern era, all previous beliefs about the self are placed in jeopardy, and with them the patterns of action they sustain. Postmodernism does not bring with it a new vocabulary for understanding ourselves, new traits or characteristics to be discovered or explored. Its impact is more apocalyptic than that: the very concept of personal essences is thrown into doubt. Selves as possessors of real and identifiable characteristics—such as rationality, emotion, inspiration, and will—are dismantled. . . .

The Process of Social Saturation

A century ago, social relationships were largely confined to the distance of an easy walk. Most were conducted in person, within small communities: family, neighbors, townspeople. Yes, the horse and carriage made longer trips possible, but even a trip of thirty miles could take all day. The railroad could speed one away, but cost and availability limited such travel. If one moved from the community, relationships were likely to end. From birth to death, one could depend on relatively even-textured social surroundings. Words, faces, gestures, and possibilities were relatively consistent, coherent, and slow to change.

For much of the world's population, especially the industrialized West, the small, face-to-face community is vanishing into the pages of history. We go to country inns for weekend outings, we decorate condominium interiors with clapboards and brass beds, and we dream of old age in a rural cottage. But as a result of the technological developments just described, contemporary life is a swirling sea of social relations. Words thunder in by radio, television, newspaper, mail, radio, telephone, fax, wire service, electronic mail, billboards, Federal Express, and more. Waves of new faces are everywhere—in town for a day, visiting for the weekend, at the Rotary lunch, at the church social—and incessantly and incandescently on television. Long weeks in a single community are unusual; a full day within a single neighborhood is becoming rare. We travel casually across town, into the countryside, to neighboring towns, cities, states; one might go thirty miles for coffee and conversation.

Through the technologies of the century, the number and variety of relationships in which we are engaged, potential frequency of contact, expressed intensity of relationship, and endurance through time all are steadily increasing. As this increase becomes extreme, we reach a state of social saturation.

In the face-to-face community, the cast of others remained relatively stable. There were changes by virtue of births and deaths, but moving from one town—much less state or country—to another was difficult. The number of relationships commonly maintained in today's world stands in stark contrast. Counting one's family, the morning television news, the car radio, colleagues on the train, and the local newspaper, the typical commuter may confront as many different persons (in terms of views or images) in the first two hours of a day as the community-based predecessor did in a month. The morning calls in a business office may connect one to a dozen different locales in a given city, often across the continent, and very possibly across national boundaries. A single hour of prime-time melodrama immerses one in the lives of a score of individuals. In an evening of television, hundreds of engaging faces insinuate themselves into our lives. It is not only the immediate community that occupies our thoughts and feelings, but a constantly changing cast of characters spread across the globe. . . .

Populating the Self

Consider the moments:

- Over lunch with friends, you discuss Northern Ireland. Although you have never spoken a word on the subject, you find yourself heatedly defending British policies.

- You work as an executive in the investments department of a bank. In the evenings, you smoke marijuana and listen to the Grateful Dead.

- You sit in a cafe and wonder what it would be like to have an intimate relationship with various strangers walking past.

- You are a lawyer in a prestigious midtown firm. On the weekends, you work on a novel about romance with a terrorist.

- You go to a Moroccan restaurant and afterward take in the latest show at a country-and-western bar.

In each case, individuals harbor a sense of coherent identity or self-sameness, only to find themselves suddenly propelled by alternative impulses. They seem securely to be one sort of person, but yet another comes bursting to the surface—in a suddenly voiced opinion, a fantasy, a turn of interests, or a private activity. Such experiences with variation and self-contradiction may be viewed as preliminary effects of social saturation. They may signal a *populating of the self,* the acquisition of multiple and disparate potentials for being. It is this process of self-population that begins to undermine the traditional commitments to both romanticist and modernist forms of being. It is of pivotal importance in setting the stage for the postmodern turn. Let us explore.

The technologies of social saturation expose us to an enormous range of persons, new forms of relationship, unique circumstances and opportunities, and special intensities of feeling. One can scarcely remain unaffected by such exposure. As child-development specialists now agree, the process of socialization is lifelong. We continue to incorporate information from the environment throughout our lives. When exposed to other persons, we change in two major ways. We increase our capacities for *knowing that* and for *knowing how*. In the first case, through exposure to others, we learn myriad details about their words, actions, dress, mannerisms, and so on. We ingest enormous amounts of information about patterns of interchange. Thus, for example, from an hour on a city street, we are informed of the clothing styles of blacks, whites, upper class, lower class, and more. We may learn the ways of Japanese businessmen, bag ladies, Sikhs, Hare Krishnas, or flute players from Chile. We see how relationships are carried out between mothers and daughters, business executives, teenage friends, and construction workers. An hour in a business office may expose us to the political views of a Texas oilman, a Chicago lawyer, and a gay activist from San Francisco. Radio commentators espouse views on boxing, pollution, and child abuse; pop music may advocate machoism, racial bigotry, and suicide. Paperback books cause hearts to race over the unjustly treated, those who strive against impossible odds, those who are brave or brilliant. And this is to say nothing of television input. Via television, myriad figures are allowed into the home who would never otherwise trespass. Millions watch as talk-show guests—murderers, rapists, women prisoners, child abusers, members of the KKK, mental patients, and others often discredited—attempt to make their lives intelligible. There are few six-year-olds who cannot furnish at least a rudimentary account of life in an African village, the concerns of divorcing parents, or drug-pushing in the ghetto. Hourly, our storehouse of social knowledge expands in range and sophistication.

This massive increase in knowledge of the social world lays the ground work for a second kind of learning, a *knowing how*. We learn how to place such knowledge into action, to shape it for social consumption, to act so that social life can proceed effectively. And the possibilities for placing this supply of information into effective action are constantly expanding. The Japanese businessman glimpsed on the street today, and on the television tomorrow, may well be confronted in one's office the following week. On these occasions, the rudiments of appropriate behavior are already in place. If a mate announces that he or she is thinking about divorce, the other's reaction is not likely to be dumb dismay. The drama has so often been played out on television and movie screens that one is already prepared with multiple options. If one wins a wonderful prize, suffers a humiliating loss, faces temptation to cheat, or learns of a sudden death in the family, the reactions are hardly random. One more or less knows how it goes, is more or less ready for action. Having seen it all before, one approaches a state of ennui.

In an important sense, as social saturation proceeds we become pastiches, imitative assemblages of each other. In memory, we carry others' patterns of being with us. If the conditions are favorable, we can place these patterns into action. Each of us becomes the other, a representative, or a replacement. To put it more broadly, as the century has progressed, selves become increasingly populated with the character of others. . . .

Multiphrenia

It is sunny Saturday morning, and he finishes breakfast in high spirits. It is a rare day in which he is free to do as he pleases. With relish, he contemplates his options. The back door needs fixing, which calls for a trip to the hardware store. This would allow a much-needed haircut; and, while in town, he could get a birthday card for his brother, leave off his shoes for repair, and pick up shirts at the cleaners. But, he ponders, he really should get some exercise; is there time for jogging in the afternoon? That reminds him of a championship game he wanted to see at the same time. To be taken more seriously was his ex-wife's repeated request for a luncheon talk. And shouldn't he also settle his vacation plans before all the best locations are taken? Slowly, his optimism gives way to a sense of defeat. The free day has become a chaos of competing opportunities and necessities.

If such a scene is vaguely familiar, it attests only further to the pervasive effects of social saturation and the populating of the self. More important, one detects amid the hurly-burly of contemporary life a new constellation of feelings or sensibilities, a new pattern of self-consciousness. This syndrome may be termed *multiphrenia*, generally referring to the splitting of the individual into a multiplicity of self-investments. This condition is partly an outcome of self-population, but partly a result of the populated self's efforts to exploit the potentials of the technologies of relationship. In this sense, there is a cyclical spiraling toward a state of multiphrenia. As one's potentials are expanded by the technologies, so one increasingly employs the technologies for self-expression; yet, as the technologies are further utilized, so do they add to the repertoire of potentials. It would be a mistake to view this multiphrenic condition as a form of illness, for it is often suffused with a sense of expansiveness and adventure. Someday, there may indeed be nothing to distinguish multiphrenia from simply "normal living."

However, before we pass into this oceanic state, let us pause to consider some prominent features of the condition. Three of these are especially noteworthy.

Vertigo of the Valued

With the technology of social saturation, two of the major factors traditionally impeding relationships—namely time and space—are both removed. The past can be continuously renewed—via voice, video, and visits, for example—and distance poses no substantial barriers to ongoing interchange. Yet this same freedom ironically leads to a form of enslavement. For each person, passion, or potential incorporated into oneself exacts a penalty—a penalty both of *being* and of *being with*. In the former case, as others are incorporated into the self, their tastes, goals, and values also insinuate themselves into one's being. Through continued interchange, one acquires, for example, a yen for Thai cooking, the desire for retirement security, or an investment in wildlife preservation. Through others, one comes to value whole-grain breads, novels from Chile, or community politics. Yet as Buddhists have long been aware, to desire is simultaneously to become a slave of the desirable. To "want" reduces one's choice to "want not." Thus, as others are incorporated into the self, and their desires become one's own, there is an expansion of goals—of "musts," wants, and needs. Attention is necessitated, effort is exerted, frustrations are encoun-

tered. Each new desire places its demands and reduces one's liberties.

There is also the penalty of being with. As relationships develop, their participants acquire local definitions—friend, lover, teacher, supporter, and so on. To sustain the relationship requires an honoring of the definitions—both of self and other. If two persons become close friends, for example, each acquires certain rights, duties, and privileges. Most relationships of any significance carry with them a range of obligations—for communication, joint activities, preparing for the other's pleasure, rendering appropriate congratulations, and so on. Thus, as relations accumulate and expand over time, there is a steadily increasing range of phone calls to make and answer, greeting cards to address, visits or activities to arrange, meals to prepare, preparations to be made, clothes to buy, makeup to apply. . . . And with each new opportunity—for skiing together in the Alps, touring Australia, camping in the Adirondacks, or snorkeling in the Bahamas—there are "opportunity costs." One must unearth information, buy equipment, reserve hotels, arrange travel, work long hours to clear one's desk, locate babysitters, dogsitters, homesitters. . . . Liberation becomes a swirling vertigo of demands.

In the professional world, this expansion of "musts" is strikingly evident. In the university of the 1950s, for example, one's departmental colleagues were often vital to one's work. One could walk but a short distance for advice, information, support, and so on. Departments were often close-knit and highly interdependent; travels to other departments or professional meetings were notable events. Today, however, the energetic academic will be linked by post, long-distance phone, fax, and electronic mail to like-minded scholars around the globe. The number of interactions possible in a day is limited only by the constraints of time. The technologies have also stimulated the development of hundreds of new organizations, international conferences, and professional meetings. A colleague recently informed me that if funds were available, he could spend his entire sabbatical traveling from one professional gathering to another. A similar condition pervades the business world. One's scope of business opportunities is no longer so limited by geography; the technologies of the age enable projects to be pursued around the world. (Colgate Tartar Control toothpaste is now sold in over forty countries.) In effect, the potential for new connection and new opportunities is practically unlimited. Daily life has become a sea of drowning demands, and there is no shore in sight.

The Expansion of Inadequacy

It is not simply the expansion of self through relationships that hounds one with the continued sense of "ought." There is also the seeping of self-doubt into everyday consciousness, a subtle feeling of inadequacy that smothers one's activities with an uneasy sense of impending emptiness. In important respects, this sense of inadequacy is a by-product of the populating of self and the presence of social ghosts. For as we incorporate others into ourselves, so does the range of proprieties expand—that is, the range of what we feel a "good," "proper," or "exemplary" person should be. Many of us carry with us the "ghost of a father," reminding us of the values of honesty and hard work, or a mother challenging us to be nurturing and understanding. We may also absorb from a friend the values of maintaining a healthy body, from a lover the goal of self-sacrifice, from a teacher the ideal of worldly knowledge, and so on. Normal development leaves most people with a rich sense of personal well-being by fulfilling these goals.

But now consider the effects of social saturation. The range of one's friends and associates expands exponentially; one's past life continues to be vivid; and the mass media

expose one to an enormous array of new criteria for self-evaluation. A friend from California reminds one to relax and enjoy life; in Ohio, an associate is getting ahead by working eleven hours a day. A relative from Boston stresses the importance of cultural sophistication, while a Washington colleague belittles one's lack of political savvy. A relative's return from Paris reminds one to pay more attention to personal appearance, while a ruddy companion from Colorado suggests that one grows soft.

Meanwhile, newspapers, magazines, and television provide a barrage of new criteria of self-evaluation. Is one sufficiently adventurous, clean, well traveled, well read, low in cholesterol, slim, skilled in cooking, friendly, odor free, coiffed, frugal, burglar proof, family oriented? The list is unending. More than once, I have heard the lament of a subscriber to the Sunday *New York Times*. Each page of this weighty tome will be read by millions. Thus, each page remaining undevoured by day's end will leave one precariously disadvantaged—a potential idiot in a thousand unpredictable circumstances.

Yet the threat of inadequacy is hardly limited to the immediate confrontation with mates and media. Because many of these criteria for self-evaluation are incorporated into the self—existing within the cadre of social ghosts—they are free to speak at any moment. The problem with values is that they are sufficient unto themselves. To value justice, for example, is to say nothing of the value of love; investing in duty will blind one to the value of spontaneity. No one value in itself recognizes the importance of any alternative value. And so it is with the chorus of social ghosts. Each voice of value stands to discredit all that does not meet its standard. All the voices at odds with one's current conduct thus stand as internal critics, scolding, ridiculing, and robbing action of its potential for fulfillment. One settles in front of the television for enjoyment, and the chorus begins: "twelve-year-old," "couch potato," "lazy," "irresponsible." . . . One sits down with a good book, and again: "sedentary," "antisocial," "inefficient," "fantasist." . . . Join friends for a game of tennis, and "skin cancer," "shirker of household duties," "underexercised," "overly competitive" come up. Work late and it is "workaholic," "heart attack-prone," "overly ambitious," "irresponsible family member." Each moment is enveloped in the guilt born of all that was possible but now foreclosed.

Rationality in Recession

A third dimension of multiphrenia is closely related to the others. The focus here is on the rationality of everyday decision-making instances in which one tries to be a "reasonable person." Why, one asks, is it important for one's children to attend college? The rational reply is that a college education increases one's job opportunities, earnings, and likely sense of personal fulfillment. Why should I stop smoking? one asks, and the answer is clear that smoking causes cancer, so to smoke is simply to invite a short life. Yet these "obvious" lines of reasoning are obvious only so long as one's identity remains fixed within a particular group.

The rationality of these replies depends altogether on the sharing of opinions—of each incorporating the views of others. To achieve identity in other cultural enclaves turns these "good reasons" into "rationalizations," "false consciousness," or "ignorance." Within some subcultures, a college education is a one-way ticket to bourgeois conventionality—a white-collar job, picket fence in the suburbs, and chronic boredom. For many, smoking is an integral part of a risky lifestyle; it furnishes a sense of intensity, offbeatness, rugged individualism. In the same way, saving money for old age is "sensible" in one family, and "oblivious to the erosions of inflation" in another. For most Westerners, marrying for love is the only reasonable (if not conceivable) thing to do. But many Japanese will point to statistics demonstrating greater longevity and happiness in arranged marriages. Rationality is a vital by-product of social participation.

Yet as the range of our relationships is expanded, the validity of each localized rationality is threatened. What is rational in one relationship is questionable or absurd from the standpoint of another. The "obvious choice" while talking with a colleague lapses into absurdity when speaking with a spouse, and into irrelevance when an old friend calls that evening. Further, because each relationship increases one's capacities for discernment, one carries with oneself a multiplicity of competing expectations, values, and beliefs about "the obvious solution." Thus, if the options are carefully evaluated, every decision becomes a leap into gray vapors. Hamlet's bifurcated decision becomes all too simple, for it is no longer being or non-being that is in question, but to which of multifarious beings one can be committed.

Conclusion

So we find a profound sea change taking place in the character of social life during the twentieth century. Through an array of newly emerging technologies, the world of relationships becomes increasingly saturated. We engage in greater numbers of relationships, in a greater variety of forms, and with greater intensities than ever before. With the multiplication of relationships also comes a transformation in the social capacities of the individual—both in knowing how and knowing that. The relatively coherent and unified sense of self inherent in a traditional culture gives way to manifold and competing potentials. A multiphrenic condition emerges in which one swims in ever-shifting, concatenating, and contentious currents of being. One bears the burden of an increasing array of oughts, of self-doubts and irrationalities. The possibility for committed romanticism or strong and single-minded modernism recedes, and the way is opened for the post-modern being. . . .

As belief in essential selves erodes, awareness expands of the ways in which personal identity can be created and re-created. . . . This consciousness of construction does not strike as a thunderbolt; rather, it eats slowly and irregularly away at the edge of consciousness. And as it increasingly colors our understanding of self and relationships, the character of this consciousness undergoes a qualitative change. . . . [P]ostmodern consciousness [brings] the erasure of the category of self. No longer can one securely determine what it is to be a specific kind of person . . . or even a person at all. As the category of the individual person fades from view, consciousness of construction becomes focal. We realize increasingly that who and what we are is not so much the result of our "person essence" (real feelings, deep beliefs, and the like), but of how we are constructed in various social groups. . . . [T]he concept of the individual self ceases to be intelligible. . . .

Reprinted from: Kenneth J. Gergen, *The Saturated Self*, pp. 6–7, 61–62, 68–71, 73–80, 146, 170. Copyright © 1991 by Basic Books, Inc. Reprinted by permission of Basic Books, a member of Perseus Books, L.L.C. ✦

37

The Self in a World of Going Concerns

Jaber F. Gubrium and James A. Holstein

In the preceding selection, Gergen argues that postmodern experience makes the very concept of the individual self unintelligible, erasing the very category of the self. This selection offers an alternative interpretation of our postmodern condition. Jaber Gubrium and James Holstein argue that, in everyday life, most people still cling to the idea of a core self, as, they argue, Gergen does. Rather than embrace what he identifies as postmodern consciousness, Gubrium and Holstein accuse Gergen, and others, of condemning it in the name of a solitary "real" self that stands apart from the "madding crowd" of postmodern experience. This is not an argument about how we should think about the self but over how we postmodern women and men actually *do* think.

According to Gubrium and Holstein, what distinguishes our postmodern social world from the modern world of the recent past is the multitude and range of opportunities for self construction. In the past, individuals' sense of their "real" selves was firmly rooted in familial and communal social roles. Today, we are presented with myriad possibilities for talking and acting a particular self into being. There are countless varieties of psychotherapy that promise to help us "find ourselves" or, in more colorful language, "discover our inner child." There has been a proliferation of self-help and support groups. Recreational activities provide not just brief respites

from the self-constraints of work life but the possibility of consuming identities. Even some employers offer employees "assistance" in repairing and refashioning their selves. Moreover, these varied opportunities for self-construction are promoted on television, in newspapers and the books that fill the shelves of the ever-expanding "self-help" sections of bookstores.

Yet, as Gubrium and Holstein suggest, when we take advantage of one of these opportunities, we do not experience it as self-construction but as self-discovery. For example, the members of Co-dependents Anonymous that Leslie Irvine described in Chapter 15 did not think that they were talking a "codependent self" into being but were discovering who and what they had always been. Despite the time and energy many of us devote to self-construction and reconstruction, we still believe that a core, "real" self lies within us. We may be confused about who and what we "really" are but that, we believe, is because our true self has been buried by the overwhelming self-presentational demands of contemporary social life. Indeed, the growing opportunities for self-construction are, in part, in response to the widespread self-confusion in the postmodern world. However confused, Gubrium and Holstein argue, we have not given up on the idea of a solitary, core self but have simply intensified our search for it.

Gubrium and Holstein also note that opportunities for self-construction are not equally distributed throughout society. For example, prisoners, like those discussed by Kathryn Fox in Chapter 33, are subtly coerced into constructing a particular kind of self while others, like the homeless who are designated mentally ill, must participate in particular programs of self-construction to obtain needed services and resources. In contrast, those in more privileged social structural positions can choose from a virtual smorgasbord of self-construction possibilities. That might explain why students of social life have offered contrasting assessments of postmodern selfhood. For those who can choose, the many opportunities for self-construction can be self empowering. For those with few if any choices, the self-constructing machinery of postmodern life may feel like an "iron cage" that prevents expression of their "real self." It may not be that some interpretations of the postmodern condition are right and others wrong, but that they address different sides of the same postmodern coin. In either case, they remind us that contemporary social life has created new ways of social being, which is to say, new ways of human being. Whether we recognize it or not, George Herbert Mead's insight is as relevant today as it was when he first proposed it: The self is essentially a social structure and arises in social experience.

Times are tough for the personal self. This stalwart social form was conceptualized as being the heart of social action. But now the self is increasingly beleaguered by claims that postmodern life decenters and trivializes its presence in experience. In this view, who we really are is constantly in question. What we can or should be swings in endless response to the demands of the moment. Postmodern life provides one identity option after another, implicating a dizzying array of possibilities for the self.

Perhaps this situation is the inevitable result of a fast-paced world. With daily living swirling about at unprecedented speed, some say that the postmodern self is simultaneously everywhere and nowhere. It is fleeting and evanescent, a mere shadow of what the self once might have been. If it was commonly viewed as the central presence in experience, some observers of the postmodern scene now tell us that the self is arbitrarily "up for grabs" (Sica 1993: 17). . . .

Oddly enough, at the same time that such commentators portray the self as having come undone, actors in the world of everyday life seem to be unflinchingly committed to the belief that a singular, authentic self resides within. This self occupies an inner sanctum, insulated from the moral ravages of today's world. Social life may shape who we are, bestow glowing or blemished identities;

it may confuse our public personas beyond recognition, but we still believe that a "true self" lies somewhere inside, in some deeply privileged space. As besieged or hidden as the self might be, in the world of everyday life it is resolutely available as a beacon to guide us. It is taken for granted that in our most private recesses we do not need to divide ourselves between countless identities but rather feel it is still possible to get in touch, and be at one, with our true selves.

Culture plays a strong hand in this belief. We place great stock in the Western notion of an inner beacon, in a self that stands fundamentally apart from the social world. We harbor this inner self as a key ingredient in our everyday lives. Although it may be socially influenced, the self ultimately exists separately from—outside of—our social transactions. It is immersed in social affairs, to be sure, but its autonomous agency is also a leading theme of those affairs. Our cultural sensibilities articulate selves virtually owned by individuals, independent and distinct from the social marketplaces in which people acquire their identities. This *personal* self repeatedly surfaces in familiar phrases such as "the individual versus society," "the core, true self," and "who *I* really am" as opposed to who I appear to be.

What are we to make, then, of the cacophony of charges that the basic contours of this subjectivity have vanished into thin air? Has the personal self really been lost in the swirling experiences of postmodernity? Has the self been battered beyond recognition or into trivialized submission? Does it indeed not amount to much anymore?

Our view is that, even while some commentators have written the personal self's epitaph, it is still the leading experiential project of our era. There is overwhelming evidence, we believe, that if these indeed are trying times for the self, it is not because the personal self has disappeared from the social landscape but just the opposite. The personal self remains our primary subjectivity—a

Chapter 37: *The Self in a World of Going Concerns*

self we live by—but it is now produced in a proliferating and variegated panorama of sites of self-knowledge. These are domains whose participants regularly turn their attention to questions of who and what they are, or could be. From counseling centers, therapy agencies of every stripe, and support groups to spiritual fellowships, Internet chat rooms, and television talk shows, personal selves have become big business, the stock-in-trade of a world of self-constituting institutions, which increasingly compete with each other for discerning and designating identities.

The Siege of the Personal Self

To set a background for discussing these issues, we turn first to exemplary commentary on the siege of the personal self. . . . Perhaps the most poignant recent account is offered in Kenneth Gergen's *The Saturated Self* (1991). . . . Gergen argues that the self desperately needs to be sheltered from the identity storms that currently overwhelm it, saturating it with endless demands. According to Gergen, this frenetic and multidimensional postmodern world is so full of meanings and messages that it routinely floods the self, leaving it with no life of its own. Filled to overflowing, the self is diluted, with little sense of a true identity. This self breathes easily only when it escapes these relationships; it is most at home when it is separated from the madding crowd. The self comes into its own by seeking haven in the quiet, private, sequestered hideaways of experience. Only there can it sustain a genuine sense of being who and what it is.

The first chapter of Gergen's book, *The Self Under Siege*, is revealing. From the start, it is apparent that it is the author himself who is overwhelmed, whose self is under fierce assault. Gergen is wrenched in all directions at once. He wants to control his affairs, but they spin out of control at every turn. He begins with a vivid account of how unraveled he

feels. Recalling the scene that awaited him after a brief trip out of town, Gergen writes:

> An urgent fax from Spain lay on the desk, asking about a paper I was months late in contributing to a conference in Barcelona. Before I could think about answering, the office hours I had postponed began. One of my favorite students arrived and began to quiz me about the ethnic biases in my course syllabus. My secretary came in holding a sheaf of telephone messages, and some accumulated mail. . . . My conversations with my students were later interrupted by phone calls from a London publisher, a colleague in Connecticut on her way to Oslo for the weekend, and an old California friend wondering if we might meet during his summer travels to Holland. By the morning's end I was drained. The hours had been wholly consumed by the process of relating—face to face, electronically, and by letter. The relations were scattered across Europe and America, and scattered points in my personal past. And so keen was the competition for "relational time" that virtually none of the interchanges seemed effective in the ways I wished. (p. 1)

While most academics would envy the attention, Gergen senses that something is missing, something that might signal a feeling of being at one with oneself. He soon tells us what that is: "I turned my attention optimistically to the afternoon. Perhaps here I would find moments of *seclusion, restoration,* and *recentering*—three remedial features of a distinctly modern self" (p. 1; emphasis added). Gergen conveys the personal shape of the self he desires, one that apparently has lost its distinct moorings to the fast pace and diverse spaces of postmodern life. This self realizes its authenticity by escaping from the daily rat race. Undoubtedly, social experience nourishes such a self, but, ironically, it is most true to itself when it is apart from the social swirl. In seclusion, it can take stock of, and restore, itself. . . .

The working struggle between the inner self and . . . exterior forces is perceptively depicted in Arlie Russell Hochschild's (1983) account of the managed heart. Hochschild's book makes extensive use of similar metaphors to chronicle how the personal self manages to stave off an increasingly commodified sociability. Focusing on the commercialization of feeling in the airline industry, Hochschild introduces her reader to the "emotion work" of flight attendants. Their job is to keep customers happy. Hochschild describes how the attendants try to safeguard their true selves in the face of nagging demands to selflessly, cheerfully serve customers.

Hochschild's presentation is not a lament over the state of the personal self, as Gergen's is. Rather, it is a story of resistance, a tale of how we protect our true selves from exploitation. Hochschild provides a strategy for combating the saturated and commercialized self, a way of preserving the authentic "me" we feel in our heart of hearts. Speaking of flight attendants, but hoping to strike a more general chord, Hochschild writes about how people might respond to a world in which feelings are bought and sold and emotion management is rife. In such a world, she explains, the true self is overrun by false selves that have been mobilized to ward off the growing demands of daily living. As outside interests inundate the self, it retreats inward, leaving only uncomfortable false personas directed toward others. We preserve our selves by seeking inner shelter from the social onslaught.

The "false self" is a necessary conspirator in this resistance. As Hochschild states, it is a "disbelieved, unclaimed self, a part of 'me' that is not 'really me'," yet necessary to protect the "real self" (1983:194).

The false self embodies our acceptance of early parental requirements that we act so as to please others, at the expense of our own needs and desires. This sociocentric, other-directed self comes to live a sepa-rate existence from the self we claim. In the extreme case, the false self may set itself up as the real self, which remains completely hidden. More commonly, the false self allows the real self a life of its own, which emerges when there is little danger of its being used by others. (p. 194)

Clearly, false selves perform an important, self-preserving function. They can be set up in service to others, protecting the authentic, core self. They serve as buffers between external demands and an internal core that may be at odds with such demands. According to Hochschild, false selves maintain the true self while living civilly among others who make so many contrary demands on us.

With the true self hidden within, how do we know it continues to exist? Emotions, Hochschild explains, are the beacons of our authentic selves. Every emotion serves a "signal function," she argues (p. 29), noting that "it is from feelings that we learn the self-relevance of what we see, remember, or imagine" (p. 196). Emotions put us in touch with the personal "me," providing us with an inner perspective for interpreting and responding to experience. Social life becomes problematic, however, in that it often demands that we harness our feelings. This emotion management, Hochschild maintains, interferes with the signal function of feelings (p. 130), diluting or confusing a person's sense of self. As emotion management is commercialized, we must manipulate our feelings and, in the process, our selves, for purely instrumental ends. Consequently, our feelings are given over "more to the organization and less to the self" (p. 198). The upshot is "burnout" and "estrangement."

Flight attendants' emotion work provides a case in point. Hochschild explains that flight attendants are not only asked to smile as they serve their customers but are actually trained to feel and project a warmth and sincerity that convinces others that the smile is genuine. But as emotions are managed to meet these demands, the distinction be-tween real and projected selves begins to blur. Hochschild questions this confusion.

> What happens to the way a person re-lates to her feelings or her face? When worked-up warmth becomes an instru-ment of service work, what can a person learn about herself from her feelings? And when a worker abandons her work smile, what kind of tie remains between her smile and her self? (Pp. 89–90)

The answer is obvious: flight attendants be-come estranged from their selves, as, by im-plication, do the rest of us in our own ways become estranged from our selves.

Still, people know that social circum-stances forever influence their behavior and feelings. We all are routinely asked to present images and emotions that do not flow from what we take to be our inner, authentic selves. We convey impressions and emotions that are shaped by interpersonal relations, organizational policies, and the like. Our emotion work, Hochschild notes, shields our true selves and deep feelings as much as it manages social situations. It is a way of resist-ing social intrusions, a technique for counter-acting the impact on our true selves.

But as we shelter the true self, we also iso-late it. As Hochschild observes, "We make up an idea of our 'real self,' an inner jewel that re-mains our unique possession no matter whose billboard we wear on our back or whose smile we paste on our face. We push the 'real self' further inside, making it more inaccessi-ble" (p. 34). The more threatened it be-comes, the further we push the true self in-ward. Ultimately, our defenses against the social siege can be the self's undoing. As we hide our personal self deep inside, we risk losing sight of who we are.

Sources of the Self

These commentaries ring familiar. We rou-tinely draw on a similar vocabulary to describe experience when the pace of life increases and demands on our time overwhelm us. Such talk concedes that the complex and var-ied circumstances of daily living are at odds with personal identity and integrity. Laments over such trying times cast social life as the personal self's ordeal, if not its antagonist.

But is social life truly so much at odds with the personal self? Must social interaction al-ways involve a holding action against the ap-parently destructive infringements of the out-side world? The central tenets of [sociological psychology] would tell us that this is short-sighted. Harkening back to George Herbert Mead (1934) . . . reassures us that the self re-mains essentially a social structure, arising and flourishing, even coming undone, within social experience. Its sources and destiny lie in the very same social world that some crit-ics view as perilously challenging it.

The Social Self

From the start, the self unfolds in and through social life, never separate from it. If a personal self exists, it is not a distinct private entity so much as it is a concoction of traits, roles, standpoints, and behaviors that individ-uals articulate and present through social in-teraction. The self is not so much the clois-tered core of our being as an important operating principle used to morally anchor thoughts and feelings about who and what we are. As we interact in everyday life, the personal self takes shape as the central narra-tive theme around which we convey identity. Indeed, commonplace experiences and ev-eryday folk psychologies tell us that the per-sonal self is the principal experiential agent of our culture. . . . It is the primary lived entity we comprehend ourselves as being as we go about everyday life.

Interaction and communication are key constituents. As we talk with ourselves or with others, we learn and inform each other about who and what we are. In a sense, we talk our selves into being. But not just any-thing goes. Social selves are not without design or restraint; they are not impromptu performances. What we say about ourselves and others is mediated by recognizable identities. We speak of ourselves in meaningful ways within the social contexts in which we communicate who we are. Selves do not just pop out of social interaction but are deftly assembled from recognizable identities in some place, at some time, for some purpose. . . .

Going Concerns

As important as social situations are in mediating who and what we are, we must take care not to focus too narrowly on strictly situational influences on self-production. Mead and others . . . remind us that the environment for meaning-making is tremendously variegated and multifaceted. Perhaps most significantly, today's postmodern scene is widely and diversely populated by groups and organizations that are explicitly or incidentally implicated in self-production. This landscape of *[going]* concerns provides much more than immediate, face-to-face contexts for designating who and what we are.

We borrow the term "going concerns" from Everett Hughes (1984) as a way of characterizing relatively stable, routinized, ongoing patterns of action and interaction. It is another way of referring to social institutions but underscores their actively discursive quality. For Hughes, going concerns could be as massive and formally structured as government bureaucracies or as modest and loosely organized as a group of friends who gather on Thursday nights to play bridge. Large or small, formal or informal, each represents an ongoing commitment to a particular moral order, a way of being who and what we are in relation to the immediate scheme of things. Hughes was careful not to reify going concerns; he did not view them as static social entities. Rather, he oriented to them as patterns of concerted activity. For Hughes, there was as much "going" in social institutions as there were "concerns."

From the myriad formal organizations in which we work, study, pray, curse, play, and recover, to the countless informal associations and networks to which we otherwise attend, to our affiliations with racial, ethnic, and gendered groupings, we multiply engage in a panoply of going concerns most of our lives. The self is a product of this engagement. Many of these going concerns explicitly structure or reconfigure personal identity. All variety of human service agencies, for example, readily delve into the deepest enclaves of the self to ameliorate personal ills. Self-help organizations seem to crop up on every street corner, and self-help literature barks at us from the book spindles of most supermarkets and the shelves of every bookstore. "Psychobabble" in the public media, radio and television talk shows, and Internet chat rooms constantly prompts us to formulate (or reformulate) who and what we are. Whatever self we might have is thus increasingly *deprivatized*, constructed, and interpreted under the auspices of these decidedly *public* going concerns . . . (Holstein and Gubrium 2000).

Interpretive Practice

Because selves are interactionally presented and constructed in the context of going concerns, they are not conjured up willy-nilly out of thin air. As strategic as it might be, we do not make just any claim about who or what we are, cavalierly ignoring time and place. Self-construction is always accountable to the institutional preferences and the pertinent biographical particulars of one's life. . . . Broadly speaking, the self emanates from the interplay among institutional demands, restraints, and resources, on the one hand, and biographically informed, self-constituting social actions, on the other.

. . . [T]his interplay constitutes what we have called *interpretive practice*—the constellation of procedures, conditions, and resources through which reality . . . is apprehended, understood, organized, and represented . . .

(Holstein and Gubrium 2000). It occupies a space now replete with going concerns, implicating both face-to-face processes of self-construction and the institutional conditioning of self-realization. . . . Employing [this] broad view of practice, it is possible to attend not only to the *discursive practices* of self-construction but also to the *discourses-in-practice* that supply the resources and interpretive possibilities for self-designation (Holstein and Gubrium 2000). These represent two reflexively related components of interpretive practice. . . .

Discursive Environments

Since the mid-twentieth century, social life has come under the purview of countless going concerns whose *discursive environments* function increasingly to assemble, alter, and reformulate our lives and selves. By "discursive environments," we mean interactional domains characterized by distinctive ways of interpreting and representing everyday realities. Schools, correctional facilities, clinics, family courts, support groups, recreational clubs, fitness centers, and self-improvement programs, among other institutions, promote particular ways of representing who and what we are, furnishing discourses of subjectivity that are accountably put into discursive practice as individuals enter into their interpretive purview.

Such going concerns pose new challenges for the concept of a personal self. They are not especially hostile to the personal, nor do they necessarily saturate a vessel already filled to overflowing. Rather, today's discursive environments for self-construction provide complex and variegated institutional options for who we could be. While, taken together, these environments might be seen as an overwhelming surfeit of self-constructive challenges by some, they may also be viewed as a burgeoning supply of possibilities for who and what we might be.

Institutional Selves in Postmodern Context

Discursive environments set the "conditions of possibility" for subjectivity, as Foucault (1977) put it. They establish general parameters for producing recognizable and accountable constructions, including even the core self. With more going concerns than ever entering the self-construction business, we might characterize today's world as increasingly populated by *institutional selves* (Gubrium and Holstein forthcoming).

In some institutions, such as psychiatric hospitals and counseling centers, selves are officially constructed in terms of "too much" or "too little" of every conceivable combination of thought, feeling, and action. This can range from too much restlessness, talkativeness, and grandiosity, which are among the diagnostic criteria for manic episodes, to too little passion about life or "not caring anymore," which are signal features for depression. Taken together, such discursive environments comprise a virtual "troubled identity" market, geared up to construct more kinds of problem-ridden selves than ever.

Needless to say, not all identities are medicalized, nor do they all become the targets of psychotherapeutic efforts. Self-construction extends across the wide variety of human service institutions and beyond, to the pastoral care and spiritual fellowships offered by churches and the behavioral rehabilitation programs imposed on violent offenders in prison. Alcoholics Anonymous (AA), for example, is decidedly nonmedical and construes uncontrollable drinking as a moral failure. Failure here entails a refusal to recognize that one's actions are not self-governed but are lodged in "higher powers."

There also are plenty of going concerns that feature mainly positive self-images, seeking to valorize or glamorize the self rather than to cement and reformulate troubled identities. Formalized avocational affiliation, for example, puts people in touch with significant resources for self-construction. From international associations like the Sierra Club to local senior centers, recreational organizations offer activities, training, and challenges that both explicitly and implicitly supply self-building opportunities. Mountain climbers, cyclists, and go-cart racers, along with martial artists, wilderness skiers, scuba divers, and myriad others, find that the social sites of their activities provide not only recreation but also diverse ways of viewing and articulating identity. Such discursive environments may be just as consequential for self-construction as those that construct and heal the troubled.

The ubiquity and variety of venues for self-construction suggest an important transformation in linkage between the personal and the social self: in a postmodern world, the traditional relationship between the personal self and society is reversed. From a *modern* point of view, while the personal self is viewed as socially influenced, it also is believed to have its own private location separate from society, a space centered in personal experience. In this context, social life is important for growth and development, but, in excess, it can be portrayed as besieging, saturating and commodifying identity. As we have noted, this view still thrives in our cultural belief system. From this perspective, the personal self is currently being inundated by the heartless intrusions of public life and its engaging social institutions. . . .

In a world understood in *postmodern* terms, however, the relationship between the personal self and society dramatically changes. Social construction moves to foreground, as the personal self is decentered from itself and relocated into myriad going concerns. The personal self, however, does not vanish from the postmodern scene. It persists in the popularly held tenet that an individual agent or subject exists inside or behind the surface appearances of our actions. Most significantly, in a postmodern context, we can see that the sense of a personal identity is being constructed in more social settings than ever. A thriving landscape of institutions serves up myriad selves, providing more and more occasions for constructing who and what we are.

. . . As with any social context, in each of these environments we must present ourselves in locally familiar terms or risk being seen as eccentric, if not outrageous, in the immediate scheme of things. If we do not proffer recognizable identities, our claims to selfhood might readily be treated as nonsense. To say, for example, "I'm a bloody warclub"—implying "That's me"—does not usually make much sense in our society. It is not a readily recognizable identity. But its meaning may be perfectly clear in a going concern whose vocabulary of identity makes frequent reference to a band of unruly warriors beset by dreams of bloody sacrifice. In fact, it might even make sense in our own society if we found ourselves among members of a survivalist group who share a premonition of enduring a battle with a world rent with evil (cf. Mitchell 1998). The conditions of possibility for self-construction . . . have been extended countless ways across the broad horizon of contemporary life's institutional encounters. While some view contemporary life as saturating the self, it also can be seen as providing countless options for what we could be, markedly expanding our potential for self-expression.

New and Diverse Options

No single discursive environment determines who and what we are. An individual who presents himself or herself for counseling at a psychoanalytically oriented therapy agency, for example, is likely to witness the self formulated in terms of the familiar Freudian idiom of psychic structures and depth understanding. Troubles for this self would be formulated in the guise of unconscious turmoil in relation to psychosexual development, embedded in the relational past. In contrast, individuals receiving counseling from a "solution-focused" therapy agency would find the self articulated in the very concrete terms of the present, relating to everyday conduct and routine competence. The vestigial past is of no concern for the self here, nor is deep-seated pathology. Troubles are viewed as solvable everyday problems of living, pure and simple. . . .

In today's world, the individual has diverse options for self-construction. To some degree, one can choose the environment(s) in which one's self will be constituted. A good deal of personal expression and empowerment is implicated, for example, in choosing between alternative psychotherapeutic modalities. Opt for psychoanalysis and one is apt to become a seething cauldron of unconscious conflicts rooted in early childhood and parental relationships. Select "brief" solution-focused therapy and one is likely to find oneself defined as a generally competent, if confused or misguided, practitioner of everyday life, who merely needs to decide on how he or she will solve surmountable problems of living in the present.

Such freedom of choice is a fairly recent development. Today's range of discursive environments was unheard of a century ago; it was hardly evident until the 1970s. Our forebears likely constructed selves within a relatively narrow range of spiritual, familial, or communal identities. They simply did not encounter the profusion of going concerns and discursive offerings that engage us today. Their lives were not spread across the plethora of sites and situations that now call for distinctive kinds of self-presentation. Self-construction was more straightforward to be sure, and its possibilities were decidedly limited. . . .

We even find some traditional parameters of self-construction newly reconfigured. For example, Hochschild's . . . book, *The Time Bind* (1997), suggests that the traditional experiential relationship between work and home has been reversed with respect to where we seek our identities. . . . Most American adults, Hochschild argues, now work

outside the home and, thus, engage daily in the institutional life of organizations large and small. This fact represents a major departure from work life earlier in the century. According to Hochschild, for some, the workplace, rather than the home, has become a preferred sanctuary for the personal self, where one finds himself or herself to be most centered and whole.

The family-friendly company called "Amerco," where Hochschild conducted her study, is a case in point. Amerco operates under a Total Quality (TQ) management system, replacing the traditional top-down, scientific framework. It provides a discursive environment that ostensibly empowers workers to make decisions on their own. Amerco's TQ principles not only offer a nurturing atmosphere for workers but also seek to heal the troubled selves that employees often bring to, or develop, in the workplace. In fact, the self itself is firmly recognized as critical to company policy and subject to redesign. . . .

Hochschild points to an unanticipated consequence of TQ's cognitive and emotional involvement in workers' personal lives: it turns the workplace into a home of sorts, a place for self-repair and recentering. This, in turn, encourages a particular kind of self-surveillance. TQ puts a premium on expressing feelings, sharing emotional labor, and cooperating in family-like corporate responsibility. This also puts TQ in the business of reconstructing its participants' personal selves for the greater good of the company and its employees.

A corporate workplace results that competes with the home as a source of identity, and extends even to the core self. According to Hochschild, the enticement to put in long hours at work—called the "time bind"—upsets the traditional work-family balance. A "third shift" emerges for workers that prompts them to distance themselves from the time-pressured and increasingly rationalized household so they can devote themselves—their selves—to the emotional allures of the company. For many of Amerco's employees, the workplace is more of an experiential haven than they find at home; Amerco offers emotional relief and interpersonal sustenance away from the tumult and turmoil of the domestic front. This arrangement inverts the traditional cultural geography of privacy, making the workplace more of a self-sustaining refuge than the household.

The inversion is not necessarily bad or good. But it cogently illustrates the changing possibilities and options for self-construction [in the] new millennium. The proliferation of going concerns and their discursive environments complicate or relocate self-construction, but it is also enabling in terms of the options presented for constructing and repairing who and what we are, both in the immediate realm of daily living and throughout the life course. . . .

Inequality of Opportunities

Lest we sound overly sanguine, we must also recognize that these institutional options are not equally distributed across the contemporary social scene. As ubiquitous and varied as self-constructing institutions have become, their discursive environments are not options for everyone. Not everyone is subjected to or has access to the same field of possibilities. For the economically and socially privileged, the landscape of contemporary self-building opportunities may appear to be a smorgasbord of identities, while the less advantaged are more likely to be selectively filtered through the self-constructive processing of going concerns of last resort such as homeless shelters and prisons. . . .

For those who are disturbed, addicted, impoverished, or otherwise destitute, such as individuals seeking admission to shelters or community mental health programs, the selves they become are soon lodged in one of the few relationships they can afford. They are left with the option of presenting selves that are socially tolerated in order to avail themselves of desperately needed services. . . .

As Michael Schwalbe (1993:341–342) notes, materially disadvantaged persons frequently must submit wholesale to institutional demands on self-presentation as a matter of sheer survival.

Dire exigencies of all sorts may force individuals into constructing particular selves. Those seeking to escape their drinking habits, for instance, may turn to AA for help. Cognizant of no plausible alternative and unaware of the demands of AA, new members may voluntarily enter the twelve-step program, but the price will be the acceptance of an "alcoholic self" that conforms to a distinctly patterned and ritualized organizational discourse. . . . For every work site like Amerco, there is a "heartless," "faceless" bureaucracy that homogenizes employee selves, consigning them to "Dilbert"-like cubicles that work to ensure that each member remains anonymous and institutionally undistinguished. For every potential client shopping the middle-class psychotherapy market, there is a coerced recipient of court-mandated behavioral therapy or prison-imposed cognitive self change. . . . This is variety, yes, but always at a price.

Analytic Challenges of a Postmodern Self

As unequally distributed as these options are, taken together they offer increasingly complex and socially differentiated opportunities to the personal self. . . . [W]e can no longer examine self-construction solely in the realm of talk and interaction. . . . To be sure, talk and interaction remain the operating vehicles through which individuals construct selves. But interactional moves—discursive practices—do not fully specify the concrete selves we live by. Neither are selves unfettered performances or situationally convenient presentations. Selves are not just locally presented but are also artifacts of discourses-in-practice, reflecting the moral agendas and material constraints of diverse going concerns and discursive environments of postmodern life.

Looking beyond but not ignoring talk and interaction, we come upon concrete sites of self-construction and the sources of identity they purvey. For better or worse, the expansion of the human service industry represents an explosion of professional self-constructive venues. Its agents and outlets can be viewed as veritable factories for the production of selves.

In the world of human services, of course, the self is usually located at the heart of social and personal problems and their solutions. In practice, these institutions construct the troubled selves that they need to do their work (Gubrium and Holstein forthcoming). Indeed, each helping profession, with its underlying disciplinary commitment to a particular view of troubles and solutions, is the source or a distinctive kind of troubled identity. . . .

This not only yields a broad spectrum of troubled selves, but an equally broad range of untroubled ones. For all the troubled selves that are being produced, there are also institutional mandates to replace each and every one of them with an untroubled self. Each organization, agency, or profession that designates a self-in-trouble is likely to be charged with repairing that troubled self, turning out its untroubled counterpart. More broadly, each instance of a troubled self also serves to show us *what we are not*, populating an equally large counterlandscape of positive identities. As Emile Durkheim (1964) taught us long ago, we need the visible presence of the "pathological" to assure us of what is "normal," suggesting that just as we have more troubled selves than ever before, we now have more untroubled ones as well.

The human service professions, of course, are not solely responsible for the propagation of troubled identities. The scientific and academic communities as well as the popular media also serve up troubled and untroubled selves. Indeed, self-construction is now

also being undertaken in opposition to professional efforts. On any given Sunday, for example, local newspapers announce literally dozens of self-help groups, which offer innumerable self-constructive opportunities for persons from all walks of life: victims of depression, parents of the troubled or gifted, alcoholics, codependents of substance abusers, cancer sufferers, survivors of cancer, Gulf War veterans, victims of sexual assault, perpetrators of domestic violence, AIDS victims, the friends and significant others of Alzheimer's disease sufferers, and transvestites and their spouses, among many others. We look for ways to structure identity on our own, so much so that Robert Wuthnow (1994) estimates that 40 percent of the U.S. population now participates in such discussion groups.

Add to this the human interest programming we see on television and in print, and it is clear that identity-conferring opportunities are amply available. Ordinary life has become an emporium of self-constructive options. Images of special or sullied selves come alive and are acted out before our very eyes on television talk shows, facilitated, if not encouraged, by the likes of Oprah Winfrey, Jenny Jones, and Ricki Lake. . . . We see models of every conceivable kind of persona one might become, from cover girls to superstar athletes to serial killers, cocaine addicts, and road ragers.

And, like it or not, the "sciences of the self"—from psychology and psychoanalysis to sociology and anthropology—have lent their voices to the popular cacophony. Public discourse often commandeers the language of the academic disciplines to describe their senses of everyday subjectivity. Roles, status, peer pressure, socialization, culture and subculture, self-esteem, reinforcement, defense mechanisms, denial, and countless other technical terms are now familiar to just about everyone, regardless of education or training. The popular discourse of the self brings the academy and the clinic right into the living room, if not fully into the bedroom. . . . What began with intellectual forays by . . . Mead and Cooley is now integral even to the self-constructive rantings of Dr. Laura and Jerry Springer. Everyday parlance echoes them all. The challenge on this front is surely obvious, the analytic implication being that we can no longer view these discursive environments in isolation. Rather, we need to consider the myriad overlapping, intersecting going concerns that shape the self.

Last but not least, these developments implicate a complex moral climate, challenging us to view them in positive as well as negative terms. For some, such as Gergen and Hochschild (especially in *The Managed Heart*), the social landscape has become a coercive, "iron cage-like" environment of options for the self. Cast this way, institutions tyrannically impose limited conditions of possibility for self-construction, bordering on molding, if not determining, the selves we become. The numerous institutional demands placed on the self heighten the sense that self-construction is now beyond personal control. This is the dark side of a postmodern world as it relates to who and what we are, and can be.

Another, more optimistic, overlay suggests that contemporary life presents us with an ever-expanding, even emancipating, horizon of possibilities. Today, we are offered unprecedented opportunities for what could be done to construct selves that comfortably accommodate the biographical particulars of our lives. A thousand going concerns provide us with these opportunities: a thousand more proffer new and different chances for further growth, as well as a basis for challenging existing constructions. This is the positive side of a postmodern world.

Going concerns play a pivotal role in how we view and express ourselves and what we accept within our deepest reaches. To the extent that we inhabit a world of multiple institutional affiliations, we encounter diverse options for discerning even what we presume to be our core identities. We might experience this as either threatening or empowering. Social life is fully penetrating and engrossing; it completely permeates our lives. We cannot escape the social because it is built *into* our very beings. But the important lesson now is that the social is also built *out of* the eminently variegated going concerns that supply us with identities. Following Gergen, we can read this situation as an indictment of the self-saturating diversification of the postmodern world. But the possibilities for self-construction offered by an unprecedented and expanding horizon of identities can also be morally compelling. Our ability to choose between the options—indeed, to use some options in order to resist others, or to construct new ones—can be as liberating as it is overwhelming and debilitating.

References

Durkheim, Emile. 1964. *The Rules of the Sociological Method*. New York: Free Press.

Foucault, Michel. 1977. *Discipline and Punish*. New York: Vintage.

Gergen, Kenneth J. 1991. *The Saturated Self*. New York: Basic Books.

Gubrium, Jaber, and James Holstein. Forthcoming. *Institutional Selves: Troubled Identities in a Postmodern World*. New York: Oxford University Press.

Hochschild, Arlie Russell. 1983. *The Managed Heart*. Berkeley: University of California Press.

——. 1997. *The Time Bind: When Work Becomes Home and Home Becomes Work*. New York: Henry Holt.

Holstein, James, and Jaber Gubrium. 2000. *The Self We Live By: Narrative Identity in a Postmodern World*. New York: Oxford University Press.

Hughes, Everett C. 1984. "Going Concerns: The Study of American Institutions." Pp. 52–64 in *The Sociological Eye: Selected Papers*. New Brunswick, NJ: Transaction Books.

Mead, George Herbert. 1934. *Mind, Self, and Society*. Chicago: University of Chicago Press.

Mitchell, Richard. 1998. "Shuffling off to Armageddon: Social Problems in Text and Context." Pp. 183–206 in *Perspectives on Social Problems,* Vol. 10, edited by J. Holstein and G. Miller. Greenwich. CT: JAI Press.

Schwalbe, Michael L. 1993. "Goffman Against Postmodernism: Emotion and the Reality of the Self." *Symbolic Interaction* 16: 333–350.

Sica, Alan. 1993. "Does PoMo Matter?" *Contemporary Sociology* 22: 16–19.

Wuthnow, Robert. 1994. *Sharing the Journey: Support Groups and America's New Quest for Community.* New York: Free Press.